HARRAP'S

Beginner's French

Edited by

Michael Janes

HARRAP

EDINBURGH PARIS

Distributed in the United States by

PRENTICE HALL

New York

Consultant Editors
Fabrice Antoine
Stuart Fortey

First published in Great Britain 1993
by Chambers Harrap Publishers Ltd
43-45 Annandale Street, Edinburgh EH7 4AZ, UK

ISBN 0 245 60478 2 UK
0 245 50240 8 France

Library of Congress Cataloging-in-Publication Data

Harrap's beginner's French / Michael Janes, editor.
p. cm.
ISBN 0 671 87468 3
1. French language – Dictionaries – English.
2. English language – Dictionaries – French.
I. Janes, Michael.
PC2640.H25 1993 93-20564
443'.21 – dc20 CIP

Dépôt légal pour cette édition: mai 1993

Printed in Great Britain by
Clays Ltd, St Ives plc

Contents/Table des matières

Preface

This dictionary, based on the text of Harrap's *Mini French-English Dictionary*, is a major new work aiming to provide a practical selection of the most frequently used words and expressions of the French and English languages of today. An invaluable learning tool for beginners, the dictionary offers reliable, up-to-date and useful translations with a clarity unparalleled in a small-format work. Every headword, written in full in clear bold type, stands on a new line. In addition, English phrasal verbs (e.g. bring down), and, normally, French pronominal verbs (e.g. se battre), as well as many English compounds (e.g. birth certificate) are given as separate entries. For greatest convenience, all headwords are arranged in strict alphabetical order.

The text of the dictionary offers the maximum amount of guidance in pinpointing and understanding translations. Different translations of the same headword or phrase are clearly identified by context words in brackets. In addition, labels are used to indicate the level of style (e.g. *Fam* for 'familiar' or colloquial) or to define a particular usage (e.g. *Am* for 'American'). Context words or explanations are also given when considered helpful for the understanding of single translations (e.g. **article** (*object, in newspaper, in grammar*) article *m*, or **putty** mastic *m* (*pour vitres*)). The user is further helped by having context indicators and labels in French in the French section and in English in the English section of the dictionary. To maintain clarity in the text, all labelling has been kept to a strict minimum.

The user will find in the text a wide coverage of American words and usage (e.g. diaper, pinkie), and a selection of important abbreviated words in English (e.g. HP, BA) and in French (e.g. PCV, OVNI). A list of countries with derived adjectives is included in the appendix.

In common with other Harrap dictionaries, when a headword appears in an example in the same form, it is represented by its initial letter (e.g. **at h.** stands for **at home** at headword **home**).

The different grammatical divisions of a headword are easily identified by means of Arabic numerals in bold (i.e. **1**, **2**, **3**, **4**), and important sense divisions within long entries are clearly marked by the use of a block (i.e. ▮).

An oblique stroke within an entry is a useful space-saving device to separate non interchangeable parts of a phrase or expression matched exactly in French and English (e.g. **to be able to swim/drive** savoir nager/conduire is to be understood as: **to be able to swim** savoir nager and **to be able to drive** savoir conduire).

The pronunciation of English is shown using the latest symbols of the International Phonetic Alphabet. In order to avoid unnecessary repetition, the pronunciation, including stress, is given of all English headwords (e.g. sleep, birth) except derived forms (e.g. sleeping, birthday). Stress is indicated in derived forms in which it differs from that of the main form (e.g. miracle, mi'raculous). American English pronunciation is given whenever it is considered to show a marked difference from that of British English (e.g. **tomato** [tə'mɑːtəʊ, *Am* tə'meɪtəʊ]). American spelling is also supplied if sufficiently different from British (e.g. **tire** and **tyre**, **plow** and **plough**).

French pronunciation is considered more regular than English, and guidance is offered to the English user in the table on p x of the symbols of the International Phonetic Alphabet. The pronunciation of French headwords is only given where it does not follow well-established rules or may cause difficulties for the user of English (e.g. dix, donc, chut).

The author wishes to express his gratitude to Monsieur P. Szczeciner for his advice and help and to Mrs H. Curties for her assistance with proofreading.

M. Janes
London, 1993

Préface

Ce dictionnaire établi à partir du *Mini Dictionnaire Anglais-Français Harrap* est un ouvrage tout à fait nouveau tant par son contenu que par sa conception: on a voulu y faire figurer les mots et les expressions les plus fréquemment utilisés en français et en anglais moderne. Il constituera un précieux outil pour le débutant dans l'une ou l'autre des deux langues, grâce à ses traductions modernes, précises et fiables, toutes présentées avec une clarté qu'aucun autre dictionnaire de petit format ne parvient à égaler. Chaque mot d'entrée, donné en toutes lettres, en caractères gras très lisibles, fait l'objet d'un article distinct. Cela concerne également les verbes à particule anglais (par exemple: bring down) et, en général, les verbes pronominaux français (par exemple: se battre), de même que de nombreux mots composés anglais (par exemple: birth certificate). Pour faciliter la recherche, tous les mots d'entrée sont strictement classés par ordre alphabétique.

Ce dictionnaire fournit le plus d'indications possible pour aider l'utilisateur à cerner et comprendre les traductions proposées. Les différentes traductions d'un même mot d'entrée ou d'une même expression sont clairement définies à l'aide d'indications de contexte entre parenthèses. Des abréviations sont par ailleurs utilisées pour indiquer le niveau de langue (par exemple: *Fam* pour 'familier') ou des domaines d'emploi particuliers (par exemple: *Am* pour 'Américain'). On a également jugé utile de fournir parfois des mots indiquant le contexte, ou des explications, pour clarifier une traduction unique (par exemple: **article** (*object, in newspaper, in grammar*) article *m*, ou: **putty** mastic *m* (*pour vitres*)). L'accès à cet ouvrage est encore facilité par l'utilisation d'indicateurs en français dans la partie français-anglais et en anglais dans la partie anglais-français. La priorité a été donnée à la clarté de l'ensemble, on a donc employé le moins d'abréviations possible.

L'utilisateur trouvera dans cet ouvrage une large sélection d'américanismes (par exemple: diaper, pinkie) ainsi que d'abréviations courantes, tant anglaises (par exemple: HP, BA) que françaises (par exemple: PCV, OVNI). Une liste de noms de pays et des adjectifs correspondants figure en appendice.

Comme il est d'usage dans les autres dictionnaires Harrap, chaque fois qu'un mot d'entrée est repris sous la même forme dans un exemple, il est remplacé par sa première lettre (ainsi, **at h.** signifie **at home** dans l'article consacré à **home**).

Les différentes catégories grammaticales d'un mot d'entrée sont clairement repérées par des chiffres arabes en gras (**1**, **2**, **3**, **4**); le symbole ▮ sert à séparer les sens principaux au sein des articles longs.

Par souci de concision, on utilise dans les articles une barre oblique pour séparer des éléments non interchangeables d'une expression ou locution, lorsque la même structure se retrouve dans les deux langues; ainsi, **to be able to swim/drive** savoir nager/conduire se lira: **to be able to swim** savoir nager et **to be able to drive** savoir conduire.

La prononciation de l'anglais est fournie; les transcriptions utilisent les symboles les plus récents de l'Alphabet Phonétique International. Afin d'éviter des répétitions inutiles, on indique la prononciation — et l'accentuation — de tous les mots d'entrée anglais (par exemple: sleep, birth), à l'exception des mots dérivés (par exemple: sleeping, birthday). Chaque fois que l'accentuation d'un dérivé diffère de celle du mot simple, cela est indiqué (par exemple: miracle, mi'raculous). Les prononciations américaines sont indiquées chaque fois qu'elles diffèrent sensiblement de celles de l'anglais britannique (par exemple: **tomato** [tə'mɑːtəʊ, *Am* tə'meɪtəʊ]). On indique également l'orthographe américaine lorsqu'elle est notablement différente de celle de l'anglais britannique (par exemple: **tire** et **tyre**, **plow** et **plough**).

On considère que la prononciation du français est plus régulière que celle de l'anglais; l'utilisateur anglophone pourra donc s'aider du tableau des symboles de l'Alphabet Phonétique International proposé à la page x. La prononciation des mots d'entrée français n'est fournie que dans les cas où elle n'obéit pas à des règles bien établies ou est susceptible de n'être pas immédiatement perçue par l'utilisateur de langue anglaise (par exemple: dix, donc, chut).

L'auteur tient à exprimer sa gratitude à Monsieur P. Szczeciner pour ses conseils et sa collaboration, et à Mrs H. Curties qui a bien voulu nous aider à relire les épreuves.

M. Janes
Londres, 1993

Grammar notes

In French, the feminine of an adjective is formed, when regular, by adding **e** to the masculine form (e.g. grand, grande; carré, carrée; fin, fine). If the masculine already ends in **e**, the feminine is the same as the masculine (e.g. utile). Both regular and irregular feminine forms of adjectives (e.g. généreux, généreuse; léger, légère; doux, douce) are given on the French-English side of the dictionary. On the English-French side, French adjectives are shown in the masculine but highly irregular feminine forms (e.g. frais, fraîche; faux, fausse) have been included as an additional help to the user.

To form the plural of a French noun or adjective **s** is usually added to the singular (e.g. arbre, arbres; taxi, taxis; petit, petits). The plural form of a noun ending in **s**, **x** or **z** (e.g. pois, croix, nez) is the same as that of the singular. Plurals of nouns and adjectives which do not follow these general rules (e.g. where **x** or **aux** is added in the plural, or where there is a highly irregular plural such as œil, yeux) are listed in the French section. Also included are the plurals of French compounds where the formation of the plural involves a change other than the addition of final **s** (e.g. chou-fleur, choux-fleurs; arc-en-ciel, arcs-en-ciel). The irregular plurals of French nouns (and irregular masculine plurals of French adjectives) ending in **al**, **eau**, **eu**, **au**, **ail** and **ou** are listed on the French-English side (e.g. cerveau, -x; général, -aux). Included on the English-French side, as an additional help to the user, are the plurals of French nouns (and adjectives) ending in **al**, **eu** and **au** where **s**, and not the usual **x**, forms the plural (e.g. pneu, pneus; naval, navals) and of those nouns in **ail** and **ou** where the plural is formed with **x**, and not the usual **s** (e.g. travail, travaux; chou, choux).

In English also, **s** is added to form the plural of a noun (e.g. cat, cats; taxi, taxis) but a noun ending in **ch**, **s**, **sh**, **x** or **z** forms its plural by the addition of **es**, pronounced [-ɪz] (e.g. glass, glasses; match, matches). When a noun ends in **y** preceded by a consonant, **y** is changed to **ies** to form the plural (e.g. army, armies). Irregular English plurals (e.g. hero, heroes; leaf, leaves) are given on the English-French side, including the plurals of English compounds where the formation of the plural involves a change other than the addition of final **s** (e.g. brother-in-law, brothers-in-law). Common English irregular plurals involving a change of vowel (e.g. tooth, teeth) are given, for convenience, at both singular and plural headword positions.

Most French verbs have regular conjugations though some display spelling anomalies (see French verb conjugations on p (i)). In the French section an asterisk is used to mark an irregular French verb, and refers the user to the table of irregular verbs on p (iii).

Most English verbs form their past tense and past participle by adding **ed** to the infinitive (e.g. look, looked) or **d** to an infinitive already ending in **e** (e.g. love, loved). When a verb ends in **y** preceded by a consonant, **y** becomes **ied** (e.g. satisfy, satisfied). To form the third person singular of a verb in the present tense **s** is added to the infinitive (e.g. know, knows) but an infinitive in **ch**, **s**, **sh**, **x** or **z** forms its third person singular by the addition of **es**, pronounced [-ɪz] (e.g. dash, dashes). When an infinitive ends in **y** preceded by a consonant, **y** is changed to **ies** to form the third person singular (e.g. satisfy, satisfies).

The English present participle is formed by the addition of **ing** to the infinitive (e.g. look, looking) but final **e** is omitted when an infinitive ends in **e** (e.g. love, loving). When the infinitive ends in a single consonant preceded by a vowel (e.g. tug), the final consonant is usually doubled in the past tense, past and present participles (e.g. tug, tugged, tugging).

An asterisk is used, in the English section as on the French side, to show an irregular English verb and to refer the user to the list of irregular verbs on p (viii).

Notes sur la grammaire

En français, le féminin d'un adjectif se forme en général en ajoutant **e** au masculin (par exemple: grand, grande; carré, carrée; fin, fine). Lorsque le masculin se termine déjà par **e**, le féminin est identique (par exemple: utile). Les féminins de tous les adjectifs, réguliers et irréguliers, (par exemple: généreux, généreuse; léger, légère; doux, douce) sont indiqués dans la partie français-anglais. Dans la partie anglais-français, seul le masculin des adjectifs est donné; cependant, par souci de fournir une information complémentaire utile, on a indiqué des féminins irréguliers remarquables (par exemple: frais, fraîche, faux, fausse).

On forme en général le pluriel d'un nom ou d'un adjectif français en ajoutant **s** au singulier (par exemple: arbre, arbres; taxi, taxis; petit, petits). Le pluriel d'un nom qui se termine par **s**, **x** ou **z** (par exemple: pois, croix, nez) est identique au singulier. Les pluriels des noms et adjectifs qui font exception à ces règles générales (par exemple: ceux qui se forment avec **x** ou **aux**, ou sont irréguliers, comme: œil, yeux) sont signalés dans la partie français-anglais. Il en est de même pour les pluriels des mots composés français dont le passage au pluriel appelle une modification autre que le simple ajout d'un **s** final (par exemple: chou-fleur, choux-fleurs; arc-en-ciel, arcs-en-ciel). Les pluriels irréguliers des noms français, de même que ceux des adjectifs masculins, qui se terminent par **al**, **eau**, **eu**, **au**, **ail** et **ou** sont indiqués dans la partie français-anglais (par exemple: cerveau, -x; général, -aux). Un complément d'information est fourni, dans la partie anglais-français, par la mention des pluriels des noms (et adjectifs) français qui se terminent par **al**, **eu** et **au** et forment leur pluriel en **-s**, au lieu de **-x** (par exemple: pneu, pneus; naval, navals); il en va de même pour ceux qui se terminent par **ail** et **ou** et qui forment leur pluriel en **-x**, au lieu de **-s** (par exemple: travail, travaux; chou, choux).

En anglais, on forme également le pluriel des noms en leur ajoutant **s** (par exemple: cat, cats; taxi, taxis) mais on ajoutera **es**, prononcé [-ɪz], aux noms qui se terminent par **ch**, **s**, **sh**, **x** ou **z** (par exemple: glass, glasses; match, matches). Lorsqu'un nom se termine par un **y** précédé d'une consonne, ce **y** devient **ies** au pluriel (par exemple: army, armies). Les pluriels irréguliers de l'anglais (par exemple: hero, heroes; leaf, leaves) sont signalés dans la partie anglais-français, de même que les pluriels des mots composés anglais dont le passage au pluriel entraîne une modification autre que le simple ajout d'un **s** final (par exemple: brother-in-law, brothers-in-law). Pour faciliter la recherche, on a fait figurer comme mots d'entrée les pluriels irréguliers de mots anglais usuels qui se forment par modification de voyelle (par exemple: tooth, teeth).

La plupart des verbes français ont des conjugaisons régulières; certains subissent cependant des variations orthographiques (voir: Conjugaisons des verbes français à la page (i)). Dans la partie français-anglais, un astérisque signale un verbe irrégulier français et renvoie à la table des verbes irréguliers donnée en page (iii).

En anglais, le passé et le participe passé des verbes se forment dans la plupart des cas en ajoutant **ed** à l'infinitif (par exemple: look, looked) ou seulement **d** lorsque l'infinitif se termine par un **e** (par exemple: love, loved). Lorsqu'un verbe se termine par un **y** précédé d'une consonne, ce **y** devient **ied** (par exemple: satisfy, satisfied). La troisième personne du singulier d'un verbe au présent se forme en ajoutant **s** à l'infinitif (par exemple: know, knows), mais on ajoutera **es**, prononcé [-ɪz], aux infinitifs qui se terminent par **ch**, **s**, **sh**, **x** ou **z** (par exemple: dash, dashes). Enfin, lorsqu'un verbe se termine par un **y** précédé d'une consonne, ce **y** devient **ies** à la troisième personne du singulier (par exemple: satisfy, satisfies).

Le participe présent en anglais se forme en ajoutant **ing** à l'infinitif (par exemple: look, looking); lorsqu'un infinitif comporte un **e** final, celui-ci disparaît (par exemple: love, loving). Lorsque l'infinitif se termine par une seule consonne précédée d'une voyelle (par exemple: tug), la consonne finale est le plus souvent doublée au passé et aux participes passé et présent (par exemple: tug, tugged, tugging).

Dans la partie anglais-français, comme dans la partie français-anglais, un astérisque signale un verbe irrégulier anglais et renvoie à la liste de verbes irréguliers donnée en page (viii).

Pronunciation of French

TABLE OF PHONETIC SYMBOLS

Vowels

[i]	vite, cygne, sortie
[e]	été, donner, légal
[ɛ]	elle, mais, père, prêt
[a]	chat, fameux, toit [twa]
[ɑ]	pas, âge, tâche
[ɔ]	donne, fort, album
[o]	dos, chaud, peau, dôme
[u]	tout, cour, roue, goût
[y]	cru, sûr, rue
[ø]	feu, meule, nœud
[œ]	œuf, jeune, cueillir [kœjir]
[ə]	le, refaire, entre
[ɛ̃]	vin, plein, faim, saint
[ɑ̃]	enfant, temps, paon
[ɔ̃]	mon, nombre, honte
[œ̃]	lundi, humble, un

Consonants

[p]	pain, absolu, taper, frapper
[b]	beau, abbé, robe
[t]	table, nette, vite
[d]	donner, sud, raide
[k]	camp, képi, qui, taxe [taks], accès [aksɛ]
[g]	garde, guerre, second, exister [ɛgziste]
[f]	feu, siffler, phrase
[v]	voir, trouver, wagon
[s]	son, cire, ça, chasse, nation
[z]	cousin, zéro, rose
[ʃ]	chose, hache, schéma
[ʒ]	gilet, jeter, âge
[l]	lait, facile, elle
[r]	rare, rhume, sortir, barreau
[m]	mon, flamme, aimer
[n]	né, canne, animal
[ɲ]	campagne, agneau
[ŋ]	jogging
[']	This symbol is placed before a word beginning with h in the headword list to show that the preceding word must not be abbreviated (e.g. la hache and not l'hache), and that the final consonant of the previous word must not be pronounced (e.g. les haches: [leaʃ] and not [lezaʃ]).

Semi-consonants

[j]	piano, voyage, fille, yeux
[w]	ouest, noir [nwar], tramway
[ɥ]	muet, lui, huile

Prononciation de l'anglais

TABLEAU DES SIGNES PHONÉTIQUES

Voyelles et diphtongues

[iː]	**bee, police**	[ɒ]	**lot, what**
[ɪə]	**beer, real**	[ɔː]	**all, saw**
[ɪ]	**bit, added**	[ɔɪ]	**boil, toy**
[e]	**bet, said**	[əʊ]	**low, soap**
[eɪ]	**date, nail**	[ʊ]	**put, wool**
[eə]	**bear, air**	[uː]	**shoe, too**
[æ]	**bat, plan**	[ʊə]	**poor, sure**
[aɪ]	**fly, life**	[ʌ]	**cut, some**
[ɑː]	**art, ask**	[ɜː]	**burn, learn**
[aʊ]	**fowl, house**	[ə]	**china, annoy**
		[(ə)]	**relation**

Consonnes

[p]	**pat, top**	[ð]	**that, breathe**
[b]	**but, tab**	[h]	**hat, rehearse**
[t]	**tap, matter**	[l]	**lad, all**
[d]	**dab, ladder**	[r]	**red, sorry**
[k]	**cat, kite**	[*r*]	**better, here** (représente un r final qui se prononce en liaison devant une voyelle, par exemple 'here is' [hɪə*r*ɪz])
[g]	**go, rogue**		
[f]	**fat, phrase**		
[v]	**veal, save**		
[s]	**sat, ace**	[m]	**mat, hammer**
[z]	**zero, houses**	[n]	**no, banner**
[ʃ]	**dish, pressure**	[ŋ]	**singing, link**
[ʒ]	**pleasure**	[j]	**yet, onion**
[tʃ]	**charm, rich**	[w]	**wall**, quite [kwaɪt]
[dʒ]	**judge, rage**	[ˈ]	marque l'accent tonique; précède la syllabe accentuée
[θ]	**thank, breath**		

Abbreviations / Abréviations

Abbreviations		Abréviations
adjective	*a*	adjectif
abbreviation	*abbr, abrév*	abréviation
adverb	*adv*	adverbe
American	*Am*	américain
article	*art*	article
auxiliary	*aux*	auxiliaire
British	*Br*	britannique
Canadian	*Can*	canadien
conjunction	*conj*	conjonction
definite	*def, déf*	défini
demonstrative	*dem, dém*	démonstratif
et cetera	*etc*	et cetera
feminine	*f*	féminin
familiar	*Fam*	familier
feminine plural	*fpl*	féminin pluriel
French	*Fr*	français
indefinite	*indef, indéf*	indéfini
interjection	*int*	interjection
invariable	*inv*	invariable
masculine	*m*	masculin
masculine and feminine	*mf*	masculin et féminin
masculine plural	*mpl*	masculin pluriel
noun	*n*	nom
plural	*pl*	pluriel
possessive	*poss*	possessif
past participle	*pp*	participe passé
preposition	*prep, prép*	préposition
present participle	*pres p*	participe présent
pronoun	*pron*	pronom
	qch	quelque chose
	qn	quelqu'un
registered trademark	®	marque déposée
relative	*rel*	relatif
singular	*sing*	singulier
someone	*s.o.*	
something	*sth*	
United States	*US*	États-Unis
auxiliary verb	*v aux*	verbe auxiliaire
intransitive verb	*vi*	verbe intransitif
pronominal verb	*vpr*	verbe pronominal
transitive verb	*vt*	verbe transitif
transitive and intransitive verb	*vti*	verbe transitif et intransitif

A

a [ə, *stressed* eɪ] (*before vowel or mute h* **an** [ən, *stressed* æn]) *indef art* un, une; **a man** un homme; **an apple** une pomme; **six pence a kilo** six pence le kilo; **50 km an hour** 50 km à l'heure; **he's a doctor** il est médecin; **twice a month** deux fois par mois.
abandon [ə'bændən] *vt* abandonner.
abbey ['æbɪ] abbaye *f*.
abbreviation [əbriːvɪ'eɪʃ(ə)n] abréviation *f*.
ability [ə'bɪlətɪ] capacité *f* (**to do** pour faire); **to the best of my a.** de mon mieux.
able ['eɪb(ə)l] *a* capable; **to be a. to do** être capable de faire, pouvoir faire; **to be a. to swim/drive** savoir nager/conduire.
abnormal [æb'nɔːm(ə)l] *a* anormal.
aboard [ə'bɔːd] **1** *adv* (*on ship*) à bord; **all a.** (*on train*) en voiture. **2** *prep* **a. the ship** à bord du navire; **a. the train** dans le train.
abolish [ə'bɒlɪʃ] *vt* supprimer.
abortion [ə'bɔːʃ(ə)n] avortement *m*; **to have an a.** se faire avorter.
about [ə'baʊt] **1** *adv* (*approximately*) à peu près, environ; **(at) a. two o'clock** vers deux heures. ▮ (*here and there*) çà et là; (*ideas, flu*) dans l'air; (*rumour*) en circulation; **there are lots a.** il en existe beaucoup; **(out and) a.** (*after illness*) sur pied; **(up and) a.** (*out of bed*) levé, debout. **2** *prep* (*around*) **a. the garden** autour du jardin; **a. the streets** par les rues. ▮ (*near to*) **a. here** par ici. ▮ (*concerning*) au sujet de; **to talk a.** parler de; **a book a.** un livre sur; **what's it (all) a.?** de quoi s'agit-il?; **what** *or* **how a. me?** et moi?; **what** *or* **how a. a drink?** que dirais-tu de prendre un verre? ▮ (+ *infinitive*) **a. to do** sur le point de faire.
above [ə'bʌv] **1** *adv* au-dessus; **from a.** d'en haut; **floor a.** étage *m* supérieur. **2** *prep* au-dessus de; **a. all** par-dessus tout; **he's a. me** (*in rank*) c'est mon supérieur.
above 'mentioned *a* susmentionné.
abreast [ə'brest] *adv* **four a.** par rangs de quatre; **to keep a. of** se tenir au courant de.
abroad [ə'brɔːd] *adv* à l'étranger; **from a.** de l'étranger.
abrupt [ə'brʌpt] *a* (*sudden, rude*) brusque.
abscess ['æbses] abcès *m*.
absence ['æbsəns] absence *f*.
absent ['æbsənt] *a* absent (**from** de).
absent-'minded *a* distrait.
absolute ['æbsəluːt] *a* absolu; (*coward etc*) parfait.
absolutely *adv* absolument.

absorb [əb'zɔːb] *vt* (*liquid*) absorber; **absorbed in one's work** absorbé dans *ou* par son travail.
absorbent cotton *Am* coton *m* hydrophile.
absurd [əb'sɜːd] *a* absurde.
abuse 1 *n* [ə'bjuːs] abus *m* (**of** de); (*of child etc*) mauvais traitements *mpl*; (*insults*) injures *fpl*. **2** *vt* [ə'bjuːz] (*use badly or wrongly*) abuser de; (*ill-treat*) maltraiter; (*insult*) injurier.
abusive [ə'bjuːsɪv] *a* grossier.
academic [ækə'demɪk] **1** *a* (*year, diploma etc*) universitaire. **2** *n* (*teacher*) universitaire *mf*.
accelerate [ək'seləreɪt] *vi* (*in vehicle*) accélérer.
accelerator accélérateur *m*.
accent ['æksənt] accent *m*.
accept [ək'sept] *vt* accepter.
acceptable *a* acceptable.
access ['ækses] accès *m* (**to sth** à qch, **to s.o.** auprès de qn).
ac'cessible *a* accessible.
accessories [ək'sesərɪz] *npl* (*objects*) accessoires *mpl*.
accident ['æksɪdənt] accident *m*; **by a.** (*without meaning to*) accidentellement.
acci'dental *a* accidentel.
acci'dentally *adv* accidentellement.
accommodation [əkɒmə'deɪʃ(ə)n] logement *m*; **accommodations** (*in hotel*) *Am* chambre(s) *f*(*pl*).
accompany [ə'kʌmpənɪ] *vt* accompagner.
accomplish [ə'kʌmplɪʃ] *vt* accomplir; (*aim*) réaliser.
accord [ə'kɔːd] **of my own a.** volontairement.
accordance in a. with conformément à.
according to [ə'kɔːdɪŋtuː] *prep* selon.
accordion [ə'kɔːdɪən] accordéon *m*.
account [ə'kaʊnt] (*with bank or firm*) compte *m*; (*report*) compte rendu *m*; **accounts** (*of firm*) comptabilité *f*; **to take into a.** tenir compte de; **on a. of** à cause de.
accountant [ə'kaʊntənt] comptable *mf*.
account for (*explain*) expliquer; (*represent*) représenter.
accumulate [ə'kjuːmjʊleɪt] **1** *vt* accumuler. **2** *vi* s'accumuler.
accurate ['ækjʊrət] *a* exact, précis.
accurately *adv* avec précision.
accu'sation accusation *f*.
accuse [ə'kjuːz] *vt* accuser (**of** de).
accustomed [ə'kʌstəmd] *a* habitué (**to sth** à qch, **to doing** à faire); **to get a. to** s'habituer à.

ace [eɪs] (*card*, *person*) as *m*.
ache [eɪk] **1** *n* douleur *f*; **to have an a. in one's arm** avoir mal au bras. **2** *vi* faire mal; **my head aches** ma tête me fait mal; **I'm aching all over** j'ai mal partout.
achieve [ə'tʃiːv] *vt* réaliser; (*success*, *result*) obtenir; (*victory*) remporter
achievement (*success*) réussite *f*.
aching *a* douloureux.
acid ['æsɪd] *a* & *n* acide (*m*).
acknowledge [ək'nɒlɪdʒ] *vt* reconnaître (**as** pour); **to a. (receipt of)** accuser réception de.
acne ['æknɪ] acné *f*.
acorn ['eɪkɔːn] gland *m*.
acquaint [ə'kweɪnt] *vt* **to be acquainted with s.o.** connaître qn; **we are acquainted** on se connaît.
acquaintance connaissance *f*.
acquire [ə'kwaɪər] *vt* acquérir.
acre ['eɪkər] acre *f* (= *0,4 hectare*).
acrobat ['ækrəbæt] acrobate *mf*.
acro'batic *a* acrobatique.
across [ə'krɒs] *adv* & *prep* (*from side to side* (*of*)) d'un côté a l'autre (de); (*on the other side* (*of*)) de l'autre côté (de); (*so as to cross*, *diagonally*) en travers (de); **to be a kilometre a.** (*wide*) avoir un kilomètre de large; **to walk** *or* **go a.** (*street*) traverser.
acrylic [ə'krɪlɪk] *n* acrylique *m*; **a. socks**/*etc* chaussettes *fpl*/*etc* en acrylique.
act [ækt] **1** *n* (*deed*, *part of play*) acte *m*; (*in circus*) numéro *m*; **caught in the a.** pris sur le fait. **2** *vt* (*role in play or film*) jouer. **3** *vi* (*do sth*, *behave*) agir; (*in play or film*) jouer; **to a. as** (*secretary etc*) faire office de; (*of object*) servir de.
act for s.o. représenter qn.
action ['ækʃ(ə)n] action *f*; (*military*) combat *m*; **to take a.** prendre des mesures; **to put into a.** (*plan*) exécuter; **out of a.** hors d'usage; (*person*) hors (de) combat.
active ['æktɪv] **1** *a* actif; (*interest*, *dislike*) vif. **2** *n Grammar* actif *m*.
ac'tivity activité *f*; (*in street*) animation *f*
act (up)on (*affect*) agir sur; (*advice*) suivre.
actor ['æktər] acteur *m*.
actress ['æktrɪs] actrice *f*.
actual ['æktʃʊəl] *a* réel; **the a. book** le livre même.
actually *adv* (*truly*) réellement; (*in fact*) en réalité.

acute [ə'kjuːt] *a* aigu; (*emotion*) vif; (*shortage*) grave.
AD [eɪ'diː] *abbr* (*anno Domini*) après Jésus-Christ.
ad [æd] *Fam* pub *f*; (*private*, *in newspaper*) annonce *f*; **small ad**, *Am* **want ad** petite annonce.
adapt [ə'dæpt] *vt* adapter (**to** à); **to a. (oneself)** s'adapter.
adaptable *a* (*person*) souple.
adaptor (*plug*) prise *f* multiple.
add [æd] *vt* ajouter (**to** à, **that** que); (*total*) additionner.
addict ['ædɪkt] **jazz/sport a.** fanatique *mf* du jazz/du sport; **drug a.** drogué, -ée *mf*.
a'ddicted *a* **to be a. to** (*music*, *sport*) se passionner pour; **a. to drink** alcoolique; **a. to cigarettes** drogué par la cigarette.
a'ddiction drug a. toxicomanie *f*.
add in (*include*) inclure.
adding machine machine *f* à calculer.
a'ddition addition *f*; **in a.** de plus; **in a. to** en plus de.
a'dditional *a* supplémentaire.
additive additif *m*.
address 1 *n* [ə'dres, *Am* 'ædres] (*on letter etc*) adresse *f*; (*speech*) allocution *f*. **2** *vt* [ə'dres] (*person*) s'adresser à; (*audience*) parler devant; (*letter*) mettre l'adresse sur.
add to (*increase*) augmenter.
add together (*numbers*) additionner.
add up 1 *vt* (*numbers*) additionner. **2** *vi* **to a. up to** (*total*) s'élever à; (*mean*) signifier; (*represent*) constituer.
adenoids ['ædɪnɔɪdz] *npl* végétations *fpl* (adénoïdes).
adequate ['ædɪkwət] *a* (*quantity etc*) suffisant; (*acceptable*) convenable; (*person*) compétent.
adequately *adv* suffisamment; convenablement.
adhesive [əd'hiːsɪv] *a* & *n* adhésif (*m*).
adjective ['ædʒɪktɪv] adjectif *m*.
adjust [ə'dʒʌst] *vt* (*machine*) régler; (*salaries*) ajuster; **to a. (oneself) to** s'adapter à.
adjustable *a* (*seat*) réglable.
adjustment réglage *m*; (*of person*) adaptation *f*.
administer [əd'mɪnɪstər] *vt* administrer.
admini'stration administration *f*; *Am* gouvernement *m*.
administrative *a* administratif.
admiral ['ædmərəl] amiral *m*.
admi'ration admiration *f*.
admire [əd'maɪər] *vt* admirer (**for** pour, **for doing** de faire).
admission (*to cinema etc*) entrée *f*; **a. charge** prix *m* d'entrée.

admit [əd'mɪt] *vt* (*let in*) laisser entrer, admettre; (*acknowledge*) reconnaître, admettre (**that** que).
admittance 'no a.' 'entrée interdite'.
admit to sth (*confess*) avouer qch.
adolescent [ædə'lesənt] adolescent, -ente *mf*.
adopt [ə'dɒpt] *vt* (*child, attitude etc*) adopter.
adopted *a* (*child*) adoptif.
adoption adoption *f*.
adorable *a* adorable.
adore [ə'dɔːr] *vt* adorer (**doing** faire).
adult ['ædʌlt, ə'dʌlt] **1** *n* adulte *mf*. **2** *a* (*animal etc*) adulte; **a. class/film/***etc* classe *f*/film *m*/*etc* pour adultes.
advance [əd'vɑːns] **1** *n* (*movement, money*) avance *f*; **advances** (*of love*) avances *fpl*; **in a.** à l'avance, d'avance. **2** *a* (*payment*) anticipé; **a. booking** réservation *f*. **3** *vt* (*put forward, lend*) avancer. **4** *vi* (*go forward, progress*) avancer.
advanced [əd'vɑːnst] *a* avancé; (*studies, level*) supérieur; (*course*) de niveau supérieur.
advantage [əd'vɑːntɪdʒ] avantage *m* (**over** sur); **to take a. of** profiter de; (*person*) exploiter.
adventure [əd'ventʃər] aventure *f*.
adventurous *a* aventureux.
adverb ['ædvɜːb] adverbe *m*.
advert ['ædvɜːt] pub *f*; (*private, in newspaper*) annonce *f*.
advertise ['ædvətaɪz] **1** *vt* (*commercially*) faire de la publicité pour; (*privately*) passer une annonce pour vendre; (*make known*) annoncer. **2** *vi* faire de la publicité; (*privately*) passer une annonce (**for** pour trouver).
advertisement [əd'vɜːtɪsmənt, *Am* ædvə'taɪzmənt] publicité *f*; (*private, in newspaper*) annonce *f*; (*poster*) affiche *f*; **classified a.** petite annonce.
advice [əd'vaɪs] conseil(s) *m*(*pl*); **a piece of a.** un conseil.
advisable *a* (*wise*) prudent (**to do** de faire).
advise [əd'vaɪz] *vt* conseiller; (*recommend*) recommander; **to a. s.o. to do** conseiller à qn de faire.
advise against déconseiller.
adviser conseiller, -ère *mf*.
aerial ['eərɪəl] antenne *f*.
aerobics [eə'rəubɪks] *npl* aérobic *f*.
aeroplane ['eərəpleɪn] avion *m*.
aerosol ['eərəsɒl] aérosol *m*.
affair [ə'feər] affaire *f*; (**love**) **a.** liaison *f*.

affect [ə'fekt] *vt* (*concern*, *move*) toucher, affecter; (*harm*) nuire à.
affection [ə'fekʃ(ə)n] affection *f* (**for** pour).
affectionate *a* affectueux.
affluent ['æfluənt] *a* riche.
afford [ə'fɔːd] *vt* (*pay for*) avoir les moyens d'acheter; (*time*) pouvoir trouver.
affordable *a* (*price etc*) abordable.
afloat [ə'fləʊt] *adv* (*ship*, *swimmer*, *business*) à flot.
afraid [ə'freɪd] *a* **to be a.** avoir peur (**of, to** de); **he's a. (that) she may be ill** il a peur qu'elle (ne) soit malade; **I'm a. he's out** (*I regret to say*) je regrette, il est sorti.
African ['æfrɪkən] *a* & *n* africain, -aine (*mf*).
after ['ɑːftər] **1** *adv* après; **the month a.** le mois suivant. **2** *prep* après; **a. all** après tout; **a. eating** après avoir mangé; **a. you!** je vous en prie!; **ten a. four** *Am* quatre heures dix; **to be a. sth/s.o.** (*seek*) chercher qch/qn. **3** *conj* après que.
aftereffects *npl* suites *fpl*.
after'noon après-midi *m or f inv*; **in the a.** l'après-midi; **good a.!** (*hello*) bonjour!; (*goodbye*) au revoir!
after'noons *adv Am* l'après-midi.
aftersales service service *m* après-vente.
aftershave (lotion) lotion *f* après-rasage.
afterward(s) ['ɑːftəwədz] *adv* après, plus tard.
again [ə'gen, ə'geɪn] *adv* de nouveau, encore une fois; **never a.** plus jamais; **a. and a., time and (time) a.** bien des fois, maintes fois.
against [ə'genst, ə'geɪnst] *prep* contre; **a. the law** illégal.
age [eɪdʒ] **1** *n* âge *m*; **(old) a.** vieillesse *f*; **the Middle Ages** le moyen âge; **five years of a.** âgé de cinq ans; **under a.** trop jeune. **2** *vti* vieillir.
aged [eɪdʒd] *a* **a. ten** âgé de dix ans.
agency (*office*) agence *f*.
agenda [ə'dʒendə] ordre *m* du jour.
agent ['eɪdʒənt] agent *m*; (*dealer*) concessionnaire *mf*.
aggravate ['ægrəveɪt] *vt* (*make worse*) aggraver; **to a. s.o.** exaspérer qn.
aggra'vation (*bother*) ennui(s) *m*(*pl*).
aggression [ə'greʃ(ə)n] agression *f*.
aggressive *a* agressif.
agile ['ædʒaɪl, *Am* 'ædʒ(ə)l] *a* agile.
agitated ['ædʒɪteɪtɪd] *a* agité.
ago [ə'gəʊ] *adv* **a year a.** il y a un an; **how long a.?** il y a combien de temps (de cela)?

agony ['ægənɪ] **to be in a.** souffrir horriblement.

agree [ə'griː] **1** *vi* (*come to an agreement*) se mettre d'accord; (*be in agreement*) être d'accord (**with** avec); (*of facts, dates*) concorder; *Grammar* s'accorder; **to a. to sth/to doing** consentir à qch/à faire; **it doesn't a. with me** (*food, climate*) ça ne me réussit pas. **2** *vt* **to a. to do** accepter de faire; **to a. that** admettre que.

agreeable *a* (*pleasant*) agréable.

agreed *a* (*time, place*) convenu; **we are a.** nous sommes d'accord; **a.!** entendu!

agreement accord *m*; **in a. with** d'accord avec.

agree (up)on (*decide*) convenir de.

agri'cultural *a* agricole.

agriculture ['ægrɪkʌltʃər] agriculture *f*.

ahead [ə'hed] *adv* (*in space*) en avant; (*leading*) en tête; (*in the future*) dans l'avenir; **a. (of time)** en avance (sur l'horaire); **to be one hour a.** avoir une heure d'avance (**of** sur); **a. of** (*space*) devant; (*time*) en avance sur; **straight a.** (*to walk*) tout droit; (*to look*) droit devant soi.

aid [eɪd] aide *f*; (*device*) accessoire *m*, support *m*; **with the a. of** (*a stick etc*) à l'aide de; **in a. of** (*charity*) au profit de.

AIDS [eɪdz] SIDA *m*.

aim [eɪm] **1** *n* but *m*; **with the a. of** dans le but de. **2** *vt* (*gun*) braquer (**at** sur); **aimed at children**/*etc* (*product*) destiné aux enfants/*etc*. **3** *vi* viser; **to a. at s.o.** viser qn; **to a. to do** *or* **at doing** avoir l'intention de faire.

air [eər] **1** *n* air *m*; **in the open a.** en plein air; **by a.** (*to travel, send*) par avion; **(up) in(to) the a.** en l'air. **2** *a* (*raid, base*) aérien. **3** *vt* (*room*) aérer.

air-conditioned *a* climatisé.

aircraft *n inv* avion(s) *m(pl)*.

aircraft carrier porte-avions *m inv*.

air fare prix *m* du billet d'avion.

air force armée *f* de l'air.

air hostess hôtesse *f* de l'air.

airing cupboard armoire *f* sèche-linge.

airline ligne *f* aérienne.

airline ticket billet *m* d'avion.

airmail poste *f* aérienne; **by a.** par avion.

airplane *Am* avion *m*.

airport aéroport *m*.

airsickness mal *m* de l'air.

air terminal aérogare *f*.

airtight *a* hermétique.
air traffic controller aiguilleur *m* du ciel.
aisle [aɪl] (*in plane*, *supermarket*, *cinema etc*) allée *f*; (*in church*) nef *f* latérale.
ajar [ə'dʒɑːr] *a* (*door*) entrouvert.
alarm [ə'lɑːm] **1** *n* (*warning*, *device in house or car*) alarme *f*; (*mechanism*) sonnerie *f* (d'alarme); **a. (clock)** réveil *m*. **2** *vt* alarmer.
album ['ælbəm] (*book*, *record*) album *m*.
alcohol ['ælkəhɒl] alcool *m*.
alco'holic 1 *a* (*drink*) alcoolisé. **2** *n* (*person*) alcoolique *mf*.
alert [ə'lɜːt] *a* (*watching carefully*) vigilant.
A level ['eɪlev(ə)l] (*exam*) *Br* = épreuve *f* de bac.
algebra ['ældʒɪbrə] algèbre *f*.
alibi ['ælɪbaɪ] alibi *m*.
alien ['eɪlɪən] étranger, -ère *mf*.
alight [ə'laɪt] *a* (*fire*) allumé; **to set a.** mettre le feu à.
alike [ə'laɪk] **1** *a* (*people*, *things*) semblables; **to look** *or* **be a.** se ressembler. **2** *adv* de la même manière.
alive [ə'laɪv] *a* vivant, en vie.
all [ɔːl] **1** *a* tout, toute, *pl* tous, toutes; **a. day** toute la journée; **a. (the) men** tous les hommes. **2** *pron* tous *mpl*, toutes *fpl*; (*everything*) tout; **my sisters are a. here** toutes mes sœurs sont ici; **he ate it a., he ate a. of it** il a tout mangé; **a. (that) he has** tout ce qu'il a; **a. of us** nous tous; **in a., a. told** en tout; **a. but** (*almost*) presque; **if there's any wind at a.** s'il y a le moindre vent; **not at a.** pas du tout; (*after 'thank you'*) pas de quoi. **3** *adv* tout; **a. alone** tout seul; **six a.** *Football* six buts partout.
allergic [ə'lɜːdʒɪk] *a* allergique (**to** à).
alley ['ælɪ] ruelle *f*; (*in park*) allée *f*.
alleyway ruelle *f*.
alliance [ə'laɪəns] alliance *f*.
alligator ['ælɪgeɪtər] alligator *m*.
all-in *a* (*price*) global.
allocate ['æləkeɪt] *vt* allouer (**to** à); (*distribute*) répartir.
allotment [ə'lɒtmənt] (*land*) lopin *m* de terre (*loué pour la culture*).
all-out *a* (*effort*) énergique.
allow [ə'laʊ] *vt* permettre; (*give*) accorder; (*as discount*) déduire; **to a. s.o. to do** permettre à qn de faire; **you're not allowed to go** on vous interdit de partir.
allowance [ə'laʊəns] allocation *f*; (*for travel*, *housing*, *food*) indemnité *f*; (*for duty-free goods*) tolérance *f*; **to make allowances for s.o.** être indulgent envers qn.

allow for sth tenir compte de qch.
all-purpose *a* (*tool*) universel.
all right [ɔːl'raɪt] **1** *a* (*satisfactory*) bien *inv*; (*unharmed*) sain et sauf; (*undamaged*) intact; (*without worries*) tranquille; **it's all r.** ça va; **I'm all r.** (*healthy*) je vais bien. **2** *adv* (*well*) bien; **all r.!** (*agreement*) d'accord!; **I got your letter all r.** (*emphatic*) j'ai bien reçu votre lettre.
all-round *a* complet.
ally ['ælaɪ] allié, -ée *mf*.
almond ['ɑːmənd] amande *f*.
almost ['ɔːlməʊst] *adv* presque; **he a. fell**/*etc* il a failli tomber/*etc*.
alone [ə'ləʊn] *a & adv* seul; **to leave a.** (*person*) laisser tranquille; (*thing*) ne pas toucher à.
along [ə'lɒŋ] **1** *prep* **(all) a.** (tout) le long de; **to go** *or* **walk a.** (*street*) passer par; **a. with** avec. **2** *adv* **all a.** (*time*) dès le début.
along'side *prep & adv* à côté (de).
aloud [ə'laʊd] *adv* à haute voix.
alphabet ['ælfəbet] alphabet *m*.
alpha'betical *a* alphabétique.
Alps [ælps] *npl* **the A.** les Alpes *fpl*.
already [ɔːl'redɪ] *adv* déjà.
alright [ɔːl'raɪt] *adv Fam* = **all right.**
Alsatian [æl'seɪʃ(ə)n] (*dog*) berger *m* allemand.
also ['ɔːlsəʊ] *adv* aussi.
altar ['ɔːltər] autel *m*.
alter ['ɔːltər] **1** *vt* changer; (*clothing*) retoucher. **2** *vi* changer.
alte'ration changement *m*; (*of clothing*) retouche *f*.
alternate **1** *a* [ɔːl'tɜːnət] alterné; **on a. days** tous les deux jours. **2** *vi* ['ɔːltəneɪt] alterner (**with** avec).
alternative [ɔːl'tɜːnətɪv] **1** *a* (*other*) autre. **2** *n* alternative *f*.
alternatively *adv* comme alternative.
although [ɔːl'ðəʊ] *adv* bien que (+ *subjunctive*).
altogether [ɔːltə'geðər] *adv* (*completely*) tout à fait; (*on the whole*) somme toute; **how much a.?** combien en tout?
aluminium [ælju'mɪnjəm] (*Am* **aluminum** [ə'luːmɪnəm]) aluminium *m*.
always ['ɔːlweɪz] *adv* toujours.
am [æm, *unstressed* əm] *see* **be.**
a.m. [eɪ'em] *adv* du matin.
amateur ['æmətər] **1** *n* amateur *m*. **2** *a* **a. painter**/*etc* peintre/*etc* amateur.
amaze [ə'meɪz] *vt* étonner.

amazed *a* stupéfait (**at sth** de qch, **at seeing** de voir); (*filled with wonder*) émerveillé.
amazing *a* stupéfiant; (*incredible*) extraordinaire.
ambassador [æm'bæsədər] ambassadeur *m*; (*woman*) ambassadrice *f*.
amber ['æmbər] **a. (light)** (*of traffic signal*) (feu *m*) orange *m*.
ambition [æm'bɪʃ(ə)n] ambition *f*.
ambitious *a* ambitieux.
ambulance ['æmbjʊləns] ambulance *f*.
ambulance driver ambulancier *m*.
American [ə'merɪkən] *a* & *n* américain, -aine (*mf*).
ammunition [æmjʊ'nɪʃ(ə)n] munitions *fpl*.
among(st) [ə'mʌŋ(st)] *prep* parmi, entre; **a. the crowd/books** parmi la foule/les livres; **a. themselves/friends** entre eux/amis.
amount [ə'maʊnt] quantité *f*; (*sum of money*) somme *f*; (*total of bill etc*) montant *m*.
amount to s'élever à; (*mean*) signifier; (*represent*) représenter.
ample ['æmp(ə)l] *a* (*enough*) largement assez de; **you have a. time** tu as largement le temps.
amplifier ['æmplɪfaɪər] amplificateur *m*.
amputate ['æmpjʊteɪt] *vt* amputer.
amuse [ə'mjuːz] *vt* amuser.
amusement amusement *m*; **amusements** (*at fair etc*) machines *fpl* à sous.
amusement arcade salle *f* de jeux.
amusing *a* amusant.
an [æn, *unstressed* ən] *see* **a.**
analyse ['ænəlaɪz] *vt* analyser.
analysis, *pl* **-yses** [ə'næləsɪs, -ɪsiːz] analyse *f*.
anarchy ['ænəkɪ] anarchie *f*.
anatomy [ə'nætəmɪ] anatomie *f*.
ancestor ['ænsestər] ancêtre *m*.
anchor ['æŋkər] ancre *f*.
anchored *a* ancré.
anchovy ['æntʃəvɪ, *Am* æn'tʃəʊvɪ] anchois *m*.
ancient ['eɪnʃənt] *a* ancien; (*pre-medieval*) antique.
and [ænd, *unstressed* ən(d)] *conj* et; **two hundred a. two** deux cent deux; **better a. better** de mieux en mieux; **go a. see** va voir.
an(a)esthetic [ænɪs'θetɪk] anesthésie *f*; (*substance*) anesthésique *m*; **general a.** anesthésie générale.
angel ['eɪndʒəl] ange *m*.
anger ['æŋgər] colère *f*.

angle ['æŋg(ə)l] angle *m*; **at an a.** en biais.
angler pêcheur, -euse *mf* à la ligne.
angling pêche *f* à la ligne.
angrily *adv* (*to speak etc*) avec colère.
angry ['æŋgrɪ] *a* fâché; (*letter*) indigné; **to get a.** se fâcher (**with** contre).
animal ['ænɪməl] *n* & *a* animal (*m*).
ankle ['æŋk(ə)l] cheville *f*.
ankle sock socquette *f*.
annex(e) ['æneks] (*building*) annexe *f*.
anniversary [ænɪ'vɜːsərɪ] (*of event*) anniversaire *m*.
announce [ə'naʊns] *vt* annoncer; (*birth*, *marriage*) faire part de.
announcement (*statement*) annonce *f*; (*notice*) avis.
announcer (*on TV*) speaker *m*, speakerine *f*.
annoy [ə'nɔɪ] *vt* (*inconvenience*) ennuyer; (*irritate*) agacer.
annoyed *a* fâché; **to get a.** se fâcher (**with** contre).
annoying *a* ennuyeux.
annual ['ænjʊəl] **1** *a* annuel. **2** *n* (*book*) annuaire *m*.
annually *adv* annuellement.
anonymous [ə'nɒnɪməs] *a* anonyme.
anorak ['ænəræk] anorak *m*.
another [ə'nʌðər] *a* & *pron* un(e) autre; **a. man** un autre homme; **a. month** (*additional*) encore un mois; **a. ten** encore dix; **one a.** l'un(e) l'autre, *pl* les un(e)s les autres; **they love one a.** ils s'aiment (l'un l'autre).
answer ['ɑːnsər] **1** *n* réponse *f*; (*to problem*) solution (**to** de). **2** *vt* (*person*, *question*, *phone*) répondre à; (*prayer*, *wish*) exaucer; **to a. the bell** *or* **the door** ouvrir la porte. **3** *vi* répondre.
answer (s.o.) back répondre (à qn).
answer for s.o./sth répondre de qn/qch.
answering machine répondeur *m*.
ant [ænt] fourmi *f*.
antelope ['æntɪləʊp] antilope *f*.
antenna [æn'tenə] (*aerial*) *Am* antenne *f*.
anthem ['ænθəm] **national a.** hymne *m* national.
anthology [æn'θɒlədʒɪ] recueil *m*.
anti- ['æntɪ, *Am* 'æntaɪ] *prefix* anti-.
antibi'otic antibiotique *m*.
antibody anticorps *m*.
anticipate [æn'tɪsɪpeɪt] *vt* (*foresee*) prévoir; (*expect*) s'attendre à.
antici'pation in a. of en prévision de.
anti'clockwise *adv* dans le sens inverse des aiguilles d'une montre.

antics ['æntɪks] *npl* singeries *fpl.*
antifreeze antigel *m.*
anti'histamine antihistaminique *m.*
antique [æn'ti:k] **1** *a* (*furniture etc*) ancien. **2** *n* antiquité *f.*
antique dealer antiquaire *mf.*
antique shop magasin *m* d'antiquités.
anti'septic *a* & *n* antiseptique (*m*).
anxiety [æŋ'zaɪətɪ] (*worry*) inquiétude *f*; (*fear*) anxiété *f.*
anxious ['æŋkʃəs] *a* (*worried*) inquiet (**about** de, pour); (*afraid*) anxieux; (*eager*) impatient (**to do** de faire).
anxiously *adv* (*to wait*) impatiemment.
any ['enɪ] **1** *a* (*with question*) du, de la, des; **have you a. milk/tickets?** avez-vous du lait/des billets? ▮ (*negative*) de; **he hasn't got a. milk/tickets** il n'a pas de lait/de billets. ▮ (*no matter which*) n'importe quel. ▮ (*every*) tout; **in a. case, at a. rate** de toute façon. **2** *pron* (*no matter which one*) n'importe lequel; (*somebody*) quelqu'un; **if a. of you** si l'un d'entre vous. ▮ (*quantity*) en; **have you a.?** en as-tu? **3** *adv* (**not**) **a. happier**/*etc* (pas) plus heureux/*etc*; **I don't see him a. more** je ne le vois plus; **a. more tea?** encore du thé?; **a. better?** (un peu) mieux?
anybody *pron* (*somebody*) quelqu'un; **do you see a.?** vois-tu quelqu'un? ▮ (*negative*) personne; **he doesn't know a.** il ne connaît personne. ▮ (*no matter who*) n'importe qui.
anyhow *adv* (*at any rate*) de toute façon; (*badly*) n'importe comment.
anyone *pron* = **anybody.**
anyplace *adv Am* = **anywhere.**
anything *pron* (*something*) quelque chose. ▮ (*negative*) rien; **he doesn't do a.** il ne fait rien. ▮ (*everything*) tout; **a. you like** (tout) ce que tu veux. ▮ (*no matter what*) **a. (at all)** n'importe quoi.
anyway *adv* (*at any rate*) de toute façon.
anywhere *adv* (*no matter where*) n'importe où. ▮ (*everywhere*) partout; **a. you go** partout où vous allez; **a. you like** là où tu veux. ▮ (*somewhere*) quelque part. ▮ (*negative*) nulle part; **he doesn't go a.** il ne va nulle part.
apart [ə'pɑ:t] *adv* **we kept them a.** (*separate*) on les tenait séparés; **with legs a.** les jambes écartées; **they are a metre a.** ils se trouvent à un mètre l'un de l'autre; **a. from** (*except for*) à part.
apartment [ə'pɑ:tmənt] *Am* appartement *m.*
apartment house *Am* immeuble *m* (*d'habitation*).
ape [eɪp] singe *m.*
aperitif [ə'perəti:f] apéritif *m.*

apologetic [əpɒlə'dʒetɪk] *a* **to be a. (about)** s'excuser (de).
apologize *vi* s'excuser (**for** de); **to a. to s.o.** faire ses excuses à qn (**for** pour).
apology [ə'pɒlədʒɪ] excuses *fpl.*
apostrophe [ə'pɒstrəfɪ] apostrophe *f.*
appal [ə'pɔːl] (*Am* **appall**) *vt* consterner.
appalling *a* épouvantable.
apparatus [æpə'reɪtəs, *Am* -'rætəs] appareil *m*; (*in gym*) agrès *mpl.*
apparent [ə'pærənt] *a* apparent; **it's a. that** il est évident que.
apparently *adv* apparemment.
appeal[1] [ə'piːl] (*charm*) attrait *m*; (*interest*) intérêt *m.*
appeal[2] **1** *n* (*in court*) appel *m.* **2** *vi* faire appel.
appeal to s.o. (*attract*) plaire à qn; (*interest*) intéresser qn.
appear [ə'pɪər] *vi* (*become visible*) apparaître; (*present oneself*) se présenter; (*seem, be published*) paraître; (*in court*) comparaître; **it appears that** il semble que (+ *subjunctive or indicative*).
appearance *n* (*act*) apparition *f*; (*look*) apparence *f.*
appendicitis [əpendɪ'saɪtɪs] appendicite *f.*
appendix, *pl* **-ixes** *or* **-ices** [ə'pendɪks, -ɪksɪz, -ɪsiːz] (*in book, body*) appendice *m.*
appetite ['æpɪtaɪt] appétit *m.*
appetizing *a* appétissant.
applaud [ə'plɔːd] *vti* (*clap*) applaudir.
applause applaudissements *mpl.*
apple ['æp(ə)l] pomme *f*; **eating/cooking a.** pomme *f* à couteau/à cuire; **a. pie** tarte *f* aux pommes.
appliance [ə'plaɪəns] appareil *m.*
'applicant candidat, -ate *mf* (**for** à).
appli'cation (*for job*) candidature *f*; (*for membership*) demande *f* d'adhésion; **a. (form)** (*for job*) formulaire *m* de candidature.
apply [ə'plaɪ] **1** *vt* appliquer; (*brake*) appuyer sur; **to a. oneself to** s'appliquer à. **2** *vi* (*be relevant*) s'appliquer (**to** à).
apply for (*job*) poser sa candidature à.
appoint [ə'pɔɪnt] *vt* (*person*) nommer (**to sth** à qch, **to do** pour faire).
appointment nomination *f*; (*meeting*) rendez-vous *m inv.*
appreciate [ə'priːʃɪeɪt] *vt* (*enjoy, value*) apprécier; (*understand*) comprendre; (*be grateful for*) être reconnaissant de.
appreci'ation (*gratitude*) reconnaissance *f.*
apprentice [ə'prentɪs] apprenti, -ie *mf.*
apprenticeship *n* apprentissage *m.*
approach [ə'prəʊtʃ] **1** *vt* (*person, door etc*) s'approcher de; (*age,*

result, *town*) approcher de; (*subject*) aborder. **2** *vi* (*of person*, *vehicle*) s'approcher; (*of date*) approcher. **3** *n* (*method*) façon *f* de s'y prendre.
appropriate [ə'prəʊprɪət] *a* convenable.
appropriately *adv* convenablement.
approval approbation *f*; **on a.** (*goods*) à l'essai.
approve of [ə'pruːv] (*conduct etc*) approuver; **I don't a. of him** il ne me plaît pas; **I a. of his going** je trouve bon qu'il y aille.
approximate [ə'prɒksɪmət] *a* approximatif.
approximately *adv* à peu près.
apricot ['eɪprɪkɒt] abricot *m*.
April ['eɪprəl] avril *m*.
apron ['eɪprən] tablier *m*.
apt [æpt] *a* (*remark*, *reply*) juste, convenable; **to be a. to** avoir tendance à.
aptitude aptitude *f* (**for** à, pour).
aquarium [ə'kweərɪəm] aquarium *m*.
Arab ['ærəb] *a* & *n* arabe (*mf*).
Arabic *a* & *n* (*language*) arabe (*m*); **A. numerals** chiffres *mpl* arabes.
arc [ɑːk] (*of circle*) arc *m*.
arcade [ɑː'keɪd] (*market*) passage *m* couvert.
arch [ɑːtʃ] (*of bridge*) arche *f*; (*of building*) voûte *f*.
archer ['ɑːtʃər] archer *m*.
archery tir *m* à l'arc.
architect ['ɑːkɪtekt] architecte *mf*.
architecture architecture *f*.
Arctic ['ɑːktɪk] **the A.** l'Arctique *m*.
are [ɑːr] *see* **be**.
area ['eərɪə] (*in geometry*) superficie *f*; (*of country*) région *f*; (*of town*) quartier *m*; **parking a.** aire *f* de stationnement.
area code (*phone number*) *Am* indicatif *m*.
argue ['ɑːgjuː] **1** *vi* (*quarrel*) se disputer (**with** avec, **about** au sujet de); (*reason*) raisonner (**with** avec, **about** sur). **2** *vt* **to a. that** (*maintain*) soutenir que.
argument (*quarrel*) dispute *f*; (*reasoning*) argument *m*; **to have an a.** se disputer.
arise* [ə'raɪz] *vi* (*of problem*, *opportunity*) se présenter; (*result*) résulter (**from** de).
arithmetic [ə'rɪθmətɪk] arithmétique *f*.
arm [ɑːm] **1** *n* bras *m*; (*weapon*) arme *f*. **2** *vt* armer (**with** de).
armband brassard *m*; (*for swimming*) manchon *m*.

armchair fauteuil *m*.
armour ['ɑːmər] (*of knight*) armure *f*; (*of tank etc*) blindage *m*.
armoured *a* (*car etc*) blindé.
armpit aisselle *f*.
army ['ɑːmɪ] **1** *n* armée *f*. **2** *a* militaire.
around [ə'raʊnd] **1** *prep* autour de; (*approximately*) environ. **2** *adv* autour; **a. here** par ici; **he's still a.** il est encore là; **there's a lot of flu a.** il y a pas mal de grippes dans l'air; **up and a.** (*after illness*) *Am* sur pied.
arrange [ə'reɪndʒ] *vt* arranger; (*time, meeting*) fixer; **to a. to do** s'arranger pour faire.
arrangement (*layout, agreement*) arrangement *m*; **arrangements** préparatifs *mpl*; (*plans*) projets *mpl*.
arrears [ə'rɪəz] *npl* **in a.** en retard dans ses paiements.
arrest [ə'rest] **1** *vt* arrêter. **2** *n* arrestation *f*; **under a.** en état d'arrestation.
arrival arrivée *f*.
arrive [ə'raɪv] *vi* arriver.
arrow ['ærəʊ] flèche *f*.
art [ɑːt] art *m*; **work of a.** œuvre *f* d'art.
artery ['ɑːtərɪ] artère *f*.
arthritis [ɑː'θraɪtɪs] arthrite *f*.
article ['ɑːtɪk(ə)l] (*object, in newspaper, in grammar*) article *m*.
articulated lorry [ɑː'tɪkjʊleɪtɪd] semi-remorque *m*.
artificial [ɑːtɪ'fɪʃ(ə)l] *a* artificiel.
artist ['ɑːtɪst] (*actor, painter etc*) artiste *mf*.
ar'tistic *a* artistique; (*person*) artiste.
as [æz, *unstressed* əz] *adv & conj* (*manner etc*) comme; **as you like** comme tu veux; **as much** *or* **as hard as I can** (au)tant que je peux; **as it is** (*to leave sth*) comme ça, tel quel; **as if, as though** comme si. ■ (*comparison*) **as tall as you** aussi grand que vous; **as white as a sheet** blanc comme un linge; **as much** *or* **as hard as you** autant que vous; **twice as big as** deux fois plus grand que. ■ (*though*) (**as**) **clever as he is** si intelligent qu'il soit. ■ (*capacity*) **as a teacher** comme professeur; **to act as a father** agir en père. ■ (*reason*) puisque; **as it's late** puisqu'il est tard. ■ (*time*) **as I was leaving** comme je partais; **as he slept** pendant qu'il dormait; **as from, as of** (*time*) à partir de. ■ (*concerning*) **as for that** quant à cela. ■ (+ *infinitive*) **so as to** de manière à; **so stupid as to** assez bête pour.
asap [eɪeseɪ'piː] *abbr* (*as soon as possible*) le plus tôt possible.
ash [æʃ] cendre *f*.
ashamed [ə'ʃeɪmd] *a* **to be a.** avoir honte (**of** de).

ashcan *Am* poubelle *f*.
ashore [ə'ʃɔːr] *adv* **to go a.** débarquer.
ashtray cendrier *m*.
Asian ['eɪʃən] **1** *a* asiatique. **2** *n* Asiatique *mf*.
aside [ə'saɪd] *adv* de côté; **a. from** *Am* en dehors de.
ask [ɑːsk] **1** *vt* demander; (*a question*) poser; (*invite*) inviter; **to a. s.o. (for) sth** demander qch à qn; **to a. s.o. to do** demander à qn de faire. **2** *vi* demander; **to a. for sth/s.o.** demander qch/qn; **to a. about sth** se renseigner sur qch; **to a. after** *or* **about s.o.** demander des nouvelles de qn; **to a. s.o. about** interroger qn sur.
asleep [ə'sliːp] *a* **to be a.** dormir; **to fall a.** s'endormir.
asparagus [ə'spærəgəs] (*for cooking*) asperges *fpl*.
aspect ['æspekt] aspect *m*.
aspirin ['æsprɪn] aspirine *f*.
assault [ə'sɔːlt] **1** *n* (*crime*) agression *f*. **2** *vt* (*attack*) agresser.
assemble [ə'semb(ə)l] **1** *vt* assembler; (*people*) rassembler; (*machine*) monter. **2** *vi* se rassembler.
assembly (*meeting*) assemblée *f*; (*in school*) rassemblement *m*.
assess [ə'ses] *vt* (*estimate*) évaluer; (*decide amount of*) fixer le montant de.
asset ['æset] (*advantage*) atout *m*; **assets** (*of business*) biens *mpl*.
assign [ə'saɪn] *vt* (*give*) attribuer (**to** à).
assignment (*task*) mission *f*.
assist [ə'sɪst] *vti* aider (**in doing, to do** à faire).
assistance aide *f*; **to be of a. to s.o.** aider qn.
assistant **1** *n* assistant, -ante *mf*; (*in shop*) vendeur, -euse *mf*. **2** *a* adjoint.
associate **1** *vt* [ə'səʊʃɪeɪt] associer; **associated with sth/s.o.** associé à qch/avec qn. **2** *n* & *a* [ə'səʊʃɪət] associé, -ée (*mf*).
associ'ation association *f*.
assorted [ə'sɔːtɪd] *a* variés; (*foods*) assortis.
assortment assortiment *m*.
assume [ə'sjuːm] *vt* (*suppose*) présumer (**that** que); (*take on*) prendre; (*responsibility, role*) assumer.
assurance assurance *f*.
assure [ə'ʃʊər] *vt* assurer (**s.o. that** à qn que, **s.o. of** qn de).
asterisk ['æstərɪsk] astérisque *m*.
asthma ['æsmə] asthme *m*.
asth'matic *a* & *n* asthmatique (*mf*).
astonish [ə'stɒnɪʃ] *vt* étonner; **to be astonished** s'étonner (**at sth** de qch).
astonishing *a* étonnant.

astray [ə'streɪ] *adv* **to go a.** s'égarer.
astrology [ə'strɒlədʒɪ] astrologie *f.*
astronaut ['æstrənɔːt] astronaute *mf.*
astronomy [ə'strɒnəmɪ] astronomie *f.*
at [æt, *unstressed* ət] *prep* à; **at work** au travail; **at six (o'clock)** à six heures. ▮ chez, **at the doctor's** chez le médecin. ▮ en; **at sea** en mer. ▮ contre; **angry at** fâché contre. ▮ sur. **to shoot at** tirer sur. ▮ de. **to laugh at** rire de. ▮ (au)près de; **at the window** (au)près de la fenêtre. ▮ par; **to come in at the door** entrer par la porte; **six at a time** six par six.
athlete ['æθliːt] athlète *mf.*
ath'letic *a* athlétique.
ath'letics *npl* athlétisme *m.*
Atlantic [ət'læntɪk] **1** *a* atlantique. **2** *n* **the A.** l'Atlantique *m.*
atlas ['ætləs] atlas *m.*
atmosphere ['ætməsfɪər] atmosphère *f.*
atom ['ætəm] atome *m.*
a'tomic *a* (*bomb etc*) atomique.
attach [ə'tætʃ] *vt* attacher (**to** à), (*document*) joindre (**to** à); **attached to** (*fond of*) attaché à.
attaché case [ə'tæʃeɪ] attaché-case *m*, mallette *f.*
attachment (*tool*) accessoire *m.*
attack [ə'tæk] **1** *n* attaque *f.* **2** *vti* attaquer.
attacker agresseur *m.*
attempt [ə'tempt] **1** *n* tentative *f*; **to make an a. to** tenter de. **2** *vt* tenter; (*task*) entreprendre; **to a. to do** tenter de faire.
attend [ə'tend] **1** *vt* (*meeting etc*) assister à; (*course*) suivre; (*school, church*) aller à. **2** *vi* assister.
attendance présence *f* (**at** à); (**school**) **a.** scolarité *f.*
attendant employé, -ée *mf*, (*in filling station*) pompiste *mf*; (*in museum*) gardien, -ienne *mf.*
attend to (*take care of*) s'occuper de (*client, tâche*)
attention [ə'tenʃ(ə)n] attention *f*; **to pay a.** faire attention (**to** à).
attentive *a* attentif (**to** à).
attic ['ætɪk] grenier *m.*
attitude ['ætɪtjuːd] attitude *f.*
attorney [ə'tɜːnɪ] (*lawyer*) *Am* avocat *m.*
attract [ə'trækt] *vt* attirer.
attraction (*charm*) attrait *m.*
attractive *a* (*price, offer etc*) intéressant; (*girl*) belle; (*boy*) beau.
aubergine ['əʊbəʒiːn] aubergine *f.*
auction ['ɔːkʃən] vente *f* (aux enchères).

auction (off) vendre (aux enchères).
auctio'neer commissaire-priseur *m*.
audible ['ɔːdɪb(ə)l] *a* perceptible.
audience ['ɔːdɪəns] (*of speaker*, *musician*) auditoire *m*; (*in theatre*, *cinema*) spectateurs *mpl*; (*of radio broadcast*) auditeurs *mpl*; **TV a.** téléspectateurs *mpl*.
audio ['ɔːdɪəʊ] *a* audio *inv*.
audiotypist dactylo *f* au magnétophone.
audio-'visual *a* audio-visuel.
August ['ɔːgəst] août *m*.
aunt [ɑːnt] tante *f*.
auntie *or* **aunty** *Fam* tata *f*.
au pair [əʊ'peər] **1** *adv* au pair. **2** *n* **au p. (girl)** jeune fille *f* au pair.
Australian [ɒ'streɪlɪən] *a* & *n* australien, -ienne (*mf*).
Austrian ['ɒstrɪən] *a* & *n* autrichien, -ienne (*mf*).
author ['ɔːθər] auteur *m*.
authority [ɔː'θɒrɪtɪ] autorité *f*; (*permission*) autorisation *f* (**to do** de faire).
authorize ['ɔːθəraɪz] *vt* autoriser (**to do** à faire).
autobiography [ɔːtəʊbaɪ'ɒgrəfɪ] autobiographie *f*.
autograph ['ɔːtəgrɑːf] **1** *n* autographe *m*. **2** *vt* dédicacer (**for** à).
automatic [ɔːtə'mætɪk] *a* automatique.
automatically *adv* automatiquement.
automobile ['ɔːtəməbiːl] *Am* auto(mobile) *f*.
autumn ['ɔːtəm] automne *m*.
auxiliary [ɔːg'zɪljərɪ] *a* & *n* **a. (verb)** (verbe *m*) auxiliaire *m*.
available [ə'veɪləb(ə)l] *a* disponible; **a. to all** accessible à tous.
avalanche ['ævəlɑːnʃ] avalanche *f*.
avenue ['ævənjuː] avenue *f*.
average ['ævərɪdʒ] **1** *n* moyenne *f*; **on a.** en moyenne. **2** *a* moyen.
aviation [eɪvɪ'eɪʃ(ə)n] aviation *f*.
avocado [ævə'kɑːdəʊ] (*pl* **-os**) **a. (pear)** avocat *m*.
avoid [ə'vɔɪd] *vt* éviter; **to a. doing** éviter de faire.
awake [ə'weɪk] **1** *vi** se réveiller. **2** *a* éveillé; **to keep s.o. a.** empêcher qn de dormir; **he's (still) a.** il ne dort pas (encore).
award [ə'wɔːd] **1** *vt* (*money*, *prize*) attribuer. **2** *n* (*prize*) prix *m*; (*scholarship*) bourse *f*.
aware [ə'weər] *a* **a. of** (*conscious*) conscient de; (*informed*) au courant de; **to become a. of** prendre conscience de.
away [ə'weɪ] *adv* (*distant*) loin; **far a.** au loin; **5 km a.** à 5 km (de distance); **to play a.** (*of team*) jouer à l'extérieur. ▮ (*in time*) **ten**

days a. dans dix jours. ▮ (*absent*) parti. ▮ (*continuously*) **to work/talk/***etc* **a.** travailler/parler/*etc* sans relâche.

awful ['ɔːfəl] *a* affreux; (*terrifying*) épouvantable; (*ill*) malade; **an a. lot of** *Fam* un nombre incroyable de.

awfully *adv* (*very*) *Fam* affreusement.

awkward ['ɔːkwəd] *a* (*clumsy*) maladroit; (*difficult*) difficile; (*tool*) peu commode; (*time*) inopportun.

awning ['ɔːnɪŋ] (*over shop*) store *m*.

axe [æks] (*Am* **ax**) **1** *n* hache *f*. **2** *vt* (*job etc*) supprimer.

axle ['æks(ə)l] essieu *m*.

B

BA *abbr* = **Bachelor of Arts**.
baby ['beɪbɪ] bébé *m*; **b. boy** petit garçon *m*; **b. girl** petite fille *f*.
baby carriage *Am* landau *m* (*pl* -aus).
baby clothes vêtements *mpl* de bébé.
baby-minder gardien, -ienne *mf* d'enfants.
baby-sit *vi* garder les enfants.
baby-sitter baby-sitter *mf*.
bachelor ['bætʃələr] célibataire *m*; **B. of Arts/of Science** licencié, -ée *mf* ès lettres/ès sciences.
back¹ [bæk] **1** *n* dos *m*; (*of chair*) dossier *m*; (*of hand*) revers *m*; (*of house*) derrière *m*, arrière *m*; (*of room*) fond *m*; (*of vehicle*) arrière *m*; (*of page*) verso *m*; **at the b. of the book** à la fin du livre; **b. to front** devant derrière; **in b. of** *Am* derrière. **2** *a* arrière *inv*, de derrière; **b. door** porte *f* de derrière; **b. number** vieux numéro *m*; **b. tooth** molaire *f*. **3** *adv* (*behind*) en arrière; **to come b.** revenir; **he's b.** il est de retour, il est revenu.
back² *vt* (*with money*) financer; (*horse etc*) parier sur.
back s.o. (up) (*support*) appuyer qn.
backache mal *m* aux reins.
back'fire *vi* (*of vehicle*) pétarader.
background fond *m*; (*events*) antécédents *mpl*; (*education*) formation *f*; (*environment*) milieu *m*; **b. music** musique *f* de fond.
backing (*aid*) soutien *m*; (*material*) support *m*.
backlog (*of work*) arriéré *m*.
back out (*withdraw*) se retirer.
back'side (*buttocks*) *Fam* derrière *m*.
back'stage *adv* dans les coulisses.
backward ['bækwəd] *a* (*retarded*) arriéré; (*glance*) en arrière.
backwards *adv* en arrière; (*to walk*) à reculons.
back'yard *Am* jardin *m*.
bacon ['beɪkən] lard *m*.
bad [bæd] *a* mauvais; (*wicked*) méchant; (*accident*, *wound*) grave; (*arm*, *leg*) malade; (*pain*) violent; **to feel b.** (*ill*) se sentir mal; **things are b.** ça va mal; **not b.!** pas mal!
badge [bædʒ] insigne *m*; (*of postman etc*) plaque *f*; (*bearing slogan*) badge *m*.
badger ['bædʒər] blaireau *m*.
badly *adv* mal; (*hurt*) grièvement; **b. affected** très touché; **to want b.** avoir grande envie de.
bad-'mannered *a* mal élevé.

badminton ['bædmɪntən] badminton *m*.
bad-'tempered *a* grincheux.
baffle ['bæf(ə)l] *vt* déconcerter.
bag [bæg] sac *m*; **bags** (*luggage*) valises *fpl*; (*under eyes*) poches *fpl*; **bags of** *Fam* beaucoup de.
baggage ['bægɪdʒ] bagages *mpl*.
baggage room *Am* consigne *f*.
baggy ['bægɪ] *a* (*trousers*) faisant des poches.
bagpipes *npl* cornemuse *f*.
bail [beɪl] (*in court*) caution *f*; **on b.** en liberté provisoire.
bait [beɪt] amorce *f*, appât *m*.
bake [beɪk] **1** *vt* (faire) cuire (au four). **2** *vi* (*of cook*) faire de la pâtisserie *or* du pain; (*of cake etc*) cuire (au four).
baked [beɪkt] *a* (*potatoes*) au four.
baked beans haricots *mpl* blancs (à la tomate).
baker boulanger, -ère *mf*.
bakery boulangerie *f*.
balance ['bæləns] **1** *n* équilibre *m*; (*of account*) solde *m*; (*remainder*) reste *m*; **to lose one's b.** perdre l'équilibre. **2** *vt* tenir en équilibre (**on** sur); (*account*) équilibrer. **3** *vi* (*of person*) se tenir en équilibre; (*of accounts*) être en équilibre.
balance sheet bilan *m*.
balcony ['bælkənɪ] balcon *m*.
bald [bɔːld] *a* chauve.
bald-'headed *a* chauve.
baldness calvitie *f*.
ball[1] [bɔːl] *n* balle *f*; (*inflated*) (*for sports*) ballon *m*; (*of string*, *wool*) pelote *f*; (*any round shape*) boule *f*; (*of meat or fish*) boulette *f*; **on the b.** *Fam* (*alert*) éveillé; (*efficient*) au point.
ball[2] (*dance*) bal *m* (*pl* bals).
ballerina [bælə'riːnə] ballerine *f*.
ballet ['bæleɪ] ballet *m*.
balloon [bə'luːn] ballon *m*.
ballot ['bælət] (*voting*) scrutin *m*.
ballpoint stylo *m* à bille.
ballroom salle *f* de danse.
ban [bæn] **1** *n* interdiction *f*. **2** *vt* interdire (**s.o. from doing** à qn de faire); (*exclude*) exclure (**from** de).
banana [bə'nɑːnə] banane *f*.
band [bænd] (*strip*) bande *f*; (*musicians*) (petit) orchestre *m*; (*pop group*) groupe *m*; **rubber** *or* **elastic b.** élastique *m*.
bandage ['bændɪdʒ] bande *f*.

bandage (up) (*arm, wound*) bander.
Band-Aid® ['bændeɪd] pansement *m* adhésif.
bang [bæŋ] **1** *n* coup *m* (violent); (*of door*) claquement *m*. **2** *vt* cogner; (*door*) (faire) claquer. **3** *vi* cogner; (*of door*) claquer.
bang down (*lid*) rabattre (violemment).
banger old b. (*car*) *Fam* tacot *m*.
bang into sth/s.o. heurter qch/qn.
bangle ['bæŋg(ə)l] bracelet *m* (rigide).
bangs [bæŋz] *npl* (*of hair*) *Am* frange *f*.
banister(s) ['bænɪstə(z)] *n(pl)* rampe *f* (d'escalier).
bank [bæŋk] (*of river*) bord *m*; (*for money*) banque *f*.
bank account compte *m* en banque.
bank card carte *f* d'identité bancaire.
banker banquier *m*.
bank holiday jour *m* férié.
banking (*activity*) la banque.
banknote billet *m* de banque.
bank on s.o./sth compter sur qn/qch.
bankrupt ['bæŋkrʌpt] *a* **to go b.** faire faillite.
bankruptcy faillite *f*.
banner ['bænər] (*at rallies, on two poles*) banderole *f*.
bar [bɑːr] **1** *n* barre *f*; (*of gold*) lingot *m*; (*of chocolate*) tablette *f*; (*on window*) barreau *m*; (*pub, counter*) bar *m*. **2** *vt* (*way*) bloquer; (*prohibit*) interdire (**s.o. from doing** à qn de faire); (*exclude*) exclure (**from** de).
barbecue ['bɑːbɪkjuː] barbecue *m*.
barbed [bɑːbd] *a* **b. wire** fil *m* de fer barbelé.
barber ['bɑːbər] coiffeur *m*.
bare [beər] *a* nu; (*tree*) dénudé; **with his b. hands** à mains nues.
barefoot *adv* nu-pieds.
barely ['beəlɪ] *adv* (*scarcely*) à peine.
bargain ['bɑːgɪn] **1** *n* (*deal*) marché *m*; **a b.** (*cheap buy*) une occasion; **b. price** prix *m* exceptionnel. **2** *vi* négocier.
bargain for sth (*expect*) s'attendre à qch.
barge [bɑːdʒ] chaland *m*.
barge in (*enter a room*) faire irruption; (*interrupt s.o.*) interrompre.
bark [bɑːk] **1** *n* (*of tree*) écorce *f*. **2** *vi* (*of dog*) aboyer.
barking aboiements *mpl*.
barley ['bɑːlɪ] orge *f*.
barmaid serveuse *f* de bar.
barman barman *m*.
barmy ['bɑːmɪ] *a Fam* dingue.

barn [bɑːn] (*for crops*) grange *f*.
barometer [bə'rɒmɪtər] baromètre *m*.
barracks ['bærəks] *npl* caserne *f*.
barrage ['bærɑːʒ, *Am* bə'rɑːʒ] (*barrier*) barrage *m*.
barrel ['bærəl] (*cask*) tonneau *m*; (*of oil*) baril *m*; (*of gun*) canon *m*.
barren ['bærən] *a* stérile.
barrette [bə'ret] (*hair slide*) *Am* barrette *f*.
barricade ['bærɪkeɪd] **1** *n* barricade *f*. **2** *vt* barricader.
barrier ['bærɪər] barrière *f*; **(ticket) b.** portillon *m*.
barrister ['bærɪstər] avocat *m*.
bartender *Am* barman *m*.
base [beɪs] **1** *n* base *f*; (*of tree*, *lamp*) pied *m*. **2** *vt* baser.
baseball base-ball *m*.
baseboard *Am* plinthe *f*.
basement ['beɪsmənt] sous-sol *m*.
bash [bæʃ] **1** *n* (*bang*) coup *m*; **to have a b.** (*try*) essayer un coup. **2** *vt* (*hit*) cogner.
bash s.o. up tabasser qn.
basic ['beɪsɪk] **1** *a* essentiel, de base; (*elementary*) élémentaire; (*pay*) de base. **2** *n* **the basics** l'essentiel *m*.
basically *adv* au fond.
basin ['beɪs(ə)n] bassin *m*; (*sink*) lavabo *m*.
basis ['beɪsɪs] (*of agreement etc*) bases *fpl*; **on the b. of** d'après; **on that b.** dans ces conditions; **on a weekly b.** chaque semaine.
bask [bɑːsk] *vi* se chauffer.
basket ['bɑːskɪt] panier *m*; (*for bread*, *laundry*, *litter*) corbeille *f*.
bat [bæt] **1** *n* (*animal*) chauve-souris *f*; *Cricket* batte *f*; *Table Tennis* raquette *f*; **off my own b.** de ma propre initiative. **2** *vt* **she didn't b. an eyelid** elle n'a pas sourcillé.
batch [bætʃ] (*of people*) groupe *m*; (*of letters*) paquet *m*; (*of papers*) liasse *f*.
bath [bɑːθ] **1** *n* bain *m*; (*tub*) baignoire *f*; **to have** *or* **take a b.** prendre un bain. **2** *vt* baigner.
bathe [beɪð] **1** *vt* baigner. **2** *vi* se baigner; *Am* prendre un bain. **3** *n* bain *m* (de mer).
bathing costume *or* **suit** maillot *m* de bain.
bathrobe *Am* robe *f* de chambre.
bathroom salle *f* de bain(s); (*toilet*) *Am* toilettes *fpl*.
bathtub baignoire *f*.
batter ['bætər] **1** *n* pâte *f* à frire. **2** *vt* (*baby*) martyriser.
batter down (*door*) défoncer.
battered *a* (*car*) cabossé.

battery ['bætərɪ] batterie *f*; (*in radio, appliance*) pile *f*.
battle ['bæt(ə)l] **1** *n* bataille *f*; (*struggle*) lutte *f*. **2** *vi* se battre.
battleship cuirassé *m*.
bawl (out) [bɔːl] *vti* beugler; **to b. s.o. out** *Am Slang* engueuler qn.
bay [beɪ] (*part of coastline*) baie *f*; (*for loading*) aire *f*.
BC [biː'siː] *abbr* (*before Christ*) avant Jésus-Christ.
be* [biː] *vi* être; **she's a doctor** elle est médecin; **it's 3 (o'clock)** il est trois heures. ▮ avoir; **to be hot/right/lucky** avoir chaud/raison/de la chance; **he's 20** il a 20 ans; **to be 2 metres high** avoir 2 mètres de haut. ▮ (*health*) aller; **how are you?** comment vas-tu? ▮ (*go, come*) **I've been to see her** je suis allé *or* j'ai été la voir; **he's (already) been** il est (déjà) venu. ▮ (*weather, calculations*) faire; **it's fine** il fait beau; **2 and 2 are 4** 2 et 2 font 4. ▮ (*cost*) faire; **how much is it?** ça fait combien? ▮ (*auxiliary*) **I am/was doing** je fais/faisais; **he was killed** il a été tué; **I've been waiting (for) two hours** j'attends depuis deux heures; **isn't it?, aren't you?** *etc* n'est-ce pas?, non? ▮ (+ *infinitive*) **he is to come** (*must*) il doit venir. ▮ **there is** *or* **are** il y a; (*pointing*) voilà; **here is** *or* **are** voici.
beach [biːtʃ] plage *f*.
beacon ['biːkən] balise *f*.
bead [biːd] perle *f*; (*of sweat*) goutte *f*; **(string of) beads** collier *m*.
beak [biːk] bec *m*.
beaker ['biːkər] gobelet *m*.
beam [biːm] (*of wood*) poutre *f*; (*of light*) rayon *m*; (*of headlight*) faisceau *m*.
beaming *a* (*radiant*) radieux.
bean [biːn] haricot *m*; (*of coffee*) grain *m*; **(broad) b.** fève *f*.
beanshoots *npl* germes *mpl* de soja.
bear[1] [beər] (*animal*) ours *m*.
bear[2]* **1** *vt* (*carry, show*) porter; (*endure*) supporter; (*responsibility*) assumer; **to b. in mind** tenir compte de. **2** *vi* **to b. left/right** tourner à gauche/droite.
bearable *a* supportable.
beard [bɪəd] barbe *f*.
bearded *a* barbu.
bearing (*relevance*) relation *f* (**on** avec); **to get one's bearings** s'orienter.
bear sth out corroborer qch.
beast [biːst] bête *f*; (*person*) brute *f*.
beastly *a Fam* (*bad*) vilain.
beat [biːt] **1** *n* (*of heart, drum*) battement *m*; (*of policeman*) ronde *f*. **2** *vt** battre.

beat down 1 *vt* (*door*) défoncer. **2** *vi* (*of rain*) tomber à verse; (*of sun*) taper.
beating (*blows*, *defeat*) raclée *f*.
beat s.o. off repousser qn.
beat s.o. up tabasser qn.
beautiful *a* (très) beau (*f* belle).
beauty ['bjuːtɪ] (*quality*, *woman*) beauté *f*.
beauty spot (*on skin*) grain *m* de beauté; (*in countryside*) endroit *m* pittoresque.
beaver ['biːvər] castor *m*.
because [bɪ'kɒz] *conj* parce que; **b. of** à cause de.
become* [bɪ'kʌm] *vi* devenir; **to b. a painter** devenir peintre; **what has b. of her?** qu'est-elle devenue?
bed [bed] lit *m*; **to go to b.** (aller) se coucher; **in b.** couché; **to get out of b.** se lever; **b. and breakfast** chambre *f* avec petit déjeuner.
bedclothes *npl* couvertures *fpl* et draps *mpl*.
bedroom chambre *f* à coucher.
bedside chevet *m*; **b. lamp/book** lampe *f*/livre *m* de chevet.
bed'sitter chambre *f* meublée.
bedtime heure *f* du coucher.
bee [biː] abeille *f*.
beech [biːtʃ] (*tree*, *wood*) hêtre *m*.
beef [biːf] bœuf *m*.
beefburger hamburger *m*.
beehive ruche *f*.
been [biːn] *pp de* **be**.
beer [bɪər] bière *f*; **b. glass** chope *f*.
beet [biːt] *Am* = **beetroot.**
beetle ['biːt(ə)l] scarabée *m*; (*any beetle shaped insect*) bestiole *f*.
beetroot betterave *f* (potagère).
before [bɪ'fɔːr] **1** *adv* avant; (*already*) déjà; (*in front*) devant; **the day b.** la veille. **2** *prep* (*time*) avant; (*place*) devant; **the year b. last** il y a deux ans. **3** *conj* avant que (+ *ne* + *subjunctive*), avant de (+ *infinitive*), **b. he goes** avant qu'il (ne) parte; **b. going** avant de partir.
beg [beg] **1** *vt* **to b. (for)** solliciter; (*bread*, *money*) mendier; **to b. s.o. to do** supplier qn de faire. **2** *vi* mendier.
beggar mendiant, -ante *mf*.
begin* [bɪ'gɪn] **1** *vt* commencer; (*campaign*) lancer; **to b. doing** *or* **to do** commencer *or* se mettre à faire. **2** *vi* commencer (**with** par, **by doing** par faire); **to b. with** (*first*) d'abord.
beginner débutant, -ante *mf*.

beginning commencement *m*, début *m*.
begrudge [bɪ'grʌdʒ] *vt* (*envy*) envier (**s.o. sth** qch à qn); **to b. doing sth** faire qch à contrecœur.
behalf [bɪ'hɑːf] *n* **on b. of** pour.
behave [bɪ'heɪv] *vi* se conduire; (*of machine*) fonctionner; **to b. (oneself)** se tenir bien; (*of child*) être sage.
behaviour conduite *f*.
behind [bɪ'haɪnd] **1** *prep* derrière; (*in making progress*) en retard sur. **2** *adv* derrière; (*late*) en retard. **3** *n* (*buttocks*) *Fam* derrière *m*.
beige [beɪʒ] *a* & *n* beige (*m*).
belch **1** *vi* faire un renvoi. **2** *n* renvoi *m*.
Belgian ['beldʒən] *a* & *n* belge (*mf*).
belief [bɪ'liːf] croyance *f* (**in** en); (*trust*) confiance *f*, foi *f*; (*opinion*) opinion *f*.
believable *a* croyable.
believe [bɪ'liːv] *vti* croire (**in sth** à qch, **in God** en Dieu); **I b. so** je crois que oui; **to b. in doing** croire qu'il faut faire.
believer (*religious*) croyant, -ante *mf*.
belittle [bɪ'lɪt(ə)l] *vt* dénigrer.
bell [bel] cloche *f*; (*small*) clochette *f*; (*in phone*) sonnerie *f*; (*on door*, *bicycle*) sonnette *f*.
bellboy *Am* groom *m*.
belly ['belɪ] ventre *m*; **b. button** *Fam* nombril *m*.
bellyache mal *m* au ventre.
belong [bɪ'lɒŋ] *vi* appartenir (**to** à); **to b. to** (*club*) être membre de.
belongings *npl* affaires *fpl*.
below [bɪ'ləʊ] **1** *prep* au-dessous de. **2** *adv* en dessous.
belt [belt] ceinture *f*; (*in machine*) courroie *f*.
belt (along) (*rush*) *Fam* filer à toute allure.
bench [bentʃ] (*seat*) banc *m*; (*work table*) établi *m*.
bend [bend] **1** *n* courbe *f*; (*in river*) coude *m*; (*in road*) virage *m*; (*of arm*, *knee*) pli *m*. **2** *vt** courber; (*leg*, *arm*) plier. **3** *vi* (*of branch*) plier; (*of road*) tourner.
bend (down) (*stoop*) se courber.
bend (over) (*lean forward*) se pencher.
beneath [bɪ'niːθ] **1** *prep* au-dessous de. **2** *adv* (au-)dessous.
beneficial [benɪ'fɪʃəl] *a* bénéfique.
benefit ['benɪfɪt] **1** *n* avantage *m*; (*money*) allocation *f*; **child b.** allocations familiales; **for your (own) b.** pour vous. **2** *vt* faire du bien à; (*be useful to*) profiter à. **3** *vi* **you'll b. from it** ça vous fera du bien.

bent *a* (*nail*) tordu; **b. on doing** résolu à faire.
bereavement [bɪ'riːvmənt] deuil *m*.
berk [bɜːk] *Slang* imbécile *mf*.
berry ['berɪ] baie *f*.
berserk [bə'zɜːk] *a* **to go b.** devenir fou.
berth [bɜːθ] (*in ship, train*) couchette *f*.
beside [bɪ'saɪd] *prep* à côté de; **that's b. the point** ça n'a rien à voir.
besides [bɪ'saɪdz] **1** *prep* en plus de; (*except*) excepté. **2** *adv* de plus; (*moreover*) d'ailleurs.
best [best] **1** *a* meilleur (**in** de); **the b. part of** (*most*) la plus grande partie de. **2** *n* **the b.** (**one**) le meilleur, la meilleure; **at b.** au mieux; **to do one's b.** faire de son mieux; **to make the b. of** s'accommoder de. **3** *adv* (**the**) **b.** (*to play, sing etc*) le mieux; **the b. loved** le plus aimé.
best man (*at wedding*) témoin *m*.
best-'seller best-seller *m*.
bet [bet] **1** *n* pari *m*. **2** *vti** parier (**on** sur, **that** que).
betray [bɪ'treɪ] *vt* trahir.
betrayal trahison *f*.
better ['betər] **1** *a* meilleur (**than** que); **she's (much) b.** (*in health*) elle va (bien) mieux; **that's b.** c'est mieux; **to get b.** (*recover*) se remettre; (*improve*) s'améliorer; **it's b. to go** il vaut mieux partir. **2** *adv* mieux; **I had b. go** il vaut mieux que je parte. **3** *vt* **to b. oneself** améliorer sa condition.
betting pari(s) *m(pl)*.
betting shop *or* **office** bureau *m* du pari mutuel.
between [bɪ'twiːn] **1** *prep* entre; **in b. sth and sth/two things** entre qch et qch/deux choses. **2** *adv* **in b.** au milieu; (*time*) dans l'intervalle.
beware [bɪ'weər] *vi* **to b. of** se méfier de; **b.!** méfiez-vous!
bewilder [bɪ'wɪldər] *vt* dérouter.
beyond [bɪ'jɒnd] **1** *prep* au-delà de; (*reach, doubt*) hors de; **b. my means** au-dessus de mes moyens; **it's b. me** ça me dépasse. **2** *adv* au-delà.
bias ['baɪəs] penchant *m* (**towards** pour); (*prejudice*) préjugé *m*.
bias(s)ed *a* partial; **to be b. against** avoir des préjugés contre.
bib [bɪb] (*baby's*) bavoir *m*.
bible ['baɪb(ə)l] bible *f*; **the B.** la Bible.
bicycle ['baɪsɪk(ə)l] bicyclette *f*.
bid* **1** *vt* (*money*) offrir. **2** *vi* faire une offre (**for** pour). **3** *n* (*at auction*) offre *f*; (*for doing a job*) soumission *f*.
big [bɪg] *a* grand, gros (*f* grosse); (*in age, generous*) grand; (*in bulk*,

amount) gros; **b. deal!** *Fam* (bon) et alors!
bighead *Fam* (*conceited*) prétentieux, -euse *mf*; (*boasting*) vantard, -arde *mf*.
bigshot *Fam* gros bonnet *m*.
bike [baɪk] *Fam* vélo *m*.
bikini [bɪ'kiːnɪ] deux-pièces *m inv*; **b. briefs** mini-slip *m*.
bile bile *f*.
bilingual [baɪ'lɪŋgwəl] *a* bilingue.
bill [bɪl] **1** *n* (*invoice*) facture *f*, note *f*; (*in restaurant*) addition *f*; (*in hotel*) note *f*; (*banknote*) *Am* billet *m*; (*proposed law*) projet *m* de loi. **2** *vt* **to b. s.o.** envoyer la facture à qn.
billboard panneau *m* d'affichage.
billfold *Am* portefeuille *m*.
billiards *npl* (jeu *m* de) billard *m*.
billion ['bɪljən] milliard *m*.
bin [bɪn] boîte *f*; (*for litter*) poubelle *f*.
bind [baɪnd] **1** *vt** lier; (*book*) relier. **2** *n* (*bore*) *Fam* plaie *f*.
binder (*for papers*) classeur *m*.
binding (*of book*) reliure *f*.
bingo ['bɪŋgəʊ] loto *m*.
binoculars [bɪ'nɒkjʊləz] *npl* jumelles *fpl*.
bio'logical *a* biologique.
biology [baɪ'ɒlədʒɪ] biologie *f*.
birch [bɜːtʃ] **(silver) b.** (*tree*) bouleau *m*.
bird [bɜːd] oiseau *m*; (*fowl*) volaille *f*; **b.'s-eye view** vue d'ensemble.
biro® ['baɪərəʊ] (*pl* **-os**) bic® *m*.
birth [bɜːθ] naissance *f*; **to give b. to** donner naissance à.
birth certificate acte *m* de naissance.
birthday anniversaire *m*; **happy b.!** bon anniversaire!
biscuit ['bɪskɪt] biscuit *m*; *Am* petit pain *m* au lait.
bishop ['bɪʃəp] évêque *m*.
bit [bɪt] morceau *m*; **a b.** (*a little*) un peu; **quite a b.** (*very*) très; (*a lot*) beaucoup; **not a b.** pas du tout; **b. by b.** petit à petit.
bite [baɪt] **1** *n* (*wound*) morsure *f*; (*from insect*) piqûre *f*; **a b. to eat** un morceau à manger. **2** *vti** mordre; **to b. one's nails** se ronger les ongles.
bitter ['bɪtər] **1** *a* amer; (*cold*, *wind*) glacial; (*conflict*) violent. **2** *n* bière *f* (pression).
bitterness amertume *f*; (*of conflict*) violence *f*.
bizarre [bɪ'zɑːr] *a* bizarre.
black [blæk] **1** *a* noir; **b. eye** œil *m* poché; **to give s.o. a b. eye**

pocher l'œil à qn; **b. and blue** (*bruised*) couvert de bleus. **2** *n* (*colour*) noir *m*; (*person*) Noir, -e *mf*.
blackberry ['blækbərɪ, *Am* -berɪ] mûre *f*.
blackbird merle *m*.
blackboard tableau *m* (noir); **on the b.** au tableau.
black'currant cassis *m*.
blacklist 1 *n* liste *f* noire. **2** *vt* mettre sur la liste noire.
blackmail 1 *n* chantage *m*. **2** *vt* faire chanter.
blackmailer maître chanteur *m*.
black out (*faint*) s'évanouir.
blackout panne *f* d'électricité; (*fainting fit*) syncope *f*.
bladder ['blædər] vessie *f*.
blade lame *f*; (*of grass*) brin *m*.
blame [bleɪm] **1** *vt* accuser; **to b. s.o. for sth** reprocher qch à qn; **you're to b.** c'est ta faute. **2** *n* faute *f*.
blameless *a* irréprochable.
bland [blænd] *a* (*food*) fade.
blank [blæŋk] **1** *a* (*paper, page*) blanc (*f* blanche); (*cheque*, *Am check*) en blanc. **2** *a* & *n* **b. (space)** blanc *m*.
blanket ['blæŋkɪt] couverture *f*.
blare (out) [bleər] (*of radio*) beugler; (*of music*) retentir.
blast [blɑːst] **1** *n* explosion *f*; (*air from explosion*) souffle *m*. **2** *int Fam* zut!
blasted *a Fam* fichu.
blast-off (*of spacecraft*) mise *f* à feu.
blaze [bleɪz] **1** *n* (*fire*) flamme *f*; (*large*) incendie *m*. **2** *vi* (*of fire*) flamber; (*of sun*) flamboyer.
blazer ['bleɪzər] blazer *m*.
blazing *a* en feu; (*sun*) brûlant.
bleach [bliːtʃ] (*household*) eau *f* de Javel.
bleak [bliːk] *a* morne.
bleed* [bliːd] *vti* saigner.
bleep [bliːp] **1** *n* bip *m*. **2** *vt* appeler au bip(-bip).
bleeper bip(-bip) *m*.
blemish ['blemɪʃ] défaut *m*; (*on reputation*) tache *f*.
blend [blend] **1** *n* mélange *m*. **2** *vt* mélanger. **3** *vi* se mélanger.
blender (*for food*) mixer *m*.
bless [bles] *vt* bénir; **b. you!** (*sneezing*) à vos souhaits!
blessing bénédiction *f*; (*benefit*) bienfait *m*.
blew [bluː] *pt de* **blow**[1].
blind [blaɪnd] **1** *a* aveugle; **b. person** aveugle *mf*. **2** *n* (*on window*) store *m*; **the b.** les aveugles *mpl*.

blindfold 1 *n* bandeau *m*. **2** *vt* bander les yeux à.
blindly *adv* aveuglément.
blindness cécité *f*.
blink [blɪŋk] **1** *vi* (*of person*) cligner des yeux; (*of eyes*) cligner. **2** *n* clignement *m*.
bliss [blɪs] félicité *f*.
blister ['blɪstər] (*on skin*) ampoule *f*.
blizzard ['blɪzəd] tempête *f* de neige.
bloat [bləʊt] *vt* gonfler.
blob [blɒb] goutte *f*; (*of ink*) tache *f*.
block [blɒk] **1** *n* (*of stone*) bloc *m*; (*of buildings*) pâté *m* (de maisons); **b. of flats** immeuble *m*. **2** *vt* (*obstruct*) bloquer.
blockage obstruction *f*.
block off (*road*) barrer.
block up (*pipe*, *hole*) bloquer.
bloke [bləʊk] *Fam* type *m*.
blond [blɒnd] *a* & *n* blond (*m*).
blonde *a* & *n* blonde (*f*).
blood [blʌd] sang *m*; **b. donor** donneur, -euse *mf* de sang; **b. group** groupe *m* sanguin; **b. pressure** tension *f* (artérielle); **to have high b. pressure** avoir de la tension.
bloodshed effusion *f* de sang.
bloodshot *a* (*eye*) injecté de sang.
bloody ['blʌdɪ] **1** *a* sanglant; (*awful*) *Fam* sacré. **2** *adv Fam* (*very*, *completely*) vachement.
bloom [blu:m] **1** *n* fleur *f*; **in b.** en fleur(s). **2** *vi* fleurir.
blossom ['blɒsəm] **1** *n* fleur(s) *f*(*pl*). **2** *vi* fleurir.
blot [blɒt] tache *f*.
blotchy ['blɒtʃɪ] *a* couvert de taches.
blotting paper buvard *m*.
blouse [blaʊz, *Am* blaʊs] chemisier *m*.
blow[1]* [bləʊ] **1** *vt* (*of wind*) pousser (*un navire*), chasser (*la pluie*); (*of person*) (*smoke*) souffler; (*bubbles*) faire; (*trumpet*) souffler dans; **to b. one's nose** se moucher; **to b. a whistle** siffler. **2** *vi* (*of wind*, *person*) souffler.
blow[2] (*with fist*, *tool etc*) coup *m*.
blow away 1 *vt* (*of wind*) emporter. **2** *vi* (*of hat etc*) s'envoler.
blow down *or* **over 1** *vt* (*chimney etc*) faire tomber. **2** *vi* tomber.
blow-dry brushing *m*.
blow off 1 *vt* (*hat etc*) emporter. **2** *vi* s'envoler.
blow out (*candle*) souffler.
blowtorch chalumeau *m*.

blow up 1 *vt* (*building*) faire sauter; (*pump up*) gonfler. **2** *vi* exploser.
blowy *a* **it's b.** *Fam* il y a du vent.
blue [bluː] **1** *a* bleu (*mpl* bleus). **2** *n* bleu *m* (*pl* bleus).
blueberry ['bluːbərɪ, *Am* -berɪ] airelle *f*.
bluff [blʌf] **1** *vti* bluffer. **2** *n* bluff *m*.
blunder 1 *n* (*mistake*) bévue *f*. **2** *vi* faire une bévue.
blunt [blʌnt] *a* (*edge*) émoussé; (*person*, *speech*) franc, brusque.
blur [blɜːr] **1** *n* tache *f* floue. **2** *vt rendre flou.*
blurred *a* flou.
blush [blʌʃ] *vi* rougir (**with** de).
blustery ['blʌstərɪ] *a* (*weather*) de grand vent.
board[1] [bɔːd] **1** *n* (*piece of wood*) planche *f*; (*for notices*) tableau *m*; (*cardboard*) carton *m*; **b. (of directors)** conseil *m* d'administration; **on b.** (*ship*, *aircraft*) à bord (de). **2** *vt* monter à bord de; (*bus*, *train*) monter dans.
board[2] (*food*) pension *f*; **b. and lodging** (chambre *f* avec) pension *f*.
boarder pensionnaire *mf*.
boarding (*of passengers*) embarquement *m*.
boarding house pension *f* (de famille).
boarding school pensionnat *m*.
boardwalk *Am* promenade *f*.
boast [bəʊst] *vi* se vanter (**about, of** de).
boat [bəʊt] bateau *m*; (*small*) barque *f*, canot *m*; (*liner*) paquebot *m*.
bobby ['bɒbɪ] (*policeman*) *Fam* flic *m*.
bobby pin *Am* pince *f* à cheveux.
bodily *a* (*need*) physique.
body ['bɒdɪ] corps *m*; (*institution*) organisme *m*.
bodyguard garde *m* du corps.
bodywork carrosserie *f*.
bogged down [bɒgd] *a* **to get b. down** s'enliser.
bogus ['bəʊgəs] *a* faux (*f* fausse).
boil[1] [bɔɪl] *n* (*pimple*) furoncle *m*.
boil[2] **1** *n* **come to the b.** bouillir. **2** *vi* bouillir.
boil (up) faire bouillir.
boiled *a* bouilli; (*potato*) à l'eau; **b. egg** œuf *m* à la coque.
boiler chaudière *f*.
boiling *a* **b. (hot)** bouillant; **it's b. (hot)** (*weather*) il fait une chaleur infernale.
boil over (*of milk*) déborder.
bold [bəʊld] *a* hardi.

boldness hardiesse *f.*
bolt [bəʊlt] **1** *n* (*on door*) verrou *m*; (*for nut*) boulon *m.* **2** *vt* (*door*) fermer au verrou. **3** *vi* (*dash*) se précipiter.
bomb [bɒm] **1** *n* bombe *f.* **2** *vt* bombarder.
bomber (*aircraft*) bombardier *m.*
bombing bombardement *m.*
bond [bɒnd] (*link*) lien *m*; (*investment certificate*) bon *m.*
bone [bəʊn] os *m*; (*of fish*) arête *f.*
bonfire ['bɒnfaɪər] (*celebration*) feu *m* de joie; (*for dead leaves*) feu *m* (de jardin).
bonnet ['bɒnɪt] (*hat*) bonnet *m*; (*of car*) capot *m.*
bonus ['bəʊnəs] prime *f.*
bony *a* (*thin*) osseux; (*fish*) plein d'arêtes.
boo [buː] **1** *vti* siffler. **2** *n* **boos** sifflets *mpl.*
booby-trap ['buːbɪtræp] *vt* piéger.
book [bʊk] *n* livre *m*; (*of tickets*) carnet *m*; **(exercise) b.** cahier *m*; **books** (*accounts*) comptes *mpl.*
book (up) 1 *vt* (*seat*) réserver; **fully booked (up)** (*hotel, concert*) complet. **2** *vi* réserver des places.
bookcase bibliothèque *f.*
booking réservation *f.*
booking office bureau *m* de location.
bookkeeper comptable *mf.*
bookkeeping comptabilité *f.*
booklet (*pamphlet*) brochure *f.*
bookmaker bookmaker *m.*
bookseller libraire *mf.*
bookshelf rayon *m.*
bookshop, *Am* **bookstore** librairie *f.*
boom [buːm] (*economic*) expansion *f.*
boost [buːst] **1** *vt* (*increase*) augmenter; (*product*) faire de la réclame pour; (*economy*) stimuler. **2** *n* **to give a b. to = to boost.**
boot [buːt] (*shoe*) botte *f*; (*of car*) coffre *m*; **(ankle) b.** bottillon *m*; **to get the b.** *Fam* être mis à la porte.
booth [buːθ] (*for phone*) cabine *f.*
boot out mettre à la porte.
booze [buːz] *Fam* **1** *n* alcool *m.* **2** *vi* boire (beaucoup).
border ['bɔːdər] (*of country*) frontière *f*; (*edge*) bord *m.*
border (on) (*country*) toucher à.
borderline case cas *m* limite.
bore [bɔːr] **1** *vt* ennuyer; **to be bored** s'ennuyer. **2** *n* (*person*) raseur, -euse *mf*; (*thing*) ennui *m.*

boredom ennui *m*.
boring *a* ennuyeux.
born [bɔːn] *a* né; **to be b.** naître; **he was b.** il est né.
borrow ['bɒrəʊ] *vt* emprunter **(from** à).
boss [bɒs] patron, -onne *mf*, chef *m*.
boss s.o. around *or* **about** commander qn.
bossy *a Fam* autoritaire.
botch (up) [bɒtʃ] (*spoil*) bâcler.
both [bəʊθ] **1** *a* les deux. **2** *pron* tous *or* toutes (les) deux; **b. of us** nous deux. **3** *adv* (*at the same time*) à la fois; **b. you and I** vous et moi.
bother ['bɒðər] **1** *vt* (*annoy, worry*) ennuyer; (*disturb*) déranger; (*pester*) importuner; **to b. doing** *or* **to do** se donner la peine de faire; **I can't be bothered!** je n'en ai pas envie! **2** *n* (*trouble*) ennui *m*; (*effort*) peine *f*; (*inconvenience*) dérangement *m*.
bother about (*worry about*) se préoccuper de.
bottle ['bɒt(ə)l] bouteille *f*; (*small*) flacon *m*; (*for baby*) biberon *m*; **(hot-water) b.** bouillotte *f*.
bottle opener ouvre-bouteilles *m inv*.
bottom ['bɒtəm] **1** *n* (*of sea, box*) fond *m*; (*of page, hill*) bas *m*; (*buttocks*) *Fam* derrière *m*; **to be at the b. of the class** être le dernier de la classe. **2** *a* (*part, shelf*) inférieur, du bas; **b. floor** rez-de-chaussée *m*.
boulder ['bəʊldər] rocher *m*.
bounce [baʊns] **1** *vi* (*of ball*) rebondir; (*of cheque, Am check*) *Fam* être sans provision. **2** *vt* faire rebondir. **3** *n* (re)bond *m*.
bound *a* **b. to do** (*obliged*) obligé de faire; (*certain*) sûr de faire; **it's b. to happen/snow/***etc* ça arrivera/il neigera/*etc* sûrement; **b. for** en route pour.
boundary ['baʊnd(ə)rɪ] limite *f*.
bounds *npl* **out of b.** (*place*) interdit.
bouquet [bəʊ'keɪ] (*of flowers*) bouquet *m*.
boutique [buː'tiːk] boutique *f* (de mode).
bow[1] [bəʊ] (*weapon*) arc *m*; (*knot*) nœud *m*.
bow[2] [baʊ] **1** *n* (*with knees bent*) révérence *f*; (*nod*) salut *m*. **2** *vi* s'incliner **(to** devant); (*nod*) incliner la tête **(to** devant).
bowels ['baʊəlz] *npl* intestins *mpl*.
bowl [bəʊl] (*for food*) bol *m*; (*for sugar*) sucrier *m*; (*for salad*) saladier *m*; (*for fruit*) coupe *f*.
bowler (hat) (chapeau *m*) melon *m*.
bowling (tenpin) b. bowling *m*.
bowling alley bowling *m*.

bowls *npl* (*game*) boules *fpl*.
bow tie nœud *m* papillon.
box [bɒks] **1** *n* boîte *f*; (*large*) caisse *f*. **2** *vi Boxing* boxer.
boxer boxeur *m*.
box in (*enclose*) enfermer.
boxing boxe *f*; **b. ring** ring *m*.
Boxing Day le lendemain de Noël.
box office bureau *m* de location.
boy [bɔɪ] garçon *m*; **English b.** jeune Anglais *m*; **oh b.!** mon Dieu!
boycott ['bɔɪkɒt] **1** *vt* boycotter. **2** *n* boycottage *m*.
boyfriend petit ami *m*.
bra [brɑː] soutien-gorge *m*.
bracelet ['breɪslɪt] bracelet *m*.
braces *npl* (*trouser straps*) bretelles *fpl*.
bracket ['brækɪt] (*round sign*) parenthèse *f*; (*square sign*) crochet *m*.
brag [bræg] *vi* se vanter (**about, of** de).
bragging vantardise *f*.
braid [breɪd] **1** *n* (*of hair*) *Am* tresse *f*. **2** *vt Am* tresser.
brain [breɪn] cerveau *m*; **to have brains** avoir de l'intelligence.
brainwash *vt* faire un lavage de cerveau à.
brainy ['breɪnɪ] *a Fam* intelligent.
brake 1 *n* frein *m*. **2** *vi* freiner.
brake light stop *m*.
branch [brɑːntʃ] branche *f*; (*of road*) embranchement *m*; (*of store, office*) succursale *f*.
branch off (*of road*) bifurquer.
branch out (*of firm, person*) étendre ses activités (**into** à).
brand [brænd] (*trademark*) marque *f*.
brand-new *a* tout neuf (*f* toute neuve).
brandy ['brændɪ] cognac *m*.
brass [brɑːs] cuivre *m*.
brave [breɪv] *a* courageux, brave.
bravery courage *m*.
brawl [brɔːl] bagarre *f*.
brawny ['brɔːnɪ] *a* musclé.
bread [bred] *n inv* pain *m*; **loaf of b.** pain *m*; **(slice** *or* **piece of) b. and butter** tartine *f*.
breadbin, *Am* **breadbox** coffre *m* à pain.
breadcrumb miette *f* (de pain); **breadcrumbs** (*in cooking*) chapelure *f*.
breadth [bretθ] largeur *f*.
breadwinner soutien *m* de famille.

break [breɪk] **1** *vt** casser; (*into pieces*) briser; (*silence*, *spell*) rompre; (*strike*, *heart*, *ice*) briser; (*sporting record*) battre; (*law*) violer; (*one's word*, *promise*) manquer à; (*journey*) interrompre; (*news*) révéler (**to** à). **2** *vi* (se) casser; se briser; se rompre; (*of news*) éclater; (*stop work*) faire la pause. **3** *n* cassure *f*; (*in bone*) fracture *f*; (*with person*, *group*) rupture *f*; (*in journey*) interruption *f*; (*rest*) repos *m*; (*in activity*, *for tea etc*) pause *f*; (*in school*) récréation *f*; **a lucky b.** une chance.
breakable *a* fragile.
break away *vi* se détacher.
break down **1** *vt* (*door*) enfoncer. **2** *vi* (*of vehicle*, *machine*) tomber en panne; (*of talks*) échouer; (*collapse*) (*of person*) s'effondrer.
breakdown panne *f*; (*in talks*) rupture *f*; (*nervous*) dépression *f*.
breakfast ['brekfəst] petit déjeuner *m*.
break in **1** *vi* (*of burglar*) entrer par effraction. **2** *vt* (*door*) enfoncer; (*vehicle*) *Am* roder.
break-in cambriolage *m*.
break into (*house*) cambrioler; (*safe*) forcer.
break loose s'échapper.
break off **1** *vt* détacher; (*relations*) rompre. **2** *vi* se détacher; (*stop*) s'arrêter; **to b. off with s.o.** rompre avec qn.
break out (*of war*, *fire*) éclater; (*escape*) s'échapper.
breakthrough percée *f*, découverte *f*.
break up **1** *vt* mettre en morceaux; (*fight*) mettre fin à. **2** *vi* (*of group*) se disperser; (*of marriage*) se briser; (*from school*) partir en vacances.
breakup (*in marriage*) rupture *f*.
breast [brest] sein *m*; (*of chicken*) blanc *m*.
breastfeed *vt* allaiter.
breaststroke brasse *f*.
breath [breθ] haleine *f*, souffle *m*; **out of b. (tout)** essoufflé.
breathalyser® alcootest® *m*.
breathe [bri:ð] *vti* respirer; **to b. in** aspirer; **to b. out** expirer.
breathing respiration *f*; **b. space** moment *m* de repos.
breathtaking *a* sensationnel.
breed [bri:d] **1** *vt** (*animals*) élever. **2** *vi* (*of animals*) se reproduire. **3** *n* race *f*.
breeder éleveur, -euse *mf*.
breeze [bri:z] brise *f*.
breezy *a* (*weather*) frais.
brew [bru:] *vi* (*of storm*) se préparer; (*of tea*) infuser; **something is**

brewing il se prépare quelque chose.
brewery brasserie *f*.
bribe [braɪb] **1** *n* pot-de-vin *m*. **2** *vt* acheter (*qn*).
brick [brɪk] brique *f*; (*child's*) cube *m*.
bricklayer maçon *m*.
bride [braɪd] mariée *f*; **the b. and groom** les mariés *mpl*.
bridegroom marié *m*.
bridesmaid demoiselle *f* d'honneur.
bridge [brɪdʒ] pont *m*.
brief [briːf] **1** *a* bref (*f* brève). **2** *vt* (*inform*) mettre au courant (**on** de). **3** *n* **briefs** (*underpants*) slip *m*.
briefcase serviette *f*.
briefing instructions *fpl*.
briefly *adv* (*quickly*) en vitesse.
bright [braɪt] **1** *a* brillant; (*weather*, *room*) clair; (*clever*) intelligent; (*idea*) génial. **2** *adv* **b. and early** de bonne heure.
brighten (up) **1** *vt* (*room*) égayer. **2** *vi* (*of weather*) s'éclaircir.
brightly *adv* avec éclat.
brightness éclat *m*.
brilliance éclat *m*; (*of person*) grande intelligence *f*.
brilliant ['brɪljənt] *a* (*light*) éclatant; (*clever*) brillant.
bring* *vt* (*person*, *vehicle*) amener; (*thing*) apporter; (*to cause*) amener; **to b. to an end** mettre fin à; **to b. to mind** rappeler.
bring about provoquer.
bring along (*object*) emporter; (*person*) emmener.
bring back (*person*) ramener; (*thing*) rapporter; (*memories*) rappeler.
bring down descendre (*qch*); (*overthrow*) faire tomber; (*reduce*) réduire.
bring in rentrer (*qch*); (*person*) faire entrer; (*introduce*) introduire.
bring out sortir (*qch*); (*person*) faire sortir; (*meaning*) faire ressortir; (*book*) publier; (*product*) lancer.
bring s.o. round *or* **to** ranimer qn.
bring together (*reconcile*) réconcilier.
bring up monter (*qch*); (*child*) élever; (*subject*) mentionner.
brink [brɪŋk] bord *m*.
brisk [brɪsk] *a* vif.
briskly *adv* (*to walk*) vite.
bristle ['brɪs(ə)l] poil *m*.
British ['brɪtɪʃ] *a* britannique; **the B.** les Britanniques *mpl*.
British Isles îles *fpl* Britanniques.
Briton Britannique *mf*.

brittle ['brɪt(ə)l] *a* fragile.
broad [brɔːd] *a* (*wide*) large; (*outline*) général; **in b. daylight** en plein jour.
broadcast 1 *vt** diffuser, retransmettre. **2** *n* émission *f*.
broccoli ['brɒkəlɪ] *n inv* brocoli *m*.
brochure ['brəʊʃər] brochure *f*.
broke [brəʊk] (*pt de* **break**) *a* (*penniless*) fauché.
broken ['brəʊk(ə)n] *pp de* **break**.
broken-'down *a* (*machine*) déglingué.
bronchitis [brɒŋ'kaɪtɪs] bronchite *f*.
bronze [brɒnz] bronze *m*.
brooch [brəʊtʃ] broche *f*.
brood [bruːd] **1** *n* couvée *f*. **2** *vi* méditer tristement (**over** sur).
broody *a* maussade.
brook [brʊk] ruisseau *m*.
broom [bruːm] balai *m*.
broomstick manche *m* à balai.
brother ['brʌðər] frère *m*.
brother-in-law (*pl* **brothers-in-law**) beau-frère *m*.
brought [brɔːt] *pt & pp de* **bring**.
brown [braʊn] **1** *a* brun; (*reddish*) marron; (*hair*) châtain; (*tanned*) bronzé. **2** *n* brun *m*; marron *m*.
browse [braʊz] *vi* (*in bookshop*) feuilleter des livres.
bruise [bruːz] **1** *vt* **to b. one's knee**/*etc* se faire un bleu au genou/*etc*. **2** *n* bleu *m* (*pl* bleus), contusion *f*.
bruised *a* couvert de bleus.
brunch [brʌntʃ] brunch *m*.
brunette [bruː'net] brunette *f*.
brush [brʌʃ] **1** *n* brosse *f*. **2** *vt* (*teeth, hair*) brosser.
brush aside écarter.
brush away *or* **off** enlever.
brush up (on) (*language*) se remettre à.
brutal ['bruːt(ə)l] *a* brutal.
bru'tality brutalité *f*.
brute [bruːt] brute *f*.
BSc, *Am* **BS** *abbr* = **Bachelor of Science.**
bubble ['bʌb(ə)l] **1** *n* bulle *f*. **2** *vi* bouillonner.
bubble over déborder.
buck [bʌk] *Am Fam* dollar *m*.
bucket ['bʌkɪt] seau *m*.
buckle ['bʌk(ə)l] **1** *n* boucle *f*. **2** *vt* boucler. **3** *vti* (*warp*) voiler.
buck up 1 *vt* remonter le moral à (*qn*). **2** *vi* (*become livelier*)

reprendre du poil de la bête.
bud [bʌd] **1** *n* (*of tree*) bourgeon *m*; (*of flower*) bouton *m*. **2** *vi* bourgeonner; pousser des boutons.
Buddhist ['bʊdɪst] *a* & *n* bouddhiste (*mf*).
budge [bʌdʒ] *vi* bouger.
budgerigar ['bʌdʒərɪgɑːr] perruche *f*.
budget ['bʌdʒɪt] budget *m*.
budget for inscrire au budget.
buffalo ['bʌfələʊ] (*pl* **-oes** *or* **-o**) buffle *m*; **(American) b.** bison *m*.
buffet ['bʊfeɪ] (*table*, *meal*) buffet *m*.
bug[1] [bʌg] punaise *f*; (*any insect*) bestiole *f*; (*germ*) microbe *m*, virus *m*; (*in machine*) défaut *m*; (*in computer program*) erreur *f*; (*listening device*) micro *m* clandestin.
bug[2] *vt* (*annoy*) *Fam* embêter.
buggy ['bʌgɪ] **(baby) b.** (*folding*) poussette-canne *f*; (*pram*) *Am* landau *m* (*pl* -aus).
bugle ['bjuːg(ə)l] clairon *m*.
build [bɪld] **1** *n* (*of person*) carrure *f*. **2** *vt** construire; (*house*) construire, bâtir.
builder maçon *m*; (*contractor*) entrepreneur *m*.
building bâtiment *m*; (*flats*, *offices*) immeuble *m*.
building society = société *f* de crédit immobilier.
build up 1 *vt* (*increase*) augmenter; (*collection*) constituer; (*business*) monter; (*speed*) prendre. **2** *vi* (*of tension*, *pressure*) augmenter.
built-in *a* (*cupboard*, *Am closet*) encastré; (*part of machine*) incorporé.
built-up area agglomération *f*.
bulb [bʌlb] (*of plant*) oignon *m*; (*of lamp*) ampoule *f*.
bulge [bʌldʒ] renflement *m*.
bulge (out) se renfler.
bulging *a* renflé.
bulk [bʌlk] *n inv* grosseur *f*; **the b. of** (*most*) la majeure partie de.
bulky *a* gros (*f* grosse).
bull [bʊl] taureau *m*.
bulldog bouledogue *m*.
bulldozer ['bʊldəʊzər] bulldozer *m*.
bullet ['bʊlɪt] balle *f* (*de revolver etc*).
bulletin ['bʊlətɪn] bulletin *m*.
bulletproof *a* (*jacket*, *Am vest*) pare-balles *inv*; (*car*) blindé.
bullfight corrida *f*.
bully ['bʊlɪ] **1** *n* (grosse) brute *f*. **2** *vt* brutaliser.

bum [bʌm] *Fam* (*loafer*) clochard, -arde *mf*; (*good-for-nothing*) propre *mf* à rien; (*buttocks*) derrière *m*.
bumblebee ['bʌmb(ə)lbiː] bourdon *m*.
bump [bʌmp] **1** *vt* (*of car*) heurter; **to b. one's head/knee** se cogner la tête/le genou. **2** *n* (*impact*) choc *m*; (*jerk*) cahot *m*; (*on road, body*) bosse *f*.
bumper pare-chocs *m inv*.
bump into se cogner contre; (*of car*) rentrer dans; (*meet*) tomber sur.
bumpy *a* (*road, ride*) cahoteux.
bun [bʌn] (*cake*) petit pain *m* au lait.
bunch [bʌntʃ] (*of flowers*) bouquet *m*; (*of keys*) trousseau *m*; (*of people*) bande *f*; **b. of grapes** grappe *f* de raisin.
bundle ['bʌnd(ə)l] **1** *n* paquet *m*; (*of papers*) liasse *f*. **2** *vt* (*put*) fourrer; (*push*) pousser (**into** dans).
bungalow ['bʌŋgələʊ] bungalow *m*.
bung up [bʌŋ] (*stop up*) boucher.
bunk [bʌŋk] couchette *f*; **b. beds** lits *mpl* superposés.
bunny ['bʌnɪ] *Fam* Jeannot *m* lapin.
buoy [bɔɪ] bouée *f*.
burden ['bɜːd(ə)n] **1** *n* fardeau *m*; (*of tax*) poids *m*. **2** *vt* accabler (**with** de).
bureaucracy [bjʊə'rɒkrəsɪ] bureaucratie *f*.
burger ['bɜːgər] hamburger *m*.
burglar ['bɜːglər] cambrioleur, -euse *mf*.
burglar alarm alarme *f* antivol.
burglarize *vt Am* cambrioler.
burglary cambriolage *m*.
burgle *vt* cambrioler.
burial ['berɪəl] enterrement *m*.
burn [bɜːn] **1** *n* brûlure *f*. **2** *vti** brûler; **burnt alive** brûlé vif.
burn down 1 *vt* détruire par le feu. **2** *vi* être détruit par le feu.
burner (*of stove*) brûleur *m*.
burning *a* en feu; (*fire, light*) allumé.
burp [bɜːp] **1** *n* rot *m*. **2** *vi* roter.
burst [bɜːst] **1** *n* (*of laughter*) éclat *m*; (*of thunder*) coup *m*. **2** *vi** (*with force*) éclater; (*of bubble, balloon, boil, tyre*) crever.
bursting *a* (*full*) plein à craquer.
burst into (*room*) faire irruption dans; **to b. into tears** fondre en larmes.
burst out to b. out laughing éclater de rire.
bury ['berɪ] *vt* enterrer; (*hide*) enfouir; (*plunge, absorb*) plonger.

bus [bʌs] (auto)bus *m*; (*long-distance*) (auto)car *m*.
bush buisson *m*.
bushy *a* broussailleux.
business ['bɪznɪs] **1** *n* affaires *fpl*, commerce *m*; (*shop*) commerce *m*; (*task, concern, matter*) affaire *f*; **on b.** pour affaires; **it's your b. to...** c'est à vous de...; **that's none of your b.!, mind your own b!** ça ne vous regarde pas!. **2** *a* commercial; (*meeting, trip*) d'affaires; **b. hours** heures *fpl* de travail; **b. card** carte *f* de visite.
businessman (*pl* **-men**) homme *m* d'affaires.
businesswoman (*pl* **-women**) femme *f* d'affaires.
bus shelter abribus *m*.
bus station gare *f* routière.
bus stop arrêt *m* d'autobus.
bust [bʌst] **1** *n* (*sculpture*) buste *m*; (*woman's breasts*) poitrine *f*. **2** *a* **to go b.** (*bankrupt*) faire faillite.
bustle ['bʌs(ə)l] **1** *vi* s'affairer. **2** *n* activité *f*.
bustling *a* (*street*) bruyant.
busy ['bɪzɪ] *a* occupé (**doing** à faire); (*active*) actif; (*day*) chargé; (*street*) animé; (*phone*) *Am* occupé; **to be b. doing** (*in the process of*) être en train de faire; **b. signal** *Am* sonnerie *f* 'occupé'.
busybody **to be a b.** faire la mouche du coche.
but [bʌt, *unstressed* bət] **1** *conj* mais. **2** *prep* (*except*) sauf; **b. for that/him** sans cela/lui. **3** *adv* (*only*) seulement.
butcher ['bʊtʃər] boucher *m*; **b.'s shop** boucherie *f*.
butler ['bʌtlər] maître *m* d'hôtel.
butt [bʌt] (*of cigarette*) mégot *m*; (*buttocks*) *Am Fam* derrière *m*.
butter ['bʌtər] **1** *n* beurre *m*. **2** *vt* beurrer.
buttercup bouton-d'or *m*.
butterfly papillon *m*.
butt in interrompre.
buttock ['bʌtək] fesse *f*.
button ['bʌtən] bouton *m*; (*of phone*) touche *f*.
button (up) (*garment*) boutonner.
buttonhole boutonnière *f*.
buy [baɪ] **1** *vt** acheter (**from s.o.** à qn, **for s.o.** à *or* pour qn). **2** *n* **a good b.** une bonne affaire.
buyer acheteur, -euse *mf*.
buzz [bʌz] **1** *vi* bourdonner. **2** *n* bourdonnement *m*.
buzz off *Fam* décamper.
by [baɪ] **1** *prep* (*agent, manner*) par; **hit**/*etc* **by** frappé/*etc* par; **surrounded**/*etc* **by** entouré/*etc* de; **by doing** en faisant; **by sea** par mer; **by car** en voiture; **by bicycle** à bicyclette; **by day** de jour; **by**

oneself tout seul. ▮ (*next to*) à côté de; (*near*) près de; **by the lake** au bord du lac. ▮ (*before in time*) avant; **by Monday** avant lundi; **by now** à cette heure-ci. ▮ (*amount*) à; **by the kilo** au kilo; **paid by the hour** payé à l'heure. **2** *adv* **close by** tout près; **to go by, pass by** passer; **by and large** en gros.
bye(-bye)! [baɪ('baɪ)] *int Fam* salut!
by-election élection *f* partielle.
bypass 1 *n* déviation *f* (routière). **2** *vt* contourner.
bystander ['baɪstændər] spectateur, -trice *mf*.

C

cab [kæb] taxi *m*.
cabbage ['kæbɪdʒ] chou *m* (*pl* choux).
cabin ['kæbɪn] (*on ship*) cabine *f*; (*hut*) cabane *f*.
cabinet[1] ['kæbɪnɪt] armoire *f*; (*for display*) vitrine *f*; **(filing) c.** classeur *m* (de bureau).
cabinet[2] (*government ministers*) gouvernement *m*; **c. meeting** conseil *m* des ministres.
cable ['keɪb(ə)l] câble *m*; **c. television** la télévision par câble.
cable car téléphérique *m*; (*on tracks*) funiculaire *m*.
cactus, *pl* **-ti** *or* **-tuses** ['kæktəs, -taɪ, -təsɪz] cactus *m*.
café ['kæfeɪ] café(-restaurant) *m*.
cafeteria [kæfɪ'tɪərɪə] cafétéria *f*.
caffeine ['kæfiːn] caféine *f*.
cage [keɪdʒ] cage *f*.
cake [keɪk] gâteau *m*; (*small*) pâtisserie *f*.
calculate ['kælkjʊleɪt] *vti* calculer.
calcu'lation calcul *m*.
calculator calculatrice *f*.
calendar ['kælɪndər] calendrier *m*.
calf [kɑːf] (*pl* **calves**) (*animal*) veau *m*; (*part of leg*) mollet *m*.
call [kɔːl] **1** *n* appel *m*; (*shout*) cri *m*; (*visit*) visite *f*; **(telephone) c.** communication *f*; **to make a c.** (*phone*) téléphoner (**to** à). **2** *vt* appeler; (*shout*) crier; (*attention*) attirer (**to** sur); **he's called David** il s'appelle David; **to c. a meeting** convoquer une assemblée; **to c. s.o. a liar**/*etc* qualifier qn de menteur/*etc*. **3** *vi* appeler; (*cry out*) crier; (*visit*) passer.
call back *vti* rappeler.
call by *vi* (*visit*) passer.
caller visiteur, -euse *mf*; (*on phone*) correspondant, -ante *mf*.
call for *vt* (*require*) demander; (*summon*) appeler; (*collect*) passer prendre.
call in 1 *vt* (*into room etc*) faire venir *or* entrer. **2** *vi* (*visit*) passer (**on** chez).
calling card *Am* carte *f* de visite.
call off (*cancel*) annuler.
call on (*visit*) passer voir; **to c. on s.o. to do** inviter qn à faire; (*urge*) presser qn de faire.
call out 1 *vt* (*shout*) crier; (*doctor*) appeler. **2** *vi* crier; **to c. out for** demander à haute voix.
call round *vi* (*visit*) passer.

call up (*phone*) appeler.
calm [kɑːm] **1** *a* calme; **keep c.!** du calme! **2** *n* calme *m*. **3** *vt* calmer.
calm down 1 *vi* se calmer. **2** *vt* calmer.
calmly *adv* calmement.
calorie ['kælərɪ] calorie *f*.
camcorder [kæm'kɔːdər] caméscope *m*.
came [keɪm] *pt de* **come**.
camel ['kæməl] chameau *m*.
camera ['kæmrə] appareil (photo) *m*; **(TV** *or* **film) c.** caméra *f*.
camp [kæmp] camp *m*; **c. bed** lit *m* de camp.
camp (out) camper.
campaign [kæm'peɪn] campagne *f*.
camper campeur, -euse *mf*; (*vehicle*) camping-car *m*.
campfire feu *m* de camp.
camping camping *m*; **c. site** camping *m*.
campsite camping *m*.
can[1] [kæn, *unstressed* kən] *v aux* (*pt* **could**) pouvoir; (*know how to*) savoir; **he couldn't help me** il ne pouvait pas m'aider; **she c. swim** elle sait nager; **you could be wrong** (*possibility*) tu as peut-être tort; **he can't be old** (*probability*) il ne doit pas être vieux; **c. I come in?** puis-je entrer?
can[2] (*for food*) boîte *f*.
Canadian [kə'neɪdɪən] *a* & *n* canadien, -ienne (*mf*).
canal [kə'næl] canal *m*.
canary [kə'neərɪ] canari *m*.
cancel ['kænsəl] *vt* (*flight, appointment etc*) annuler; (*goods, taxi*) décommander; (*train*) supprimer; **to c. a ticket** (*punch*) composter un billet.
cance'llation annulation *f*; (*of train*) suppression *f*.
cancer ['kænsər] cancer *m*.
candid ['kændɪd] *a* franc (*f* franche).
candidate ['kændɪdeɪt] candidat, -ate *mf*.
candle ['kænd(ə)l] bougie *f*; (*in church*) cierge *m*.
candlestick bougeoir *m*; (*tall*) chandelier *m*.
candy ['kændɪ] *Am* bonbon(s) *m*(*pl*).
cane [keɪn] **1** *n* (*stick*) canne *f*; (*for punishing s.o.*) baguette *f*. **2** *vt* (*punish*) fouetter.
cannabis ['kænəbɪs] (*drug*) haschisch *m*.
canned *a* en boîte; **c. food** conserves *fpl*.
cannibal cannibale *mf*.
canoe [kə'nuː] canoë *m*.

canoeing to go c. faire du canoë.
can-opener ouvre-boîtes *m inv*.
canopy ['kænəpɪ] (*hood of pram or Am baby carriage*) capote *f*; (*small roof*) auvent *m*.
cantaloup(e) ['kæntəlu:p, *Am* -ləʊp] (*melon*) cantaloup *m*.
canteen [kæn'ti:n] (*place*) cantine *f*.
canvas ['kænvəs] toile *f*.
canyon ['kænjən] canyon *m*.
cap [kæp] (*hat*) casquette *f*; (*for shower*) bonnet *m*; (*of soldier*) képi *m*; (*of bottle, tube*) bouchon *m*; (*of milk or beer bottle*) capsule *f*; (*of pen*) capuchon *m*; (*of child's gun*) amorce *f*.
capa'bility capacité *f*.
capable ['keɪpəb(ə)l] *a* (*person*) capable (**of sth** de qch, **of doing** de faire).
capacity [kə'pæsətɪ] (*of container*) capacité *f*; (*ability*) aptitude *f*; **in my c. as** en ma qualité de.
cape [keɪp] (*cloak*) cape *f*; (*of cyclist*) pèlerine *f*.
capital ['kæpɪtəl] (*money*) capital *m*; **c. (city)** capitale *f*; **c. (letter)** majuscule *f*.
capsize [kæp'saɪz] *vti* chavirer.
capsule ['kæpsju:l] capsule *f*.
captain ['kæptɪn] capitaine *m*.
capture ['kæptʃər] *vt* (*person, town*) prendre.
car [kɑ:*r*] voiture *f*, auto *f*; (*train carriage*) wagon *m*; **c. radio** autoradio *m*.
caramel ['kærəməl] caramel *m*.
caravan caravane *f*; (*horse-drawn*) roulotte *f*; **c. site** camping *m* pour caravanes.
carbon ['kɑ:bən] carbone *m*; **c. copy** double *m* (au carbone).
carbon paper (papier *m*) carbone *m*.
carburettor [kɑ:bjʊ'retər] (*Am* **carburetor** ['kɑ:bəreɪtər]) carburateur *m*.
card [kɑ:d] carte *f*; (*cardboard*) carton *m*; **(index) c.** fiche *f*; **to play cards** jouer aux cartes.
cardboard carton *m*.
cardigan ['kɑ:dɪgən] gilet *m*.
cardinal ['kɑ:dɪn(ə)l] *a* (*number, point*) cardinal.
card index fichier *m*.
care [keər] **1** *vi* (*like*) aimer; **would you c. to try?** aimeriez-vous essayer?; **I don't c.** ça m'est égal; **who cares?** qu'est-ce que ça fait? **2** *n* (*attention*) soin(s) *m(pl)*; (*protection*) garde *f*; (*anxiety*) souci *m*; **to take c. not to do** faire attention à ne pas faire; **to take c. to do**

veiller à faire; **to take c. of** s'occuper de (*qch*, *qn*); (*sick person*) prendre soin de; **to take c. of oneself** (*manage*) se débrouiller; (*keep healthy*) faire bien attention à soi.
care about se soucier de (*qch*); (*person*) avoir de la sympathie pour.
career [kə'rɪər] carrière *f*.
care for (*a drink etc*) avoir envie de; **to c. for s.o.** s'occuper de qn; (*sick person*) soigner qn; (*like*) avoir de la sympathie pour qn; **I don't c. for it** je n'aime pas ça.
carefree *a* insouciant.
careful *a* (*exact*, *thorough*) soigneux (**about** de); (*cautious*) prudent; **to be c. of** *or* **with** faire attention à.
carefully *adv* avec soin; (*cautiously*) prudemment.
careless *a* négligent; (*absent-minded*) étourdi.
caretaker gardien, -ienne *mf*.
carfare *Am* frais *mpl* de voyage.
car ferry ferry boat *m*.
cargo ['kɑːgəʊ] (*pl* **-oes**, *Am* **-os**) cargaison *f*.
caring *a* (*loving*) aimant; (*understanding*) très humain.
carnation [kɑː'neɪʃən] œillet *m*.
carnival ['kɑːnɪvəl] carnaval *m* (*pl* -als).
carol ['kærəl] chant *m* (de Noël).
carp [kɑːp] (*fish*) carpe *f*.
car park parking *m*.
carpenter ['kɑːpɪntər] charpentier *m*; (*for light woodwork*) menuisier *m*.
carpentry charpenterie *f*; menuiserie *f*.
carpet ['kɑːpɪt] tapis *m*; (*fitted*) moquette *f*.
carpeting (wall-to-wall) c. *Am* moquette *f*.
carpet sweeper balai *m* mécanique.
carriage ['kærɪdʒ] (*of train*, *horse-drawn*) voiture *f*.
carriageway (*of road*) chaussée *f*.
carrier (bag) ['kærɪər] sac *m* (en plastique).
carrot ['kærət] carotte *f*.
carry ['kærɪ] *vt* porter; (*goods*) transporter; (*sell*) stocker; (*in calculation*) retenir.
carryall *Am* fourre-tout *m inv*.
carry away *vt* emporter; **to get carried away** (*excited*) s'emballer.
carry back *vt* rapporter; (*person*) ramener.
carrycot porte-bébé *m*.
carry off *vt* emporter; (*prize*) remporter; **to c. it off** réussir.
carry on 1 *vt* continuer; (*conduct*) diriger; (*sustain*) soutenir. **2** *vi*

continuer (**doing** à faire).
carry out *vt* (*plan*, *order*, *promise*) exécuter; (*repair*, *reform*) effectuer; (*duty*) accomplir; (*meal*) *Am* emporter.
carry through *vt* (*plan*) mener à bonne fin.
cart [kɑːt] (*horse-drawn*) charrette *f*; (*in supermarket*) *Am* caddie® *m*; (**serving**) **c.** *Am* table *f* roulante.
cart (around) *vt Fam* trimbal(l)er.
cart away *vt* emporter.
carton ['kɑːtən] (*box*) carton *m*; (*of milk etc*) brique *f*; (*cigarettes*) cartouche *f*; (*cream*) pot *m*.
cartoon [kɑː'tuːn] dessin *m* (humoristique); (*film*) dessin *m* animé; (**strip**) **c.** bande *f* dessinée.
cartridge ['kɑːtrɪdʒ] cartouche *f*.
carve [kɑːv] *vt* tailler (**out of** dans); (*initials etc*) graver.
carve (up) (*meat*) découper.
car wash (*machine*) lave-auto *m*.
case[1] [keɪs] (*instance*, *in hospital*) cas *m*; (*in court*) affaire *f*; **in any c.** en tout cas; **in c. it rains** pour le cas où il pleuvrait; **in c. of** en cas de; **(just) in c.** à tout hasard.
case[2] (*bag*) valise *f*; (*crate*) caisse *f*; (*for pen*, *glasses*, *camera*, *cigarettes*) étui *m*; (*for jewels*) coffret *m*.
cash [kæʃ] **1** *n* argent *m*; **to pay (in) c.** payer en espèces. **2** *vt* **to c. a cheque** *or Am* **check** encaisser un chèque; (*of bank*) payer un chèque.
cash desk caisse *f*.
ca'shier caissier, -ière *mf*.
cash machine distributeur *m* de billets.
cash price prix *m* (au) comptant.
cash register caisse *f* enregistreuse.
casino [kə'siːnəʊ] (*pl* **-os**) casino *m*.
casserole ['kæsərəʊl] cocotte *f*; (*stew*) ragoût *m* en cocotte.
cassette [kə'set] (*audio*, *video*) cassette *f*; (*film*) cartouche *f*.
cassette player lecteur *m* de cassettes.
cassette recorder magnétophone *m* à cassettes.
cast[1] [kɑːst] (*actors*) acteurs *mpl*; (*list of actors*) distribution *f*; (*for broken bone*) plâtre *m*.
cast[2]* *vt* jeter; (*light*, *shadow*) projeter; (*doubt*) exprimer; **to c. a vote** voter.
caster sugar sucre *m* en poudre.
castle ['kɑːs(ə)l] château *m*; *Chess* tour *f*.
castor ['kɑːstər] (*wheel*) roulette *f*.
casual ['kæʒjʊəl] *a* (*remark*) fait en passant; (*stroll*) sans but;

(*offhand*) désinvolte; (*worker*) temporaire; (*work*) irrégulier; **c. clothes** vêtements *mpl* sport.
casualty (*dead*) mort *m*, morte *f*; (*wounded*) blessé, -ée *mf*; **c. (department)** (*of hospital*) (service *m* des) urgences *fpl*.
cat [kæt] chat *m*; (*female*) chatte *f*; **c. food** pâtée *f*.
catalogue ['kætəlɒg] (*Am* **catalog**) catalogue *m*.
catapult ['kætəpʌlt] lance-pierres *m inv*.
catastrophe [kə'tæstrəfɪ] catastrophe *f*.
catch* [kætʃ] **1** *vt* (*ball*, *thief*, *illness*, *train etc*) attraper; (*grab*, *surprise*) prendre; (*understand*) saisir; (*attention*) attirer; (*on nail etc*) accrocher (**on** à); (*finger etc*) se prendre (**in** dans); **to c. fire** prendre feu; **to c. one's breath** (*rest*) reprendre haleine. **2** *vi* **her skirt (got) caught in the door** sa jupe s'est prise dans la porte. **3** *n* (*trick*) piège *m*; (*on door*) loquet *m*.
catching *a* contagieux.
catch on (*become popular*) prendre; (*understand*) saisir.
catch s.o. out prendre qn en défaut.
catch up 1 *vt* **to c. s.o. up** rattraper qn. **2** *vi* se rattraper; **to c. up with s.o.** rattraper qn.
category ['kætɪgərɪ] catégorie *f*.
cater for *or* **to** ['keɪtər] (*need*, *taste*) satisfaire.
caterpillar ['kætəpɪlər] chenille *f*.
cathedral [kə'θiːdrəl] cathédrale *f*.
Catholic ['kæθlɪk] *a* & *n* catholique (*mf*).
cauliflower ['kɒlɪflaʊər] chou-fleur *m*.
cause [kɔːz] **1** *n* cause *f*. **2** *vt* causer; **to c. sth to move**/*etc* faire bouger/*etc* qch.
caution ['kɔːʃ(ə)n] (*care*) prudence *f*; (*warning*) avertissement *m*.
cautious *a* prudent.
cautiously *adv* prudemment.
cave [keɪv] caverne *f*.
cave in (*fall in*) s'effondrer.
cavity ['kævɪtɪ] cavité *f*.
CD [siː'diː] *abbr* (*compact disc*) CD *m*.
cease [siːs] *vti* cesser (**doing** de faire).
cease-fire cessez-le-feu *m inv*.
ceiling ['siːlɪŋ] plafond *m*.
celebrate ['selɪbreɪt] **1** *vt* fêter; (*mass*) célébrer. **2** *vi* faire la fête.
cele'bration fête *f*.
ce'lebrity (*person*) célébrité *f*.
celery ['selərɪ] céleri *m*.
cell [sel] cellule *f*.

cellar ['selər] cave *f*.
cellophane® ['seləfeın] cellophane® *f*.
cement [sı'ment] **1** *n* ciment *m*. **2** *vt* cimenter.
cement mixer bétonnière *f*.
cemetery ['semətrı, *Am* 'semәterı] cimetière *m*.
cent [sent] (*coin*) cent *m*.
centigrade ['sentıgreıd] *a* centigrade.
centimetre ['sentımi:tər] centimètre *m*.
centipede ['sentıpi:d] mille-pattes *m inv*.
central *a* central.
centre ['sentər] (*Am* **center**) centre *m*.
century ['sentʃərı] siècle *m*.
ceramic [sə'ræmık] *a* (*tile*) de céramique.
cereal ['sıərıəl] céréale *f*.
ceremony ['serımənı] cérémonie *f*.
certain ['sɜ:tən] *a* (*sure, particular*) certain; **she's c. to come** c'est certain qu'elle viendra; **I'm not c. what to do** je ne sais pas très bien ce qu'il faut faire; **to be c. of sth/that** être certain de qch/que; **to make c. of** (*fact*) s'assurer de; (*seat etc*) s'assurer.
certainly *adv* certainement; (*yes*) bien sûr.
certainty certitude *f*.
certificate [sə'tıfıkıt] certificat *m*; (*from university*) diplôme *m*.
certify ['sɜ:tıfaı] *vt* (*document etc*) certifier.
chain [tʃeın] (*of rings, mountains*) chaîne *f*.
chain (up) (*dog*) mettre à l'attache.
chain saw tronçonneuse *f*.
chain store magasin *m* à succursales multiples.
chair [tʃeər] chaise *f*; (*armchair*) fauteuil *m*.
chair lift télésiège *m*.
chairman (*pl* **-men**) président, -ente *mf*.
chalet ['ʃæleı] chalet *m*.
chalk [tʃɔ:k] **1** *n* craie *f*. **2** *vti* écrire à la craie.
challenge ['tʃælındʒ] **1** *n* défi *m*; (*task*) challenge *m*, gageure *f*. **2** *vt* défier (**s.o. to do** qn de faire); (*dispute*) contester.
challenging *a* (*job*) exigeant.
chamber ['tʃeımbər] **c. of commerce** chambre *f* de commerce.
champagne [ʃæm'peın] champagne *m*.
champion ['tʃæmpıən] champion, -onne *mf*.
championship championnat *m*.
chance [tʃɑ:ns] **1** *n* (*luck*) hasard *m*; (*possibility*) chances *fpl*; (*opportunity*) occasion *f*; **by c.** par hasard. **2** *vt* **to c. doing** prendre le risque de faire; **to c. it** risquer le coup.

chandelier [ʃændə'lɪər] lustre *m*.
change [tʃeɪndʒ] **1** *n* changement *m*; (*money*) monnaie *f*; **for a c.** pour changer; **it makes a c. from** ça change de; **a c. of clothes** des vêtements de rechange. **2** *vt* changer; (*exchange*) échanger (**for** contre); (*money*) changer; **to c. trains/one's skirt**/*etc* changer de train/de jupe/*etc*; **to c. gear/the subject** changer de vitesse/sujet. **3** *vi* changer; (*change clothes*) se changer.
changeable *a* changeant.
change over *vi* passer (**from** de, **to** à).
changeover passage *m* (**from** de, **to** à).
changing room vestiaire *m*.
channel ['tʃæn(ə)l] (*on television*) chaîne *f*; (*for inquiry etc*) voie *f*; **the C.** la Manche; **to go through the normal channels** passer par la voie normale.
chant [tʃɑːnt] **1** *vt* (*slogan*) scander. **2** *vi* (*of demonstrators*) scander des slogans.
chaos ['keɪɒs] chaos *m*.
cha'otic *a* sens dessus dessous.
chap [tʃæp] (*fellow*) type *m*; (*on skin*) gerçure *f*.
chapel ['tʃæp(ə)l] chapelle *f*.
chapped [tʃæpt] *a* gercé.
chapter ['tʃæptər] chapitre *m*.
char [tʃɑːr] *vt* carboniser; (*scorch*) brûler légèrement.
character ['kærɪktər] caractère *m*; (*in book, film*) personnage *m*; (*strange person*) numéro *m*.
characte'ristic *a* & *n* caractéristique (*f*).
charge[1] [tʃɑːdʒ] **1** *n* (*cost*) prix *m*; **charges** (*expenses*) frais *mpl*; **there's a c. (for it)** c'est payant; **free of c.** gratuit. **2** *vt* (*amount*) demander (**for** pour); (*person*) faire payer.
charge[2] **1** *n* (*in court*) accusation *f*; (*care*) garde *f*; **to take c. of** prendre en charge; **to be in c. of** (*child*) avoir la garde de; (*office*) être responsable de; **the person in c.** le *or* la responsable. **2** *vt* (*battery, soldiers*) charger; (*accuse*) accuser (**with** de). **3** *vi* (*rush*) se précipiter.
charity ['tʃærɪtɪ] (*society*) fondation *f* charitable; **to give to c.** faire la charité.
charm [tʃɑːm] **1** *n* charme *m*; (*trinket*) amulette *f*. **2** *vt* charmer.
charming *a* charmant.
chart [tʃɑːt] (*map*) carte *f*; (*graph*) graphique *m*; **(pop) charts** hit-parade *m*.
chartered accountant expert-comptable *m*.
charter flight ['tʃɑːtər] charter *m*.

chase [tʃeɪs] **1** *n* poursuite *f*. **2** *vt* poursuivre.
chase after s.o./sth courir après qn/qch.
chase s.o. away *or* **off** chasser qn.
chasm ['kæzəm] *n* abîme *m*, gouffre *m*.
chassis ['ʃæsɪ, *Am* 'tʃæsɪ] (*of vehicle*) châssis *m*.
chat [tʃæt] **1** *n* petite conversation *f*; **to have a c.** bavarder. **2** *vi* causer.
chatter ['tʃætər] **1** *vi* (*of person*) bavarder; **his teeth are chattering** il claque des dents. **2** *n* bavardage *m*.
chatterbox bavard, -arde *mf*.
chatty *a* bavard.
chat s.o. up *Fam* baratiner qn.
chauffeur ['ʃəʊfər] chauffeur *m* (de maître).
cheap [tʃiːp] **1** *a* bon marché *inv*; (*rate*) réduit; (*worthless*) sans valeur; **cheaper** meilleur marché. **2** *adv* (*to buy*) (à) bon marché.
cheaply *adv* (à) bon marché.
cheat [tʃiːt] **1** *vt* tromper; **to c. s.o. out of sth** escroquer qch à qn. **2** *vi* (*at games etc*) tricher. **3** *n* tricheur, -euse *mf*; (*crook*) escroc *m*.
cheater *n Am* = **cheat.**
check[1] [tʃek] **1** *vt* (*examine*) vérifier; (*inspect*) contrôler; (*stop*) arrêter; (*baggage*) *Am* mettre à la consigne. **2** *vi* vérifier. **3** *n* vérification *f*; (*inspection*) contrôle *m*; *Chess* échec *m*; (*tick*) *Am* = croix *f*; (*receipt*) *Am* reçu *m*; (*bill in restaurant*) *Am* addition *f*; (*cheque*) *Am* chèque *m*.
check[2] *a* à carreaux; **c. (pattern)** carreaux *mpl*.
checkbook *Am* carnet *m* de chèques.
checkers *npl Am* jeu *m* de dames.
check-in enregistrement *m* (des bagages).
check in 1 *vt* (*luggage*) enregistrer. **2** *vi* (*at hotel*) signer le registre; (*arrive*) arriver; (*at airport*) se présenter (à l'enregistrement).
checkmate *Chess* échec et mat *m*.
check off (*names on list etc*) cocher.
check on sth vérifier qch.
checkout (*in supermarket*) caisse *f*.
check out 1 *vt* confirmer. **2** *vi* (*at hotel*) régler sa note.
checkroom *Am* vestiaire *m*; (*left-luggage office*) *Am* consigne *f*.
checkup bilan *m* de santé.
check up *vi* vérifier.
cheddar ['tʃedər] (*cheese*) cheddar *m*.
cheek [tʃiːk] joue *f*; (*impudence*) culot *m*.
cheeky *a* effronté.
cheer [tʃɪər] **1** *n* **cheers** acclamations *fpl*; **cheers!** *Fam* à votre santé!

2 *vt* (*applaud*) acclamer. **3** *vi* applaudir.
cheerful *a* gai.
cheering acclamations *fpl*.
cheerio! [tʃɪərɪ'əʊ] *int* salut!
cheer up 1 *vt* donner du courage à (*qn*); (*amuse*) égayer. **2** *vi* prendre courage; s'égayer; **c. up!** (du) courage!
cheese [tʃi:z] fromage *m*.
cheeseburger cheeseburger *m*.
cheesecake tarte *f* au fromage blanc.
chef [ʃef] (*cook*) chef *m*.
chemical 1 *a* chimique. **2** *n* produit *m* chimique.
chemist pharmacien, -ienne *mf*; (*scientist*) chimiste *mf*; **c.'s shop** pharmacie *f*.
chemistry ['kemɪstrɪ] chimie *f*.
cheque [tʃek] chèque *m*.
chequebook carnet *m* de chèques.
cherry ['tʃerɪ] cerise *f*.
cherry brandy cherry *m*.
chess [tʃes] échecs *mpl*.
chessboard échiquier *m*.
chest [tʃest] (*part of body*) poitrine *f*; (*box*) coffre *m*; **c. of drawers** commode *f*.
chestnut ['tʃestnʌt] châtaigne *f*.
chew [tʃu:] **1** *vt* **to c. (up)** mâcher. **2** *vi* mastiquer.
chewing gum chewing-gum *m*.
chick [tʃɪk] poussin *m*.
chicken 1 *n* poulet *m*. **2** *a* (*cowardly*) *Fam* froussard.
chicken out *vi Fam* se dégonfler.
chickenpox varicelle *f*.
chickpea pois *m* chiche.
chicory ['tʃɪkərɪ] (*for salad*) endive *f*.
chief 1 *n* chef *m*; **in c.** en chef. **2** *a* principal.
chiefly *adv* principalement.
chilblain ['tʃɪlbleɪn] engelure *f*.
child, *pl* **children** [tʃaɪld, 'tʃɪldrən] enfant *mf*.
child care (*for working parents*) crèches *fpl* et garderies *fpl*.
childhood enfance *f*.
childish *a* puéril.
child minder nourrice *f*, assistante *f* maternelle.
chill [tʃɪl] **1** *n* froid *m*; (*illness*) refroidissement *m*; **to catch a c.** prendre froid. **2** *vt* (*wine, melon*) faire rafraîchir; (*meat*) réfrigérer.
chilled *a* (*wine*) frais.

chilli ['tʃɪlɪ] (*pl* **-ies**) piment *m* (de Cayenne).
chilly *a* froid; **it's c.** il fait (un peu) froid.
chime [tʃaɪm] *vi* (*of clock*) sonner.
chimney ['tʃɪmnɪ] cheminée *f.*
chimneypot tuyau *m* de cheminée.
chimpanzee [tʃɪmpæn'zɪː] chimpanzé *m.*
chin [tʃɪn] menton *m.*
china ['tʃaɪnə] **1** *n inv* porcelaine *f.* **2** *a* en porcelaine.
Chinese [tʃaɪ'niːz] **1** *a* & *n inv* chinois, -oise (*mf*). **2** *n* (*language*) chinois *m.*
chip [tʃɪp] **1** *vt* (*cup etc*) ébrécher; (*paint*) écailler. **2** *n* (*break*) ébréchure *f*; (*microchip*) puce *f*; (*counter*) jeton *m*; **chips** (*French fries*) frites *fpl*; (*crisps*) *Am* chips *mpl.*
chipboard (bois *m*) aggloméré *m.*
chiropodist [kɪ'rɒpədɪst] pédicure *mf.*
chisel ['tʃɪz(ə)l] ciseau *m.*
chives [tʃaɪvz] *npl* ciboulette *f.*
choc-ice ['tʃɒkaɪs] (*ice cream*) esquimau *m.*
chock-a-block [tʃɒkə'blɒk] *a Fam* archiplein.
chocolate ['tʃɒklɪt] **1** *n* chocolat *m*; **milk c.** chocolat au lait; **plain** *or Am* **bittersweet c.** chocolat à croquer. **2** *a* (*cake*) au chocolat.
choice [tʃɔɪs] choix *m.*
choir ['kwaɪər] chœur *m.*
choke [tʃəʊk] **1** *vt* (*person*) étrangler; (*clog*) boucher. **2** *vi* s'étrangler (**on** avec).
cholesterol [kə'lestərɒl] cholestérol *m.*
choose* [tʃuːz] **1** *vt* choisir; **to c. to do** (*decide*) juger bon de faire. **2** *vi* choisir.
choos(e)y *a* difficile.
chop [tʃɒp] **1** *n* (*of lamb, pork*) côtelette *f.* **2** *vt* couper (à la hache); (*food*) hacher.
chop down (*tree*) abattre.
chop off (*branch, finger etc*) couper.
chopper hachoir *m.*
chopsticks baguettes *fpl.*
chop up couper en morceaux.
chord [kɔːd] (*in music*) accord *m.*
chore [tʃɔːr] travail *m* (routinier); (*unpleasant*) corvée *f*; **chores** travaux *mpl* du ménage.
chorus ['kɔːrəs] (*of song*) refrain *m.*
christen ['krɪs(ə)n] *vt* baptiser.
christening baptême *m.*

Christian ['krɪstʃən] *a & n* chrétien, -ienne (*mf*).
Christian name prénom *m*.
Christmas ['krɪsməs] **1** *n* Noël *m*; **Merry** *or* **Happy C.** Joyeux Noël; **Father C.** le père Noël; **C. Eve** la veille de Noël. **2** *a* (*tree etc*) de Noël.
chrome chrome *m*.
chrysanthemum [krɪ'sænθəməm] chrysanthème *m*.
chubby ['tʃʌbɪ] *a* potelé.
chuck [tʃʌk] *vt* (*throw*) *Fam* jeter.
chuck away *or* **out** (*old clothes etc*) *Fam* balancer.
chuck in *or* **up** (*job etc*) *Fam* laisser tomber.
chum [tʃʌm] *Fam* copain *m*, copine *f*.
chunk [tʃʌŋk] (gros) morceau *m*.
church [tʃɜːtʃ] église *f*.
chute [ʃuːt] (*for refuse*) vide-ordures *m inv*; (*in pool*) toboggan *m*.
cider ['saɪdər] cidre *m*.
cigar [sɪ'gɑːr] cigare *m*.
ciga'rette cigarette *f*.
cigarette end mégot *m*.
cigarette lighter briquet *m*.
cine-camera ['sɪnɪkæmrə] caméra *f*.
cinema ['sɪnəmə] cinéma *m*.
cinnamon ['sɪnəmən] cannelle *f*.
circle ['sɜːk(ə)l] **1** *n* cercle *m*; **circles** (*political etc*) milieux *mpl*. **2** *vt* faire le tour de; (*word*) encadrer. **3** *vi* (*of aircraft etc*) décrire des cercles.
circuit ['sɜːkɪt] (*electrical path, in sport etc*) circuit *m*.
circular **1** *a* circulaire. **2** *n* (*letter*) circulaire *f*; (*advertisement*) prospectus *m*.
circulate ['sɜːkjʊleɪt] **1** *vi* (*of blood etc*) circuler. **2** *vt* (*pass round*) faire circuler.
circu'lation (*of newspaper*) tirage *m*.
circumference [sɜː'kʌmfərəns] circonférence *f*.
circumstance ['sɜːkəmstæns] circonstance *f*; **in** *or* **under no circumstances** en aucun cas.
circus ['sɜːkəs] cirque *m*.
citizen ['sɪtɪz(ə)n] citoyen, -enne *mf*; (*of town*) habitant, -ante *mf*.
city ['sɪtɪ] (grande) ville *f*.
city centre centre-ville *m inv*.
city hall *Am* hôtel *m* de ville.
civil ['sɪv(ə)l] *a* civil.
ci'vilian *a & n* civil, -ile (*mf*).

civilization [sɪvɪlaɪ'zeɪʃ(ə)n] civilisation *f*.
civil servant fonctionnaire *mf*.
civil service fonction *f* publique.
claim [kleɪm] **1** *vt* réclamer; **to c. that** prétendre que. **2** *n* (*demand*) revendication *f*; (*statement*) affirmation *f*; (*right*) droit *m* (**to** à); (**insurance**) **c.** demande *f* d'indemnité.
clam [klæm] (*shellfish*) palourde *f*.
clamp [klæmp] (**wheel**) **c.** sabot *m* (de Denver).
clap [klæp] *vti* applaudir; **to c.** (**one's hands**) battre des mains.
clapping applaudissements *mpl*.
clarinet [klærɪ'net] clarinette *f*.
clash [klæʃ] **1** *vi* (*of plates*) s'entrechoquer; (*of interests*) se heurter; (*of colours*) jurer (**with** avec); (*of people*) se bagarrer; (*coincide*) tomber en même temps (**with** que). **2** *n* (*noise*) choc *m*; (*of interests*) conflit *m*.
clasp [klɑːsp] **1** *vt* serrer. **2** *n* (*fastener*) fermoir *m*; (*of belt*) boucle *f*.
class [klɑːs] **1** *n* classe *f*; (*lesson*) cours *m*; (*university grade*) mention *f*. **2** *vt* classer.
classic ['klæsɪk] **1** *a* classique. **2** *n* (*work etc*) classique *m*.
classical *a* classique.
classmate camarade *mf* de classe.
classroom (salle *f* de) classe *f*.
clause [klɔːz] (*in sentence*) proposition *f*.
claw [klɔː] griffe *f*; (*of lobster*) pince *f*.
clay [kleɪ] argile *f*.
clean [kliːn] **1** *a* (*not dirty*) propre; (*clear-cut*) net (*f* nette). **2** *adv* (*utterly*) complètement; (*to break, cut*) net. **3** *n* **to give sth a c**[lean] nettoyer qch. **4** *vt* nettoyer; (*wash*) laver; (*wipe*) essuyer; **to c**[lean] **one's teeth** se brosser les dents. **5** *vi* faire le nettoyage.
cleaner femme *f* de ménage; (**dry**) **c.** teinturier, -ière *mf*.
cleaning nettoyage *m*; (*housework*) ménage *m*.
cleaning woman femme *f* de ménage.
cleanly *adv* (*to break, cut*) net.
clean out (*room etc*) nettoyer; (*empty*) vider.
cleansing cream ['klenzɪŋ] crème *f* démaquillante.
clean up 1 *vt* nettoyer. **2** *vi* faire le nettoyage.
clear 1 *a* (*sky, outline, sound, thought etc*) clair; (*glass*) transparent; (*road*) libre; (*profit*) net; (*obvious*) évident, clair; **to be c. of** (*free of*) être libre de; **to make oneself c.** se faire comprendre. **2** *adv* **to keep** *or* **steer c. of** se tenir à l'écart de; **to get c. of** s'éloigner de. [3] *vt* (*path, table*) débarrasser; (*fence*) franchir; (*accused person*)

disculper; (*cheque*, *Am check*) faire passer (sur un compte); (*through customs*) dédouaner; **to c. one's throat** s'éclaircir la gorge. **4** *vi* (*of weather*) s'éclaircir; (*of fog*) se dissiper.
clearance (*sale*) soldes *mpl*; (*space*) dégagement *m*.
clear away (*remove*) enlever.
clear-'cut *a* net (*f* nette).
clearly *adv* clairement; (*obviously*) évidemment.
clear off (*go*) *Fam* filer.
clear out *vt* vider; (*clean*) nettoyer; (*remove*) enlever.
clear up 1 *vt* (*mystery*) éclaircir. **2** *vti* (*tidy*) ranger.
clearway route *f* à stationnement interdit.
clementine ['klemәntaɪn] clémentine *f*.
clench [klentʃ] *vt* (*fist*) serrer.
clerical ['klerɪk(ә)l] *a* (*job*) d'employé; (*work*) de bureau.
clerk [klɑːk, *Am* klɜːk] employé, -ée *mf* (de bureau), (*in store*) *Am* vendeur, -euse *mf*.
clever ['klevәr] *a* intelligent; (*smart*) astucieux; (*skilful*) habile (**at sth** à qch, **at doing** à faire); (*machine*, *book etc*) ingénieux; **c. at** (*English etc*) fort en.
click [klɪk] **1** *n* déclic *m*. **2** *vi* (*of machine etc*) faire un déclic.
client ['klaɪәnt] client, -ente *mf*.
cliff [klɪf] falaise *f*.
climate ['klaɪmɪt] climat *m*.
climax ['klaɪmæks] point *m* culminant.
climb (over) [klaɪm] (*wall*) escalader.
climb (up) 1 *vt* (*stairs*, *steps*) monter; (*hill*, *mountain*) gravir; (*tree*, *ladder*) monter à. **2** *vi* monter.
climb down 1 *vt* (*wall*, *tree*, *hill*) descendre de. **2** *vi* descendre (**from** de).
climber (*mountaineer*) alpiniste *mf*.
cling* [klɪŋ] *vi* se cramponner; (*stick*) adhérer (**to** à).
clingfilm film *m* plastique.
clinic ['klɪnɪk] (*private*) clinique *f*; (*health centre*) centre *m* médical.
clip [klɪp] **1** *vt* couper; (*hedge*) tailler; (*ticket*) poinçonner; (*attach*) attacher. **2** *n* (*for paper*) attache *f*; (*of brooch*, *of cyclist*, *for hair*) pince *f*.
clip on *vt* attacher (**to** à).
clippers *npl* (*for hair*) tondeuse *f*; (*for nails*) coupe-ongles *m inv*.
clipping (*newspaper article*) *Am* coupure *f*.
cloak [klәʊk] (grande) cape *f*.
cloakroom vestiaire *m*; (*lavatory*) toilettes *fpl*.
clock [klɒk] horloge *f*; (*small*) pendule *f*; **round the c.** vingt-quatre

heures sur vingt-quatre.
clockwise *adv* dans le sens des aiguilles d'une montre.
close[1] [kləʊs] **1** *a* (*place, relative etc*) proche (**to** de); (*collaboration, connection*) étroit; (*friend*) intime; (*atmosphere*) lourd. **2** *adv* **c.** (**by**) (tout) près; **c. to** près de; **c. behind** juste derrière.
close[2] [kləʊz] **1** *n* (*end*) fin *f*. **2** *vt* (*door, shop etc*) fermer; (*road*) barrer; (*deal*) conclure. **3** *vi* se fermer; (*of shop*) fermer.
close down *vti* (*for good*) fermer (définitivement).
close in *vi* approcher.
closely ['kləʊslɪ] *adv* (*to follow, guard*) de près; (*to listen*) attentivement.
closet ['klɒzɪt] *Am* (*cupboard*) placard *m*; (*wardrobe*) penderie *f*.
close up 1 *vt* fermer. **2** *vi* (*of shopkeeper*) fermer; (*of line of people*) se rapprocher.
closing time heure *f* de fermeture.
clot [klɒt] **1** *n* (*of blood*) caillot *m*. **2** *vi* se coaguler.
cloth [klɒθ] tissu *m*; (*for dusting*) chiffon *m*; (*for dishes*) torchon *m*; (*tablecloth*) nappe *f*.
clothes [kləʊðz] *npl* vêtements *mpl*; **to put one's c. on** s'habiller.
clothes brush brosse *f* à habits.
clothes line corde *f* à linge.
clothes peg, *Am* **clothes pin** pince *f* à linge.
clothes shop magasin *m* d'habillement.
clothing ['kləʊðɪŋ] vêtements *mpl*; **an article of c.** un vêtement.
cloud [klaʊd] nuage *m*.
cloud over (*of sky*) se couvrir.
cloudy *a* (*weather*) couvert.
clove [kləʊv] **c. of garlic** gousse *f* d'ail.
clown [klaʊn] clown *m*.
club [klʌb] (*society, stick for golf*) club *m*; **club(s)** (*at cards*) trèfle *m*.
club soda *Am* eau *f* gazeuse.
clue [kluː] indice *m*; (*of crossword*) définition *f*; **I don't have a c.** *Fam* je n'en ai pas la moindre idée.
clumsy ['klʌmzɪ] *a* maladroit; (*tool*) peu commode.
clutch [klʌtʃ] **1** *vt* (*hold*) serrer; (*grasp*) saisir. **2** *n* (*in vehicle*) embrayage *m*; (*pedal*) pédale *f* d'embrayage.
clutter up ['klʌtər] (*room etc*) encombrer (**with** de).
cm *abbr* (*centimetre*) cm.
Co [kəʊ] *abbr* (*company*) Cie.
coach [kəʊtʃ] **1** *n* (*train carriage*) voiture *f*; (*bus*) autocar *m*. **2** *vt* (*pupil*) donner des leçons (particulières) à.
coal [kəʊl] charbon *m*.

coalmine mine *f* de charbon.
coarse [kɔːs] *a* (*person*, *fabric*) grossier.
coast [kəʊst] côte *f*.
coat [kəʊt] **1** *n* manteau *m*; (*jacket*) veste *f*; (*of animal*) pelage *m*; (*of paint*) couche *f*. **2** *vt* couvrir (**with** de).
coathanger cintre *m*.
coating couche *f*.
cob [kɒb] **corn on the c.** épi *m* de maïs.
cobbled ['kɒb(ə)ld] *a* pavé.
cobweb toile *f* d'araignée.
cocaine [kəʊ'keɪn] cocaïne *f*.
cock [kɒk] (*fowl*) coq *m*.
cockle ['kɒk(ə)l] (*shellfish*) coque *f*.
cockpit poste *m* de pilotage.
cockroach ['kɒkrəʊtʃ] (*beetle*) cafard *m*.
cocktail cocktail *m*; **(fruit) c.** macédoine *f* (de fruits); **prawn c.** crevettes *fpl* à la mayonnaise.
cocktail party cocktail *m*.
cocoa ['kəʊkəʊ] cacao *m*.
coconut ['kəʊkənʌt] noix *f* de coco.
cod [kɒd] morue *f*.
code [kəʊd] code *m*.
cod-liver 'oil huile *f* de foie de morue.
co-edu'cational *a* (*school etc*) mixte.
coffee ['kɒfɪ] café *m*; **white c.** café *m* au lait; (*in restaurant*) (café *m*) crème *m*.
coffee bar café *m*.
coffee break pause-café *f*.
coffeepot cafetière *f*.
coffee table table *f* basse.
coffin ['kɒfɪn] cercueil *m*.
cognac ['kɒnjæk] cognac *m*.
coil [kɔɪl] **1** *n* (*of wire, rope etc*) rouleau *m*. **2** *vt* enrouler.
coin [kɔɪn] pièce *f* (de monnaie).
coin bank *Am* tirelire *f*.
coincide [kəʊɪn'saɪd] *vi* coïncider (**with** avec).
co'incidence coïncidence *f*.
coke [kəʊk] (*Coca-Cola*®) coca *m*.
colander ['kʌləndər] passoire *f*.
cold [kəʊld] **1** *n* froid *m*; (*illness*) rhume *m*; **to catch c.** prendre froid. **2** *a* froid; **to be** *or* **feel c.** avoir froid; **my hands are c.** j'ai froid aux mains; **it's c.** (*of weather*) il fait froid; **to get c.** (*of wea-

ther) se refroidir; (*of food*) refroidir.
cold cuts *Am* assiette *f* anglaise.
coldness froideur *f*.
coleslaw ['kəʊlslɔː] salade *f* de chou cru.
collaborate [kə'læbəreɪt] *vi* collaborer (**on** à).
collabo'ration collaboration *f*.
collapse [kə'læps] **1** *vi* (*of person, building*) s'effondrer. **2** *n* effondrement *m*.
collar ['kɒlər] col *m*; (*of dog*) collier *m*.
collarbone clavicule *f*.
colleague ['kɒliːg] collègue *mf*.
collect [kə'lekt] **1** *vt* (*pick up*) ramasser; (*gather*) rassembler; (*taxes*) percevoir; (*rent*) encaisser; (*stamps etc*) collectionner; (*fetch*) (passer) prendre; **to c. (money)** (*in street, church*) quêter. **2** *vi* (*of dust*) s'accumuler. **3** *adv* **to call c.** *Am* téléphoner en PCV.
collection (*group of objects*) collection *f*; (*of poems etc*) recueil *m*; (*of money in church etc*) quête *f*; (*of mail*) levée *f*.
collector (*of stamps etc*) collectionneur, -euse *mf*.
college ['kɒlɪdʒ] université *f*; (*within university*) collège *m*.
collide [kə'laɪd] *vi* entrer en collision (**with** avec).
collision collision *f*.
colloquial [kə'ləʊkwɪəl] *a* (*word etc*) familier.
cologne [kə'ləʊn] eau *f* de Cologne.
colon ['kəʊlən] *Grammar* deux-points *m inv*.
colonel ['kɜːn(ə)l] colonel *m*.
colony ['kɒlənɪ] colonie *f*.
colour ['kʌlər] (*Am* **color**) **1** *n* couleur *f*. **2** *a* (*photo, TV set*) en couleurs. **3** *vt* colorer.
colour (in) (*drawing*) colorier.
coloured *a* (*person, pencil*) de couleur.
colourful *a* coloré; (*person*) pittoresque.
colouring book album *m* de coloriages.
column ['kɒləm] colonne *f*; (*newspaper feature*) chronique *f*.
coma ['kəʊmə] coma *m*; **in a c.** dans le coma.
comb [kəʊm] **1** *n* peigne *m*. **2** *vt* **to c. one's hair** se peigner.
combi'nation combinaison *f*.
combine [kəm'baɪn] **1** *vt* joindre (**with** à); **our combined efforts achieved a result** en joignant nos efforts nous avons obtenu un résultat. **2** *vi* s'unir.
come* [kʌm] *vi* venir (**from** de, **to** à); **to c. first** (*in race*) arriver premier; (*in exam*) être le premier; **to c. close to doing** faillir faire.
come about (*happen*) se faire, arriver.

come across (*thing*, *person*) tomber sur.
come along venir (**with** avec); (*progress*) avancer; **c. along!** allons!
come apart (*of two objects*) se séparer.
come away (*leave*, *come off*) partir.
come back revenir; (*return home*) rentrer.
come by obtenir; (*find*) trouver.
co'median (acteur *m*) comique *m*, actrice *f* comique.
come down descendre; (*of rain*, *price*) tomber.
comedy ['kɒmɪdɪ] comédie *f*.
come for sth/s.o. venir chercher qch/qn.
come forward (*volunteer*) se présenter; **to c. forward with sth** offrir qch.
come in entrer; (*of tide*) monter; (*of train*) arriver.
come into (*room etc*) entrer dans; (*money*) hériter de.
come off 1 *vi* (*of button etc*) se détacher; (*succeed*) réussir. **2** *vt* (*fall from*) tomber de; (*get down from*) descendre de.
come on (*progress*) avancer; **c. on!** allez!
come out sortir; (*of sun*, *book*) paraître; (*of stain*) partir; **to c. out (on strike)** se mettre en grève.
come over 1 *vi* (*visit*) venir. **2** *vt* (*of feeling*) saisir (*qn*).
come round (*visit*) venir; (*of date*) revenir; (*regain consciousness*) revenir à soi.
come through 1 *vi* (*survive*) s'en tirer. **2** *vt* (*crisis etc*) se tirer indemne de.
come to (*regain consciousness*) revenir à soi; (*amount to*) revenir à; (*a decision*) parvenir à.
come under (*heading*) être classé sous; (*s.o.'s influence*) tomber sous.
come up (*rise*) monter; (*of plant*) sortir; (*of question*, *job*) se présenter.
come up against (*wall*, *problem*) se heurter à.
come up to (*reach*) arriver jusqu' à.
come up with (*idea*, *money*) trouver.
comfort ['kʌmfət] **1** *n* confort *m*; (*consolation*) réconfort *m*. **2** *vt* consoler.
comfortable *a* (*chair etc*) confortable; (*rich*) aisé; **he's c.** (*in chair etc*) il est à l'aise; **make yourself c.** mets-toi à l'aise.
comforter (*quilt*) *Am* édredon *m*.
comic ['kɒmɪk] **1** *a* comique. **2** *n* (*magazine*) bande *f* dessinée.
comic strip bande *f* dessinée.
comings *npl* **c. and goings** allées *fpl* et venues.
comma ['kɒmə] virgule *f*.

command [kə'mɑːnd] **1** *vt* (*order*) commander (**s.o. to do** à qn de faire); (*ship etc*) commander. **2** *n* (*order*) ordre *m*; (*mastery*) maîtrise *f* (**of** de); **to be in c. (of)** (*army etc*) commander; (*situation*) être maître (de).
commemorate [kə'meməreɪt] *vt* commémorer.
commence [kə'mens] *vti* commencer (**doing** à faire).
comment ['kɒment] commentaire *m*.
commentary commentaire *m*; **(live) c.** reportage *m*.
commentator reporter *m*.
comment on (*event etc*) commenter.
commerce ['kɒmɜːs] commerce *m*.
co'mmercial **1** *a* commercial. **2** *n* **commercial**(s) (*on television*) publicité *f*.
commission [kə'mɪʃ(ə)n] (*fee*, *group*) commission *f*.
commit [kə'mɪt] *vt* (*crime*) commettre; **to c. suicide** se suicider.
commitment (*promise*) engagement *m*.
committee [kə'mɪtɪ] comité *m*.
commodity [kə'mɒdɪtɪ] produit *m*.
common ['kɒmən] **1** *a* (*shared*, *frequent etc*) commun; **in c.** (*shared*) en commun (**with** avec); **in c. with** (*like*) comme. **2** *n* **House of Commons** Chambre *f* des Communes.
commonly *adv* (*generally*) en général.
Common Market Marché *m* commun.
commonplace *a* banal (*mpl* banals).
common room salle *f* commune.
common'sense sens *m* commun.
commotion [kə'məʊʃ(ə)n] agitation *f*.
communal [kə'mjuːn(ə)l] *a* (*bathroom etc*) commun.
communicate [kə'mjuːnɪkeɪt] *vti* communiquer.
communi'cation communication *f*.
communion [kə'mjuːnjən] communion *f*.
community [kə'mjuːnɪtɪ] communauté *f*.
community centre centre *m* socio-culturel.
commute [kə'mjuːt] *vi* faire la navette (**to work** pour se rendre à son travail).
commuter banlieusard, -arde *mf*.
commuting trajets *mpl* journaliers.
compact **1** *a* [kəm'pækt] compact. **2** *n* ['kɒmpækt] (*for face powder*) poudrier *m*.
compact disc *or Am* **disk** ['kɒmpækt] disque *m* compact.
companion [kəm'pænjən] compagnon *m*.
company ['kʌmpənɪ] (*being with others*, *firm*) compagnie *f*; (*guests*)

invités, -ées *mfpl*; **to keep s.o. c.** tenir compagnie à qn.
comparatively *adv* relativement.
compare [kəm'peər] *vt* comparer (**with, to** à); **compared to** *or* **with** en comparaison de.
comparison comparaison *f* (**with** avec).
compartment [kəm'pɑːtmənt] compartiment *m*.
compass ['kʌmpəs] (*for direction*) boussole *f*; (*on ship*) compas *m*; **(pair of) compasses** (*for drawing etc*) compas *m*.
compatible [kəm'pætɪb(ə)l] *a* compatible.
compel [kəm'pel] *vt* forcer, contraindre (**to do** à faire).
compensate ['kɒmpənseɪt] **1** *vt* **to c. s.o.** dédommager qn (**for** de). **2** *vi* compenser (**for sth** qch).
compen'sation dédommagement *m*.
compère ['kɒmpeər] animateur, -trice *mf*.
compete [kəm'piːt] *vi* (*take part*) concourir (**in** à, **for** pour); **to c. (with s.o.)** rivaliser (avec qn); (*in business*) faire concurrence (à qn).
competent ['kɒmpɪtənt] *a* compétent (**to do** pour faire).
competently *adv* avec compétence.
competition [kɒmpə'tɪʃ(ə)n] (*rivalry*) compétition *f*; **a c.** (*contest*) un concours; (*in sport*) une compétition.
com'petitive *a* (*price etc*) compétitif; (*person*) aimant la compétition.
com'petitor concurrent, -ente *mf*.
compile [kəm'paɪl] *vt* (*dictionary*) rédiger; (*list*) dresser.
complain [kəm'pleɪn] *vi* se plaindre (**of, about** de; **that** que).
complaint plainte *f*; (*in shop etc*) réclamation *f*; (*illness*) maladie *f*.
complete [kəm'pliːt] **1** *a* (*total*) complet; (*finished*) achevé; **a c. idiot** un parfait imbécile. **2** *vt* compléter; (*finish*) achever; (*a form*) remplir.
completely *adv* complètement.
complex ['kɒmpleks] **1** *a* complexe. **2** *n* (*feeling, buildings*) complexe *m*.
complexion [kəm'plekʃ(ə)n] (*of the face*) teint *m*.
complicate ['kɒmplɪkeɪt] *vt* compliquer.
complicated *a* compliqué.
compli'cation complication *f*.
compliment ['kɒmplɪmənt] compliment *m*.
comply [kəm'plaɪ] *vi* obéir (**with** à).
compose [kəm'pəʊz] *vt* composer; **to c. oneself** se calmer.
composed *a* calme.
composer compositeur, -trice *mf*.

compo'sition (*school essay*) rédaction *f*.
compound (*substance*, *word*) composé *m*.
comprehensive *a* complet; (*insurance*) tous risques; **c. (school)** = collège *m* d'enseignement secondaire.
comprise [kəm'praɪz] *vt* comprendre.
compromise ['kɒmprəmaɪz] compromis *m*.
compulsive *a* (*smoker etc*) invétéré; **c. liar** mythomane *mf*.
compulsory [kəm'pʌlsərɪ] *a* obligatoire.
computer [kəm'pjuːtər] ordinateur *m*; **c. operator** opérateur, -trice *mf* sur ordinateur.
computerized *a* informatisé.
computer science informatique *f*.
con [kɒn] *vt* (*deceive*) *Slang* escroquer.
conceal [kən'siːl] *vt* dissimuler (**from s.o.** à qn); (*plan*) tenir secret.
conceited [kən'siːtɪd] *a* vaniteux.
conceivable [kən'siːvəb(ə)l] *a* concevable.
concentrate ['kɒnsəntreɪt] **1** *vt* concentrer. **2** *vi* se concentrer (**on** sur); **to c. on doing** s'appliquer à faire.
concen'tration concentration *f*.
concern [kən'sɜːn] **1** *vt* concerner; **to be concerned with/about** s'occuper de/s'inquiéter de. **2** *n* (*matter*) affaire *f*; (*anxiety*) inquiétude *f*; **his c. for** son souci de; **(business) c.** entreprise *f*.
concerned *a* (*anxious*) inquiet.
concerning *prep* en ce qui concerne.
concert ['kɒnsət] concert *m*.
concise [kən'saɪs] *a* concis.
conclude [kən'kluːd] **1** *vt* conclure; **to c. that** conclure que. **2** *vi* se terminer (**with** par); (*of speaker*) conclure.
conclusion conclusion *f*.
concrete ['kɒŋkriːt] **1** *n* béton *m*. **2** *a* en béton; (*real*) concret.
condemn [kən'dem] *vt* condamner (*qn*) (**to** à).
condensation [kɒnden'seɪʃ(ə)n] (*mist*) buée *f*.
condition [kən'dɪʃ(ə)n] condition *f*; **on c. that one does** à condition de faire, à condition que l'on fasse.
conditioner (hair) c. après-shampooing *m*.
condo ['kɒndəʊ] *abbr* (*pl* **-os**) *Am* = **condominium.**
condom ['kɒndəm] préservatif *m*.
condominium [kɒndə'mɪnɪəm] *Am* (*building*) copropriété *f*; (*apartment*) appartement *m* dans une copropriété.
conduct **1** *n* ['kɒndʌkt] conduite *f*. **2** *vt* [kən'dʌkt] conduire; (*orchestra*) diriger.
conducted tour excursion *f* accompagnée.

conductor (*of orchestra*) chef *m* d'orchestre; (*on bus*) receveur, -euse *mf*; (*on train*) *Am* chef *m* de train.
cone [kəʊn] cône *m*; (*of ice cream*) cornet *m*.
conference ['kɒnfərəns] conférence *f*; (*scientific etc*) congrès *m*.
confess [kən'fes] **1** *vt* avouer (**that** que). **2** *vi* **to c.** (**to**) avouer.
confession aveu(x) *m*(*pl*).
confetti [kən'fetɪ] confettis *mpl*.
confidence ['kɒnfɪdəns] (*trust*) confiance *f*; (**self-**)**c.** confiance *f* en soi; **in c.** en confidence.
confident *a* sûr; (**self-**)**c.** sûr de soi.
confi'dential *a* confidentiel.
confidently *adv* avec confiance.
confine [kən'faɪn] *vt* limiter (**to** à); **to c. oneself to doing** se limiter à faire.
confined *a* (*space*) réduit; **c. to bed** cloué au lit.
confirm [kən'fɜːm] *vt* confirmer (**that** que).
confir'mation confirmation *f*.
confirmed *a* (*bachelor*) endurci.
confiscate ['kɒnfɪskeɪt] *vt* confisquer (**from s.o.** à qn).
conflict 1 *n* ['kɒnflɪkt] conflit *m*. **2** *vi* [kən'flɪkt] être en contradiction (**with** avec).
conflicting *a* (*views etc*) contradictoires; (*dates*) incompatibles.
conform [kən'fɔːm] *vi* (*of person*) se conformer (**to** à).
confront [kən'frʌnt] *vt* (*problems, danger*) faire face à; **to c. s.o.** (*be face to face with*) se trouver en face de qn; (*oppose*) s'opposer à qn.
confuse [kən'fjuːz] *vt* (*make unsure*) embrouiller; **to c. with** (*mistake for*) confondre avec.
confused *a* (*situation*) confus; **to be c.** (*of person*) s'y perdre; **to get c.** s'embrouiller.
confusing *a* déroutant.
confusion confusion *f*.
congested [kən'dʒestɪd] *a* (*street*) encombré.
congestion (*traffic*) encombrement(s) *m*(*pl*).
congratulate [kən'grætʃʊleɪt] *vt* féliciter (**s.o. on sth** qn de qch).
congratu'lations *npl* félicitations *fpl* (**on** pour).
congregate ['kɒŋgrɪgeɪt] *vi* se rassembler.
congress ['kɒŋgres] congrès *m*; **C.** (*political body*) *Am* le Congrès.
Congressman (*pl* **-men**) *Am* membre *m* du Congrès.
conjugate ['kɒndʒʊgeɪt] *vt* (*verb*) conjuguer.
conju'gation conjugaison *f*.
conjunction [kən'dʒʌŋkʃ(ə)n] *Grammar* conjonction *f*.
conjurer ['kʌndʒərər] prestidigitateur, -trice *mf*.

conjuring trick tour *m* de prestidigitation.
con man escroc *m*.
connect [kə'nekt] **1** *vt* relier (**with, to** à); (*telephone etc*) brancher **to c. s.o. with s.o.** (*by phone*) mettre qn en communication avec qn **2** *vi* **to c. with** (*of train, bus*) assurer la correspondance avec.
connected *a* (*facts*) liés; **to be c. with** (*have dealings with, relate to*) être lié à.
connection (*link*) rapport *m* (**with** avec); (*train etc*) correspondance *f*; (*phone call*) communication *f*; **connections** (*contacts*) relations *fpl* **in c. with** à propos de.
conquer ['kɒŋkər] *vt* (*country*) conquérir; (*enemy, habit*) vaincre.
conscience ['kɒnʃəns] conscience *f*.
conscientious [kɒnʃɪ'enʃəs] *a* consciencieux.
conscious ['kɒnʃəs] *a* (*awake*) conscient; **c. of sth** (*aware*) conscient de qch; **to be c. of doing** avoir conscience de faire.
consent [kən'sent] **1** *vi* consentir (**to** à). **2** *n* consentement *m*.
consequence ['kɒnsɪkwəns] (*result*) conséquence *f*.
consequently *adv* par conséquent.
conser'vation économies *fpl* d'énergie; (*of nature*) protection *f* de l'environnement.
Conservative [kən'sɜːvətɪv] *a & n* conservateur, -trice (*mf*).
conservatory [kən'sɜːvətrɪ] (*room*) véranda *f*.
conserve [kən'sɜːv] *vt* **to c. energy** faire des économies d'énergie.
consider [kən'sɪdər] *vt* considérer (**that** que); (*take into account*) tenir compte de; **to c. doing** envisager de faire.
considerable *a* (*large*) considérable; (*much*) beaucoup de.
considerate [kən'sɪdərət] *a* plein d'égards (**to** pour).
conside'ration considération *f*; **to take into c.** prendre en considération.
considering *prep* compte tenu de.
consignment [kən'saɪnmənt] (*goods*) arrivage *m*.
consist [kən'sɪst] *vi* consister (**of** en, **in** dans, **in doing** à faire).
consistent [kən'sɪstənt] *a* (*unchanging*) constant; (*ideas*) logique; **c. with** compatible avec.
consistently *adv* (*always*) constamment.
conso'lation consolation *f*; **c. prize** lot *m* de consolation.
console[1] [kən'səʊl] *vt* consoler.
console[2] ['kɒnsəʊl] (*control desk*) console *f*.
consonant ['kɒnsənənt] consonne *f*.
conspicuous [kən'spɪkjʊəs] *a* visible; (*striking*) remarquable.
constable ['kɒnstəb(ə)l] **(police) c.** agent *m* (de police).
constant ['kɒnstənt] *a* (*frequent*) incessant; (*unchanging*) constant.

constantly *adv* constamment.
constipated ['kɒnstɪpeɪtɪd] *a* constipé.
constitution [kɒnstɪ'tjuːʃ(ə)n] constitution *f*.
construct [kən'strʌkt] *vt* construire.
construction construction *f*; **under c.** en construction.
consul ['kɒnsəl] consul *m*.
consulate consulat *m*.
consult [kən'sʌlt] **1** *vt* consulter. **2** *vi* **to c. with** discuter avec.
consultancy (firm) cabinet *m* d'experts-conseils.
consultant (*doctor*) spécialiste *mf*; (*financial, legal*) expert-conseil *m*.
consul'tation consultation *f*.
consume [kən'sjuːm] *vt* (*food, supplies*) consommer.
consumer consommateur, -trice *mf*.
con'sumption consommation *f* (**of** de).
contact ['kɒntækt] **1** *n* contact *m*; (*person*) contact *m*, relation *f*; **in c. with** en contact avec. **2** *vt* contacter.
contact lenses lentilles *fpl or* verres *mpl* de contact.
contagious [kən'teɪdʒəs] *a* contagieux.
contain [kən'teɪn] *vt* contenir.
container récipient *m*; (*for goods*) conteneur *m*.
contemporary [kən'tempərərɪ] *a* & *n* contemporain, -aine (*mf*).
contempt [kən'tempt] mépris *m*.
contend with [kən'tend] (*problem*) faire face à; (*person*) avoir affaire à.
content[1] [kən'tent] *a* satisfait (**with** de).
content[2] ['kɒntent] (*of text etc*) contenu *m*; **contents** (*of container*) contenu *m*; **(table of) contents** (*of book*) table *f* des matières.
con'tented *a* satisfait.
contest ['kɒntest] concours *m*; (*fight*) lutte *f*.
con'testant concurrent, -ente *mf*; (*in fight*) adversaire *mf*.
context ['kɒntekst] contexte *m*.
continent ['kɒntɪnənt] continent *m*; **the C.** l'Europe *f* (continentale).
conti'nental *a* (*European*) européen; **c. breakfast** petit déjeuner *m* à la française.
continual *a* continuel.
continually *adv* continuellement.
continue [kən'tɪnjuː] **1** *vt* continuer (**to do** *or* **doing** à *or* de faire); **to c. (with)** (*work etc*) poursuivre; (*resume*) reprendre. **2** *vi* continuer; (*resume*) reprendre.
continuous *a* continu; **c. performance** (*at cinema*) spectacle *m*

permanent.
continuously *adv* sans interruption.
contraceptive *a* & *n* contraceptif (*m*).
contract ['kɒntrækt] contrat *m*.
contradict [kɒntrə'dɪkt] *vt* contredire.
contradiction contradiction *f*.
contrary ['kɒntrərɪ] **1** *adv* **c. to** contrairement à. **2** *n* **on the c.** au contraire.
contrast ['kɒntrɑːst] contraste *m*; **in c. to** par opposition à.
contrasting *a* (*colours, opinions*) opposés.
contribute [kən'trɪbjuːt] **1** *vt* donner (**to** à); (*article*) écrire (**to** pour); **to c. money to** contribuer à. **2** *vi* **to c. to** contribuer à; (*publication*) collaborer à.
contri'bution contribution *f*; (*to fund etc*) cotisation(s) *f*(*pl*).
contrive [kən'traɪv] *vt* **to c. to do** trouver moyen de faire.
contrived *a* artificiel.
control [kən'trəʊl] **1** *vt* (*organization*) diriger; (*traffic*) régler; (*prices, quality, situation, emotion*) contrôler; **to c. oneself** se contrôler. **2** *n* autorité *f* (**over** sur); (*over prices, quality*) contrôle *m*; **controls** (*of train etc*) commandes *fpl*; (*of TV set etc*) boutons *mpl*; **everything is under c.** tout est en ordre; **in c. of** maître de; **to lose c. of** perdre le contrôle de.
control tower tour *f* de contrôle.
convalesce [kɒnvə'les] *vi* être en convalescence.
convalescence convalescence *f*.
convalescent home maison *f* de convalescence.
convenience commodité *f*; **c. foods** plats *mpl* tout préparés; **(public) conveniences** toilettes *fpl*.
convenient [kən'viːnɪənt] *a* commode; (*well-situated*) bien situé (**for the shops**/*etc* par rapport aux magasins/*etc*); (*moment*) convenable; **to be c. (for)** (*suit*) convenir (à).
convent ['kɒnvənt] couvent *m*.
conversation [kɒnvə'seɪʃ(ə)n] conversation *f*.
converse [kən'vɜːs] *vi* s'entretenir (**with** avec).
convert [kən'vɜːt] *vt* convertir (**into** en, **to** à); (*building*) aménager (**into** en).
con'vertible (*car*) (voiture *f*) décapotable *f*.
convey [kən'veɪ] *vt* (*goods, people*) transporter; (*sound, message*) transmettre; (*idea*) communiquer.
conveyor belt tapis *m* roulant.
convict [kən'vɪkt] *vt* déclarer coupable.
con'viction (*for crime*) condamnation *f*; (*belief*) conviction *f*.

convince [kən'vɪns] *vt* convaincre (**of** de).
convincing *a* convaincant.
convoy ['kɒnvɔɪ] (*cars*) convoi *m*.
cook [kʊk] **1** *vt* (*food*) (faire) cuire. **2** *vi* (*of food*) cuire; (*of person*) faire la cuisine. **3** *n* cuisinier, -ière *mf*.
cookbook livre *m* de cuisine.
cooker (*stove*) cuisinière *f*.
cookery cuisine *f*.
cookie ['kʊkɪ] *Am* biscuit *m*.
cooking cuisine *f*.
cooking apple pomme *f* à cuire.
cool [kuːl] **1** *a* (*weather, place, drink etc*) frais (*f* fraîche); (*manner*) calme; (*unfriendly*) froid; **to keep sth c.** tenir qch au frais. **2** *n* (*of evening*) fraîcheur *f*, **to lose one's c.** perdre son sang-froid.
cool (down) 1 *vi* (*of angry person*) se calmer; (*of hot liquid*) refroidir. **2** *vt* refroidir.
cooler (*for food*) glacière *f*.
cool-'headed *a* calme.
coolness fraîcheur *f*; (*unfriendliness*) froideur *f*.
cool off (*refresh oneself*) se rafraîchir.
co-op ['kəʊɒp] *Am* appartement *m* en copropriété.
co-operate [kəʊ'ɒpəreɪt] *vi* coopérer (**in** à, **with** avec).
co-ope'ration coopération *f*.
coop up [kuːp] (*person*) enfermer.
cop [kɒp] (*policeman*) *Fam* flic *m*.
cope [kəʊp] *vi* **to c. with** s'occuper de; (*problem*) faire face à; **(to be able) to c.** (savoir) se débrouiller.
copper ['kɒpəɪ] (*metal*) cuivre *m*.
copy ['kɒpɪ] **1** copie *f*; (*of book, magazine etc*) exemplaire *m*. **2** *vti* copier.
copy out *or* **down** (*letter etc*) (re)copier.
cord [kɔːd] cordon *m*; (*electrical*) cordon *m* électrique.
cordial ['kɔːdɪəl] **(fruit) c.** sirop *m*.
cordon off ['kɔːdən] (*of police etc*) interdire l'accès de.
corduroy ['kɔːdərɔɪ] velours *m* côtelé; **corduroys** pantalon *m* en velours (côtelé).
core [kɔːr] (*of apple etc*) trognon *m*.
cork [kɔːk] liège *m*; (*for bottle*) bouchon *m*.
cork (up) (*bottle*) boucher.
corkscrew tire-bouchon *m*.
corn [kɔːn] (*wheat*) blé *m*; (*maize*) *Am* maïs *m*; (*hard skin on foot*) cor *m*.

corned beef corned-beef *m.*

corner ['kɔːnər] **1** *n* coin *m*; (*bend in road*) virage *m*; *Football* corner *m.* **2** *vt* (*person in corridor etc*) coincer; (*market*) monopoliser.

cornet ['kɔːnɪt] (*of ice cream*) cornet *m.*

cornflakes *npl* céréales *fpl.*

corny ['kɔːnɪ] *a* (*joke*) rebattu.

coronary ['kɒrənərɪ] infarctus *m.*

corporal ['kɔːpərəl] caporal(-chef) *m.*

corpse [kɔːps] cadavre *m.*

correct [kə'rekt] **1** *a* exact, correct; (*proper*) correct; **he's c.** (*right*) il a raison. **2** *vt* corriger.

correction correction *f.*

correctly *adv* correctment.

correspond [kɒrɪ'spɒnd] correspondre (**to**, **with** à); (*by letter*) correspondre (**with** avec).

correspondence correspondance *f*; **c. course** cours *m* par correspondance.

corresponding *a* (*matching*) correspondant.

corridor ['kɒrɪdɔːr] couloir *m.*

corrugated ['kɒrəgeɪtɪd] *a* **c. iron** tôle *f* ondulée.

corrupt [kə'rʌpt] *a* corrompu.

cosmetic [kɒz'metɪk] produit *m* de beauté.

cosmonaut ['kɒzmənɔːt] cosmonaute *mf.*

cost [kɒst] **1** *vti* coûter; **how much does it c.?** ça coûte combien? **2** *n* prix *m*; **at all costs** à tout prix.

costly *a* coûteux.

costume ['kɒstjuːm] costume *m*; (*woman's suit*) tailleur *m*; **(swimming) c.** maillot *m* (de bain).

costume jewellery *or Am* **jewelry** bijoux *mpl* de fantaisie.

cosy ['kəʊzɪ] *a* douillet; **make yourself c.** mets-toi à l'aise.

cot [kɒt] lit *m* d'enfant; (*camp bed*) *Am* lit *m* de camp.

cottage ['kɒtɪdʒ] petite maison *f* de campagne; **(thatched) c.** chaumière *f.*

cottage cheese fromage *m* blanc (maigre).

cotton ['kɒtən] coton *m*; (*yarn*) fil *m* (de coton); **c. wool**, *Am* **absorbent c.** coton *m* hydrophile.

couch [kaʊtʃ] canapé *m.*

couchette [kuː'ʃet] (*on train*) couchette *f.*

cough [kɒf] **1** *n* toux *f*; **c. mixture** sirop *m* contre la toux. **2** *vi* tousser.

cough up 1 *vt* (*blood*) cracher. **2** *vti* (*pay*) *Slang* casquer.

could [kʊd, *unstressed* kəd] *see* **can**[1].
council ['kaʊns(ə)l] conseil *m*; **(town) c.** conseil municipal, municipalité *f*; **c. house** maison *f* louée à la municipalité.
councillor (town) c. conseiller *m* municipal.
count[1] [kaʊnt] **1** *vt* compter. **2** *vi* (*calculate, be important*) compter. **3 he's lost c. of the books he has** il ne sait plus combien il a de livres.
count[2] (*title*) comte *m*.
countdown compte *m* à rebours.
counter ['kaʊntər] (*in shop, bar etc*) comptoir *m*; (*in bank etc*) guichet *m*; (*in games*) jeton *m*.
counter- ['kaʊntər] *prefix* contre-.
counterattack contre-attaque *f*.
counter'clockwise *a & adv Am* dans le sens inverse des aiguilles d'une montre.
counterfoil souche *f*.
count in inclure.
count on s.o./sth (*rely on*) compter sur qn/qch; **to c. on doing** compter faire.
count out exclure; (*money*) compter.
country ['kʌntrɪ] pays *m*; (*regarded with affection*) patrie *f*; (*opposed to town*) campagne *f*; **c. house** maison *f* de campagne.
countryside campagne *f*.
county ['kaʊntɪ] comté *m*.
couple ['kʌp(ə)l] (*of people*) couple *m*; **a c. of** deux ou trois; (*a few*) quelques.
coupon ['kuːpɒn] (*voucher*) bon *m*.
courage ['kʌrɪdʒ] courage *m*.
courageous [kə'reɪdʒəs] *a* courageux.
courgette [kʊə'ʒet] courgette *f*.
courier ['kʊrɪər] (*for tourists*) guide *m*; (*messenger*) messager *m*.
course [kɔːs] **1** *n* (*duration, movement*) cours *m*; (*of ship*) route *f*; **c. (of action)** ligne *f* de conduite; (*option*) parti *m*; **in the c. of** au cours de. ■ (*lessons*) cours *m*; **c. of lectures** série *f* de conférences. ■ **c. (of treatment)** traitement *m*. ■ (*of meal*) plat *m*; **first c.** entrée *f*. ■ **(golf) c.** terrain *m* (de golf). **2** *adv* **of c.!** bien sûr!; **of c. not!** bien sûr que non!
court [kɔːt] (*of king etc, for trials*) cour *f*; **(tennis) c.**, court *m* (de tennis); **to take s.o. to c.** poursuivre qn en justice.
courteous ['kɜːtɪəs] *a* poli.
courtroom salle *f* du tribunal.
courtyard cour *f*.

cousin ['kʌz(ə)n] cousin, -ine *mf*.
cover ['kʌvər] **1** *n* (*lid*) couvercle *m*; (*of book*) couverture *f*; (*for furniture etc*) housse *f*; **the covers** (*on bed*) les couvertures *fpl* et les draps *mpl*; **to take c.** se mettre à l'abri. **2** *vt* couvrir (**with** de); (*insure*) assurer.
coveralls *npl Am* bleus *mpl* de travail.
cover charge (*in restaurant*) couvert *m*.
covering (*wrapping*) enveloppe *f*; (*layer*) couche *f*.
covering letter lettre *f* jointe (*à un document*).
cover over (*floor etc*) recouvrir.
cover up 1 *vt* recouvrir; (*truth*, *tracks*) dissimuler; (*scandal*) étouffer. **2** *vi* **to c. (oneself) up** (*wrap up*) se couvrir.
cover up for s.o. couvrir qn.
cow [kaʊ] vache *f*.
coward ['kaʊəd] lâche *mf*.
cowardice lâcheté *f*.
cowardly *a* lâche.
cowboy cow-boy *m*.
cozy ['kəʊzɪ] *a Am* douillet; **make yourself c.** mets-toi à l'aise.
crab [kræb] crabe *m*.
crack [kræk] **1** *n* fente *f*; (*in glass*, *china*, *bone*) fêlure *f*; (*noise*) craquement *m*; (*of whip*) claquement *m*; (*joke*) *Fam* plaisanterie *f*. **2** *vt* (*glass*, *ice*) fêler; (*nut*) casser; (*whip*) faire claquer; (*joke*) lancer. **3** *vi* se fêler; (*of branch*, *wood*) craquer; **to get cracking** (*get to work*) *Fam* s'y mettre.
cracker (*biscuit*) biscuit *m* (salé); **Christmas c.** diablotin *m*.
crackpot *Fam* cinglé, -ée *mf*.
crack up *vi* (*mentally*) *Fam* craquer.
cradle ['kreɪd(ə)l] berceau *m*.
craft [krɑːft] (*skill*) art *m*; (*job*) métier *m* (artisanal).
craftsman (*pl* **-men**) artisan *m*.
crafty *a* astucieux.
cram [kræm] **1** *vt* **to c. into** (*force*) fourrer dans; **to c. with** (*fill*) bourrer de. **2** *vi* **to c. into** (*of people*) s'entasser dans; **to c. (for an exam)** bachoter.
cramp (*muscle pain*) crampe *f* (**in** à).
cramped [kræmpt] *a* à l'étroit.
crane [kreɪn] (*machine*) grue *f*.
crash [kræʃ] **1** *n* accident *m*; (*of firm*) faillite *f*; (*noise*) fracas *m*. **2** *int* (*of fallen object*) patatras! **3** *vt* (*car*) avoir un accident avec; **to c. one's car into** faire rentrer sa voiture dans. **4** *vi* (*of car*, *plane*) s'écraser; **to c. into** rentrer dans.

crash course/diet cours *m*/régime *m* intensif.
crash down (*fall*) tomber; (*break*) se casser.
crash helmet casque *m* (anti-choc).
crash-land *vi* atterrir en catastrophe.
crash landing atterrissage *m* en catastrophe.
crate [kreɪt] caisse *f*.
craving ['kreɪvɪŋ] désir *m* (**for** de).
crawl [krɔːl] **1** *vi* ramper; (*of child*) marcher à quatre pattes; (*of vehicle*) avancer au pas; **to be crawling with** grouiller de. **2** *n* (*swimming stroke*) crawl *m*.
crayon ['kreɪən] crayon *m* de couleur (*en cire*).
craze [kreɪz] manie *f* (**for** de).
crazy ['kreɪzɪ] *a* fou (*f* folle); **c. about sth** fana de qch; **c. about s.o.** fou de qn.
creak [kriːk] *vi* (*of hinge*) grincer.
cream [kriːm] crème *f*; **c. cake** gâteau *m* à la crème.
cream cheese fromage *m* blanc.
creamy *a* crémeux.
crease [kriːs] **1** *vt* froisser. **2** *vi* se froisser. **3** *n* pli *m*.
create [kriː'eɪt] *vt* créer; (*impression, noise*) faire.
creation création *f*.
creative *a* créatif.
creature ['kriːtʃər] animal *m*; (*person*) créature *f*.
crèche [kreʃ] (*nursery*) crèche *f*.
credible ['kredɪb(ə)l] *a* croyable; (*politician etc*) crédible.
credit ['kredɪt] **1** *n* (*financial*) crédit *m*; (*merit*) mérite *m*; (*from university*) unité *f* de valeur; **to be a c. to** faire honneur à; **on c.** à crédit; **in c.** (*account*) créditeur. **2** *vt* (*of bank*) créditer (**s.o. with sth** qn de qch).
credit card carte *f* de crédit.
credit facilities facilités *fpl* de paiement.
creditworthy *a* solvable.
creek [kriːk] (*stream*) *Am* ruisseau *m*.
creep* [kriːp] *vi* ramper; (*silently*) se glisser; (*slowly*) avancer lentement.
creepy *a* (*causing fear*) *Fam* terrifiant.
cremate [krɪ'meɪt] *vt* incinérer.
cremation crémation *f*.
crema'torium (*Am* **'crematory**) crématorium *m*.
crêpe paper [kreɪp] papier *m* crêpon.
cress [kres] cresson *m*.
crest [krest] (*of wave etc*) crête *f*; (*of hill*) sommet *m*.

crew [kruː] (*of ship, plane*) équipage *m*.
crew cut (coupe *f* en) brosse *f*.
crib [krɪb] (*cot*) *Am* lit *m* d'enfant; (*list of answers*) pompe *f* antisèche.
cricket ['krɪkɪt] (*game*) cricket *m*; (*insect*) grillon *m*.
crime [kraɪm] crime *m*; (*not serious*) délit *m*; (*criminal practice*) criminalité *f*.
criminal *a* & *n* criminel, -elle (*mf*).
cripple ['krɪpəl] (*disabled person*) infirme *mf*.
crisis, *pl* **-ses** ['kraɪsɪs, -siːz] crise *f*.
crisp [krɪsp] **1** *a* (*biscuit*) croustillant; (*apple*) croquant. **2** *npl* **(potato) crisps** chips *mpl*.
crispbread pain *m* suédois.
critic ['krɪtɪk] critique *m*.
critical *a* critique.
critically *adv* (*ill*) gravement.
criticism critique *f*.
criticize *vti* critiquer.
crochet ['krəʊʃeɪ] **1** *vt* faire au crochet. **2** *vi* faire du crochet. **3** *n* (travail *m* au) crochet *m*.
crockery ['krɒkərɪ] (*cups etc*) vaisselle *f*.
crocodile ['krɒkədaɪl] crocodile *m*.
crocus ['krəʊkəs] crocus *m*.
crook [krʊk] (*thief*) escroc *m*.
crooked ['krʊkɪd] *a* (*stick*) courbé; (*path*) tortueux; (*hat*, *picture*) de travers.
crop [krɒp] (*harvest*) récolte *f*; (*produce*) culture *f*.
crop up *vi* se présenter.
croquet ['krəʊkeɪ] croquet *m*.
cross[1] [krɒs] **1** *n* croix *f*; **a c. between** (*animal*) un croisement entre *or* de. **2** *vt* (*street*, *room etc*) traverser; (*barrier*) franchir; (*legs*) croiser; (*cheque*, *Am check*) barrer. **3** *vi* (*of paths*) se croiser.
cross[2] *a* (*angry*) fâché (**with** contre).
cross-country 'race cross(-country) *m*.
cross-eyed *a* qui louche.
crossing (*by ship*) traversée *f*; **(pedestrian) c.** passage *m* clouté.
cross off *or* **out** (*word*, *name etc*) rayer.
cross over *vti* traverser.
cross-'reference renvoi *m*.
crossroads carrefour *m*.
cross-section coupe *f* transversale; (*sample*) échantillon *m*.
crosswalk *Am* passage *m* clouté.

crossword (puzzle) mots *mpl* croisés.
crouch (down) [krautʃ] *vi* s'accroupir.
crow [krəu] corbeau *m*.
crowbar levier *m*.
crowd [kraud] foule *f*; (*particular group*) bande *f*.
crowded *a* plein (**with** de).
crowd into (*of people*) s'entasser dans.
crowd round s.o./sth se presser autour de qn/qch.
crown [kraun] couronne *f*.
crucial ['kruːʃəl] *a* crucial.
crude [kruːd] *a* (*manners*, *language*) grossier; (*work*) rudimentaire.
cruel [kruəl] *a* cruel.
cruelty cruauté *f*; **an act of c.** une cruauté.
cruet (stand) ['kruːɪt] salière *f*, poivrière *f* et huilier *m*.
cruise [kruːz] **1** *vi* (*of ship*) croiser; (*of car*) rouler; (*of plane*) voler; (*of tourists*) faire une croisière. **2** *n* croisière *f*.
crumb [krʌm] miette *f*.
crumble ['krʌmb(ə)l] **1** *vt* (*bread*) émietter. **2** *vi* (*in small pieces*) s'effriter; (*of bread*) s'émietter; (*become ruined*) tomber en ruine.
crumbly *a* friable.
crummy ['krʌmɪ] *a Fam* moche.
crumpet ['krʌmpɪt] petite crêpe *f* grillée (*servie beurrée*).
crumple ['krʌmp(ə)l] *vt* froisser.
crunch [krʌntʃ] *vt* (*food*) croquer.
crunchy *a* (*apple etc*) croquant; (*bread*, *biscuit*, *Am cookie*) croustillant.
crush [krʌʃ] **1** *n* (*crowd*) cohue *f*; (*rush*) bousculade *f*. **2** *vt* écraser; (*clothes*) froisser; (*cram*) entasser (**into** dans).
crust [krʌst] croûte *f*.
crusty *a* (*bread*) croustillant.
crutch [krʌtʃ] (*of invalid*) béquille *f*.
cry [kraɪ] **1** *n* (*shout*) cri *m*; **to have a c.** *Fam* pleurer. **2** *vi* pleurer; (*shout*) pousser un cri.
crying (*weeping*) pleurs *mpl*.
cry off *vi* abandonner.
cry out 1 *vi* pousser un cri; (*exclaim*) s'écrier. **2** *vt* crier.
cry out for sth demander qch (à grands cris); **to be crying out for sth** avoir grand besoin de qch.
cry over sth/s.o. pleurer (sur) qch/qn.
crystal ['krɪst(ə)l] cristal *m*.
cub [kʌb] (*scout*) louveteau *m*.
cube [kjuːb] cube *m*; (*of meat etc*) dé *m*.

cubic *a* (*metre etc*) cube.
cubicle ['kju:bɪk(ə)l] (*for changing*) cabine *f*; (*in hospital*) box *m*.
cuckoo ['kʊku:] (*bird*) coucou *m*.
cucumber ['kju:kʌmbər] concombre *m*.
cuddle ['kʌd(ə)l] **1** *vt* (*hug*) serrer; (*caress*) câliner. **2** *vi* se serrer. **3** *n* caresse *f*.
cuddle up to s.o. se serrer contre qn.
cuddly *a* câlin; (*toy*) doux (*f* douce).
cue [kju:] (*in theatre*) réplique *f*; (*signal*) signal *m*.
cuff [kʌf] (*of shirt*) poignet *m*; (*of trousers*, *Am pants*) *Am* revers *m*.
cuff link bouton *m* de manchette.
cul-de-sac ['kʌldəsæk] impasse *f*.
culprit ['kʌlprɪt] coupable *mf*.
cultivate ['kʌltɪveɪt] *vt* cultiver.
cultivated *a* cultivé.
cultural *a* culturel.
culture ['kʌltʃər] culture *f*.
cultured *a* cultivé.
cumbersome ['kʌmbəsəm] *a* encombrant.
cunning ['kʌnɪŋ] **1** *a* astucieux. **2** *n* astuce *f*.
cup [kʌp] tasse *f*; (*prize*) coupe *f*.
cupboard ['kʌbəd] armoire *f*; (*built-in*) placard *m*.
cupful tasse *f*.
curable *a* guérissable.
curb [kɜ:b] (*kerb*) *Am* bord *m* du trottoir.
curd cheese [kɜ:d] fromage *m* blanc (maigre).
cure [kjʊər] **1** *vt* guérir (*qn*) (**of** de). **2** *n* remède *m* (**for** contre); **rest c.** cure *f* de repos.
curi'osity curiosité *f*.
curious ['kjʊərɪəs] *a* (*odd*) curieux; (*inquisitive*) curieux (**about** de).
curl [kɜ:l] **1** *vti* (*hair*) boucler. **2** *n* boucle *f*.
curler bigoudi *m*.
curl (oneself) up se pelotonner.
curly *a* (*hair*) bouclé.
currant ['kʌrənt] (*dried grape*) raisin *m* de Corinthe.
currency ['kʌrənsɪ] monnaie *f*; (*foreign*) devises *fpl* (étrangères).
current ['kʌrənt] **1** *a* actuel; (*opinion*) courant; (*year*) courant. **2** *n* (*of river*, *electric*) courant *m*.
current affairs questions *fpl* d'actualité.
currently *adv* actuellement.
curriculum [kə'rɪkjʊləm] programme *m* (scolaire).
curry ['kʌrɪ] curry *m*.

curse [kɜːs] *vi* (*swear*) jurer.
cursor ['kɜːsər] (*of computer*) curseur *m*.
curtain ['kɜːt(ə)n] rideau *m*.
curts(e)y ['kɜːtsɪ] **1** *n* révérence *f*. **2** *vi* faire une révérence.
curve [kɜːv] **1** *n* courbe *f*; (*in road*) virage *m*. **2** *vi* se courber; (*of road*) faire une courbe.
cushion ['kʊʃən] coussin *m*.
custard ['kʌstəd] crème *f* anglaise; (*when set*) crème *f* renversée.
custom ['kʌstəm] coutume *f*; (*customers*) clientèle *f*.
customer client, -ente *mf*.
customs *n(pl)* **(the) c.** la douane; **c. (duties)** droits *mpl* de douane; **c. officer** douanier *m*.
cut [kʌt] **1** *n* (*mark*) coupure *f*; (*stroke*) coup *m*; (*of clothes, hair*) coupe *f*; (*in salary, prices etc*) réduction *f*; (*of meat*) morceau *m*. **2** *vt** couper; (*meat*) découper; (*glass, tree*) tailler; (*salary etc*) réduire; **to c. open** ouvrir (*au couteau etc*). **3** *vi* (*of person, scissors*) couper.
cut away (*remove*) enlever.
cutback réduction *f*.
cut back (on) *vti* réduire.
cut down (*tree*) abattre.
cut down (on) *vti* réduire.
cute [kjuːt] *a Fam* (*pretty*) mignon (*f* mignonne).
cut into (*cake*) entamer.
cutlery ['kʌtlərɪ] couverts *mpl*.
cutlet ['kʌtlɪt] côtelette *f*.
cut off *vt* couper; (*isolate*) isoler.
cut out 1 *vi* (*of engine*) caler. **2** *vt* (*article*) découper; (*remove*) enlever; **to c. out drinking** s'arrêter de boire; **c. it out!** *Fam* ça suffit!; **c. out to be a doctor/***etc* fait pour être médecin/*etc*.
cutout (*picture*) découpage *m*.
cut-'price *a* à prix réduit.
cutting (*newspaper article*) coupure *f*.
cut up *vt* couper (en morceaux).
cv [siː'viː] *abbr* curriculum (vitae) *m inv*.
cycle ['saɪk(ə)l] **1** *n* (*bicycle*) bicyclette *f*; (*series, period*) cycle *m*. **2** *vi* aller à bicyclette (**to** à).
cycle path *or* **track** piste *f* cyclable.
cycling cyclisme *m*.
cyclist cycliste *mf*.
cylinder ['sɪlɪndər] cylindre *m*.
cymbal ['sɪmbəl] cymbale *f*.

D

dab [dæb] *vt* (*wound*) tamponner; **to d. sth on sth** appliquer qch sur qch.
Dacron® ['dækrɒn] *Am* tergal® *m*.
daddy [dæd(ɪ)] *Fam* papa *m*.
daffodil ['dæfədɪl] jonquille *f*.
daft [dɑːft] *a Fam* idiot, bête.
daily ['deɪlɪ] **1** *a* quotidien. **2** *adv* quotidiennement. **3** *n* **d. (paper)** quotidien *m*; **d. (help)** femme *f* de ménage.
dairy ['deərɪ] *a* (*product*) laitier.
daisy ['deɪzɪ] pâquerette *f*.
dam [dæm] barrage *m*.
damage ['dæmɪdʒ] **1** *n* dégâts *mpl*; (*harm*) préjudice *m*. **2** *vt* (*spoil*) abîmer; (*harm*) nuire à.
damn [dæm] *Fam* **1** *int* **d. (it)!** zut!; **d. him!** qu'il aille au diable! **2** *a* (*awful*) fichu. **3** *adv* (*very*) vachement.
damp [dæmp] **1** *a* humide. **2** *n* humidité *f*.
damp(en) *vt* humecter.
dampness humidité *f*.
dance [dɑːns] **1** *n* danse *f*; (*social event*) bal *m* (*pl* bals). **2** *vti* danser.
dance hall salle *f* de danse.
dancer danseur, -euse *mf*.
dandelion ['dændɪlaɪən] pissenlit *m*.
dandruff ['dændrʌf] pellicules *fpl*.
Dane [deɪn] Danois, -oise *mf*.
danger ['deɪndʒər] danger *m* (**to** pour); **in d.** en danger; **to be in d. of falling**/*etc* risquer de tomber/*etc*.
dangerous *a* dangereux (**to** pour).
Danish ['deɪnɪʃ] **1** *a* danois. **2** *n* (*language*) danois *m*.
dare [deər] *vt* oser (**do** faire); **to d. s.o. to do** défier qn de faire.
daring *a* audacieux.
dark [dɑːk] **1** *a* obscur, noir; (*colour*, *eyes*) foncé; (*skin*, *hair*) brun; **it's d.** il fait nuit *or* noir; **d. glasses** lunettes *fpl* noires. **2** *n* noir *m*, obscurité *f*.
dark-'haired *a* aux cheveux bruns.
darkness obscurité *f*, noir *m*.
dark-'skinned *a* brun.
darling ['dɑːlɪŋ] **(my) d.** (mon) chéri, (ma) chérie.
dart [dɑːt] fléchette *f*; **darts** (*game*) fléchettes *fpl*.
dartboard cible *f*.

dash [dæʃ] **1** *vi* se précipiter. **2** *n* (*stroke*) trait *m*.
dash away *or* **off** partir en vitesse.
dashboard (*of car*) tableau *m* de bord.
data ['deɪtə] *npl* données *fpl*.
data processing informatique *f*.
date[1] [deɪt] **1** *n* (*time*) date *f*; (*meeting*) *Fam* rendez-vous *m inv*; (*person*) *Fam* copain, -ine *mf*; **up to d.** moderne; (*information*) à jour; (*well-informed*) au courant (**on** de); **out of d.** (*old-fashioned*) démodé; (*expired*) périmé. **2** *vt* (*letter etc*) dater; (*girl, boy*) *Fam* sortir avec.
date[2] [deɪt] (*fruit*) datte *f*.
datebook *Am* agenda *m*.
date stamp (tampon *m*) dateur *m*; (*mark*) cachet *m*.
daughter ['dɔːtər] fille *f*.
daughter-in-law (*pl* **daughters-in-law**) belle-fille *f*.
dawdle ['dɔːd(ə)l] *vi* traîner.
dawn [dɔːn] aube *f*.
day [deɪ] jour *m*; (*whole day long*) journée *f*; **all d. (long)** toute la journée; **the following** *or* **next d.** le lendemain; **the d. before** la veille; **the d. before yesterday** avant-hier; **the d. after tomorrow** après-demain.
daylight (lumière *f* du) jour *m*.
day return (*on train*) aller et retour *m* (*pour une journée*).
daytime journée *f*, jour *m*.
dead [ded] **1** *a* mort. **2** *adv* (*completely*) absolument; (*very*) très.
dead end (*street*) impasse *f*.
deadline date *f* limite; (*hour*) heure *f* limite.
deaf [def] *a* sourd; **d. and dumb** sourd-muet.
deafness surdité *f*.
deal[1] [diːl] **a good** *or* **great d.** (*a lot*) beaucoup (**of** de).
deal[2] **1** *n* (*in business*) marché *m*, affaire *f*; **it's a d.** d'accord. **2** *vi** (*trade*) traiter (**with s.o.** avec qn); **to d. in** faire le commerce de; **to d. with** s'occuper de; (*concern*) traiter de.
deal (out) (*cards*) donner.
dealer marchand, -ande *mf* (**in** de); (*agent*) dépositaire *mf*; (*for cars*) concessionnaire *mf*.
dealings *npl* relations *fpl* (**with** avec); (*in business*) transactions *fpl*.
dear [dɪər] **1** *a* (*loved, expensive*) cher; **D. Sir** (*in letter*) Monsieur; **oh d.!** oh là là! **2** *n* **(my) d.** (*darling*) (mon) chéri, (ma) chérie; (*friend*) mon cher, ma chère.
death [deθ] mort *f*.
death certificate acte *m* de décès.

debate [dɪ'beɪt] **1** *vti* discuter. **2** *n* débat *m*, discussion *f*.
debit ['debɪt] **1** *n* débit *m*; **in d.** (*account*) débiteur. **2** *vt* débiter (**s.o. with sth** qn de qch).
debt [det] dette *f*; **to be in d.** avoir des dettes.
decade ['dekeɪd] décennie *f*.
decaffeinated [diː'kæfɪneɪtɪd] *a* décaféiné.
decal ['diːkæl] *Am* décalcomanie *f*.
decay [dɪ'keɪ] (*of tooth*) carie(s) *f*(*pl*).
deceive [dɪ'siːv] *vti* tromper.
December [dɪ'sembər] décembre *m*.
decent ['diːsənt] *a* (*respectable*) convenable, décent; (*good*) *Fam* bon; (*kind*) *Fam* gentil.
decide [dɪ'saɪd] **1** *vt* (*question etc*) décider; **to d. to do** décider de faire; **to d. that** décider que. **2** *vi* (*make decisions*) décider (**on** de); (*make up one's mind*) se décider (**on doing** à faire); (*choose*) se décider (**on** pour).
decimal ['desɪməl] **1** *a* **d. point** virgule *f*. **2** *n* décimale *f*.
decision [dɪ'sɪʒ(ə)n] décision *f*.
decisive [dɪ'saɪsɪv] *a* décisif; (*victory*) net (*f* nette).
deck [dek] (*of ship*) pont *m*.
deckchair chaise *f* longue.
declare [dɪ'kleər] *vt* déclarer (**that** que); (*verdict*, *result*) proclamer.
decline [dɪ'klaɪn] *vi* (*become less*) (*of popularity etc*) être en baisse.
decorate ['dekəreɪt] *vt* (*cake*, *house*, *soldier*) décorer (**with** de); (*hat*, *skirt etc*) orner (**with** de); (*paint etc*) peindre (et tapisser); (*pièce*, *maison*).
deco'ration décoration *f*.
decorative *a* décoratif.
decorator peintre *m* décorateur; **(interior) d.** décorateur, -trice *mf*.
decrease **1** *vti* [dɪ'kriːs] diminuer. **2** *n* ['diːkriːs] diminution *f* (**in** de).
dedicated ['dedɪkeɪtɪd] *a* (*teacher etc*) consciencieux.
deduct [dɪ'dʌkt] *vt* déduire (**from** de); (*from wage*, *account*) prélever (**from** sur).
deduction déduction *f*.
deed [diːd] action *f*, acte *m*; (*document*) acte *m* (notarié).
deep [diːp] *a* profond; (*voice*) grave; **to be six metres**/*etc* **d.** avoir six mètres/*etc* de profondeur; **the d. end** (*in pool*) le grand bain.
deep-'freeze **1** *vt* surgeler. **2** *n* congélateur *m*.
deer [dɪər] *n inv* cerf *m*.
defeat [dɪ'fiːt] **1** *vt* battre. **2** *n* défaite *f*.
defect ['diːfekt] défaut *m*.

de'fective *a* défectueux.
defence [dɪ'fens] (*Am* **defense**) défense *f*.
defend [dɪ'fend] *vt* défendre.
defendant (*accused*) prévenu, -ue *mf*.
defiant [dɪ'faɪənt] *a* (*tone, attitude*) de défi; (*person*) rebelle.
deficiency manque *m*; (*of vitamins etc*) carence *f*.
deficient [dɪ'fɪʃənt] *a* insuffisant; **to be d. in** manquer de.
deficit ['defɪsɪt] déficit *m*.
define [dɪ'faɪn] *vt* définir.
definite ['defɪnɪt] *a* (*date, plan*) précis; (*reply, improvement*) net (*f* nette); (*order, offer*) ferme; (*certain*) certain; **d. article** *Grammar* article *m* défini.
definitely *adv* certainement; (*considerably*) nettement; (*to say*) catégoriquement.
defi'nition définition *f*.
deformed [dɪ'fɔːmd] *a* (*body*) difforme.
defrost [diː'frɒst] *vt* (*fridge*) dégivrer; (*food*) décongeler.
defy [dɪ'faɪ] *vt* défier (*qn*); **to d. s.o. to do** défier qn de faire.
degenerate [dɪ'dʒenəreɪt] *vi* dégénérer (**into** en).
degree [dɪ'griː] (*angle, temperature*) degré *m*; (*from university*) diplôme *m*; (*Bachelor's*) licence *f*; (*Master's*) maîtrise *f*; (*PhD*) doctorat *m*; **to such a d.** à tel point (**that** que).
de-ice [diː'aɪs] *vt* (*car window etc*) dégivrer.
de-icer (*substance*) dégivreur *m*.
dejected [dɪ'dʒektɪd] *a* abattu.
delay [dɪ'leɪ] **1** *vt* retarder; (*payment*) différer. **2** *vi* (*be slow*) tarder (**doing** à faire); (*linger*) s'attarder. **3** *n* retard *m*; (*waiting period*) délai *m*; **without d.** sans tarder.
delegate 1 *vt* ['delɪgeɪt] déléguer (**to** à). **2** *n* ['delɪgət] délégué, -ée *mf*.
dele'gation délégation *f*.
delete [dɪ'liːt] *vt* rayer.
deliberate [dɪ'lɪbərət] *a* (*intentional*) intentionnel.
deliberately *adv* (*intentionally*) exprès.
delicacy (*food*) mets *m* délicat.
delicate ['delɪkət] *a* délicat.
delica'tessen traiteur *m* et épicerie *f* fine.
delicious [dɪ'lɪʃəs] *a* délicieux.
delight [dɪ'laɪt] **1** *n* délice *m*; **to take d. in sth/in doing** se délecter de qch/à faire. **2** *vt* réjouir. **3** *vi* **to d. in doing** se délecter à faire.
delighted *a* ravi (**with sth** de qch, **to do** de faire, **that** que).
delightful *a* charmant; (*meal*) délicieux.

delinquent [dɪ'lɪŋkwənt] délinquant, -ante *mf*.
deliver [dɪ'lɪvər] *vt* (*goods etc*) livrer; (*letters*) distribuer; (*hand over*) remettre (**to** à); (*speech*) prononcer; (*warning*) lancer.
delivery livraison *f*; (*of letters*) distribution *f*; (*handing over*) remise *f*; (*birth*) accouchement *m*.
delude [dɪ'lu:d] *vt* tromper; **to d. oneself** se faire des illusions.
de luxe [dɪ'lʌks] *a* de luxe.
demand [dɪ'mɑ:nd] **1** *vt* exiger (**sth from s.o.** qch de qn); (*rights, more pay*) revendiquer; **to d. that** exiger que. **2** *n* exigence *f*; (*claim*) revendication *f*; (*for goods*) demande *f*; **in great d.** très demandé.
demanding *a* exigeant.
demerara (sugar) [demə'reərə] sucre *m* roux.
democracy [dɪ'mɒkrəsɪ] démocratie *f*.
demo'cratic *a* démocratique; (*person*) démocrate.
demolish [dɪ'mɒlɪʃ] *vt* démolir.
demo'lition démolition *f*.
demonstrate ['demənstreɪt] **1** *vt* démontrer; (*machine*) faire une démonstration de. **2** *vi* manifester.
demon'stration démonstration *f*; (*protest*) manifestation *f*.
de'monstrative *a* & *n Grammar* démonstratif (*m*).
demonstrator (*protester*) manifestant, -ante *mf*.
demoralize [dɪ'mɒrəlaɪz] *vt* démoraliser.
den tanière *f*.
denial [dɪ'naɪəl] (*of rumour*) démenti *m*.
denim ['denɪm] (toile *f* de) coton *m*; **denims** (*jeans*) (blue-)jean *m*.
denounce [dɪ'naʊns] *vt* (*person, injustice etc*) dénoncer (**to** à).
dense [dens] *a* dense; (*stupid*) *Fam* lourd, bête.
dent [dent] **1** *n* (*in car etc*) bosse *f*. **2** *vt* cabosser.
dental ['dent(ə)l] *a* dentaire.
dentist dentiste *mf*.
dentures *npl* dentier *m*.
deny [dɪ'naɪ] *vt* nier (**doing** avoir fait, **that** que); (*rumour*) démentir; **to d. s.o. sth** refuser qch à qn.
deodorant [di:'əʊdərənt] déodorant *m*.
depart [dɪ'pɑ:t] *vi* partir; (*deviate*) s'écarter (**from** de).
department [dɪ'pɑ:tmənt] département *m*; (*in office*) service *m*; (*in shop*) rayon *m*.
department store grand magasin *m*.
departure départ *m*; **a d. from** (*rule*) un écart par rapport à.
depend [dɪ'pend] *vi* dépendre (**on, upon** de); **to d. (up)on** (*rely on*) compter sur (**for sth** pour qch).

dependable *a* sûr.
dependant personne *f* à charge.
depict [dɪ'pɪkt] *vt* (*describe*) dépeindre; (*in pictures*) représenter.
deplorable *a* déplorable.
deplore [dɪ'plɔːr] *vt* déplorer.
deposit [dɪ'pɒzɪt] **1** *vt* déposer. **2** *n* dépôt *m*; (*part payment*) acompte *m*; (*against damage*) caution *f*; (*on bottle*) consigne *f*.
depot [*Am* 'diːpəʊ] (*railroad station*) *Am* gare *f*; **(bus) d.** *Am* gare *f* routière.
depress [dɪ'pres] *vt* (*discourage*) déprimer.
depressed [dɪ'prest] *a* déprimé; **to get d.** se décourager.
depression dépression *f*.
deprive [dɪ'praɪv] *vt* priver (**of** de).
deprived *a* (*child etc*) déshérité.
depth [depθ] profondeur *f*.
deputy ['depjʊtɪ] (*replacement*) remplaçant, -ante *mf*; (*assistant*) adjoint, -ointe *mf*.
derailment déraillement *m*.
derelict ['derɪlɪkt] *a* abandonné.
derive [dɪ'raɪv] *vt* **to d. from sth** (*pleasure etc*) tirer de qch; **to be derived from** (*of word etc*) dériver de.
descend [dɪ'send] **1** *vi* descendre (**from** de). **2** *vt* (*stairs*) descendre.
descendant descendant, -ante *mf*.
descend upon (*of tourists*) envahir.
descent (*of aircraft etc*) descente *f*.
describe [dɪ'skraɪb] *vt* décrire.
description description *f*; (*on passport*) signalement *m*; **of every d.** de toutes sortes.
desert[1] ['dezət] désert *m*; **d. island** île *f* déserte.
desert[2] [dɪ'zɜːt] *vt* abandonner.
deserted *a* (*place*) désert.
deserve [dɪ'zɜːv] *vt* mériter (**to do** de faire).
design [dɪ'zaɪn] **1** *vt* (*car etc*) dessiner; **designed to do/for s.o.** conçu pour faire/pour qn; **well designed** bien conçu. **2** *n* (*pattern*) motif *m*; (*sketch*) plan *m*, dessin *m*; (*type of dress or car*) modèle *m*.
designer dessinateur, -trice *mf*.
designer clothes vêtements *mpl* griffés.
desirable *a* désirable.
desire [dɪ'zaɪər] **1** *n* désir *m*; **I've no d. to** je n'ai aucune envie de. **2** *vt* désirer (**to do** faire).
desk [desk] (*in school*) table *f*; (*in office*) bureau *m*; (*in shop*) caisse *f*; **(reception) d.** réception *f*.

desk clerk (*in hotel*) *Am* réceptionniste *mf*.
despair [dɪ'speər] **1** *n* désespoir *m*; **to be in d.** être au désespoir. **2** *vi* désespérer (**of s.o.** de qn, **of doing** de faire).
despatch [dɪ'spætʃ] *see* **dispatch.**
'desperate *a* désespéré; **to be d. for** avoir désespérément besoin de; (*cigarette, baby*) mourir d'envie d'avoir.
despicable [dɪ'spɪkəb(ə)l] *a* méprisable.
despise [dɪ'spaɪz] *vt* mépriser.
despite [dɪ'spaɪt] *prep* malgré.
dessert [dɪ'zɜːt] dessert *m*.
dessertspoon cuillère *f* à dessert.
destination [destɪ'neɪʃ(ə)n] destination *f*.
destitute ['destɪtjuːt] *a* indigent.
destroy [dɪ'strɔɪ] *vt* détruire.
destruction destruction *f*.
destructive *a* destructeur.
detach [dɪ'tætʃ] *vt* détacher (**from** de).
detachable *a* (*lining*) amovible.
detached house maison *f* individuelle.
detail ['diːteɪl, *Am* dɪ'teɪl] détail *m*; **in d.** en détail.
detailed *a* détaillé.
detain [dɪ'teɪn] *vt* retenir; (*prisoner*) détenir.
detect [dɪ'tekt] (*find*) découvrir; (*see, hear*) distinguer.
detective [dɪ'tektɪv] inspecteur *m* de police; (*private*) détective *m*; **d. film/novel** film *m*/roman *m* policier.
detector détecteur *m*.
detention (*school punishment*) retenue *f*.
deter [dɪ'tɜːr] *vt* **to d. s.o.** dissuader qn (**from doing** de faire, **from sth** de qch).
detergent [dɪ'tɜːdʒənt] détergent *m*.
deteriorate [dɪ'tɪərɪəreɪt] *vi* se détériorer.
deterio'ration détérioration *f*.
determi'nation (*intention*) ferme intention *f*.
determine [dɪ'tɜːmɪn] *vt* déterminer; (*price*) fixer.
determined *a* déterminé; **d. to do** *or* **on doing** décidé à faire.
deterrent [dɪ'terənt, *Am* dɪ'tɜːrənt] **to be a d.** être dissuasif.
detest [dɪ'test] *vt* détester (**doing** faire).
detour ['diːtʊər] détour *m*.
develop [dɪ'veləp] **1** *vt* développer; (*area, land*) mettre en valeur; (*habit, illness*) contracter. **2** *vi* se développer.
develop into devenir.
development développement *m*; **housing d.** lotissement *m*; (*large*)

grand ensemble *m*; **a (new) d.** (*in situation*) un fait nouveau.
deviate ['diːvɪeɪt] *vi* dévier (**from** de).
device [dɪ'vaɪs] dispositif *m*; **left to one's own devices** livré à soi-même.
devil ['dev(ə)l] diable *m*; **what/where/why the d.?** que/où/pourquoi diable?
devise [dɪ'vaɪz] *vt* (*a plan*) combiner; (*invent*) inventer.
devote [dɪ'vəʊt] *vt* consacrer (**to** à).
devoted *a* dévoué.
devotion dévouement *m* (**to s.o.** à qn).
dew [djuː] rosée *f*.
diabetes [daɪə'biːtiːz] diabète *m*.
diabetic diabétique *mf*.
diagnosis, *pl* **-oses** [daɪəg'nəʊsɪs, -əʊsiːz] diagnostic *m*.
diagonal [daɪ'ægən(ə)l] **1** *a* diagonal. **2** *n* **d. (line)** diagonale *f*.
diagonally *adv* en diagonale.
diagram ['daɪəgræm] schéma *m*.
dial ['daɪəl] **1** *n* cadran *m*. **2** *vt* (*phone number*) faire; (*person*) appeler.
dialect ['daɪəlekt] dialecte *m*.
dialling code indicatif *m*.
dialling tone, *Am* **dial tone** tonalité *f*.
dialogue ['daɪəlɒg] (*Am* **dialog**) dialogue *m*.
diameter [daɪ'æmɪtər] diamètre *m*.
diamond ['daɪəmənd] diamant *m*; (*shape*) losange *m*; *Baseball* terrain *m*; **diamond(s)** (*at cards*) carreau *m*; **d. necklace** rivière *f* de diamants.
diaper ['daɪəpər] (*for baby*) *Am* couche *f*.
diarrh(o)ea [daɪə'riːə] diarrhée *f*.
diary ['daɪərɪ] (*calendar*) agenda *m*; (*private*) journal *m* (intime).
dice [daɪs] **1** *n inv* dé *m* (à jouer). **2** *vt* (*food*) couper en dés.
dictate [dɪk'teɪt] *vti* dicter (**to** à).
dictation dictée *f*.
dictionary ['dɪkʃənərɪ] dictionnaire *m*.
did [dɪd] *pt de* **do**[1].
die [daɪ] *vi* (*pt & pp* **died**, *pres p* **dying**) mourir (**of, from** de); **to be dying to do** mourir d'envie de faire; **to be dying for sth** avoir une envie folle de qch.
die away (*of noise*) mourir.
die down (*of storm*) se calmer.
die out (*of custom*) mourir.
diesel ['diːzəl] *a* & *n* **d. (engine)** (moteur *m*) diesel *m*; **d. (oil)**

gazole *m*.

diet ['daɪət] **1** *n* (*for slimming*) régime *m*; (*usual food*) alimentation *f*; **to go on a d.** faire un régime. **2** *vi* suivre un régime.

differ ['dɪfər] *vi* différer (**from** de); (*disagree*) ne pas être d'accord (**from** avec).

difference différence *f* (**in** de); **d. (of opinion)** différend *m*; **it makes no d.** ça n'a pas d'importance; **it makes no d. to me** ça m'est égal.

different différent (**from, to** de); (*another*) autre; (*various*) divers.

differently *adv* autrement (**from, to** que).

difficult ['dɪfɪkəlt] *a* difficile (**to do** à faire); **it's d. for us to** il nous est difficile de.

difficulty difficulté *f*; **to have d. doing** avoir du mal à faire.

dig* [dɪg] **1** *vt* (*ground*) bêcher; (*hole*) creuser. **2** *vi* creuser.

digest [daɪ'dʒest] *vti* digérer.

digestion digestion *f*.

digger (*machine*) pelleteuse *f*.

dig sth into (*push*) enfoncer qch dans.

digit ['dɪdʒɪt] (*number*) chiffre *m*.

digital *a* numérique.

dig out (*from ground*) déterrer; (*accident victim*) dégager; (*find*) dénicher.

dig up (*from ground*) déterrer; (*weed*) arracher; (*earth*) retourner; (*street*) piocher.

dilapidated [dɪ'læpɪdeɪtɪd] *a* délabré.

dilute [daɪ'luːt] *vt* diluer.

dim [dɪm] **1** *a* (*light*) faible; (*room*) sombre; (*memory, outline*) vague; (*person*) stupide. **2** *vt* (*light*) baisser.

dime [daɪm] *US Can* (pièce *f* de) dix cents *mpl*; **a d. store** = un Prisunic®.

dimension [daɪ'menʃ(ə)n] dimension *f*.

din [dɪn] vacarme *m*.

dine [daɪn] *vi* dîner (**on** de).

dine out dîner en ville.

diner dîneur, -euse *mf*; (*train carriage*) wagon-restaurant *m*; (*restaurant*) *Am* petit restaurant *m*.

dinghy ['dɪŋgɪ] petit canot *m*; **(rubber) d.** canot *m* pneumatique.

dingy ['dɪndʒɪ] *a* (*room etc*) minable; (*colour*) terne.

dining car wagon-restaurant *m*.

dining room salle *f* à manger.

dinner ['dɪnər] dîner *m*; (*lunch*) déjeuner *m*; **to have d.** dîner.

dinner jacket smoking *m*.

dinner party dîner *m* (à la maison).

dinner service *or* **set** service *m* de table.
dinosaur ['daɪnəsɔːr] dinosaure *m*.
dip [dɪp] **1** *vt* plonger; **to d. one's headlights** se mettre en code. **2** *vi* (*of road*) plonger; **to d. into** (*pocket*, *savings*) puiser dans. **3** *n* (*in road*) petit creux *m*; **to go for a d.** (*swim*) faire trempette.
diphthong ['dɪfθɒŋ] diphtongue *f*.
diploma [dɪ'pləʊmə] diplôme *m*.
dipped headlights (*of vehicle*) codes *mpl*.
direct [daɪ'rekt] **1** *a* direct. **2** *adv* directement. **3** *vt* diriger; (*remark*) adresser (**to** à); **to d. s.o. to** (*place*) indiquer à qn le chemin de.
direction direction *f*; **directions (for use)** mode *m* d'emploi; **in the opposite d.** en sens inverse.
directly 1 *adv* directement; (*at once*) tout de suite. **2** *conj* aussitôt que + *indicative*.
director directeur, -trice *mf*; (*board member in firm*) administrateur, -trice *mf*; (*of film*) metteur *m* en scène.
directory [daɪ'rektərɪ] **(telephone) d.** annuaire *m* (téléphonique).
directory inquiries renseignements *mpl*.
dirt [dɜːt] saleté *f*; (*earth*) terre *f*; **d. cheap** *Fam* très bon marché.
dirty 1 *a* sale; (*job*) salissant; (*word*) grossier; **to get d.** se salir; **to get sth d.** salir qch; **a d. joke** une histoire cochonne. **2** *vt* salir.
dis- [dɪs] *prefix* dé-, dés-.
disa'bility infirmité *f*.
disabled [dɪ'seɪb(ə)ld] **1** *a* handicapé. **2** *n* **the d.** les handicapés *mpl*.
disadvantage désavantage *m*.
disagree *vi* ne pas être d'accord (**with** avec); **to d. with s.o.** (*of food etc*) ne pas réussir à qn.
disagreeable *a* désagréable.
disagreement désaccord *m*; (*quarrel*) différend *m*.
disappear *vi* disparaître.
disappearance disparition *f*.
disappoint [dɪsə'pɔɪnt] *vt* décevoir; **I'm disappointed with it** ça m'a déçu.
disappointing *a* décevant.
disappointment déception *f*.
disapproval désapprobation *f*.
disapprove *vi* **to d. of s.o./sth** désapprouver qn/qch; **I d.** je suis contre.
disarm *vt* désarmer.
disaster [dɪ'zɑːstər] désastre *m*.

disastrous *a* désastreux.
disc [dɪsk] (*Am* **disk**) disque *m*; **identity d.** plaque *f* d'identité.
discard [dɪs'kɑːd] *vt* se débarrasser de.
discharge [dɪs'tʃɑːdʒ] (*patient*, *employee*) renvoyer; (*soldier*) libérer.
discipline ['dɪsɪplɪn] **1** *n* discipline *f*. **2** *vt* discipliner; (*punish*) punir.
disc jockey disc-jockey *m*.
disclose [dɪs'kləʊz] *vt* révéler.
disco ['dɪskəʊ] (*pl* **-os**) disco *f*.
discomfort douleur *f*; **I get d. from my wrist** mon poignet me gêne.
disconnect *vt* détacher; (*unplug*) débrancher; (*wires*) déconnecter; (*gas*, *telephone*) couper.
discontented *a* mécontent.
discontinued *a* (*article*) qui ne se fait plus.
discotheque ['dɪskətek] (*club*) discothèque *f*.
discount ['dɪskaʊnt] (*on article*) remise *f*, réduction *f*; **at a d.** à prix réduit.
discount store solderie *f*.
discourage *vt* décourager; **to get discouraged** se décourager.
discover *vt* découvrir (**that** que).
discovery découverte *f*.
discreet [dɪ'skriːt] *a* discret.
discriminate [dɪ'skrɪmɪneɪt] *vi* **to d. against** faire de la discrimination contre.
discrimi'nation (*against s.o.*) discrimination *f*.
discuss [dɪ'skʌs] *vt* discuter de; (*plan*, *question*, *price*) discuter.
discussion discussion *f*.
disease [dɪ'ziːz] maladie *f*.
disembark *vti* débarquer.
disfigured [dɪs'fɪgəd] *a* défiguré.
disgrace **1** *n* (*shame*) honte *f* (**to** à). **2** *vt* déshonorer.
disgraceful *a* honteux.
disguise [dɪs'gaɪz] **1** *vt* déguiser (**as** en). **2** *n* déguisement *m*; **in d.** déguisé.
disgust [dɪs'gʌst] **1** *n* dégoût *m* (**for, at, with** de); **in d.** dégoûté. **2** *vt* dégoûter.
disgusted *a* dégoûté (**at, by, with** de); **d. with s.o.** (*annoyed*) fâché contre qn.
disgusting *a* dégoûtant.
dish [dɪʃ] (*container*, *food*) plat *m*; **the dishes** la vaisselle.
dishcloth (*for washing*) lavette *f*; (*for drying*) torchon *m*.

dishevelled [dɪ'ʃevəld] *a* hirsute.
dishonest *a* malhonnête.
dish out *or* **up** (*food*) servir.
dishwasher (*machine*) lave-vaisselle *m inv*.
disillusioned *a* déçu (**with** de).
disincentive mesure *f* dissuasive.
disinfect *vt* désinfecter.
disinfectant désinfectant *m*.
disk [dɪsk] *Am* = **disc**; (*of computer*) disque *m*.
dislike 1 *vt* ne pas aimer (**doing** faire). **2** *n* aversion *f* (**for, of** pour); **to take a d. to s.o./sth** prendre qn/qch en grippe.
dislocate ['dɪsləkeɪt] *vt* (*limb*) démettre.
dismal ['dɪzməl] *a* morne.
dismantle [dɪs'mænt(ə)l] *vt* (*machine*) démonter.
dismay [dɪs'meɪ] *vt* consterner.
dismiss [dɪs'mɪs] *vt* (*from job*) renvoyer (**from** de).
dismissal renvoi *m*.
disobedience désobéissance *f*.
disobedient *a* désobéissant.
disobey 1 *vt* désobéir à. **2** *vi* désobéir.
disorder (*confusion*) désordre *m*; (*illness*) troubles *mpl*.
disorganized *a* désorganisé.
dispatch [dɪs'pætʃ] *vt* expédier; (*troops, messenger*) envoyer.
dispel [dɪs'pel] *vt* dissiper.
dispenser [dɪs'pensər] (*device*) distributeur *m*; **cash d.** distributeur *m* de billets.
disperse [dɪ'spɜːs] **1** *vt* disperser. **2** *vi* se disperser.
display [dɪ'spleɪ] **1** *vt* montrer; (*notice, electronic data*) afficher; (*painting, goods*) exposer; (*courage etc*) faire preuve de. **2** *n* (*in shop*) étalage *m*; (*of data*) affichage *m*; **on d.** exposé.
displeased *a* mécontent (**with** de).
disposable *a* (*plate etc*) à jeter, jetable.
disposal at the d. of à la disposition de.
dispose [dɪ'spəʊz] *vi* **to d. of** (*get rid of*) se débarrasser de; (*sell*) vendre.
dispute [dɪ'spjuːt] **1** *n* (*quarrel*) dispute *f*; (*industrial*) conflit *m*. **2** *vt* contester.
disqualify *vt* rendre inapte (**from** à); (*in sport*) disqualifier; **to d. s.o. from driving** retirer son permis à qn.
disregard *vt* ne tenir aucun compte de.
disrupt [dɪs'rʌpt] *vt* (*traffic, class etc*) perturber; (*plan, s.o.'s books etc*) déranger.

disruption perturbation *f*; (*of plan etc*) dérangement *m*.
disruptive *a* (*child*) turbulent.
dissatis'faction mécontentement *m*.
dissatisfied *a* mécontent (**with** de).
dissolve [dɪ'zɒlv] **1** *vt* dissoudre. **2** *vi* se dissoudre.
dissuade [dɪ'sweɪd] *vt* dissuader (**from doing** de faire).
distance ['dɪstəns] distance *f*; **in the d.** au loin; **from a d.** de loin; **it's within walking d.** on peut y aller à pied; **to keep one's d.** garder ses distances.
distant *a* éloigné; (*reserved*) distant.
distaste aversion *f* (**for** pour).
distasteful *a* désagréable.
distinct [dɪ'stɪŋkt] *a* (*voice*, *light*) distinct; (*difference*, *improvement*) net (*f* nette); (*different*) distinct (**from** de).
distinction distinction *f*; (*in university exam*) mention *f* très bien.
distinctive *a* distinctif.
distinctly *adv* distinctement; (*definitely*) sensiblement.
distinguish [dɪ'stɪŋgwɪʃ] *vti* distinguer (**from** de, **between** entre).
distinguished [dɪ'stɪŋgwɪʃt] *a* distingué.
distort [dɪ'stɔːt] *vt* déformer.
distract [dɪ'strækt] *vt* distraire (**from** de).
distraction distraction *f*.
distress [dɪ'stres] (*pain*) douleur *f*; (*anguish*) détresse *f*; **in d.** (*ship*) en détresse.
distressing *a* affligeant.
distribute [dɪ'strɪbjuːt] *vt* distribuer; (*spread evenly*) répartir.
distri'bution distribution *f*.
distributor (*in car*) distributeur *m*; (*of goods*) concessionnaire *mf*.
district ['dɪstrɪkt] région *f*; (*of town*) quartier *m*; **postal d.** division postale; **d. attorney** *Am* = procureur *m* (de la République).
distrust *vt* se méfier de.
disturb [dɪ'stɜːb] *vt* (*sleep*) troubler; (*papers*, *belongings*) déranger; **to d. s.o.** (*bother*) déranger qn; (*worry*) troubler qn.
disturbance (*noise*) tapage *m*; **disturbances** (*riots*) troubles *mpl*.
disturbing *a* (*worrying*) inquiétant.
ditch [dɪtʃ] fossé *m*.
ditto ['dɪtəʊ] *adv* idem.
divan [dɪ'væn] divan *m*.
dive* [daɪv] **1** *vi* plonger; (*rush*) se précipiter. **2** *n* (*of swimmer*, *goalkeeper*) plongeon *m*; (*of aircraft*) piqué *m*.
diver plongeur, -euse *mf*.
diversion (*on road*) déviation *f*; (*distraction*) diversion *f*.

divert [daɪ'vɜːt] *vt* (*traffic*) dévier; (*aircraft*) dérouter.
divide [dɪ'vaɪd] *vt* diviser (**into** en); (*share out*) partager; (*separate*) séparer (**from** de).
divide sth off séparer qch (**from sth** de qch).
divide sth up (*share out*) partager qch.
diving plongée *f* sous-marine.
diving board plongeoir *m*.
division [dɪ'vɪʒ(ə)n] division *f*.
divorce [dɪ'vɔːs] **1** *n* divorce *m*. **2** *vt* (*husband*, *wife*) divorcer d'avec.
divorced [dɪ'vɔːst] *a* divorcé (**from** d'avec); **to get d.** divorcer.
DIY [diːaɪ'waɪ] *abbr* (*do-it-yourself*) bricolage *m*.
dizziness vertige *m*.
dizzy ['dɪzɪ] *a* **to be** *or* **feel d.** avoir le vertige; **to make s.o. (feel) d.** donner le vertige à qn.
DJ [diː'dʒeɪ] *abbr* = **disc jockey.**
do[1]* [duː] **1** *v aux* **do you know?** savez-vous?, est-ce que vous savez?; **I do not** *or* **don't see** je ne vois pas; **he** *did* **say so** (*emphasis*) il l'a bien dit; **do stay** reste donc; **you know him, don't you?** tu le connais, n'est-ce pas?; **neither do I** moi non plus; **so do I** moi aussi. **2** *vt* faire; **what does she do?** (*in general*), **what is she doing?** (*now*) qu'est-ce qu'elle fait?; **what have you done (with)...?** qu'as-tu fait (de)...?; **well done** (*congratulations*) bravo!; (*steak*) bien cuit; **to do s.o. out of sth** escroquer qch à qn; **he's done for** *Fam* il est fichu. **3** *vi* (*get along*) aller; (*suit*) faire l'affaire; (*be enough*) suffire; (*finish*) finir; **how do you do?** (*introduction*) enchanté; (*greeting*) bonjour; **he did well** *or* **right to leave** il a bien fait de partir; **do as I do** fais comme moi; **to have to do with** (*relate to*) avoir à voir avec; (*concern*) concerner.
do[2] *n* (*pl* **dos** *or* **do's**) (*party*) *Fam* soirée *f*.
do away with sth/s.o. supprimer qch/qn.
dock [dɒk] **1** *n* (*for ship*) dock *m*. **2** *vi* (*at quayside*) se mettre à quai.
docker docker *m*.
dockyard chantier *m* naval.
doctor ['dɒktər] médecin *m*; (*academic*) docteur *m*.
doctorate doctorat *m*.
document ['dɒkjʊmənt] document *m*.
docu'mentary (*film*) documentaire *m*.
dodge [dɒdʒ] **1** *vt* esquiver; (*pursuer*) échapper à; (*tax*) éviter de payer. **2** *vi* **to d. through** (*crowd*) se faufiler dans.
dodgems ['dɒdʒəmz] *npl* autos *fpl* tamponneuses.

does [dʌz] *see* **do**[1].
dog [dɒg] chien *m*; (*female*) chienne *f*; **d. food** pâtée *f*.
doggy bag (*in restaurant*) *Am* petit sac *m* pour emporter les restes.
doghouse *Am* niche *f*.
doing ['du:ɪŋ] **that's your d.** c'est toi qui as fait ça.
do-it-yourself 1 *n* bricolage *m*. **2** *a* (*store*, *book*) de bricolage.
dole [dəʊl] **d. (money)** allocation *f* de chômage; **to go on the d.** s'inscrire au chômage.
doll [dɒl] poupée *f*.
dollar ['dɒlər] dollar *m*.
doll's house, *Am* **dollhouse** maison *f* de poupée.
dolphin ['dɒlfɪn] dauphin *m*.
dome [dəʊm] dôme *m*.
domestic [də'mestɪk] *a* domestique; (*trade*, *flight*) intérieur.
domestic science arts *mpl* ménagers.
dominant ['dɒmɪnənt] *a* dominant; (*person*) dominateur.
dominate *vti* dominer.
domino ['dɒmɪnəʊ] domino *m*; **dominoes** (*game*) dominos *mpl*.
donate [dəʊ'neɪt] **1** *vt* faire don de; (*blood*) donner. **2** *vi* donner.
donation don *m*.
done [dʌn] *pp de* **do**[1].
donkey ['dɒŋkɪ] âne *m*.
door [dɔ:r] porte *f*; **out of doors** dehors.
doorbell sonnette *f*.
doorknob poignée *f* de porte.
doorknocker marteau *m*.
doorman (*pl* **-men**) (*of hotel*) portier *m*.
doormat paillasson *m*.
doorstep seuil *m*.
doorstop(per) butoir *m* (de porte).
doorway in the d. dans l'encadrement de la porte.
do sth out (*clean*) nettoyer qch.
do sth over (*redecorate*) refaire qch.
dope [dəʊp] (*drugs*) *Fam* drogue *f*.
dormitory ['dɔ:mɪtrɪ, *Am* 'dɔ:mɪtɔ:rɪ] dortoir *m*; *Am* résidence *f* (universitaire).
dosage (*amount*) dose *f*.
dose [dəʊs] dose *f*.
dot [dɒt] point *m*.
dotted line pointillé *m*.
double ['dʌb(ə)l] **1** *a* double; **a d. bed** un grand lit; **a d. room** une chambre pour deux personnes. **2** *adv* (*twice*) deux fois, le double;

(*to fold*) en deux. **3** *n* double *m*. **4** *vti* doubler.
double back (*of person*) revenir en arrière.
double-'breasted *a* (*jacket*) croisé.
double-'decker (bus) autobus *m* à impériale.
double-'glazing double vitrage *m*.
double up (*with pain, laughter*) être plié en deux.
doubt [daʊt] **1** *n* doute *m*; **no d.** (*probably*) sans doute. **2** *vt* douter de; **to d. whether** *or* **that** *or* **if** douter que (+ *subjunctive*).
doubtful *a* **to be d. (about sth)** avoir des doutes (sur qch); **it's d. whether** *or* **that** *or* **if** ce n'est pas sûr que (+ *subjunctive*).
dough [dəʊ] pâte *f*; (*money*) *Fam* fric *m*.
doughnut beignet *m* (rond).
do up (*coat, button*) boutonner; (*zip, Am zipper*) fermer; (*house*) refaire; (*goods*) emballer.
dove [dʌv] colombe *f*.
do with sth (*want*) **I could do with that** j'aimerais bien ça.
do without sth/s.o. se passer de qch/qn.
down [daʊn] **1** *adv* en bas; (*to the ground*) par terre; (*of curtain, temperature*) baissé; (*in writing*) inscrit; (*out of bed*) descendu; **to come** *or* **go d.** descendre; **d. there** *or* **here** en bas; **d. with flu** grippé; **to feel d.** avoir le cafard. **2** *prep* (*at bottom of*) en bas de; (*from top to bottom of*) du haut en bas de; (*along*) le long de; **to go d.** (*hill, street, stairs*) descendre.
down-and-out clochard, -arde *mf*.
down'hill *adv* **to go d.** descendre; (*of sick person, business*) aller de plus en plus mal.
down payment acompte *m*.
downpour averse *f*.
downright **1** *a* (*rogue etc*) véritable; (*refusal*) catégorique. **2** *adv* (*rude etc*) franchement.
downstairs **1** *a* ['daʊnsteəz] (*room, neighbours*) d'en bas. **2** *adv* [daʊn'steəz] *adv* en bas; **to come** *or* **go d.** descendre l'escalier.
down'town *adv* en ville; **d. Chicago** le centre de Chicago
downward(s) ['daʊnwəd(z)] *adv* vers le bas.
doze [dəʊz] **1** *n* petit somme *m*. **2** *vi* sommeiller.
dozen ['dʌz(ə)n] douzaine *f*; **a d.** (*books etc*) une douzaine de.
doze off s'assoupir.
Dr *abbr* (*Doctor*) Docteur.
drab [dræb] *a* terne; (*weather*) gris.
drag [dræg] *vti* traîner.
drag s.o./sth along (en)traîner qn/qch.
drag s.o. away from s.o./sth arracher qn à qn/qch.

drag on *or* **out** (*last a long time*) se prolonger.
dragon ['drægən] dragon *m*.
drain [dreɪn] **1** *n* (*sewer*) égout *m*; (*outside house*) puisard *m*; (*in street*) bouche *f* d'égout. **2** *vt* (*tank*) vider; (*vegetables*) égoutter.
drain (off) **1** *vt* (*liquid*) faire écouler. **2** *vi* (*of liquid*) s'écouler.
drainboard *Am* paillasse *f*.
drainer (*board*) paillasse *f*; (*rack, basket*) égouttoir *m*.
draining board paillasse *f*.
drainpipe tuyau *m* d'évacuation.
drama ['drɑːmə] (*event*) drame *m*; (*dramatic art*) théâtre *m*.
dra'matic *a* dramatique; (*very great, striking*) spectaculaire.
dra'matically *adv* (*to change etc*) de façon spectaculaire.
drapes [dreɪps] *npl* (*heavy curtains*) *Am* rideaux *mpl*.
drastic ['dræstɪk] *a* radical.
drastically *adv* radicalement.
draught [drɑːft] courant *m* d'air; **draughts** (*game*) dames *fpl*.
draught beer bière *f* pression.
draughtboard damier *m*.
draughty *a* (*room*) plein de courants d'air.
draw[1] [drɔː] **1** *n* (*in sport*) match *m* nul. **2** *vt** (*pull*) tirer; (*money from bank*) retirer (**from** de); (*attract*) attirer. **3** *vi* (*in sport*) faire match nul.
draw[2]***** [drɔː] **1** *vt* (*picture*) dessiner; (*circle*) tracer. **2** *vi* dessiner.
drawback inconvénient *m*.
drawer [drɔːr] tiroir *m*.
draw in (*of train*) arriver (en gare).
drawing dessin *m*.
drawing pin punaise *f*.
drawing room salon *m*.
drawn *a* **d. match** *or* **game** match *m* nul.
draw near (to) s'approcher (de); (*of time*) approcher (de).
draw on (*savings*) puiser dans.
draw out (*money*) retirer.
draw up **1** *vt* (*chair*) approcher; (*list, plan*) dresser. **2** *vi* (*of vehicle*) s'arrêter.
dread [dred] **1** *vt* (*exam etc*) appréhender; **to d. doing** appréhender de faire. **2** *n* crainte *f*.
dreadful *a* épouvantable; (*child*) insupportable; (*ill*) malade.
dreadfully *adv* terriblement; **to be d. sorry** regretter infiniment.
dream [driːm] **1** *vi** rêver (**of** de, **of doing** de faire). **2** *vt* rêver (**that** que). **3** *n* rêve *m*; **to have a d.** faire un rêve (**about** de); **a d. house**/*etc* une maison/*etc* de rêve.

dream sth up imaginer qch.
dreary ['drɪərɪ] *a* (*gloomy*) morne; (*boring*) ennuyeux.
drench [drentʃ] *vt* tremper; **to get drenched** se faire tremper.
dress [dres] **1** *n* (*woman's*) robe *f*; (*style of dressing*) tenue *f*. **2** *vt* (*person*) habiller; (*wound*) panser; **to get dressed** s'habiller. **3** *vi* s'habiller.
dresser (*furniture*) *Am* coiffeuse *f*.
dressing (*for wound*) pansement *m*; (*seasoning*) assaisonnement *m*.
dressing gown robe *f* de chambre.
dressing table coiffeuse *f*.
dressmaker couturière *f*.
dress up (*smartly*) bien s'habiller; (*in disguise*) se déguiser (**as** en).
drew [dru:] *pt de* **draw**[1,2].
dribble ['drɪb(ə)l] **1** *vi* (*of baby*) baver. **2** *vti Football* dribbler.
dried [draɪd] *a* (*fruit*) sec (*f* sèche); (*flowers*) séché.
drier ['draɪər] = **dryer.**
drift [drɪft] *vi* être emporté par le vent *or* le courant.
drill [drɪl] **1** *n* (*tool*) perceuse *f*; (*bit*) mèche *f*; (*pneumatic*) marteau *m* piqueur; (*dentist's*) roulette *f*. **2** *vt* (*hole*) percer.
drink [drɪŋk] **1** *n* boisson *f*; (*glass of sth*) verre *m*; **to give s.o. a d.** donner (quelque chose) à boire à qn. **2** *vt** boire. **3** *vi* boire (**out of** dans); **to d. to s.o.** boire à la santé de qn.
drinkable *a* potable; (*not unpleasant*) buvable.
drink sth down boire qch.
drinking water eau *f* potable.
drink up 1 *vt* boire. **2** *vi* finir son verre.
drip [drɪp] **1** *vi* dégouliner; (*of washing, vegetables*) s'égoutter; (*of tap, Am faucet*) fuir. **2** *vt* (*paint etc*) laisser couler. **3** *n* goutte *f*; (*fool*) *Fam* nouille *f*.
drip-dry *a* (*shirt etc*) sans repassage.
dripping *a & adv* **d. (wet)** dégoulinant.
drive [draɪv] **1** *n* promenade *f* en voiture; (*energy*) énergie *f*; (*road to house*) allée *f*; **an hour's d.** une heure de voiture; **left-hand d.** (véhicule *m* à) conduite *f* à gauche. **2** *vt** (*vehicle, train, passenger*) conduire; (*machine*) actionner; (*chase away*) chasser; **to d. s.o. to do** pousser qn à faire; **to d. s.o. mad** *or* **crazy** rendre qn fou. **3** *vi* (*drive a car*) conduire; (*go by car*) rouler; **to d. on the left** rouler à gauche.
drive along (*in car*) rouler.
drive away 1 *vt* (*chase*) chasser. **2** *vi* partir (en voiture).
drive back 1 *vt* (*enemy*) repousser; (*passenger*) ramener (en voiture). **2** *vi* revenir (en voiture).

drive in (*nail*) enfoncer.
drivel ['drɪv(ə)l] idioties *fpl*.
drive off *vi* partir (en voiture).
drive on *vi* (*in car*) continuer.
drive s.o./sth out (*chase away*) chasser qn/qch.
driver conducteur, -trice *mf*; **(train** *or* **engine) d.** mécanicien *m*; **she's a good d.** elle conduit bien.
driver's license *Am* permis *m* de conduire.
drive to aller (en voiture) à.
drive up *vi* arriver (en voiture).
driving conduite *f*.
driving lesson leçon *f* de conduite.
driving licence permis *m* de conduire.
driving school auto-école *f*.
driving test examen *m* du permis de conduire.
drizzle ['drɪz(ə)l] **1** *n* bruine *f*. **2** *vi* bruiner.
droop [druːp] *vi* (*of flower*) se faner.
drop [drɒp] **1** *n* (*of liquid*) goutte *f*; (*fall*) baisse *f* (**in** de). **2** *vt* laisser tomber; (*price*, *voice*) baisser; (*passenger*, *goods from vehicle*) déposer; (*put*) mettre; (*leave out*) omettre; **to d. a line to** écrire un petit mot à. **3** *vi* tomber; (*of price*) baisser.
drop back *or* **behind** rester en arrière.
drop in (*visit s.o.*) passer (chez qn).
drop off **1** *vi* (*fall asleep*) s'endormir; (*fall off*) tomber; (*of sales*) diminuer. **2** *vt* (*passenger*) déposer.
drop out (*withdraw*) se retirer.
drought [draʊt] sécheresse *f*.
drown [draʊn] **1** *vi* se noyer. **2** *vt* **to d. oneself, be drowned** se noyer.
drowsy ['draʊzɪ] *a* **to be** *or* **feel d.** avoir sommeil.
drug [drʌg] **1** *n* médicament *m*; (*narcotic*) stupéfiant *m*; **drugs** (*narcotics in general*) la drogue; **to be on drugs, take drugs** se droguer. **2** *vt* droguer (*qn*).
drug addict drogué, -ée *mf*.
druggist *Am* pharmacien, -ienne *mf*.
drugstore *Am* drugstore *m*.
drum [drʌm] tambour *m*; (*for oil*) bidon *m*; **the drums** (*of orchestra etc*) la batterie.
drummer (joueur, -euse *mf* de) tambour *m*; (*in pop or jazz group*) batteur *m*.
drumstick baguette *f* (de tambour).
drunk [drʌŋk] (*pp de* **drink**) **1** *a* ivre; **to get d.** s'enivrer. **2** *n*

ivrogne *mf*.
drunkard ivrogne *mf*.
drunken *a* (*driver*) ivre; **d. driving** conduite *f* en état d'ivresse.
dry [draɪ] **1** *a* sec (*f* sèche); (*well*, *river*) à sec; (*day*) sans pluie; (*book*) aride; **to keep sth d.** tenir qch au sec; **to feel** *or* **be d.** (*thirsty*) avoir soif. **2** *vt* sécher; (*by wiping*) essuyer.
dry-'clean *vt* nettoyer à sec.
dry-'cleaner teinturier, -ière *mf*.
dryer séchoir *m*; (*helmet-style for hair*) casque *m*.
dry off *vti* sécher.
dry up **1** *vt* sécher. **2** *vi* sécher; (*dry the dishes*) essuyer la vaisselle.
dual ['djuːəl] *a* double.
dual carriageway route *f* à deux voies (séparées).
dub [dʌb] *vt* (*film*) doubler.
dubious ['djuːbɪəs] *a* douteux; **I'm d. about going** je me demande si je dois y aller.
duchess ['dʌtʃɪs] duchesse *f*.
duck [dʌk] **1** *n* canard *m*. **2** *vi* se baisser (vivement).
due [djuː] *a* (*money*) dû (*f* due) (**to** à); (*rent*, *bill*) à payer; **to fall d.** échoir; **he's d. (to arrive)** il doit arriver; **in d. course** en temps utile; (*finally*) à la longue; **d. to** dû à; (*because of*) à cause de.
duel ['djuːəl] duel *m*.
duffel *or* **duffle coat** ['dʌf(ə)l] duffel-coat *m*.
duke [djuːk] duc *m*.
dull [dʌl] *a* (*boring*) ennuyeux; (*colour*) terne; (*weather*) maussade; (*sound*, *ache*) sourd.
dullness (*of life*, *town*) monotonie *f*.
dumb [dʌm] *a* muet (*f* muette); (*stupid*) idiot.
dummy [dʌmɪ] (*of baby*) sucette *f*; (*for clothes*) mannequin *m*.
dump [dʌmp] **1** *vt* (*rubbish*) déposer. **2** *n* (*dull town*) *Fam* trou *m*; (**rubbish**) **d.** tas *m* d'ordures; (*place*) dépôt *m* d'ordures; (*room*) dépotoir *m*.
dump truck camion *m* à benne basculante.
dungarees [dʌŋgə'riːz] *npl* (*of child*, *workman*) salopette *f*; (*jeans*) *Am* jean *m*.
duplex ['duːpleks] (*apartment*) *Am* duplex *m*.
duplicate ['djuːplɪkət] double *m*; **in d.** en deux exemplaires; **a d. copy** une copie en double.
durable ['djʊərəb(ə)l] *a* (*material*) résistant.
duration [djʊə'reɪʃ(ə)n] durée *f*.
during ['djʊərɪŋ] *prep* pendant.
dusk [dʌsk] crépuscule *m*.

dust [dʌst] **1** *n* poussière *f*. **2** *vt* (*furniture etc*) essuyer (la poussière de). **3** *vi* faire la poussière.
dustbin poubelle *f*.
dustcart camion-benne *m*.
dust cover (*for furniture*) housse *f*; (*for book*) jaquette *f*.
duster chiffon *m* (à poussière).
dustman (*pl* **-men**) éboueur *m*.
dusty *a* poussiéreux.
Dutch [dʌtʃ] **1** *a* hollandais; **the D.** les Hollandais *mpl*. **2** *n* (*language*) hollandais *m*.
Dutchman (*pl* **-men**) Hollandais *m*.
Dutchwoman (*pl* **-women**) Hollandaise *f*.
duty ['djuːtɪ] devoir *m*; (*tax*) droit *m*; **duties** (*responsibilities*) fonctions *fpl*; **on d.** (*policeman, teacher*) de service; (*doctor*) de garde; **off d.** libre.
duty-'free *a* (*goods, shop*) hors-taxe *inv*.
duvet [duː'veɪ] couette *f*.
dwarf [dwɔːf] nain *m*, naine *f*.
dye [daɪ] **1** *n* teinture *f*. **2** *vt* teindre; **to d. green** teindre en vert.
dynamic [daɪ'næmɪk] *a* dynamique.
dynamite ['daɪnəmaɪt] dynamite *f*.
dynamo ['daɪnəməʊ] (*pl* **-os**) dynamo *f*.
dyslexic [dɪs'leksɪk] *a* & *n* dyslexique (*mf*).

E

each 1 *a* chaque. **2** *pron*; **e. (one)** chacun, -une; **e. other** l'un(e) l'autre, *pl* les un(e)s les autres; **e. of us** chacun, -une d'entre nous.
eager ['iːgər] *a* impatient (**to do** de faire); (*enthusiastic*) plein d'enthousiasme; **to be e. to do** (*want*) tenir (beaucoup) à faire.
eagerly *adv* avec enthousiasme; (*to await*) avec impatience.
eagerness impatience *f* (**to do** de faire).
eagle ['iːg(ə)l] aigle *m*.
ear [ɪər] oreille *f*.
earache mal *m* d'oreille; **to have an e.** avoir mal à l'oreille.
early ['ɜːlɪ] **1** *a* (*first*) premier; (*age*) jeune; **it's e.** (*on clock*) il est tôt; (*referring to meeting*) c'est tôt; **it's too e. to get up** il est trop tôt pour se lever; **to be e.** (*ahead of time*) être en avance; **to have an e. meal/night** manger/se coucher de bonne heure; **in e. summer** au début de l'été. **2** *adv* tôt, de bonne heure; (*ahead of time*) en avance; **as e. as possible** le plus tôt possible; **earlier (on)** plus tôt.
earn [ɜːn] *vt* gagner; (*interest*) rapporter.
earnings *npl* (*wages*) rémunérations *fpl*.
earphones *npl* casque *m*.
earplug boule *f* Quiès®.
earring boucle *f* d'oreille.
earth [ɜːθ] (*world, ground*) terre *f*; **where/what on e.?** où/que diable?
earthquake ['ɜːθkweɪk] tremblement *m* de terre.
ease [iːz] **1** *n* facilité *f*; **with e.** facilement; **(ill) at e.** (mal) à l'aise. **2** *vt* (*pain*) soulager; (*mind*) calmer.
ease (off *or* **up)** (*become less*) diminuer; (*of pain*) se calmer; (*not work so hard*) se relâcher.
easel ['iːz(ə)l] chevalet *m*.
ease sth off enlever qch doucement.
easily *adv* facilement; **e. the best**/*etc* de loin le meilleur/*etc*.
east [iːst] **1** *n* est *m*; **(to the) e. of** à l'est de. **2** *a* (*coast*) est *inv*; (*wind*) d'est. **3** *adv* à l'est.
eastbound *a* en direction de l'est.
Easter ['iːstər] Pâques *m sing or fpl*; **Happy E.!** joyeuses Pâques!
eastern *a* (*coast*) est *inv*; **E. Europe** Europe *f* de l'Est.
eastward(s) ['iːstwədz] *a & adv* vers l'est.
easy ['iːzɪ] **1** *a* facile; (*life*) tranquille; **it's e. to do** c'est facile à faire. **2** *adv* doucement; **go e. on** (*sugar etc*) vas-y doucement avec; (*person*) ne sois pas trop dur avec; **take it e.** calme-toi; (*rest*) repose-toi; (*work less*) ne te fatigue pas.

easy chair fauteuil *m*.
easy'going *a* (*carefree*) insouciant; (*easy to get on with*) facile à vivre.
eat* [iːt] **1** *vt* manger; (*meal*) prendre. **2** *vi* manger.
eater big e. gros mangeur *m*, grosse mangeuse *f*.
eating apple pomme *f* à couteau.
eat out *vi* manger dehors.
eat sth up (*finish*) finir qch.
eau de Cologne [əʊdəkə'ləʊn] eau *f* de Cologne.
EC [iː'siː] *abbr* (*European Community*) CEE *f*.
eccentric [ɪk'sentrɪk] *a* & *n* excentrique (*mf*).
echo ['ekəʊ] **1** *n* (*pl* **-oes**) écho *m*. **2** *vi* **the explosion/*etc* echoed** l'écho de l'explosion/*etc* se répercuta.
economic [iːkə'nɒmɪk] *a* économique; (*profitable*) rentable.
economical *a* économique.
economize *vti* économiser (**on** sur).
economy [ɪ'kɒnəmɪ] économie *f*.
economy class (*on aircraft*) classe *f* touriste.
edge [edʒ] bord *m*; (*of forest*) lisière *f*; (*of town*) abords *mpl*; (*of page*) marge *f*; (*of knife*) tranchant *m*; **on e.** énervé; (*nerves*) tendu.
edge forward avancer doucement.
edible ['edɪb(ə)l] *a* comestible; (*not unpleasant*) mangeable.
edit ['edɪt] *vt* (*newspaper*) diriger; (*article*) mettre au point; (*film*) monter; (*text*) éditer; (*compile*) rédiger.
edition [ɪ'dɪʃ(ə)n] édition *f*.
editor (*of newspaper*) rédacteur *m* en chef; (*compiler*) rédacteur, -trice *mf*.
edi'torial e. staff rédaction *f*.
educate ['edjʊkeɪt] *vt* éduquer; (*pupil*, *mind*) former.
educated *a* **(well-)e.** instruit.
edu'cation éducation *f*; (*teaching*, *training*) formation *f*.
edu'cational *a* (*establishment*) d'enseignement; (*game*) éducatif.
EEC [iːiː'siː] *abbr* (*European Economic Community*) CEE *f*.
eel [iːl] anguille *f*.
effect [ɪ'fekt] effet *m* (**on** sur); **to put into e.** mettre en application; **to come into e., take e.** (*of law*) entrer en vigueur; **to take e.** (*of drug*) agir; **to have an e.** (*of medicine*) faire de l'effet.
effective [ɪ'fektɪv] *a* (*efficient*) efficace; (*striking*) frappant.
effectively *adv* efficacement; (*in fact*) effectivement.
efficiency efficacité *f*; (*of machine*) performances *fpl*.
efficient [ɪ'fɪʃ(ə)nt] *a* efficace; (*machine*) performant.
efficiently *adv* efficacement; **to work e.** (*of machine*) bien

fonctionner.

effort ['efət] effort *m*; **to make an e.** faire un effort (**to** pour); **it isn't worth the e.** ça ne *or* n'en vaut pas la peine.

e.g. [iː'dʒiː] *abbr* par exemple.

egg [eg] œuf *m*.

eggcup coquetier *m*.

eggplant *Am* aubergine *f*.

egg timer sablier *m*.

Egyptian [ɪ'dʒɪpʃən] *a* & *n* égyptien, -ienne (*mf*).

eh? [eɪ] *int Fam* hein?

eiderdown ['aɪdədaʊn] édredon *m*.

eight [eɪt] *a* & *n* huit (*m*).

eigh'teen *a* & *n* dix-huit (*m*).

eighth *a* & *n* huitième (*mf*).

eighty *a* & *n* quatre-vingts (*m*); **e.-one** quatre-vingt-un.

either ['aɪðər] **1** *a* & *pron* (*one or other*) l'un(e) ou l'autre; (*with negative*) ni l'un(e) ni l'autre; (*each*) chaque; **on e. side** de chaque côté. **2** *adv* **she can't swim e.** elle ne sait pas nager non plus; **I don't e.** (ni) moi non plus. **3** *conj* **e....or** ou (bien)... ou (bien); (*with negative*) ni...ni.

elastic [ɪ'læstɪk] *a* & *n* élastique (*m*).

elastic band élastique *m*.

elbow ['elbəʊ] **1** *n* coude *m*. **2** *vt* **to e. one's way** se frayer un chemin (à coups de coude) (**through** à travers).

elder ['eldər] *a* & *n* (*of two people*) aîné, -ée (*mf*).

elderly *a* assez âgé.

eldest *a* & *n* aîné, -ée (*mf*); **his** *or* **her e. brother** l'aîné de ses frères.

elect [ɪ'lekt] *vt* élire (*qn*) (**to** à).

election 1 *n* élection *f*; **general e.** élections *fpl* législatives. **2** *a* (*campaign*) électoral; (*day*, *results*) du scrutin.

electric(al) [ɪ'lektrɪk, -ɪk(ə)l] *a* électrique.

electric blanket couverture *f* chauffante.

elec'trician électricien *m*.

elec'tricity électricité *f*.

electrocute [ɪ'lektrəkjuːt] *vt* électrocuter.

electronic [ɪlek'trɒnɪk] *a* électronique.

elegance élégance *f*.

elegant ['elɪgənt] *a* élégant.

elegantly *adv* avec élégance.

element ['eləmənt] élément *m*; (*of heater*) résistance *f*.

ele'mentary *a* élémentaire; (*school*) *Am* primaire.

elephant ['elɪfənt] éléphant *m.*
elevator ['elɪveɪtər] *Am* ascenseur *m.*
eleven [ɪ'lev(ə)n] *a* & *n* onze (*m*).
eleventh *a* & *n* onzième (*mf*).
eligible ['elɪdʒəb(ə)l] *a* (*for post*) admissible (**for** à); **to be e. for** (*entitled to*) avoir droit à.
eliminate [ɪ'lɪmɪneɪt] *vt* supprimer; (*applicant*, *possibility*) éliminer.
else [els] *adv* d'autre; **everybody e.** tous les autres; **somebody/nobody/nothing e.** quelqu'un/personne/rien d'autre; **something e.** autre chose; **anything e.?** encore quelque chose?; **somewhere e.** ailleurs; **how e.?** de quelle autre façon?; **or e.** ou bien.
elsewhere *adv* ailleurs.
elude [ɪ'luːd] *vt* (*of word*, *name*) échapper à (*qn*).
embark [ɪm'bɑːk] *vi* (s')embarquer.
embark on (*start*) commencer.
embarrass [ɪm'bærəs] *vt* embarrasser.
embarrassing *a* embarrassant.
embarrassment embarras *m.*
embassy ['embəsɪ] ambassade *f.*
emblem ['embləm] emblème *m.*
embrace [ɪm'breɪs] **1** *vt* (*hug*) étreindre. **2** *vi* s'étreindre. **3** *n* étreinte *f.*
embroider [ɪm'brɔɪdər] *vt* (*cloth*) broder.
embroidery broderie *f.*
emerald ['emərəld] émeraude *f.*
emerge [ɪ'mɜːdʒ] *vi* apparaître (**from** de); (*from hole*) sortir; (*of truth*, *from water*) émerger.
emergency [ɪ'mɜːdʒənsɪ] **1** *n* urgence *f*; **in an e.** en cas d'urgence. **2** *a* (*measure*) d'urgence; (*exit*, *brake*) de secours; **e. ward** *or Am* **room** salle *f* des urgences; **e. landing** atterrissage *m* forcé.
emigrate *vi* émigrer.
emotion [ɪ'məʊʃ(ə)n] (*strength of feeling*) émotion *f*; (*joy*, *love etc*) sentiment *m.*
emotional *a* (*person*, *reaction*) émotif; (*story*) émouvant.
emperor ['empərər] empereur *m.*
emphasis (*in word or phrase*) accent *m*; **to lay** *or* **put e. on** mettre l'accent sur.
emphasize ['emfəsaɪz] *vt* souligner (**that** que).
empire ['empaɪər] empire *m.*
employ [ɪm'plɔɪ] *vt* employer.
employee employé, -ée *mf.*
employer patron, -onne *mf.*

employment emploi *m*; **place of e.** lieu *m* de travail.
employment agency bureau *m* de placement.
empty ['emptɪ] **1** *a* vide; (*stomach*) creux; (*threat, promise*) vain; **to return e.-handed** revenir les mains vides. **2** *vi* (*of building, tank etc*) se vider.
empty (out) (*box, liquid etc*) vider; (*vehicle*) décharger; (*objects in box etc*) sortir (**from**, de).
emulsion [ɪ'mʌlʃ(ə)n] (*paint*) peinture *f* acrylique.
enable [ɪ'neɪb(ə)l] *vt* **to e. s.o. to do** permettre à qn de faire.
enamel [ɪ'næm(ə)l] **1** *n* émail *m* (*pl* émaux). **2** *a* en émail.
enchanting [ɪn'tʃɑːntɪŋ] *a* charmant, enchanteur (*f* -eresse).
enclose [ɪn'kləʊz] *vt* (*send with letter*) joindre (**in, with** à); (*fence off*) clôturer.
enclosed *a* (*space*) clos; (*receipt etc*) ci-joint.
enclosure (*in letter*) pièce *f* jointe; (*place*) enceinte *f*.
encounter [ɪn'kaʊntər] **1** *vt* rencontrer. **2** *n* rencontre *f*.
encourage [ɪn'kʌrɪdʒ] *vt* encourager (**to do** à faire).
encouragement encouragement *m*.
encyclop(a)edia [ɪnsaɪklə'piːdɪə] encyclopédie *f*.
end [end] **1** *n* (*of street, box etc*) bout *m*; (*of meeting, month, book etc*) fin *f*; (*purpose*) fin *f*, but *m*; **at an e.** (*discussion etc*) fini; (*patience*) à bout; **in the e.** à la fin; **to come to an e.** prendre fin; **to put an e. to, bring to an e.** mettre fin à; **no e. of** *Fam* beaucoup de; **for days on e.** pendant des jours et des jours. **2** *vt* finir (**with** par); (*rumour*) mettre fin à. **3** *vi* finir; **to e. in failure** se solder par un échec.
endanger [ɪn'deɪndʒər] *vt* mettre en danger.
ending ['endɪŋ] fin *f*; (*of word*) terminaison *f*.
endive ['endɪv, *Am* 'endaɪv] (*curly*) chicorée *f*; (*smooth*) endive *f*.
endless *a* interminable.
endorse [ɪn'dɔːs] *vt* (*cheque, Am check*) endosser; (*action*) approuver.
endorsement (*on driving licence*) contravention *f*.
end up *vi* **to e. up doing** finir par faire; **to e. up in** (*London etc*) se retrouver à; **he ended up in prison/a doctor** il a fini en prison/par devenir médecin.
endurance endurance *f*.
endure [ɪn'djʊər] *vt* supporter (**doing** de faire).
enemy ['enəmɪ] *n & a* ennemi, -ie (*mf*).
ener'getic *a* énergique.
energy ['enədʒɪ] **1** *n* énergie *f*. **2** *a* (*crisis, resources etc*) énergétique.

enforce [ɪn'fɔːs] *vt* (*law*) faire respecter.
engaged [ɪn'geɪdʒd] *a* (*person*, *toilet*, *phone*) occupé; **e. (to be married)** fiancé; **to get e.** se fiancer.
engagement (*to marry*) fiançailles *fpl*; (*meeting*) rendez-vous *m inv*; **e. ring** bague *f* de fiançailles.
engine ['endʒɪn] (*of vehicle*) moteur *m*; (*of train*) locomotive *f*.
engineer [endʒɪ'nɪər] ingénieur *m*; (*repairer*) dépanneur, -euse *mf*.
engineering ingénierie *f*.
English ['ɪŋglɪʃ] **1** *a* anglais; (*teacher*) d'anglais; **the E. Channel** la Manche; **the E.** les Anglais *mpl*. **2** *n* (*language*) anglais *m*.
Englishman (*pl* **-men**) Anglais *m*.
English-speaking *a* anglophone.
Englishwoman (*pl* **-women**) Anglaise *f*.
engrave [ɪn'greɪv] *vt* graver.
engraving gravure *f*.
enjoy [ɪn'dʒɔɪ] *vt* aimer (**doing** faire); (*meal*) apprécier; **to e. the evening** passer une bonne soirée; **to e. oneself** s'amuser; **to e. being in London** se plaire à Londres.
enjoyable *a* agréable.
enjoyment plaisir *m*.
enlarge [ɪn'lɑːdʒ] *vt* agrandir.
enlighten [ɪn'laɪt(ə)n] *vt* éclairer (**s.o. on** *or* **about sth** qn sur qch).
enormous [ɪ'nɔːməs] *a* énorme.
enormously *adv* (*very much*) énormément; (*very* extrêmement.
enough [ɪ'nʌf] **1** *a* & *n* assez (de); **e. time/cups**/*etc* assez de temps/de tasses/*etc*; **to have e. to live on** avoir de quoi vivre; **e. to drink** assez à boire; **to have had e. of** en avoir assez de; **that's e.** ça suffit. **2** *adv* assez; **big/good**/*etc* **e.** assez grand/bon/*etc* (**to** pour).
enquire [ɪn'kwaɪər] *vi* = **inquire.**
enquiry [ɪn'kwaɪərɪ] *n* = **inquiry.**
enrol [ɪn'rəʊl] (*Am* **enroll**) *vi* s'inscrire (**in**, **for** à).
enrolment (*Am* **enrollment**) inscription *f*.
ensure [ɪn'ʃʊər] *vt* assurer; **to e. that** s'assurer que.
entail [ɪn'teɪl] *vt* supposer.
enter ['entər] **1** *vt* (*room*, *vehicle etc*) entrer dans; (*university*) s'inscrire à; (*write down*) inscrire (**in** dans); **to e. s.o. for** (*exam*) présenter qn à; **to e. sth in** (*competition*) présenter qch à; **it didn't e. my head** *or* **mind** ça ne m'est pas venu à l'esprit. **2** *vi* entrer.
enter for (*race*, *exam*) s'inscrire pour.
enter into (*conversation*) entrer en; (*career*) entrer dans; (*agreement*) conclure.
enterprise ['entəpraɪz] (*undertaking*, *firm*) entreprise *f*; (*spirit*)

initiative *f*.
enterprising *a* plein d'initiative.
entertain [entə'teɪn] **1** *vt* amuser; (*guest*) recevoir. **2** *vi* (*receive guests*) recevoir.
entertainer artiste *mf*.
entertaining *a* amusant.
entertainment amusement *m*; (*show*) spectacle *m*.
enthusiasm [ɪn'θjuːzɪæz(ə)m] enthousiasme *m*.
enthusiast enthousiaste *mf*; **jazz/*etc* e.** passionné, -ée *mf* du jazz/*etc*.
enthusi'astic *a* enthousiaste; (*golfer etc*) passionné; **to be e. about** (*hobby*) être passionné de; (*gift*) être emballé par; **to get e.** s'emballer (**about** pour).
enthusi'astically *adv* avec enthousiasme.
entire [ɪn'taɪər] *a* entier.
entirely *adv* tout à fait.
entitle [ɪn'taɪt(ə)l] *vt* **to e. s.o. to do** donner à qn le droit de faire; **to e. s.o. to sth** donner à qn (le) droit à qch.
entitled *a* **to be e. to do** avoir le droit de faire; **to be e. to sth** avoir droit à qch.
entrance ['entrəns] entrée *f* (**to** de); (*to university*) admission *f* (**to** à); **e. exam** examen *m* d'entrée.
entrant ['entrənt] (*in race*) concurrent, -ente *mf*; (*for exam*) candidat, -ate *mf*.
entry ['entrɪ] (*way in, action*) entrée *f*; (*bookkeeping item*) écriture *f*; (*dictionary term*) entrée *f*; (*in competition*) objet *m* (*or* œuvre *f or* projet *m*) soumis au jury; **'no e.'** 'entrée interdite'; (*road sign*) 'sens interdit'.
entry form feuille *f* d'inscription.
envelope ['envələʊp] enveloppe *f*.
envious ['envɪəs] *a* envieux (**of sth** de qch); **e. of s.o.** jaloux de qn.
environment [ɪn'vaɪərənmənt] milieu *m*; (*natural*) environnement *m*.
environ'mental *a* du milieu; de l'environnement.
envy ['envɪ] **1** *n* envie *f*. **2** *vt* envier (**s.o. sth** qch à qn).
epidemic [epɪ'demɪk] épidémie *f*.
episode ['epɪsəʊd] épisode *m*.
equal ['iːkwəl] **1** *a* égal (**to** à); **to be e. to** (*number*) égaler; **she's e. to** (*task*) elle est à la hauteur de. **2** *n* (*person*) égal, -ale *mf*.
e'quality égalité *f*.
equalize *vi* (*score*) égaliser.
equally *adv* également; (*to divide*) en parts égales.

equation [ɪ'kweɪʒ(ə)n] équation *f*.
equator [ɪ'kweɪtər] équateur *m*.
equip [ɪ'kwɪp] *vt* équiper (**with** de); **(well-)equipped with** pourvu de; **(well-)equipped to do** compétent pour faire.
equipment équipement *m*.
equivalent [ɪ'kwɪvələnt] *a* & *n* équivalent (*m*).
erase [ɪ'reɪz, *Am* ɪ'reɪs] *vt* effacer.
eraser (*rubber for pencil marks*) gomme *f*.
erect [ɪ'rekt] **1** *a* (*upright*) (bien) droit. **2** *vt* construire; (*statue etc*) ériger; (*scaffolding*, *tent*) monter.
errand ['erənd] commission *f*.
erratic [ɪ'rætɪk] *a* (*service*, *machine etc*) capricieux; (*person*) lunatique.
error ['erər] erreur *f*; **to do sth in e.** faire qch par erreur.
escalator ['eskəleɪtər] escalier *m* roulant.
escape [ɪ'skeɪp] **1** *vi* s'échapper; **to e. from** (*person*) échapper à; (*place*) s'échapper de. **2** *vt* (*death*) échapper à; (*punishment*) éviter; **that name escapes me** ce nom m'échappe. **3** *n* (*of gas*) fuite *f*; (*of person*) évasion *f*.
escort ['eskɔːt] **1** *n* (*soldiers etc*) escorte *f*. **2** *vt* [ɪ'skɔːt] escorter.
Eskimo ['eskɪməʊ] (*pl* **-os**) Esquimau, -aude *mf*.
especially [ɪ'speʃəlɪ] *adv* (tout) spécialement; **e. as** d'autant plus que.
espresso [e'spresəʊ] (*pl* **-os**) (café *m*) express *m inv*.
essay ['eseɪ] (*at school*) rédaction *f*; (*at university*) dissertation *f*.
essential [ɪ'senʃ(ə)l] *a* essentiel.
essentially *adv* essentiellement.
establish [ɪ'stæblɪʃ] *vt* établir.
establishment (*institution*, *firm*) établissement *m*.
estate [ɪ'steɪt] (*land*) terre(s) *f*(*pl*); (*property after death*) succession *f*; **housing e.** lotissement *m*; (*workers'*) cité *f* (ouvrière); **industrial e.** zone *f* industrielle.
estate agent agent *m* immobilier.
estate car break *m*.
estimate **1** *vt* ['estɪmeɪt] estimer (**that** que). **2** *n* ['estɪmət] évaluation *f*; (*price for work to be done*) devis *m*.
etiquette ['etɪket] bienséances *fpl*.
Euro- ['jʊərəʊ] *prefix* euro-.
Euro'pean [jʊərə'piːən] *a* & *n* européen, -éenne (*mf*).
evacuate [ɪ'vækjʊeɪt] *vt* évacuer.
evade [ɪ'veɪd] *vt* éviter; (*pursuer*, *tax*) échapper à; (*law*, *question*) éluder.

evaluate [ɪ'væljʊeɪt] *vt* évaluer (**at** à).
evaporated milk [ɪ'væpəreɪtɪd] lait *m* concentré.
eve [iːv] **on the e. of** à la veille de.
even ['iːv(ə)n] **1** *a* (*flat*) uni; (*equal*) égal; (*regular*) régulier; (*number*) pair; **to get e. with s.o.** se venger de qn; **we're e.** nous sommes quittes; (*in score*) nous sommes à égalité; **to break e.** (*financially*) s'y retrouver. **2** *adv* même; **e. better/more** encore mieux/plus; **e. if** *or* **though** même si; **e. so** quand même.
evening ['iːvnɪŋ] soir *m*; (*whole evening, event*) soirée *f*; **in the e.** le soir; **at seven in the e.** à sept heures du soir; **every Tuesday e.** tous les mardis soir; **all e. (long)** toute la soirée.
evening dress tenue *f* de soirée; (*of woman*) robe *f* du soir.
evenly *adv* de manière égale; (*regularly*) régulièrement.
even sth out *or* **up** égaliser qch.
event [ɪ'vent] événement *m*; (*in sport*) épreuve *f*; **in the e. of death** en cas de décès; **in any e.** en tout cas.
eventual [ɪ'ventʃʊəl] *a* final.
eventually *adv* finalement; (*some day or other*) un jour ou l'autre.
ever ['evər] *adv* jamais; **more than e.** plus que jamais; **nothing e.** jamais rien; **hardly e.** presque jamais; **the first e.** le tout premier; **e. since** (*that event etc*) depuis; **e. since then** depuis lors; **for e.** pour toujours; (*continually*) sans cesse; **e. so happy**/*etc* vraiment heureux/*etc*; **it's e. such a pity** c'est vraiment dommage; **why e. not?** pourquoi pas donc?
every ['evrɪ] *a* chaque; **e. one** chacun, -une; **e. single one** tous *or* toutes (sans exception); **e. other day** tous les deux jours; **e. so often, e. now and then** de temps en temps.
everybody *pron* tout le monde; **e. in turn** chacun *or* chacune à son tour.
everyday *a* (*life*) de tous les jours; (*ordinary*) banal (*mpl* banals); **in e. use** d'usage courant.
everyone *pron* = **everybody.**
everyplace *adv Am* = **everywhere.**
everything *pron* tout; **e. I have** tout ce que j'ai.
everywhere *adv* partout; **e. she goes** où qu'elle aille.
evidence ['evɪdəns] *n* preuve(s) *f(pl)*; (*given by witness etc*) témoignage *m*; **e. of** (*wear etc*) des signes *mpl* de.
evident *a* évident (**that** que).
evidently *adv* évidemment; (*apparently*) apparemment.
evil ['iːv(ə)l] **1** *a* (*influence, person*) malfaisant; (*deed, system*) mauvais. **2** *n* mal *m*.
ewe [juː] brebis *f*.

ex- [eks] *prefix* ex-; **ex-wife** ex-femme *f*.
exact [ɪg'zækt] *a* exact; **to be e. about sth** préciser qch.
exactly *adv* exactement.
exaggerate [ɪg'zædʒəreɪt] *vti* exagérer.
exagge'ration exagération *f*.
exam [ɪg'zæm] examen *m*.
exami'nation (*in school etc*) examen *m*; (*of passport*) contrôle *m*; **class e.** devoir *m* sur table.
examine [ɪg'zæmɪn] *vt* examiner; (*accounts, luggage*) vérifier; (*passport*) contrôler; (*question*) interroger (*élève*).
examiner examinateur, -trice *mf*.
example [ɪg'zɑːmp(ə)l] exemple *m*; **for e.** par exemple; **to set an e.** donner l'exemple (**to** à).
exceed [ɪk'siːd] *vt* dépasser.
excel [ɪk'sel] *vi* **to e. in sth** être excellent en qch.
excellent ['eksələnt] *a* excellent.
except [ɪk'sept] *prep* sauf, excepté; **e. for** à part; **e. that** sauf que.
exception exception *f*; **with the e. of** à l'exception de.
exceptional *a* exceptionnel.
exceptionally *adv* exceptionnellement.
excerpt ['eksɜːpt] extrait *m*.
excess ['ekses] **1** *n* excès *m*; (*surplus*) excédent *m*. **2** *a* **e. fare** supplément *m* (de billet); **e. luggage** *or Am* **baggage** excédent *m* de bagages.
ex'cessive *a* excessif.
ex'cessively *adv* (*too, too much*) excessivement; (*very*) extrêmement.
exchange [ɪks'tʃeɪndʒ] **1** *vt* échanger (**for** contre). **2** *n* échange *m*; (*of foreign currencies*) change *m*; **(telephone) e.** central *m* (téléphonique); **in e.** en échange (**for** de).
excite [ɪk'saɪt] *vt* (*enthuse*) passionner.
excited *a* (*happy*) surexcité; (*nervous*) énervé; **to get e.** (*nervous, enthusiastic*) s'exciter; **to be e. about** (*new car etc*) se réjouir de.
excitement agitation *f*; (*emotion*) vive émotion *f*.
exciting *a* (*book etc*) passionnant.
exclaim [ɪk'skleɪm] *vti* s'exclamer (**that** que).
excla'mation mark *or Am* **point** point *m* d'exclamation.
exclude [ɪks'kluːd] *vt* exclure (**from** de).
exclusive *a* exclusif; (*club*) fermé; **e. of wine/***etc* vin/*etc* non compris.
excursion [ɪk'skɜːʃ(ə)n] excursion *f*.
excuse 1 *vt* [ɪk'skjuːz] excuser (**s.o. for doing** qn d'avoir fait, qn de

faire); (*exempt*) dispenser (**from** de). **2** *n* [ɪk'skjuːs] excuse *f*.
ex-directory *a* sur la liste rouge.
execute ['eksɪkjuːt] *vt* (*criminal*) exécuter.
exe'cution exécution *f*.
executive [ɪg'zekjʊtɪv] **1** *a* (*job*) de cadre; (*car, plane*) de direction. **2** *n* (*person*) cadre *m*; **senior e.** cadre *m* supérieur; **junior e.** jeune cadre *m*; **sales e.** cadre *m* commercial.
exempt [ɪg'zempt] **1** *a* dispensé (**from** de). **2** *vt* dispenser (**from** de).
exemption dispense *f*.
exercise ['eksəsaɪz] **1** *n* exercice *m*. **2** *vt* (*muscles, rights*) exercer; (*dog, horse*) promener; (*tact, judgment*) faire preuve de. **3** *vi* faire de l'exercice.
exercise book cahier *m*.
exert [ɪg'zɜːt] *vt* exercer; **to e. oneself** (*physically*) se dépenser; **don't e. yourself!** ne te fatigue pas!
exertion effort *m*.
exhaust [ɪg'zɔːst] **1** *vt* épuiser; **to become exhausted** s'épuiser. **2** *n* **e. (pipe)** tuyau *m* d'échappement.
exhausting *a* épuisant.
exhibit [ɪg'zɪbɪt] **1** *vt* (*put on display*) exposer. **2** *n* objet *m* exposé.
exhi'bition exposition *f*.
exhibitor exposant, -ante *mf*.
exist [ɪg'zɪst] *vi* exister; (*live*) vivre (**on** de).
existence existence *f*; **to be in e.** exister.
existing *a* (*situation*) actuel.
exit ['eksɪt, 'egzɪt] sortie *f*.
exorbitant [ɪg'zɔːbɪtənt] *a* exorbitant.
expand [ɪk'spænd] **1** *vt* (*trade, ideas*) développer; (*production*) augmenter; (*gas, metal*) dilater. **2** *vi* se développer; (*of production*) augmenter; (*of gas, metal*) se dilater.
expanse [ɪk'spæns] étendue *f*.
expansion (*of trade etc*) développement *m*.
expect [ɪk'spekt] *vt* s'attendre à; (*think*) penser (**that** que); (*suppose*) supposer (**that** que); (*await*) attendre; **to e. sth from s.o./sth** attendre qch de qn/qch; **to e. to do** compter faire; **to e. that** s'attendre à ce que (+ *subjunctive*); **I e. you to come** (*want*) je compte que vous viendrez; **it was expected** c'était prévu; **she's expecting (a baby)** elle attend un bébé.
expec'tation attente *f*.
expedition [ekspɪ'dɪʃ(ə)n] expédition *f*.
expel [ɪk'spel] *vt* (*from school*) renvoyer.

expenditure [ɪk'spendɪtʃər] (*money*) dépenses *fpl*.
expense [ɪk'spens] frais *mpl*; **business expenses** frais *mpl* généraux; **at s.o.'s e.** (*doing s.o. no good*) aux dépens de qn.
expensive [ɪk'spensɪv] *a* cher.
experience [ɪk'spɪərɪəns] **1** *n* expérience *f*; **he's had e. of driving** il a déjà conduit. **2** *vt* connaître; (*difficulty*) éprouver.
experienced [-ənst] *a* expérimenté; **to be e. in** s'y connaître en.
experiment 1 *n* [ɪk'sperɪmənt] expérience *f*. **2** *vi* [ɪk'sperɪment] faire une expérience *or* des expériences.
expert ['ekspɜːt] expert *m* (**on, in** en); **e. advice** le conseil d'un expert.
exper'tise compétence *f* (**in** en).
expire [ɪk'spaɪər] *vi* expirer.
expired *a* (*ticket, passport etc*) périmé.
expiry date date *f* expiration.
explain [ɪk'spleɪn] *vt* expliquer (**to** à, **that** que).
explain sth away justifier qch.
expla'nation explication *f*.
explode [ɪk'spləʊd] *vi* exploser.
exploit 1 *vt* [ɪk'splɔɪt] exploiter. **2** *n* ['eksplɔɪt] exploit *m*.
explo'ration exploration *f*.
explore [ɪk'splɔːr] *vt* explorer; (*causes etc*) examiner.
explorer explorateur, -trice *mf*.
explosion [ɪk'spləʊʒ(ə)n] explosion *f*.
explosive explosif *m*.
export 1 *n* ['ekspɔːt] exportation *f*. **2** *vt* [ɪk'spɔːt] exporter (**to** vers, **from** de).
expose [ɪk'spəʊz] *vt* exposer (**to** à); (*plot etc*) révéler; (*crook etc*) démasquer.
express [ɪk'spres] **1** *vt* exprimer; **to e. oneself** s'exprimer. **2** *a* (*letter, delivery*) exprès *inv*; (*train*) rapide. **3** *adv* (*to send*) par exprès. **4** *n* (*train*) rapide *m*.
expression (*phrase, look*) expression *f*.
expressway *Am* autoroute *f*.
extend [ɪk'stend] **1** *vt* (*arm, business*) étendre; (*line, visit*) prolonger (**by** de); (*house*) agrandir; (*time limit*) reculer. **2** *vi* s'étendre (**to** jusqu'à); (*in time*) se prolonger.
extension (*for table*) rallonge *f*; (*to building*) agrandissement(s) *m(pl)*; (*of phone*) appareil *m* supplémentaire; (*of office phone*) poste *m*; **e. (cable** *or* **lead)** rallonge *f*.
extensive *a* étendu; (*repairs, damage*) important.
extensively *adv* (*very much*) énormément, considérablement.

extent [ɪk'stent] (*scope*) étendue *f*; (*size*) importance *f*; **to a large/certain e.** dans une large/certaine mesure; **to such an e. that** à tel point que.
exterior [ɪks'tɪərɪər] *a* & *n* extérieur (*m*).
external [ek'stɜːn(ə)l] *a* extérieur; **for e. use** (*medicine*) à usage externe.
extinguisher [ɪk'stɪŋgwɪʃər] **(fire) e.** extincteur *m*.
extra ['ekstrə] **1** *a* supplémentaire; **one e. glass** un verre de *or* en plus; **to be e.** (*spare*) être en trop; (*cost more*) être en supplément; **e. charge** *or* **portion** supplément *m*. **2** *adv* **to pay e.** payer un supplément; **wine costs** *or* **is 3 francs e.** il y a un supplément de 3F pour le vin. **3** *n* (*perk*) à-côté *m*; **extras** (*expenses*) frais *mpl* supplémentaires.
extra- ['ekstrə] *prefix* extra-.
extract 1 *vt* [ɪk'strækt] extraire (**from** de). **2** *n* ['ekstrækt] extrait *m*.
extra-curricular [-kə'rɪkjʊlər] *a* extrascolaire.
extraordinary [ɪk'strɔːdən(ə)rɪ] *a* extraordinaire.
extra-special *a* (*occasion*) très spécial.
extravagant [ɪk'strævəgənt] *a* (*wasteful with money*) dépensier.
extreme [ɪk'striːm] **1** *a* extrême; (*danger, poverty*) très grand. **2** *n* extrême *m*.
extremely *adv* extrêmement.
eye [aɪ] œil *m* (*pl* yeux); **to keep an e. on** surveiller; **to lay** *or* **set eyes on** voir; **to take one's eyes off s.o./sth** quitter qn/qch des yeux.
eyebrow sourcil *m*.
eyeglasses *npl Am* lunettes *fpl*.
eyelash cil *m*.
eyelid paupière *f*.
eyeliner eye-liner *m*.
eye shadow fard *m* à paupières.
eyesight vue *f*.

F

fabulous ['fæbjʊləs] *a* (*wonderful*) *Fam* formidable.

face [feɪs] **1** *n* (*of person*) visage *m*, figure *f*; (*of clock*) cadran *m*; **f. down** face contre terre; (*thing*) tourné à l'envers; **f. to f.** face à face; **to make** *or* **pull faces** faire des grimaces. **2** *vt* (*danger*, *problem etc*) faire face à; (*accept*) accepter; (*look in the face*) regarder (*qn*) bien en face; (*be opposite*) être en face de; (*of window*) donner sur; **faced with** (*problem*) confronté à; **he can't f. leaving** il n'a pas le courage de partir. **3** *vi* (*of house*) être orienté (**north**/*etc* au nord/*etc*); (*be turned*) être tourné (**towards** vers).

facecloth gant *m* de toilette.

face up to (*danger*, *problem*) faire face à; (*fact*) accepter.

facilities [fə'sɪlɪtɪz] *npl* (*for sports*, *cooking etc*) équipements *mpl*; (*in harbour*, *airport*) installations *fpl*.

fact [fækt] fait *m*; **as a matter of f., in f.** en fait.

factor ['fæktər] facteur *m*.

factory ['fækt(ə)rɪ] usine *f*.

fade [feɪd] *vi* (*of flower*) se faner; (*of light*) baisser; (*of colour*) passer; (*of fabric*) se décolorer.

fade (away) (*of sound*) s'affaiblir.

fag [fæg] (*cigarette*) *Fam* clope *m or f*.

fail [feɪl] **1** *vi* échouer; (*of business*) faire faillite; (*of health*, *sight*) baisser; (*of brakes*) lâcher; **to f. in an exam** échouer à un examen. **2** *vt* (*exam*) rater, échouer à; (*candidate*) refuser, recaler; **to f. to do** (*forget*) manquer de faire; (*not be able*) ne pas arriver à faire. **3** *n* **without f.** à coup sûr.

failed *a* (*attempt*, *poet*) manqué.

failing **1** *n* défaut *m*. **2** *prep* **f. that** à défaut.

failure échec *m*; (*of business*) faillite *f*; (*person*) raté, -ée *mf*; **f. to do** incapacité *f* de faire.

faint [feɪnt] **1** *a* faible; (*colour*) pâle; **I haven't got the faintest idea** je n'en ai pas la moindre idée; **to feel f.** se trouver mal. **2** *vi* s'évanouir.

faintly *adv* faiblement; (*slightly*) légèrement.

fair[1] [feər] foire *f*; (*for charity*) fête *f*; (*funfair*) fête *f* foraine.

fair[2] *a* (*just*) juste; (*game*, *fight*) loyal; **f. enough!** très bien! ▮ (*rather good*) passable; (*weather*) beau; (*price*) raisonnable; **a f. amount (of)** pas mal (de).

fair[3] *a* (*hair*, *person*) blond.

fair copy copie *f* au propre.

fair-'haired *a* blond.

fairly *adv* (*to treat*) équitablement; (*rather*) assez.
fairness justice *f*; (*of person*) impartialité *f*.
fair play fair-play *m inv*.
fair-'sized *a* assez grand.
fairy ['feərɪ] fée *f*; **f. tale** *or* **story** conte *m* de fées.
faith [feɪθ] foi *f*; **to have f. in s.o.** avoir confiance en qn.
faithful *a* fidèle (**to** à).
faithfully yours f. (*in letter*) veuillez agréer l'expression de mes salutations distinguées.
fake [feɪk] **1** *n* faux *m*; (*person*) imposteur *m*. **2** *vt* (*document etc*) falsifier. **3** *vi* faire semblant. **4** *a* faux (*f* fausse).
fall [fɔːl] **1** *n* chute *f*; (*in price etc*) baisse *f* (**in** de); (*season*) *Am* automne *m*. **2** *vi** tomber; **to f. off** *or* **out of** *or* **down sth** tomber de qch; **to f. over** (*chair*) tomber en butant contre; (*balcony*) tomber de; **to f. ill** tomber malade.
fall apart (*of machine*) tomber en morceaux; (*of group*) se désagréger.
fall back on sth (*as last resort*) se rabattre sur qch.
fall behind rester en arrière; (*in work, payments*) prendre du retard.
fall down *vi* tomber; (*of building*) s'effondrer.
fall for tomber amoureux de; (*trick*) se laisser prendre à.
fall in (*collapse*) s'écrouler.
fall off (*come off*) se détacher; (*of numbers*) diminuer.
fall out (*quarrel*) se brouiller (**with** avec).
fall over *vi* tomber; (*of table, vase*) se renverser.
fall through (*of plan*) tomber à l'eau.
false [fɔːls] *a* faux (*f* fausse).
fame [feɪm] renommée *f*.
familiar [fə'mɪljər] *a* familier (**to** à); **f. with s.o.** (*too friendly*) familier avec qn; **to be f. with** (*know*) connaître.
famili'arity familiarité *f* (**with** avec).
familiarize *vt* **to f. oneself with** se familiariser avec.
family ['fæmɪlɪ] famille *f*.
famous ['feɪməs] *a* célèbre (**for** pour).
fan[1] [fæn] (*held in hand*) éventail *m*; (*mechanical*) ventilateur *m*.
fan[2] (*of person*) fan *mf*; (*of team etc*) supporter *m*; **to be a jazz/sports f.** être passionné de jazz/de sport.
fancy ['fænsɪ] **1** *n* **I took a f. to it, it took my f.** j'en ai eu envie. **2** *a* (*hat, button etc*) fantaisie *inv*. **3** *vt* (*want*) avoir envie de; **f. (that)!** tiens (donc)!
fancy dress travesti *m*; **f.-dress ball** bal *m* masqué.

fan heater radiateur *m* soufflant.
fantastic [fæn'tæstɪk] *a* fantastique.
far [fɑːr] **1** *adv* (*distance*) loin; **f. bigger**/*etc* beaucoup plus grand/*etc* (**than** que); **how f. is it to?** combien y a-t-il d'ici à?; **so f.** (*time*) jusqu'ici; **as f. as** (*place*) jusqu'à; **as f. as I know** autant que je sache; **as f. as I'm concerned** en ce qui me concerne; **f. from doing** loin de faire; **f. away** *or* **off** au loin; **by f.** de loin. **2** *a* (*side, end*) autre.
faraway *a* (*country*) lointain.
farce [fɑːs] farce *f*.
fare [feər] (*price*) prix *m* du billet.
farewell [feə'wel] *int* adieu.
far-'fetched *a* tiré par les cheveux.
farm [fɑːm] **1** *n* ferme *f*. **2** *a* (*worker, produce*) agricole; **f. land** terres *fpl* cultivées. **3** *vt* cultiver.
farmer fermier, -ière *mf*.
farmhouse ferme *f*.
farming agriculture *f*.
farmyard basse-cour *f*, cour *f* de ferme.
far-'off *a* lointain.
farther ['fɑːðər] *adv* plus loin; **to get f. away** s'éloigner.
farthest **1** *a* le plus éloigné. **2** *adv* le plus loin.
fascinate ['fæsɪneɪt] *vt* fasciner.
fasci'nation fascination *f*.
fashion ['fæʃ(ə)n] (*style in clothes*) mode *f*; (*manner*) façon *f*; **in f.** à la mode; **out of f.** démodé.
fashionable *a* à la mode; (*place*) chic *inv*.
fashion show présentation *f* de collections.
fast [fɑːst] **1** *a* rapide; **to be f.** (*of clock*) avancer (**by** de). **2** *adv* (*quickly*) vite; **f. asleep** profondément endormi.
fasten ['fɑːs(ə)n] *vt* attacher (**to** à); (*door, window*) fermer (bien).
fasten sth down *or* **up** attacher qch.
fastener (*clip*) attache *f*; (*of garment*) fermeture *f*; (*of bag*) fermoir *m*; (*hook*) agrafe *f*.
fat [fæt] **1** *n* graisse *f*; (*on meat*) gras *m*. **2** *a* gras (*f* grasse); (*cheek, salary*) gros (*f* grosse); **to get f.** grossir.
fatal ['feɪt(ə)l] *a* mortel; (*mistake etc*) fatal (*mpl* fatals).
fate [feɪt] destin *m*, sort *m*.
father ['fɑːðər] père *m*.
father-in-law (*pl* **fathers-in-law**) beau-père *m*.
fatigue [fə'tiːg] fatigue *f*.
fattening ['fæt(ə)nɪŋ] *a* (*food*) qui fait grossir.

fatty *a* (*food*) gras (*f* grasse).
faucet ['fɔːsɪt] (*tap*) *Am* robinet *m*.
fault faute *f*; (*defect*) défaut *m*; (*mistake*) erreur *f*; **it's your f.** c'est ta faute; **to find f. (with)** critiquer.
faulty *a* défectueux.
favour ['feɪvər] (*Am* **favor**) **1** *n* (*act of kindness*) service *m*; **to do s.o. a f.** rendre service à qn; **to be in f. of** (*support*) être pour; (*prefer*) préférer. **2** *vt* (*encourage*) favoriser; (*prefer*) préférer.
favourable *a* favorable (**to** à).
favourite *a* & *n* favori, -ite (*mf*).
fax [fæks] **1** *n* (*machine*) télécopieur *m*, fax *m*; (*message*) télécopie *f*, fax *m*. **2** *vt* (*message*) faxer; **to f. s.o.** envoyer une télécopie *or* un fax à qn.
fear [fɪər] **1** *n* crainte *f*, peur *f*; **for f. of doing** de peur de faire. **2** *vt* craindre.
fearless *a* intrépide.
feast [fiːst] festin *m*.
feat [fiːt] exploit *m*.
feather ['feðər] plume *f*.
feature ['fiːtʃər] (*of face, person*) trait *m*; (*of thing, place*) caractéristique *f*.
February ['februərɪ] février *m*.
fed up [fed'ʌp] *a* **to be f. up** *Fam* en avoir marre (**with** de).
fee [fiː] prix *m*; **fee(s)** (*professional*) honoraires *mpl*; (*for registration*) droits *mpl*; **school** *or* **tuition fees** frais *mpl* de scolarité.
feeble ['fiːb(ə)l] *a* faible.
feed* [fiːd] *vt* donner à manger à; (*breast-feed*) allaiter; (*bottle-feed*) donner le biberon à (*un bébé*).
feedback réaction(s) *f(pl)*.
feel [fiːl] **1** *n* toucher *m*; (*feeling*) sensation *f*. **2** *vt** (*be aware of*) sentir; (*experience*) éprouver; (*touch*) tâter; **to f. that** avoir l'impression que. **3** *vi* (*tired, old etc*) se sentir; **I f. hot/sleepy/***etc* j'ai chaud/sommeil/*etc*; **she feels better** elle va mieux; **to f. like sth** (*want*) avoir envie de qch.
feel about tâtonner; (*in pocket etc*) fouiller.
feeling sentiment *m*; (*physical*) sensation *f*.
feel up to doing être en forme pour faire.
feet [fiːt] *see* **foot.**
fell [fel] *pt de* **fall.**
fellow ['feləʊ] (*man*) type *m*.
felt[1] [felt] *pt & pp de* **feel.**
felt[2] feutre *m*.

felt-tip (pen) (crayon *m*) feutre *m*.
female ['fiːmeɪl] **1** *a* (*voice etc*) féminin; (*animal*) femelle; **f. student** étudiante *f*. **2** *n* femme *f*; (*animal*) femelle *f*.
feminine ['femɪnɪn] *a* féminin.
fence [fens] **1** *n* barrière *f*; (*in race*) obstacle *m*. **2** *vi* (*with sword*) faire de l'escrime.
fence (in) (*land*) clôturer.
fencing (*sport*) escrime *f*.
fend [fend] *vi* **to f. for oneself** se débrouiller.
fender (*on car*) *Am* aile *f*.
fern [fɜːn] fougère *f*.
ferocious [fə'rəʊʃəs] *a* féroce.
ferry ['ferɪ] ferry-boat *m*; (*small, for river*) bac *m*.
fertile ['fɜːtaɪl, *Am* 'fɜːt(ə)l] *a* (*land*) fertile.
fertilizer engrais *m*.
festival ['festɪv(ə)l] festival *m* (*pl* -als).
fe'stivities *npl* festivités *fpl*.
fetch¹ [fetʃ] *vt* (*bring*) amener (*qn*); (*object*) apporter; **to (go and) f.** aller chercher.
fetch² *vt* (*be sold for*) rapporter.
fetch sth in/out rentrer/sortir qch.
fête [feɪt] fête *f*.
fever ['fiːvər] fièvre *f*; **to have a f.** avoir de la fièvre.
feverish *a* fiévreux.
few [fjuː] *a & pron* peu (de); **f. towns**/*etc* peu de villes/*etc*; **a f. towns**/*etc* quelques villes/*etc*; **f. of them** peu d'entre eux; **a f.** quelques-un(e)s (**of** de); **a f. of us** quelques-uns d'entre nous; **quite a f., a good f.** bon nombre (de); **a f. more books**/*etc* encore quelques livres/*etc*; **every f. days** tous les trois ou quatre jours.
fewer *a & pron* moins (de) (**than** que).
fiancé(e) [fɪ'ɒnseɪ] fiancé, -ée *mf*.
fibre ['faɪbər] (*Am* **fiber**) fibre *f*.
fiction ['fɪkʃ(ə)n] **(works of) f.** romans *mpl*.
fiddle ['fɪd(ə)l] (*dishonest act*) *Fam* combine *f*.
fiddle (about) with (*pen etc*) tripoter; (*cars etc*) bricoler.
fidget (about) ['fɪdʒɪt] *vi* gigoter.
field [fiːld] champ *m*; (*for sport*) terrain *m*.
fierce [fɪəs] *a* féroce; (*attack*) furieux.
fifteen [fɪf'tiːn] *a & n* quinze (*m*).
fifteenth *a & n* quinzième (*mf*).
fifth *a & n* cinquième (*mf*).
fiftieth *a & n* cinquantième (*mf*).

fifty ['fɪftɪ] *a & n* cinquante (*m*).
fig [fɪg] figue *f*.
fight [faɪt] **1** *n* bagarre *f*; *Boxing* combat *m*; (*struggle*) lutte *f*; (*quarrel*) dispute *f*. **2** *vi** se battre (**against** contre); (*struggle*) lutter (**for** pour); (*quarrel*) se disputer. **3** *vt* se battre avec (*qn*).
fight back *vi* se défendre.
fighter (*determined person*) battant, -ante *mf*.
fight off (*attacker*) repousser.
fight over sth se disputer qch.
figure[1] ['fɪgər, *Am* 'fɪgjər] (*numeral*) chiffre *m*; (*price*) prix *m*; (*of woman*) ligne *f*; (*diagram, important person*) figure *f*.
figure[2] *vt* **to f. that** (*guess*) penser que.
figure on doing compter faire.
figure out arriver à comprendre; (*problem*) résoudre.
file [faɪl] (*tool*) lime *f*; (*folder, information*) dossier *m*; (*computer data*) fichier *m*; **in single f.** en file.
file (away) (*document*) classer.
file (down) limer.
file in/out entrer/sortir à la queue leu leu.
filing cabinet classeur *m*.
fill [fɪl] **1** *vt* remplir (**with** de); (*tooth*) plomber. **2** *vi* se remplir.
fillet ['fɪlɪt, *Am* fɪ'leɪ] filet *m*.
fill in (*form, hole*) remplir.
filling 1 *a* (*meal*) nourrissant. **2** *n* (*in tooth*) plombage *m*; (*in food*) garniture *f*.
fill out (*form*) remplir.
fill up 1 *vt* (*container, form*) remplir. **2** *vi* se remplir; (*with petrol or Am gas*) faire le plein.
film [fɪlm] **1** *n* film *m*; (*for camera*) pellicule *f*. **2** *vt* filmer.
film star vedette *f* (de cinéma).
filter ['fɪltər] filtre *m*; **f.-tipped cigarette** cigarette *f* (à bout) filtre.
filth [fɪlθ] saleté *f*.
filthy *a* sale.
fin (*of fish*) nageoire *f*.
final ['faɪn(ə)l] **1** *a* (*last*) dernier. **2** *n* (*match*) finale *f*.
finalize *vt* mettre au point; (*date*) fixer.
finally *adv* enfin.
finance ['faɪnæns] **1** *n* finance *f*. **2** *vt* financer.
fi'nancial *a* financier.
find [faɪnd] **1** *n* trouvaille *f*. **2** *vt** trouver; (*sth or s.o. lost*) retrouver.
find out 1 *vt* (*secret etc*) découvrir; (*person*) démasquer. **2** *vi*

(*inquire*) se renseigner (**about** sur); **to f. out about sth** (*discover*) découvrir qch.

fine[1] [faɪn] **1** *n* amende *f*; (*for driving offence*) contravention *f*. **2** *vt* **to f. s.o.** (**£10**/*etc*) infliger une amende (de dix livres/*etc*) à qn.

fine[2] [faɪn] **1** *a* (*thin, not coarse*) fin; (*very good*) excellent; (*weather*) beau; **it's fine** (*weather*) il fait beau; **he's f.** (*healthy*) il va bien. **2** *adv* (*well*) très bien.

finger ['fɪŋgər] doigt *m*; **little f.** petit doigt *m*; **f. mark** trace *f* de doigt.

fingernail ongle *m*.

fingerprint empreinte *f* (digitale).

fingertip bout *m* du doigt.

finish ['fɪnɪʃ] **1** *n* fin *f*; (*of race*) arrivée *f*. **2** *vt* finir; **to f. doing** finir de faire. **3** *vi* finir; **to have finished with** ne plus avoir besoin de; (*situation, person*) en avoir fini avec.

finish off *vti* finir.

finish up 1 *vt* finir. **2** *vi* **to f. up in** se retrouver à; **to f. up doing** finir par faire.

Finn [fɪn] Finlandais, -aise *mf*.

Finnish *a* finlandais.

fir [fɜːr] sapin *m*.

fire[1] ['faɪər] feu *m*; (*accidental*) incendie *m*; (*electric*) radiateur *m*; **on f.** en feu; **(there's a) f.!** au feu!

fire[2] **1** *vt* **to f. a gun** tirer un coup de fusil *or* de revolver; **to f. s.o.** (*dismiss*) renvoyer qn. **2** *vi* tirer (**at** sur).

fire alarm alarme *f* d'incendie.

fire brigade, *Am* **fire department** pompiers *mpl*.

firecracker pétard *m*.

fire engine voiture *f* de pompiers.

fire escape escalier *m* de secours.

fireman (*pl* **-men**) pompier *m*.

fireplace cheminée *f*.

fire station caserne *f* de pompiers.

firewood bois *m* de chauffage.

firework fusée *f*; (*firecracker*) pétard *m*; **f. display** feu *m* d'artifice.

firm [fɜːm] **1** *n* entreprise *f*. **2** *a* ferme.

firmly *adv* fermement.

first [fɜːst] **1** *a* premier. **2** *adv* (*firstly*) premièrement; (*for the first time*) pour la première fois; **(at) f.** d'abord. **3** *n* premier, -ière *mf*; **f. (gear)** (*of vehicle*) première *f*.

first aid premiers secours *mpl*.

first-'class 1 *a* excellent; (*ticket, seat*) de première; (*mail*) ordi-

naire. **2** *adv* (*to travel*) en première.
firstly *adv* premièrement.
fish [fɪʃ] **1** *n inv* poisson *m*. **2** *vi* pêcher.
fisherman (*pl* **-men**) pêcheur *m*.
fish fingers, *Am* **fish sticks** bâtonnets *mpl* de poisson.
fishing pêche *f*; **to go f.** aller à la pêche.
fishing rod canne *f* à pêche.
fishmonger poissonnier, -ière *mf*.
fish shop poissonnerie *f*.
fist [fɪst] poing *m*.
fit[1] [fɪt] *a* en bonne santé; (*in good shape*) en forme; (*suitable*) propre (**for** à, **to do** à faire); (*worthy*) digne (**for** de, **to do** de faire); (*able*) apte (**for** à, **to do** à faire); **f. to eat** bon à manger; **to keep f.** se maintenir en forme.
fit[2] **1** *vt* (*of clothes*) aller (bien) à (*qn*). **2** *vi* **this shirt fits** (*fits me*) cette chemise me va (bien).
fit[3] [fɪt] (*attack*) accès *m*.
fit (in) 1 *vt* (*object*) faire entrer; **to f. s.o. in** (*find time to see*) prendre qn. **2** *vti* **to f. (in) sth** (*go in*) aller dans qch; **he doesn't f. in** il ne peut pas s'intégrer.
fit (on) 1 *vt* **to f. sth (on) to sth** (*put*) poser qch sur qch; (*fix*) fixer qch à qch. **2** *vti* **to f. (on) sth** (*go on sth*) aller sur qch.
fitness (*health*) santé *f*.
fit (out *or* **up) with sth** (*house etc*) équiper de qch.
fitted carpet moquette *f*.
fitting room cabine *f* d'essayage.
five [faɪv] *a* & *n* cinq (*m*).
fiver *Fam* billet *m* de cinq livres.
fix [fɪks] *vt* (*make firm, decide*) fixer; (*mend*) réparer; (*deal with*) arranger; (*prepare, cook*) préparer.
fix (on) (*lid etc*) mettre en place.
fix up (*trip etc*) arranger; **to f. s.o. up with a job**/*etc* procurer un travail/*etc* à qn.
fizzy ['fɪzɪ] *a* pétillant.
flag [flæg] drapeau *m*; (*on ship*) pavillon *m*.
flake [fleɪk] (*of snow*) flocon *m*; (*of soap*) paillette *f*.
flake (off) (*of paint*) s'écailler.
flame [fleɪm] flamme *f*; **to burst into f., go up in flames** prendre feu.
flammable ['flæməb(ə)l] *a* inflammable.
flan [flæn] tarte *f*.
flannel ['flænəl] **(face) f.** gant *m* de toilette.
flap [flæp] **1** *vi* (*of wings etc*) battre. **2** *vt* **to f. its wings** battre des

ailes. **3** *n* (*of pocket*, *envelope*) rabat *m*.
flare up [fleər] (*of fire*) prendre; (*of violence*) éclater.
flash [flæʃ] **1** *n* (*of light*) éclat *m*; (*for camera*) flash *m*. **2** *vi* (*shine*) briller; (*on and off*) clignoter. **3** *vt* (*a light*) projeter; (*aim*) diriger (**on, at** sur); **to f. one's headlights** faire un appel de phares.
flashlight (*torch*) lampe *f* électrique.
flask [flɑːsk] thermos® *m or f inv*.
flat[1] [flæt] **1** *a* plat; (*tyre or Am tire*, *battery*) à plat; (*beer*) éventé; (*rate*, *fare*) fixe; **to put sth (down) f.** mettre qch à plat; **f. (on one's face)** à plat ventre. **2** *adv* **f. out** (*to work*) d'arrache-pied; (*to run*) à toute vitesse. **3** *n* (*puncture*) crevaison *f*.
flat[2] (*rooms*) appartement *m*.
flatly *adv* (*to deny*, *refuse*) catégoriquement.
flatten (out) aplatir.
flatter ['flætər] *vt* flatter.
flavour ['fleɪvər] (*Am* **flavor**) goût *m*; (*of ice cream etc*) parfum *m*.
flavouring (*in cake etc*) parfum *m*.
flaw [flɔː] défaut *m*.
flea [fliː] puce *f*.
flea market marché *m* aux puces.
flee* [fliː] **1** *vi* s'enfuir. **2** *vt* (*place*) s'enfuir de.
fleet [fliːt] (*of ships*) flotte *f*.
Flemish ['flemɪʃ] **1** *a* flamand. **2** *n* (*language*) flamand *m*.
flesh [fleʃ] chair *f*.
flex [fleks] **1** *vt* (*limb*) fléchir. **2** *n* (*wire*) fil *m* (souple); (*for telephone*) cordon *m*.
flexible ['fleksɪb(ə)l] *a* souple.
flick [flɪk] (*with finger*) chiquenaude *f*.
flick off enlever (d'une chiquenaude).
flick through (*pages*) feuilleter.
flies [flaɪz] *npl* (*on trousers*) braguette *f*.
flight [flaɪt] (*of bird*, *aircraft*) vol *m*; (*escape*) fuite *f*; **f. of stairs** escalier *m*.
flimsy ['flɪmzɪ] *a* (*light*) (trop) léger; (*thin*) (trop) mince.
fling* [flɪŋ] *vt* lancer.
flint [flɪnt] (*for lighter*) pierre *f*.
flip-flops ['flɪpflɒps] *npl* tongs *fpl*.
flipper ['flɪpər] (*of swimmer*) palme *f*.
flip through [flɪp] (*book*) feuilleter.
float [fləʊt] **1** *n Fishing* flotteur *m*. **2** *vi* flotter (**on** sur).
flock [flɒk] **1** *n* (*of sheep*) troupeau *m*; (*of birds*) volée *f*. **2** *vi* venir en foule.

flood [flʌd] **1** *n* inondation *f*; (*of letters, tears*) flot *m*. **2** *vt* (*field, house etc*) inonder. **3** *vi* (*of river*) déborder.
flood in (*of tourists etc*) affluer.
flood into (*of tourists etc*) envahir (*un pays etc*).
floodlight projecteur *m*.
floor [flɔːr] (*ground*) sol *m*; (*wooden etc in building*) plancher *m*; (*storey, Am story*) étage *m*; **on the f.** par terre; **on the first f.** au premier étage; *Am* au rez-de-chaussée.
floorboard planche *f*.
flop [flɒp] **1** *vi* (*of play etc*) faire un four. **2** *n* four *m*.
floppy ['flɒpɪ] *a* (*soft*) mou (*f* molle).
floppy disk disquette *f*.
florist ['flɒrɪst] fleuriste *mf*.
floss [flɒs] **(dental) f.** fil *m* dentaire.
flour ['flaʊər] farine *f*.
flow [fləʊ] **1** *vi* couler; (*of electric current, information*) circuler; (*of traffic*) s'écouler. **2** *n* (*of river*) courant *m*; (*of current, information*) circulation *f*.
flow chart organigramme *m*.
flower ['flaʊər] **1** *n* fleur *f*; **in f.** en fleur(s). **2** *vi* fleurir.
flower bed parterre *m*.
flower shop (boutique *f* de) fleuriste *mf*.
flu [fluː] grippe *f*.
fluent ['fluːənt] *a* **he's f. in Russian, his Russian is f.** il parle couramment le russe.
fluently (*to speak a language*) couramment.
fluff (*of material*) peluche(s) *f*(*pl*); (*on floor*) moutons *mpl*.
fluid ['fluːɪd] *a* & *n* fluide (*m*).
flunk [flʌŋk] *vt* (*exam*) *Am Fam* être collé à.
fluorescent [flʊə'res(ə)nt] *a* fluorescent.
flush *vt* **to f. the toilet** tirer la chasse d'eau.
flute [fluːt] flûte *f*.
flutter ['flʌtər] *vi* (*of bird*) voltiger; (*of flag*) flotter.
fly[1] [flaɪ] (*insect*) mouche *f*.
fly[2]* **1** *vi* voler; (*of passenger*) aller en avion; (*of time*) passer vite; (*of flag*) flotter. **2** *vt* (*aircraft*) piloter; (*airline*) voyager par.
fly[3] (*on trousers or Am pants*) braguette *f*.
fly across *or* **over** (*country etc*) survoler.
fly away *or* **off** s'envoler.
flying vol *m*; (*air travel*) l'avion *m*; **f. saucer** soucoupe *f* volante.
flyover (*bridge*) toboggan *m*.
foam [fəʊm] écume *f*; (*on beer*) mousse *f*; **f. rubber** caoutchouc *m*

mousse; **f. mattress**/*etc* matelas *m*/*etc* mousse.

focus ['fəʊkəs] **1** *n* (*of attention*) centre *m*; **in f.** au point. **2** *vt* (*image*) mettre au point. **3** *vti* **to f. (one's attention) on** se tourner vers.

fog [fɒg] brouillard *m*.

foggy *a* **it's f.** il y a du brouillard; **f. weather** brouillard *m*.

foil (*for cooking*) papier *m* alu(minium).

fold [fəʊld] **1** *n* (*in paper etc*) pli *m*. **2** *vt* plier; (*wrap*) envelopper (**in** dans); **to f. one's arms** (se) croiser les bras. **3** *vi* (*of chair etc*) se plier.

fold away *or* **down** *or* **up 1** *vt* (*chair etc*) plier. **2** *vi* se plier.

fold back *or* **over 1** *vt* (*blanket etc*) replier. **2** *vi* se replier.

folder (*file holder*) chemise *f*.

folding *a* (*chair etc*) pliant.

folk [fəʊk] **1** *npl* (*Am* **folks**) gens *mpl or fpl*. **2** *a* (*dance etc*) folklorique; **f. music** (musique *f*) folk *m*.

follow ['fɒləʊ] **1** *vt* suivre; (*career*) poursuivre; **followed by** suivi de. **2** *vi* suivre.

follow s.o. around suivre qn partout.

follower partisan *m*.

following 1 *a* suivant. **2** *prep* à la suite de.

follow on (*come after*) suivre.

follow through (*plan etc*) poursuivre jusqu'au bout.

follow up (*idea, story*) creuser; (*clue*) suivre.

fond [fɒnd] *a* **to be (very) f. of** aimer (beaucoup).

food [fuːd] nourriture *f*; (*particular substance*) aliment *m*; (*for cats, dogs*) pâtée *f*.

fool [fuːl] **1** *n* imbécile *mf*; **to play the f.** faire l'imbécile. **2** *vt* (*trick*) rouler.

fool (about *or* **around)** faire l'imbécile; (*waste time*) perdre son temps.

foolish *a* bête.

foolishly *adv* bêtement.

foot, *pl* **feet** [fʊt, fiːt] pied *m*; (*of animal*) patte *f*; (*measure*) pied *m* (= *30,48 cm*); **at the f. of** (*page, stairs*) au bas de; **on f.** à pied.

football ['fʊtbɔːl] (*game*) football *m*; (*ball*) ballon *m*.

footballer joueur, -euse *mf* de football.

footbridge passerelle *f*.

footpath sentier *m*.

footprint empreinte *f* (de pied *or* de pas).

footstep pas *m*.

for [fɒr, *unstressed* fər] *prep* pour; (*in exchange for*) contre; (*for a* *distance of*) pendant; **what's it f.?** ça sert à quoi?; **the road f. London** la route de Londres; **he was away f. a month** il a été absent pendant un mois; **he won't be back f. a month** il ne sera pas de retour avant un mois; **he's been here/I haven't seen him f. a month** il est ici/je ne l'ai pas vu depuis un mois; **I haven't seen him f. ten years** voilà dix ans que je ne l'ai vu; **it's f. you to say** c'est à toi de dire; **f. that to be done** pour que ça soit fait.

forbid* [fə'bɪd] *vt* interdire (**s.o. to do** à qn de faire); **she is forbidden to leave** il lui est interdit de partir.

force 1 *n* force *f*; **the (armed) forces** les forces armées. **2** *vt* forcer (*qn*) (**to do** à faire); (*door*) forcer; **forced to do** obligé *or* forcé de faire; **to f. one's way into** entrer de force dans.

forecast ['fɔːkɑːst] **1** *vt** prévoir. **2** *n* prévision *f*; (*of weather*) prévisions *fpl*.

forehead ['fɒrɪd, 'fɔːhed] front *m*.

foreign ['fɒrən] *a* étranger; (*trade*) extérieur; (*travel*) à l'étranger.

foreigner étranger, -ère *mf*.

foreman ['fɔːmən] (*pl* **-men**) (*worker*) contremaître *m*.

foremost ['fɔːməʊst] *a* principal.

forerunner ['fɔːrʌnər] précurseur *m*.

foresee* [fɔː'siː] *vt* prévoir.

forest ['fɒrɪst] forêt *f*.

forever [fə'revər] *adv* pour toujours; (*continually*) sans cesse.

forge [fɔːdʒ] *vt* (*signature*, *money*) contrefaire; (*document*) falsifier.

forge ahead (*progress*) aller de l'avant.

forgery faux *m*.

forget* [fə'get] *vti* oublier (**to do** de faire).

forget about oublier.

forgetful *a* **he's f.** il n'a pas de mémoire.

forgive* [fə'gɪv] *vt* pardonner (**s.o. sth** qch à qn).

fork 1 *n* (*for eating*) fourchette *f*; (*for garden*) fourche *f*; (*in road*) bifurcation *f*. **2** *vi* (*of road*) bifurquer.

fork out (*money*) *Fam* allonger.

form [fɔːm] **1** *n* forme *f*; (*document*) formulaire *m*; (*in school*) classe *f*; **on f., in good f.** en (pleine) forme. **2** *vt* (*group*, *basis etc*) former; (*habit*) contracter; (*an opinion*) se former; **to f. part of** faire partie de. **3** *vi* (*appear*) se former.

formal ['fɔːm(ə)l] *a* (*person*, *tone etc*) cérémonieux; (*stuffy*) compassé; (*official*) officiel; **f. dress** tenue de cérémonie.

for'mality formalité *f*.

for'mation formation *f*.

former ['fɔːmər] **1** *a* (*previous*) ancien; (*of two*) premier. **2** *pron*

the f. celui-là, celle-là.
formerly *adv* autrefois.
formula ['fɔːmjʊlə] (*pl* **-as** *or* **-ae** [-iː]) formule *f*; (*pl* **-as**) (*baby food*) lait *m* maternisé.
fort [fɔːt] fort *m*.
fortieth ['fɔːtɪəθ] *a* & *n* quarantième (*mf*).
fortnight ['fɔːtnaɪt] quinze jours *mpl*.
fortress ['fɔːtrɪs] forteresse *f*.
fortunate ['fɔːtʃənɪt] *a* (*choice etc*) heureux; **to be f.** (*of person*) avoir de la chance; **it's f. that** c'est heureux que (+ *subjunctive*).
fortunately *adv* heureusement.
fortune ['fɔːtʃuːn] *n* fortune *f*; **to make one's f.** faire fortune; **to have the good f. to do** avoir la chance de faire.
forty ['fɔːtɪ] *a* & *n* quarante (*m*).
forward ['fɔːwəd] **1** *adv* **forward(s)** en avant; **to go f.** avancer. **2** *vt* (*letter*) faire suivre; (*goods*) expédier.
foul [faʊl] **1** *a* (*smell*, *taste*) infect; (*language*) grossier. **2** *n Football* faute *f*.
found[1] [faʊnd] *pt* & *pp de* **find.**
found[2] *vt* (*town etc*) fonder.
fountain ['faʊntɪn] fontaine *f*.
fountain pen stylo(-plume) *m*.
four [fɔːr] *a* & *n* quatre (*m*).
four'teen *a* & *n* quatorze (*m*).
fourth *a* & *n* quatrième (*mf*).
fowl [faʊl] volaille *f*.
fox [fɒks] renard *m*.
foyer ['fɔɪeɪ] (*in theatre*) foyer *m*.
fraction ['frækʃ(ə)n] fraction *f*.
fracture ['fræktʃər] **1** *n* fracture *f*. **2** *vt* **to f. one's leg**/*etc* se fracturer la jambe/*etc*.
fragile ['frædʒaɪl, *Am* 'frædʒ(ə)l] *a* fragile.
fragment ['frægmənt] fragment *m*.
fragrance ['freɪgrəns] parfum *m*.
frail [freɪl] *a* fragile.
frame [freɪm] **1** *n* (*of picture*, *bicycle*) cadre *m*; (*of window*) châssis *m*; **f. of mind** humeur *f*. **2** *vt* (*picture*) encadrer.
framework structure *f*; **in the f. of** dans le cadre de.
franc [fræŋk] franc *m*.
frank [fræŋk] *a* franc (*f* franche).
frankly *adv* franchement.
frankness franchise *f*.

frantic ['fræntɪk] *a* (*activity*) frénétique; (*rush*) effréné; (*person*) hors de soi.
frantically *adv* comme un fou.
fraud [frɔːd] (*crime*) fraude *f*; (*person*) imposteur *m*.
fray [freɪ] *vi* (*of garment*) s'effilocher.
freckle ['frek(ə)l] tache *f* de rousseur.
freckled *a* couvert de taches de rousseur.
free [friː] **1** *a* libre; (*lavish*) généreux (**with** de); **f. (of charge)** gratuit; **to get f.** se libérer; **f. to do** libre de faire; **f. of** (*pain etc*) débarrassé de. **2** *adv* **f. (of charge)** gratuitement. **3** *vt* (*pt* & *pp* **freed**) (*prisoner*) libérer; (*trapped person*) dégager.
freedom ['friːdəm] liberté *f*; **f. from** (*worry*) absence *f* de.
Freefone® = numéro *m* vert.
free kick *Football* coup *m* franc.
freely ['friːlɪ] *adv* librement; (*to give*) libéralement.
free-range egg œuf *m* de ferme.
freeway *Am* autoroute *f*.
freeze* [friːz] **1** *vi* geler. **2** *vt* (*food*) congeler; (*prices*) bloquer.
freezer congélateur *m*; (*in fridge*) freezer *m*.
freeze up *or* **over** *vi* geler; (*of window*) se givrer.
freezing *a* (*weather*) glacial; (*hands, person*) gelé; **it's f.** on gèle.
French [frentʃ] **1** *a* français; (*teacher*) de français; (*embassy*) de France; **the F.** les Français *mpl*. **2** *n* (*language*) français *m*.
French fries *Am* frites *fpl*.
Frenchman (*pl* **-men**) Français *m*.
French-speaking *a* francophone.
Frenchwoman (*pl* **-women**) Française *f*.
frequent ['friːkwənt] *a* fréquent; **f. visitor** habitué, -ée *mf* (**to** de).
frequently *adv* fréquemment.
fresh [freʃ] *a* frais (*f* fraîche); (*new*) nouveau (*f* nouvelle); **to get some f. air** prendre l'air.
freshener air f. désodorisant *m*.
freshen up (*have a wash*) faire un brin de toilette.
fret [fret] *vi* (*worry*) se faire du souci.
Friday ['fraɪdɪ] vendredi *m*; **Good F.** Vendredi Saint.
fridge [frɪdʒ] frigo *m*.
fried [fraɪd] (*pt* & *pp de* **fry**) *a* (*fish*) frit; **f. egg** œuf *m* sur le plat.
friend [frend] ami, -ie *mf*; (*from school, work*) camarade *mf*; **to be friends with s.o.** être ami avec qn.
friendly *a* aimable (**to** avec); **to be f. with** être ami avec.
friendship amitié *f*.
fright [fraɪt] peur *f*; **to have a f.** avoir peur; **to give s.o. a f.** faire

peur à qn.
frighten *vt* effrayer.
frighten away *or* **off** (*animal*, *person*) fair fuir.
frightened *a* effrayé; **to be f.** avoir peur (**of** de, **to do** de faire).
frightening *a* effrayant.
frill [frɪl] (*on dress etc*) volant *m*.
fringe [frɪndʒ] (*of hair*) frange *f*.
fro [frəʊ] *adv* **to go to and f.** aller et venir.
frock [frɒk] (*dress*) robe *f*.
frog [frɒg] grenouille *f*.
from [frɒm, *unstressed* frəm] *prep* de; **where are you f.?** d'où êtes-vous?; **a train f.** un train en provenance de. ▮ (*time onwards*) à partir de, dès; **f. today (on), as f. today** à partir d'aujourd'hui, dès aujourd'hui. ▮ (*numbers*, *prices onwards*) à partir de. ▮ (*away from*) à; **to take/borrow f.** prendre/emprunter à. ▮ (*out of*) dans; sur; **to take f.** (*box*) prendre dans; (*table*) prendre sur; **to drink f. a cup/the bottle** boire dans une tasse/à la bouteille. ▮ (*according to*) d'après. ▮ (*cause*) par; **f. habit**/*etc* par habitude/*etc*. ▮ (*on behalf of*) de la part de; **tell her f. me** dis-lui de ma part.
front [frʌnt] **1** *n* (*of garment*, *building*) devant *m*; (*of boat*, *car*) avant *m*; (*of book*) début *m*; **in f. (of)** devant; **in f.** (*ahead*) en avant; (*in race*) en tête; **in the f.** (*in vehicle*) à l'avant. **2** *a* (*tooth*) de devant; (*part*, *wheel*, *car seat*) avant *inv*; (*row*, *page*) premier; **f. door** porte *f* d'entrée.
frost [frɒst] gel *m*; (*on window*) givré *m*.
frostbite gelure *f*.
frost up (*of window etc*) se givrer.
frosty *a* (*window*) givré; **it's f.** il gèle.
froth [frɒθ] mousse *f*.
frown [fraʊn] *vi* froncer les sourcils.
frozen ['frəʊz(ə)n] *a* (*vegetables etc*) surgelé; **f. food** surgelés *mpl*.
fruit [fruːt] fruit *m*; **(some) f.** (*one item*) un fruit; (*more than one*) des fruits; **f. drink** boisson *f* aux fruits; **f. salad** salade *f* de fruits; **f. tree** arbre *m* fruitier.
fruitcake cake *m*.
fruit machine machine *f* à sous.
frustrated [frʌ'streɪtɪd] *a* frustré.
frustrating *a* irritant.
fry [fraɪ] **1** *vt* faire frire. **2** *vi* frire.
frying pan poêle *f* (à frire).
fudge [fʌdʒ] (*sweet*, *Am candy*) caramel *m* mou.
fuel [fjʊəl] combustible *m*; (*for vehicle*) carburant *m*.

fugitive ['fjuːdʒɪtɪv] fugitif, -ive *mf*.
fulfil, *Am* **fulfill** [fʊl'fɪl] *vt* (*ambition*) réaliser; (*condition*) remplir; (*desire*) satisfaire.
fulfilling *a* satisfaisant.
full [fʊl] **1** *a* plein (**of** de); (*bus, theatre etc*) complet; (*life, day*) rempli; **the f. price** le prix fort; **to pay f. fare** payer plein tarif; **to be f. (up)** (*of person*) n'avoir plus faim; (*of hotel*) être complet; **f. name** (*on form*) nom et prénom. **2** *n* **in f.** (*to read sth etc*) en entier.
full-'scale *a*, **full-'sized** *a* (*model*) grandeur nature *inv*.
full stop point *m*.
full-'time *a* & *adv* à plein temps.
fully *adv* entièrement.
fumes [fjuːmz] *npl* vapeurs *fpl*; (*from car exhaust*) gaz *m inv*.
fun [fʌn] amusement *m*; **to be (good) f.** être très amusant; **to have (some) f.** s'amuser; **to make f. of** se moquer de; **for f.** pour le plaisir.
function ['fʌŋkʃ(ə)n] fonction *f*; (*meeting*) réunion *f*.
fund [fʌnd] **1** *n* (*for pension etc*) caisse *f*; **funds** (*money resources*) fonds *mpl*. **2** *vt* fournir des fonds à.
funeral ['fjuːnərəl] enterrement *m*.
funfair fête *f* foraine.
funnel ['fʌn(ə)l] (*of ship*) cheminée *f*; (*for pouring*) entonnoir *m*.
funny ['fʌnɪ] *a* drôle; (*strange*) bizarre; **a f. idea** une drôle d'idée; **to feel f.** ne pas se sentir très bien.
fur [fɜːr] fourrure *f*.
furious ['fjʊərɪəs] *a* furieux (**with, at** contre).
furnish ['fɜːnɪʃ] *vt* (*room*) meubler.
furniture ['fɜːnɪtʃər] meubles *mpl*; **a piece of f.** un meuble.
further ['fɜːðər] **1** *adv* = **farther**; (*more*) davantage. **2** *a* supplémentaire; **f. details** de plus amples détails; **a f. case**/*etc* un autre cas/*etc*.
further education enseignement *m* post-scolaire.
furthermore *adv* en outre.
furthest *a* & *adv* = **farthest**.
fury ['fjʊərɪ] fureur *f*.
fuse [fjuːz] **1** *vt* **to f. the lights** *etc* faire sauter les plombs. **2** *vi* **the lights** *etc* **have fused** les plombs ont sauté. **3** *n* (*wire*) fusible *m*; (*of bomb*) amorce *f*.
fuss [fʌs] **1** *n* chichis *mpl*; **what a f.!** quelle histoire!; **to make a f. of** = **fuss over**. **2** *vi* faire des chichis.
fuss (about) *vi* s'agiter.

fuss over s.o. être aux petits soins pour qn.
fussy *a* tatillon; (*difficult*) difficile (**about** sur).
future ['fjuːtʃər] **1** *n* avenir *m*; *Grammar* futur *m*; **in f.** à l'avenir; **in the f.** (*one day*) un jour (futur). **2** *a* futur; (*date*) ultérieur.
fuzzy ['fʌzɪ] *a* (*picture*, *idea*) flou.

G

gadget ['gædʒɪt] gadget *m*.
Gaelic ['geɪlɪk, 'gælɪk] *a* & *n* gaélique (*m*).
gag [gæg] **1** *n* (*over mouth*) bâillon *m*; (*joke*) gag *m*. **2** *vt* (*victim*) bâillonner. **3** *vi* (*choke*) s'étouffer (**on** avec).
gaiety ['geɪɪtɪ] gaieté *f*.
gaily *adv* gaiement.
gain [geɪn] **1** *vt* (*obtain*) gagner; (*experience*) acquérir; **to g. speed/weight** prendre de la vitesse/du poids. **2** *n* (*increase*) augmentation *f* (**in** de); (*profit*) bénéfice *m*.
gain on (*catch up with*) rattraper.
gala ['gɑːlə, *Am* 'geɪlə] gala *m*; **swimming g.** concours *m* de natation.
galaxy ['gæləksɪ] galaxie *f*.
gale [geɪl] grand vent *m*.
gallant ['gælənt] *a* (*chivalrous*) galant.
gallery ['gælərɪ] galerie *f*; (*for public*) tribune *f*; **art g.** (*private*) galerie *f* d'art; (*public*) musée *m* d'art.
gallivant (about) ['gælɪvænt] *Fam* vadrouiller.
gallon ['gælən] gallon *m*.
gallop ['gæləp] **1** *vi* galoper. **2** *n* galop *m*.
gamble ['gæmb(ə)l] **1** *vi* jouer (**on** sur, **with** avec). **2** *vt* jouer. **3** *n* coup *m* risqué.
gamble (away) (*lose*) perdre (au jeu).
gambler joueur, -euse *mf*.
gambling jeu *m*.
game [geɪm] jeu *m*; (*of football, cricket etc*) match *m*; (*of tennis, chess, cards*) partie *f*; **to have a g. of** jouer un match de; faire une partie de; **games** (*in school*) le sport.
gammon ['gæmən] jambon *m* fumé.
gang [gæŋ] (*of children, criminals*) bande *f*; (*of workers*) équipe *f*.
gangster gangster *m*.
gang up on se mettre à plusieurs contre.
gangway passage *m*; (*in train*) couloir *m*; (*in bus, cinema*) allée *f*; (*to ship, aircraft*) passerelle *f*.
gaol [dʒeɪl] *n* & *vt* = **jail**.
gap [gæp] (*empty space*) trou; (*in time*) intervalle *m*; (*in knowledge*) lacune *f*; **the g. between** (*difference*) l'écart *m* entre.
gape [geɪp] *vi* rester bouche bée.
gape at regarder bouche bée.
garage ['gærɑː(d)ʒ, *Am* gə'rɑːʒ] garage *m*.

garbage ['gɑːbɪdʒ] *Am* ordures *fpl*; **g. can** poubelle *f*; **g. man** éboueur *m*; **g. truck** camion-benne *m*.
garden ['gɑːd(ə)n] **1** *n* jardin *m*; **the gardens** (*park*) le parc. **2** *vi* jardiner.
gardener jardinier, -ière *mf*.
gardening jardinage *m*.
gargle ['gɑːg(ə)l] *vi* se gargariser.
garland ['gɑːlənd] guirlande *f*.
garlic ['gɑːlɪk] ail *m*.
garment ['gɑːmənt] vêtement *m*.
gas [gæs] **1** *n* gaz *m inv*; (*gasoline*) *Am* essence *f*; **g. mask/meter/***etc* masque *m*/compteur *m*/*etc* à gaz; **g. fire** *or* **heater** appareil *m* de chauffage à gaz; **g. heating** chauffage *m* au gaz; **g. stove** cuisinière *f* à gaz; (*portable*) réchaud *m* à gaz. **2** *vt* (*poison*) asphyxier (*qn*).
gash [gæʃ] **1** *n* entaille *f*. **2** *vt* entailler.
gasman (*pl* **-men**) employé *m* du gaz.
gasoline *Am* essence *f*.
gasp [gɑːsp] **1** *vi* **to g. (for breath)** haleter. **2** *n* halètement *m*.
gas station *Am* station-service *f*.
gassy ['gæsɪ] *a* (*drink*) gazeux.
gasworks usine *f* à gaz.
gate [geɪt] (*at level crossing*, *field etc*) barrière *f*; (*metal*) grille *f*; (*of castle*, *in airport*) porte *f*; (*at stadium*) entrée *f*.
gatecrash *vi* s'inviter (de force).
gather ['gæðər] **1** *vt* (*people*, *objects*) rassembler; (*pick up*) ramasser; (*information*) recueillir; **I g. that...** je crois comprendre que...; **to g. speed** prendre de la vitesse. **2** *vi* (*of people*) se rassembler.
gathering (*group*) réunion *f*.
gather round (*come closer*) s'approcher.
gaudy ['gɔːdɪ] *a* voyant.
gauge [geɪdʒ] **1** *n* (*instrument*) jauge *f*. **2** *vt* (*estimate*) évaluer.
gaunt [gɔːnt] *a* décharné.
gauze [gɔːz] gaze *f*.
gave [geɪv] *pt de* **give.**
gay [geɪ] **1** *a* homo(sexuel); (*cheerful*) gai. **2** *n* homo(sexuel) *m*.
gaze [geɪz] **1** *n* regard *m* (fixe). **2** *vi* regarder.
gaze at regarder (fixement).
GB [dʒiː'biː] Grande-Bretagne *f*.
GCE [dʒiːsiː'iː] *abbr Br* (*General Certificate of Education*) = épreuve *f* de bac.
GCSE [dʒiːsiːes'iː] *abbr Br* (*General Certificate of Secondary Educa-*

tion) = épreuve *f* de brevet.
gear [gɪər] **1** *n* équipement *m*; (*belongings*) affaires *fpl*; (*clothes*) *Fam* vêtements *mpl*; (*speed in vehicle*) vitesse *f*; **in g.** en prise; **not in g.** au point mort. **2** *vt* adapter (**to** à).
gearbox boîte *f* de vitesses.
gear up geared up to do prêt à faire; **to g. oneself up for** se préparer pour.
geese [giːs] *see* **goose.**
gel [dʒel] gel *m*.
gem [dʒem] pierre *f* précieuse.
gen [dʒen] (*information*) *Fam* tuyaux *mpl*.
gender ['dʒendər] *Grammar* genre *m*.
general ['dʒenərəl] **1** *a* général; **in g.** en général; **the g. public** le (grand) public; **for g. use** à l'usage du public. **2** *n* (*in army*) général *m*.
generally *adv* généralement.
generation [dʒenə'reɪʃ(ə)n] génération *f*.
generator ['dʒenəreɪtər] groupe *m* électrogène.
gene'rosity générosité *f*.
generous ['dʒenərəs] *a* généreux (**with** de); (*helping*) copieux.
generously *adv* généreusement.
genius ['dʒiːnɪəs] (*ability, person*) génie *m*.
gentle ['dʒent(ə)l] *a* (*person, slope etc*) doux (*f* douce); (*touch*) léger; (*exercise, speed*) modéré.
gentleman (*pl* **-men**) monsieur *m*.
gentleness douceur *f*.
gently *adv* doucement.
gents [dʒents] *npl* **the g.** *Fam* les toilettes *fpl* pour hommes.
genuine ['dʒenjʊɪn] *a* véritable, authentique; (*sincere*) sincère.
genuinely *adv* véritablement, sincèrement.
geo'graphical *a* géographique.
geography [dʒɪ'ɒgrəfɪ] géographie *f*.
geo'metric(al) *a* géométrique.
geometry [dʒɪ'ɒmɪtrɪ] géométrie *f*.
germ [dʒɜːm] (*in body, food etc*) microbe *m*.
German ['dʒɜːmən] **1** *a* allemand. **2** *n* (*person*) Allemand, -ande *mf*; (*language*) allemand *m*.
German measles rubéole *f*.
German shepherd (*dog*) *Am* berger *m* allemand.
gesture ['dʒestʃər] geste *m*.
get* **1** *vt* (*obtain*) obtenir; (*find*) trouver; (*buy*) acheter; (*receive*) recevoir; (*catch*) attraper; (*bus, train*) prendre; (*seize*) saisir; (*fetch*)

aller chercher (*qn*, *qch*); (*put*) mettre; (*derive*) tirer (**from** de); (*understand*) comprendre; (*prepare*) préparer; (*hit with fist, stick etc*) atteindre; (*reputation*) se faire; **I have got,** *Am* **I have gotten** j'ai; **to g. s.o. to do sth** faire faire qch à qn; **to g. sth built**/*etc* faire construire/*etc* qch. **2** *vi* (*go*) aller; (*arrive*) arriver (**to** à); (*become*) devenir; **to g. caught**/*etc* se faire prendre/*etc*; **to g. washed** se laver; **where have you got** *or Am* **gotten to?** où en es-tu?; **you've got to stay** (*must*) tu dois rester; **to g. working** se mettre à travailler.

get about *or* **(a)round** se déplacer.

get across 1 *vt* (*road*) traverser; (*message*) communiquer. **2** *vi* traverser.

get along (*manage*) se débrouiller; (*be on good terms*) s'entendre (**with** avec).

get at (*reach*) parvenir à.

get away (*leave*) partir; (*escape*) s'échapper.

get back 1 *vt* (*recover*) récupérer; (*replace*) remettre. **2** *vi* (*return*) revenir; (*move back*) reculer.

get by passer; (*manage*) se débrouiller.

get down *vti* descendre.

get in 1 *vt* (*washing etc*) rentrer; (*call for*) faire venir (*qn*). **2** *vi* (*enter*) entrer; (*come home*) rentrer; (*enter vehicle or train*) monter; (*of plane, train*) arriver.

get in(to) entrer dans; (*vehicle, train*) monter dans; **to g. in(to) bed** se mettre au lit.

get off 1 *vi* (*leave*) partir; (*from vehicle or train*) descendre (**from** de); (*in court*) être acquitté. **2** *vt* (*remove*) enlever; (*send*) expédier; **to g. off a chair** se lever d'une chaise; **to g. off a bus** descendre d'un bus.

get on 1 *vt* (*shoes, clothes*) mettre; (*bus, train*) monter dans. **2** *vi* (*progress*) marcher; (*manage*) se débrouiller; (*succeed*) réussir; (*enter bus or train*) monter; (*be on good terms*) s'entendre (**with** avec); **how are you getting on?** comment ça va?; **to g. on to s.o.** (*on phone*) contacter qn; **to g. on with** (*task*) continuer.

get out 1 *vi* sortir; (*from vehicle or train*) descendre (**of** de); **to g. out of** (*danger*) se tirer de; (*habit*) perdre. **2** *vt* (*remove*) enlever; (*bring out*) sortir (*qch*), faire sortir (*qn*).

get over 1 *vt* (*road*) traverser; (*obstacle*) surmonter; (*fence*) franchir; (*illness*) se remettre de. **2** *vi* (*cross*) traverser; (*visit*) passer.

get round *vi* (*visit*) passer; **to g. round to doing** en venir à faire.

get through 1 *vi* passer; (*finish*) finir; **to g. through to s.o.** (*on phone*) contacter qn. **2** *vt* passer par; (*meal*) venir à bout de; (*exam*) être reçu à.

get to (*send*) faire parvenir (*qch*) à; (*bring*) amener (*qn*) à.

get-together réunion *f*.

get up 1 *vi* (*rise*) se lever (**from** de); **to g. up to something** *or* **to mischief** faire des bêtises. **2** *vt* (*bring up*) monter (*qch*); (*wake up*) réveiller.

ghastly ['gɑːstlɪ] *a* (*horrible*) affreux.

gherkin ['gɜːkɪn] cornichon *m*.

ghetto ['getəʊ] (*pl* **-os**) ghetto *m*.

ghost [gəʊst] fantôme *m*.

giant ['dʒaɪənt] **1** *n* géant *m*. **2** *a* (*tree*, *packet*) géant.

giddy ['gɪdɪ] *a* **to be** *or* **feel g.** avoir le vertige; **to make g.** donner le vertige à.

gift ['gɪft] cadeau *m*; (*talent*) don *m*.

gifted *a* doué.

gift voucher *or* **token** chèque-cadeau *m*.

gigantic [dʒaɪ'gæntɪk] *a* gigantesque.

giggle ['gɪg(ə)l] *vi* rire (bêtement).

gills [gɪlz] *npl* (*of fish*) ouïes *fpl*.

gimmick ['gɪmɪk] truc *m*.

gin [dʒɪn] (*drink*) gin *m*.

ginger ['dʒɪndʒər] *a* (*hair*) roux (*f* rousse).

giraffe [dʒɪ'ræf] girafe *f*.

girl [gɜːl] (jeune) fille *f*; (*daughter*) fille *f*; **English g.** jeune Anglaise *f*.

girlfriend amie *f*; (*of boy*) petite amie *f*.

girl guide éclaireuse *f*.

give* [gɪv] *vt* donner (**to** à); (*support*) apporter; (*a smile*) faire; (*a sigh*) pousser; (*a look*) jeter.

give away (*free of charge*) donner; (*prizes*) distribuer; (*betray*) trahir (*qn*).

give back (*return*) rendre.

give in 1 *vi* (*surrender*) céder (**to** à). **2** *vt* (*hand in*) remettre.

give out (*hand out*) distribuer.

give over (*devote*) consacrer (**to** à).

give up 1 *vi* abandonner. **2** *vt* abandonner; (*seat*) céder (**to** à); (*prisoner*) livrer (**to** à); **to g. up smoking** cesser de fumer.

give way (*of branch*, *person etc*) céder (**to** à); (*in vehicle*) céder la priorité (**to** à).

glad [glæd] *a* content (**of, about** de).

gladly *adv* volontiers.

glamorous *a* séduisant.

glamour ['glæmər] (*charm*) enchantement *m*; (*splendour*) éclat *m*.

glance [glɑːns] **1** *n* coup *m* d'œil. **2** *vi* jeter un coup d'œil (**at** à, sur).
gland [glænd] glande *f*.
glaring ['gleərɪŋ] *a* (*light*) éblouissant; (*injustice*) flagrant.
glass [glɑːs] verre *m*; (*mirror*) miroir *m*; **a pane of g.** une vitre.
glasses *npl* (*for eyes*) lunettes *fpl*.
glee [gliː] joie *f*.
glen [glen] vallon *m*.
glide [glaɪd] *vi* glisser; (*of aircraft*, *bird*) planer.
gliding (*sport*) vol *m* à voile.
glimmer ['glɪmər] (*of hope*) lueur *f*.
glimpse [glɪmps] aperçu *m*; **to catch** *or* **get a g. of** entrevoir.
glittering ['glɪtərɪŋ] *a* scintillant.
globe [gləʊb] globe *m*.
gloom [gluːm] (*sadness*) tristesse *f*.
gloomy *a* triste; (*pessimistic*) pessimiste.
glorified *a* **it's a glorified barn**/*etc* ce n'est guère plus qu'une grange/*etc*.
glorious *a* glorieux; (*splendid*) magnifique.
glory ['glɔːrɪ] gloire *f*.
gloss [glɒs] (*shine*) brillant *m*; **g. paint** peinture *f* brillante.
glossy *a* brillant; (*magazine*) de luxe.
glove [glʌv] gant *m*.
glove compartment (*in car*) vide-poches *m inv*.
glow [gləʊ] *vi* (*of sky*, *fire*) rougeoyer.
glue [gluː] **1** *n* colle *f*. **2** *vt* coller (**to, on** à); **with eyes glued to** les yeux fixés sur.
glum [glʌm] *a* triste.
glut [glʌt] (*of oil etc*) surplus *m*.
glutton ['glʌt(ə)n] glouton, -onne *mf*.
gnat [næt] (*insect*) cousin *m*.
gnaw [nɔː] *vti* ronger.
go¹* [gəʊ] *vi* aller (**to** à, **from** de); (*depart*) partir, s'en aller; (*disappear*) disparaître, partir; (*function*) marcher; (*become*) devenir; (*of fuse*, *bulb*) sauter; (*of material*) s'user; **to go well/badly** (*of event*) se passer bien/mal; **she's going to do** (*is about to*, *intends to*) elle va faire; **it's all gone** il n'y en a plus; **to go and get** aller chercher; **to go riding/on a trip**/*etc* faire du cheval/un voyage/*etc*; **to let go of** lâcher; **to go to a doctor**/*etc* aller voir un médecin/*etc*; **two hours**/*etc* **to go** encore deux heures/*etc*.
go² (*pl* **goes**) (*attempt*) coup *m*; **to have a go at (doing) sth** essayer (de faire) qch; **at one go** d'un seul coup; **on the go** actif.

go about *or* **(a)round 1** *vi* se déplacer; (*of news*) circuler. **2** *vt* **to know how to go about it** savoir s'y prendre.

go across *vti* (*cross*) traverser.

go after (*chase*) poursuivre; (*seek*) (re)chercher.

go ahead *vi* avancer; (*continue*) continuer; (*start*) commencer; **go ahead!** allez-y!; **to go ahead with** (*plan etc*) poursuivre.

go-ahead to get the go-ahead avoir le feu vert.

goal [gəʊl] but *m*.

goalkeeper gardien *m* de but.

go along aller; **to go along with** (*agree*) être d'accord avec.

goat [gəʊt] chèvre *f*.

go away partir, s'en aller.

go back retourner; (*in time*) remonter; (*step back*) reculer; **to go back on** (*promise*) revenir sur.

go-between intermédiaire *mf*.

god [gɒd] dieu *m*; **G.** Dieu *m*.

goddaughter filleule *f*.

godfather parrain *m*.

godmother marraine *f*.

go down 1 *vi* descendre; (*fall down*) tomber; (*of ship*) couler; (*of sun*) se coucher; (*of price etc*) baisser. **2** *vt* **to go down the stairs/street** descendre l'escalier/la rue.

godsend to be a g. tomber à pic.

godson filleul *m*.

goes [gəʊz] *see* **go**[1].

go for (*fetch*) aller chercher.

goggles ['gɒg(ə)lz] *npl* lunettes *fpl* (*de protection*, *de plongée*).

go in 1 *vi* (r)entrer; (*of sun*) se cacher. **2** *vt* **to go in a room**/*etc* entrer dans une pièce/*etc*.

go in for (*exam*) se présenter à.

going 1 *n* (*conditions*) conditions *fpl*; **it's hard** *or* **heavy g.** c'est difficile. **2** *a* **the g. price** le prix pratiqué (**for** pour).

goings-'on *npl* activités *fpl*.

go into (*room etc*) entrer dans.

gold [gəʊld] or *m*; **g. watch**/*etc* montre/*etc* en or.

golden *a* (*in colour*) doré; (*rule*) d'or.

goldfish poisson *m* rouge.

goldmine mine *f* d'or.

gold-'plated *a* plaqué or.

golf [gɒlf] golf *m*.

golfer golfeur, -euse *mf*.

gone [gɒn] *pp de* **go**[1].

good [gʊd] **1** *a* bon (*f* bonne); (*kind*) gentil; (*weather*) beau (*f* belle); (*well-behaved*) sage; **very g.!** (*all right*) très bien!; **to feel g.** se sentir bien; **g. at French**/*etc* (*at school*) bon en français/*etc*; **to be g. with** (*children*) savoir s'y prendre avec; **it's a g. thing (that)...** heureusement que...; **a g. many, a g. deal (of)** beaucoup (de); **g. morning** bonjour; (*on leaving*) au revoir; **g. evening** bonsoir; **g. night** bonsoir; (*going to bed*) bonne nuit. **2** *n* (*advantage*, *virtue*) bien *m*; **for her own g.** pour son bien; **it's no g. crying**/*etc* ça ne sert à rien de pleurer/*etc*; **that's no g.** (*worthless*) ça ne vaut rien; (*bad*) ça ne va pas; **what's the g.?** à quoi bon?; **for g.** pour de bon.

goodbye *int* au revoir.

good-'looking *a* beau (*f* belle).

goods *npl* marchandises *fpl*; (*articles for sale*) articles *mpl*.

good'will bonne volonté *f*.

go off (*leave*) partir; (*go bad*) se gâter; (*of alarm*) se déclencher.

go on continuer (**doing** à faire); (*happen*) se passer; (*last*) durer.

goose, *pl* **geese** [guːs, giːs] oie *f*.

gooseberry ['gʊzbərɪ, *Am* 'guːsberɪ] groseille *f* à maquereau.

goose pimples *or* **bumps** chair *f* de poule.

go out sortir; (*of light*, *fire*) s'éteindre.

go over 1 *vi* aller (**to** à); (*to enemy*) passer (**to** à); **to go over to s.o.('s)** faire un saut chez qn. **2** *vt* examiner; (*in one's mind*) repasser.

gorge [gɔːdʒ] (*ravine*) gorge *f*.

gorgeous ['gɔːdʒəs] *a* magnifique.

gorilla [gə'rɪlə] gorille *m*.

go round 1 *vi* (*turn*) tourner; (*be sufficient*) suffire. **2** *vt* (*corner*) tourner; (*world*) faire le tour de.

Gospel ['gɒspəl] Évangile *m*.

gossip ['gɒsɪp] (*talk*) bavardage(s) *m*(*pl*); (*person*) commère *f*.

got [gɒt] *pt & pp de* **get.**

go through 1 *vi* passer. **2** *vt* (*suffer*) subir; (*examine*) examiner; (*search*) fouiller; (*spend*) dépenser; (*wear out*) user.

gotten ['gɒt(ə)n] *Am pp de* **get**.

go under *vi* (*of ship*, *firm*) couler.

go up 1 *vi* monter. **2** *vt* **to go up the stairs/street** monter l'escalier/la rue.

gourmet ['gʊəmeɪ] gourmet *m*.

govern ['gʌvən] **1** *vt* (*rule*) gouverner; (*city*) administrer; (*influence*) déterminer. **2** *vi* gouverner.

government gouvernement *m*; (*local*) administration *f*.

governor gouverneur *m*; (*of school*) administrateur, -trice *mf*.

go without sth se passer de qch.
gown [gaʊn] (*of woman*) robe *f*.
GP [dʒiːˈpiː] *abbr* (*general practitioner*) généraliste *m*.
grab [græb] *vt* **to g. (hold of)** saisir; **to g. sth from s.o.** arracher qch à qn.
grace [greɪs] (*charm*) grâce *f*.
graceful *a* gracieux.
grade [greɪd] **1** *n* catégorie *f*; (*in exam etc*) note *f*; (*class in school*) *Am* classe *f*. **2** *vt* (*classify*) classer; (*school paper*) noter.
grade school *Am* école *f* primaire.
gradual [ˈgrædʒʊəl] *a* progressif.
gradually *adv* progressivement.
graduate **1** *vi* [ˈgrædʒʊeɪt] obtenir son diplôme; *Am* obtenir son baccalauréat. **2** *n* [ˈgrædʒʊət] *n* diplômé, -ée *mf*.
gradu'ation remise *f* des diplômes.
graffiti [grəˈfiːtɪ] *npl* graffiti *mpl*.
graft [grɑːft] **1** *n* greffe *f*. **2** *vt* greffer.
grain [greɪn] (*seed*) grain *m*; (*cereal*) céréales *fpl*.
gram(me) [græm] gramme *m*.
grammar [ˈgræmər] grammaire *f*.
grammar school lycée *m*.
gra'mmatical *a* grammatical.
grand [grænd] *a* (*spendid*) magnifique.
grand(d)ad *Fam* papi *m*.
grandchild (*pl* **-children**) petit(e)-enfant *mf*.
granddaughter petite-fille *f*.
grandfather grand-père *m*.
grandma [-mɑː] *Fam* mamie *f*.
grandmother grand-mère *f*.
grandparents grands-parents *mpl*.
grandson petit-fils *m*.
granny [ˈgrænɪ] *Fam* mamie *f*.
grant [grɑːnt] **1** *vt* accorder (**to** à); (*request*) accéder à; **to take sth for granted** considérer qch comme acquis; **I take it for granted that** je présume que. **2** *n* subvention *f*; (*for study*) bourse *f*.
grape [greɪp] grain *m* de raisin; **grapes** le raisin, les raisins *mpl*; **to eat (some) grapes** manger du raisin *or* des raisins.
grapefruit pamplemousse *m*.
graph [græf] courbe *f*; **g. paper** papier *m* millimétré.
grasp [grɑːsp] **1** *vt* (*seize, understand*) saisir. **2** *n* (*hold*) prise *f*; (*understanding*) compréhension *f*.
grass [grɑːs] herbe *f*; (*lawn*) gazon *m*.

grasshopper sauterelle *f*.
grate [greɪt] **1** *n* (*for fireplace*) grille *f* de foyer. **2** *vt* (*cheese etc*) râper.
grateful ['greɪtful] *a* reconnaissant (**to** à, **for** de); **I'm g. (to you) for your help** je vous suis reconnaissant de votre aide.
grater râpe *f*.
gratifying ['grætɪfaɪɪŋ] *a* très satisfaisant *or* agréable.
gratitude ['grætɪtju:d] reconnaissance *f*, gratitude *f* (**for** de).
grave[1] [greɪv] tombe *f*.
grave[2] *a* (*serious*) grave.
gravel ['græv(ə)l] gravier *m*.
graveyard cimetière *m*.
gravity ['grævɪtɪ] (*force*) pesanteur *f*.
gravy ['greɪvɪ] jus *m* de viande.
gray [greɪ] *Am* = **grey**.
graze [greɪz] **1** *vi* (*of cattle*) paître. **2** *vt* (*skin*) écorcher. **3** *n* (*wound*) écorchure *f*.
grease [gri:s] **1** *n* graisse *f*. **2** *vt* graisser.
greaseproof (paper) papier *m* sulfurisé.
greasy *a* plein de graisse; (*hair*) gras.
great [greɪt] *a* grand; (*excellent*) *Fam* magnifique; **a g. deal (of), a g. many** beaucoup (de); **the greatest team**/*etc* (*best*) la meilleure équipe/*etc*.
great-'grandfather arrière-grand-père *m*.
great-'grandmother arrière-grand-mère *f*.
greatly (*much*) beaucoup; (*very*) très.
greed [gri:d] avidité *f*; (*for food*) gourmandise *f*.
greedy *a* avide; (*for food*) gourmand.
Greek [gri:k] **1** *a* grec (*f* grecque). **2** *n* Grec *m*, Greque *f*; (*language*) grec *m*.
green [gri:n] **1** *a* vert; **to turn** *or* **go g.** verdir. **2** *n* (*colour*) vert *m*; (*lawn*) pelouse *f*; **greens** légumes *mpl* verts.
greengrocer marchand, -ande *mf* de légumes.
greenhouse serre *f*.
greet [gri:t] *vt* saluer.
greeting salutation *f*; **greetings** (*for birthday*, *festival*) vœux *mpl*.
grenade [grə'neɪd] (*bomb*) grenade *f*.
grey [greɪ] *a* gris; **to be going g.** grisonner.
greyhound lévrier *m*.
grief [gri:f] chagrin *m*.
grieve [gri:v] *vi* **to g. for s.o.** pleurer qn.
grill [grɪl] **1** *n* (*utensil*) gril *m*; (*dish*) grillade *f*. **2** *vti* griller.

grim [grɪm] *a* (*face, future*) sombre; (*bad*) *Fam* affreux.
grime [graɪm] crasse *f*.
grimy *a* crasseux.
grin [grɪn] **1** *vi* avoir un large sourire. **2** *n* large sourire *m*.
grind* [graɪnd] *vt* moudre; **to g. one's teeth** grincer des dents.
grinder coffee g. moulin *m* à café.
grip [grɪp] **1** *vt* saisir; (*hold*) tenir serré. **2** *n* (*hold*) prise *f*; (*with hand*) poigne *f*; **in the g. of** en proie à.
gripping *a* (*book etc*) prenant.
groan [grəʊn] **1** *vi* gémir. **2** *n* gémissement *m*.
grocer ['grəʊsər] épicier, -ière *mf*; **g.'s shop** épicerie *f*.
grocery (*shop*) *Am* épicerie *f*; **groceries** (*food*) épicerie *f*.
groin [grɔɪn] aine *f*.
groom [gruːm] (*bridegroom*) marié *m*.
groove [gruːv] (*slot*) rainure *f*.
grope about [grəʊp] *vi* tâtonner.
grope for chercher à tâtons.
gross [grəʊs] *a* (*total*) (*income etc*) brut.
grossly *adv* (*very*) extrêmement.
grotty ['grɒtɪ] *a Fam* (*ugly*) moche; (*of poor quality*) nul.
ground [graʊnd] terre *f*, sol *m*; (*for camping, football etc*) terrain *m*; **grounds** (*reasons*) raisons *fpl*; (*gardens*) parc *m*; **on the g.** (*lying, sitting*) par terre.
ground floor rez-de-chaussée *m inv*.
ground meat *Am* hachis *m* (de viande).
groundwork préparation *f*.
group [gruːp] groupe *m*.
group (together) *vti* (se) grouper.
grow* [grəʊ] **1** *vi* (*of person*) grandir; (*of plant, hair*) pousser; (*increase*) augmenter, grandir; (*of firm, town*) se développer. **2** *vt* (*plant, crops*) cultiver; (*beard*) laisser pousser.
grow into devenir.
growl [graʊl] *vi* grogner (**at** contre).
grown *a* (*man, woman*) adulte.
grown-up grande personne *f*.
grow out of (*clothes*) devenir trop grand pour; (*habit*) perdre.
growth croissance *f*; (*increase*) augmentation *f* (**in** de); (*lump*) tumeur *f* (**on** à).
grow up devenir adulte.
grub [grʌb] (*food*) *Fam* bouffe *f*.
grubby ['grʌbɪ] *a* sale.
grudge [grʌdʒ] rancune *f*; **to have a g. against** garder rancune à.

gruelling, *Am* **grueling** ['grʊəlɪŋ] *a* éprouvant.
gruesome ['gru:səm] *a* horrible.
grumble ['grʌmb(ə)l] *vi* râler, grogner (**about, at** contre).
grumpy ['grʌmpɪ] *a* grincheux.
grunt [grʌnt] **1** *vti* grogner. **2** *n* grognement *m*.
guarantee [gærən'ti:] **1** *n* garantie *f*. **2** *vt* garantir (**against** contre, **s.o. that** à qn que).
guard [gɑ:d] **1** *n* (*vigilance, soldiers*) garde *f*; (*individual person*) garde *m*; (*on train*) chef *m* de train; **to keep a g. on** surveiller; **under g.** sous surveillance; **on one's g.** sur ses gardes; **on g. (duty)** de garde; **to stand g.** monter la garde. **2** *vt* protéger; (*watch over*) surveiller.
guess [ges] **1** *n* conjecture *f*; (*intuition*) intuition *f*; **to make a g.** (essayer de) deviner. **2** *vt* deviner (**that** que); (*length, number*) estimer; (*suppose*) *Am* supposer; (*think*) *Am* croire (**that** que).
guesswork hypothèse *f*; **by g.** au jugé.
guest [gest] invité, -ée *mf*; (*in hotel*) client, -ente *mf*; (*at meal*) convive *mf*.
guesthouse pension *f* de famille.
guidance conseils *mpl*.
guide [gaɪd] **1** *n* guide *m*; **g. (book)** guide *m*. **2** *vt* guider; **guided tour** visite *f* guidée.
guidelines *npl* indications *fpl* (à suivre).
guilt [gɪlt] culpabilité *f*.
guilty *a* coupable; **g. person** coupable *mf*.
guinea pig ['gɪnɪpɪg] cobaye *m*.
guitar [gɪ'tɑ:r] guitare *f*.
guitarist guitariste *mf*.
gulf [gʌlf] (*in sea*) golfe *m*; **a g. between** un abîme entre.
gull [gʌl] (*bird*) mouette *f*.
gulp [gʌlp] (*of drink*) gorgée *f*.
gulp down avaler (vite).
gum[1] [gʌm] (*around teeth*) gencive *f*.
gum[2] **1** *n* (*for chewing*) chewing-gum *m*; (*glue*) colle *f*. **2** *vt* coller.
gun [gʌn] pistolet *m*; (*rifle*) fusil *m*; (*firing shells*) canon *m*.
gun down abattre.
gunfire coups *mpl* de feu.
gunman (*pl* **-men**) bandit *m* armé.
gunpoint at g. sous la menace d'une arme.
gunpowder poudre *f* à canon.
gunshot coup *m* de feu.
gush (out) [gʌʃ] jaillir (**of** de).

gust [gʌst] **g. (of wind)** rafale *f* (de vent).
guts [gʌts] *npl Fam* (*insides*) ventre *m*.
gutter ['gʌtər] (*on roof*) gouttière *f*; (*in street*) caniveau *m*.
guy [gaɪ] *Fam* type *m*.
gym [dʒɪm] gym(nastique) *f*; (*gymnasium*) gymnase *m*.
gym'nasium gymnase *m*.
gym'nastics gymnastique *f*.
gynaecologist, *Am* **gynecologist** gynécologue *mf*.

H

habit ['hæbɪt] habitude *f*; **to be in/get into the h. of doing** avoir/prendre l'habitude de faire.
hack [hæk] *vt* (*cut*) tailler.
had [hæd] *pt & pp de* **have**.
haddock ['hædək] (*fish*) aiglefin *m*; **smoked h.** haddock *m*.
haemorrhage ['hemərɪdʒ] hémorragie *f*.
hag [hæg] **(old) h.** (vieille) sorcière *f*.
haggle ['hæg(ə)l] *vi* marchander; **to h. over the price** discuter le prix.
hail [heɪl] **1** *n* grêle *f*. **2** *vi* grêler; **it's hailing** il grêle.
hailstone grêlon *m*.
hair [heər] (*on head*) cheveux *mpl*; (*on body*, *of animal*) poils *mpl*; **a h.** (*on head*) un cheveu; (*on body*, *of animal*) un poil.
hairbrush brosse *f* à cheveux.
haircut coupe *f* de cheveux; **to have a h.** se faire couper les cheveux.
hairdo (*pl* **-dos**) *Fam* coiffure *f*.
hairdresser coiffeur, -euse *mf*.
hair dryer sèche-cheveux *m inv*.
-haired *suffix* **long-/red-h.** aux cheveux longs/roux.
hairgrip pince *f* à cheveux.
hairpin épingle *f* à cheveux.
hair-raising *a* effrayant.
hair spray (bombe *f* de) laque *f*.
hairstyle coiffure *f*.
hairy *a* (*person*, *animal*, *body*) poilu.
half [hɑːf] **1** *n* (*pl* **halves**) moitié *f*, demi, -ie *mf*; **h. (of) the apple**/*etc* la moitié de la pomme/*etc*; **ten and a h.** dix et demi; **ten and a h. weeks** dix semaines et demie; **to cut in h.** couper en deux. **2** *a* demi; **h. a day, a h.-day** une demi-journée; **h. a dozen, a h.-dozen** une demi-douzaine; **at h. price** à moitié prix. **3** *adv* (*full etc*) à demi, à moitié; **h. past one** une heure et demie.
half-'hour demi-heure *f*.
half-'term (*in British school*) petites vacances *fpl*.
half-'time (*in game*) mi-temps *f*.
half'way *adv* à mi-chemin (**between** entre); **to fill**/*etc* **h.** remplir/*etc* à moitié.
halibut ['hælɪbət] (*fish*) flétan *m*.
hall [hɔːl] salle *f*; (*house entrance*) entrée *f*; (*of hotel*) hall *m*; **halls of residence** cité *f* universitaire; **lecture h.** amphithéâtre *m*.

hallo! [hə'ləʊ] *int* = **hello.**
Hallowe'en [hæləʊ'iːn] la veille de la Toussaint.
hallstand portemanteau *m.*
hallway entrée *f.*
halt [hɔːlt] halte *f*; **to call a h. to** mettre fin à.
halve [hɑːv] *vt* (*time, expense*) réduire de moitié.
ham [hæm] jambon *m*; **h. and eggs** œufs *mpl* au jambon.
hamburger hamburger *m.*
hammer ['hæmər] **1** *n* marteau *m.* **2** *vt* (*nail*) enfoncer (**into** dans).
hammering (*defeat*) *Fam* raclée *f.*
hammock ['hæmək] hamac *m.*
hamper ['hæmpər] **1** *vt* gêner. **2** *n* panier *m*; (*laundry basket*) *Am* panier *m* à linge.
hamster ['hæmstər] hamster *m.*
hand[1] [hænd] main *f*; (*of clock*) aiguille *f*; *Cards* jeu *m*; **to hold in one's h.** tenir à la main; **to give s.o. a (helping) h.** donner un coup de main à qn; **by h.** (*to make, sew etc*) à la main; **at** *or* **to h.** sous la main; **on h.** disponible; **out of h.** (*situation*) incontrôlable.
hand[2] *vt* (*give*) donner (**to** à).
handbag sac *m* à main.
handbook manuel *m*; (*guide*) guide *m.*
handbrake frein *m* à main.
handcuff *vt* passer les menottes à.
handcuffs *npl* menottes *fpl.*
handful (*group*) poignée *f.*
handicap ['hændɪkæp] **1** *n* handicap *m.* **2** *vt* handicaper; **to be handicapped** (*after an accident etc*) rester handicapé.
handicapped [-kæpt] *a* handicapé.
hand in remettre.
handkerchief ['hæŋkətʃɪf] (*pl* **-fs**) mouchoir *m.*
handle ['hænd(ə)l] **1** *n* (*of door*) poignée *f*; (*of knife*) manche *m*; (*of bucket*) anse *f*; (*of saucepan*) queue *f.* **2** *vt* (*manipulate*) manier; (*touch*) toucher à; (*vehicle*) manœuvrer; (*deal with*) s'occuper de.
handlebars *npl* guidon *m.*
hand luggage bagages *mpl* à main.
hand'made *a* fait à la main.
hand out distribuer.
handout (*leaflet*) prospectus *m*; (*money*) aumône *f.*
hand over remettre.
handrail rampe *f.*
hand round (*cakes*) passer.

handshake poignée *f* de main.
handsome ['hænsəm] *a* beau (*f* belle); (*profit*) considérable.
handwriting écriture *f*.
handy ['hændɪ] *a* commode, pratique; (*skilful*) habile (**at doing** à faire); (*within reach*) sous la main; (*place*) accessible.
handyman (*pl* **-men**) bricoleur *m*.
hang[1]* [hæŋ] **1** *vt* (*pt & pp* **hung**) suspendre (**on, from** à); (*let dangle*) laisser pendre (**from, out of** de). **2** *vi* pendre; (*of fog*) flotter. **3** *n* **to get the h. of sth** *Fam* arriver à comprendre qch.
hang[2] *vt* (*pt & pp* **hanged**) (*criminal*) pendre (**for** pour).
hang about traîner; (*wait*) attendre.
hangar ['hæŋər] hangar *m*.
hang down *vi* pendre.
hanger (**coat**) **h.** cintre *m*.
hang-glider delta-plane® *m*.
hanging *a* suspendu (**from** à).
hang on résister; (*wait*) attendre; **to h. on to** ne pas lâcher; (*keep*) garder.
hang out 1 *vt* (*washing*) étendre; (*flag*) arborer. **2** *vi* (*of tongue, shirt*) pendre.
hangover gueule *f* de bois.
hang up 1 *vt* (*picture*) accrocher. **2** *vi* (*on phone*) raccrocher.
hangup complexe *m*.
happen ['hæpən] *vi* arriver, se passer; **to h. to s.o./sth** arriver à qn/qch; **I h. to know** il se trouve que je le sais; **do you h. to have...?** est-ce que par hasard vous avez...?
happening événement *m*.
happily *adv* joyeusement; (*contentedly*) tranquillement; (*fortunately*) heureusement.
happiness bonheur *m*.
happy ['hæpɪ] *a* heureux (**to do** de faire, **about sth** de qch); **I'm not h. about it** ça ne me plaît pas beaucoup; **H. New Year!** bonne année!
harass ['hærəs, *Am* hə'ræs] *vt* harceler.
harbour ['hɑːbər] port *m*.
hard [hɑːd] **1** *a* (*not soft, severe, difficult*) dur; **h. worker** gros travailleur *m*; **h. on s.o.** dur avec qn; **h. of hearing** malentendant. **2** *adv* (*to work, hit*) dur; (*to pull*) fort; (*to rain*) à verse; **to think h.** réfléchir bien.
hard-'boiled *a* (*egg*) dur.
hard core (*group*) noyau *m*.
harden *vti* durcir; **to become hardened to** s'endurcir à.

hardly *adv* à peine; **h. anyone** presque personne; **h. ever** presque jamais.
hardness dureté *f.*
hardship épreuve(s) *f(pl).*
hard up *a* (*broke*) *Fam* fauché.
hardware ['hɑːdweər] *n inv* quincaillerie *f*; (*of computer*) matériel *m.*
hard'wearing *a* résistant.
hard-'working *a* travailleur.
hare [heər] lièvre *m.*
harm [hɑːm] **1** *n* (*hurt*) mal *m*; (*wrong*) tort *m.* **2** *vt* (*physically*) faire du mal à; (*health, interests etc*) nuire à.
harmful *a* nuisible.
harmless *a* inoffensif.
harmonica [hɑː'mɒnɪkə] harmonica *m.*
har'monious *a* harmonieux.
harmony ['hɑːmənɪ] harmonie *f.*
harness ['hɑːnɪs] (*for horse, baby*) harnais *m.*
harp [hɑːp] harpe *f.*
harp on about sth *Fam* ne pas s'arrêter de parler de qch.
harsh [hɑːʃ] *a* dur, sévère; (*sound, taste*) âpre.
harshly *adv* durement.
harshness dureté *f.*
harvest ['hɑːvɪst] **1** *n* moisson *f*; (*of fruit*) récolte *f.* **2** *vt* moissonner; récolter.
has [hæz] *see* **have.**
hassle ['hæs(ə)l] *Fam* (*trouble*) histoires *fpl*; (*bother*) mal *m*, peine *f.*
haste [heɪst] hâte *f*; **to make h.** se hâter.
hasten 1 *vi* se hâter (**to do** de faire). **2** *vt* hâter.
hastily *adv* à la hâte.
hasty *a* précipité; (*visit*) rapide.
hat [hæt] chapeau *m*; (*of child*) bonnet *m*; (*cap*) casquette *f.*
hatch [hætʃ] **1** *vi* (*of chick, egg*) éclore. **2** *n* (*in kitchen wall*) passe-plats *m inv.*
hatchback (*car*) trois-portes *f inv*, cinq-portes *f inv.*
hate [heɪt] *vt* détester, haïr; **to h. doing** *or* **to do** détester faire.
hateful *a* haïssable.
hatred haine *f.*
haul [hɔːl] *vt* (*pull*) tirer.
haunted ['hɔːntɪd] *a* hanté.
have* [hæv] **1** *vt* avoir; (*meal, drink, shower etc*) prendre; **to h. a**

walk/dream faire une promenade/un rêve; **will you h....?** (*a cake, some tea etc*) est-ce que tu veux...?; **to let s.o. h. sth** donner qch à qn; **you've had it!** *Fam* tu es fichu! **2** *v aux* avoir; (*with monter, sortir etc & pronominal verbs*) être; **to h. decided/been** avoir décidé/été; **to h. gone** être allé; **to h. cut oneself** s'être coupé; **I've got to go, I h. to go** je dois partir, je suis obligé de partir; **to h. sth done** faire faire qch; **he's had his suitcase brought up** il a fait monter sa valise; **haven't I?, hasn't she?** *etc* n'est-ce pas?; **no I haven't!** non!; **yes I h.!** oui!; (*after negative question*) si!

havoc ['hævək] ravages *mpl*.

hawk [hɔːk] faucon *m*.

hay [heɪ] foin *m*.

hay fever rhume *m* des foins.

haystack meule *f* de foin.

hazard ['hæzəd] risque *m*.

haze [heɪz] brume *f*.

hazelnut noisette *f*.

hazy *a* (*weather*) brumeux; (*photo, idea*) flou; **I'm h. about my plans** je ne suis pas sûr de mes projets.

he [hiː] *pron* il; (*stressed*) lui; **he's a happy man** c'est un homme heureux.

head [hed] **1** *n* (*of person, hammer etc*) tête *f*; (*leader*) chef *m*; **it didn't enter my h.** ça ne m'est pas venu à l'esprit; **heads or tails?** pile ou face?; **per h., a h.** (*each*) par personne. **2** *a* (*salesperson etc*) principal; **h. waiter** maître *m* d'hôtel. **3** *vt* (*group, firm*) être à la tête de; (*list*) être en tête de.

headache mal *m* de tête; **to have a h.** avoir mal à la tête.

head for, be heading *or Am* **headed for** (*place*) se diriger vers; (*ruin*) aller à.

heading (*of chapter etc*) titre *m*; (*of subject*) rubrique *f*.

headlight (*of vehicle*) phare *m*.

headline (*of newspaper*) manchette *f*; **the headlines** les titres *mpl*.

head'master (*of school*) directeur *m*.

head'mistress directrice *f*.

headphones *npl* casque *m* (à écouteurs).

headquarters *npl* siège *m* (central); (*military*) quartier *m* général.

head waiter maître *m* d'hôtel.

headway progrès *mpl*.

heal [hiːl] *vi* (*of wound*) se cicatriser; (*of bruise*) disparaître; (*of bone*) se ressouder.

health [helθ] santé *f*; **the (National) H. Service** = la Sécurité Sociale.

health food aliment *m* naturel; **h. food shop** *or Am* **store** magasin

m diététique.
healthy *a* (*person*) en bonne santé; (*food, attitude etc*) sain.
heap [hiːp] **1** *n* tas *m*; **heaps of** (*money, people*) *Fam* des tas de. **2** *vt* entasser.
heap on s.o. (*praise*) couvrir qn de; (*insults*) accabler qn de.
hear* [hɪər] **1** *vt* entendre; (*listen to*) écouter; (*learn*) apprendre (**that** que). **2** *vi* entendre; (*get news*) recevoir des nouvelles (**from** de); **I've heard of** *or* **about him** j'ai entendu parler de lui.
hearing (*sense*) ouïe *f*.
hearing aid appareil *m* auditif.
hearse [hɜːs] corbillard *m*.
heart [hɑːt] cœur *m*; **heart(s)** *Cards* cœur *m*; **(off) by h.** par cœur.
heart attack crise *f* cardiaque.
heartbeat battement *m* de cœur.
heartbreaking *a* navrant.
heartening *a* encourageant.
hearty ['hɑːtɪ] *a* (*appetite*) gros (*f* grosse).
heat [hiːt] chaleur *f*; (*heating*) chauffage *m*.
heat (up) *vti* chauffer.
heater radiateur *m*.
heath [hiːθ] lande *f*.
heather ['heðər] bruyère *f*.
heating chauffage *m*.
heat wave vague *f* de chaleur.
heave [hiːv] **1** *vt* (*lift*) soulever; (*pull*) tirer; (*a sigh*) pousser. **2** (*feel sick*) avoir des haut-le-cœur.
heaven ['hev(ə)n] ciel *m*; **h. knows when** Dieu sait quand.
heavily *adv* lourdement; (*to smoke, drink*) beaucoup; **to rain h.** pleuvoir à verse.
heavy ['hevɪ] *a* lourd; (*rain*) fort; (*traffic*) dense; (*smoker, drinker*) grand.
Hebrew ['hiːbruː] (*language*) hébreu *m*.
hectic ['hektɪk] *a* fiévreux; (*period*) très agité.
hedge [hedʒ] haie *f*.
hedgehog hérisson *m*.
heel [hiːl] talon *m*.
heel bar cordonnerie *f* express.
hefty ['heftɪ] *a* gros (*f* grosse).
height [haɪt] hauteur *f*; (*of person*) taille *f*; (*of success etc*) sommet *m*; **at the h. of** (*summer*) au cœur de.
heir [eər] héritier *m*.
heiress héritière *f*.

held [held] *pt & pp de* **hold.**
helicopter ['helɪkɒptər] hélicoptère *m*.
hell [hel] enfer *m*; **a h. of a lot (of)** (*very many, very much*) *Fam* énormément (de); **h.!** *Fam* zut!
hello! [hə'ləʊ] *int* bonjour!; (*answering phone*) allô!; (*surprise*) tiens!
helm [helm] (*of boat*) barre *f*.
helmet ['helmɪt] casque *m*.
help [help] **1** *n* aide *f*, secours *m*; (*cleaning woman*) femme *f* de ménage; (*office or shop workers*) employés, -ées *mfpl*; **h.!** au secours! **2** *vt* aider (**do, to do** à faire); **to h. oneself (to)** se servir (de); **I can't h. laughing**/*etc* je ne peux m'empêcher de rire/*etc*.
helper assistant, -ante *mf*.
helpful *a* utile; (*person*) serviable.
helping (*serving*) portion *f*.
helpless *a* (*powerless*) impuissant; (*disabled*) impotent.
help out *vti* aider.
hem [hem] ourlet *m*.
hemmed in *a* enfermé; (*surrounded*) cerné.
hemorrhage ['hemərɪdʒ] hémorragie *f*.
hen [hen] poule *f*.
hepatitis [hepə'taɪtɪs] hépatite *f*.
her [hɜːr] **1** *pron* la, l'; (*after prep, 'than', 'it is'*) elle; **(to) h.** lui; **I see h.** je la vois; **I give (to) h.** je lui donne. **2** *poss a* son, sa, *pl* ses.
herb [hɜːb, *Am* ɜːb] herbe *f*; **herbs** (*in cooking*) fines herbes *fpl*.
herd [hɜːd] troupeau *m*.
here [hɪər] *adv.* ici; **h. is, h. are** voici; **h. she is** la voici; **summer is h.** l'été est là; **h.!** (*calling attention*) holà!, **h. (you are)!** (*take this*) tenez!
hermit ['hɜːmɪt] solitaire *mf*.
hero ['hɪərəʊ] (*pl* **-oes**) héros *m*.
he'roic *a* héroïque.
heroin ['herəʊɪn] (*drug*) héroïne *f*.
heroine ['herəʊɪn] héroïne *f*.
herring ['herɪŋ] hareng *m*.
hers [hɜːz] *poss pron* le sien, la sienne, *pl* les sien(ne)s; **this hat is h.** ce chapeau est à elle *or* est le sien.
her'self *pron* elle-même; (*reflexive*) se, s'; (*after prep*) elle.
hesitant *a* hésitant.
hesitate ['hezɪteɪt] *vi* hésiter (**over, about** sur; **to do** à faire).
hesi'tation hésitation *f*.
het up [het'ʌp] *a* énervé.
hey! [heɪ] *int* hé!

hi! [haɪ] *int Fam* salut!
hiccups ['hɪkʌps] *npl* **to have (the) h.** avoir le hoquet.
hide[1]* [haɪd] **1** *vt* cacher (**from** à). **2** *vi* se cacher (**from** de).
hide[2] (*skin*) peau *f*.
hide-and-'seek cache-cache *m inv*.
hideous ['hɪdɪəs] *a* horrible.
hideously *adv* horriblement.
hide-out cachette *f*.
hiding a good h. (*thrashing*) une bonne raclée.
hiding place cachette *f*.
hi-fi ['haɪfaɪ] hi-fi *f inv*.
high [haɪ] **1** *a* haut; (*speed*) grand; (*price, number*) élevé; (*on drugs*) *Fam* défoncé; **h. fever** forte fièvre *f*; **to be five metres h.** avoir cinq mètres de haut. **2** *adv* **h. (up)** (*to fly, throw etc*) haut. **3** *n* **an all-time h.** un nouveau record.
high-chair chaise *f* haute.
high-'class *a* (*service*) de premier ordre; (*building*) de luxe.
higher *a* supérieur (**than** à).
highlands ['haɪləndz] *npl* régions *fpl* montagneuses.
highlight 1 *n* (*of visit, day*) point *m* culminant; (*of show*) clou *m*. **2** *vt* souligner.
highly *adv* (*very*) très; (*to recommend*) chaudement; **h. paid** très bien payé.
high-'pitched *a* (*sound*) aigu.
high-rise *a* **h.-rise flats** tour *f*.
highroad grand-route *f*.
high school = collège *m* d'enseignement secondaire.
high-'speed *a* ultra-rapide; **h.-speed train** rapide *m*
high street grand-rue *f*.
highway *Am* autoroute *f*; **public h.** voie *f* publique; **H. Code** Code *m* de la route.
hijack 1 *vt* (*aircraft*) détourner. **2** *n* détournement *m*.
hijacker pirate *m* de l'air.
hijacking piraterie *f* aérienne; (*hijack*) détournement *m*.
hike [haɪk] **1** *n* excursion *f* à pied. **2** *vi* marcher à pied.
hiker excursionniste *mf*.
hilarious [hɪ'leərɪəs] *a* désopilant.
hill [hɪl] colline *f*.
hillside on the h. à flanc de colline.
hilly *a* accidenté.
him [hɪm] *pron* le, l'; (*after prep, 'than', 'it is'*) lui; **(to) h.** lui; **I see h.** je le vois; **I give (to) h.** je lui donne.

him'self *pron* lui-même; (*reflexive*) se, s'; (*after prep*) lui.
hinder ['hɪndər] *vt* gêner.
Hindu ['hɪnduː] *a* & *n* hindou, -oue (*mf*).
hinge [hɪndʒ] charnière *f*.
hint [hɪnt] **1** *n* allusion *f*; (*sign*) indication *f*; **hints** (*advice*) conseils *mpl*. **2** *vt* laisser entendre (**that** que).
hint at faire allusion à.
hip hanche *f*.
hippopotamus [hɪpə'pɒtəməs] hippopotame *m*.
hire ['haɪər] **1** *vt* (*vehicle etc*) louer; (*worker*) engager. **2** *n* location *f*; **for h.** à louer.
hire out donner en location, louer.
hire purchase vente *f* à crédit.
his [hɪz] **1** *poss a* son, sa, *pl* ses. **2** *poss pron* le sien, la sienne, *pl* les sien(ne)s; **this hat is h.** ce chapeau est à lui *or* est le sien.
Hispanic [hɪs'pænɪk] *a* & *n Am* hispano-américain, -aine (*mf*).
hiss [hɪs] **1** *vti* siffler. **2** *n* sifflement *m*.
hi'storic(al) *a* historique.
history ['hɪstərɪ] histoire *f*.
hit* [hɪt] **1** *vt* (*beat etc*) frapper; (*bump into*) heurter; (*reach*) atteindre; (*affect*) toucher. **2** *n* (*blow*) coup *m*; (*play*, *film*) succès *m*; **h. (song)** chanson *f* à succès.
hit-and-run driver chauffard *m*.
hitch [hɪtʃ] **1** *n* (*snag*) problème *m*. **2** *vti* **to h. (a ride)** *Fam* faire du stop (**to** jusqu'à).
hitchhike *vi* faire de l'auto-stop (**to** jusqu'à).
hitchhiker auto-stoppeur, -euse *mf*.
hitchhiking auto-stop *m*.
hit (up)on (*find*) tomber sur.
hit out (at) *Fam* attaquer.
hive [haɪv] ruche *f*.
hoard [hɔːd] *vt* amasser.
hoarding panneau *m* d'affichage.
hoarse [hɔːs] *a* enroué.
hoax [həʊks] canular *m*.
hobby ['hɒbɪ] passe-temps *m inv*.
hobo ['həʊbəʊ] (*pl* **-os**) *Am* vagabond, -onde *mf*.
hockey ['hɒkɪ] hockey *m*; **ice h.** hockey sur glace.
hold [həʊld] **1** *n* (*grip*) prise *f*; (*of ship*) cale *f*; (*of aircraft*) soute *f*; **to get h. of** saisir; (*contact*) joindre; (*find*) trouver. **2** *vt** tenir; (*breath*, *interest*, *attention*) retenir; (*a post*) occuper; (*a record*) détenir; (*possess*) posséder; (*contain*) contenir; **to h. hands** se tenir

par la main; **h. the line!** (*on phone*) ne quittez pas!; **to be held** (*of event*) avoir lieu. **3** *vi* (*of nail, rope*) tenir; **if the rain holds off** s'il ne pleut pas.

holdall fourre-tout *m inv*.

hold back (*crowd*) contenir; (*hide*) cacher.

hold down (*price*) maintenir bas; (*keep*) garder (*un emploi*).

holder (*of passport*) titulaire *mf*; (*of record*) détenteur, -trice *mf*; (*container*) support *m*.

hold on attendre; (*stand firm*) tenir bon; **h. on!** (*on phone*) ne quittez pas! **h. on (tight)!** tenez bon!

hold onto (*cling to*) tenir bien; (*keep*) garder.

hold out 1 *vt* offrir; (*arm*) étendre. **2** *vi* résister; (*last*) durer.

hold up lever; (*support*) soutenir; (*delay*) retarder; (*bank*) attaquer.

holdup (*attack*) hold-up *m inv*; (*traffic jam*) bouchon *m*.

hole [həʊl] trou *m*.

holiday ['hɒlɪdeɪ] **holiday(s)** (*from work, school etc*) vacances *fpl*; **a h.** (*day off*) un congé; **a (public** *or* **bank) h.,** *Am* **a legal h.** un jour férié; **on h.** en vacances.

holidaymaker vacancier, -ière *mf*.

hollow ['hɒləʊ] *a* creux.

holy ['həʊlɪ] *a* saint; (*water*) bénit.

home [həʊm] **1** *n* maison *f*; (*country*) pays *m* (natal); **at h.** à la maison, chez soi; **to make oneself at h.** se mettre à l'aise; **a good h.** une bonne famille; **(old people's) h.** maison *f* de retraite; **h. life/cooking/***etc* la vie/cuisine/*etc* familiale. **2** *adv* à la maison, chez soi; **to go** *or* **come (back) h.** rentrer; **to be h.** être rentré.

home help aide *f* ménagère.

homeless *a* sans abri.

home'made *a* (fait à la) maison *inv*.

homesick *a* **to be h.** avoir envie de rentrer chez soi.

home town ville *f* natale.

homework devoir(s) *m(pl)*.

homosexual [həʊmə'sekʃʊəl] *a* & *n* homosexuel, -elle (*mf*)

honest ['ɒnɪst] *a* honnête; (*frank*) franc (*f* franche) (**with** avec).

honesty honnêteté *f*; franchise *f*.

honey ['hʌnɪ] miel *m*; (*person*) *Fam* chéri, -ie *mf*.

honeymoon lune *f* de miel; (*trip*) voyage *m* de noces.

honk [hɒŋk] *vi* (*in vehicle*) klaxonner.

honour ['ɒnər] **1** *n* honneur *m*; **in h. of** en l'honneur de. **2** *vt* honorer (**with** de).

honourable *a* honorable.

honours degree = licence *f*.

hood [hʊd] capuchon *m*; (*mask of robber*) cagoule *f*; (*car or pram roof, Am baby carriage roof*) capote *f*; (*car bonnet*) *Am* capot *m*.
hoof, *pl* **-fs** *or* **-ves** [huːf, -fs, -vz] (*Am* [hʊf, -fs, huːvz]) sabot *m*.
hook [hʊk] crochet *m*; (*on clothes*) agrafe *f*; *Fishing* hameçon *m*; **off the h.** (*phone*) décroché.
hooked [hʊkt] *a* (*nose, object*) recourbé; **h. on** (*drugs, chess etc*) *Fam* accro de.
hook (on *or* **up)** accrocher (**to** à).
hook(e)y ['hʊkɪ] **to play h.** *Am* sécher (la classe).
hooligan ['huːlɪgən] vandale *m*.
hoop [huːp] cerceau *m*.
hoot [huːt] *vi* (*in vehicle*) klaxonner.
hooter klaxon® *m*.
hoover® ['huːvər] **1** *n* aspirateur *m*. **2** *vt* passer à l'aspirateur.
hop [hɒp] **1** *vi* sauter (à cloche-pied); (*of bird*) sautiller; **h. in!** (*in car*) montez! **2** *n* saut *m*.
hope [həʊp] **1** *n* espoir *m*. **2** *vi* espérer; **I h. so** j'espère que oui. **3** *vt* espérer (**to do** faire, **that** que).
hope for espérer.
hopeful *a* optimiste; (*promising*) prometteur; **to be h. that** avoir bon espoir que.
hopefully (*one hopes*) on espère (que).
hopeless *a* désespéré; (*useless*) nul.
hopelessly (*extremely*) complètement.
hops *npl* houblon *m*.
hopscotch marelle *f*.
horizon [hə'raɪz(ə)n] horizon *m*; **on the h.** à l'horizon.
horizontal [hɒrɪ'zɒnt(ə)l] *a* horizontal.
horn [hɔːn] (*of animal*) corne *f*; (*on vehicle*) klaxon® *m*.
horrible *a* horrible.
horribly *adv* horriblement.
ho'rrific *a* horrible.
horrify *vt* horrifier.
horror ['hɒrər] horreur *f*.
horse [hɔːs] cheval *m*; **h. chestnut** marron *m* (d'Inde).
horseback **on h.** à cheval.
horseracing courses *fpl*.
horseshoe fer *m* à cheval.
hose [həʊz] tuyau *m*.
hosepipe tuyau *m*.
hospitable [hɒ'spɪtəb(ə)l] *a* accueillant.
hospital ['hɒspɪt(ə)l] hôpital *m*; **in h.**, *Am* **in the h.** à l'hôpital.

hospi'tality hospitalité *f.*
hospitalize *vt* hospitaliser.
host [həʊst] hôte *m*; (*of TV show*) présentateur, -trice *mf.*
hostage ['hɒstɪdʒ] otage *m*; **to take s.o. h.** prendre qn en otage.
hostel ['hɒst(ə)l] foyer *m*; **youth h.** auberge *f* de jeunesse.
hostess hôtesse *f.*
hostile ['hɒstaɪl, *Am* 'hɒst(ə)l] *a* hostile (**to, towards** à).
ho'stility hostilité *f* (**to, towards** envers).
hot [hɒt] *a* chaud; (*spice*) fort; **to be** *or* **feel h.** avoir chaud; **it's h.** (*of weather*) il fait chaud.
hot dog hot-dog *m.*
hotel [həʊ'tel] hôtel *m.*
hot-'water bottle bouillotte *f.*
hound [haʊnd] *vt* (*pursue*) traquer.
hour ['aʊər] heure *f*; **half an h.** une demi-heure; **a quarter of an h.** un quart d'heure.
hourly 1 *a* (*pay*) horaire; **an h. bus/***etc* un bus/*etc* toutes les heures. **2** *adv* toutes les heures.
house[1], *pl* **-ses** [haʊs, -zɪz] maison *f*; (*audience in theatre*) salle *f.*
house[2] [haʊz] *vt* loger; (*of building*) abriter.
household famille *f.*
housekeeping ménage *m* (*entretien*).
housewarming to have a h.-warming (party) pendre la crémaillère.
housewife (*pl* **-wives**) ménagère *f.*
housework (travaux *mpl* de) ménage *m.*
housing logement *m*; (*houses*) logements *mpl.*
hovel ['hɒv(ə)l] taudis *m.*
hover ['hɒvər] *vi* (*of bird etc*) planer.
hovercraft aéroglisseur *m.*
how [haʊ] *adv* comment; **h. kind!** comme c'est gentil!; **h. do you do?** bonjour; **h. long/high is?** quelle est la longueur/hauteur de?; **h. much?, h. many?** combien?; **h. much time/***etc*? combien de temps/*etc*?; **h. many apples/***etc*? combien de pommes/*etc*?; **h. about some coffee?** du café?
however 1 *adv* **h. big he may be** quelque grand qu'il soit; **h. she may do it** de quelque manière qu'elle le fasse. **2** *conj* cependant.
howl [haʊl] **1** *vi* hurler. **2** *n* hurlement *m.*
HP [eɪtʃ'piː] *abbr* = **hire purchase.**
HQ [eɪtʃ'kjuː] *abbr* = **headquarters.**
hubcap enjoliveur *m.*
huddle ['hʌd(ə)l] *vi* se blottir.
hug [hʌg] **1** *vt* serrer (dans ses bras). **2** *n* **to give s.o. a h.** serrer qn

(dans ses bras).

huge [hjuːdʒ] *a* énorme.

hull (*of ship*) coque *f*.

hullo! [hʌ'ləʊ] *int* = **hello.**

hum [hʌm] **1** *vi* (*of insect*) bourdonner; (*of person*) fredonner. **2** *vt* (*tune*) fredonner.

human ['hjuːmən] *a* humain; **h. being** être *m* humain.

hu'manity humanité *f*.

humble ['hʌmb(ə)l] *a* humble.

humid ['hjuːmɪd] *a* humide.

hu'midity humidité *f*.

humiliate [hjuː'mɪlɪeɪt] *vt* humilier.

humili'ation humiliation *f*.

humorous *a* (*book etc*) humoristique; (*person*) plein d'humour.

humour ['hjuːmər] (*fun*) humour *m*.

hump [hʌmp] (*lump*) bosse *f*.

hunch [hʌntʃ] *Fam* intuition *f*.

hundred ['hʌndrəd] *a* & *n* cent (*m*); **a h. pages** cent pages; **hundreds of** des centaines de.

hundredth *a* & *n* centième (*mf*).

hunger ['hʌŋgər] faim *f*.

hungry *a* **to be** *or* **feel h.** avoir faim; **to make h.** donner faim à.

hunt [hʌnt] **1** *n* (*search*) recherche *f* (**for** de). **2** *vt* (*animals*) chasser; (*pursue*) poursuivre; (*seek*) chercher. **3** *vi* chasser.

hunt down traquer.

hunter chasseur *m*.

hunt for sth (re)chercher qch.

hunting chasse *f*.

hurdle ['hɜːd(ə)l] (*fence*) haie *f*; (*problem*) obstacle *m*.

hurl [hɜːl] *vt* lancer.

hurray! [hʊ'reɪ] *int* hourra!

hurricane ['hʌrɪkən, *Am* 'hʌrɪkeɪn] ouragan *m*.

hurry ['hʌrɪ] **1** *n* hâte *f*; **in a h.** à la hâte; **to be in a h.** être pressé. **2** *vi* se dépêcher (**to do** de faire); **to h. towards** se précipiter vers. **3** *vt* (*person*) bousculer; **to h. one's meal** manger à toute vitesse.

hurry up (*go faster*) se dépêcher.

hurt* [hɜːt] **1** *vt* faire du mal à; (*emotionally*) faire de la peine à; (*reputation etc*) nuire à; **to h. s.o.'s feelings** blesser qn. **2** *vi* faire mal. **3** *n* mal *m*.

husband ['hʌzbənd] mari *m*.

hush [hʌʃ] silence *m*.

hustle ['hʌs(ə)l] **1** *vt* (*shove*) bousculer (*qn*). **2** *n* **h. and bustle**

tourbillon *m*.
hut [hʌt] cabane *f*.
hygiene ['haɪdʒiːn] hygiène *f*.
hy'gienic *a* hygiénique.
hymn [hɪm] cantique *m*.
hypermarket ['haɪpəmɑːkɪt] hypermarché *m*.
hyphen ['haɪf(ə)n] trait *m* d'union.
hyphenated *a* (*word*) à trait d'union.
hypocrisy [hɪ'pɒkrɪsɪ] hypocrisie *f*.
'hypocrite hypocrite *mf*.
hysterical [hɪ'sterɪk(ə)l] *a* (*upset*) qui a une crise de nerfs; (*funny*) *Fam* désopilant.
hysterically *adv* (*to cry*) sans pouvoir s'arrêter.

I

I [aɪ] *pron* je, j'; (*stressed*) moi.
ice [aɪs] glace *f*; (*on road*) verglas *m*.
iceberg iceberg *m*.
ice-'cold *a* glacial; (*drink*) glacé.
ice cream glace *f*.
ice cube glaçon *m*.
ice-skating patinage *m* (sur glace).
ice up (*of windscreen or Am windshield*) givrer.
icicle glaçon *m*.
icing (*on cake*) glaçage *m*.
icy ['aɪsɪ] *a* glacé; (*weather*) glacial; (*road*) verglacé.
ID [aɪ'diː] pièce *f* d'identité.
idea [aɪ'dɪə] idée *f*; **I have an i. that** j'ai l'impression que.
ideal [aɪ'dɪəl] **1** *a* idéal (*mpl* -aux *or* -als). **2** *n* idéal *m* (*pl* -aux *or* -als).
ideally *adv* idéalement; **i. we should stay** l'idéal, ce serait que nous restions.
identical [aɪ'dentɪk(ə)l] *a* identique (**to, with** à).
identifi'cation (*document*) pièce *f* d'identité.
identify *vt* identifier; **to i. (oneself) with** s'identifier avec.
identity identité *f*.
idiom ['ɪdɪəm] expression *f* idiomatique.
idiot ['ɪdɪət] idiot, -ote *mf*.
idi'otic *a* idiot.
idle ['aɪd(ə)l] *a* (*unoccupied*) inactif; (*lazy*) paresseux.
idler paresseux, -euse *mf*.
idol ['aɪd(ə)l] idole *f*.
idolize *vt* (*adore*) traiter comme une idole.
i.e. [aɪ'iː] *abbr* c'est-à-dire.
if [ɪf] *conj* si; **if he comes** s'il vient; **even if** même si; **if only I were rich** si seulement j'étais riche.
igloo ['ɪgluː] igloo *m*.
ignorance ['ɪgnərəns] ignorance *f* (**of** de).
ignorant *a* ignorant (**of** de).
ignore [ɪg'nɔːr] *vt* ne prêter aucune attention à (*qch*); (*pretend not to recognize*) faire semblant de ne pas reconnaître (*qn*).
ill [ɪl] **1** *a* (*sick*) malade; (*bad*) mauvais. **2** *n* **ills** maux *mpl*.
illegal [ɪ'liːg(ə)l] *a* illégal.
illegible [ɪ'ledʒəb(ə)l] *a* illisible.
illiterate [ɪ'lɪtərət] *a* illettré.

illness maladie *f*.
ill-'treat *vt* maltraiter.
illusion [ɪ'luːʒ(ə)n] illusion *f* (**about** sur).
illustrate ['ɪləstreɪt] *vt* illustrer (**with** de).
illu'stration illustration *f*.
image ['ɪmɪdʒ] image *f*; (**public**) **i.** (*of firm*) image *f* de marque.
imaginary *a* imaginaire.
imagi'nation imagination *f*.
imagine [ɪ'mædʒɪn] *vt* (s')imaginer (**that** que).
imitate ['ɪmɪteɪt] *vt* imiter.
imi'tation imitation *f*; **i. jewellery** *or Am* **jewelry** bijoux *mpl* fantaisie.
immaculate [ɪ'mækjʊlət] *a* impeccable.
immature [ɪmə'tʃʊər] *a* (*person*) qui manque de maturité.
immediate [ɪ'miːdɪət] *a* immédiat.
immediately 1 *adv* (*at once*) tout de suite, immédiatement. **2** *conj* (*as soon as*) dès que.
immense [ɪ'mens] *a* immense.
immensely *adv* extraordinairement.
immigrant ['ɪmɪgrənt] *n* & *a* immigré, -ée (*mf*).
immi'gration immigration *f*.
immortal [ɪ'mɔːt(ə)l] *a* immortel.
immune [ɪ'mjuːn] *a* (*naturally*) immunisé (**to** contre); (*vaccinated*) vacciné.
'immunize *vt* vacciner (**against** contre).
impact ['ɪmpækt] effet (**on** sur).
impatience impatience *f*.
impatient [ɪm'peɪʃ(ə)nt] *a* impatient (**to do** de faire).
impatiently *adv* avec impatience.
imperative [ɪm'perətɪv] *Grammar* impératif *m*.
impersonate [ɪm'pɜːsəneɪt] *vt* se faire passer pour; (*on TV etc*) imiter.
impersonator (*on TV etc*) imitateur, -trice *mf*.
impertinent [ɪm'pɜːtɪnənt] *a* impertinent (**to** envers).
impetus ['ɪmpɪtəs] impulsion *f*.
implement[1] ['ɪmplɪmənt] (*tool*) instrument *m*; (*utensil*) ustensile *m*.
implement[2] [-ment] *vt* mettre en œuvre.
implication [ɪmplɪ'keɪʃ(ə)n] conséquence *f*; (*impact*) portée *f*.
imply [ɪm'plaɪ] *vt* laisser entendre (**that** que); (*assume*) impliquer.
impolite [ɪmpə'laɪt] *a* impoli.
import 1 [ɪm'pɔːt] *vt* importer (**from** de). **2** *n* ['ɪmpɔːt] importation *f*.

importance [ɪm'pɔːtəns] importance *f*; **of no i.** sans importance.
important *a* important.
im'porter importateur, -trice *mf*.
impose [ɪm'pəʊz] **1** *vt* imposer (**on** à); (*fine*) infliger (**on** à). **2** *vi* (*cause trouble*) déranger; **to i. on s.o.** déranger qn.
imposing *a* (*building*) impressionnant.
impo'sition (*inconvenience*) dérangement *m*.
impossi'bility impossibilité *f*.
impossible [ɪm'pɒsəb(ə)l] *a* impossible (**to do** à faire); **it is i. (for us) to do it** il (nous) est impossible de le faire.
impostor [ɪm'pɒstər] imposteur *m*.
impractical [ɪm'præktɪk(ə)l] *a* peu réaliste.
impress [ɪm'pres] *vt* impressionner (*qn*).
impression impression *f*.
impressive *a* impressionnant.
imprison [ɪm'prɪz(ə)n] *vt* emprisonner.
improbable [ɪm'prɒbəb(ə)l] *a* peu probable.
improper [ɪm'prɒpər] *a* indécent.
improve [ɪm'pruːv] **1** *vt* améliorer. **2** *vi* s'améliorer; (*of business*) reprendre.
improvement amélioration *f*.
improve on faire mieux que.
improvise ['ɪmprəvaɪz] *vti* improviser.
impudent ['ɪmpjʊdənt] *a* impudent.
impulse ['ɪmpʌls] impulsion *f*; **on i.** sur un coup de tête.
im'pulsive *a* impulsif.
im'pulsively *adv* de manière impulsive.
impurity [ɪm'pjʊərɪtɪ] impureté *f*.
in [ɪn] **1** *prep* dans; **in the box**/*etc* dans la boîte/*etc*; **in an hour('s time)** dans une heure. ▮ à; **in school** à l'école; **in Paris** à Paris; **in Portugal** au Portugal; **in ink** à l'encre. ▮ en; **in summer/May/French** en été/mai/français; **in Spain** en Espagne; **in an hour** (*within that period*) en une heure; **in doing** en faisant. ▮ de; **in a soft voice** d'une voix douce; **the best in** le meilleur de. ▮ **in the morning** le matin; **one in ten** un sur dix. **2** *adv* **to be in** (*home*) être là, être à la maison; (*of train*) être arrivé; (*in fashion*) être en vogue.
in- [ɪn] *prefix* in-.
inability incapacité *f* (**to do** de faire).
inaccessible *a* inaccessible.
inaccuracy (*error*) inexactitude *f*.
inaccurate *a* inexact.
inadequacy insuffisance *f*.

inadequate *a* insuffisant; (*person*) pas à la hauteur.
inappropriate *a* peu approprié.
inaugurate [ɪ'nɔːgjʊreɪt] *vt* (*building*) inaugurer.
inaugu'ration inauguration *f*.
Inc [ɪŋk] *abbr* (*Incorporated*) *Am* SA, SARL.
incapable *a* incapable (**of doing** de faire).
incense [ɪn'sens] *vt* mettre en colère.
incentive [ɪn'sentɪv] encouragement *m*, motivation *f*.
inch [ɪntʃ] pouce *m* (= *2,54 cm*).
incident ['ɪnsɪdənt] incident *m*; (*in film etc*) épisode *m*.
inci'dently (*by the way*) à propos.
incite [ɪn'saɪt] *vt* inciter (**to do** à faire).
incitement incitation *f*.
incli'nation (*desire*) envie *f* (**to do** de faire).
incline [ɪn'klaɪn] *vt* (*bend*) incliner; **to be inclined to do** (*feel a wish to*) avoir bien envie de faire; (*tend to*) avoir tendance à faire.
include [ɪn'kluːd] *vt* (*contain*) comprendre; **to be included** être compris; (*on list*) être inclus.
including *prep* y compris; **i. service** service *m* compris; **up to and including Monday** jusqu'à lundi inclus.
inclusive *a* inclus; **to be i. of** comprendre.
income ['ɪŋkʌm] revenu *m* (**from** de); **private i.** rentes *fpl*.
income tax impôt *m* sur le revenu.
incompatible *a* incompatible (**with** avec).
incompetent *a* incompétent.
incomplete *a* incomplet.
inconceivable *a* inconcevable.
inconsiderate *a* (*remark*) irréfléchi; (*person*) pas très gentil (**towards** avec).
inconsistency incohérence *f*.
inconsistent *a* en contradiction (**with** avec).
inconspicuous *a* peu en évidence.
inconvenience 1 *n* (*bother*) dérangement *m*; (*disadvantage*) inconvénient *m*. **2** *vt* déranger, gêner.
inconvenient *a* (*moment, situation etc*) gênant; (*house*) mal situé; **it's i. (for me) to** ça me dérange de.
incorporate [ɪn'kɔːpəreɪt] *vt* (*contain*) contenir.
incorrect *a* inexact; **you're i.** vous avez tort.
increase 1 *vi* [ɪn'kriːs] augmenter; (*of effort, noise*) s'intensifier. **2** *vt* augmenter; intensifier. **3** *n* ['ɪnkriːs] augmentation *f* (**in, of** de); intensification *f*; **on the i.** en hausse.
increasing *a* (*amount*) croissant.

increasingly *adv* de plus en plus.
incredible *a* incroyable.
incredibly *adv* incroyablement.
incubator ['ɪŋkjʊbeɪtər] (*for baby, eggs*) couveuse *f*.
incur [ɪn'kɜːr] *vt* (*expenses*) faire; (*loss*) subir.
incurable *a* incurable.
indecent *a* (*obscene*) indécent.
indecisive *a* indécis.
indeed [ɪn'diːd] *adv* en effet; **very good**/*etc* **i.** vraiment très bon/*etc*; **yes i.**! bien sûr!; **thank you very much i.**! merci infiniment!
indefinite *a* indéfini.
indefinitely *adv* indéfiniment.
independence indépendance *f*.
independent *a* indépendant (**of** de).
independently *adv* de façon indépendante; **i. of** indépendamment de.
index ['ɪndeks] **1** *n* (*in book*) index *m*; (*in library*) catalogue *m*. **2** *vt* (*classify*) classer.
index card fiche *f*.
index finger index *m*.
index-'linked *a* indexé (**to** sur).
Indian *a* & *n* indien, -ienne (*mf*).
indicate ['ɪndɪkeɪt] *vt* indiquer (**that** que); **I was indicating right** (*in vehicle*) j'avais mis mon clignotant droit.
indi'cation (*sign*) indice *m*, indication *f*.
indicator (*instrument*) indicateur *m*; (*in vehicle*) clignotant *m*.
indifference indifférence *f* (**to** à).
indifferent *a* indifférent (**to** à).
indigestion [ɪndɪ'dʒestʃ(ə)n] problèmes *mpl* de digestion; **(an attack of) i.** une indigestion.
indignant [ɪn'dɪgnənt] *a* indigné (**at** de).
indig'nation indignation *f*.
indirect *a* indirect.
indirectly *adv* indirectement.
indiscreet *a* indiscret.
indiscriminately *adv* (*at random*) au hasard.
indiscriminate [ɪndɪ'skrɪmɪnət] (*random*) fait, donné *etc* au hasard.
indistinguishable *a* indifférenciable (**from** de).
individual [ɪndɪ'vɪdʒʊəl] **1** *a* individuel; (*specific*) particulier. **2** *n* (*person*) individu *m*.
individually *adv* (*separately*) individuellement.
indoor ['ɪndɔːr] *a* (*games, shoes etc*) d'intérieur; (*swimming pool*)

couvert.
in'doors *adv* à l'intérieur.
induce [ɪn'djuːs] *vt* persuader (**to do** de faire); (*cause*) provoquer.
indulge [ɪn'dʌldʒ] *vt* (*s.o.'s wishes*) satisfaire; (*child etc*) gâter.
indulge in (*ice cream etc*) se permettre.
indulgent *a* indulgent (**to** envers).
industrial [ɪn'dʌstrɪəl] *a* industriel; (*conflict*) du travail; **i. action** mouvement *m* revendicatif; **i. estate**, *Am* **i. park** zone *f* industrielle.
industry ['ɪndəstrɪ] industrie *f*.
inedible *a* immangeable.
ineffective *a* (*measure*) inefficace.
inefficiency inefficacité *f*.
inefficient *a* (*person, measure*) inefficace.
inept [ɪ'nept] *a* (*unskilled*) peu habile (**at** à); (*incompetent*) incapable.
inequality inégalité *f*.
inevitable [ɪn'evɪtəb(ə)l] *a* inévitable.
inevitably *adv* inévitablement.
inexcusable [ɪnɪk'skjuːzəb(ə)l] *a* inexcusable.
inexpensive *a* bon marché *inv*.
inexperience inexpérience *f*.
inexperienced *a* inexpérimenté.
inexplicable [ɪnɪk'splɪkəb(ə)l] *a* inexplicable.
infallible [ɪn'fæləb(ə)l] *a* infaillible.
infamous ['ɪnfəməs] *a* (*evil*) infâme.
infancy petite enfance *f*.
infant ['ɪnfənt] petit(e) enfant *mf*; (*baby*) nourrisson *m*.
infantry ['ɪnfəntrɪ] infanterie *f*.
infant school classes *fpl* préparatoires.
infatuated [ɪn'fætʃʊeɪtɪd] *a* amoureux (**with** de).
infatu'ation engouement *m* (**for, with** pour).
infect [ɪn'fekt] *vt* infecter; **to get infected** s'infecter.
infection infection *f*.
infectious *a* contagieux.
inferior [ɪn'fɪərɪər] *a* inférieur (**to** à); (*goods, work*) de qualité inférieure.
inferi'ority infériorité *f*.
infernal [ɪn'fɜːn(ə)l] *a* infernal.
infest [ɪn'fest] *vt* infester (**with** de).
infinite ['ɪnfɪnɪt] *a* infini.
infinitely *adv* infiniment.
infinitive [ɪn'fɪnɪtɪv] *Grammar* infinitif *m*.

in'finity infini *m*.
infirm [ɪn'fɜːm] *a* infirme.
inflamed [ɪn'fleɪmd] *a* (*throat etc*) enflammé.
infla'mmation inflammation *f*.
inflate [ɪn'fleɪt] *vt* gonfler.
inflation inflation *f*.
inflexible *a* inflexible.
inflict [ɪn'flɪkt] *vt* (*a wound*) occasionner (**on** à); **to i. pain on s.o.** faire souffrir qn.
influence ['ɪnflʊəns] **1** *n* influence *f*; **under the i. (of drink)** en état d'ébriété. **2** *vt* influencer.
influ'ential *a* **to be i.** avoir une grande influence.
influenza [ɪnflʊ'enzə] grippe *f*.
influx ['ɪnflʌks] flot *m*.
info ['ɪnfəʊ] *Fam* renseignements *mpl* (**on** sur).
inform [ɪn'fɔːm] *vt* informer (**of** de, **that** que).
informal *a* simple, décontracté; (*expression*) familier; (*meeting*) non-officiel.
informally *adv* sans cérémonie; (*to dress*) simplement; (*to discuss*) à titre non-officiel.
information [ɪnfə'meɪʃ(ə)n] renseignements *mpl* (**about, on** sur); **a piece of i.** un renseignement.
informative *a* instructif.
inform on dénoncer.
infuriate [ɪn'fjʊərɪeɪt] *vt* exaspérer.
infuriating *a* exaspérant.
ingenious [ɪn'dʒiːnɪəs] *a* ingénieux.
ingratitude ingratitude *f*.
ingredient [ɪn'griːdɪənt] ingrédient *m*.
inhabit [ɪn'hæbɪt] *vt* habiter.
inhabitant habitant, -ante *mf*.
inhale [ɪn'heɪl] *vt* aspirer.
inherit [ɪn'herɪt] *vt* hériter (de).
inheritance héritage *m*.
inhibit [ɪn'hɪbɪt] *vt* (*hinder*) gêner; **to be inhibited** avoir des inhibitions.
inhi'bition inhibition *f*.
inhospitable *a* peu accueillant, inhospitalier.
inhuman *a* inhumain.
initial [ɪ'nɪʃ(ə)l] **1** *a* premier. **2** *n* **initials** initiales *fpl*; (*signature*) paraphe *m*. **3** *vt* parapher.
initially *adv* au début.

inject [ɪn'dʒekt] *vt* injecter (**into** à).
injection injection *f*, piqûre *f*.
injure ['ɪndʒər] *vt* (*physically*) blesser, faire du mal à.
injured 1 *a* blessé. **2** *n* **the i.** les blessés *mpl*.
injury blessure *f*; (*fracture*) fracture *f*; (*sprain*) foulure *f*.
injustice injustice *f*.
ink [ɪŋk] encre *f*.
inkling ['ɪŋklɪŋ] (petite) idée *f*.
inland 1 *a* ['ɪnlænd] intérieur. **2** *adv* [ɪn'lænd] à l'intérieur.
Inland Revenue service *m* des impôts.
in-laws ['ɪnlɔːz] *npl* belle-famille *f*.
inmate ['ɪnmeɪt] (*of prison*) détenu, -ue *mf*.
inn [ɪn] auberge *f*.
inner ['ɪnər] *a* intérieur; **the i. city** les quartiers du centre-ville.
inner tube (*of tyre*, *Am tire*) chambre *f* à air.
innkeeper aubergiste *mf*.
innocence innocence *f*.
innocent ['ɪnəs(ə)nt] *a* innocent.
inoculate [ɪ'nɒkjʊleɪt] *vt* vacciner (**against** contre).
inocu'lation vaccination *f*.
input ['ɪnpʊt] (*computer operation*) entrée *f*; (*data*) données *fpl*.
inquire [ɪn'kwaɪər] **1** *vi* se renseigner (**about** sur). **2** *vt* demander; **to i. how to get to** demander le chemin de.
inquire into faire une enquête sur.
inquiry demande *f* de renseignements; (*investigation*) enquête *f*.
inquisitive [ɪn'kwɪzɪtɪv] *a* curieux.
insane *a* fou (*f* folle).
insanity folie *f*.
inscription [ɪn'skrɪpʃ(ə)n] inscription *f*; (*in book*) dédicace *f*.
insect ['ɪnsekt] insecte *m*.
in'secticide insecticide *m*.
insecure *a* (*not securely fixed*) mal fixé; (*uncertain*) incertain; (*person*) qui manque d'assurance.
insensitive *a* insensible (**to** à).
insensi'tivity insensibilité *f*.
insert [ɪn'sɜːt] *vt* introduire, insérer (**in, into** dans).
inside 1 *adv* [ɪn'saɪd] dedans, à l'intérieur. **2** *prep* à l'intérieur de. **3** *n* dedans *m*, intérieur *m*; **on the i.** à l'intérieur (**of** de); **i. out** (*socks etc*) à l'envers. **4** *a* ['ɪnsaɪd] intérieur; **the i. lane** la voie de gauche, *Am* la voie de droite.
insight ['ɪnsaɪt] (*into question*) aperçu *m* (**into** de).
insignificant *a* insignifiant.

insincere *a* peu sincère.
insist [ɪn'sɪst] **1** *vi* insister (**on doing** pour faire). **2** *vt* (*order*) insister (**that** pour que + *subjunctive*); (*declare*) affirmer (**that** que).
insistence insistance *f*; **her i. on seeing me** l'insistance qu'elle met à vouloir me voir.
insistent *a* **to be i.** insister (**that** pour que + *subjunctive*).
insist on sth (*demand*) exiger qch; (*assert*) affirmer qch.
insolence insolence *f*.
insolent ['ɪnsələnt] *a* insolent.
insomnia [ɪn'sɒmnɪə] insomnie *f*.
inspect [ɪn'spekt] *vt* inspecter; (*tickets*) contrôler.
inspection inspection *f*; (*of tickets*) contrôle *m*.
inspector inspecteur, -trice *mf*; (*on train*) contrôleur, -euse *mf*.
inspi'ration inspiration *f*.
inspire [ɪn'spaɪər] *vt* inspirer (**s.o. with sth** qch à qn).
install [ɪn'stɔːl] *vt* installer.
instalment (*Am* **installment**) (*of money*) acompte *m*; (*of serial*) épisode *m*.
instance ['ɪnstəns] (*example*) cas *m*; **for i.** par exemple.
instant ['ɪnstənt] **1** *a* immédiat; **i. coffee** café *m* soluble. **2** (*moment*) instant *m*.
instantly *adv* immédiatement.
instead [ɪn'sted] *adv* plutôt; **i. of (doing) sth** au lieu de (faire) qch; **i. of s.o.** à la place de qn; **i. (of him** *or* **her)** à sa place.
instinct ['ɪnstɪŋkt] instinct *m*.
in'stinctive *a* instinctif.
in'stinctively *adv* instinctivement.
institution [ɪnstɪ'tjuːʃ(ə)n] institution *f*.
instruct [ɪn'strʌkt] *vt* (*teach*) enseigner (**s.o. in sth** qch à qn); **to i. s.o. to do** (*order*) charger qn de faire.
instructions *npl* (*for use*) mode *m* d'emploi; (*orders*) instructions *fpl*.
instructive *a* instructif.
instructor (*for skiing etc*) moniteur, -trice *mf*; **driving i.** moniteur, -trice *mf* d'auto-école.
instrument ['ɪnstrʊmənt] instrument *m*.
insufficient *a* insuffisant.
insulate ['ɪnsjʊleɪt] *vt* (*against cold and electrically*) isoler; **insulating tape** chatterton *m*.
insu'lation (*material*) isolant *m*.
insult 1 *vt* [ɪn'sʌlt] insulter. **2** *n* ['ɪnsʌlt] insulte *f* (**to** à).
insurance assurance *f*; **i. company** compagnie *f* d'assurances.

insure [ɪn'ʃʊər] *vt* assurer (**against** contre); *Am* = **ensure.**
intact [ɪn'tækt] *a* intact.
intellect ['ɪntɪlekt] intelligence *f*.
inte'llectual *a* & *n* intellectuel, -elle (*mf*).
intelligence [ɪn'telɪdʒəns] intelligence *f*.
intelligent *a* intelligent.
intelligible [ɪn'telɪdʒəb(ə)l] *a* compréhensible.
intend [ɪn'tend] *vt* (*gift etc*) destiner (**for** à); **to be intended to do/for s.o.** être destiné à faire/à qn; **to i. to do** avoir l'intention de faire.
intense [ɪn'tens] *a* intense; (*interest*) vif.
intensify 1 *vt* intensifier. **2** *vi* s'intensifier.
intensity intensité *f*.
intensive *a* intensif; **in i. care** en réanimation.
intent [ɪn'tent] *a* **i. on doing** résolu à faire.
intention intention *f* (**of doing** de faire).
intentional *a* **it wasn't i.** ce n'était pas fait exprès.
intentionally *adv* exprès.
intercept [ɪntə'sept] *vt* intercepter.
interchange ['ɪntətʃeɪndʒ] (*on road*) échangeur *m*.
inter'changeable *a* interchangeable.
intercom ['ɪntəkɒm] interphone *m*.
interconnected [ɪntəkə'nektɪd] *a* (*facts etc*) liés.
interest ['ɪnt(ə)rɪst] **1** *n* intérêt *m*; (*money*) intérêts *mpl*; **to take an i. in** s'intéresser à; **to be of i. to s.o.** intéresser qn. **2** *vt* intéresser.
interested *a* intéressé; **to be i. in sth/s.o.** s'intéresser à qch/qn; **I'm i. in doing** ça m'intéresse de faire.
interesting *a* intéressant.
interfere [ɪntə'fɪər] *vi* se mêler des affaires d'autrui.
interfere in s'ingérer dans.
interference ingérence *f*; (*on radio*) parasites *mpl*.
interfere with (*upset*) déranger.
interior [ɪn'tɪərɪər] **1** *a* intérieur. **2** *n* intérieur *m*.
interjection [ɪntə'dʒekʃ(ə)n] *Grammar* interjection *f*.
interlude ['ɪntəluːd] (*on TV*) interlude *m*; (*in theatre*) entracte *m*.
intermediary [ɪntə'miːdɪərɪ] intermédiaire *mf*.
intermediate [ɪntə'miːdɪət] *a* intermédiaire; (*course*) de niveau moyen.
intern ['ɪntɜːn] *Am* interne *mf* (des hôpitaux).
internal [ɪn'tɜːn(ə)l] *a* interne; (*flight*) intérieur.
Internal Revenue Service *Am* service *m* des impôts.
international [ɪntə'næʃ(ə)nəl] *a* international.
interpret [ɪn'tɜːprɪt] *vt* interpréter.

interpreter interprète *mf*.
interrogate [ɪn'terəgeɪt] *vt* interroger.
interro'gation (*by police*) interrogatoire *m*.
interrogative [ɪntə'rɒgətɪv] *a* & *n Grammar* interrogatif (*m*).
interrupt [ɪntə'rʌpt] *vt* interrompre.
interruption interruption *f*.
intersect [ɪntə'sekt] **1** *vt* couper. **2** *vi* s'entrecouper.
intersection (*of roads, lines*) intersection *f*.
interval ['ɪntəv(ə)l] intervalle *m*; (*in theatre*) entracte *m*.
intervene [ɪntə'viːn] *vi* (*of person*) intervenir; (*of event*) survenir.
intervention intervention *f*.
interview ['ɪntəvjuː] **1** *n* entrevue *f* (**with** avec); (*on TV etc*) interview *f*. **2** *vt* avoir une entrevue avec; (*on TV etc*) interviewer [-vjuve].
interviewer (*on TV etc*) interviewer *m* [-vjuvœr].
intimate ['ɪntɪmət] *a* intime.
intimidate [ɪn'tɪmɪdeɪt] *vt* intimider.
into ['ɪntuː, *unstressed* 'ɪntə] *prep* dans; **to put i.** mettre dans. ▮ en; **to translate i.** traduire en; **i. pieces** en morceaux. ▮ **to be i. yoga**/*etc Fam* être à fond dans le yoga/*etc*.
intolerable *a* intolérable (**that** que + *subjunctive*).
intoxicate [ɪn'tɒksɪkeɪt] *vt* enivrer.
intoxicated *a* ivre.
intransitive *a Grammar* intransitif.
intricate ['ɪntrɪkət] *a* complexe.
introduce [ɪntrə'djuːs] *vt* (*bring in*) introduire (**into** dans); (*programme*) présenter; **to i. s.o. to s.o.** présenter qn à qn.
introduction introduction *f*; (*of person to person*) présentation *f*; **i. to** (*initiation*) premier contact avec.
intrude [ɪn'truːd] *vi* déranger (**on s.o.** qn).
intruder intrus, -use *mf*.
intrusion (*bother*) dérangement *m*.
intuition [ɪntjuː'ɪʃ(ə)n] intuition *f*.
inundated ['ɪnʌndeɪtɪd] *a* submergé (**with work/letters**/*etc* de travail/lettres/*etc*).
invade [ɪn'veɪd] *vt* envahir.
invader envahisseur, -euse *mf*.
invalid[1] ['ɪnvəlɪd] malade *mf*; (*through injury*) infirme *mf*.
invalid[2] [ɪn'vælɪd] *a* non valable.
invaluable *a* inestimable.
invariably [ɪn'veərɪəblɪ] *adv* (*always*) toujours.
invent [ɪn'vent] *vt* inventer.

invention invention *f*.
inventor inventeur, -trice *mf*.
inventory ['ɪnvənt(ə)rɪ] inventaire *m*.
inverted commas [ɪn'vɜːtɪd] guillemets *mpl*.
invest [ɪn'vest] *vt* (*money*) placer, investir (**in** dans).
investigate [ɪn'vestɪgeɪt] *vt* examiner; (*crime*) enquêter sur.
investi'gation examen *m*; (*inquiry by journalist, police etc*) enquête *f* (**of, into** sur).
investigator enquêteur, -euse *mf*.
invest in placer son argent dans; (*firm*) investir dans.
investment investissement *m*, placement *m*.
investor (*in shares*) actionnaire *mf*; (*saver*) épargnant, -ante *mf*.
invigorating [ɪn'vɪgəreɪtɪŋ] *a* stimulant.
invisible *a* invisible.
invi'tation invitation *f*.
invite [ɪn'vaɪt] *vt* inviter (**to do** à faire); (*ask for*) demander; (*give occasion for*) provoquer.
inviting *a* engageant.
invoice ['ɪnvɔɪs] **1** *n* facture *f*. **2** *vt* facturer.
involve [ɪn'vɒlv] *vt* (*include*) mêler (*qn*) (**in** à); (*entail*) entraîner; **the job involves...** le poste nécessite....
involved *a* (*concerned*) concerné; (*committed*) engagé (**in** dans); (*complicated*) compliqué; (*at stake*) en jeu; **the person i.** la personne en question; **i. with s.o.** mêlé aux affaires de qn.
involvement participation *f* (**in** à); (*commitment*) engagement *m*; (*emotional*) liaison *f*.
inward(s) ['ɪnwəd(z)] *adv* vers l'intérieur.
IOU [aɪəʊ'juː] *abbr* (*I owe you*) reconnaissance *f* de dette.
IQ [aɪ'kjuː] *abbr* (*intelligence quotient*) QI *m inv*.
iris ['aɪərɪs] (*plant, of eye*) iris *m*.
Irish ['aɪərɪʃ] *a* irlandais; **the I.** les Irlandais *mpl*.
Irishman (*pl* **-men**) Irlandais *m*.
Irishwoman (*pl* **-women**) Irlandaise *f*.
iron ['aɪən] **1** *n* fer *m*; (*for clothes*) fer *m* (à repasser). **2** *vt* (*clothes*) repasser.
i'ronic(al) *a* ironique.
ironing repassage *m*.
ironing board planche *f* à repasser.
ironmonger quincaillier, -ière *mf*.
irony ['aɪərənɪ] ironie *f*.
irrational [ɪ'ræʃən(ə)l] *a* (*person*) peu rationnel.
irregular [ɪ'regjʊlər] *a* irrégulier.

irrelevance manque *m* de rapport.
irrelevant [ɪ'reləvənt] *a* sans rapport (**to** avec); **that's i.** ça n'a rien à voir.
irresistible [ɪrɪ'zɪstəb(ə)l] *a* irrésistible.
irrespective of [ɪrɪ'spektɪvəv] *prep* sans tenir compte de.
irrigate ['ɪrɪgeɪt] *vt* irriguer.
irritable *a* irritable.
irritate ['ɪrɪteɪt] *vt* (*annoy, inflame*) irriter.
irritating *a* irritant.
irri'tation irritation *f*.
is [ɪz] *see* **be**.
Islamic [ɪz'læmɪk] *a* islamique.
island ['aɪlənd] île *f*.
isolate ['aɪsəleɪt] *vt* isoler (**from** de).
isolated *a* isolé.
iso'lation isolement *m*; **in i.** isolément.
issue ['ɪʃuː] **1** *vt* publier; (*tickets*) distribuer; (*passport*) délivrer; (*an order*) donner; (*warning*) lancer; (*supply*) fournir (**with** de, **to** à). **2** *n* (*matter*) question *f*; (*newspaper*) numéro *m*.
it [ɪt] *pron* (*subject*) il, elle; (*object*) le, la, l'; **(to) it** (*indirect object*) lui; **it bites** il mord; **I've done it** je l'ai fait. ▮ (*impersonal*) il; **it's snowing** il neige. ▮ (*non specific*) ce, cela, ça; **who is it?** qui est-ce?; **it was Paul who...** c'est Paul qui.... ▮ **of it, from it, about it** en; **in it, to it, at it** y; **on it** dessus; **under it** dessous.
Italian [ɪ'tæljən] **1** *a* & *n* italien, -ienne (*mf*). **2** *n* (*language*) italien *m*.
italics [ɪ'tælɪks] *npl* italique *m*.
itch [ɪtʃ] **1** *n* démangeaison(s) *f(pl)*. **2** *vi* démanger; **his arm itches** son bras le démange.
itching démangeaison(s) *f(pl)*.
itchy *a* **an i. hand** une main qui me démange.
item ['aɪtəm] (*object*) article *m*; (*matter*) question *f*; **(news) i.** information *f*.
its [ɪts] *poss a* son, sa, *pl* ses.
it'self *pron* lui-même, elle-même; (*reflexive*) se, s'.
ivory ['aɪvərɪ] ivoire *m*.
ivy ['aɪvɪ] lierre *m*.

J

jab [dʒæb] **1** *vt* enfoncer (**into** dans); (*prick*) piquer (*qn*) (**with sth** du bout de qch). **2** *n* (*injection*) piqûre *f*.
jack [dʒæk] (*for car*) cric *m*; *Cards* valet *m*; **j. of all trades** homme *m* à tout faire.
jacket ['dʒækɪt] veste *f*; (*man's suit*) veston *m*; (*bulletproof*) gilet *m*; **j. potato** pomme *f* de terre en robe des champs.
jacuzzi [dʒə'kuːzɪ] jacousi *m*.
jagged ['dʒægɪd] *a* déchiqueté.
jaguar ['dʒægjʊər, *Am* -wɑːr] jaguar *m*.
jail [dʒeɪl] **1** *n* prison *f*. **2** *vt* emprisonner.
jam¹ [dʒæm] confiture *f*.
jam² **1** *n* (**traffic**) **j.** embouteillage *m*. **2** *vt* (*squeeze, make stuck*) coincer; (*street etc*) encombrer. **3** *vi* (*get stuck*) se coincer.
jam into (*of crowd*) s'entasser dans.
jam sth/s.o. into (*cram*) (en)tasser qch/qn dans.
jamjar pot *m* à confiture.
jammed *a* (*machine etc*) coincé, bloqué; (*street etc*) encombré.
jam-'packed *a* bourré de monde.
January ['dʒænjʊərɪ] janvier *m*.
Japanese [dʒæpə'niːz] **1** *a* & *n inv* japonais, -aise (*mf*). **2** *n* (*language*) japonais *m*.
jar [dʒɑːr] pot *m*; (*large, glass*) bocal *m*.
jaundice ['dʒɔːndɪs] jaunisse *f*.
javelin ['dʒævlɪn] javelot *m*.
jaw [dʒɔː] mâchoire *f*.
jazz [dʒæz] jazz *m*.
jealous ['dʒeləs] *a* jaloux (*f* -ouse) (**of** de).
jealousy jalousie *f*.
jeans [dʒiːnz] *npl* (**pair of**) **j.** (blue-)jean *m*.
jeep® [dʒiːp] jeep® *f*.
jeer (at) [dʒɪər] *vti* railler; (*boo*) huer.
jeering (*of crowd*) huées *fpl*.
jeers *npl* huées *fpl*.
jello® ['dʒeləʊ] *n inv Am* gelée *f*.
jelly (*preserve, dessert*) gelée *f*.
jeopardize *vt* mettre en danger.
jeopardy ['dʒepədɪ] danger *m*.
jerk [dʒɜːk] **1** *vt* donner une secousse à. **2** *n* secousse *f*; (**stupid**) **j.** *Fam* crétin, -ine *mf*.
jersey ['dʒɜːzɪ] (*garment*) maillot *m*.

jet [dʒet] (*plane*) avion *m* à réaction.
jet lag fatigue *f* (due au décalage horaire).
jet-lagged *a* qui souffre du décalage horaire.
jetty ['dʒetɪ] jetée *f*.
Jew [dʒuː] (*man*) Juif *m*; (*woman*) Juive *f*.
jewel ['dʒuːəl] bijou *m* (*pl* -oux); (*in watch*) rubis *m*.
jeweller bijoutier, -ière *mf*.
jewellery, *Am* **jewelry** bijoux *mpl*.
Jewish *a* juif.
jigsaw ['dʒɪgsɔː] **j. (puzzle)** puzzle *m*.
jingle ['dʒɪŋg(ə)l] *vi* (*of keys*) tinter.
jittery ['dʒɪtərɪ] *a* **to be j.** *Fam* avoir la frousse.
job [dʒɒb] (*task*) travail *m*; (*post*) poste *m*; **to have a (hard) j. doing** *or* **to do** *Fam* avoir du mal à faire; **it's a good j. (that)** *Fam* heureusement que.
jobcentre = agence *f* nationale pour l'emploi.
jobless *a* au chômage.
jockey ['dʒɒkɪ] jockey *m*.
jog [dʒɒg] **1** *n* (*shake*) secousse *f*. **2** *vt* secouer; (*push*) pousser; (*memory*) rafraîchir. **3** *vi* faire du jogging.
john [dʒɒn] *Am Slang* cabinets *mpl*.
join[1] [dʒɔɪn] **1** *vt* (*put together*) joindre; (*wires*, *pipes*) raccorder; (*words*, *towns*) relier; **to j. s.o.** (*catch up with*, *meet*) rejoindre qn; (*go with*) se joindre à qn (**in doing** pour faire). **2** *vi* (*of roads etc*) se rejoindre; (*of objects*) se joindre. **3** *n* raccord *m*.
join[2] **1** *vt* (*become a member of*) s'inscrire à (*club*, *parti*); (*firm*, *army*) entrer dans. **2** *vi* devenir membre.
join in prendre part; **to join in sth** prendre part à qch.
joint [dʒɔɪnt] **1** *n* (*in body*) articulation *f*; (*meat*) rôti *m*. **2** *a* (*account*) joint; (*effort*) conjugué.
joke [dʒəʊk] **1** *n* plaisanterie *f*; (*trick*) tour *m*. **2** *vi* plaisanter (**about** sur).
joker plaisantin *m*; *Cards* joker *m*.
jolly ['dʒɒlɪ] **1** *a* gai. **2** *adv* (*very*) *Fam* rudement.
jolt [dʒɒlt] *vti* secouer.
jostle ['dʒɒs(ə)l] **1** *vti* (*push*) bousculer. **2** *vi* (*push each other*) se bousculer.
jot down [dʒɒt] noter.
journalist journaliste *mf*.
journey ['dʒɜːnɪ] voyage *m*; (*distance*) trajet *m*.
joy [dʒɔɪ] joie *f*.
joyful *a* joyeux.

joystick manche *m* à balai.
judge [dʒʌdʒ] **1** *n* juge *m.* **2** *vti* juger.
judg(e)ment jugement *m.*
judo ['dʒuːdəʊ] judo *m.*
jug [dʒʌg] cruche *f*; (*for milk*) pot *m.*
juggernaut ['dʒʌgənɔːt] (*truck*) poids *m* lourd.
juggle ['dʒʌg(ə)l] *vi* jongler (**with** avec).
juggler jongleur, -euse *mf.*
juice [dʒuːs] jus *m.*
juicy *a* (*fruit*) juteux.
July [dʒuː'laɪ] juillet *m.*
jumble (up) ['dʒʌmb(ə)l] mélanger.
jumble sale vente *f* de charité.
jumbo ['dʒʌmbəʊ] *a* géant.
jumbo jet gros porteur *m.*
jump [dʒʌmp] **1** *n* saut; (*start*) sursaut *m*; (*increase*) hausse *f.* **2** *vi* sauter; (*start*) sursauter; **to j. off sth** sauter de qch. **3** *vt* **to j. the queue** passer avant son tour; *Am* **to j. rope** sauter à la corde.
jumper pull(-over) *m*
jump in *or* **on** **1** *vt* (*train, vehicle*) monter dans. **2** *vi* monter.
jumpy *a* nerveux.
junction ['dʒʌŋkʃ(ə)n] carrefour *m.*
June [dʒuːn] juin *m.*
jungle ['dʒʌŋg(ə)l] jungle *f.*
junior ['dʒuːnɪər] **1** *a* (*younger*) plus jeune; (*in rank*) subalterne; (*doctor*) jeune. **2** *n* cadet, -ette *mf*; (*in school*) petit(e) élève *mf.*
junior high school *Am* = collège *m* d'enseignement secondaire.
junior school école *f* primaire.
junk [dʒʌŋk] bric-à-brac *m inv*; (*metal*) ferraille *f*; (*inferior goods*) camelote *f*; (*waste*) ordures *fpl.*
jury ['dʒʊərɪ] jury *m.*
just [dʒʌst] *adv* (*exactly, only*) juste; **she has/had j. left** elle vient/venait de partir; **he'll (only) j. catch the bus** il aura son bus de justesse; **he j. missed it** il l'a manqué de peu; **j. as big**/*etc* tout aussi grand/*etc* (**as** que); **j. over ten** un peu plus de dix; **j. one** un(e) seul(e); **j. about** à peu près; (*almost*) presque; **j. about to do** sur le point de faire.
justice ['dʒʌstɪs] justice *f.*
justify ['dʒʌstɪfaɪ] *vt* justifier; **to be justified in doing** être fondé à faire.
jut out [dʒʌt] faire saillie.

K

kangaroo [kæŋgə'ruː] (*pl* **-oos**) kangourou *m*.
karate [kə'rɑːtɪ] karaté *m*.
kebab [kə'bæb] brochette *f*.
keen [kiːn] *a* (*eager*) plein d'enthousiasme; (*interest*) vif; **k. eyesight** vue *f* perçante; **he's k. on sport, he's a k. sportsman** c'est un passionné de sport; **to be k. to do** *or* **on doing** (*want*) tenir (beaucoup) à faire; **to be k. on doing** (*like*) aimer (beaucoup) faire.
keep* **1** *vt* garder; (*shop*, *car*) avoir; (*diary*, *promise*) tenir; (*family*) entretenir; (*rule*) respecter; (*delay*) retenir; **to k. doing** continuer à faire; **to k. s.o. waiting/working** faire attendre/travailler qn; **to k. s.o. in/out** empêcher qn de sortir/d'entrer. **2** *vi* (*remain*) rester; (*of food*) se garder; **to k. going** continuer; **to k. (to the) left** tenir la gauche. **3** *n* (*food*) nourriture *f*, subsistance *f*.
keep away **1** *vt* (*person*) éloigner (**from** de). **2** *vi* ne pas s'approcher (**from** de).
keep back **1** *vt* (*crowd*) contenir; (*delay*) retenir; (*hide*) cacher (**from** à). **2** *vi* ne pas s'approcher (**from** de).
keep down (*restrict*) limiter; (*price*) maintenir bas.
keeper (*in park*, *zoo*) gardien, -ienne *mf*.
keep from (*hide*) cacher à; **to k. s.o. from doing** (*prevent*) empêcher qn de faire.
keep off (*not go near*) ne pas s'approcher; **the rain kept off** il n'a pas plu.
keep on (*hat*, *employee*) garder; **to k. on doing** continuer à faire.
keep up *vti* continuer (**doing sth** à faire qch); **to k. up (with s.o.)** (*follow*) suivre (qn).
kennel ['ken(ə)l] niche *f*.
kept [kept] *pt* & *pp de* **keep**.
kerb [kɜːb] bord *m* du trottoir.
kerosene ['kerəsiːn] (*paraffin*) *Am* pétrole *m* (lampant).
ketchup ['ketʃəp] ketchup *m*.
kettle ['ket(ə)l] bouilloire *f*; **the k. is boiling** l'eau bout.
key [kiː] **1** *n* clef *f*; (*of piano*, *typewriter*, *computer*) touche *f*. **2** *a* (*industry*, *post etc*) clef (*f inv*).
keyboard clavier *m*.
key ring porte-clefs *m inv*.
kick [kɪk] **1** *n* coup *m* de pied. **2** *vt* donner un coup de pied à. **3** *vi* donner des coups de pied.
kick down *or* **in** (*door etc*) démolir à coups de pied.
kick-off *Football* coup *m* d'envoi.

kick out (*throw out*) *Fam* flanquer dehors.
kid [kɪd] **1** *n* (*child*) *Fam* gosse *mf*. **2** *vti* (*joke, tease*) *Fam* blaguer.
kidnap ['kɪdnæp] *vt* kidnapper.
kidnapper ravisseur, -euse *mf*.
kidney ['kɪdnɪ] rein *m*; (*as food*) rognon *m*.
kill [kɪl] *vti* tuer.
killer tueur, -euse *mf*.
kilo ['kiːləʊ] (*pl* **-os**) kilo *m*.
kilogram(me) ['kɪləʊgræm] kilogramme *m*.
kilometre [kɪ'lɒmɪtər] kilomètre *m*.
kind[1] [kaɪnd] (*sort*) sorte *f*, genre *m*, espèce *f* (**of** de); **all kinds of** toutes sortes de; **what k. of drink**/*etc* **is it?** qu'est-ce que c'est comme boisson/*etc*?; **k. of worried**/*etc* plutôt inquiet/*etc*.
kind[2] *a* (*pleasant*) gentil (**to** avec).
kindergarten ['kɪndəgɑːt(ə)n] jardin *m* d'enfants.
kindness gentillesse *f*.
king [kɪŋ] roi *m*.
kingdom royaume *m*.
kiosk ['kiːɒsk] kiosque *m*; (**telephone**) **k.** cabine *f* (téléphonique).
kiss [kɪs] **1** *n* baiser *m*. **2** *vt* (*person*) embrasser; **to k. s.o.'s hand** baiser la main de qn. **3** *vi* s'embrasser.
kit [kɪt] équipement *m*; (*set of articles*) trousse *f*; (*belongings*) affaires *fpl;* (**do-it-yourself**) **k.** kit *m*; **tool k.** trousse *f* à outils.
kitchen ['kɪtʃɪn] cuisine *f*.
kite [kaɪt] (*toy*) cerf-volant *m*.
kitten ['kɪt(ə)n] chaton *m*.
knack [næk] **to have a** *or* **the k. of doing** avoir le don de faire.
knee [niː] genou *m* (*pl* genoux).
kneel* **(down)** [niːl] *vi* s'agenouiller; **to be kneeling (down)** être à genoux.
knew [n(j)uː] *pt de* **know.**
knickers ['nɪkəz] *npl* slip *m*; (*longer*) culotte *f*.
knife [naɪf] (*pl* **knives**) couteau *m*; (*penknife*) canif *m*.
knight [naɪt] chevalier *m*; *Chess* cavalier *m*.
knit [nɪt] *vti* tricoter.
knitting (*activity, material*) tricot *m*; **k. needle** aiguille *f* à tricoter.
knob [nɒb] (*on door etc*) bouton *m*.
knock [nɒk] **1** *vt* (*strike*) frapper; (*collide with*) heurter; **to k. one's head on sth** se cogner la tête contre qch. **2** *vi* frapper. **3** *n* coup *m*; **there's a k. at the door** quelqu'un frappe; **I heard a k.** j'ai entendu frapper.
knock against *or* **into** (*bump into*) heurter.

knock down (*vase*, *pedestrian etc*) renverser; (*house*, *wall etc*) abattre.
knocker ['nɒkər] (*for door*) marteau *m*.
knock in (*nail*) enfoncer.
knock off (*person*, *object*) faire tomber (**from** de).
knock out (*make unconscious*) assommer; *Boxing* mettre k.-o.; (*beat in competition*) éliminer.
knock over (*pedestrian*, *vase etc*) renverser.
knot [nɒt] **1** *n* nœud *m*. **2** *vt* nouer.
know* [nəʊ] **1** *vt* (*facts*, *language etc*) savoir; (*person*, *place etc*) connaître; (*recognize*) reconnaître (**by** à); **to k. that** savoir que; **to k. how to do** savoir faire; **I'll let you k.** je te le ferai savoir; **to k. (a lot) about** (*person*, *event*) en savoir long sur; (*cars*, *sewing etc*) s'y connaître en; **to get to k. s.o.** faire la connaissance de qn. **2** *vi* savoir; **I wouldn't k.** je n'en sais rien; **I k. about that** je suis au courant; **do you k. of a good dentist/*etc*?** connais-tu un bon dentiste/*etc*?
know-how savoir-faire *m inv*.
knowledge ['nɒlɪdʒ] connaissance *f* (**of** de); (*learning*) connaissances *fpl*.
known *a* connu; **well k.** (bien) connu (**that** que); **she is k. to be** on sait qu'elle est.
knuckle articulation *f* (du doigt).
Koran [kə'rɑːn] **the K.** le Coran *m*.

L

lab [læb] *Fam* labo *m*.
label ['leɪb(ə)l] **1** *n* étiquette *f*. **2** *vt* (*goods*) étiqueter.
laboratory [lə'bɒrət(ə)rɪ, *Am* 'læbrətɔrɪ] laboratoire *m*.
labor union *Am* syndicat *m*.
labour ['leɪbər] (*Am* **labor**) **1** *n* (*work*) travail *m*; (*workers*) main-d'œuvre *f*; **L.** (*political party*) les travaillistes *mpl*; **in l.** en train d'accoucher. **2** *a* (*market, situation*) du travail.
labourer manœuvre *m*; (*on farm*) ouvrier *m* agricole.
lace [leɪs] (*cloth*) dentelle *f*; (*of shoe*) lacet *m*.
lace (up) (*shoe*) lacer.
lack **1** *n* manque *m*. **2** *vt* manquer de. **3** *vi* **to be lacking** manquer (**in** de).
lad [læd] gamin *m*.
ladder ['lædər] échelle *f*.
ladle ['leɪd(ə)l] louche *f*.
lady ['leɪdɪ] dame *f*; **a young l.** une jeune fille; (*married*) une jeune femme; **l. doctor** femme *f* médecin; **the ladies' room, the ladies** les toilettes *fpl* pour dames.
ladybird, *Am* **ladybug** coccinelle *f*.
lager ['lɑːgər] bière *f* blonde.
lake [leɪk] lac *m*.
lamb [læm] agneau *m*.
lame [leɪm] *a* **to be l.** boiter.
lamp [læmp] lampe *f*.
lamppost réverbère *m*.
lampshade abat-jour *m inv*.
land [lænd] **1** *n* terre *f*; (*country*) pays *m*; **(plot of) l.** terrain *m*. **2** *vi* (*of aircraft*) atterrir; (*of passengers*) débarquer. **3** *vt* (*aircraft*) poser.
landing (*of aircraft*) atterrissage *m*; (*at top of stairs*) palier *m*.
landlady propriétaire *f*; (*of pub*) patronne *f*.
landlord propriétaire *m*; (*of pub*) patron *m*.
landscape ['lændskeɪp] paysage *m*.
landslide éboulement *m*.
lane [leɪn] (*in country*) chemin *m*; (*in town*) ruelle *f*; (*division of road*) voie *f*.
language ['læŋgwɪdʒ] **1** *n* (*English etc*) langue *f*; (*means of expression, style*) langage *m*. **2** *a* (*laboratory*) de langues; (*teacher, studies*) de langue(s).
lantern ['læntən] lanterne *f*.

lap [læp] (*of person*) genoux *mpl*; (*in race*) tour *m* (de piste).
lapel [lə'pel] (*of coat etc*) revers *m*.
larder ['lɑːdər] (*storeroom*) garde-manger *m inv*.
large [lɑːdʒ] *a* grand; (*in volume*) gros (*f* grosse).
largely *adv* en grande mesure.
lark [lɑːk] (*bird*) alouette *f*; (*joke*) *Fam* rigolade *f*.
laser ['leɪzər] laser *m*.
last[1] [lɑːst] **1** *a* dernier; **l. but one** avant-dernier. **2** *adv* (*lastly*) en dernier lieu; (*on the last occasion*) (pour) la dernière fois; **to leave l.** sortir en dernier. **3** *n* (*person*, *object*) dernier, -ière *mf*; **the l. of the beer**/*etc* le reste de la bière/*etc*; **at (long) l.** enfin.
last[2] *vi* durer; (*endure*) tenir.
lastly *adv* en dernier lieu, enfin.
latch [lætʃ] loquet *m*; **the door is on the l.** la porte n'est pas fermée à clef.
late [leɪt] **1** *a* (*not on time*) en retard (**for** à); (*meal*, *hour*) tardif; **he's an hour l.** il a une heure de retard; **it's l.** il est tard; **at a later date** à une date ultérieure; **at the latest** au plus tard; **of l.** dernièrement. **2** *adv* (*in the day*, *season etc*) tard; (*not on time*) en retard; **it's getting l.** il se fait tard; **later (on)** plus tard.
latecomer retardataire *mf*.
lately *adv* dernièrement.
Latin ['lætɪn] **1** *a* latin. **2** *n* (*language*) latin *m*.
latter ['lætər] **1** *a* (*last-named*) dernier; (*second*) deuxième. **2** *n* dernier, -ière *mf*; second, -onde *mf*.
laugh [lɑːf] **1** *n* rire *m*. **2** *vi* rire (**at, about** de).
laughter rire(s) *m*(*pl*).
launch [lɔːntʃ] **1** *vt* (*rocket*, *fashion etc*) lancer. **2** *n* lancement *m*.
launderette [lɔːndə'ret], *Am* **'laundromat** laverie *f* automatique.
'laundry (*place*) blanchisserie *f*; (*clothes*) linge *m*.
lavatory ['lævətrɪ] cabinets *mpl*.
law [lɔː] loi *f*; (*study*, *profession*) droit *m*; **court of l., l. court** cour *f* de justice.
lawn [lɔːn] pelouse *f*, gazon *m*; **l. mower** tondeuse *f* (à gazon).
lawsuit procès *m*.
lawyer ['lɔːjər] avocat *m*; (*for wills*, *sales*) notaire *m*.
lay* [leɪ] *vt* (*put down*) poser; (*table*) mettre; (*blanket*) étendre (**over** sur); (*trap*) tendre; (*egg*) pondre.
layabout *Fam* fainéant, -ante *mf*.
lay-by (*pl* **-bys**) aire *f* de stationnement.
lay down (*put down*) poser.
layer couche *f*.

lay off (*worker*) licencier.
lay on installer; (*supply*) fournir.
lay out (*garden*) dessiner; (*display*) disposer; (*money*) *Fam* mettre (**on** dans).
layout disposition *f*.
lazy ['leɪzɪ] *a* paresseux.
lead[1] [li:d] **1** *vt** (*conduct*) mener, conduire (**to** à); (*team*, *government etc*) diriger; (*life*) mener; **to l. s.o. in/out/***etc* faire entrer/sortir/*etc* qn; **to l. s.o. to do** amener qn à faire. **2** *vi* (*of street*, *door etc*) mener (**to** à); (*in race*) être en tête; (*in match*) mener; (*go ahead*) aller devant. **3** *n* (*distance or time ahead*) avance *f* (**over** sur); (*example*) exemple *m*; (*leash*) laisse *f*; (*electric wire*) fil *m*; **to be in the l.** (*in race*) être en tête; (*in match*) mener.
lead[2] [led] (*metal*) plomb *m*; (*of pencil*) mine *f*.
lead s.o. away *or* **off** emmener qn.
leader chef *m*; (*of country*, *party*) dirigeant, -ante *mf*.
leading *a* (*main*) principal.
lead to (*result in*) aboutir à; (*cause*) causer.
lead up to (*of street etc*) conduire à; (*precede*) précéder.
leaf [li:f] (*pl* **leaves**) feuille *f*; (*of book*) feuillet *m*
leaflet prospectus *m*; (*containing instructions*) notice *f*.
leaf through (*book*) feuilleter.
leak [li:k] **1** *n* (*of gas etc*) fuite *f*. **2** *vi* (*of liquid*, *pipe etc*) fuir.
lean* [li:n] **1** *vi* (*of object*) pencher; (*of person*) se pencher; **to l. against/on sth** (*of person*) s'appuyer contre/sur qch. **2** *vt* appuyer (**against** contre); **to l. one's head on/out of sth** pencher la tête sur/par qch.
lean forward (*of person*) se pencher (en avant).
lean over (*of person*) se pencher; (*of object*) pencher.
leap [li:p] **1** *n* bond *m*. **2** *vi** bondir.
leap year année *f* bissextile.
learn* [lɜ:n] **1** *vt* apprendre (**that** que); **to l. (how) to do** apprendre à faire. **2** *vi* apprendre; **to l. about** (*study*) étudier; (*hear about*) apprendre.
learner débutant, -ante *mf*.
learning (*of language*) apprentissage *m* (**of** de).
leash [li:ʃ] laisse *f*.
least [li:st] **1** *a* **the l.** (*smallest amount of*) le moins de; (*slightest*) le *or* la moindre. **2** *n* **the l.** le moins; **at l.** du moins; (*with quantity*) au moins. **3** *adv* (*to work etc*) le moins; (*with adjective*) le *or* la moins.
leather ['leðər] cuir *m*; **(wash) l.** peau *f* de chamois.

leave [liːv] **1** *n* (*holiday*) congé *m*. **2** *vt** laisser; (*go away from*) quitter; **to be left (over)** rester; **there's no bread/***etc* **left** il ne reste plus de pain/*etc*; **to l. go (of)** (*release*) lâcher. **3** *vi* (*go away*) partir (**from** de, **for** pour).
leave behind (*not take*) laisser; (*in race, at school*) distancer.
leave on (*hat, gloves*) garder.
leave out (*forget to put*) oublier (de mettre) (*accent etc*); (*word, line*) sauter; (*exclude*) exclure.
lecture ['lektʃər] **1** *n* (*public speech*) conférence *f*; (*as part of series at university*) cours *m*. **2** *vi* faire une conférence *or* un cours.
lecturer conférencier, -ière *mf*; (*at university*) professeur *m*.
leek [liːk] poireau *m*.
left[1] [left] *pt & pp de* **leave**.
left[2] **1** *a* (*side, hand etc*) gauche. **2** *adv* à gauche. **3** *n* gauche *f*; **on** *or* **to the l.** à gauche (**of** de).
left-hand *a* à *or* de gauche; **on the l.-hand side** à gauche (**of** de).
left-'handed *a* (*person*) gaucher.
left luggage office consigne *f*.
leftovers *npl* restes *mpl*.
leg [leg] jambe *f*; (*of dog etc*) patte *f*; (*of table*) pied *m*; **l. (of chicken)** cuisse *f* (de poulet); **l. of lamb** gigot *m* (d'agneau).
legal ['liːg(ə)l] *a* légal.
legend ['ledʒənd] légende *f*.
legible ['ledʒəb(ə)l] *a* lisible.
leisure ['leʒər, *Am* 'liːʒər] **l. (time)** loisirs *mpl*; **l. activities** loisirs *mpl*.
lemon ['lemən] citron *m*; **l. drink** citronnade *f*; **l. tea** thé *m* au citron.
lemo'nade (*fizzy*) limonade *f*; (*still*) *Am* citronnade *f*.
lend* [lend] *vt* prêter (**to** à); (*colour, charm etc*) donner (**to** à).
length [leŋθ] longueur *f*; (*section of rope etc*) morceau *m*; (*duration*) durée *f*; **l. of time** temps *m*.
lengthen *vt* allonger; (*in time*) prolonger.
lenient ['liːnɪənt] *a* indulgent (**to** envers).
lens [lenz] lentille *f*; (*in spectacles*) verre *m*; (*of camera*) objectif *m*.
lentil ['lent(ə)l] lentille *f* (*graine*).
leopard ['lepəd] léopard *m*.
leotard ['liːətɑːd] collant *m* (*de danse*).
less [les] **1** *a & n* moins (de) (**than** que); **l. time/***etc* moins de temps/*etc*; **l. than a kilo/ten** (*with quantity, number*) moins d'un kilo/de dix. **2** *adv* moins (**than** que); **l. (often)** moins souvent; **l. and l.** de moins en moins; **one l.** un(e) de moins. **3** *prep* moins.

lesson ['les(ə)n] leçon *f*.
let* [let] *vt* (*allow*) laisser (**s.o. do** qn faire); **to l. s.o. have sth** donner qch à qn; **l. us** *or* **l.'s eat**/*etc* mangeons/*etc*; **l.'s go for a stroll** allons nous promener; **l. him come** qu'il vienne.
let (out) (*room etc*) louer.
let down (*lower*) baisser; **to l. s.o. down** (*disappoint*) décevoir qn.
letdown déception *f*.
let in (*person*) faire entrer; (*noise*, *light*) laisser entrer.
let off (*firework*, *gun*) faire partir; **to l. s.o. off** (*not punish*) ne pas punir qn; **to l. s.o. off doing** dispenser qn de faire.
let out (*person*) laisser sortir; (*cry*, *secret*) laisser échapper.
letter ['letər] lettre *f*.
letterbox boîte *f* aux *or* à lettres.
lettuce ['letɪs] laitue *f*.
let up (*of rain etc*) s'arrêter.
level ['lev(ə)l] **1** *n* niveau *m*; (*rate*) taux *m*. **2** *a* (*surface*) plat; (*object on surface*) d'aplomb; (*equal in score*) à égalité (**with** avec); (*in height*) au même niveau (**with** que).
level crossing passage *m* à niveau
lever ['liːvər, *Am* 'levər] levier *m*.
liable ['laɪəb(ə)l] *a* **to be l. to do** être capable *or* susceptible de faire.
liar ['laɪər] menteur, -euse *mf*.
liberty ['lɪbətɪ] liberté *f*; **at l. to do** libre de faire.
li'brarian bibliothécaire *mf*.
library ['laɪbrərɪ] bibliothèque *f*.
lice [laɪs] *npl* poux *mpl*.
licence, *Am* **license** ['laɪsəns] (*document*) permis *m*; **licence plate/number** plaque *f*/numéro *m* d'immatriculation.
lick [lɪk] *vt* lécher.
licorice ['lɪkərɪʃ] *Am* réglisse *f*.
lid [lɪd] (*of box etc*) couvercle *m*.
lie[1]* [laɪ] *vi* (*in flat position*) s'allonger; (*remain*) rester; (*be*) être; **to be lying** (*on the grass etc*) être allongé.
lie[2] **1** *vi* (*pt & pp* **lied**, *present* + **lying**) (*tell lies*) mentir. **2** *n* mensonge *m*.
lie about *or* **around** (*of objects*, *person*) traîner.
lie down s'allonger; **lying down** allongé.
life [laɪf] (*pl* **lives**) vie *f*; **to come to l.** s'animer.
lifebelt ceinture *f* de sauvetage.
lifeboat canot *m* de sauvetage.
lifeguard maître nageur *m* (sauveteur).
life insurance assurance-vie *f*.

life jacket gilet *m* de sauvetage.
life preserver *Am* ceinture *f* de sauvetage.
lifetime in my l. de mon vivant.
lift [lɪft] **1** *vt* lever. **2** *n* (*elevator*) ascenseur *m*; **to give s.o. a l.** emmener qn (en voiture) (**to** à).
lift down *or* **off** (*take down*) descendre (**from** de).
lift out (*take out*) sortir (**of** de).
lift up (*arm*, *object*) lever.
light¹ [laɪt] lumière *f*; (*on vehicle*) feu *m*; (*vehicle headlight*) phare *m*; **do you have a l.?** (*for cigarette*) est-ce que vous avez du feu?; **to set l. to** mettre le feu à.
light²* *vt* (*match*, *fire*, *gas*) allumer.
light³ *a* (*not dark*) clair; **a l. green jacket** une veste vert clair.
light⁴ *a* (*in weight*, *quantity etc*) léger; **to travel l.** voyager avec peu de bagages.
light (up) (*room*) éclairer; (*cigarette*) allumer.
light bulb ampoule *f* (électrique).
lighter (*for cigarettes*) briquet *m*; (*for cooker*, *Am stove*) allume-gaz *m inv*.
lighthouse phare *m*.
lighting (*lights*) éclairage *m*.
lightning ['laɪtnɪŋ] (*charge*) foudre *f*; **(flash of) l.** éclair *m*.
like¹ [laɪk] **1** *prep* comme; **l. this** comme ça; **what's he l.?** comment est-il?; **to be** *or* **look l.** ressembler à; **what was the book l.?** comment as-tu trouvé le livre? **2** *conj* (*as*) *Fam* comme; **do l. I do** fais comme moi.
like² *vt* aimer (bien) (**to do, doing** faire); **she likes it here** elle se plaît ici; **to l. sth best** aimer mieux qch; **I'd l. to come** je voudrais (bien) *or* j'aimerais (bien) venir; **I'd l. a kilo of apples** je voudrais un kilo de pommes; **would you l. an apple?** voulez-vous une pomme?; **if you l.** si vous voulez.
likeable *a* sympathique.
likelihood there's isn't much l. that il y a peu de chances que (+ *subjunctive*).
likely ['laɪklɪ] **1** *a* probable; (*excuse*) vraisemblable; **it's l. (that) she'll come, she's l. to come** il est probable qu'elle viendra. **2** *adv* **very l.** très probablement; **not l.!** pas question!
likewise *adv* de même.
liking a l. for (*person*) de la sympathie pour; (*thing*) du goût pour.
lily ['lɪlɪ] lis *m*.
limb [lɪm] membre *m*.
lime [laɪm] (*fruit*) citron *m* vert.

limit ['lɪmɪt] **1** *n* limite *f* (**to** à). **2** *vt* limiter (**to** à).

limousine [lɪmə'ziːn] (*airport shuttle*) *Am* voiture-navette *f*.

limp [lɪmp] **1** *vi* (*of person*) boiter. **2** *n* **to have a l.** boiter.

line[1] [laɪn] **1** *n* ligne *f*; (*of poem*) vers *m*; (*wrinkle*) ride *f*; (*track*) voie *f*; (*rope*) corde *f*; (*row*) rangée *f*; (*of vehicles, people*) file *f*; **on the l.** (*phone*) au bout du fil; **to stand in l.** *Am* faire la queue; **to drop a l.** (*send a letter*) envoyer un mot (**to** à). **2** *vt* **to l. the street** (*of trees*) border la rue; (*of people*) faire la haie le long de la rue.

line[2] *vt* (*clothes*) doubler.

linen ['lɪnɪn] (*sheets etc*) linge *m*.

liner ['laɪnər] **(ocean) l.** paquebot *m*; **(dust)bin l.** sac *m* poubelle.

line up 1 *vt* (*children, objects*) aligner; (*arrange*) organiser. **2** *vi* s'aligner; (*queue up*) *Am* faire la queue.

lining (*of clothes*) doublure *f*.

link [lɪŋk] **1** *vt* (*connect*) relier; (*relate*) lier (**to** à). **2** *n* lien *m*; (*of chain*) maillon *m*; (*by road, rail*) liaison *f*.

link up (*of firms etc*) s'associer; (*of roads*) se rejoindre.

lino ['laɪnəʊ] (*pl* **-os**) lino *m*.

lion ['laɪən] lion *m*.

lip [lɪp] lèvre *f*.

lipstick bâton *m* de rouge; (*substance*) rouge *m* (à lèvres).

liqueur [lɪ'kjʊər] liqueur *f*.

liquid ['lɪkwɪd] *n* & *a* liquide (*m*).

liquor ['lɪkər] alcool *m*.

liquorice ['lɪkərɪʃ, -rɪs] réglisse *f*.

list [lɪst] **1** *n* liste *f*. **2** *vt* faire la liste de; (*names*) mettre sur la liste, inscrire; (*name one by one*) énumérer.

listen (to) ['lɪsən] écouter.

listener (*to radio*) auditeur, -trice *mf*.

listen (out) for guetter (le bruit *ou* les cris *etc* de).

liter ['liːtər] *Am* litre *m*.

literary *a* littéraire.

literature ['lɪt(ə)rɪtʃər] littérature *f*; (*pamphlets etc*) documentation *f*.

litre ['liːtər] litre *m*.

litter ['lɪtər] (*rubbish*) détritus *m*; (*papers*) papiers *mpl*; (*young animals*) portée *f*.

litter bin boîte *f* à ordures.

little ['lɪt(ə)l] **1** *a* (*small*) petit. **2** *a* & *n* (*not much*) peu (de); **l. time**/*etc* peu de temps/*etc*; **she eats l.** elle mange peu; **as l. as possible** le moins possible; **a l. money**/*etc* (*some*) un peu d'argent/*etc*. **3** *adv* **a l. heavy**/*etc* un peu lourd/*etc*; **to work**/*etc* **a l.**

travailler/*etc* un peu; **l. by l.** peu à peu.

live[1] [lɪv] **1** *vi* vivre; (*reside*) habiter, vivre. **2** *vt* (*life*) mener.

live[2] [laɪv] **1** *a* (*electric wire*) sous tension; (*switch*) mal isolé. **2** *a & adv* (*broadcast*) en direct.

lively ['laɪvlɪ] *a* (*person, style, interest, mind*) vif; (*discussion*) animé.

live off *or* **on** (*eat*) vivre de.

liver ['lɪvər] foie *m*.

live through (*experience*) vivre; (*survive*) survivre à.

living ['lɪvɪŋ] **1** *a* (*alive*) vivant. **2** *n* vie *f*; **to make** *or* **earn a** *or* **one's l.** gagner sa vie; **the cost of l.** le coût de la vie.

living room salle *f* de séjour.

lizard ['lɪzəd] lézard *m*.

load [ləʊd] **1** *n* charge *f*; (*weight*) poids *m*; **a l. of, loads of** (*people, money etc*) *Fam* un tas de. **2** *vt* (*truck, gun etc*) charger (**with** de).

load up 1 *vt* (*car, ship etc*) charger (**with** de). **2** *vi* charger la voiture, le navire *etc*.

loaf [ləʊf] (*pl* **loaves**) pain *m*; **French l.** baguette *f*.

loan [ləʊn] **1** *n* (*money lent*) prêt *m*; (*money borrowed*) emprunt *m*. **2** *vt* (*lend*) prêter (**to** à).

lobby ['lɒbɪ] (*of hotel*) hall *m*.

lobster ['lɒbstər] homard *m*.

local ['ləʊk(ə)l] *a* local; (*regional*) régional; (*of the neighbourhood*) du *or* de quartier; (*of the region*) de la région.

locally *adv* dans le coin.

locate [ləʊ'keɪt] *vt* (*find*) trouver, repérer; **to be located** être situé.

location (*site*) emplacement *m*.

lock [lɒk] **1** *vt* (*door etc*) fermer à clef. **2** *n* (*on door etc*) serrure *f*; (*on canal*) écluse *f*; (*of hair*) mèche *f*.

lock away (*prisoner, jewels etc*) enfermer.

locker (*for luggage*) casier *m* de consigne automatique; (*for clothes*) vestiaire *m* (métallique).

locket ['lɒkɪt] (*jewel*) médaillon *m*.

lock s.o. in enfermer qn; **to l. s.o. in sth** enfermer qn dans qch.

lock s.o. out (*accidentally*) enfermer qn dehors.

lock up 1 *vt* (*house etc*) fermer à clef; (*prisoner, jewels etc*) enfermer. **2** *vi* fermer à clef.

lodger (*room and meals*) pensionnaire *mf*; (*room only*) locataire *mf*.

lodgings ['lɒdʒɪŋz] *npl* (*flat*) logement *m*; (*room*) chambre *f*; **in lodgings** en meublé.

loft [lɒft] (*attic*) grenier *m*.

log [lɒg] (*tree trunk*) tronc *m* d'arbre; (*for fire*) bûche *f*.

logical ['lɒdʒɪk(ə)l] *a* logique.

lollipop ['lɒlɪpɒp], *Fam* **lolly** sucette *f*; (*ice*) esquimau *m*.
loneliness solitude *f*.
lonely ['ləʊnlɪ] *a* solitaire.
long [lɒŋ] **1** *a* long (*f* longue); **to be ten metres l.** avoir dix mètres de long; **to be six weeks l.** durer six semaines; **a l. time** longtemps. **2** *adv* longtemps; **has he been here l.?** il y a longtemps qu'il est ici?; **how l. ago?** il y a combien de temps?; **before l.** sous peu; **she no longer swims** elle ne nage plus; **I won't be l.** je n'en ai pas pour longtemps; **all summer l.** tout l'été; **as l. as, so l. as** (*provided that*) pourvu que (+ *subjunctive*).
long-'distance (*phone call*) interurbain; (*flight*) long-courrier.
long-'term *a* à long terme.
loo [luː] (*toilet*) *Fam* toilettes *fpl*, cabinets *mpl*.
look [lʊk] **1** *n* regard *m*; (*appearance*) air *m*; **to have a l. (at)** jeter un coup d'œil (à); **to have a l. (for)** chercher; **to have a l. (a)round** regarder; (*walk*) faire un tour; **let me have a l.** fais voir. **2** *vi* regarder; **to l. tired**/*etc* sembler *or* avoir l'air fatigué/*etc*; **you l. like** *or* **as if you're tired** on dirait que tu es fatigué; **to l. well** *or* **good** (*of person*) avoir bonne mine; **you l. good in that hat**/*etc* ce chapeau/*etc* te va très bien.
look after (*deal with*) s'occuper de (*qch*, *qn*); (*sick person*) soigner; (*keep safely*) garder (**for s.o.** pour qn); **to l. after oneself** (*keep healthy*) faire bien attention à soi; (*manage*) se débrouiller.
look around **1** *vt* visiter. **2** *vi* regarder; (*walk round*) faire un tour.
look at regarder.
look down *vi* baisser les yeux; (*from a height*) regarder en bas.
look for chercher.
look forward to (*event*) attendre avec impatience; **to l. forward to doing** avoir hâte de faire.
look into examiner; (*find out about*) se renseigner sur.
look (out) on to (*of window etc*) donner sur.
look out (*be careful*) faire attention (**for** à).
lookout (*high place*) observatoire *m*; **to be on the l.** faire le guet; **to be on the l. for** guetter.
look over *or* **through** examiner; (*briefly*) parcourir; (*region, town*) parcourir.
look round **1** *vt* visiter. **2** *vi* regarder; (*walk round*) faire un tour; (*look back*) se retourner.
look up **1** *vi* lever les yeux; (*into the air*) regarder en l'air; (*improve*) s'améliorer. **2** *vt* (*word*) chercher.
loose [luːs] **1** *a* (*screw, belt, knot*) desserré; (*tooth*) branlant; (*page*) détaché; (*clothes*) flottant; (*tea etc*) au poids; (*having escaped*)

(*animal*) échappé; (*prisoner*) évadé; **l. change** petite monnaie *f*; **to set** *or* **turn l.** (*dog etc*) lâcher. **2** *n* **on the l.** (*prisoner*) évadé; (*animal*) échappé.

loosen *vt* (*knot*, *belt*, *screw*) desserrer.

lord [lɔːd] seigneur *m*; (*title*) lord *m*.

lorry ['lɒrɪ] camion *m*.

lorry driver camionneur *m*; **long-distance l. driver** routier *m*.

lose* **1** *vt* perdre; **to get lost** (*of person*) se perdre; **the ticket/***etc* **got lost** on a perdu le billet/*etc*. **2** *vi* perdre.

loser (*in contest etc*) perdant, -ante *mf*.

lose to s.o. *vi* être battu par qn.

loss [lɒs] perte *f*.

lost *a* perdu.

lost property, *Am* **lost and found** objets *mpl* trouvés.

lot [lɒt] **the l.** (*everything*) (le) tout; **a l. of, lots of** beaucoup de; **a l.** beaucoup; **quite a l.** pas mal (**of** de); **such a l.** tellement (**of** de); **what a l. of flowers/water/***etc***!** regarde toutes ces fleurs/toute cette eau/*etc*!

lotion ['ləʊʃ(ə)n] lotion *f*.

lottery ['lɒtərɪ] loterie *f*.

loud [laʊd] **1** *a* (*voice*, *music*) fort; (*noise*, *cry*) grand; **the radio/TV is too l.** le son de la radio/télé est trop fort. **2** *adv* (*to shout etc*) fort; **out l.** tout haut.

loudly *adv* (*to speak etc*) fort.

loud'speaker haut-parleur *m*; (*for speaking to crowd*) porte-voix *m inv*.

lounge [laʊndʒ] salon *m*.

lousy ['laʊzɪ] *a* (*food*, *weather etc*) *Fam* infect.

love [lʌv] **1** *n* amour *m*; **in l.** amoureux (**with** de); **they're in l.** ils s'aiment. **2** *vt* aimer (beaucoup) (**to do, doing** faire).

lovely *a* agréable; (*excellent*) excellent; (*pretty*) joli; (*charming*) charmant; (*kind*) gentil; **l. and warm/***etc* bien chaud/*etc*.

lover a l. of music/*etc*, un amateur de musique/*etc*.

loving *a* affectueux.

low [ləʊ] **1** *a* bas (*f* basse); (*speed*, *income*, *intelligence*) faible; (*opinion*, *quality*) mauvais; **to feel l.** être déprimé; **in a l. voice** à voix basse; **lower** inférieur. **2** *adv* bas; **to turn (down) l.** mettre plus bas.

low beams (*of vehicle*) *Am* codes *mpl*.

lower *vt* baisser; (*by rope*) descendre.

low-'fat *a* (*milk*) écrémé; (*cheese*) allégé.

loyal ['lɔɪəl] *a* fidèle (**to** à), loyal (**to** envers).

lozenge ['lɒzɪndʒ] (*tablet*) pastille *f*.
LP [el'piː] 33 tours *m inv*.
luck [lʌk] (*chance*) chance *f*; **bad l.** malchance *f*.
luckily *adv* heureusement.
lucky *a* (*person*) chanceux; (*guess, event*) heureux; **to be l.** avoir de la chance (**to do** de faire); **it's l. that** c'est une chance que; **l. charm** porte-bonheur *m inv*; **l. number/***etc* chiffre *m/etc* porte-bonheur.
ludicrous ['luːdɪkrəs] *a* ridicule.
luggage ['lʌgɪdʒ] bagages *mpl*.
lukewarm ['luːkwɔːm] *a* tiède.
lullaby ['lʌləbaɪ] berceuse *f*.
luminous ['luːmɪnəs] *a* (*colour etc*) fluo *inv*.
lump [lʌmp] morceau *m*; (*bump*) bosse *f*; (*swelling*) grosseur *f*.
lump sum somme *f* forfaitaire.
lunatic ['luːnətɪk] fou *m*, folle *f*.
lunch [lʌntʃ] déjeuner *m*; **to have l.** déjeuner; **l. break, l. hour, l. time** heure *f* du déjeuner.
luncheon voucher chèque-déjeuner *m*.
lung [lʌŋ] poumon *m*.
luxurious [lʌg'ʒʊərɪəs] *a* luxueux.
luxury ['lʌkʃərɪ] **1** *n* luxe *m*. **2** *a* (*goods etc*) de luxe.

M

MA *abbr* = **Master of Arts.**
mac [mæk] (*raincoat*) imper *m*.
macaroni [mækə'rəʊnɪ] macaroni(s) *m*(*pl*).
machine [mə'ʃiːn] machine *f*.
machinegun (*heavy*) mitrailleuse *f*; (*portable*) mitraillette *f*.
machinery machines *fpl*; (*works*) mécanisme *m*.
mackerel ['mækrəl] *n inv* maquereau *m*.
mackintosh ['mækɪntɒʃ] imperméable *m*.
mad [mæd] *a* fou (*f* folle); **m. (at)** (*angry*) furieux (contre); **m. about** (*person*) fou de; (*films etc*) passionné de; **like m.** comme un fou *or* une folle.
madam ['mædəm] madame *f*; (*unmarried*) mademoiselle *f*.
made [meɪd] *pt & pp de* **make.**
madman (*pl* **-men**) fou *m*.
madness folie *f*.
magazine [mægə'ziːn] magazine *m*, revue *f*.
maggot ['mægət] ver *m*.
magic ['mædʒɪk] **1** *n* magie *f*. **2** *a* (*wand etc*) magique.
magical *a* magique.
ma'gician magicien, -ienne *mf*.
magistrate ['mædʒɪstreɪt] magistrat *m*.
magnet ['mægnɪt] aimant *m*.
magnificent [mæg'nɪfɪsənt] *a* magnifique.
magnifying glass ['mægnɪfaɪɪŋ] loupe *f*.
mahogany [mə'hɒgənɪ] acajou *m*.
maid [meɪd] (*servant*) bonne *f*.
mail [meɪl] **1** *n* (*system*) poste *f*; (*letters*) courrier *m*. **2** *a* (*bag etc*) postal. **3** *vt* (*letter*) poster.
mailbox *Am* boîte *f* aux *or* à lettres.
mailman (*pl* **-men**) *Am* facteur *m*.
main[1] [meɪn] *a* principal; **the m. thing is to** l'essentiel est de; **m. road** grand-route *f*.
main[2] **water/gas m.** conduite *f* d'eau/de gaz; **the mains** (*electricity*) le secteur.
mainly *adv* surtout.
maintain [meɪn'teɪn] *vt* (*vehicle etc*) entretenir; (*law and order*) faire respecter; **to m. that** affirmer que.
maisonette [meɪzə'net] duplex *m*.
maître d' [meɪtrə'diː] *Am* maître *m* d'hôtel.
maize [meɪz] maïs *m*.

majesty ['mædʒəstɪ] **Your M.** Votre Majesté.
major ['meɪdʒər] **1** *a* majeur; **a m. road** une grande route. **2** *n* (*officer*) commandant *m*.
majo'rette majorette *f*.
majority [mə'dʒɒrɪtɪ] majorité *f* (**of** de); **the m. of people** la plupart des gens.
make* [meɪk] **1** *vt* faire; (*tool, vehicle etc*) fabriquer; (*decision*) prendre; (*friends, salary*) se faire; (*destination*) arriver à; **to m. happy**/*etc* rendre heureux/*etc*; **to m. s.o. do sth** faire faire qch à qn; **to m. do** (*manage*) se débrouiller (**with** avec); **to m. do with** (*be satisfied with*) se contenter de; **to m. it** arriver; (*succeed*) réussir; **what do you m. of it?** qu'en penses-tu? **2** *n* (*brand*) marque *f*.
make for aller vers.
make good (*loss*) compenser; (*damage*) réparer.
make off (*run away*) se sauver.
make out 1 *vt* (*see*) distinguer; (*understand*) comprendre; (*write*) faire (*chèque, liste*); (*claim*) prétendre (**that** que). **2** *vi* se débrouiller.
maker (*of product*) fabricant, -ante *mf*.
make up 1 *vt* (*story*) inventer; (*put together*) faire (*collection, liste etc*); (*form*) former; (*loss*) compenser; (*quantity*) compléter; (*quarrel*) régler; (*one's face*) maquiller. **2** *vti* **to m. (it) up** (*of friends*) se réconcilier.
make-up (*for face*) maquillage *m*.
make up for (*loss, damage*) compenser; (*lost time, mistake*) rattraper.
malaria [mə'leərɪə] malaria *f*.
male [meɪl] **1** *a* mâle; (*clothes, sex*) masculin. **2** *n* mâle *m*.
malice ['mælɪs] méchanceté *f*.
ma'licious *a* malveillant.
mall [mɔːl] **(shopping) m.** galerie *f* marchande.
mammal ['mæm(ə)l] mammifère *m*.
man [mæn] (*pl* **men** [men]) homme *m*.
manage ['mænɪdʒ] **1** *vt* (*run*) diriger; (*handle*) manier; **to m. to do** (*succeed*) réussir à faire; (*by being smart*) se débrouiller pour faire; **I'll m. it** j'y arriverai. **2** *vi* (*succeed*) y arriver; (*make do*) se débrouiller (**with** avec); **to m. without sth** se passer de qch.
management (*running, managers*) direction *f*.
manager directeur *m*; (*of shop, café*) gérant *m*.
manage'ress directrice *f*; gérante *f*.
managing director PDG *m*.
mane [meɪn] crinière *f*.

maneuver [mə'nuːvər] *Am* = **manoeuvre**.
maniac ['meɪnɪæk] fou *m*, folle *f*.
man-'made *a* artificiel.
manner ['mænər] (*way*) manière *f*; (*behaviour*) attitude *f*; **manners** (*social habits*) manières *fpl*; **to have no manners** être mal élevé.
manoeuvre [mə'nuːvər] **1** *n* manœuvre *f*. **2** *vti* manœuvrer.
mantelpiece ['mænt(ə)lpiːs] (*shelf*) cheminée *f*.
manual ['mænjʊəl] **1** *a* manuel. **2** *n* (*book*) manuel *m*.
manufacture [mænjʊ'fæktʃər] **1** *vt* fabriquer. **2** *n* fabrication *f*.
manufacturer fabricant, -ante *mf*.
manure [mə'njʊər] fumier *m*.
many ['menɪ] *a* & *n* beaucoup (de); **m. things** beaucoup de choses; **I don't have m.** je n'en ai pas beaucoup; **m. came** beaucoup sont venus; (**a good** *or* **great**) **m. of** un (très) grand nombre de; **m. times** bien des fois; **as m. books**/*etc* **as** autant de livres/*etc* que.
map [mæp] (*of country*, *region*) carte *f*; (*of town etc*) plan *m*.
marathon ['mærəθən] marathon *m*.
marble ['mɑːb(ə)l] marbre *m*; (*toy*) bille *f*.
March [mɑːtʃ] mars *m*.
march [mɑːtʃ] **1** *n* marche *f* (*militaire*). **2** *vi* (*of soldiers*) défiler.
mare [meər] jument *f*.
margarine [mɑːdʒə'riːn] margarine *f*.
margin ['mɑːdʒɪn] (*of page*) marge *f*.
mark [mɑːk] **1** *n* (*symbol*) marque *f*; (*stain*, *trace*) trace *f*; (*token*, *sign*) signe *m*; (*for school exercise etc*) note *f*; (*target*) but *m*. **2** *vt* marquer; (*exam etc*) corriger.
marker (*pen*) marqueur *m*.
market ['mɑːkɪt] marché *m*.
marketing marketing *m*.
mark off (*area*) délimiter.
marmalade ['mɑːməleɪd] confiture *f* d'oranges.
marriage mariage *m*.
married *a* marié; **to get m.** se marier.
marrow ['mærəʊ] (*of bone*) moelle *f*; (*vegetable*) courge *f*.
marry ['mærɪ] **1** *vt* épouser, se marier avec; (*of priest etc*) marier. **2** *vi* se marier.
marsh [mɑːʃ] marais *m*.
Martian ['mɑːʃ(ə)n] *n* & *a* martien, -ienne (*mf*).
marvellous ['mɑːv(ə)ləs] *a* merveilleux.
marzipan ['mɑːzɪpæn] pâte *f* d'amandes.
mascara [mæ'skɑːrə] mascara *m*.
mascot ['mæskɒt] mascotte *f*.

masculine ['mæskjʊlɪn] *a* masculin.
mashed potatoes [mæʃt] purée *f* (de pommes de terre).
mask [mɑːsk] masque *m*.
mass[1] [mæs] **1** *n* (*quantity*) masse *f*; **a m. of** (*many*) une multitude de; (*pile*) un tas de; **masses of** des masses de. **2** *a* (*protests, departure*) en masse.
mass[2] (*church service*) messe *f*.
massacre ['mæsəkər] **1** *n* massacre *m*. **2** *vt* massacrer.
massage ['mæsɑːʒ] **1** *n* massage *m*. **2** *vt* masser.
ma'sseur masseur *m*.
ma'sseuse masseuse *f*.
massive ['mæsɪv] *a* (*huge*) énorme.
mast [mɑːst] (*of ship*) mât *m*.
master ['mɑːstər] **1** *n* maître *m*; (*in secondary school*) professeur *m*; **M. of Arts/Science** (*person*) Maître *m* ès lettres/sciences. **2** *vt* (*control*) maîtriser; (*subject, situation*) dominer; **she has mastered Latin** elle possède le latin.
masterpiece chef-d'œuvre *m*.
mat [mæt] tapis *m*; (*of straw*) natte *f*; (*at door*) paillasson *m*; **(place) m.** set *m* (de table).
match[1] [mætʃ] (*stick*) allumette *f*.
match[2] **1** *n* (*game*) match *m*; (*equal*) égal, -ale *mf*; **to be a good m.** (*of colours, people etc*) être bien assortis. **2** *vt* (*of clothes, colour etc*) aller (bien) avec; **to be well-matched** être (bien) assortis. **3** *vi* être assortis.
match (up) (*plates etc*) assortir.
match (up to) égaler; (*s.o.'s hopes or expectations*) répondre à.
matchbox boîte *f* d'allumettes.
matching *a* (*dress etc*) assorti.
matchstick allumette *f*.
mate [meɪt] (*friend*) camarade *mf*.
material [mə'tɪərɪəl] matière *f*; (*cloth*) tissu *m*; **material(s)** (*equipment*) matériel *m*; **building materials** matériaux *mpl* de construction.
maternal [mə'tɜːn(ə)l] *a* maternel.
maternity hospital maternité *f*.
mathematical [mæθə'mætɪk(ə)l] *a* mathématique.
mathematics mathématiques *fpl*.
maths, *Am* **math** maths *fpl*.
matinée ['mætɪneɪ] (*in theatre*) matinée *f*.
matt [mæt] *a* (*paint, paper*) mat.
matter ['mætər] **1** *n* matière *f*; (*subject, affair*) affaire *f*; **no m.!** peu

importe!; **what's the m.?** qu'est-ce qu'il y a?; **what's the m. with you?** qu'est-ce que tu as?; **there's sth the m.** il y a qch qui ne va pas; **there's sth the m. with my leg** j'ai qch à la jambe. **2** *vi* importer (**to** à); **it doesn't m. if/who/***etc* peu importe si/qui/*etc*; **it doesn't m.!** ça ne fait rien!

mattress ['mætrəs] matelas *m*.

mature [mə'tʃʊər] *a* mûr; (*cheese*) fait.

maximum ['mæksɪməm] *a* & *n* maximum (*m*).

May mai *m*.

may [meɪ] *v aux* (*pt* **might**) (*possibility*) pouvoir; **he m. come** il peut arriver; **he might come** il pourrait arriver; **I m.** *or* **might have forgotten it** je l'ai peut-être oublié; **we m.** *or* **might as well go** nous ferions aussi bien de partir. ▮ (*permission*) pouvoir; **m. I stay?** puis-je rester?; **m. I?** vous permettez?; **you m. go** tu peux partir. ▮ (*wish*) **m. you be happy** (que tu) sois heureux.

maybe *adv* peut-être.

mayonnaise [meɪə'neɪz] mayonnaise *f*.

mayor [meər] maire *m*.

maze [meɪz] labyrinthe *m*.

me [miː] *pron* me, m'; (*after prep*, *'than'*, *'it is'*) moi; **(to) me** me, m'; **she knows me** elle me connaît; **he gives (to) me** il me donne.

meadow ['medəʊ] pré *m*.

meal [miːl] repas *m*.

mean¹* [miːn] *vt* (*signify*) vouloir dire; (*intend*) destiner (**for** à); (*result in*) entraîner; **to m. to do** avoir l'intention de faire; **I m. it** je suis sérieux; **to m. sth to s.o.** avoir de l'importance pour qn; **I didn't m. to!** je ne l'ai pas fait exprès!

mean² [miːn] (*with money etc*) avare; (*nasty*) méchant.

meaning sens *m*.

meaningless *a* qui n'a pas de sens.

meanness avarice *f*; (*nastiness*) méchanceté *f*.

means [miːnz] *n*(*pl*) (*method*) moyen(s) *m*(*pl*) (**to do, of doing** de faire); (*wealth*) moyens *mpl*; **by m. of** (*stick etc*) au moyen de; (*work etc*) à force de; **by all m.!** très certainement!; **by no m.** nullement.

meantime *adv* & *n* **(in the) m.** entre-temps.

meanwhile *adv* entre-temps.

measles ['miːz(ə)lz] rougeole *f*.

measure 1 *n* (*action*, *amount*) mesure *f*. **2** *vt* mesurer.

measurement (*of chest etc*) tour *m*; **measurements** mesures *fpl*.

measure up (*plank etc*) mesurer.

measure up to (*task*) être à la hauteur de.

meat [mi:t] viande *f*.
mechanic [mɪ'kænɪk] mécanicien, -ienne *mf*.
mechanical *a* mécanique.
'mechanism mécanisme *m*.
medal ['med(ə)l] médaille *f*.
medallist **to be a gold m.** être médaille d'or.
media ['mi:dɪə] *npl* **the (mass) m.** les médias *mpl*.
mediaeval [medɪ'i:v(ə)l] *a* médiéval.
medical ['medɪk(ə)l] *a* médical; (*school, studies*) de médecine; (*student*) en médecine.
medi'cation médicaments *mpl*.
medicine médicament *m*; (*science*) médecine *f*.
medicine cabinet *or* **chest** (armoire *f* à) pharmacie *f*.
medieval [medɪ'i:v(ə)] *a* médiéval.
Mediterranean [medɪtə'reɪnɪən] **1** *a* méditerranéen. **2** *n* **the M.** la Méditerranée.
medium ['mi:dɪəm] *a* moyen.
medium-sized *a* moyen.
meet* [mi:t] **1** *vt* (*person, team*) rencontrer; (*person by arrangement*) retrouver; (*pass in street etc*) croiser; (*fetch*) (aller *or* venir) chercher; (*wait for*) attendre; (*be introduced to*) faire la connaissance de. **2** *vi* (*of people, teams*) se rencontrer; (*of people by arrangement*) se retrouver; (*be introduced*) se connaître; (*of club etc*) se réunir.
meeting réunion *f*; (*large*) assemblée *f*; (*between two people*) rencontre *f*; (*arranged*) rendez-vous *m inv*.
meet up (*of people*) se rencontrer; (*by arrangement*) se retrouver.
meet up with s.o. rencontrer qn; retrouver qn.
meet with (*accident*) avoir; (*difficulty*) rencontrer; (*person*) *Am* rencontrer; retrouver.
melody ['melədɪ] mélodie *f*.
melon ['melən] melon *m*.
melt [melt] **1** *vi* fondre. **2** *vt* (faire) fondre.
member ['membər] membre *m*.
memo ['meməʊ] (*pl* **-os**) note *f*.
memory ['memərɪ] mémoire *f*; (*recollection*) souvenir *m*; **in m. of** à la mémoire de.
men [men] *see* **man.**
mend [mend] *vt* réparer; (*clothes*) raccommoder.
mental ['ment(ə)l] *a* mental.
mentally *adv* **he's m. handicapped** c'est un handicapé mental; **she's m. ill** c'est une malade mentale.

mention ['menʃ(ə)n] **1** *vt* mentionner; **not to m....** sans parler de...; **don't m. it!** il n'y a pas de quoi! **2** *n* mention *f*.
menu ['menjuː] menu *m*.
mercy ['mɜːsɪ] pitié *f*; **at the m. of** à la merci de.
mere [mɪər] *a* simple; (*only*) ne... que; **she's a m. child** ce n'est qu'une enfant.
merely *adv* (tout) simplement.
merge [mɜːdʒ] *vi* (*blend*) se mêler (**with** à); (*of roads*) se (re)joindre; (*of firms*) fusionner.
merger fusion *f*.
merry ['merɪ] *a* gai; (*drunk*) éméché.
merry-go-round (*at funfair*) manège *m*.
mesh [meʃ] (*of net*) maille *f*.
mess [mes] (*confusion*) désordre *m*; (*dirt*) saleté *f*; **in a m.** sens dessus dessous; (*trouble*) dans le pétrin.
mess about (*have fun*) s'amuser; (*play the fool*) faire l'idiot.
mess about with sth (*fiddle with*) s'amuser avec qch.
message ['mesɪdʒ] message *m*.
messenger messager *m*; (*in office, hotel*) coursier, -ière *mf*.
mess up (*spoil*) gâcher; (*dirty*) salir; (*room*) mettre sens dessus dessous.
messy *a* (*untidy*) en désordre; (*dirty*) sale.
metal ['met(ə)l] métal *m*; **m. ladder**/*etc* échelle *f*/*etc* métallique.
meter[1] ['miːtər] (*device*) compteur *m*; **(parking) m.** parcmètre *m*.
meter[2] *Am* mètre *m*.
method ['meθəd] méthode *f*.
me'thodical *a* méthodique.
metre ['miːtər] mètre *m*.
metric ['metrɪk] *a* métrique.
miaow [miː'aʊ] (*of cat*) miauler.
mice [maɪs] *see* **mouse.**
micro- ['maɪkrəʊ] *prefix* micro-.
microchip puce *f*.
microphone ['maɪkrəfəʊn] micro *m*.
microscope ['maɪkrəskəʊp] microscope *m*.
microwave (oven) four *m* à micro-ondes.
mid [mɪd] *a* **(in) m.-June** (à) la mi-juin; **in m. air** en plein ciel.
mid'day midi *m*.
middle ['mɪd(ə)l] **1** *n* milieu *m*; (*waist*) taille *f*; **(right) in the m. of** au (beau) milieu de; **in the m. of saying**/*etc* en train de dire/*etc*. **2** *a* du milieu; (*class*) moyen; (*name*) deuxième.
middle-'aged *a* d'un certain âge.

middle-'class *a* bourgeois.
midnight minuit *f*.
midst [mɪdst] **in the m. of** au milieu de.
midwife (*pl* **-wives**) sage-femme *f*.
might [maɪt] *see* **may.**
mild [maɪld] *a* doux (*f* douce); (*beer, punishment*) léger; (*medicine, illness*) bénin (*f* bénigne).
mile [maɪl] mile *m* (= *1,6 km*).
mileage = kilométrage *m*.
military ['mɪlɪt(ə)rɪ] *a* militaire.
milk [mɪlk] **1** *n* lait *m*. **2** *a* (*chocolate*) au lait; (*bottle*) à lait. **3** *vt* (*cow*) traire.
milkman (*pl* **-men**) laitier *m*.
milk shake milk-shake *m*.
mill [mɪl] moulin *m*; (*factory*) usine *f*.
millimetre ['mɪlɪmiːtər] millimètre *m*.
million ['mɪljən] million *m*; **a m. men**/*etc* un million d'hommes/*etc*.
millio'naire millionnaire *mf*.
mime [maɪm] *vti* mimer.
mimic ['mɪmɪk] *vt* (**-ck-**) imiter.
mince(meat) ['mɪns(miːt)] hachis *m* (de viande).
mincer hachoir *m*.
mind [maɪnd] **1** *n* esprit *m*; (*sanity*) raison *f*; (*memory*) mémoire *f*; **to change one's m.** changer d'avis; **to make up one's m.** se décider; **to be on s.o.'s m.** préoccuper qn; **to have in m.** (*person, plan*) avoir en vue. **2** *vti* faire attention à; (*look after*) garder; (*noise etc*) être gêné par; **do you m. if?** (*I smoke*) ça vous gêne si?; (*I leave*) ça ne vous fait rien si?; **I don't m.** ça m'est égal; **I wouldn't m. a cup of tea** j'aimerais bien une tasse de thé; **never m.!** ça ne fait rien!; (*don't worry*) ne vous en faites pas!; **m. (out)!** attention!
minder child m. nourrice *f*.
mine[1] [maɪn] *poss pron* le mien, la mienne, *pl* les mien(ne)s; **this hat is m.** ce chapeau est à moi *or* est le mien.
mine[2] (*for coal etc, explosive*) mine *f*.
miner mineur *m*.
mineral ['mɪnərəl] *a* & *n* minéral (*m*).
mini ['mɪnɪ] *prefix* mini-.
miniature ['mɪnɪtʃər] *a* (*train etc*) miniature *inv*; **in m.** en miniature.
minibus minibus *m*.
minicab (radio-)taxi *m*.
minimum ['mɪnɪməm] *a* & *n* minimum (*m*).

minister ['mɪnɪstər] (*politician*, *priest*) ministre *m*.
ministry ministère *m*.
minor ['maɪnər] *a* (*detail*, *operation*) petit.
minority [maɪ'nɒrɪtɪ] minorité *f*.
mint [mɪnt] (*herb*) menthe *f*; (*sweet*, *Am candy*) bonbon *m* à la menthe; **m. tea**/*etc* thé *m*/*etc* à la menthe.
minus ['maɪnəs] *prep* moins; (*without*) sans.
minute[1] ['mɪnɪt] minute *f*.
minute[2] [maɪ'nju:t] *a* (*tiny*) minuscule.
miracle ['mɪrək(ə)l] miracle *m*.
mi'raculous *a* miraculeux.
mirror ['mɪrər] miroir *m*, glace *f*; (*in vehicle*) rétroviseur *m*.
misbehave [mɪsbɪ'heɪv] *vi* se conduire mal.
miscellaneous [mɪsɪ'leɪnɪəs] *a* divers.
mischief ['mɪstʃɪf] espièglerie *f*; (*malice*) méchanceté *f*; **to get into m.** faire des bêtises.
mischievous *a* espiègle; (*malicious*) méchant.
miser ['maɪzər] avare *mf*.
miserable *a* (*wretched*) misérable; (*unhappy*) malheureux.
miserly *a* avare.
misery ['mɪzərɪ] souffrances *fpl*; (*sadness*) tristesse *f*.
misfortune [mɪs'fɔ:tʃu:n] malheur *m*.
mishap ['mɪshæp] contretemps *m*.
mislay* [mɪs'leɪ] *vt* égarer.
mislead* [mɪs'li:d] *vt* tromper.
misleading *a* trompeur.
miss[1] [mɪs] **1** *vt* (*train*, *opportunity etc*) manquer; (*not see*) ne pas voir; (*not understand*) ne pas comprendre; **he misses Paris/her** Paris/elle lui manque. **2** *vi* manquer.
miss[2] (*woman*) mademoiselle *f*; **Miss Brown** Mademoiselle *or* Mlle Brown.
missile ['mɪsaɪl, *Am* 'mɪs(ə)l] (*rocket*) missile *m*; (*object thrown*) projectile *m*.
missing *a* absent; (*after disaster*) disparu; (*object*) manquant; **there are two cups m.** il manque deux tasses.
mission ['mɪʃ(ə)n] mission *f*.
miss out 1 *vt* (*leave out*) sauter. **2** *vi* rater l'occasion.
miss out on (*opportunity etc*) rater.
mist [mɪst] (*fog*) brume *f*; (*on glass*) buée *f*.
mistake [mɪ'steɪk] **1** *n* erreur *f*, faute *f*; **to make a m.** se tromper; **by m.** par erreur. **2** *vt** (*meaning etc*) se tromper sur; **to m. the date**/*etc* se tromper de date/*etc*; **to m. s.o./sth for** prendre qn/qch

pour; **you're mistaken** tu te trompes.
mistakenly *adv* par erreur.
mistress ['mɪstrɪs] maîtresse *f*; (*in secondary school*) professeur *m*.
mistrust [mɪs'trʌst] **1** *n* méfiance *f*. **2** *vt* se méfier de.
misty ['mɪstɪ] *a* brumeux.
misunderstand* [mɪsʌndə'stænd] *vt* mal comprendre.
misunderstanding malentendu *m*.
mitten ['mɪt(ə)n] (*glove*) moufle *f*.
mix [mɪks] **1** *vt* mélanger, mêler; (*cake*) préparer; (*salad*) remuer. **2** *vi* se mêler; **she doesn't m.** elle n'est pas sociable.
mixed [mɪkst] *a* (*school*) mixte; (*chocolates etc*) assortis.
mixer (*electric, for cooking*) mixe(u)r *m*.
mixture mélange *m*.
mix-up confusion *f*.
mix up (*drink, papers etc*) mélanger; (*make confused*) embrouiller (*qn*); (*mistake*) confondre (**with** avec).
mix with s.o. fréquenter qn.
moan [məʊn] *vi* (*groan*) gémir; (*complain*) se plaindre (**to** à, **about** de, **that** que).
mob [mɒb] **1** *n* foule *f*. **2** *vt* assiéger.
mobile ['məʊbaɪl, *Am* 'məʊb(ə)l] *a* mobile.
model ['mɒd(ə)l] **1** *n* (*example etc*) modèle *m*; **(fashion) m.** mannequin *m*; **(scale) m.** modèle *m* (réduit). **2** *a* (*car, plane etc*) modèle réduit *inv*; **m. railway** train *m* miniature.
moderate ['mɒdərət] *a* modéré.
mode'ration modération *f*.
modern ['mɒd(ə)n] *a* moderne; **m. languages** langues *fpl* vivantes.
modernize **1** *vt* moderniser. **2** *vi* se moderniser.
modest ['mɒdɪst] *a* modeste.
modesty modestie *f*.
modifi'cation modification *f*.
modify ['mɒdɪfaɪ] *vt* modifier.
moist [mɔɪst] *a* humide; (*sticky*) moite.
moisture humidité *f*, (*on glass*) buée *f*.
mold [məʊld] *Am* = **mould.**
mole [məʊl] (*on skin*) grain *m* de beauté; (*animal*) taupe *f*.
mom [mɒm] *Am Fam* maman *f*.
moment ['məʊmənt] moment *m*; **the m. she leaves** dès qu'elle partira.
Monday ['mʌndɪ, *Am* -deɪ] lundi *m*.
money ['mʌnɪ] argent *m*.
moneybox tirelire *f*.

money order mandat *m*.
monk [mʌŋk] moine *m*.
monkey ['mʌŋkɪ] singe *m*.
monopolize *vt* monopoliser.
monotonous *a* monotone.
monotony [mə'nɒtənɪ] monotonie *f*.
monster ['mɒnstər] monstre *m*.
month [mʌnθ] mois *m*.
monthly **1** *a* mensuel. **2** *adv* mensuellement.
monument ['mɒnjʊmənt] monument *m*.
moo [muː] *vi* meugler.
mood [muːd] (*of person*) humeur *f*; *Grammar* mode *m*; **in a good/bad m.** de bonne/mauvaise humeur; **to be in the m. to do** être d'humeur à faire.
moody *a* (*bad-tempered*) de mauvaise humeur.
moon [muːn] lune *f*.
moonlight clair *m* de lune.
moor [mʊər] lande *f*.
mop [mɒp] **1** *n* balai *m* (à laver). **2** *vt* (*floor etc*) essuyer.
moped ['məʊped] mobylette® *f*.
mop up (*liquid*) éponger.
moral ['mɒrəl] (*of story*) morale *f*.
morale [mə'rɑːl, *Am* mə'ræl] moral *m*.
more [mɔːr] **1** *a* & *n* plus (de) (**than** que); (*other*) d'autres; **m. cars/***etc* plus de voitures/*etc*; **he has m. (than you)** il en a plus (que toi); **a few m. months** encore quelques mois; **(some) m. tea/***etc* encore du thé/*etc*; **m. than a kilo/ten** (*with quantity, number*) plus d'un kilo/de dix; **many m., much m.** beaucoup plus (de). **2** *adv* plus (**than** que); **m. and m.** de plus en plus; **m. or less** plus ou moins; **she doesn't have any m.** elle n'en a plus.
mo'reover *adv* de plus.
morning ['mɔːnɪŋ] matin *m*; (*duration of morning*) matinée *f*; **in the m.** le matin; (*tomorrow*) demain matin; **at seven in the m.** à sept heures du matin; **every Tuesday m.** tous les mardis matin.
mortal ['mɔːt(ə)l] *a* & *n* mortel, -elle (*mf*).
mortgage ['mɔːgɪdʒ] prêt-logement *m*.
Moslem ['mɒzlɪm] *a* & *n* musulman, -ane (*mf*).
mosque [mɒsk] mosquée *f*.
mosquito [mɒ'skiːtəʊ] (*pl* **-oes**) moustique *m*.
moss [mɒs] mousse *f* (*plante*).
most [məʊst] **1** *a* & *n* **the m.** le plus (de); **I have (the) m. books** j'ai le plus de livres; **I have (the) m.** j'en ai le plus; **m. (of the) books/***etc*

la plupart des livres/*etc*; **m. of the cake**/*etc* la plus grande partie du gâteau/*etc*; **at (the very) m.** tout au plus. **2** *adv* (le) plus; (*very*) très; **the m. beautiful** le plus beau, la plus belle (**in, of** de); **to talk (the) m.** parler le plus; **m. of all** surtout.

mostly *adv* surtout.

motel [məʊ'tel] motel *m*.

moth [mɒθ] papillon *m* de nuit; (*in clothes*) mite *f*.

mother ['mʌðər] mère *f*; **M.'s Day** la fête des Mères.

mother-in-law (*pl* **mothers-in-law**) belle-mère *f*.

motion ['məʊʃ(ə)n] **1** *n* (*of arm etc*) mouvement *m*. **2** *vti* **to m. (to) s.o. to do** faire signe à qn de faire.

motivated *a* motivé.

motive ['məʊtɪv] motif *m* (**for** de).

motor ['məʊtər] (*engine*) moteur *m*.

motorbike moto *f*.

motor boat canot *m* automobile.

motorcar automobile *f*.

motorcycle moto *f*.

motorcyclist motocycliste *mf*.

motorist automobiliste *mf*.

motorway autoroute *f*.

mould [məʊld] **1** *n* (*shape*) moule *m*; (*growth*) moisissure *f*. **2** *vt* (*clay etc*) mouler.

mouldy *a* moisi; **to go m.** moisir.

mount [maʊnt] **1** *n* (*frame for photo*) cadre *m*. **2** *vt* (*horse, photo*) monter. **3** *vi* (*on horse*) se mettre en selle.

mountain ['maʊntɪn] montagne *f*; **m. bike** VTT *m inv*.

mountai'neer alpiniste *mf*.

mountai'neering alpinisme *m*.

mountainous *a* montagneux.

mount up *vi* (*add up*) chiffrer (**to** à); (*accumulate*) s'accumuler.

mourn [mɔːn] *vt* **to m. (for) s.o., m. the loss of s.o.** pleurer (la perte de) qn; **she's mourning** elle est en deuil.

mourning deuil *m*; **in m.** en deuil.

mouse, *pl* **mice** [maʊs, maɪs] souris *f*.

mousse [muːs] mousse *f* (*dessert*).

moustache [mə'stɑːʃ, *Am* 'mʌstæʃ] moustache *f*.

mouth [maʊθ] (*pl* **-s** [maʊðz]) bouche *f*; (*of dog, lion etc*) gueule *f*; (*of river*) embouchure *f*.

mouthorgan harmonica *m*.

mouthwash bain *m* de bouche.

move [muːv] **1** *n* mouvement *m*; (*change of house*) déménagement *m*; (*in game*) coup *m*, (*one's turn*) tour *m*; (*act*) démarche *f*; **to make a m.** (*leave*) se préparer à partir. **2** *vt* déplacer; (*arm*, *leg*) remuer; (*put*) mettre; (*transport*) transporter; (*piece in game*) jouer; **to m. s.o.** (*emotionally*) émouvoir qn; (*transfer in job*) muter qn; **to m. house** déménager. **3** *vi* bouger; (*go*) aller (**to** à); (*out of house*) déménager; (*change seats*) changer de place; (*play*) jouer; **to m. to a new house/***etc* aller habiter une nouvelle maison/*etc*; **to m. into a house** emménager dans une maison.

move about *vi* se déplacer; (*fidget*) remuer.

move along *vi* avancer.

move away *vi* s'éloigner; (*move house*) déménager.

move back 1 *vt* (*chair etc*) reculer; (*to its position*) remettre. **2** *vi* reculer; (*return*) retourner.

move sth down descendre qch.

move forward *vti* avancer.

move in *vi* (*into house*) emménager.

movement (*action*, *group etc*) mouvement *m*.

move off (*go away*) s'éloigner; (*of vehicle*) démarrer.

move on *vi* avancer; **move on!** circulez!

move out *vi* (*out of house*) déménager.

move over 1 *vt* pousser. **2** *vi* se pousser.

move up *vi* (*on seats etc*) se pousser.

movie ['mu:vɪ] film *m*.

movie camera caméra *f*.

moving *a* en mouvement; (*touching*) émouvant.

mow [məʊ] *vt* (*pp* **mown** *or* **mowed**) **to m. the lawn** tondre le gazon.

mower (lawn) m. tondeuse *f* (à gazon).

MP [em'pi:] *abbr* (*Member of Parliament*) député *m*.

Mr ['mɪstər] **Mr Brown** Monsieur Brown.

Mrs ['mɪsɪz] **Mrs Brown** Madame *or* Mme Brown.

Ms [mɪz] **Ms Brown** Madame *or* Mme Brown.

MSc, *Am* **MS** *abbr* = **Master of Science.**

much [mʌtʃ] **1** *a* & *n* beaucoup (de); **not m. time/***etc* pas beaucoup de temps/*etc*; **I don't have m.** je n'en ai pas beaucoup; **as m. as** autant que; **as m. wine/***etc* **as** autant de vin/*etc* que; **twice as m.** deux fois plus (de). **2** *adv* **very m.** beaucoup; **not (very) m.** pas beaucoup.

mud [mʌd] boue *f*.

muddle ['mʌd(ə)l] (*mix-up*) confusion *f*; (*mess*) désordre *m*; **in a m.** (*person*) désorienté; (*mind*, *ideas*) embrouillé.

muddle (up) (*person*, *facts*) embrouiller; (*papers*) mélanger.

muddy *a* (*water*, *road*) boueux; (*hands etc*) couvert de boue.

muesli ['mju:zlɪ] muesli *m*.
muffin ['mʌfɪn] *sorte de petite brioche*.
mug¹ [mʌg] (*cup*) grande tasse *f*; **(beer) m.** chope *f*.
mug *vt* (*in street*) agresser, attaquer.
mugger agresseur *m*.
mule [mju:l] (*male*) mulet *m*; (*female*) mule *f*.
multiple ['mʌltɪp(ə)l] *a* & *n* multiple (*m*).
multipli'cation multiplication *f*.
multiply *vt* multiplier.
mum [mʌm] *Fam* maman *f*.
mumble ['mʌmb(ə)l] *vti* marmotter.
mummy ['mʌmɪ] *Fam* maman *f*.
mumps [mʌmps] oreillons *mpl*.
murder ['mɜ:dər] **1** *n* meurtre *m*, assassinat *m*. **2** *vt* tuer, assassiner.
murderer meurtrier, -ière *mf*, assassin *m*.
murmur ['mɜ:mər] *vti* murmurer.
muscle ['mʌs(ə)l] muscle *m*.
muscular *a* (*arm etc*) musclé.
museum [mju:'zɪəm] musée *m*.
mushroom ['mʌʃrʊm] champignon *m*.
music ['mju:zɪk] musique *f*.
musical 1 *a* musical; (*instrument*) de musique; **to be m.** être musicien. **2** *n* comédie *f* musicale.
mu'sician musicien, -ienne *mf*.
Muslim ['mʊzlɪm] *a* & *n* musulman, -ane (*mf*).
mussel ['mʌs(ə)l] moule *f*.
must [mʌst] *v aux* (*necessity*) devoir; **you m. obey** tu dois obéir, il faut que tu obéisses. ▮ (*certainty*) devoir; **she m. be clever** elle doit être intelligente; **I m. have seen it** j'ai dû le voir.
mustache ['mʌstæʃ] *Am* moustache *f*.
mustard ['mʌstəd] moutarde *f*.
musty ['mʌstɪ] **to smell m.** sentir le moisi.
mutter ['mʌtər] *vti* marmonner.
mutton ['mʌt(ə)n] (*meat*) mouton *m*.
mutual ['mju:tʃʊəl] *a* (*help etc*) mutuel; (*friend*) commun.
muzzle ['mʌz(ə)l] (*for animal*) muselière *f*.
my [maɪ] *poss a* mon, ma, *pl* mes.
my'self *pron* moi-même; (*reflexive*) me, m'; (*after prep*) moi.
my'sterious *a* mystérieux.
mystery ['mɪstərɪ] mystère *m*.

N

nail [neɪl] (*of finger*, *toe*) ongle *m*; (*metal*) clou *m*.
nail (down) *vt* clouer.
nail file/polish lime *f*/vernis *m* à ongles.
naïve [naɪ'iːv] *a* naïf.
naked ['neɪkɪd] *a* nu.
name [neɪm] **1** *n* nom *m*; (*reputation*) réputation *f*; **my n. is...** je m'appelle...; **first n.** prénom *m*; **last n.** nom *m* de famille. **2** *vt* nommer; (*date*, *price*) fixer; **he was named after** *or Am* **for** il a reçu le nom de.
nanny ['nænɪ] nurse *f*; (*grandmother*) *Fam* mamie *f*.
nap [næp] (*sleep*) petit somme *m*; **to have** *or* **take a n.** faire un petit somme.
napkin ['næpkɪn] (*at table*) serviette *f*.
nappy (*for baby*) couche *f*.
narrow ['nærəʊ] *a* étroit.
narrow (down) (*choice etc*) limiter.
narrowly he n. escaped being killed/*etc* il a failli être tué/*etc*.
nastily *adv* (*to behave*) méchamment; (*to rain*) horriblement.
nasty ['nɑːstɪ] *a* mauvais; (*spiteful*) méchant (**to(wards)** avec).
nation ['neɪʃ(ə)n] nation *f*.
national *a* national.
natio'nality nationalité *f*.
native ['neɪtɪv] **1** *a* (*country*) natal (*mpl* -als); **to be an English n. speaker** parler l'anglais comme langue maternelle. **2** *n* **to be a n. of** être originaire de.
natural ['nætʃ(ə)rəl] *a* naturel; (*actor etc*) né.
naturally *adv* (*as normal*, *of course*) naturellement; (*to behave etc*) avec naturel.
nature ['neɪtʃər] (*natural world*, *character*) nature *f*.
nature study sciences *fpl* naturelles.
naughty ['nɔːtɪ] *a* (*child*) vilain.
nauseous ['nɔːʃəs] *a* **to feel n.** *Am* avoir envie de vomir.
naval ['neɪv(ə)l] *a* naval (*mpl* -als); (*officer*) de marine.
navel ['neɪv(ə)l] nombril *m*.
navigate ['nævɪgeɪt] **1** *vi* naviguer. **2** *vt* (*boat*) diriger.
navi'gation navigation *f*.
navy ['neɪvɪ] **1** *n* marine *f*. **2** *a* **n. (blue)** bleu marine *inv*.
near [nɪər] **1** *adv* près; **quite n.** tout près; **n. to** près de; **to come n. to being killed**/*etc* faillir être tué/*etc*; **n. enough** (*more or less*) plus ou moins. **2** *prep* **n. (to)** près de; **n. (to) the end** vers la fin; **to come**

n. s.o. s'approcher de qn. **3** *a* proche; **in the n. future** dans un avenir proche.

nearby [nɪə'baɪ] **1** *adv* tout près. **2** *a* ['nɪəbaɪ] proche.

nearly ['nɪəlɪ] *adv* presque; **she (very) n. fell** elle a failli tomber; **not n. as clever/*etc* as** loin d'être aussi intelligent/*etc* que.

neat [niːt] *a* (*clothes, work*) soigné; (*room*) bien rangé.

neatly *adv* avec soin.

nece'ssarily *adv* **not n.** pas forcément.

necessary ['nesɪs(ə)rɪ] *a* nécessaire (**to do** de faire); **to do what's n.** faire le nécessaire.

necessity [nɪ'sesɪtɪ] nécessité *f*.

neck [nek] cou *m*; (*of dress, horse*) encolure *f*.

necklace ['nekləs] collier *m*.

nectarine ['nektəriːn] nectarine *f*.

need [niːd] **1** *n* besoin *m*; **to be in n. of** avoir besoin de; **there's no n. (for you) to do** tu n'as pas besoin de faire; **if n. be** si besoin est. **2** *vt* avoir besoin de; **her hair needs cutting** il faut qu'elle se fasse couper les cheveux; **n. he wait?** a-t-il besoin d'attendre?; **I needn't have rushed** ce n'était pas la peine de me presser.

needle ['niːd(ə)l] aiguille *f*; (*of record player*) saphir *m*.

needlessly *adv* inutilement.

needlework couture *f*; (*object*) ouvrage *m*.

negative ['negətɪv] **1** *a* négatif. **2** *n* (*of photo*) négatif *m*; *Grammar* forme *f* négative.

neglect [nɪ'glekt] *vt* (*person, work, duty etc*) négliger; (*garden, car*) ne pas s'occuper de.

neglected *a* (*appearance*) négligé; (*garden, house*) mal tenu; **to feel n.** sentir qu'on vous néglige.

negligence négligence *f*.

negligent ['neglɪdʒənt] *a* négligent.

negotiate [nɪ'gəʊʃɪeɪt] *vti* (*discuss*) négocier.

negoti'ation négociation *f*.

neigh [neɪ] *vi* (*of horse*) hennir.

neighbour ['neɪbər] (*Am* **neighbor**) voisin, -ine *mf*.

neighbourhood quartier *m*; (*neighbours*) voisinage *m*.

neighbouring *a* voisin.

neither ['naɪðər, *Am* 'niːðər] **1** *adv* **n....nor** ni...ni; **he n. sings nor dances** il ne chante ni ne danse. **2** *conj* (*not either*) **n. shall I go** je n'y irai pas non plus; **n. do I, n. can I** *etc* (ni) moi non plus. **3** *a* **n. boy (came)** aucun des deux garçons (n'est venu). **4** *pron* **n. (of them)** ni l'un(e) ni l'autre.

neon ['niːɒn] *a* (*lighting etc*) au néon.

nephew ['nevju:, 'nefju:] neveu *m*.

nerve [nɜ:v] nerf *m*; (*courage*) courage *m* (**to do** de faire); (*calm*) sang-froid *m*; (*cheek*) culot *m* (**to do** de faire); **you get on my nerves** tu me tapes sur les nerfs.

nervous *a* (*tense*) nerveux; (*worried*) inquiet (**about** de); (*uneasy*) mal à l'aise; **to be** *or* **feel n.** (*before exam etc*) avoir le trac.

nest [nest] nid *m*.

net [net] **1** *n* filet *m*. **2** *a* (*profit*, *weight etc*) net (*f* nette).

netting (**wire**) **n.** grillage *m*.

nettle ['net(ə)l] ortie *f*.

network ['netwɜ:k] réseau *m*.

neutral ['nju:trəl] **1** *a* neutre. **2** *n* **in n.** (**gear**) au point mort.

never ['nevər] *adv* (ne...) jamais; **she n. lies** elle ne ment jamais; **n. again** plus jamais.

never-'ending *a* interminable.

neverthe'less *adv* néanmoins.

new [nju:] *a* nouveau (*f* nouvelle); (*brand-new*) neuf (*f* neuve); **a n. glass**/*etc* (*different*) un autre verre/*etc*; **what's n.?** *Fam* quoi de neuf?; **a n.-born baby** un nouveau-né, une nouveau-née.

newcomer nouveau-venu *m*, nouvelle-venue *f*.

newly *adv* (*recently*) nouvellement.

news [nju:z] nouvelle(s) *f*(*pl*); (*in the media*) informations *fpl*; **sports n.** (*newspaper column*) chronique *f* sportive; **a piece of n., some n.** une nouvelle; (*in the media*) une information.

newsagent marchand, -ande *mf* de journaux.

news flash flash *m*.

newsletter bulletin *m*.

newspaper journal *m*.

next [nekst] **1** *a* prochain; (*room*, *house*) d'à-côté; (*following*) suivant; **n. month** (*in the future*) le mois prochain; **the n. day** le lendemain; **the n. morning** le lendemain matin; **(by) this time n. week** d'ici (à) la semaine prochaine; **to live n. door** habiter à côté (**to** de); **n.-door neighbour** voisin *m* d'à-côté. **2** *n* suivant, -ante *mf*. **3** *adv* (*afterwards*) ensuite; (*now*) maintenant; **when you come n.** la prochaine fois que tu viendras. **4** *prep* **n. to** (*beside*) à côté de.

NHS [eneɪtʃ'es] *abbr* (*National Health Service*) = la Sécurité Sociale.

nib [nɪb] (*of pen*) plume *f*.

nibble ['nɪb(ə)l] *vti* (*eat*) grignoter; (*bite*) mordiller.

nice [naɪs] *a* (*pleasant*) agréable; (*pretty*) joli; (*kind*) gentil (**to** avec); **it's n. here** c'est bien ici; **n. and easy**/*etc* (*very*) bien facile/*etc*.

nicely *adv* agréablement; (*kindly*) gentiment.

nickel ['nɪk(ə)l] (*coin*) *Am* pièce *f* de cinq cents.
nickname ['nɪkneɪm] surnom *m*.
niece [niːs] nièce *f*.
night [naɪt] nuit *f*; (*evening*) soir *m*; **last n.** (*evening*) hier soir; (*night*) la nuit dernière; **to have an early/late n.** se coucher tôt/tard; **to have a good night('s sleep)** bien dormir.
nightclub boîte *f* de nuit.
nightdress, nightgown, *Fam* **nightie** chemise *f* de nuit.
nightingale ['naɪtɪŋgeɪl] rossignol *m*.
nightmare cauchemar *m*.
nighttime nuit *f*.
night watchman veilleur *m* de nuit.
nil [nɪl] zéro *m*.
nine [naɪn] *a* & *n* neuf (*m*).
nine'teen *a* & *n* dix-neuf (*m*).
ninetieth *a* & *n* quatre-vingt-dixième (*mf*).
ninety *a* & *n* quatre-vingt-dix (*m*).
ninth *a* & *n* neuvième (*mf*).
nip [nɪp] *vt* pincer.
nip in/out (*dash*) *Fam* entrer/sortir un instant.
nipple ['nɪp(ə)l] bout *m* de sein.
nip round to s.o. *Fam* faire un saut chez qn.
nitrogen ['naɪtrədʒən] azote *m*.
no [nəʊ] **1** *adv* & *n* non (*m inv*); **no more than ten**/*etc* pas plus de dix/*etc*; **no more time**/*etc* plus de temps/etc. **2** *a* aucun(e); pas de; **I have no idea** je n'ai aucune idée; **no child came** aucun enfant n'est venu; **I have no time**/*etc* je n'ai pas de temps/*etc*; **of no importance**/*etc* sans importance/*etc*; **'no smoking'** 'défense de fumer'; **no way!** *Fam* pas question!; **no one = nobody.**
noble ['nəʊb(ə)l] *a* noble.
nobody ['nəʊbɒdɪ] *pron* (ne...) personne; **n. came** personne n'est venu; **n.!** personne!
nod [nɒd] **1** *vti* **to n. (one's head)** faire un signe de tête. **2** *n* signe *m* de tête.
nod off s'assoupir.
noise [nɔɪz] bruit *m*; (*of bell, drum*) son *m*; **to make a n.** faire du bruit.
noisily *adv* bruyamment.
noisy *a* bruyant.
nominate ['nɒmɪneɪt] *vt* (*appoint*) nommer.
non- [nɒn] *prefix* non-.
none [nʌn] *pron* aucun(e) *mf*; (*in filling out a form*) néant; **she has**

n. (at all) elle n'en a pas (du tout); **n. (at all) came** pas un(e) seul(e) n'est venu(e); **n. of the cake**/*etc* pas une seule partie du gâteau/*etc*; **n. of the trees**/*etc* aucun des arbres/*etc*.

nonethe'less *adv* néanmoins.

non-ex'istent *a* inexistant.

non-'fiction (*in library*) ouvrages *mpl* généraux.

nonsense ['nɒnsəns] absurdités *fpl*; **that's n.** c'est absurde.

non-'smoker non-fumeur, -euse *mf*.

non-'stick *a* (*pan*) anti-adhésif.

non-'stop 1 *a* sans arrêt; (*train, flight*) direct. **2** *adv* sans arrêt; (*to fly*) sans escale.

noodles ['nuːd(ə)lz] *npl* nouilles *fpl*; (*in soup*) vermicelle(s) *m*(*pl*).

noon [nuːn] midi *m*; **at n.** à midi.

nor [nɔːr] *conj* ni; **neither you n. me** ni toi ni moi; **she neither drinks n. smokes** elle ne fume ni ne boit; **n. do I, n. can I** *etc* (ni) moi non plus.

normal ['nɔːm(ə)l] **1** *a* normal. **2** *n* **above/below n.** au-dessus/au-dessous de la normale.

normally *adv* normalement.

north [nɔːθ] **1** *n* nord *m*; **(to the) n. of** au nord de. **2** *a* (*coast*) nord *inv*. **3** *adv* au nord.

North American *a* & *n* nord-américain, -aine (*mf*).

northbound *a* en direction du nord.

north-'east *n* & *a* nord-est *m* & *a inv*.

northern ['nɔːðən] *a* (*coast*) nord *inv*; (*town*) du nord.

northerner habitant, -ante *mf* du Nord.

northward(s) ['nɔːθwəd(z)] *a* & *adv* vers le nord.

north-'west *n* & *a* nord-ouest *m* & *a inv*.

Norwegian [nɔː'wiːdʒən] *a* & *n* norvégien, -ienne (*mf*).

nose [nəʊz] nez *m*; **her n. is bleeding** elle saigne du nez.

nosebleed saignement *m* de nez.

nostril ['nɒstr(ə)l] (*of person*) narine *f*; (*horse*) naseau *m*.

nos(e)y ['nəʊzɪ] *a* indiscret.

not [nɒt] *adv* (ne...) pas; **he's n. there, he isn't there** il n'est pas là; **n. yet** pas encore; **why n.?** pourquoi pas?; **n. one reply**/*etc* pas une seule réponse/*etc*; **n. at all** pas du tout; (*after 'thank you'*) je vous en prie. ■ non; **I think/hope n.** je pense/j'espère que non; **isn't she?, don't you?** *etc* non?

note [nəʊt] **1** *n* (*comment, musical etc*) note *f*; (*banknote*) billet *m*; (*message*) petit mot *m*; **to make a n. of** prendre note de. **2** *vt* noter.

notebook carnet *m*; (*for school*) cahier *m*.

note down (*word etc*) noter.

notepad bloc-notes *m*.
notepaper papier *m* à lettres.
nothing ['nʌθɪŋ] *pron* (ne...) rien; **he knows n.** il ne sait rien; **n. to eat**/*etc* rien à manger/*etc*; **n. big**/*etc* rien de grand/*etc*; **n. much** pas grand-chose; **I've got n. to do with it** je n'y suis pour rien; **to come to n.** (*of efforts etc*) ne rien donner; **for n.** (*in vain*, *free of charge*) pour rien; **to have n. on** être tout nu.
notice ['nəʊtɪs] **1** *n* avis *m*, (*sign*) pancarte *f*; (*poster*) affiche *f*; **to give (in) one's n.** donner sa démission; **to give s.o. (advance) n.** avertir qn (**of** de); **to take n.** faire attention (**of** à); **until further n.** jusqu'à nouvel ordre. **2** *vt* remarquer (**that** que).
noticeable *a* visible.
notice board tableau *m* d'affichage.
notifi'cation avis *m*.
notify ['nəʊtɪfaɪ] *vt* avertir (**s.o. of sth** qn de qch).
notion ['nəʊʃ(ə)n] idée *f*.
nought [nɔːt] zéro *m*.
noun [naʊn] nom *m*.
nourishing ['nʌrɪʃɪŋ] *a* nourrissant.
novel ['nɒv(ə)l] **1** *n* roman *m*. **2** *a* nouveau (*f* nouvelle).
novelist romancier, -ière *mf*.
November [nəʊ'vembər] novembre *m*.
now [naʊ] **1** *adv* maintenant; **just n., right n.** en ce moment; **I saw her just n.** je l'ai vue à l'instant; **for n.** pour le moment; **from n. on** désormais; **before n.** avant; **n. and then** de temps à autre; **n. (then)!** bon!; (*telling s.o. off*) allons! **2** *conj* **n. (that)** maintenant que.
nowadays *adv* aujourd'hui.
nowhere ['nəʊweər] *adv* nulle part; **n. near the house** loin de la maison; **n. near enough** loin d'être assez.
nozzle ['nɒz(ə)l] (*of hose*) jet *m*.
nuclear ['njuːklɪər] *a* nucléaire.
nude [njuːd] **in the n.** (tout) nu.
nudge [nʌdʒ] **1** *vt* pousser du coude. **2** *n* coup *m* de coude.
nuisance ['njuːs(ə)ns] embêtement *m*; (*person*) peste *f*; **that's a n.** c'est embêtant.
numb [nʌm] *a* (*hand etc*) engourdi.
number ['nʌmbər] **1** *n* nombre *m*; (*of page, house, telephone etc*) numéro *m*; **a n. of** un certain nombre de. **2** *vt* (*page etc*) numéroter.
number plate plaque *f* d'immatriculation.
numeral ['njuːm(ə)rəl] chiffre *m*.
numerous *a* nombreux.

nun [nʌn] religieuse *f*.
nurse [nɜːs] **1** *n* infirmière *f*; **(male) n.** infirmier *m*. **2** *vt* (*look after*) soigner.
nursery ['nɜːsərɪ] chambre *f* d'enfants; (*for plants*) pépinière *f*; **(day) n.** (*school*) crèche *f*, garderie *f*.
nursery rhyme chanson *f* enfantine.
nursery school école *f* maternelle.
nut[1] [nʌt] (*walnut*) noix *f*; (*hazelnut*) noisette *f*; (*peanut*) cacah(o)uète *f*.
nut[2] (*for bolt*) écrou *m*.
nutcracker(s) *n*(*pl*) casse-noix *m inv*.
nylon ['naɪlɒn] **1** *n* nylon *m*; **nylons** bas *mpl* nylon. **2** *a* (*shirt etc*) en nylon.

O

oak [əʊk] chêne *m*.
OAP [əʊeɪ'piː] *abbr* (*old age pensioner*) retraité, -ée *mf*.
oar [ɔːr] aviron *m*.
oats [əʊts] *npl* avoine *f*; **(porridge) o.** flocons *mpl* d'avoine.
obedience obéissance *f* (**to** à).
obedient [ə'biːdɪənt] *a* obéissant.
obey [ə'beɪ] **1** *vt* obéir à (*qn*); **to be obeyed** être obéi. **2** *vi* obéir.
object¹ ['ɒbdʒɪkt] (*thing, aim*) objet *m*; *Grammar* complément *m* (d'objet).
object² [əb'dʒekt] *vi* **to o. to sth/s.o.** désapprouver qch/qn; **I o. to you(r) doing that** ça me gêne que tu fasses ça.
objection [əb'dʒekʃ(ə)n] objection *f*.
objective [əb'dʒektɪv] (*aim*) objectif *m*.
obligation [ɒblɪ'geɪʃ(ə)n] obligation *f*.
oblige [ə'blaɪdʒ] *vt* (*compel*) contraindre (**s.o. to do** qn à faire); (*help*) rendre service à.
obliging *a* serviable.
oblique [ə'bliːk] *a* oblique.
obscene [əb'siːn] *a* obscène.
observant *a* observateur.
obser'vation observation *f*.
observe [əb'zɜːv] *vt* observer; (*say*) remarquer (**that** que).
obstacle ['ɒbstək(ə)l] obstacle *m*.
obstinate ['ɒbstɪnət] *a* (*person, resistance*) obstiné.
obstruct [əb'strʌkt] *vt* (*block*) boucher; (*hinder*) gêner.
obtain [əb'teɪn] *vt* obtenir.
obtainable *a* disponible.
obvious ['ɒbvɪəs] *a* évident (**that** que).
obviously *adv* évidemment.
occasion [ə'keɪʒ(ə)n] (*time, opportunity*) occasion *f*; (*event, ceremony*) événement *m*.
occasional *a* (*odd*) qu'on fait, voit *etc* de temps en temps; **she drinks the o. whisky** elle boit un whisky de temps en temps.
occasionally *adv* de temps en temps.
occupant occupant, -ante *mf*.
occu'pation (*activity*) occupation *f*; (*job*) emploi *m*; (*trade*) métier *m*; (*profession*) profession *f*.
occupy ['ɒkjʊpaɪ] *vt* occuper; **to keep oneself occupied** s'occuper (**doing** à faire).
occur [ə'kɜːr] *vi* (*happen*) avoir lieu; (*be found*) se rencontrer; **it**

occurs to me that... il me vient à l'esprit que...

occurrence [ə'kʌrəns] (*event*) événement *m*.

ocean ['əʊʃ(ə)n] océan *m*.

o'clock [ə'klɒk] *adv* **(it's) three o'c.**/*etc* (il est) trois heures/*etc*.

October [ɒk'təʊbər] octobre *m*.

octopus ['ɒktəpəs] pieuvre *f*.

odd [ɒd] *a* (*strange*) bizarre. ▮ (*number*) impair. ▮ (*left over*) **I have an o. penny** il me reste un penny; **a few o. stamps** quelques timbres (qui restent); **the o. man out** l'exception *f*; **sixty o.** soixante et quelques; **an o. glove**/*etc* un gant/*etc* dépareillé. ▮ = **occasional**; **o. jobs** menus travaux *mpl*; **o. job man** homme *m* à tout faire.

oddly *adv* bizarrement.

odds [ɒdz] *npl* (*in betting*) cote *f*; (*chances*) chances *fpl*; **at o.** en désaccord (**with** avec); **o. and ends** des petites choses.

odour ['əʊdər] (*Am* **odor**) odeur *f*.

of [əv, *stressed* ɒv] *prep* de, d' (de + le = du, de + les = des); **of the table** de la table; **of a book** d'un livre; **she has a lot of it** *or* **of them** elle en a beaucoup; **a friend of his** un ami à lui; **there are ten of us** nous sommes dix; **that's nice of you** c'est gentil de ta part.

off [ɒf] **1** *adv* (*gone away*) parti; (*light, radio etc*) éteint; (*tap, Am faucet*) fermé; (*detached*) détaché; (*removed*) enlevé; (*cancelled*) annulé; (*not fit to eat or drink*) mauvais; (*milk, meat*) tourné; **2 km o.** à 2 km (d'ici *or* de là); **to be** *ou* **go o.** (*leave*) partir; **a day o.** un jour de congé; **time o.** du temps libre; **5% o.** une réduction de 5%; **hands o.!** pas touche!; **to be better o.** être mieux. **2** *prep* (*from*) de; (*distant*) éloigné de; **to get o. the bus**/*etc* descendre du bus/*etc*; **to take sth o. the table**/*etc* prendre qch sur la table/*etc*; **o. Dover** au large de Douvres.

off-'colour *a* (*ill*) patraque.

offence [ə'fens] (*crime*) délit *m*; **to take o.** s'offenser (**at** de).

offend *vt* froisser (*qn*); **to be offended (at)** se froisser (de).

offensive [ə'fensɪv] *a* (*words etc*) insultant (**to s.o.** pour qn); **o. to s.o.** (*of person*) insultant avec qn.

offer ['ɒfər] **1** *n* offre *f*; **on (special) o.** (*in shop*) en promotion. **2** *vt* offrir (**to do** de faire).

off'hand **1** *a* (*abrupt*) brusque, impoli. **2** *adv* (*to say, know etc*) comme ça.

office ['ɒfɪs] (*room*) bureau *m*; (*post*) fonction *f*; **head o.** siège *m* central; **o. block** immeuble *m* de bureaux.

officer ['ɒfɪsər] (*in the army etc*) officier *m*; **(police) o.** agent *m* (de police).

official [ə'fɪʃ(ə)l] **1** *a* officiel. **2** *n* (*civil servant*) fonctionnaire *mf*.

officially *adv* officiellement.
off-licence magasin *m* de vins et de spiritueux.
often ['ɒf(t)ən] *adv* souvent; **how o.?** combien de fois?; **how o. do they run?** (*train etc*) il y en a tous les combien?; **every so o.** de temps en temps.
oh! [əʊ] *int* oh!, ah!; **oh yes!** mais oui!; **oh yes?** ah oui?
oil [ɔɪl] **1** *n* huile *f*; (*extracted from ground*) pétrole *m*; (*fuel*) mazout *m*. **2** *vt* (*machine*) graisser.
oilcan burette *f*.
oil change (*in vehicle*) vidange *f*.
ointment ['ɔɪntmənt] pommade *f*.
OK, okay [əʊ'keɪ] *see* **all right**.
old [əʊld] *a* vieux (*f* vieille); (*former*) ancien; **how o. is he?** quel âge a-t-il?; **he's ten years o.** il a dix ans; **he's older than me** il est plus âgé que moi; **an older son** un fils aîné; **the oldest son** le fils aîné; **o. man** vieillard *m*; **o. woman** vieille femme *f*; **to get** *or* **grow old(er)** vieillir; **o. age** vieillesse *f*.
old-'fashioned *a* démodé; (*person*) rétro *inv*.
olive ['ɒlɪv] olive *f*; **o. oil** huile *f* d'olive.
Olympic [ə'lɪmpɪk] *a* (*games etc*) olympique.
omelet(te) ['ɒmlɪt] omelette *f*; **cheese**/*etc* **o.** omelette au fromage/*etc*.
on [ɒn] **1** *prep* (*position*) sur; **to put on (to)** mettre sur. ▮ (*about*) sur; **to speak on** parler sur. ▮ (*manner, means*) **on foot** à pied; **on the train**/*etc* dans le train/*etc*; **to be on** (*course*) suivre; (*salary*) toucher; (*team*) être membre de; **to keep** *or* **stay on** (*path etc*) suivre. ▮ (*time*) **on Monday** lundi; **on Mondays** le lundi; **on May 3rd** le 3 mai. ▮ (+ *present participle*) en; **on seeing this** en voyant ceci. **2** *adv* (*ahead*) en avant; (*in progress*) en cours; (*lid, brake*) mis; (*light, radio*) allumé; (*gas, tap, Am faucet*) ouvert; **on (and on)** sans cesse; **to play**/*etc* **on** continuer à jouer/*etc*; **what's on?** (*television*) qu'y a-t-il à la télé?; (*cinema etc*) qu'est-ce qu'on joue?; **from then on** à partir de là.
once [wʌns] **1** *adv* une fois; (*formerly*) autrefois; **o. a month** une fois par mois; **o. again, o. more** encore une fois; **at o.** tout de suite; **all at o.** tout à coup; (*at the same time*) à la fois. **2** *conj* une fois que.
one [wʌn] **1** *a* un, une; **o. man** un homme; **o. woman** une femme; **page o.** la page un; **twenty-o.** vingt-et-un. ▮ (*only*) seul; **my o. (and only) aim** mon seul (et unique) but. ▮ (*same*) même; **in the o. bus** dans le même bus. **2** *pron* un, une; **do you want o.?** en veux-tu (un)?; **o. of them** l'un d'eux, l'une d'elles; **a big**/*etc* **o.** un grand/*etc*; **that o.** celui-là, celle-là; **the o. who** *or* **which** celui *or* celle qui;

another o. un(e) autre. ■ (*impersonal*) on; **o. knows** on sait; **it helps o.** ça nous *or* vous aide; **one's family** sa famille.
one'self *pron* soi-même; (*reflexive*) se, s'.
one-'way *a* (*street*) à sens unique; (*ticket*) simple.
onion ['ʌnjən] oignon *m*.
onlooker ['ɒnlʊkər] spectateur, -trice *mf*.
only ['əʊnlɪ] **1** *a* seul; **the o. one** le seul, la seule; **an o. son** un fils unique. **2** *adv* seulement, ne...que; **I o. have ten** je n'en ai que dix, j'en ai dix seulement; **not o.** non seulement; **I have o. just seen it** je viens tout juste de le voir; **o. he knows** lui seul le sait. **3** *conj* (*but*) *Fam* seulement.
onto ['ɒntuː, *unstressed* 'ɒntə] *prep* = **on to.**
onward(s) ['ɒnwəd(z)] *adv* en avant; **from that time o.** à partir de là.
opaque [əʊ'peɪk] *a* opaque.
open ['əʊpən] **1** *a* ouvert; (*ticket*) open *inv*; **wide o.** grand ouvert. **2** *n* **(out) in the o.** en plein air. **3** *vt* ouvrir. **4** *vi* (*of flower*, *door*, *eyes etc*) s'ouvrir; (*of shop*, *office*, *person*) ouvrir.
open-'air *a* (*pool*, *market etc*) en plein air.
opening ouverture *f*; (*career prospect*) débouché *m*.
openly *adv* ouvertement.
openness franchise *f*.
open out 1 *vt* ouvrir. **2** *vi* s'ouvrir; (*widen*) s'élargir.
open up 1 *vt* ouvrir. **2** *vi* s'ouvrir; (*open the door*) ouvrir.
opera ['ɒprə] opéra *m*.
operate ['ɒpəreɪt] **1** *vi* (*of surgeon*) opérer (**on s.o.** qn, **for** de); (*of machine etc*) fonctionner; (*proceed*) opérer. **2** *vt* faire fonctionner; (*business*) gérer.
ope'ration opération *f*; (*working*) fonctionnement *m*.
operator (*on phone*) standardiste *mf*.
opinion [ə'pɪnjən] opinion *f*, avis *m*; **in my o.** à mon avis.
opponent [ə'pəʊnənt] adversaire *mf*.
opportunity [ɒpə'tjuːnɪtɪ] occasion *f* (**to do** de faire); **opportunities** (*prospects*) perspectives *fpl*.
oppose [ə'pəʊz] *vt* s'opposer à.
opposed *a* opposé (**to** à).
opposing *a* (*team*) opposé.
opposite ['ɒpəzɪt] **1** *a* (*direction*, *opinion etc*) opposé; (*house*) d'en face. **2** *adv* (*to sit etc*) en face. **3** *prep* **o. (to)** en face de. **4** *n* **the o.** le contraire.
oppo'sition opposition *f* (**to** à).
opt [ɒpt] *vi* **to o. for sth** décider pour qch.

optician [ɒp'tɪʃ(ə)n] opticien, -ienne *mf*.
optimist ['ɒptɪmɪst] **to be an o.** être optimiste.
opti'mistic *a* optimiste.
option (*choice*) choix *m*.
optional *a* facultatif.
or [ɔːr] *conj* ou; **he doesn't drink or smoke** il ne boit ni ne fume.
oral ['ɔːrəl] **1** *a* oral. **2** *n* (*exam*) oral *m*.
orange ['ɒrɪndʒ] **1** *n* (*fruit*) orange *f*; **o. juice** jus *m* d'orange. **2** *a* & *n* (*colour*) orange *a* & *m inv*.
orangeade orangeade *f*.
orbit ['ɔːbɪt] orbite *f*.
orchard ['ɔːtʃəd] verger *m*.
orchestra ['ɔːkɪstrə] orchestre *m*.
ordeal [ɔː'diːl] épreuve *f*.
order ['ɔːdər] **1** *n* (*command, arrangement*) ordre *m*; (*purchase*) commande; **in o.** (*passport etc*) en règle; **in o. to do** pour faire; **in o. that** pour que (+ *subjunctive*), **out of o.** (*machine*) en panne; (*telephone*) en dérangement. **2** *vt* ordonner (**s.o. to do** à qn de faire); (*meal, goods etc*) commander; (*taxi*) appeler. **3** *vi* (*in café etc*) commander.
order s.o. around commander qn.
ordinary ['ɔːd(ə)nrɪ] *a* (*usual, commonplace*) ordinaire; (*average*) moyen; **it's out of the o.** ça sort de l'ordinaire.
ore [ɔːr] minerai *m*.
organ ['ɔːgən] (*in body*) organe *m*; (*instrument*) orgue *m*, orgues *fpl*.
organic [ɔː'gænɪk] *a* (*vegetables etc*) biologique.
organi'zation organisation *f*.
organize ['ɔːgənaɪz] *vt* organiser.
organizer organisateur, -trice *mf*.
oriental [ɔːrɪ'ent(ə)l] *a* oriental.
origin ['ɒrɪdʒɪn] origine *f*.
original [ə'rɪdʒɪn(ə)l] **1** *a* (*idea, artist etc*) original; (*first*) premier; (*copy, version*) original. **2** *n* (*document etc*) original *m*.
origi'nality originalité *f*.
originally *adv* (*at first*) au départ.
ornament ['ɔːnəmənt] (*on dress etc*) ornement *m*; (*vase etc*) bibelot *m*.
orphan ['ɔːf(ə)n] orphelin, -ine *mf*.
orphanage orphelinat *m*.
ostrich ['ɒstrɪtʃ] autruche *f*.
other ['ʌðər] **1** *a* autre; **o. doctors** d'autres médecins; **the o. one**

l'autre *mf*. **2** *pron* **the o.** l'autre *mf*; **(some) others** d'autres; **some do, others don't** les uns le font, les autres ne le font pas. **3** *adv* **o. than** autrement que.

otherwise *adv* autrement.

ouch! [aʊtʃ] *int* aïe!

ought [ɔːt] *v aux* (*obligation*, *desirability*) devoir; **you o. to leave** tu devrais partir; **I o. to have done it** j'aurais dû le faire; **he said he o. to stay** il a dit qu'il devait rester. ▮ (*probability*) devoir; **it o. to be ready** ça devrait être prêt.

ounce [aʊns] once *f* (= *28,35 g*).

our [aʊər] *poss a* notre, *pl* nos.

ours *pron* le nôtre, la nôtre, *pl* les nôtres; **this book is o.** ce livre est à nous *or* est le nôtre.

our'selves *pron* nous-mêmes; (*reflexive* & *after prep*) nous.

out [aʊt] **1** *adv* (*outside*) dehors; (*not at home etc*) sorti; (*light*, *fire*) éteint; (*news*, *secret*) connu; (*book*) publié; (*eliminated from game*) éliminé; **to be** *or* **go o. a lot** sortir beaucoup; **to have a day o.** sortir pour la journée; **the tide's o.** la marée est basse; **o. there** là-bas. **2** *prep* **o. of** en dehors de; (*danger*, *water*) hors de; (*without*) sans; **o. of pity**/*etc* par pitié/*etc*; **o. of the window** par la fenêtre; **to drink/take/copy o. of sth** boire/prendre/copier dans qch; **made o. of** (*wood etc*) fait en; **to make sth o. of a box**/*etc* faire qch avec une boîte/*etc*; **she's o. of town** elle n'est pas en ville; **four o. of five** quatre sur cinq; **to feel o. of place** ne pas se sentir intégré.

outbreak ['aʊtbreɪk] (*of war*) début *m*; (*of violence*) éruption *f*.

outburst ['aʊtbɜːst] (*of anger*, *joy*) explosion *f*.

outcome ['aʊtkʌm] résultat *m*.

outdated [aʊt'deɪtɪd] *a* démodé.

outdo* [aʊt'duː] *vt* surpasser (**in** en).

outdoor ['aʊtdɔːr] *a* (*pool*, *market*) en plein air; **o. clothes** tenue *f* pour sortir.

out'doors *adv* dehors.

outer ['aʊtər] *a* extérieur.

outer space l'espace *m* (cosmique).

outfit ['aʊtfɪt] (*clothes*) costume *m*; (*for woman*) toilette *f*; (*toy*) panoplie *f* (*de cow-boy etc*); **ski**/*etc* **o.** tenue *f* de ski/*etc*.

outing ['aʊtɪŋ] sortie *f*, excursion *f*.

outlet ['aʊtlet] (*market for goods*) débouché *m*.

outline ['aʊtlaɪn] (*shape*) contour *m*.

outlook ['aʊtlʊk] *n inv* (*for future*) perspective(s) *f*(*pl*); (*point of view*) perspective *f* (**on** sur).

outnumber [aʊt'nʌmbər] *vt* être plus nombreux que.

out-of-'date *a* (*expired*) périmé; (*old-fashioned*) démodé.
out-of-'doors *adv* dehors.
output ['aʊtpʊt] rendement *m*; (*computer data*) données *fpl* de sortie.
outrage ['aʊtreɪdʒ] **1** *n* scandale *m*; (*anger*) indignation *f*. **2** *vt* **outraged by sth** indigné de qch.
out'rageous (*shocking*) scandaleux.
outright [aʊt'raɪt] *adv* (*to say, tell*) franchement.
outside [aʊt'saɪd] **1** *adv* (au) dehors; **to go o.** sortir. **2** *prep* en dehors de. **3** *n* extérieur *m*. **4** *a* ['aʊtsaɪd] extérieur; **the o. lane** la voie de droite *or Am* de gauche.
outskirts ['aʊtskɜːts] *npl* banlieue *f*.
outstanding [aʊt'stændɪŋ] *a* remarquable; (*problem*) non réglé; (*debt*) impayé.
outward ['aʊtwəd] *a* (*sign, appearance*) extérieur; **o. journey** *or* **trip** aller *m*.
outward(s) *adv* vers l'extérieur.
oval ['əʊv(ə)l] *a* & *n* ovale (*m*).
oven ['ʌv(ə)n] four *m*.
oven glove gant *m* isolant.
over ['əʊvər] **1** *prep* (*on*) sur; (*above*) au-dessus de; (*on the other side of*) de l'autre côté de; **to jump/look/***etc* **o. sth** sauter/regarder/*etc* par-dessus qch; **o. it** (*on*) dessus; (*above*) au-dessus; (*to jump etc*) par-dessus; **to criticize/***etc* **o. sth** (*about*) critiquer/*etc* à propos de qch; **o. the phone** au téléphone; **o. the holidays** pendant les vacances; **o. ten days** (*more than*) plus de dix jours; **men o. sixty** les hommes de plus de soixante ans; **all o. Spain** dans toute l'Espagne; **all o. the carpet** partout sur le tapis. **2** *adv* (*above*) (par-)dessus; **o. here** ici; **o. there** là-bas; **to come** *or* **go o.** (*visit*) passer; **to ask o.** inviter (à venir); **all o.** (*everywhere*) partout; **it's (all) o.** (*finished*) c'est fini; **a kilo or o.** un kilo ou plus; **I have ten o.** il m'en reste dix; **o. and o. (again)** à plusieurs reprises; **o. pleased/***etc* trop content/*etc*.
overall [əʊvər'ɔːl] *a* (*length etc*) total.
'overalls *npl* bleus *mpl* de travail.
overboard ['əʊvəbɔːd] *adv* à la mer.
over'charge to o. s.o. for sth faire payer qch trop cher à qn.
'overcoat pardessus *m*.
over'come *vt* (*problem*) surmonter.
overdo* [əʊvə'duː] *vt* **to o. it** ne pas y aller doucement; **don't o. it!** vas-y doucement!
overdraft ['əʊvədrɑːft] découvert *m*.
over'due *a* (*train etc*) en retard.

over'eat *vi* manger trop.
overex'cited *a* surexcité.
over'flow *vi* (*of river*, *bath etc*) déborder.
over'head *adv* au-dessus.
over'hear *vt* (*pt & pp* **overheard**) surprendre.
over'heat *vi* (*of engine*) chauffer.
over'joyed *a* fou (*f* folle) de joie.
over'lap 1 *vi* se chevaucher. **2** *vt* chevaucher.
over'leaf *adv* au verso.
over'load *vt* surcharger.
over'look *vt* ne pas remarquer; (*forget*) oublier; (*ignore*) passer sur; (*of window etc*) donner sur.
overnight 1 *adv* [əʊvə'naɪt] (pendant) la nuit; **to stay o.** passer la nuit. **2** *a* ['əʊvənaɪt] *a* (*train*) de nuit.
overpass ['əʊvəpæs] (*bridge*) *Am* toboggan *m*.
over'rated *a* surfait.
overseas 1 *adv* [əʊvə'siːz] (*abroad*) à l'étranger. **2** *a* ['əʊvəsiːz] (*visitor etc*) étranger; (*trade*) extérieur.
'oversight oubli *m*.
over'sleep *vi* (*pt & pp* **overslept**) dormir trop longtemps.
over'spend *vi* dépenser trop.
over'take* *vti* (*in vehicle*) dépasser.
'overtime 1 *n* heures *fpl* supplémentaires. **2** *adv* **to work o.** faire des heures supplémentaires.
over'turn *vi* (*of car*, *boat*) se retourner.
over'weight *a* **to be o.** (*of person*) avoir des kilos en trop.
overwhelm [əʊvə'welm] *vt* accabler; **overwhelmed with** (*work*, *offers*) submergé de.
over'work 1 *n* surmenage *m*. **2** *vi* se surmener.
owe [əʊ] *vt* (*money etc*) devoir (**to** à).
owing *prep* **o. to** à cause de.
owl [aʊl] hibou *m* (*pl* hiboux).
own [əʊn] **1** *a* propre; **my o. house** ma propre maison. **2** *pron* **it's my (very) o.** c'est à moi (tout seul); **a house of his o.** sa propre maison; **(all) on one's o.** tout seul; **to get one's o. back** se venger. **3** *vt* posséder; **who owns this ball**/*etc*? à qui appartient cette balle/*etc*?
owner propriétaire *mf*.
own up avouer (**to sth** qch).
ox, *pl* **oxen** [ɒks, 'ɒks(ə)n] bœuf *m*.
oxygen ['ɒksɪdʒ(ə)n] oxygène *m*.
oyster ['ɔɪstər] huître *f*.

P

pa [pɑː] *Fam* papa *m*.
pace [peɪs] pas *m*.
Pacific [pə'sɪfɪk] **1** *a* pacifique. **2** *n* **the P.** le Pacifique.
pacifier ['pæsɪfaɪər] *Am* (*of baby*) sucette *f*.
pack [pæk] **1** *n* paquet *m*; (*rucksack*) sac *m* (à dos); (*of wolves*) meute *f*; (*of cards*) jeu *m*; (*of lies*) tissu *m*. **2** *vt* (*fill*) remplir (**with** de); (*suitcase*) faire; (*object into box etc*) emballer; (*object into suitcase*) mettre dans sa valise.
pack (down) (*crush*) tasser.
package ['pækɪdʒ] paquet *m*; (*computer programs*) progiciel *m*.
package tour voyage *m* organisé.
packaging emballage *m*.
pack away (*tidy away*) ranger.
packed [pækt] *a* (*bus etc*) bourré.
packed lunch panier-repas *m*.
packet ['pækɪt] paquet *m*.
pack sth in *Fam* laisser tomber qch.
packing emballage *m*.
pack into **1** *vt* (*cram*) entasser dans. **2** *vi* (*crowd into*) s'entasser dans.
pack up **1** *vt* (*put into box*) emballer; (*give up*) *Fam* laisser tomber. **2** *vi* *Fam* (*stop*) s'arrêter; (*of machine*) tomber en panne.
pad [pæd] (*of cloth etc*) tampon *m*; (*for writing etc*) bloc *m*.
padded *a* (*armchair etc*) rembourré.
paddle ['pæd(ə)l] **1** *vi* (*dip one's feet*) se mouiller les pieds. **2** *n* (*pole*) pagaie *f*. **3** *vt* **to p. a canoe** pagayer.
paddling pool (*small, inflatable*) piscine *f* gonflable.
padlock cadenas *m*; (*on bicycle*) antivol *m*.
page [peɪdʒ] (*of book etc*) page *f*; **p. (boy)** (*in hotel*) groom.
pain [peɪn] douleur *f*; (*grief*) peine *f*; **pains** (*efforts*) efforts *mpl*; **to be in p.** souffrir; **to take (great) pains to do** se donner du mal à faire.
painful *a* douloureux.
pain-killer calmant *m*; **on painkillers** sous calmants.
paint [peɪnt] **1** *n* peinture *f*; **paints** (*in box, tube*) couleurs *fpl*. **2** *vti* peindre; **to p. sth blue**/*etc* peindre qch en bleu/*etc*.
paintbrush pinceau *m*.
painter peintre *m*.
painting (*activity, picture*) peinture *f*.
paint stripper décapant *m*.

pair [peər] (*two*) paire *f*; (*man and woman*) couple *m*.
pajamas [pə'dʒɑːməz] *npl Am* = **pyjamas.**
Pakistani *a* & *n* pakistanais, -aise (*mf*).
pal [pæl] *Fam* copain *m*, copine *f*.
palace ['pælɪs] palais *m*.
palate ['pælɪt] (*in mouth*) palais *m*.
pale [peɪl] *a* pâle.
palette ['pælɪt] (*of artist*) palette *f*.
palm [pɑːm] (*of hand*) paume *f*; **p. (tree)** palmier *m*; **p. (leaf)** palme *f*.
pamphlet ['pæmflɪt] brochure *f*.
pan [pæn] casserole *f*; (*for frying*) poêle *f*.
pancake crêpe *f*.
pane [peɪn] vitre *f*.
panel ['pæn(ə)l] (*of door etc*) panneau *m*; (*of judges*) jury *m*; (*of experts*) groupe *m*; **(control) p.** console *f*.
panic ['pænɪk] **1** *n* panique *f*. **2** *vi* s'affoler.
pant [pænt] *vi* haleter.
panties ['pæntɪz] *npl* (*female*) slip *m*; (*longer*) culotte *f*.
pantomime ['pæntəmaɪm] spectacle *m* de Noël.
pantry ['pæntrɪ] (*larder*) garde-manger *m inv*.
pants [pænts] *npl* (*male*) slip *m*; (*long*) caleçon *m*; (*trousers*) *Am* pantalon *m*.
pantyhose ['pæntɪhəʊz] *Am* collant(s) *m*(*pl*).
paper ['peɪpər] **1** *n* papier *m*; (*newspaper*) journal *m*; (*wallpaper*) papier *m* peint; (*exam*) épreuve *f* (écrite); **brown p.** papier *m* d'emballage; **to put down on p.** mettre par écrit. **2** *a* (*bag, towel etc*) en papier; (*cup, plate*) en carton.
paperback livre *m* de poche.
paper clip trombone *m*.
paper knife coupe-papier *m inv*.
parachute ['pærəʃuːt] parachute *m*.
parade [pə'reɪd] (*procession*) défilé *m*; (*street*) avenue *f*.
paradise ['pærədaɪs] paradis *m*.
paraffin ['pærəfɪn] pétrole *m* (lampant).
paragraph ['pærəgrɑːf] paragraphe *m*; **'new p.'** 'à la ligne'.
parakeet ['pærəkiːt] perruche *f*.
parallel ['pærəlel] *a* parallèle (**with, to** à).
paralyse ['pærəlaɪz] (*Am* **-lyze**) *vt* paralyser.
parasite ['pærəsaɪt] parasite *m*.
parasol ['pærəsɒl] (*over table, on beach*) parasol *m*.
parcel ['pɑːs(ə)l] colis *m*, paquet *m*.

pardon ['pɑːd(ə)n] **1** *n* **I beg your p.** je vous prie de m'excuser; (*not hearing*) vous dites?; **p.?** (*not hearing*) comment?; **p. (me)!** (*sorry*) pardon! **2** *vt* pardonner (**s.o. for sth** qch à qn).

parent ['peərənt] père *m*, mère *f*; **one's parents** ses parents *mpl*.

parish ['pærɪʃ] paroisse *f*; (*civil*) commune *f*.

Parisian [pə'rɪzɪən, *Am* pə'riːʒən] *a* & *n* parisien, -ienne (*mf*).

park [pɑːk] **1** *n* parc *m*. **2** *vt* (*vehicle*) garer. **3** *vi* se garer; (*remain parked*) stationner.

parking stationnement *m*; **'no p.'** 'défense de stationner'.

parking light veilleuse *f*.

parking lot *Am* parking *m*.

parking meter parcmètre *m*.

parking place *or* **space** place *f* de parking.

parking ticket contravention *f*.

parliament ['pɑːləmənt] parlement *m*.

parrot ['pærət] perroquet *m*.

parsley ['pɑːslɪ] persil *m*.

parsnip ['pɑːsnɪp] panais *m*.

part [pɑːt] **1** *n* partie *f*; (*of machine*) pièce *f*; (*of serial*) épisode *m*; (*role*) rôle *m*; **to take p.** participer (**in** à); **in p.** en partie; **for the most p.** dans l'ensemble; **to be a p. of sth** faire partie de qch; **in these parts** dans ces parages. **2** *adv* (*partly*) en partie. **3** *vi* (*of friends etc*) se quitter; (*of married couple*) se séparer.

part exchange reprise *f*; **to take in p. exchange** reprendre.

partial ['pɑːʃəl] *a* partiel; **to be p. to sth** (*fond of*) *Fam* avoir un faible pour qch.

participant participant, -ante *mf*.

participate [pɑː'tɪsɪpeɪt] *vi* participer (**in** à).

partici'pation participation *f*.

participle [pɑː'tɪsɪp(ə)l] *Grammar* participe *m*.

particular [pə'tɪkjʊlər] **1** *a* particulier; (*fussy*) difficile (**about** sur); (*showing care*) méticuleux; **in p.** en particulier. **2** *npl* **particulars** détails *mpl*; **s.o.'s particulars** les coordonnées *fpl* de qn.

particularly *adv* particulièrement.

parting (*in hair*) raie *f*.

partition [pɑː'tɪʃ(ə)n] (*in room*) cloison *f*.

partly *adv* en partie.

partner ['pɑːtnər] partenaire *mf*; (*in business*) associé, -ée *mf*; (**dancing**) **p.** cavalier, -ière *mf*.

partnership association *f*.

partridge ['pɑːtrɪdʒ] perdix *f*.

part-'time *a* & *adv* à temps partiel.

part with sth (*get rid of*) se séparer de qch.

party ['pɑːtɪ] (*formal*) réception *f*; (*with friends*) soirée *f*; (*for birthday*) fête *f*; (*group*) groupe *m*; (*political*) parti *m*.

pass [pɑːs] **1** *n* (*entry permit*) laissez-passer *m inv*; (*over mountains*) col *m*; *Football etc* passe *f*; **to get a p.** (*in exam*) être reçu (**in French**/*etc* en français/*etc*). **2** *vi* passer (**to** à, **through** par); (*overtake*) dépasser; (*in exam*) être reçu (**in French**/*etc* en français/*etc*). **3** *vt* passer (**to** à); (*go past*) passer devant (*immeuble etc*); (*vehicle*) dépasser; (*exam*) être reçu à; **to p. s.o.** (*in street*) croiser qn.

passable ['pɑːsəb(ə)l] *a* (*not bad*) passable; (*road*) praticable.

passage ['pæsɪdʒ] (*of text etc*) passage *m*; (*corridor*) couloir *m*.

passageway (*corridor*) couloir *m*.

pass away (*die*) mourir.

passbook livret *m* de caisse d'épargne.

pass by 1 *vi* passer (à côté). **2** *vt* (*building etc*) passer devant; **to p. by s.o.** (*in street*) croiser qn.

passenger ['pæsɪndʒər] passager, -ère *mf*; (*on train*) voyageur, -euse *mf*.

passer-'by (*pl* **passers-by**) passant, -ante *mf*.

passion ['pæʃ(ə)n] passion *f*.

passionate *a* passionné.

passive ['pæsɪv] **1** *a* passif. **2** *n Grammar* passif *m*.

pass mark (*in exam*) moyenne *f*.

pass off 1 *vi* (*happen*) se passer. **2** *vt* **to p. oneself off as** se faire passer pour.

pass on *vt* (*message etc*) transmettre (**to** à).

pass out (*faint*) s'évanouir.

pass over sth (*ignore*) passer sur qch.

passport passeport *m*.

pass round (*cakes etc*) faire passer.

pass through *vi* passer.

pass up (*chance*) laisser passer.

past [pɑːst] **1** *n* passé *m*; **in the p.** (*formerly*) dans le temps. **2** *a* (*gone by*) passé; (*former*) ancien; **these p. months** ces derniers mois; **in the p. tense** au passé. **3** *prep* (*in front of*) devant; (*after*) après; (*further than*) plus loin que; **p. four o'clock** quatre heures passées. **4** *adv* devant; **to go p.** passer.

pasta ['pæstə] pâtes *fpl*.

paste [peɪst] **1** *n* (*of meat*) pâté *m*; (*of fish*) beurre *m*; (*glue*) colle *f*. **2** *vt* coller.

pasteurized ['pæstəraɪzd] *a* (*milk*) pasteurisé.

pastille ['pæstɪl, *Am* pæ'stiːl] pastille *f*.

pastime ['pɑːstaɪm] passe-temps *m inv*.
pastry ['peɪstrɪ] pâte *f*; (*cake*) pâtisserie *f*.
pasture ['pɑːstʃər] pâturage *m*.
pat [pæt] *vt* (*cheek etc*) tapoter; (*animal*) caresser.
patch [pætʃ] (*for clothes*) pièce *f*; (*over eye*) bandeau *m*; (*of colour*) tache *f*; **cabbage p.** carré *m* de choux; **bad p.** mauvaise période *f*.
patch (up) (*clothing*) rapiécer.
path [pɑːθ] (*pl* **-s** [pɑːðz]) sentier *m*; (*in park*) allée *f*.
pathetic [pə'θetɪk] *a* (*results etc*) lamentable.
pathway sentier *m*.
patience patience *f*; **to lose p.** perdre patience (**with s.o.** avec qn).
patient ['peɪʃ(ə)nt] **1** *a* patient. **2** *n* malade *mf*; (*on doctor's or dentist's list*) patient, -ente *mf*.
patiently *adv* patiemment.
patio ['pætɪəʊ] (*pl* **-os**) patio *m*.
patriotic [pætrɪ'ɒtɪk] *a* patriotique; (*person*) patriote.
patrol [pə'trəʊl] **1** *n* patrouille *f*. **2** *vi* patrouiller. **3** *vt* patrouiller dans.
pattern ['pæt(ə)n] dessin *m*; (*paper model for garment*) patron *m*.
pause [pɔːz] **1** *n* pause *f*; (*in conversation*) silence *m*. **2** *vi* faire une pause; (*hesitate*) hésiter.
paved [peɪvd] *a* pavé.
pavement trottoir *m*; (*roadway*) *Am* chaussée *f*.
pavilion [pə'vɪljən] pavillon *m*.
paving stone pavé *m*.
paw [pɔː] patte *f*.
pawn [pɔːn] *Chess* pion *m*.
pay [peɪ] **1** salaire *m*; (*of workman, soldier*) paie *f*; **p. slip** bulletin *m* de paie. **2** *vt* (*pt & pp* **paid**) (*person, sum*) payer; (*deposit*) verser; (*of investment*) rapporter; (*compliment, visit*) faire (**to** à); **to p. s.o. to do** *or* **for doing** payer qn pour faire; **to p. s.o. for sth** payer qch à qn; **to p. money into one's account** verser de l'argent sur son compte. **3** *vi* payer; **to p. a lot** payer cher.
payable *a* payable; **a cheque** *or Am* **check p. to** un chèque à l'ordre de.
pay back (*person, loan*) rembourser.
pay cheque, *Am* **paycheck** chèque *m* de règlement de salaire.
pay for sth payer qch.
pay in (*cheque, Am check*) verser (**to one's account** sur son compte).
payment paiement *m*; (*of deposit*) versement *m*.
pay off (*debt, person*) rembourser.

pay out (*spend*) dépenser.
payphone téléphone *m* public.
pay up *vti* payer.
pea [piː] pois *m*; **peas, garden** *or* **green peas** petits pois *mpl*; **p. soup** soupe *f* aux pois.
peace [piːs] paix *f*; **p. of mind** tranquillité *f* d'esprit; **in p.** en paix; **to have (some) p. and quiet** avoir la paix.
peaceful *a* paisible; (*demonstration*) pacifique.
peach [piːtʃ] pêche *f*.
peacock paon *m*.
peak [piːk] **1** *n* (*mountain top*) sommet *m*; (*mountain*) pic *m*; **to be at its p.** être à son maximum. **2** *a* (*hours*, *period*) de pointe.
peaky ['piːkɪ] *a Fam* (*ill*) patraque.
peanut cacah(o)uète *f*.
pear [peər] poire *f*; **p. tree** poirier *m*.
pearl [pɜːl] perle *f*.
pebble ['peb(ə)l] caillou *m* (*pl* cailloux); (*on beach*) galet *m*.
pecan ['piːkæn] *Am* noix *f* de pécan.
peck [pek] *vti* **to p. (at)** (*of bird*) picorer (*du pain etc*); donner un coup de bec à (*qn*).
peckish ['pekɪʃ] *a* **to be p.** *Fam* avoir un petit creux.
peculiar [pɪ'kjuːlɪər] *a* bizarre; (*special*) particulier (**to** à).
peculi'arity (*feature*) particularité *f*.
pedal ['ped(ə)l] **1** *n* pédale *f*. **2** *vi* pédaler. **3** *vt* **to p. a bicycle** faire marcher un vélo; (*ride*) rouler en vélo.
pedal boat pédalo *m*.
pedestrian [pə'destrɪən] piéton *m*; **p. crossing** passage *m* pour piétons; **p. street** rue *f* piétonne.
peek [piːk] **to have a p.** jeter un petit coup d'œil (**at** à).
peel [piːl] **1** *n* épluchure(s) *f(pl)*; **a piece of p., some p.** une épluchure. **2** *vt* (*apple*, *potato etc*) éplucher. **3** *vi* (*of sunburnt skin*) peler; (*of paint*) s'écailler.
peeler **(potato) p.** éplucheur *m*.
peel off (*label etc*) décoller.
peep [piːp] **1** *n* coup *m* d'œil (furtif). **2** *vi* **to p. (at)** regarder furtivement.
peer [pɪər] *vi* **to p. (at)** regarder attentivement.
peg [peg] (*for tent*) piquet *m*; (*for clothes*) pince *f* (à linge); (*for coat*, *hat*) patère *f*.
pen [pen] (*fountain*, *ballpoint*) stylo *m*; (*enclosure*) parc *m*.
penalty ['pen(ə)ltɪ] (*prison sentence*) peine *f*; (*fine*) amende *f*; *Football* penalty *m*.

pence [pens] *see* **penny.**
pencil ['pens(ə)l] crayon *m*; **in p.** au crayon.
pencil case trousse *f*.
pencil in (*note down*) noter provisoirement.
pencil sharpener taille-crayon(s) *m inv*.
penetrate ['penɪtreɪt] *vt* (*substance*) pénétrer; (*forest*) pénétrer dans.
pen friend *or Am* **pal** correspondant, -ante *mf*.
penguin ['peŋgwɪn] manchot *m*.
penicillin [penɪ'sɪlɪn] pénicilline *f*.
peninsula [pə'nɪnsjʊlə] presqu'île *f*.
penknife (*pl* **-knives**) canif *m*.
penniless *a* sans le sou.
penny ['penɪ] (*pl* **pennies**) (*coin*) penny *m*; *Am* cent *m*; **not a p.!** pas un sou! ■ (*pl* **pence** [pens]) (*value, currency*) penny *m*.
pension ['penʃ(ə)n] pension *f*; **(retirement) p.** retraite *f*.
pensioner (old age) p. retraité, -ée *mf*
people ['pi:p(ə)l] **1** *npl* gens *mpl or fpl*; (*specific persons*) personnes *fpl*; **the p.** (*citizens*) le peuple; **old p.** les personnes *fpl* âgées; **old people's home** hospice *m* de vieillards; (*private*) maison *f* de retraite; **English p.** les Anglais *mpl*. **2** *n* (*nation*) peuple *m*.
pepper ['pepər] poivre *m*; (*vegetable*) poivron *m*.
peppermint (*flavour*) menthe *f*; (*sweet, Am candy*) bonbon *m* à la menthe.
per [pɜ:r] *prep* par; **p. annum** par an; **p. person** par personne; **p. cent** pour cent; **50 pence p. kilo** 50 pence le kilo.
per'centage pourcentage *m*.
perch [pɜ:tʃ] **1** *n* (*for bird*) perchoir *m*. **2** *vi* (*of bird, person*) se percher.
percolater ['pɜ:kəleɪtər] cafetière *f*; (*in café etc*) percolateur *m*.
perfect ['pɜ:fɪkt] **1** *a* parfait. **2** *a & n Grammar* **p. (tense)** parfait *m*. **3** *vt* [pə'fekt] (*technique*) mettre au point; (*one's French etc*) parfaire ses connaissances en.
per'fection perfection *f*.
'perfectly *adv* parfaitement.
perform [pə'fɔ:m] **1** *vt* (*task, miracle*) accomplir; (*one's duty*) remplir; (*surgical operation*) pratiquer (**on** sur); (*a play, piece of music*) jouer. **2** *vi* (*act, play*) jouer; (*sing*) chanter; (*dance*) danser; (*of machine*) fonctionner.
performance (*in theatre*) représentation *f*; (*in cinema, concert hall*) séance *f*; (*of actor, musician*) interprétation *f*; (*of athlete, machine*) performance *f*.

performer (*entertainer*) artiste *mf*.
perfume ['pɜːfjuːm] parfum *m*.
perhaps [pə'hæps] *adv* peut-être; **p. not** peut-être que non.
peril ['perɪl] péril *m*.
period ['pɪərɪəd] période *f*; (*historical*) époque *f*; (*lesson*) leçon *f*; (*full stop*) *Am* point *m*; **(monthly) period(s)** (*of woman*) règles *fpl*.
peri'odical périodique *m*.
perk [pɜːk] (*in job*) avantage *m* en nature.
perk up (*become livelier*) reprendre du poil de la bête.
perm [pɜːm] **1** *n* permanente *f*. **2** *vt* **to have one's hair permed** se faire faire une permanente.
permanent ['pɜːmənənt] *a* permanent; (*address*) fixe.
permanently *adv* à titre permanent.
per'mission *f* (**to do** de faire); **to ask p.** demander la permission.
permit 1 *vt* [pə'mɪt] permettre (**s.o. to do** à qn de faire). **2** *n* ['pɜːmɪt] permis *m*; (*entrance pass*) laissez-passer *m inv*.
perpendicular [pɜːpən'dɪkjʊlər] *a* perpendiculaire (**to** à).
persecute ['pɜːsɪkjuːt] *vt* persécuter.
perse'cution persécution *f*.
perseverance persévérance *f*.
persevere [pɜːsɪ'vɪər] *vi* persévérer (**in** dans).
persist [pə'sɪst] *vi* persister (**in doing** à faire, **in sth** dans qch).
persistent *a* (*person*) obstiné; (*noise etc*) continuel.
person ['pɜːs(ə)n] personne *f*; **in p.** en personne.
personal ['pɜːsən(ə)l] *a* personnel; (*application*) en personne; (*friend*) intime; (*life*) privé; (*indiscreet*) indiscret.
perso'nality personnalité *f*.
personally *adv* personnellement; (*in person*) en personne.
personnel [pɜːsə'nel] personnel *m*.
persuade [pə'sweɪd] *vt* persuader (**s.o. to do** qn de faire).
persuasion persuasion *f*.
pessimist ['pesɪmɪst] **to be a p.** être pessimiste.
pessi'mistic *a* pessimiste.
pest [pest] animal *m or* insecte *m* nuisible; (*person*) casse-pieds *mf inv*.
pester ['pestər] *vt* harceler (**with questions** de questions); **to p. s.o. to do sth/for sth** harceler qn pour qu'il fasse qch/jusqu'à ce qu'il donne qch.
pet [pet] **1** *n* animal *m* (domestique); (*favourite person*) chouchou, -oute *mf*. **2** *a* (*dog, cat etc*) domestique; (*favourite*) favori (*f* -ite).
petal ['pet(ə)l] pétale *m*.
petition [pə'tɪʃ(ə)n] (*signatures*) pétition *f*.

petrol ['petrəl] essence *f*.
petrol station station-service *f*.
petticoat ['petɪkəʊt] jupon *m*.
petty ['petɪ] *a* (*minor*) petit; (*mean*) mesquin; **p. cash** petite caisse *f*.
pharmacist pharmacien, -ienne *mf*.
pharmacy ['fɑːməsɪ] pharmacie *f*.
phase [feɪz] phase *f*.
phase sth in/out introduire/supprimer qch progressivement.
PhD [piːeɪtʃ'diː] *abbr* (*university degree*) doctorat *m*.
pheasant ['fezənt] faisan *m*.
phenomenal *a* phénoménal.
phenomenon, *pl* **-ena** [fɪ'nɒmɪnən, -ɪnə] phénomène *m*.
philosopher philosophe *mf*.
philo'sophical *a* philosophique; (*resigned*) philosophe.
philosophy [fɪ'lɒsəfɪ] philosophie *f*.
phlegm [flem] (*in throat*) glaires *fpl*.
phone [fəʊn] téléphone *m*; **on the p.** au téléphone; (*at other end*) au bout du fil.
phone (up) 1 *vt* téléphoner à. **2** *vi* téléphoner.
phone back *vti* rappeler.
phone book annuaire *m*.
phone booth *or* **box** cabine *f* téléphonique.
phone call coup *m* de fil; **to make a p. call** téléphoner (**to** à).
phonecard télécarte *f*.
phone number numéro *m* de téléphone.
phonetic [fə'netɪk] *a* phonétique.
photo ['fəʊtəʊ] (*pl* **-os**) photo *f*; **to take a p. of** prendre une photo de; **to have one's p. taken** se faire prendre en photo.
photocopier photocopieuse *f*.
photocopy 1 *n* photocopie *f*. **2** *vt* photocopier.
photograph photographie *f*.
photographer [fə'tɒgrəfər] photographe *mf*.
photo'graphic *a* photographique.
photography [fə'tɒgrəfɪ] photographie *f*.
phrase [freɪz] expression *f*; (*idiom*) locution *f*.
phrasebook manuel *m* de conversation.
physical ['fɪzɪk(ə)l] *a* physique; **p. examination** examen *m* médical.
physics physique *f*.
'pianist pianiste *mf*.
piano [pɪ'ænəʊ] (*pl* **-os**) piano *m*.
pick [pɪk] **1** *n* **to take one's p.** faire son choix. **2** *vt* choisir; (*flower, fruit*) cueillir; (*hole*) faire (**in** dans); **to p. one's nose** se mettre les

doigts dans le nez.
pick(axe) (*Am* (**-ax**)) pioche *f*.
pickled *a* (*onion etc*) au vinaigre.
pickles ['pɪk(ə)lz] *npl* pickles *mpl*; *Am* concombres *mpl*.
pick sth off enlever qch.
pick on s.o. s'en prendre à qn.
pick out choisir; (*identify*) reconnaître.
pickpocket pickpocket *m*.
pick up 1 *vt* (*sth dropped*) ramasser; (*fallen person or chair*) relever; (*person into air*, *weight*) soulever; (*a cold*) attraper; (*habit*, *accent*, *speed*) prendre; (*fetch*) (passer) prendre; (*find*) trouver; (*learn*) apprendre. **2** *vi* (*improve*) s'améliorer; (*of business*) reprendre; (*of patient*) aller mieux.
picnic ['pɪknɪk] pique-nique *m*.
picture ['pɪktʃər] **1** *n* image *f*; (*painting*) tableau *m*; (*photo*) photo *f*; (*film*) film *m*; **the pictures** *Fam* le cinéma. **2** *vt* (*imagine*) s'imaginer (**that** que).
picture frame cadre *m*.
picturesque [pɪktʃə'resk] *a* pittoresque.
pie [paɪ] (*open*) tarte *f*; (*with pastry on top*) tourte *f*; **meat p.** pâté *m* en croûte.
piece [piːs] morceau *m*; (*of fabric*, *machine*, *in game*) pièce *f*; (*coin*) pièce *f*; **in pieces** en morceaux; **to take to pieces** (*machine*) démonter; **a p. of news**/*etc* une nouvelle/*etc*; **in one p.** intact; (*person*) indemne.
pier [pɪər] jetée *f*.
pierce [pɪəs] *vt* percer (*qch*).
piercing *a* (*cry*, *cold*) perçant.
pig [pɪg] cochon *m*.
pigeon ['pɪdʒɪn] pigeon *m*.
pigeonhole casier *m*.
piggyback to give s.o. a p. porter qn sur le dos.
pigtail (*hair*) natte *f*.
pilchard ['pɪltʃəd] pilchard *m* (*grosse sardine*).
pile [paɪl] **1** *n* tas *m*; (*neatly arranged*) pile *f*; **piles of** *Fam* beaucoup de. **2** *vt* entasser; (*neatly*) empiler.
pile into (*crowd into*) s'entasser dans.
piles *npl* (*illness*) hémorroïdes *fpl*.
pile up 1 *vt* entasser; (*neatly*) empiler. **2** *vi* s'accumuler.
pileup (*on road*) carambolage *m*.
pill [pɪl] pilule *f*; **to be on the p.** prendre la pilule.
pillar ['pɪlər] pilier *m*.

pillar-box boîte *f* aux *or* à lettres.
pillow ['pɪləʊ] oreiller *m*.
pillowcase taie *f* d'oreiller.
pilot ['paɪlət] pilote *m*.
pimple ['pɪmp(ə)l] bouton *m*.
pin [pɪn] épingle *f*; (*drawing pin*) punaise *f*.
pin (on) épingler (**to** sur, à); (*to wall*) punaiser (**to, on** à).
pinafore ['pɪnəfɔːr] (*apron*) tablier *m*.
'pinball flipper *m*; **p. machine** flipper *m*.
pincers ['pɪnsəz] *npl* (*tool*) tenailles *fpl*.
pinch [pɪntʃ] **1** *n* (*of salt*) pincée *f*; **to give s.o. a p.** pincer qn. **2** *vt* pincer; (*steal*) *Fam* piquer (**from** à).
pincushion pelote *f* (à épingles).
pine [paɪn] pin *m*.
pineapple ananas *m*.
pink [pɪŋk] *a* & *n* (*colour*) rose (*m*).
pinkie ['pɪŋkɪ] *Am* petit doigt *m*
pint [paɪnt] pinte *f* (*Br = 0, 57 litre, Am = 0, 47 litre*); **a p. of beer** = un demi.
pin up (*on wall*) punaiser (**on** à); (*notice*) afficher.
pip [pɪp] (*of fruit*) pépin *m*.
pipe [paɪp] tuyau *m*; (*of smoker*) pipe *f*; **to smoke a p.** fumer la pipe.
pirate ['paɪərət] pirate *m*.
pistachio [pɪ'stæʃɪəʊ] pistache *f*.
pistol ['pɪstəl] pistolet *m*.
pit [pɪt] (*hole*) trou *m*; (*coalmine*) mine *f*; (*quarry*) carrière *f*; (*stone of fruit*) *Am* noyau *m*; (*smaller*) pépin *m*.
pitch [pɪtʃ] **1** *n Football etc* terrain *m*. **2** *vt* (*tent*) dresser; (*ball*) lancer.
pitch-'black, pitch-'dark *a* noir comme dans un four.
pity ['pɪtɪ] **1** *n* pitié *f*; **(what) a p.!** (quel) dommage!; **it's a p.** c'est dommage (**that** que (+ *subjunctive*), **to do** de faire). **2** *vt* plaindre.
pizza ['piːtsə] pizza *f*.
placard ['plækɑːd] (*notice*) affiche *f*.
place [pleɪs] **1** *n* endroit *m*, lieu *m*; (*house*) maison *f*; (*seat, position, rank*) place *f*; **in the first p.** en premier lieu; **to take p.** avoir lieu; **p. of work** lieu *m* de travail; **market p.** place *f* du marché; **at my p., to my p.** (*house*) chez moi; **all over the p.** partout; **to take the p. of** remplacer; **in p. of** à la place de. **2** *vt* placer; (*an order*) passer (**with s.o.** à qn); **to p. s.o.** (*identify*) remettre qn.
place mat set *m* (de table).

place setting couvert *m*.
plague [pleɪg] **1** *n* peste *f*; (*nuisance*) plaie *f*. **2** *vt* harceler (**with** de).
plaice [pleɪs] carrelet *m*.
plain[1] [pleɪn] *a* (*clear*) clair; (*simple*) simple; (*madness*) pur; (*without pattern*) uni; (*woman*, *man*) sans beauté; **to make it p. to s.o. that** faire comprendre à qn que.
plain[2] plaine *f*.
plainly *adv* clairement; (*frankly*) franchement.
plait [plæt] **1** *n* tresse *f*. **2** *vt* tresser.
plan [plæn] **1** *n* projet *m*; (*economic*, *of house etc*) plan *m*; **according to p.** comme prévu. **2** *vt* (*foresee*) prévoir; (*organize*) organiser; (*design*) concevoir; **to p. to do** *or* **on doing** avoir l'intention de faire; **as planned** comme prévu.
plane [pleɪn] (*aircraft*) avion *m*; (*tool*) rabot *m*.
planet ['plænɪt] planète *f*.
plane tree platane *m*.
plan for (*rain*, *disaster*) prévoir.
plank [plæŋk] planche *f*.
plant [plɑːnt] **1** *n* plante *f*; (*factory*) usine *f*; **house p.** plante verte. **2** *vt* (*flower etc*) planter.
plaster ['plɑːstər] plâtre *m*; **(sticking) p.** sparadrap *m*; **in p.** dans le plâtre.
plaster cast (*for broken arm etc*) plâtre *m*.
plastic ['plæstɪk] **1** *a* (*object*) en plastique. **2** *n* plastique *m*.
plasticine® ['plæstɪsiːn] pâte *f* à modeler.
plastic surgery chirurgie *f* esthétique.
plate [pleɪt] (*dish*) assiette *f*; (*metal sheet*) plaque *f*.
platform ['plætfɔːm] (*at train station*) quai *m*; (*on bus etc*) plateforme *f*; (*for speaker etc*) estrade *f*.
play [pleɪ] **1** *n* (*in theatre*) pièce *f* (de théâtre). **2** *vt* (*part*, *tune etc*) jouer; (*game*) jouer à; (*instrument*) jouer de; (*team*) jouer contre; (*record*, *compact disc*) passer; **to p. a part in doing/in sth** contribuer à faire/à qch. **3** *vi* jouer (**at** à); (*of tape recorder etc*) marcher; **what are you playing at?** qu'est-ce que tu fais?
play about *or* **around** *vi* jouer.
play back (*tape*) réécouter.
play down minimiser.
player (*in game*, *of instrument*) joueur, -euse *mf*; **cassette/CD p.** lecteur *m* de cassettes/CD.
playground (*in school*) cour *f* de récréation; (*with swings etc*) terrain *m* de jeux.

playgroup = **playschool.**
playing card carte *f* à jouer.
playing field terrain *m* de jeux.
playpen parc *m* (pour enfants).
playschool garderie *f* (d'enfants).
playtime récréation *f*.
pleasant ['plezənt] *a* agréable.
pleasantly *adv* agréablement.
please [pli:z] **1** *adv* s'il vous plaît, s'il te plaît. **2** *vt* **to p. s.o.** plaire à qn; (*satisfy*) contenter qn. **3** *vi* plaire; **do as you p.** fais comme tu veux.
pleased *a* content (**with** de, **that** que (+ *subjunctive*), **to do** de faire); **p. to meet you!** enchanté!
pleasing *a* agréable.
pleasure ['pleʒər] plaisir *m*.
pleat [pli:t] (*in skirt*) pli *m*.
pleated *a* plissé.
plentiful *a* abondant.
plenty ['plentɪ] **p. of** beaucoup de; **that's p.** c'est assez.
pliers ['plaɪəz] *npl* pince(s) *f(pl)*
plimsoll ['plɪmsəʊl] (chaussure *f* de) tennis *m*.
plot [plɒt] **1** *n* complot *m* (**against** contre); **p. (of land)** terrain *m*. **2** *vti* comploter (**to do** de faire).
plot (out) (*route*) déterminer.
plough [plaʊ] (*Am* **plow**) **1** *n* charrue *f*. **2** *vt* (*field*) labourer.
pluck [plʌk] *vt* (*fowl*) plumer; (*flower*) cueillir.
plug [plʌg] (*of cotton wool*, *Am absorbent cotton*) tampon *m*; (*for sink*, *bath*) bonde *f*; (*electrical*) fiche *f*, prise *f* (*mâle*); (*socket*) prise *f* de courant; (**wall**) **p.** (*for screw*) cheville *f*.
plug (up) boucher.
plug in (*radio etc*) brancher.
plum [plʌm] prune *f*.
plumber ['plʌmər] plombier *m*.
plumbing plomberie *f*.
plump [plʌmp] *a* potelé.
plunge [plʌndʒ] **1** *vt* plonger (**into** dans). **2** *vi* (*dive*) plonger (**into** dans); (*fall*) tomber (**from** de).
plural ['plʊərəl] **1** *a* (*form*) pluriel; (*noun*) au pluriel. **2** *n* pluriel *m*; **in the p.** au pluriel.
plus [plʌs] **1** *prep* plus; **two p. two** deux plus deux. **2** *a* **twenty p.** vingt et quelques.
p.m. [pi:'em] *adv* de l'après-midi; (*evening*) du soir.

pneumatic drill [njuː'mætɪk] marteau *m* piqueur.
poach [pəʊtʃ] *vt* (*egg*) pocher.
PO Box [piːəʊ'bɒks] boîte *f* postale.
pocket ['pɒkɪt] poche *f*; **p. money**/*etc* argent *m*/*etc* de poche.
pocketbook (*notebook*) carnet *m*; (*handbag*) *Am* sac *m* à main.
pocketful a **p. of** une pleine poche de.
poem ['pəʊɪm, *Am* 'pəʊəm] poème *m*.
poet poète *m*.
po'etic *a* poétique.
poetry poésie *f*.
point [pɔɪnt] **1** *n* (*position, score etc*) point *m*; (*decimal*) virgule *f*; (*meaning*) sens *m*; (*of knife etc*) pointe *f*; **(power) p.** prise *f* (de courant); **points** (*for train*) aiguillage *m*; **p. of view** point *m* de vue; **at this p. (in time)** en ce moment; **what's the p.?** à quoi bon? **(of waiting**/*etc* attendre/*etc*); **there's no p. (in) staying**/*etc* ça ne sert à rien de rester/*etc*. **2** *vt* (*aim*) pointer (**at** sur); **to p. one's finger (at)** montrer du doigt.
point (at *or* **to)** (*with finger*) montrer du doigt.
pointed *a* pointu.
pointless *a* inutile.
point out (*show*) indiquer; (*mention*) signaler (**that** que).
point to (*indicate*) indiquer.
poison ['pɔɪz(ə)n] **1** *n* poison *m*; (*of snake*) venin *m*. **2** *vt* empoisonner.
poisonous *a* toxique; (*snake*) venimeux; (*plant*) vénéneux.
poke [pəʊk] *vt* pousser (*du doigt etc*); (*fire*) tisonner; **to p. sth into sth** fourrer qch dans qch; **to p. one's head out of the window** passer la tête par la fenêtre.
poke about *or* **around in** (*drawer etc*) fouiner dans.
poker (*for fire*) tisonnier *m*.
polar bear ours *m* blanc.
Pole *n* Polonais, -aise *mf*.
pole [pəʊl] (*rod*) perche *f*; (*fixed*) poteau *m*; (*for flag*) mât *m*; **North/South P.** pôle Nord/Sud.
police [pə'liːs] police *f*.
police car voiture *f* de police.
police force police *f*.
policeman (*pl* **-men**) agent *m* de police.
policewoman (*pl* **-women**) femme-agent *f*.
policy ['pɒlɪsɪ] (*plan etc*) politique *f*; **(insurance) p.** police *f* (d'assurance).
polio ['pəʊlɪəʊ] polio *f*.

Polish ['pəʊlɪʃ] **1** *a* polonais. **2** *n* (*language*) polonais *m*.
polish ['pɒlɪʃ] **1** *vt* cirer; (*metal*) astiquer; (*rough surface*) polir. **2** *n* (*for shoes*) cirage *m*; (*for floor etc*) cire *f*; (*shine*) vernis *m*; **to give sth a p.** faire briller qch.
polish off (*food etc*) *Fam* liquider.
polish up (*one's French etc*) travailler.
polite [pə'laɪt] *a* poli (**to, with** avec).
politely *adv* poliment.
politeness politesse *f*.
political [pə'lɪtɪk(ə)l] *a* politique.
poli'tician homme *m or* femme *f* politique.
'politics politique *f*.
poll [pəʊl] (*voting*) scrutin *m*; **to go to the polls** aller aux urnes; **(opinion) p.** sondage *m* (d'opinion).
pollen ['pɒlən] pollen *m*.
polling station bureau *m* de vote.
pollute [pə'lu:t] *vt* polluer.
pollution pollution *f*.
polo neck ['pəʊləʊ] (*sweater*) col *m* roulé.
polyester [pɒlɪ'estər] **1** *n* polyester *m*. **2** *a* (*shirt etc*) en polyester.
polytechnic [pɒlɪ'teknɪk] institut *m* universitaire de technologie.
polythene ['pɒlɪθi:n] *a* **p. bag** sac *m* en plastique.
pomegranate ['pɒmɪgrænɪt] (*fruit*) grenade *f*.
pond [pɒnd] étang *m*; (*artificial*) bassin *m*.
pony ['pəʊnɪ] poney *m*.
ponytail (*hair*) queue *f* de cheval.
poodle ['pu:d(ə)l] caniche *m*.
pool [pu:l] (*puddle*) flaque *f*; (*for swimming*) piscine *f*; (*billiards*) billard *m* américain.
pooped [pu:pt] *a* (*tired*) *Am Fam* vanné.
poor [pʊər] **1** *a* pauvre; (*bad*) mauvais; (*weak*) faible. **2** *n* **the p.** les pauvres *mpl*.
poorly *adv* (*badly*) mal.
pop[1] [pɒp] **1** *vti* (*burst*) crever. **2** *vt* (*put*) *Fam* mettre.
pop[2] **1** *n* (*music*) pop *m*; (*drink*) soda *m*; (*father*) *Am Fam* papa *m*. **2** *a* (*concert etc*) pop *inv*.
popcorn pop-corn *m*.
pope [pəʊp] pape *m*.
pop in/out entrer/sortir un instant.
pop over *or* **round** faire un saut (**to** chez).
poppy ['pɒpɪ] coquelicot *m*.
popsicle® ['pɒpsɪk(ə)l] (*ice lolly*) *Am* = esquimau *m*.

popular ['pɒpjʊlər] *a* populaire; (*fashionable*) à la mode; **to be p. with** plaire beaucoup à.
populated *a* **highly/sparsely/***etc* **p.** très/peu/*etc* peuplé; **p. by** peuplé de.
population [pɒpjʊ'leɪʃ(ə)n] population *f.*
porch [pɔːtʃ] porche *m*; (*veranda*) *Am* véranda *f.*
pork [pɔːk] (*meat*) porc *m.*
porridge ['pɒrɪdʒ] porridge *m* (*bouillie de flocons d'avoine*).
port [pɔːt] (*harbour*) port *m.*
portable ['pɔːtəb(ə)l] *a* portable, portatif.
porter ['pɔːtər] (*for luggage*) porteur *m.*
porthole hublot *m.*
portion ['pɔːʃ(ə)n] (*share*) portion *f*; (*of train, book etc*) partie *f.*
portrait ['pɔːtreɪt] portrait *m.*
Portuguese [pɔːtjʊ'giːz] **1** *a & n inv* portugais, -aise (*mf*). **2** *n* (*language*) portugais *m.*
pose [pəʊz] **1** *n* (*of model*) pose *f.* **2** *vi* poser (**for** pour).
posh [pɒʃ] *a Fam* (*smart*) chic *inv.*
position [pə'zɪʃ(ə)n] position *f*; (*job, circumstances*) situation *f*; **in a p. to do** en mesure de faire.
positive ['pɒzɪtɪv] *a* positif; (*progress, change*) réel; (*answer*) affirmatif; (*sure*) certain (**of** de, **that** que).
possess [pə'zes] *vt* posséder.
possessions *npl* biens *mpl.*
possessive *a & n Grammar* possessif (*m*).
possi'bility possibilité *f.*
possible ['pɒsəb(ə)l] *a* possible; **it is p. (for us) to do it** il (nous) est possible de le faire; **it is p. that** il est possible que (+ *subjunctive*); **as far as p.** autant que possible; **if p.** si possible; **as much** *or* **as many as p.** le plus possible.
possibly *adv* (*perhaps*) peut-être; **if you p. can** si cela t'est possible; **to do all one p. can** faire tout son possible.
post[1] [pəʊst] **1** *n* (*system*) poste *f*; (*letters*) courrier *m*; **by p.** par la poste; **to catch/miss the p.** avoir/manquer la levée. **2** *vt* (*put in postbox or Am mailbox*) poster; (*send*) envoyer.
post[2] (*job, place*) poste *m.*
post[3] (*pole*) poteau *m*; (*of door*) montant *m*; **winning p.** poteau *m* d'arrivée.
post (up) (*notice etc*) afficher.
postage tarif *m* (postal) (**to** pour).
postage stamp timbre-poste *m.*
postal *a* (*services etc*) postal; **p. order** mandat *m* postal.

postbox boîte *f* aux *or* à lettres.
postcard carte *f* postale.
postcode code *m* postal.
poster ['pəʊstər] affiche *f*; (*for decoration*) poster *m*.
post'graduate étudiant, -ante *mf* de troisième cycle.
postman ['pəʊstmən] (*pl* **-men**) facteur *m*.
postmark cachet *m* de la poste.
post office (bureau *m* de) poste *f*.
postpone [pəʊ'spəʊn] *vt* remettre (**for** de, **until** à).
postponement remise *f*.
pot [pɒt] pot *m*; (*for cooking*) marmite *f*; (*drug*) *Fam* hasch *m*; **pots and pans** casseroles *fpl*.
potato [pə'teɪtəʊ] (*pl* **-oes**) pomme *f* de terre.
potential [pə'tenʃ(ə)l] **1** *a* (*client, sales*) éventuel. **2** *n* **to have p.** (*of firm etc*) avoir de l'avenir.
potter ['pɒtər] potier *m*.
pottery (*art*) poterie *f*; (*objects*) poteries *fpl*; **a piece of p.** une poterie.
potty ['pɒtɪ] pot *m* (de bébé).
pouch [paʊtʃ] petit sac *m*; (*of kangaroo*) poche *f*.
pouf(fe) [puːf] (*seat*) pouf *m*.
poultry ['pəʊltrɪ] volaille *f*.
pounce [paʊns] *vi* sauter (**on** sur).
pound [paʊnd] (*weight*) livre *f* (= *453,6 grammes*); (*money*) livre *f* (sterling); (*for cars, dogs*) fourrière *f*.
pour [pɔːr] *vt* (*liquid*) verser; **to p. money into sth** investir beaucoup d'argent dans qch.
pour (down) it's pouring (down) il pleut à verse.
pour away *or* **off** (*liquid*) vider.
pour in 1 *vt* (*liquid*) verser. **2** *vi* (*of water, rain*) entrer à flots; (*of people*) affluer.
pour out 1 *vt* (*liquid*) verser; (*cup etc*) vider. **2** *vi* (*of liquid*) couler à flots; (*of people*) sortir en masse.
poverty ['pɒvətɪ] pauvreté *f*.
powder ['paʊdər] **1** *n* poudre *f*. **2** *vt* **to p. one's face** se poudrer.
powdered *a* (*milk, eggs*) en poudre.
power ['paʊər] (*ability, authority*) pouvoir *m*; (*strength, nation*) puissance *f*; (*energy*) énergie *f*; (*current*) courant *m*; **in p.** au pouvoir; **p. cut** coupure *f* de courant.
powerful *a* puissant.
power station, *Am* **power plant** centrale *f* (électrique).
practical ['præktɪk(ə)l] *a* pratique.

practical joke farce *f*.
practically *adv* (*almost*) pratiquement.
practice ['præktɪs] (*exercise*, *way of proceeding*) pratique *f*; (*habit*) habitude *f*; (*sports training*) entraînement *m*; (*rehearsal*) répétition *f*; **to be out of p.** avoir perdu la pratique.
practise (*Am* **practice**) **1** *vt* (*sport*, *art etc*) pratiquer; (*medicine*, *law*) exercer; (*flute*, *piano etc*) s'exercer à; (*language*) (s'exercer à) parler (**on** avec). **2** *vi* s'exercer; (*of doctor*, *lawyer*) exercer.
praise [preɪz] **1** *vt* louer (**for sth** de qch); **to p. s.o. for doing** louer qn d'avoir fait. **2** *n* louange(s) *f*(*pl*).
pram [præm] landau *m* (*pl* -aus).
prank [præŋk] (*trick*) farce *f*.
prawn [prɔːn] crevette *f* (rose).
pray [preɪ] **1** *vi* prier; **to p. for good weather/a miracle** prier pour avoir du beau temps/pour un miracle. **2** *vt* **to p. that** prier pour que (+ *subjunctive*).
prayer [preər] prière *f*.
precaution [prɪ'kɔːʃ(ə)n] précaution *f* (**of doing** de faire); **as a p.** par précaution.
precede [prɪ'siːd] *vti* précéder.
preceding *a* précédent.
precious ['preʃəs] *a* précieux.
precise [prɪ'saɪs] *a* précis; (*person*) minutieux.
precocious [prɪ'kəʊʃəs] *a* (*child*) précoce.
predecessor ['priːdɪsesər] prédécesseur *m*.
predicament [prɪ'dɪkəmənt] situation *f* fâcheuse.
predict [prɪ'dɪkt] *vt* prédire.
predictable *a* prévisible.
prediction prédiction *f*.
preface ['prefɪs] préface *f*.
prefer [prɪ'fɜːr] *vt* préférer (**to** à); **to p. to do** préférer faire.
preferable ['prefərəb(ə)l] *a* préférable (**to** à).
'preferably *adv* de préférence.
'preference préférence *f* (**for** pour).
prefix ['priːfɪks] préfixe *m*.
pregnancy grossesse *f*.
pregnant ['pregnənt] *a* (*woman*) enceinte; **five months p.** enceinte de cinq mois.
prehistoric [priːhɪ'stɒrɪk] *a* préhistorique.
prejudice ['predʒədɪs] préjugé *m*; **to be full of p.** être plein de préjugés.
preliminary [prɪ'lɪmɪnərɪ] *a* préliminaire.

premises ['premɪsɪz] *npl* locaux *mpl*; **on the p.** sur les lieux.
premium ['priːmɪəm] **(insurance) p.** prime *f* (d'assurance).
prepa'ration préparation *f*; **preparations** préparatifs *mpl* (**for** de).
prepare [prɪ'peər] **1** *vt* préparer (**sth for** qch pour, **s.o. for** qn à); **to p. to do** se préparer à faire. **2** *vi* **to p. for** (*journey*, *occasion*) faire des préparatifs pour; (*exam*) préparer.
prepared *a* (*ready*) prêt (**to do** à faire); **to be p. for sth** (*expect*) s'attendre à qch.
preposition [prepə'zɪʃ(ə)n] *Grammar* préposition *f*.
prep school [prep] école *f* primaire privée; *Am* école *f* secondaire privée.
prescribe [prɪ'skraɪb] *vt* (*of doctor*) prescrire.
prescription (*for medicine*) ordonnance *f*.
presence ['prezəns] présence *f*; **in the p. of** en présence de.
present[1] ['prezənt] **1** *a* (*not absent*) présent (**at** à, **in** dans); (*year*, *state*, *job*, *house etc*) actuel. **2** *n* (*gift*) cadeau *m*; **present (tense)** présent *m*; **at p.** à présent.
present[2] [prɪ'zent] *vt* présenter (**to** à); **to p. s.o. with** (*gift*) offrir à qn; (*prize*) remettre à qn.
presen'tation présentation *f*; (*of prize*) remise *f*.
presently *adv* (*soon*) tout à l'heure; (*now*) à présent.
preser'vation conservation *f*.
preservative agent *m* de conservation.
preserve [prɪ'zɜːv] **1** *vt* (*keep*) conserver. **2** *n* (*jam*) confiture *f*.
presidency présidence *f*.
president ['prezɪdənt] président, -ente *mf*.
presi'dential *a* présidentiel.
press[1] [pres] **1** *n* (*newspapers*, *machine*)) presse *f*. **2** *a* (*conference etc*) de presse.
press[2] **1** *vt* (*button etc*) appuyer sur; (*tube*, *lemon*) presser; (*clothes*) repasser; **to p. s.o. to do** (*urge*) presser qn de faire. **2** *vi* (*with finger*) appuyer (**on** sur); (*of weight*) faire pression (**on** sur).
press down (*button etc*) appuyer sur.
press on (*carry on*) continuer (**with sth** qch).
pressure ['preʃər] pression *f*; **the p. of work** le surmenage; **under p.** (*worker*, *to work*) sous pression.
pressure cooker cocotte-minute® *f*.
presume [prɪ'zjuːm] *vt* présumer (**that** que).
pretend [prɪ'tend] *vti* (*make believe*) faire semblant (**to do** de faire, **that** que).
pretext ['priːtekst] prétexte *m*; **on the p. of/that** sous prétexte de/ que.

pretty ['prɪtɪ] **1** *a* joli. **2** *adv* (*rather*, *quite*) assez; **p. well, p. much** (*almost*) pratiquement.
prevent [prɪ'vent] *vt* empêcher (**from doing** de faire).
prevention prévention *f*.
previous ['priːvɪəs] *a* précédent; (*experience*) préalable; **p. to** avant.
previously *adv* avant.
prey [preɪ] proie *f*; **bird of p.** rapace *m*.
price [praɪs] prix *m*.
price list tarif *m*.
prick [prɪk] *vt* piquer (**with** avec); (*burst*) crever.
prickly ['prɪk(ə)lɪ] *a* (*plant*, *beard*) piquant.
pride [praɪd] (*satisfaction*) fierté *f*; (*exaggerated*) orgueil *m*; (*self-respect*) amour-propre *m*; **to take p. in** être fier de; (*look after*) prendre soin de.
pride oneself on sth/on doing s'enorgueillir de qch/de faire.
priest [priːst] prêtre *m*.
primarily [praɪ'merɪlɪ] *adv Am* essentiellement.
primary school ['praɪmərɪ] école *f* primaire.
Prime Minister [praɪm] Premier ministre *m*.
prime number nombre *m* premier.
primitive ['prɪmɪtɪv] *a* primitif.
primrose ['prɪmrəʊz] primevère *f*.
prince [prɪns] prince *m*.
prin'cess princesse *f*.
principal ['prɪnsɪp(ə)l] (*of school*) directeur, -trice *mf*; (*of university*) président, -ente *mf*.
print [prɪnt] **1** *n* (*of finger*, *foot etc*) empreinte *f*; (*letters*) caractères *mpl*; (*engraving*) gravure *f*; (*photo*) épreuve *f*; **out of p.** épuisé; **p. shop** *Am* imprimerie *f*. **2** *vt* (*book etc*) imprimer; (*photo*) tirer; (*write*) écrire en caractères d'imprimerie; **printing works** imprimerie *f*.
printer (*of computer*) imprimante *f*.
print out *vti* (*of computer*) imprimer.
print-out (*of computer*) sortie *f* sur imprimante.
prior ['praɪər] *a* précédent; (*experience*) préalable.
priority [praɪ'ɒrɪtɪ] priorité *f* (**over** sur).
prison ['prɪz(ə)n] prison *f*; **in p.** en prison.
prisoner prisonnier, -ière *mf*; **to take s.o. p.** faire qn prisonnier.
privacy ['praɪvəsɪ] intimité *f*.
private **1** *a* privé; (*lesson*, *car*, *secretary etc*) particulier; (*report*) confidentiel; (*dinner etc*) intime. **2** *n* (*soldier*) (simple) soldat *m*; **in p.** en privé; (*to have dinner etc*) dans l'intimité.

privately *adv* en privé; (*to have dinner etc*) dans l'intimité.
prize [praɪz] prix *m*; (*in lottery*) lot *m*.
prize-giving distribution *f* des prix.
prize-winner lauréat, -ate *mf*; (*in lottery*) gagnant, -ante *mf*.
probable ['prɒbəb(ə)l] *a* probable (**that** que); (*convincing*) vraisemblable.
probably *adv* probablement.
problem ['prɒbləm] problème *m*; **no p.!** *Fam* pas de problème!; **to have a p. doing** avoir du mal à faire.
proceed [prə'si:d] *vi* (*go*) avancer; (*act*) procéder; (*continue*) continuer.
process ['prəʊses] (*method*) procédé *m* (**for doing** pour faire); (*chemical, economic etc*) processus *m*; **in the p. of doing** en train de faire.
processed cheese = fromage *m* fondu.
procession [prə'seʃ(ə)n] cortège *m*.
produce 1 *vt* [prə'dju:s] (*manufacture, cause etc*) produire; (*bring out*) sortir (*pistolet, mouchoir etc*); (*passport*) présenter. **2** *n* ['prɒdju:s] produits *mpl*.
pro'ducer (*of goods, film*) producteur, -trice *mf*.
product ['prɒdʌkt] produit *m*.
production [prə'dʌkʃ(ə)n] production *f*; (*of play*) mise *f* en scène.
profession [prə'feʃ(ə)n] profession *f*.
professional 1 *a* professionnel; (*piece of work*) de professionnel. **2** *n* professionnel, -elle *mf*.
professor [prə'fesər] professeur *m* (d'université).
profit ['prɒfɪt] **1** *n* profit *m*, bénéfice *m*; **to sell at a p.** vendre à profit. **2** *vi* **to p. by** *or* **from sth** tirer profit de qch.
profitable *a* rentable.
program ['prəʊgræm] **1** *n* (*of computer*) programme *m*. **2** *vt* programmer.
programme, *Am* **program** programme *m*; (*broadcast*) émission *f*.
progress 1 *n* ['prəʊgres] progrès *m(pl)*; **to make p.** faire des progrès; (*when driving etc*) bien avancer; **in p.** en cours. **2** *vi* [prə'gres] progresser; (*of story, meeting*) se dérouler.
prohibit [prə'hɪbɪt] *vt* interdire (**s.o. from doing** à qn de faire).
project ['prɒdʒekt] projet *m* (**for sth** pour qch); (*at school*) étude *f*.
pro'jector (*for films etc*) projecteur *m*.
prolong [prə'lɒŋ] *vt* prolonger.
promenade [prɒmə'nɑ:d] (*at seaside*) promenade *f*.
prominent ['prɒmɪnənt] *a* (*person*) important.
promise ['prɒmɪs] **1** *n* promesse *f*; **to show p.** être prometteur. **2** *vt*

promettre (**s.o. sth, sth to s.o.** qch à qn; **to do** de faire; **that** que). **3** *vi* **I p.!** je te le promets!; **p.?** promis?

promising *a* (*situation*) prometteur (*f* -euse).

promote [prə'məʊt] *vt* **to p. s.o.** (*in job etc*) donner de l'avancement à qn.

promotion (*of person*) avancement *m*.

prompt [prɒmpt] **1** *a* (*speedy*) rapide. **2** *adv* **at 8 o'clock p.** à 8 heures pile.

prone [prəʊn] *a* **p. to** (*illnesses, accidents*) prédisposé à.

pronoun ['prəʊnaʊn] pronom *m*.

pronounce [prə'naʊns] *vt* prononcer.

pronunci'ation prononciation *f*.

proof [pruːf] (*evidence*) preuve(s) *f*(*pl*).

propeller [prə'pelər] hélice *f*.

proper ['prɒpər] *a* (*suitable, respectable*) convenable; (*downright*) véritable; (*noun, meaning*) propre; **the p. address/method/***etc* (*correct*) la bonne adresse/méthode/*etc*.

properly *adv* comme il faut, convenablement.

property ['prɒpətɪ] (*building, possessions*) propriété *f*.

proportion [prə'pɔːʃ(ə)n] (*ratio*) proportion *f*; (*portion*) partie *f*; **proportions** (*size*) dimensions *fpl*.

proposal proposition *f*; (*of marriage*) demande *f* (en mariage).

propose [prə'pəʊz] **1** *vt* (*suggest*) proposer (**to** à, **that** que (+ *subjunctive*)). **2** *vi* faire une demande (en mariage) (**to** à).

props [prɒps] *npl* (*in theatre*) accessoires *mpl*.

prop up (*ladder etc*) appuyer (**against** contre); (*one's head*) caler; (*wall*) étayer.

prose [prəʊz] *n* prose *f*.

prospect ['prɒspekt] (*outlook, possibility*) perspective *f* (**of** de); (**future**) **prospects** perspectives *fpl* d'avenir.

prosperous ['prɒspərəs] *a* riche.

protect [prə'tekt] *vt* protéger (**from** de, **against** contre).

protection protection *f*.

protective *a* (*clothes etc*) de protection.

protest 1 *n* ['prəʊtest] protestation *f* (**against** contre). **2** *vi* [prə'test] protester (**against** contre); (*of students etc*) contester.

Protestant ['prɒtɪstənt] *a* & *n* protestant, -ante (*mf*).

protester (*student etc*) contestataire *mf*.

protractor [prə'træktər] (*for measuring*) rapporteur *m*.

proud [praʊd] *a* fier (**of** de, **to do** de faire); (*superior to others*) orgueilleux.

proudly *adv* fièrement; orgueilleusement.

prove [pruːv] **1** *vt* prouver (**that** que). **2** *vi* **to p. difficult**/*etc* s'avérer difficile/*etc.*

proverb ['prɒvɜːb] proverbe *m.*

provide [prə'vaɪd] *vt* (*supply*) fournir (**s.o. with sth** qch à qn); **to p. s.o. with sth** (*equip*) pourvoir qn de qch.

provided, providing *conj* **p. (that)** pourvu que (+ *subjunctive*).

provide for s.o. pourvoir aux besoins de qn; (*s.o.'s future*) assurer l'avenir de qn.

province ['prɒvɪns] province *f*; **the provinces** la province.

pro'vincial *a* provincial.

provoke [prə'vəʊk] *vt* (*annoy*) agacer.

prowl (around) [praʊl] *vi* rôder.

prowler rôdeur, -euse *mf.*

prune [pruːn] **1** *n* pruneau *m.* **2** *vt* (*tree, bush*) tailler.

pruning shears sécateur *m.*

psychiatrist [saɪ'kaɪətrɪst] psychiatre *mf.*

psycho'logical *a* psychologique.

psychologist [saɪ'kɒlədʒɪst] psychologue *mf.*

pub [pʌb] pub *m* [pœb].

public ['pʌblɪk] **1** *a* public (*f* ique); (*library, swimming pool*) municipal. **2** *n* public *m*; **in p.** en public.

publication [pʌblɪ'keɪʃ(ə)n] publication *f.*

publicity [pʌb'lɪsɪtɪ] publicité *f.*

publish ['pʌblɪʃ] *vt* publier; (*book, author*) éditer.

publisher éditeur, -trice *mf.*

publishing (*profession*) édition *f.*

pudding ['pʊdɪŋ] pudding *m*; **Christmas p.** pudding *m*; **rice p.** riz *m* au lait.

puddle ['pʌd(ə)l] flaque *f* (d'eau).

puff [pʌf] **1** *n* (*of smoke, wind*) bouffée *f.* **2** *vi* souffler.

puff at (*cigar etc*) tirer sur.

pull [pʊl] **1** *n* **to give sth a p.** tirer qch. **2** *vt* tirer; (*trigger*) appuyer sur; (*muscle*) se claquer; **to p. apart** *or* **to bits** mettre en pièces; **to p. a face** faire la moue. **3** *vi* tirer (**at, on** sur); (*go, move*) aller.

pull along traîner (**to** jusqu'à).

pull away 1 *vt* (*move*) éloigner; (*snatch*) arracher (**from** à). **2** *vi* (*in vehicle*) démarrer; **to p. away from** s'éloigner de.

pull back 1 *vi* se retirer. **2** *vt* retirer; (*curtains*) ouvrir.

pull down baisser; (*knock down*) faire tomber; (*demolish*) démolir.

pull in 1 *vt* (*into room etc*) faire entrer (de force); (*crowd*) attirer. **2** *vi* arriver; (*stop in vehicle*) se garer.

pull off (*remove*) enlever.

pull on (*boots etc*) mettre.
pull out 1 *vt* (*tooth*, *hair*) arracher; (*cork*, *pin*) enlever; (*from pocket etc*) tirer, sortir (**from** de). **2** *vi* (*move out in vehicle*) déboîter; (*withdraw*) se retirer (**from**, **of** de).
pull over 1 *vt* traîner (**to** jusqu'à); (*knock down*) faire tomber. **2** *vi* (*in vehicle*) se ranger (sur le côté).
pullover ['pʊləʊvər] pull(-over) *m*.
pull through *vi* s'en tirer.
pull up 1 *vt* (*socks*, *sleeve*, *collar*, *blind*, *Am shade*) remonter, relever; (*plant*, *tree*) arracher. **2** *vi* (*in vehicle*) s'arrêter.
pulse [pʌls] pouls *m*.
pump [pʌmp] **1** *n* pompe *f*; **(air) p.** (*in service station*) gonfleur *m*. **2** *vt* pomper.
pumpkin ['pʌmpkɪn] potiron *m*.
pump up (*mattress etc*) gonfler.
punch[1] [pʌntʃ] **1** *n* (*blow*) coup *m* de poing. **2** *vt* donner un coup de poing à (*qn*).
punch[2] **1** *n* (*for paper*) perforeuse *f*. **2** *vt* (*ticket*) poinçonner; (*with date*) composter; **to p. a hole in sth** faire un trou dans qch.
punctual ['pʌŋktʃʊəl] *a* (*on time*) à l'heure; (*regularly*) ponctuel.
punctuation [pʌŋktʃʊ'eɪʃ(ə)n] ponctuation *f*.
puncture ['pʌŋktʃər] **1** *n* (*in tyre*, *Am tire*) crevaison *f*; **to have a p.** crever. **2** *vti* (*burst*) crever.
punish ['pʌnɪʃ] *vt* punir (**for sth** de qch, **for doing** pour avoir fait).
punishment punition *f*.
pupil ['pju:p(ə)l] élève *mf*; (*of eye*) pupille *f*.
puppet ['pʌpɪt] marionnette *f*.
pup(py) ['pʌp(ɪ)] (*dog*) chiot *m*.
purchase ['pɜ:tʃɪs] **1** *n* achat *m*. **2** *vt* acheter (**from s.o.** à qn, **for s.o.** à *or* pour qn).
pure [pjʊər] *a* pur.
purely *adv* (*only*) strictement.
purple ['pɜ:p(ə)l] **1** *a* violet (*f* -ette). **2** *n* violet *m*.
purpose ['pɜ:pəs] (*aim*) but *m*; **for this p.** dans ce but; **on p.** exprès.
purposely *adv* exprès.
purse [pɜ:s] (*for coins*) porte-monnaie *m inv*; (*handbag*) *Am* sac *m* à main.
pursue [pə'sju:] *vt* (*inquiry*, *aim etc*) poursuivre.
push [pʊʃ] **1** *n* **to give s.o./sth a p.** pousser qn/qch. **2** *vt* pousser (**to, as far as** jusqu'à); **to p. sth into/between** enfoncer qch dans/entre; **to p. s.o. into doing** pousser qn à faire. **3** *vi* pousser.
push (down) (*button*) appuyer sur; (*lever*) abaisser.

push about *or* **around** (*bully*) marcher sur les pieds à (*qn*).
push aside écarter.
push away *or* **back** *vt* repousser.
push-button bouton *m*; (*of phone*) touche *f*; **p.-button phone** téléphone *m* à touches.
pushchair poussette *f*.
pushed [pʊʃt] *a* **to be p.** (**for time**) être très bousculé.
push in *vi* (*in queue*, *Am line*) resquiller.
push on continuer (**with sth** qch).
push over renverser.
push (one's way) through se frayer un chemin (**a crowd** à travers une foule).
push up (*lever*, *sleeve*, *collar*) relever; (*increase*) augmenter.
puss [pʊs] (*cat*) minou *m*.
put* [pʊt] *vt* mettre; (*money*) placer (**into** dans); (*question*) poser (**to** à); (*say*) dire.
put across *vt* (*message etc*) communiquer (**to** à).
put aside (*money*, *object*) mettre de côté.
put away *vt* (*book*, *car etc*) ranger; (*criminal*) mettre en prison.
put back (*replace*, *postpone*) remettre; (*telephone receiver*) raccrocher; (*clock*, *date*) retarder.
put by (*money*) mettre de côté.
put down (*on floor etc*) poser; (*passenger*) déposer; (*a deposit*) verser; (*write down*) inscrire.
put forward (*clock*, *meeting*) avancer; (*candidate*) proposer (**for** à).
put in (*sth into box etc*) mettre dedans; (*insert*) introduire; (*add*) ajouter; (*install*) installer; (*application*) faire.
put off renvoyer (à plus tard); (*gas*, *radio*) fermer; **to p. s.o. off** dissuader qn (**doing** de faire); (*disgust*) dégoûter qn (**sth** de qch); **to p. s.o. off doing** (*disgust*) ôter à qn l'envie de faire.
put on (*clothes etc*) mettre; (*weight*) prendre; (*gas*, *radio*) mettre; (*record*, *cassette*) passer; (*clock*) avancer.
put out (*take outside*) sortir; (*arm*, *leg*) étendre; (*hand*) tendre; (*tongue*) tirer; (*gas*, *light*) éteindre; (*bother*) déranger.
put s.o. through (*on phone*) passer qn (**to** à).
put together mettre ensemble; (*assemble*) assembler; (*compose*) composer.
putty ['pʌtɪ] mastic *m* (*pour vitres*).
put up 1 *vi* (*stay*) descendre (**at a hotel** à un hôtel). **2** *vt* (*lift*) lever; (*window*) remonter; (*tent*, *statue*, *ladder*) dresser; (*building*) construire; (*umbrella*) ouvrir; (*picture*) mettre; (*price*) augmenter; (*candidate*) proposer (**for** à); (*guest*) loger.

put up with sth/s.o. supporter qch/qn.
puzzle ['pʌz(ə)l] **1** *n* mystère *m*; (*jigsaw*) puzzle *m*. **2** *vt* laisser perplexe.
puzzled *a* perplexe.
puzzling *a* curieux.
pyjamas *npl* pyjama *m*; **a pair of p.** un pyjama.
pylon ['paɪlən] pylône *m*.
pyramid ['pɪrəmɪd] pyramide *f*.

Q

qualification [kwɒlɪfɪ'keɪʃ(ə)n] diplôme *m*; **qualifications** (*skills*) qualités *fpl* nécessaires (**for** pour, **to do** pour faire).
qualified *a* (*able*) qualifié (**to do** pour faire); (*teacher etc*) diplômé.
qualify ['kwɒlɪfaɪ] *vi* obtenir son diplôme (**as a doctor**/*etc* de médecin/*etc*); (*in sport*) se qualifier (**for** pour).
quality ['kwɒlɪtɪ] qualité *f*.
quantity ['kwɒntɪtɪ] quantité *f*.
quarrel ['kwɒrəl] **1** *n* dispute *f*; **to pick a q.** chercher des histoires (**with s.o.** à qn). **2** *vi* se disputer (**with s.o.** avec qn).
quarrelling, *Am* **quarreling** disputes *fpl*.
quarry ['kwɒrɪ] (*to extract stone etc*) carrière *f*.
quart [kwɔːt] litre *m* (*mesure approximative*) (*Br = 1,14 litres*, *Am = 0,95 litre*).
quarter[1] quart *m*; (*money*) *Am Can* quart *m* de dollar; (*of fruit*) quartier *m*; **to divide sth into quarters** diviser qch en quatre; **q. (of a) pound** quart *m* de livre; **a q. past nine,** *Am* **a q. after nine** neuf heures et quart *or* un quart; **a q. to nine** neuf heures moins le quart.
quarter[2] (*district*) quartier *m*.
quartz [kwɔːts] *a* (*watch etc*) à quartz.
quay [kiː] quai *m*, débarcadère *m*.
queen [kwiːn] reine *f*; *Chess Cards* dame *f*.
queer [kwɪər] *a* (*odd*) bizarre; (*ill*) *Fam* patraque.
quench [kwentʃ] *vt* **to q. one's thirst** se désaltérer.
query ['kwɪərɪ] (*question*) question *f*.
question ['kwestʃ(ə)n] **1** *n* question *f*; **it's out of the q.** il n'en est pas question. **2** *vt* interroger (*qn*) (**about** sur); (*doubt*) mettre (*qch*) en question.
question mark point *m* d'interrogation.
questio'nnaire questionnaire *m*.
queue [kjuː] queue *f*; (*of cars*) file *f*; **to form a q.** faire la queue.
queue (up) *vi* faire la queue.
quibble ['kwɪb(ə)l] *vi* ergoter (**over** sur).
quiche [kiːʃ] quiche *f*.
quick [kwɪk] **1** *a* rapide; **be q.!** fais vite!; **to have a q. meal**/*etc* manger/*etc* en vitesse. **2** *adv* vite.
quickly *adv* vite.
quiet ['kwaɪət] *a* (*silent*, *peaceful*) tranquille; (*machine*, *vehicle*) silencieux; (*voice*, *sound*) doux (*f* douce); **to be** *or* **keep q.** (*shut up*) se taire; (*make no noise*) ne pas faire de bruit; **q.!** silence!; **to keep**

q. about sth ne pas parler de qch.

quietly *adv* tranquillement; (*not loudly*) doucement; (*silently*) silencieusement.

quilt [kwɪlt] édredon *m*; **(continental) q.** (*duvet*) couette *f*.

quit* [kwɪt] **1** *vt* (*leave*) quitter; **to q. doing** arrêter de faire. **2** *vi* abandonner; (*resign*) démissionner.

quite [kwaɪt] *adv* (*entirely*) tout à fait; (*really*) vraiment; (*rather*) assez; **q. a lot** pas mal (**of** de).

quiz [kwɪz] (*pl* **quizzes**) **q. (programme)** jeu(-concours) *m*.

quo'tation citation *f*; (*estimate*) devis *m*.

quotation marks guillemets *mpl*; **in q. marks** entre guillemets.

quote [kwəʊt] **1** *vt* citer; (*reference*) rappeler; (*price*) indiquer. **2** *vi* **to q. from** citer. **3** *n* = **quotation**.

R

rabbi ['ræbaɪ] rabbin *m*.
rabbit ['ræbɪt] lapin *m*.
rabies ['reɪbiːz] rage *f*.
race[1] [reɪs] **1** *n* (*contest*) course *f*. **2** *vt* (*horse*) faire courir; **to r. (against** *or* **with) s.o.** faire une course avec qn. **3** *vi* (*run*) courir.
race[2] (*group*) race *f*.
racecourse, *Am* **racetrack** champ *m* de courses.
racehorse cheval *m* de course.
racial *a* racial.
racialism, racism racisme *m*.
racing courses *fpl*.
racing car voiture *f* de course.
racing driver coureur *m* automobile.
racist *a* & *n* raciste (*mf*).
rack [ræk] (*for bottles, letters etc*) casier *m*; (*for drying dishes*) égouttoir *m*; **(luggage) r.** (*on bus, train*) filet *m* à bagages.
racket ['rækɪt] (*for tennis*) raquette *f*; (*din*) vacarme *m*.
radar ['reɪdɑːr] radar *m*.
radiator ['reɪdɪeɪtər] radiateur *m*.
radio ['reɪdɪəʊ] (*pl* **-os**) radio *f*; **on** *or* **over the r.** à la radio; **r. set** poste *m* de radio.
radio'active *a* radioactif.
radish ['rædɪʃ] radis *m*.
radius, *pl* **-dii** ['reɪdɪəs, -dɪaɪ] (*of circle*) rayon *m*.
raffle ['ræf(ə)l] tombola *f*.
raft [rɑːft] (*boat*) radeau *m*.
rag [ræg] (*old clothing*) haillon *m*; (*for dusting etc*) chiffon *m*; **in rags** (*clothes*) en loques; (*person*) en haillons.
rage [reɪdʒ] rage *f*; **to fly into a r.** se mettre en rage.
ragged ['rægɪd] *a* (*clothes*) en loques; (*person*) en haillons.
raid [reɪd] **1** *n* (*military*) raid *m*; (*by police*) descente *f*; (*by thieves*) hold-up *m inv*; **air r.** raid *m* aérien. **2** *vt* faire un raid *or* une descente *or* un hold-up dans.
rail [reɪl] (*for train*) rail *m*; (*rod on balcony*) balustrade *f*; (*on stairs*) rampe *f*; (*curtain rod*) tringle *f*; **(towel) r.** porte-serviettes *m inv*; **by r.** (*to travel*) par le train; (*to send*) par chemin de fer.
railing (*of balcony*) balustrade *f*; **railings** (*fence*) grille *f*.
railroad *Am* = **railway**; **r. track** voie *f* ferrée.
railway 1 *n* chemin *m* de fer; (*track*) voie *f* ferrée. **2** *a* (*ticket*) de chemin de fer; **r. line** ligne *f* de chemin de fer; (*track*) voie *f* ferrée.

railway station gare *f*.
rain [reɪn] **1** *n* pluie *f*; **in the r.** sous la pluie. **2** *vi* pleuvoir; **it's raining** il pleut.
rainbow arc-en-ciel *m*.
raincoat imper(méable) *m*.
rainy *a* pluvieux.
raise [reɪz] **1** *vt* (*lift*) lever; (*child*, *family*, *voice*) élever; (*salary*, *price*) augmenter; (*question*) soulever; **to r. money** réunir des fonds. **2** *n Am* augmentation *f* (de salaire).
raisin ['reɪz(ə)n] raisin *m* sec.
rake [reɪk] **1** *n* râteau *m*. **2** *vt* (*garden*) ratisser.
rake (up) (*leaves*) ratisser.
rally ['rælɪ] (*political*) rassemblement *m*.
rally round (s.o.) venir en aide (à qn).
ram [ræm] **1** *n* (*animal*) bélier *m*. **2** *vt* (*vehicle*) emboutir; **to r. sth into sth** enfoncer qch dans qch.
ramble ['ræmb(ə)l] randonnée *f*.
ramp [ræmp] (*slope for wheelchair etc*) rampe *f* (d'accès).
ran [ræn] *pt de* **run.**
ranch [ræntʃ, rɑːntʃ] *Am* ranch *m*.
random ['rændəm] **1** *n* **at r.** au hasard. **2** *a* (*choice*) (fait) au hasard; (*sample*) prélevé au hasard; **r. check** (*by police*) contrôle-surprise *m*.
range [reɪndʒ] **1** *n* (*of gun*, *voice etc*) portée *f*; (*of singer's voice*) étendue *f*; (*of colours*, *prices*, *products*) gamme *f*; (*of sizes*) choix *m*; (*of mountains*) chaîne *f*; (*stove*) *Am* cuisinière *f*. **2** *vi* (*vary*) varier (**from** de, **to** à).
rank [ræŋk] rang *m*.
ransom ['ræns(ə)m] (*money*) rançon *f*.
rape [reɪp] **1** *vt* violer. **2** *n* viol *m*.
rapid ['ræpɪd] *a* rapide.
rapidly *adv* rapidement.
rapist violeur *m*.
rare [reər] *a* rare; (*meat*) saignant.
rarely *adv* rarement.
rascal ['rɑːsk(ə)l] coquin, -ine *mf*.
rash [ræʃ] **1** *n* éruption *f*. **2** *a* irréfléchi.
rashly *adv* sans réfléchir.
raspberry ['rɑːzbərɪ, *Am* -berɪ] framboise *f*; **r. jam** confiture *f* de framboise.
rat [ræt] rat *m*.
rate [reɪt] **1** *n* (*level*) taux *m*; (*speed*) vitesse *f*; (*price*) tarif *m*; **at the**

r. of à une vitesse de; (*amount*) à raison de; **at this r.** (*slow speed*) à ce train-là; **at any r.** en tout cas. **2** *vt* évaluer (**at** à); (*regard*) considérer (**as** comme); (*deserve*) mériter.

rather ['rɑːðər] *adv* (*preferably*, *quite*) plutôt; **I'd r. stay** j'aimerais mieux rester (**than** que); **r. than leave**/*etc* plutôt que de partir/*etc*.

ratio ['reɪʃɪəʊ] (*pl* **-os**) proportion *f*.

ration ['ræʃ(ə)n, *Am* 'reɪʃ(ə)n] **1** *n* ration *f*; **rations** (*food*) vivres *mpl*. **2** *vt* rationner.

rational ['ræʃən(ə)l] *a* (*person*) raisonnable.

rationing rationnement *m*.

rattle ['ræt(ə)l] **1** *n* (*baby's toy*) hochet *m*; (*of sports fan*) crécelle *f*. **2** *vi* faire du bruit; (*of window*) trembler. **3** *vt* (*shake*) secouer.

ravenous ['rævənəs] *a* **I'm r.** j'ai une faim de loup.

raw [rɔː] *a* (*vegetable etc*) cru; (*skin*) écorché; **r. material** matière *f* première.

ray [reɪ] (*of light*, *sun*) rayon *m*.

razor ['reɪzər] rasoir *m*.

re- [riː, rɪ] *prefix* ré-, re-, r-.

reach [riːtʃ] **1** *vt* (*place*, *distant object*, *aim*) atteindre; (*gain access to*) accéder à; (*of letter*) parvenir à (*qn*); (*contact*) joindre (*qn*); (*conclusion*) arriver à. **2** *vi* s'étendre (**to** à); (*with arm*) (é)tendre le bras (**for** pour prendre). **3** *n* portée *f*; **within r. of** à portée de; (*near*) à proximité de; **within (easy) r.** (*object*) à portée de main.

reach s.o. (over) sth passer qch à qn.

reach out *vi* (é)tendre le bras (**for** pour prendre).

react [rɪ'ækt] *vi* réagir (**against** contre, **to** à).

reaction réaction *f*.

reactor réacteur *m* (*nucléaire*).

read* [riːd] **1** *vt* lire; (*meter*) relever; (*of instrument*) indiquer. **2** *vi* lire; **to r. to s.o.** faire la lecture à qn.

read about s.o./sth lire qch sur qn/qch.

read sth back *or* **over** relire qch.

reader lecteur, -trice *mf*; (*book*) livre *m* de lecture.

readily ['redɪlɪ] *adv* (*willingly*) volontiers; (*easily*) facilement.

reading lecture *f*; (*of meter*) relevé *m*; (*by instrument*) indication *f*.

read sth out lire qch (à haute voix).

read sth through parcourir qch.

read up (on) sth étudier qch.

ready ['redɪ] *a* prêt (**to do** à faire, **for sth** à *or* pour qch); **to get sth/s.o. r.** préparer qch/qn; **to get r.** se préparer (**for sth** à *or* pour qch, **to do** à faire); **r. cash** argent *m* liquide.

ready-'cooked *a* tout cuit.

ready-'made *a* tout fait; **r.-made clothes** prêt-à-porter *m inv*.
real [rɪəl] *a* vrai; (*life*, *world*) réel.
real estate *Am* biens *mpl* immobiliers; **r. estate agent** agent *m* immobilier.
rea'listic *a* réaliste.
reality [rɪ'ælətɪ] réalité *f*.
realize ['rɪəlaɪz] *vt* (*know*) se rendre compte de; (*understand*) comprendre (**that** que).
really ['rɪəlɪ] *adv* vraiment.
rear [rɪər] **1** *n* (*back part*) arrière *m*; **in** *or* **at the r.** à l'arrière. **2** *a* arrière *inv*, de derrière. **3** *vt* (*family*, *animals*) élever.
rear (up) (*of horse*) se cabrer.
rearrange *vt* (*hair*, *room*) réarranger; (*plans*) changer.
reason ['riːz(ə)n] **1** *n* raison *f*; **the r. for/why...** la raison de/pour laquelle...; **for no r.** sans raison. **2** *vi* raisonner.
reasonable *a* raisonnable.
reasonably *adv* (*fairly*, *rather*) assez.
reasoning raisonnement *m*.
reason with s.o. raisonner qn.
reassure *vt* rassurer.
reassuring *a* rassurant.
rebel 1 *n* ['reb(ə)l] rebelle *mf*; (*against parents etc*) révolté, -ée *mf*. **2** *vi* [rɪ'bel] se revolter (**against** contre).
re'bellion révolte *f*.
rebound 1 *vi* [rɪ'baʊnd] (*of ball*) rebondir; (*of stone*) ricocher. **2** *n* ['riːbaʊnd] rebond *m*; ricochet *m*.
rebuild *vt* reconstruire.
recall *vt* (*remember*) se rappeler (**that** que, **doing** avoir fait); **to r. sth to s.o.** rappeler qch à qn.
receipt [rɪ'siːt] (*for payment*, *object left etc*) reçu *m* (**for** de); **on r. of** dès réception de.
receive [rɪ'siːv] *vt* recevoir.
receiver (*of phone*) combiné *m*; **to pick up the r.** (*of phone*) décrocher.
recent ['riːsənt] *a* récent; **in r. months** ces mois-ci.
recently *adv* récemment.
reception [rɪ'sepʃ(ə)n] (*party*, *of radio etc*) réception *f*; **r. (desk)** réception *f*, accueil *m*.
receptionist secrétaire *mf*, réceptionniste *mf*.
recharge *vt* (*battery*) recharger.
recipe ['resɪpɪ] recette *f* (**for** de).
recite [rɪ'saɪt] *vt* (*poem*) réciter; (*list*) énumérer.

reckless ['rekləs] *a* (*rash*) imprudent.
reckon ['rek(ə)n] *vt* (*calculate*) calculer; (*think*) *Fam* penser (**that** que).
reckon on sth/s.o. (*rely on*) compter sur qch/qn; **to r. on doing** compter faire.
reckon with sth/s.o. (*take into account*) compter avec qch/qn.
reclaim *vt* (*luggage at airport*) récupérer.
recognize ['rekəgnaɪz] *vt* reconnaître (**by** à).
recollect [rekə'lekt] *vt* se souvenir de; **to r. that** se souvenir que.
recollection souvenir *m*.
recommend [rekə'mend] *vt* recommander (**to** à, **for** pour); **to r. s.o. to do** recommander à qn de faire.
recommen'dation recommandation *f*.
record 1 *n* ['rekɔːd] (*disc*) disque *m*; (*best performance*) record *m*; (*register*) registre *m*; (*mention*) mention *f*; (*background*) antécédents *mpl*; **(public) records** archives *fpl*; **to keep a r. of** noter. **2** *a* (*time, number etc*) record *inv*. **3** *vt* [rɪ'kɔːd] (*on tape, in register*) enregistrer; (*in diary*) noter. **4** *vi* enregistrer.
recorder flûte *f* à bec; **(tape) r.** magnétophone *m*; **(video) r.** magnétoscope *m*.
recording enregistrement *m*.
record player électrophone *m*.
recover 1 *vt* (*get back*) retrouver. **2** *vi* (*from illness etc*) se remettre (**from** de); (*of economy*) se redresser.
recruit [rɪ'kruːt] recrue *f*.
rectangle ['rektæŋg(ə)l] rectangle *m*.
rec'tangular *a* rectangulaire.
recycle *vt* recycler.
red [red] **1** *a* rouge; (*hair*) roux (*f* rousse); **to turn** *or* **go r.** rougir; **r. light** (*traffic light*) feu *m* rouge. **2** *n* (*colour*) rouge *m*; **in the r.** (*firm, account*) dans le rouge, en déficit.
red-'handed *a* **caught r.-handed** pris en flagrant délit.
redhead roux *m*, rousse *f*.
red-'hot *a* brûlant.
redirect *vt* (*mail*) faire suivre.
redo* [riː'duː] *vt* (*exercise, house etc*) refaire.
reduce [rɪ'djuːs] *vt* réduire (**to** à, **by** de); **at a reduced price** (*ticket, goods*) à prix réduit.
reduction réduction *f* (**in** de).
redundancy licenciement *m*.
redundant [rɪ'dʌndənt] *a* **to make r.** (*worker*) mettre au chômage, licencier.

reed [riːd] (*plant*) roseau *m*.
reef [riːf] récif *m*.
reel [riːl] (*of thread*, *film*) bobine *f*; (*film itself*) bande *f*.
refectory [rɪ'fektərɪ] réfectoire *m*.
refer [rɪ'fɜːr] **1** *vi* **to r. to** (*mention*) faire allusion à; (*speak of*) parler de; (*apply to*) s'appliquer à. **2** *vt* **to r. sth to s.o.** soumettre qch à qn.
refe'ree 1 *n Football Boxing* arbitre *m*. **2** *vt* arbitrer.
'reference (*in book*, *for job*) référence *f*; (*mention*) mention *f* (**to** de); **with r. to** concernant; **r. book** ouvrage *m* de référence.
refill 1 *vt* [riː'fɪl] remplir (à nouveau); (*lighter*, *pen*) recharger. **2** *n* ['riːfɪl] recharge *f*; **a r.** (*drink*) un autre verre.
reflect [rɪ'flekt] *vt* (*light etc*) refléter; **to be reflected** se refléter.
reflection (*image*) reflet *m*.
reflex ['riːfleks] réflexe *m*.
reform réforme *f*.
refrain [rɪ'freɪn] *vi* s'abstenir (**from doing** de faire).
refresh *vt* (*of bath*, *drink*) rafraîchir; (*of sleep*, *rest*) délasser.
refresher course cours *m* de recyclage.
refreshing *a* (*drink*) rafraîchissant.
refreshments *npl* (*drinks*) rafraîchissements *mpl*; (*snacks*) petites choses *fpl* à grignoter.
refrigerate [rɪ'frɪdʒəreɪt] *vt* (*food*) conserver au frais.
refrigerator réfrigérateur *m*.
refuge ['refjuːdʒ] refuge *m*; **to take r.** se réfugier.
refu'gee réfugié, -ée *mf*.
refund 1 *vt* [rɪ'fʌnd] rembourser. **2** *n* ['riːfʌnd] remboursement *m*.
refusal refus *m*.
refuse [rɪ'fjuːz] **1** *vt* refuser (**s.o. sth** qch à qn, **to do** de faire). **2** *vi* refuser.
regain [rɪ'geɪn] *vt* (*lost ground*) regagner; (*health*, *strength*) retrouver.
regard [rɪ'gɑːd] **1** *vt* considérer; **as regards** en ce qui concerne. **2** *n* considération *f* (**for** pour); **to have (a) high r. for s.o.** estimer qn; **to give one's regards to s.o.** transmettre son meilleur souvenir à qn.
regarding *prep* en ce qui concerne.
regardless 1 *a* **r. of** sans tenir compte de. **2** *adv* (*all the same*) quand même.
regiment ['redʒɪmənt] régiment *m*.
region ['riːdʒ(ə)n] région *f*; **in the r. of £50**/*etc* (*about*) dans les 50 livres/*etc*.
regional *a* régional.

register ['redʒɪstər] **1** *n* registre *m*; (*in school*) cahier *m* d'appel; **to take the r.** faire l'appel. **2** *vt* (*birth etc*) déclarer; **registered letter** lettre recommandée; **to send by registered post** envoyer en recommandé. **3** *vi* (*enrol*) s'inscrire (**for a course** à un cours); (*in hotel*) signer le registre.

regi'stration (*enrolment*) inscription *f*; **r. (number)** (*of vehicle*) numéro *m* d'immatriculation.

regret [rɪ'gret] **1** *vt* regretter (**doing, to do** de faire; **that** que (+ *subjunctive*)). **2** *n* regret *m*.

regular ['regjʊlər] *a* (*steady*) régulier; (*surface*) uni; (*usual*) habituel; (*price, size*) normal; (*listener*) fidèle.

regularly *adv* régulièrement.

regulations [regjʊ'leɪʃ(ə)nz] *npl* (*rules*) règlement *m*.

rehearsal répétition *f*.

rehearse [rɪ'hɜːs] **1** *vt* (*a play etc*) répéter. **2** *vi* répéter.

reign [reɪn] **1** *n* règne *m*; **in the r. of** sous le règne de. **2** *vi* régner (**over** sur).

reindeer ['reɪndɪər] *n inv* renne *m*.

reinforce [riːɪn'fɔːs] *vt* renforcer (**with** de).

reinforcements *npl* (*troops*) renforts *mpl*.

reins [reɪnz] *npl* (*for horse*) rênes *fpl*; (*for baby*) bretelles *fpl* de sécurité (avec laisse).

reject [rɪ'dʒekt] *vt* rejeter.

rejection rejet *m*; (*of candidate*) refus *m*.

rejoice [rɪ'dʒɔɪs] *vi* (*celebrate*) faire la fête; (*be delighted*) se réjouir (**over** *or* **at sth** de qch).

related *a* (*linked*) lié (**to** à); **to be r. to s.o.** (*by family*) être parent de qn.

relate to (*apply to*) se rapporter à.

relation [rɪ'leɪʃ(ə)n] (*relative*) parent, -ente *mf*; (*relationship*) rapport *m*; **international relations** relations *fpl* internationales.

relationship (*in family*) lien(s) *m(pl)* de parenté; (*relations*) relations *fpl*; (*connection*) rapport *m*.

relative ['relətɪv] **1** *n* (*person*) parent, -ente *mf*. **2** *a* relatif; (*qualities etc of two or more people*) respectif.

relatively *adv* relativement.

relax [rɪ'læks] **1** *vt* (*person*) détendre; (*grip, pressure*) relâcher. **2** *vi* se détendre; **r.!** (*calm down*) du calme!

rela'xation (*rest*) détente *f*.

relaxed [rɪ'lækst] *a* décontracté.

release [rɪ'liːs] **1** *vt* (*free*) libérer (**from** de); (*bomb*) lâcher; (*brake*) desserrer; (*film, record*) sortir; (*trapped person*) dégager. **2** *n* (*of*

prisoner) libération *f*; (*of film etc*) sortie *f*; **press r.** communiqué *m* de presse.
relevant ['reləvənt] *a* pertinent (**to** à); (*useful*) utile; **that's not r.** ça n'a rien à voir.
relia'bility fiabilité *f*; (*of person*) sérieux *m*.
reliable [rɪ'laɪəb(ə)l] *a* fiable; (*person*) sérieux.
relief [rɪ'liːf] (*from pain etc*) soulagement *m* (**from** à); (*help*) secours *m*; (*in geography etc*) relief *m*.
relieve *vt* (*pain, person etc*) soulager; (*take over from*) relayer (*qn*).
religion [rɪ'lɪdʒ(ə)n] religion *f*.
religious *a* religieux.
relish ['relɪʃ] (*seasoning*) assaisonnement *m*.
reload *vt* (*gun, camera*) recharger.
reluctance manque *m* d'enthousiasme (**to do** à faire).
reluctant [rɪ'lʌktənt] *a* peu enthousiaste (**to do** pour faire).
reluctantly *adv* sans enthousiasme.
rely (up)on (*count on*) compter sur; (*be dependent on*) dépendre de.
remain *vi* rester.
remaining *a* qui reste(nt).
remark 1 *n* remarque *f*. **2** *vt* (faire) remarquer (**that** que). **3** *vi* **to r. on sth** faire des remarques sur qch.
remarkable *a* remarquable (**for** par).
remarkably *adv* remarquablement.
remedial [rɪ'miːdɪəl] *a* **r. class** cours *m* de rattrapage.
remember 1 *vt* se souvenir de, se rappeler; **to r. that/doing** se rappeler que/d'avoir fait; **to r. to do** penser à faire. **2** *vi* se souvenir, se rappeler.
remind *vt* rappeler (**s.o. of sth** qch à qn, **s.o. that** à qn que); **to r. s.o. to do** faire penser à qn à faire.
reminder (*of event & letter*) rappel *m*; **to give s.o. a r. to do** faire penser à qn à faire.
remorse [rɪ'mɔːs] remords *m*(*pl*).
remote [rɪ'məʊt] *a* (*far-off*) lointain; (*isolated*) isolé; (*slight*) petit.
remote control télécommande *f*.
removal enlèvement *m*; suppression *f*.
removal man déménageur *m*.
removal van camion *m* de déménagement.
remove *vt* (*clothes, stain etc*) enlever (**from s.o.** à qn, **from sth** de qch); (*obstacle, word*) supprimer.
renew *vt* renouveler; (*resume*) reprendre; (*library book*) renouveler le prêt de.

rent [rent] **1** *n* (*for house etc*) loyer *m*. **2** *vt* louer.
rental (*of television*) (prix *m* de) location *f*; (*of telephone*) abonnement *m*.
rent out louer.
reorganize *vt* (*firm etc*) réorganiser.
repair [rɪ'peər] **1** *vt* réparer. **2** *n* réparation *f*; **in bad r.** en mauvais état.
repairman (*pl* **-men**)réparateur *m*, dépanneur *m*.
repay *vt* (*pt* & *pp* **repaid**) (*pay back*) rembourser; (*reward*) récompenser (**for** de).
repayment remboursement *m*; récompense *f*.
repeat [rɪ'piːt] **1** *vt* répéter (**that** que); (*promise*, *threat*) réitérer; (*class*) redoubler; **to r. oneself** se répéter. **2** *n* (*on TV*, *radio*) rediffusion *f*.
repeated *a* (*attempts etc*) répétés.
repeatedly *adv* à maintes reprises, de nombreuses fois.
repeat on s.o. (*of food*) *Fam* revenir à qn.
repel [rɪ'pel] *vt* repousser.
repetition [repɪ'tɪʃ(ə)n] répétition *f*.
re'petitive *a* répétitif.
replace *vt* (*take the place of*) remplacer (**by, with** par); (*put back*) remettre; (*telephone receiver*) raccrocher.
replacement (*person*) remplaçant, -ante *mf*; (*machine part*) pièce *f* de rechange.
replica ['replɪkə] copie *f* exacte.
reply [rɪ'plaɪ] **1** *vti* répondre (**to** à, **that** que). **2** *n* réponse *f*.
report **1** *n* (*account*) rapport *m*; (*of meeting*) compte rendu *m*; (*in media*) reportage *m*; (*of pupil*) bulletin *m*; (*rumour*) rumeur *f*. **2** *vt* rapporter; (*announce*) annoncer (**that** que); (*notify*) signaler (**to** à); (*inform on*) dénoncer (**to** à). **3** *vi* faire un rapport; (*of journalist*) faire un reportage (**on** sur); (*go*) se présenter (**to** à, **to s.o.** chez qn).
report card *Am* bulletin *m* (scolaire).
reported *a* (*speech*) indirect.
reporter reporter *m*.
represent [reprɪ'zent] *vt* représenter.
representative représentant, -ante *mf*.
reptile ['reptaɪl] reptile *m*.
republic [rɪ'pʌblɪk] république *f*.
reputable ['repjʊtəb(ə)l] *a* de bonne réputation.
reputation [repjʊ'teɪʃ(ə)n] réputation *f*; **to have a r. for being** avoir la réputation d'être.
request [rɪ'kwest] **1** *n* demande *f* (**for** de). **2** *vt* demander (**sth**

from s.o. qch à qn, **s.o. to do** à qn de faire).

require [rɪ'kwaɪər] *vt* (*of thing*) demander; (*of person*) avoir besoin de; **if required** s'il le faut.

required *a* **the r. qualities/***etc* les qualités/*etc* qu'il faut.

rescue ['reskjuː] **1** *vt* (*save*) sauver; (*set free*) délivrer (**from** de). **2** *n* sauvetage *m* (**of** de); (*help*) secours *mpl*; **to go to s.o.'s r.** aller au secours de qn.

research **1** *n* recherches *fpl* (**on, into** sur). **2** *vi* faire des recherches.

researcher chercheur, -euse *mf*.

resemblance ressemblance *f* (**to** avec).

resemble [rɪ'zemb(ə)l] *vt* ressembler à.

reser'vation (*booking*) réservation *f*; (*doubt*) réserve *f*.

reserve [rɪ'zɜːv] **1** *vt* réserver; (*right*) se réserver. **2** *n* **r. (player)** remplaçant, -ante *mf*; **nature r.** réserve *f* naturelle; **in r.** en réserve.

reserved *a* (*person*, *place*) réservé.

reserve tank réservoir *m* de secours.

residence ['rezɪdəns] (*home*) résidence *f*; (*of students*) foyer *m*.

resident **1** *n* habitant, -ante *mf*; (*of hotel*) pensionnaire *mf*. **2** *a* **to be r. in London** résider à Londres.

resi'dential *a* (*district*) résidentiel.

resign [rɪ'zaɪn] **1** *vt* **to r. oneself to sth/to doing** se résigner à qch/à faire. **2** *vi* démissionner; **to r. from one's job** démissionner.

resig'nation (*from job*) démission *f*.

resist [rɪ'zɪst] **1** *vt* (*attack etc*) résister à; **to r. doing sth** se retenir de faire qch; **she can't r. cakes** elle ne peut pas résister devant des gâteaux. **2** *vi* résister.

resistance résistance *f* (**to** à).

resit* *vt* (*exam*) repasser.

resort[1] [rɪ'zɔːt] **1** *vi* **to r. to doing** en venir à faire; **to r. to sth** avoir recours à qch. **2** *n* **as a last r.** en dernier ressort.

resort[2] **(holiday** *or Am* **vacation) r.** station *f* de vacances; **seaside** *or Am* **beach r.** station *f* balnéaire; **ski r.** station de ski.

resources [rɪ'sɔːsɪz] *npl* (*wealth*, *means*) ressources *fpl*.

respect [rɪ'spekt] **1** *n* respect *m* (**for** pour, de); **with r. to** en ce qui concerne. **2** *vt* respecter.

respectable *a* (*honourable*, *quite good*) respectable; (*clothes*, *behaviour*) convenable.

respond [rɪ'spɒnd] *vi* répondre (**to** à); **to r. to treatment** bien réagir au traitement.

response réponse *f*.

responsi'bility responsabilité *f*.

responsible [rɪ'spɒnsəb(ə)l] *a* responsable (**for** de, **to s.o.** devant qn); (*job*) à responsabilités.
rest[1] [rest] **1** *n* repos *m*; (*support*) support *m*; **to have** *or* **take a r.** se reposer. **2** *vi* (*relax*) se reposer; **to be resting on sth** (*of hand etc*) être posé sur qch. **3** *vt* (*lean*) appuyer (**on** sur, **against** contre).
rest[2] (*remaining part*) reste *m* (**of** de); **the r.** (*others*) les autres *mfpl*; **the r. of the men**/*etc* les autres hommes/*etc*.
restaurant ['restərɒnt] restaurant *m*.
restful *a* reposant.
restless *a* agité.
restore *vt* (*give back*) rendre (**to** à); (*building etc*) restaurer.
restrict *vt* restreindre (**to** à).
restricted *a* restreint.
restriction restriction *f*.
rest room *Am* toilettes *fpl*.
result [rɪ'zʌlt] résultat *m*; **as a r. of** par suite de.
resume [rɪ'zjuːm] *vti* reprendre.
résumé ['rezjʊmeɪ] *Am* curriculum vitae *m inv*.
retail ['riːteɪl] **1** *a* (*price*, *shop*) de détail. **2** *adv* (*to sell*) au détail.
retailer détaillant, -ante *mf*.
retain [rɪ'teɪn] *vt* (*freshness etc*) conserver.
retire *vi* (*from work*) prendre sa retraite; (*withdraw*) se retirer (**from** de, **to** à); (*go to bed*) aller se coucher.
retired *a* (*no longer working*) retraité.
retirement retraite *f*.
return **1** *vi* (*come back*) revenir; (*go back*) retourner; (*go back home*) rentrer. **2** *vt* (*give back*) rendre; (*put back*) remettre; (*send back*) renvoyer. **3** *n* retour *m*; (*on investment*) rendement *m*; **r. (ticket)** (billet *m* d')aller et retour *m*; **tax r.** déclaration *f* de revenus; **in r.** en échange (**for** de). **4** *a* (*flight etc*) (de) retour; **r. game** revanche *f*.
returnable *a* (*bottle*) consigné.
reveal [rɪ'viːl] *vt* (*make known*) révéler (**that** que).
revenge [rɪ'vendʒ] vengeance *f*; **to get one's r.** se venger (**on s.o.** de qn, **for sth** de qch); **in r.** pour se venger.
reverse [rɪ'vɜːs] **1** *a* (*order*) inverse. **2** *n* contraire *m*; **in r. (gear)** en marche arrière. **3** *vt* **to r. the charges** (*when telephoning*) téléphoner en PCV. **4** *vti* **to r. (the car)** faire marche arrière; **to r. in/out** rentrer/sortir en marche arrière.
review **1** *vt* (*book*) faire la critique de. **2** *n* critique *f*.
revise [rɪ'vaɪz] **1** *vt* (*opinion*, *notes*, *text*) réviser. **2** *vi* (*for exam*) réviser (**for** pour).

revision révision *f.*
revive [rɪ'vaɪv] *vt* (*unconscious person*) ranimer.
revolt [rɪ'vəʊlt] révolte *f.*
revolting *a* dégoûtant.
revolution [revə'luːʃ(ə)n] révolution *f.*
revolutionary *a* & *n* révolutionnaire (*mf*).
revolve [rɪ'vɒlv] *vi* tourner (**around** autour de).
revolver [rɪ'vɒlvər] revolver *m.*
revolving door(s) (porte *f* à) tambour *m.*
reward [rɪ'wɔːd] **1** *n* récompense *f* (**for** de, pour). **2** *vt* récompenser (**s.o. for sth** qn de *or* pour qch).
rewind* **1** *vt* (*tape*) rembobiner. **2** *vi* se rembobiner.
rheumatism ['ruːmətɪz(ə)m] rhumatisme *m*; **to have r.** avoir des rhumatismes.
rhinoceros [raɪ'nɒsərəs] rhinocéros *m.*
rhubarb ['ruːbɑːb] rhubarbe *f.*
rhyme [raɪm] **1** *n* rime *f*; (*poem*) vers *mpl.* **2** *vi* rimer (**with** avec).
rhythm ['rɪð(ə)m] rythme *m.*
rhythmical *a* rythmé.
rib [rɪb] (*in body*) côte *f.*
ribbon ['rɪbən] ruban *m.*
rice [raɪs] riz *m.*
rich [rɪtʃ] **1** *a* riche. **2** *n* **the r.** les riches *mpl.*
riches *npl* richesses *fpl.*
rid [rɪd] *a* **to get r. of** se débarrasser de.
riddle ['rɪd(ə)l] (*puzzle*) énigme *f.*
ride [raɪd] **1** *n* (*on bicycle, by car, on horse etc*) promenade *f*; (*distance*) trajet *m*; **to go for a (car) r.** faire une promenade (en voiture); **to give s.o. a r.** (*in car*) emmener qn en voiture. **2** *vi** aller (à bicyclette, à moto, à cheval *etc*) (**to** à); **to r., go riding** (*on horse*) monter (à cheval). **3** *vt* (*a particular horse*) monter; (*distance*) faire (à cheval *etc*); **to r. a horse** *or* **horses** monter à cheval; **I was riding (on) a bicycle** j'étais à bicyclette; **to r. a bicycle to** aller à bicylette à.
rider (*on horse*) cavalier, -ière *mf.*
ridiculous [rɪ'dɪkjʊləs] *a* ridicule.
riding (**horse**) **r.**, *Am* (**horseback**) **r.** équitation *f.*
rifle ['raɪf(ə)l] fusil *m.*
rig [rɪg] (**oil**) **r.** derrick *m*; (*at sea*) plate-forme *f* pétrolière.
right[1] [raɪt] **1** *a* (*correct*) bon (*f* bonne); (*fair*) juste; (*angle*) droit; **to be r.** (*of person*) avoir raison (**to do** de faire); **the r. choice/time** le bon choix/moment; **it's the r. time** (*accurate*) c'est l'heure exacte;

the clock's r. la pendule est à l'heure; **it's not r. to steal** ce n'est pas bien de voler; **to put r.** (*error*) corriger; **r.!** bien!; **that's r.** c'est ça. **2** *adv* (*straight*) (tout) droit; (*completely*) tout à fait; (*correctly*) juste; (*well*) bien; **she did r.** elle a bien fait; **r. round** tout autour (**sth** de qch); **r. here** ici même; **r. away, r. now** tout de suite. **3** *n* **r. and wrong** le bien et le mal.

right² **1** *a* (*hand, side etc*) droit. **2** *adv* à droite. **3** *n* droite *f*; **on** *or* **to the r.** à droite (**of** de).

right³ (*claim*) droit *m* (**to do** de faire); **to have a r. to sth** avoir droit à qch.

right-hand *a* à *or* de droite; **on the r.-hand side** à droite (**of** de).

right-'handed *a* (*person*) droitier.

rightly *adv* à juste titre.

rigid ['rɪdʒɪd] *a* rigide.

rim [rɪm] (*of cup etc*) bord *m*.

rind [raɪnd] (*of cheese*) croûte *f*.

ring¹ [rɪŋ] (*on finger, curtain etc*) anneau *m*; (*with jewel*) bague *f*; (*of people, chairs*) cercle *m*; *Boxing* ring *m*; (*burner on stove*) brûleur *m*; **diamond r.** bague *f* de diamants.

ring² **1** *n* (*sound*) sonnerie *f*; **there's a r.** on sonne; **to give s.o. a r.** (*phone call*) passer un coup de fil à qn. **2** *vi** (*of bell, phone, person*) sonner. **3** *vt* sonner; **to r. the (door)bell** sonner (à la porte).

ring (round) entourer (**with** de); (*item on list etc*) encadrer.

ring (up) **1** *vt* (*phone*) téléphoner à. **2** *vi* téléphoner.

ring back *vti* (*phone*) rappeler.

ringing tone (*on phone*) sonnerie *f*.

ring off *vi* (*after phoning*) raccrocher.

ring out *vi* (*of bell*) sonner; (*of sound*) retentir.

ring road route *f* de ceinture; (*motorway*) périphérique *m*.

rinse [rɪns] **1** *vt* rincer; **to r. one's hands** se rincer les mains. **2** *n* **to give sth a r.** rincer qch.

rinse out rincer.

riot ['raɪət] **1** *n* (*uprising*) émeute *f*; (*fight*) bagarre *f*. **2** *vi* faire une émeute; (*fight*) se bagarrer.

rip [rɪp] **1** *vt* déchirer. **2** *vi* (*of fabric*) se déchirer. **3** *n* déchirure *f*.

ripe [raɪp] *a* mûr; (*cheese*) fait.

ripen *vti* mûrir.

rip off *vt* (*button etc*) arracher (**from** de); **to r. s.o. off** *Fam* rouler qn.

'rip-off *Fam* **it's a r.-off** c'est du vol organisé.

rip sth out arracher qch (**from** de).

rip sth up déchirer qch.

rise [raɪz] **1** *vi** (*of temperature*, *balloon*, *price*) monter; (*of sun*, *curtain*, *person*) se lever; **to r. in price** augmenter de prix. **2** *n* (*in price etc*) hausse *f* (**in** de); (*slope in ground*) montée *f*; (**pay**) **r.** augmentation *f* (de salaire); **to give r. to sth** donner lieu à qch.
risk [rɪsk] **1** *n* risque *m* (**of doing** de faire, **in doing** à faire); **at r.** (*person*) en danger; (*job*) menacé. **2** *vt* risquer; **she won't r. leaving** elle ne se risquera pas à partir.
risky *a* risqué.
rival ['raɪv(ə)l] **1** *a* (*firm etc*) rival. **2** *n* rival, -ale *mf*. **3** *vt* (*compete with*) rivaliser avec (**in** de); (*equal*) égaler (**in** en).
river ['rɪvər] rivière *f*; (*flowing into sea*) fleuve *m*.
Riviera [rɪvɪ'eərə] **the (French) R.** la Côte d'Azur.
roach [rəutʃ] *Am* (*cockroach*) cafard *m*.
road [rəud] **1** *n* route *f* (**to** qui va à); (*small*) chemin *m*; (*in town*) rue *f*; (*roadway*) chaussée *f*; **across** *or* **over the r.** (*building etc*) en face; **by r.** par la route. **2** *a* (*map*, *safety*) routier; (*accident*) de la route; **r. sign** panneau *m* (routier).
roadside *a* & *n* (**by the**) **r.** au bord de la route.
roadway chaussée *f*.
roadworks, *Am* **roadwork** travaux *mpl*.
roam [rəum] *vt* parcourir; **to r. the streets** (*of child*, *dog etc*) traîner dans les rues.
roar [rɔːr] **1** *vi* (*of lion*) rugir; (*of person*) hurler. **2** *n* (*of lion*) rugissement *m*.
roast [rəust] **1** *vt* rôtir; (*coffee*) griller. **2** *vi* (*of meat*) rôtir. **3** *n* (*meat*) rôti *m*. **4** *a* (*chicken etc*) rôti; **r. beef** rosbif *m*.
rob [rɒb] *vt* (*person*) voler; (*bank*) attaquer; (*by breaking in*) cambrioler; **to r. s.o. of sth** voler qch à qn.
robber voleur, -euse *mf*.
robbery vol *m*.
robe [rəub] (*dressing gown*) robe *f* de chambre.
robin ['rɒbɪn] rouge-gorge *m*.
robot ['rəubɒt] robot *m*.
rock¹ [rɒk] **1** *vt* (*baby*, *boat*) bercer. **2** *vi* (*sway*) se balancer; (*of building*) trembler. **3** *n* (*music*) rock *m*.
rock² (*substance*) roche *f*; (*boulder*, *rock face*) rocher *m*; (*stone*) *Am* pierre *f*; **r. face** paroi *f* rocheuse.
rocket ['rɒkɪt] fusée *f*.
rocking chair fauteuil *m* à bascule.
rod [rɒd] (*wooden*) baguette *f*; (*metal*) tige *f*; (*of curtain*) tringle *f*; (*for fishing*) canne *f* (à pêche).
rogue [rəug] (*dishonest*) crapule *f*; (*mischievous*) coquin, -ine *mf*.

role [rəʊl] rôle *m*.

roll [rəʊl] **1** *n* (*of paper etc*) rouleau *m*; (*small bread loaf*) petit pain *m*; (*of drum*) roulement *m*. **2** *vi* (*of ball etc*) rouler; (*of person, animal*) se rouler. **3** *vt* rouler.

roll down (*car window etc*) baisser; (*slope*) descendre (en roulant).

roller (*for hair, painting etc*) rouleau *m*.

roller-skate 1 *n* patin *m* à roulettes. **2** *vi* faire du patin à roulettes.

rolling pin rouleau *m* à pâtisserie.

roll over 1 *vi* (*many times*) se rouler; (*once*) se retourner. **2** *vt* retourner.

roll up (*map, cloth*) rouler; (*sleeve, trousers, Am pants*) retrousser.

Roman ['rəʊmən] *a* & *n* romain, -aine (*mf*).

Roman Catholic *a* & *n* catholique (*mf*).

romance [rəʊ'mæns] (*love*) amour *m*; (*affair*) aventure *f* amoureuse.

romantic *a* romantique.

roof [ru:f] toit *m*; (*of tunnel, cave*) plafond *m*.

roof rack (*of car*) galerie *f*.

room [ru:m] (*in house etc*) pièce *f*; (*bedroom*) chambre *f*; (*large, public*) salle *f*; (*space*) place *f* (**for** pour); **men's r., ladies' r.** *Am* toilettes *fpl*.

roommate camarade *mf* de chambre.

roomy *a* spacieux; (*clothes*) ample.

root [ru:t] racine *f*; (*origin*) origine *f*; **to take r.** (*of plant*) prendre racine.

root for *Fam* encourager.

rope [rəʊp] corde *f*.

rope off (*of police etc*) interdire l'accès de.

rose [rəʊz] (*flower*) rose *f*; **r. bush** rosier *m*.

rot (away) [rɒt] *vti* pourrir.

rota ['rəʊtə] liste *f* (de service).

rotten ['rɒt(ə)n] *a* (*fruit, weather etc*) pourri; (*bad*) *Fam* moche; **to feel r.** (*ill*) être mal fichu.

rough[1] [rʌf] *a* (*surface, plank*) rugueux; (*ground*) inégal; (*brutal*) brutal; (*sea*) agité.

rough[2] *a* (*calculation etc*) approximatif; **r. guess** approximation *f*; **r. copy, r. draft** brouillon *m*; **(some) r. paper** du (papier) brouillon; **r. book** cahier *m* de brouillon.

roughly[1] *adv* (*not gently*) rudement; (*brutally*) brutalement.

roughly[2] *adv* (*more or less*) à peu (de choses) près.

round[1] [raʊnd] **1** *adv* autour; **all r., right r.** tout autour; **to go r. to**

s.o.('s) passer chez qn; **to ask r.** inviter chez soi; **r. here** par ici. **2** *prep* autour de; **r. about** (*approximately*) environ.

round² **1** *a* rond. **2** *n* (*slice*) tranche *f*; *Boxing* round *m*; (*of drinks, visits*) tournée *f*; (*of policeman*) ronde *f*.

roundabout **1** *a* indirect. **2** *n* (*at funfair*) manège *m*; (*junction*) rond-point *m* (à sens giratoire).

round off (*meal etc*) terminer (**with** par); (*figure*) arrondir.

round trip *Am* aller (et) retour *m*.

round up (*people, animals*) rassembler.

route [ruːt] itinéraire *m*; (*of ship, aircraft*) route *f*; **bus r.** ligne *f* d'autobus.

routine [ruː'tiːn] train-train *m*.

row¹ [rəʊ] **1** *n* (*line*) rang *m*, rangée *f*; (*one behind another*) file *f*; **two days in a r.** deux jours de suite. **2** *vi* (*in boat*) ramer. **3** *vt* (*boat*) faire aller à la rame.

row² [raʊ] **1** *n Fam* (*noise*) vacarme *m*; (*quarrel*) dispute *f*. **2** *vi Fam* se disputer (**with** avec).

rowing boat, *Am* **row boat** bateau *m* à rames.

royal ['rɔɪəl] *a* royal.

royalty personnages *mpl* royaux.

rub [rʌb] *vti* frotter; (*person*) frictionner.

rubber ['rʌbər] caoutchouc *m*; (*eraser*) gomme *f*.

rubber stamp tampon *m*.

rubbish ['rʌbɪʃ] (*waste*) ordures *fpl*; (*junk*) saletés *f*; (*nonsense*) idioties *fpl*.

rubbish bin poubelle *f*.

rubbish dump décharge *f* (publique); (*untidy place*) dépotoir *m*.

rubbishy *a* (*book, film*) nul; (*goods*) de mauvaise qualité.

rubble ['rʌb(ə)l] décombres *mpl*.

rub down (*person*) frictionner; (*with sandpaper*) poncer (*qch*).

rub in (*cream*) faire pénétrer (en massant).

rub off *or* **out** (*mark*) effacer.

ruby ['ruːbɪ] rubis *m*.

rucksack ['rʌksæk] sac *m* à dos.

rudder ['rʌdər] gouvernail *m*.

rude [ruːd] *a* impoli (**to** envers); (*coarse, insolent*) grossier (**to** envers); (*indecent*) obscène.

rudeness impolitesse *f*; grossièreté *f*.

rug [rʌg] carpette *f*.

rugby ['rʌgbɪ] rugby *m*.

ruin ['ruːɪn] **1** *n* ruine *f*; **in ruins** (*building*) en ruine. **2** *vt* (*health, person etc*) ruiner; (*clothes*) abîmer.

rule [ruːl] **1** *n* règle *f*; **against the rules** *or Am* **rule** contraire au règlement; **as a r.** en règle générale. **2** *vt* (*country*) gouverner. **3** *vi* (*of king etc*) régner (**over** sur).
rule sth out exclure qch.
ruler (*for measuring*) règle *f*; (*king, queen etc*) souverain, -aine *mf*.
rum [rʌm] rhum *m*.
rumour ['ruːmər] (*Am* **rumor**) bruit *m*, rumeur *f*.
run [rʌn] **1** *n* (*period*) période *f*; (*for skiing*) piste *f*; **to go for a r.** (aller) faire une course à pied; (*in car*) (aller) faire un tour; **on the r.** (*prisoner*) en fuite; **in the long r.** à la longue. **2** *vi** courir; (*of river, nose, tap or Am faucet*) couler; (*of colour in washing*) déteindre; (*of play, film*) se jouer; (*function*) marcher; (*of car engine*) tourner; **to r. down/in/***etc* descendre/entrer/*etc* en courant; **to go running** faire du jogging. **3** *vt* (*race, risk*) courir; (*temperature, errand*) faire; (*business, country etc*) diriger; (*bath*) faire couler; **to r. a car** avoir une voiture.
run across s.o. (*meet*) tomber sur qn.
run along! filez!
run away s'enfuir (**from** de).
run down (*pedestrian*) renverser.
rung [rʌŋ] (*of ladder*) barreau *m*.
run into (*meet*) tomber sur; (*crash into*) percuter.
runner (*athlete*) coureur *m*.
runner-'up second, -onde *mf*.
running 1 *n* (*on foot*) course *f*; (*of firm, country*) direction *f*. **2** *a* **r. water** eau *f* courante; **six days/***etc* **r.** six jours/*etc* de suite.
runny *a* (*nose*) qui coule.
run off (*flee*) s'enfuir.
run out (*of stocks*) s'épuiser; (*of lease*) expirer; **to r. out of** (*time, money*) manquer de; **we've r. out of coffee** on n'a plus de café.
run over *vt* (*kill pedestrian*) écraser; (*knock down pedestrian*) renverser.
runway piste *f* (d'envol)
rush [rʌʃ] **1** *vi* se précipiter (**at** sur, **towards** vers); (*hurry*) se dépêcher (**to do** de faire). **2** *vt* (*hurry*) bousculer (*qn*); **to r. s.o. to hospital** *or Am* **to the hospital** transporter qn d'urgence à l'hôpital; **to r. (through) sth** (*job, meal etc*) faire, manger *etc* qch en vitesse. **3** *n* ruée *f* (**for** vers); (*confusion*) bousculade *f*; (*hurry*) hâte *f*; **in a r.** pressé (**to do** de faire).
rush hour heure *f* d'affluence.
rush out *vi* partir en vitesse.
Russian ['rʌʃ(ə)n] **1** *a* & *n* russe (*mf*). **2** *n* (*language*) russe *m*.

rust [rʌst] **1** *n* rouille *f*. **2** *vi* (se) rouiller.
rusty *a* (*metal*, *memory etc*) rouillé.
rye bread [raɪ] pain *m* de seigle.

S

sack [sæk] **1** *n* (*bag*) sac *m*; **to get the s.** (*from one's job*) se faire virer; **to give s.o. the s.** virer qn. **2** *vt* (*dismiss*) virer.
sacrifice ['sækrɪfaɪs] **1** *n* sacrifice *m*. **2** *vt* sacrifier (**to** à, **for** pour).
sad [sæd] *a* triste.
sadden *vt* attrister.
saddle ['sæd(ə)l] selle *f*.
sadly *adv* tristement; (*unfortunately*) malheureusement.
sadness tristesse *f*.
safe¹ [seɪf] *a* (*person*) en sécurité; (*equipment*, *toy*, *animal*) sans danger; (*place*, *investment*, *method*) sûr; (*bridge*, *ladder*) solide; **s. (and sound)** sain et sauf; **it's s. to go out** on peut sortir sans danger; **s. from** à l'abri de.
safe² (*for money etc*) coffre-fort *m*.
safely *adv* (*without accident*) sans accident; (*without risk*) sans risque; (*in a safe place*) en lieu sûr.
safety sécurité *f*.
safety belt ceinture *f* de sécurité.
safety pin épingle *f* de sûreté.
sag [sæg] *vi* (*of roof*, *ground*) s'affaisser.
said [sed] *pt & pp de* **say**.
sail [seɪl] **1** *vi* naviguer; (*leave*) partir; (*as sport*) faire de la voile; **to s. round the world/an island** faire le tour du monde/d'une île en bateau. **2** *vt* (*boat*) piloter. **3** *n* voile *f*.
sailboard planche *f* (à voile).
sailboat *Am* voilier *m*.
sailing navigation *f*; (*sport*) voile *f*; (*departure*) départ *m*.
sailing boat voilier *m*.
sailor marin *m*.
saint [seɪnt] saint *m*, sainte *f*.
sake [seɪk] **for my/your/his/***etc* **s.** pour moi/toi/lui/*etc*; **(just) for the s. of eating/***etc* simplement pour manger/*etc*.
salad ['sæləd] salade *f*.
salad bowl saladier *m*.
salad dressing sauce *f* de salade.
salary ['sælərɪ] (*professional*) traitement *m*; (*wage*) salaire *m*.
sale [seɪl] vente *f*; **sale(s)** (*at reduced prices*) soldes *mpl*; **in a** *or* **the s.**, *Am* **on s.** (*cheaply*) en solde; **on s.** (*available*) en vente; **(up) for s.** à vendre.
salesclerk *Am* vendeur, -euse *mf*.
salesman (*pl* **-men**) (*in shop*) vendeur *m*; **(travelling) s.**, *Am* **(tra-**

veling) s. représentant *m* (de commerce).

saleswoman (*pl* **-women**) vendeuse *f*; (*who travels*) représentante *f* (de commerce).

saliva [sə'laɪvə] salive *f*.

salmon ['sæmən] saumon *m*.

salt [sɔːlt] **1** *n* sel *m*; **bath salts** sels *mpl* de bain. **2** *vt* saler.

saltcellar, *Am* **saltshaker** salière *f*.

salty *a* salé.

same [seɪm] **1** *a* même; **the (very) s. house as** (exactement) la même maison que. **2** *pron* **the s.** le *or* la même, *pl* les mêmes; **it's all the s. to me** ça m'est égal; **all** *or* **just the s.** tout de même; **to do the s.** en faire autant.

sample ['sɑːmp(ə)l] **1** *n* échantillon *m*; (*of blood*) prélèvement *m*. **2** *vt* (*wine etc*) goûter.

sand [sænd] **1** *n* sable *m*. **2** *vt* (*road*) sabler.

sandal ['sænd(ə)l] sandale *f*.

sandcastle château *m* de sable.

sandpaper papier *m* de verre.

sandwich ['sænwɪdʒ] sandwich *m*; **cheese**/*etc* **s.** sandwich au fromage/*etc*; **s. bar** sandwicherie *f*.

sandy *a* (*beach*) de sable; (*road*) sablonneux.

sanitary towel *or Am* **napkin** ['sænɪtərɪ] serviette *f* hygiénique.

Santa Claus ['sæntəklɔːz] le père Noël.

sardine [sɑː'diːn] sardine *f*.

sat [sæt] *pt & pp de* **sit.**

satchel ['sætʃ(ə)l] cartable *m*.

satellite ['sætəlaɪt] satellite *m*.

satin ['sætɪn] satin *m*.

satisfaction [sætɪs'fækʃ(ə)n] satisfaction *f*.

satisfactory *a* satisfaisant.

'satisfy *vt* satisfaire (*qn*); **to s. oneself that** s'assurer que; **satisfied (with)** satisfait (de).

'satisfying *a* satisfaisant.

satsuma [sæt'suːmə] (*fruit*) mandarine *f*, satsuma *f*.

saturate ['sætʃəreɪt] *vt* (*soak*) tremper.

Saturday ['sætədɪ, -deɪ] samedi *m*.

sauce [sɔːs] sauce *f*; *Am* (*stewed fruit*) compote *f*; **tomato s.** sauce *f* tomate.

saucepan ['sɔːspən, *Am* -pæn] casserole *f*.

saucer ['sɔːsər] soucoupe *f*.

sauna ['sɔːnə] sauna *m*.

sausage ['sɒsɪdʒ] saucisse *f*; (*dried, for slicing*) saucisson *m*.

save [seɪv] **1** *vt* (*rescue*) sauver (**from** de); (*keep*) garder; (*money, time*) économiser; (*stamps*) collectionner; **to s. s.o. from doing** empêcher qn de faire; **that will s. him** *or* **her (the bother of) going** ça lui évitera d'y aller. **2** *n Football* arrêt *m*.
save up **1** *vt* (*money*) économiser. **2** *vi* faire des économies (**for sth, to buy sth** pour acheter qch).
savings ['seɪvɪŋz] *npl* (*money*) économies *fpl*.
savings bank caisse *f* d'épargne.
saw[1] [sɔː] **1** *n* scie *f*. **2** *vt** scier.
saw[2] *pt de* **see.**
sawdust sciure *f*.
saw sth off scier qch.
saxophone ['sæksəfəʊn] saxophone *m*.
say* [seɪ] *vt* dire (**to** à, **that** que); (*of dial etc*) marquer; **to s. again** répéter; **(let's) s. tomorrow** disons demain; **that's to s.** c'est-à-dire.
saying proverbe *m*.
scab [skæb] (*of wound*) croûte *f*.
scaffolding ['skæfəldɪŋ] échafaudage *m*.
scald [skɔːld] *vt* ébouillanter.
scale [skeɪl] (*of map, wages etc*) échelle *f*; (*on fish*) écaille *f*; (*in music*) gamme *f*.
scales [skeɪlz] *npl* (*for weighing*) balance *f*; **(bathroom) s.** pèse-personne *m*.
scallion ['skæljən] *Am* oignon *m* vert.
scandal ['skænd(ə)l] scandale *m*; (*gossip*) médisances *fpl*.
Scandinavian [skændɪ'neɪvɪən] *a & n* scandinave (*mf*).
scanner ['skænər] scanner *m*.
scar [skɑːr] cicatrice *f*.
scarce [skeəs] *a* rare.
scarcely *adv* à peine.
scare [skeər] *vt* faire peur à.
scarecrow épouvantail *m*.
scared *a* effrayé; **to be s. (stiff)** avoir (très) peur.
scarf [skɑːf] (*pl* **scarves**) (*long*) écharpe *f*; (*square, for women*) foulard *m*.
scarlet fever ['skɑːlət] scarlatine *f*.
scary *a* **it's s.** ça fait peur.
scatter ['skætər] **1** *vt* (*crowd, clouds etc*) disperser; (*throw or dot about*) éparpiller (*papiers etc*). **2** *vi* (*of crowd*) se disperser.
scene [siːn] (*setting, fuss, part of play or film*) scène *f*; (*of crime, accident*) lieu *m*; (*view*) vue *f*.
scenery paysage *m*; (*for play or film*) décor(s) *m*(*pl*).

scent [sent] (*fragrance*, *perfume*) parfum *m*.
schedule ['ʃedju:l, *Am* 'skedjʊl] **1** *n* (*of work etc*) programme *m*; (*timetable*) horaire *m*; **on s.** (*on time*) à l'heure; **according to s.** comme prévu. **2** *vt* (*to plan*) prévoir; (*event*) fixer le programme de.
scheduled *a* (*planned*) prévu; (*service*, *flight*) régulier.
scheme [ski:m] plan *m* (**to do** pour faire); (*dishonest trick*) combine *f*.
scholarship ['skɒləʃɪp] (*grant*) bourse *f* (d'études).
school [sku:l] **1** *n* école *f*; (*teaching*, *lessons*) classe *f*; **in** *or* **at s.** à l'école; **secondary s.**, *Am* **high s.** collège *m*; **public s.** école *f* privée; *Am* école publique; **summer s.** cours *mpl* d'été. **2** *a* (*year etc*) scolaire.
schoolboy écolier *m*.
schoolgirl écolière *f*.
schoolmate camarade *mf* de classe.
schoolteacher (*primary*) instituteur, -trice *mf*; (*secondary*) professeur *m*.
science ['saɪəns] science *f*; **to study s.** étudier les sciences.
science fiction science-fiction *f*.
scien'tific *a* scientifique.
scientist scientifique *mf*, savant *m*.
scissors ['sɪzəz] *npl* ciseaux *mpl*.
scold [skəʊld] *vt* gronder (**for doing** pour avoir fait).
scone [skəʊn] petit pain *m* au lait.
scooter ['sku:tər] (*child's*) trottinette *f*; (*motorcycle*) scooter *m*.
scope [skəʊp] (*range*) étendue *f*; (*limits*) limites *fpl*; **s. for sth/for doing** (*opportunity*) des possibilités *fpl* de qch/de faire.
scorch [skɔ:tʃ] *vt* roussir.
score[1] [skɔ:r] **1** *n* (*in sport*) score *m*; (*at cards*) marque *f*; (*music*) partition *f*. **2** *vt* (*point*, *goal*) marquer. **3** *vi* marquer un point *or* un but; (*count points*) marquer les points.
score[2] **a s. (of)** (*twenty*) une vingtaine (de).
scorn [skɔ:n] mépris *m*.
Scot [skɒt] Écossais, -aise *mf*.
Scotch (*whisky*) scotch *m*.
scotch (tape)® [skɒtʃ] *Am* scotch® *m*.
Scotsman (*pl* **-men**) Écossais *m*.
Scotswoman (*pl* **-women**) Écossaise *f*.
Scottish *a* écossais.
scoundrel ['skaʊndr(ə)l] vaurien *m*.

scout [skaʊt] **(boy) s.** scout *m*; **girl s.** *Am* éclaireuse *f*.
scrambled ['skræmb(ə)ld] *a* (*egg*) brouillé.
scrap [skræp] **1** *n* petit morceau *m* (**of** de); (*of information*) fragment *m*; (*metal*) ferraille *f*; **scraps** (*food*) restes *mpl*. **2** *vt* se débarrasser de; (*vehicle*) mettre à la ferraille; (*plan*) abandonner.
scrapbook album *m* (*pour collages etc*).
scrape [skreɪp] **1** *vt* racler; (*skin, knee etc*) érafler. **2** *vi* **to s. against sth** frotter contre qch. **3** *n* (*on skin*) éraflure *f*.
scrape away *or* **off** (*mud etc*) racler.
scrape through (*in exam*) réussir de justesse.
scrape together (*money, people*) réunir (difficilement).
scrap metal ferraille *f*.
scrap paper (papier *m*) brouillon *m*.
scratch [skrætʃ] **1** *n* (*mark, injury*) éraflure *f*; **to start from s.** (re)partir de zéro; **it isn't up to s.** ce n'est pas au niveau. **2** *vt* (*arm etc that itches*) gratter; (*skin, furniture etc*) érafler; (*one's name*) graver (**on** sur). **3** *vi* (*relieve an itch*) se gratter.
scream [skriːm] **1** *vti* crier; **to s. at s.o.** crier après qn. **2** *n* cri *m* (perçant).
screen [skriːn] écran *m*; **(folding) s.** paravent *m*.
screw [skruː] **1** *n* vis *f*. **2** *vt* visser (**to** à).
screw sth down *or* **on** visser qch.
screwdriver tournevis *m*.
screw up (*paper*) chiffonner; (*eyes*) plisser.
scribble ['skrɪb(ə)l] *vti* griffonner.
script [skrɪpt] (*of film*) scénario *m*; (*of play*) texte *m*; (*in exam*) copie *f*.
scrub [skrʌb] *vt* nettoyer (à la brosse); (*pan*) récurer.
scrubbing brush brosse *f* dure.
scrum [skrʌm] *Rugby* mêlée *f*.
scuba diving ['skuːbə] plongée *f* sous-marine.
sculptor ['skʌlptər] sculpteur *m*.
sculpture (*art, object*) sculpture *f*.
sea [siː] mer *f*; (**out**) **at s.** en mer; **by s.** par mer; **by** *or* **beside the s.** au bord de la mer.
seafood fruits *mpl* de mer.
seafront bord *m* *or* front *m* de mer.
seagull mouette *f*.
seal [siːl] **1** *n* (*animal*) phoque *m*; (*mark, design*) sceau *m*; (*of wax*) cachet *m* (de cire). **2** *vt* (*document, container*) sceller; (*envelope*) cacheter; (*with putty*) boucher.

sea lion otarie *f*.
seal off (*of police etc*) interdire l'accès de.
seam [siːm] (*in cloth*) couture *f*.
search [sɜːtʃ] **1** *n* recherche *f* (**for** de); (*of person*, *place*) fouille *f*; **in s. of** à la recherche de. **2** *vt* (*person*, *place*) fouiller (**for** pour trouver); **to s. (through) one's papers**/*etc* **for sth** chercher qch dans ses papiers/*etc*. **3** *vi* chercher; **to s. for sth** chercher qch.
seashell coquillage *m*.
seashore bord *m* de la mer.
seasick *a* **to be s.** avoir le mal de mer.
seasickness mal *m* de mer.
seaside bord *m* de la mer.
season ['siːz(ə)n] **1** *n* saison *f*. **2** *vt* (*food*) assaisonner.
seasoning assaisonnement *m*.
season ticket carte *f* d'abonnement.
seat [siːt] **1** *n* siège *m*; (*on train*, *bus*) banquette *f*; (*in cinema*, *theatre*) fauteuil *m*; (*place*) place *f*; **to take** *or* **have a s.** s'asseoir. **2** *vt* (*at table*) placer (*qn*); **the room seats 50** la salle a 50 places (assises); **be seated!** asseyez-vous!
seat belt ceinture *f* de sécurité.
seated *a* (*sitting*) assis.
seating (*seats*) places *fpl* assises.
seaweed algue(s) *f*(*pl*).
second[1] ['sekənd] **1** *a* deuxième, second; **every s. week** une semaine sur deux; **in s. (gear)** en seconde. **2** *adv* **to come s.** se classer deuxième. **3** *n* (*person*, *object*) deuxième *mf*, second, -onde *mf*.
second[2] (*part of minute*) seconde *f*.
secondary *a* secondaire.
second-'class *a* (*ticket*) de seconde (classe); (*mail*) non urgent.
second'hand *a* & *adv* (*not new*) d'occasion.
secondly *adv* deuxièmement.
secret ['siːkrɪt] *a* & *n* secret (*m*); **in s.** en secret.
secretary ['sekrət(ə)rɪ] secrétaire *mf*.
section ['sekʃ(ə)n] (*of town*, *book etc*) partie *f*; (*of machine*, *furniture*) élément *m*; (*in store*) rayon *m*; **the sports**/*etc* **s.** (*of newspaper*) la page des sports/*etc*.
secure [sɪ'kjʊər] **1** *a* (*person*, *valuables*) en sûreté; (*place*) sûr; (*solid*) solide; (*door*, *window*) bien fermé. **2** *vt* (*fasten*) attacher; (*window etc*) bien fermer.
securely *adv* (*firmly*) solidement; (*safely*) en sûreté.
security sécurité *f*; (*for loan*) caution *f*.
sedation [sɪ'deɪʃ(ə)n] **under s.** sous calmants.

'sedative calmant *m*.
see* [siː] *vti* voir; **we'll s.** on verra (bien); **I saw him run(ning)** je l'ai vu courir; **s. you (later)!** à tout à l'heure!; **s. you (soon)!** à bientôt!; **to s. that** (*take care that*) = **to see to it that.**
see about sth s'occuper de qch; (*consider*) songer à qch.
seed [siːd] graine *f*; (*in grape*) pépin *m*.
seeing *conj* **s. (that)** vu que
seek* [siːk] *vt* chercher (**to do** à faire); (*ask for*) demander (**from** à).
seem [siːm] *vi* sembler (**to do** faire); **it seems that** (*impression*) il semble que (+ *subjunctive or indicative*); (*rumour*) il paraît que (+ *indicative*); **it seems to me that** il me semble que (+ *indicative*).
see s.o. off accompagner qn (*à la gare etc*).
see s.o. out raccompagner qn.
seesaw (jeu *m* de) bascule *f*.
see to sth (*deal with*) s'occuper de qch; (*mend*) réparer qch; **to see to it that** veiller à ce que (+ *subjunctive*); (*check*) s'assurer que.
see s.o. to (*accompany*) raccompagner qn à.
segment ['segmənt] segment *m*; (*of orange*) quartier *m*.
seize [siːz] *vt* saisir; (*power, land*) s'emparer de.
seldom ['seldəm] *adv* rarement.
select [sɪ'lekt] *vt* choisir (**from** parmi); (*candidates, players etc*) sélectionner.
selection sélection *f*.
self-assurance assurance *f*.
self-assured *a* sûr de soi.
self-confidence assurance *f*.
self-confident *a* sûr de soi.
self-conscious *a* gêné.
self-control maîtrise *f* de soi.
self-defence légitime défense *f*.
self-employed *a* qui travaille à son compte.
selfish ['selfɪʃ] *a* égoïste.
self-respect amour propre *m*.
self-service *n* & *a* libre-service (*m inv*)
sell* [sel] **1** *vt* vendre; **to have** *or* **be sold out of sth** n'avoir plus de qch. **2** *vi* (*of product*) se vendre.
seller vendeur, -euse *mf*.
sellotape® ['seləteɪp] scotch® *m*.
semester [sɪ'mestər] semestre *m*.
semi- ['semɪ] *prefix* demi-, semi-.
semi(trailer) *Am* semi-remorque *m*.
semicircle demi-cercle *m*.

semi'colon point-virgule *m*.
semide'tached house maison *f* jumelle.
semi'final demi-finale *f*.
semolina [semə'liːnə] semoule *f*.
senator ['senətər] *Am* sénateur *m*.
send* [send] *vt* envoyer (**to** à); **to s. s.o. for sth/s.o.** envoyer qn chercher qch/qn; **to s. s.o. mad** rendre qn fou.
send away *or* **off 1** *vt envoyer* (**to** à); (*dismiss*) renvoyer. **2** *vi* **to s. away** *or* **off for sth** commander qch (par courrier).
send back renvoyer.
sender expéditeur, -trice *mf*.
send for (*doctor etc*) faire venir; (*by mail*) commander (par courrier).
send in (*form etc*) envoyer; (*person*) faire entrer.
send on (*letter, luggage*) faire suivre.
send out (*invitation etc*) envoyer; (*from room etc*) faire sortir (*qn*); **to s. out for** (*meal*) envoyer chercher.
send up (*luggage*) faire monter.
senior ['siːnɪər] **1** *a* (*older*) plus âgé; (*position, rank*) supérieur. **2** *n* aîné, -ée *mf*; (*in school*) grand *m*, grande *f*, *Am* étudiant, -ante *mf* de dernière année; (*in sport*) senior *mf*.
sensation [sen'seɪʃ(ə)n] sensation *f*.
sensational *a* (*terrific*) *Fam* sensationnel.
sense [sens] **1** *n* (*meaning*) sens *m*; **s. of smell** odorat *m*; **a s. of** (*shame etc*) un sentiment de; **to have a s. of humour** avoir de l'humour; **to have (good) s.** avoir du bon sens; **to have the s. to do** avoir l'intelligence de faire; **to make s.** (*of story*) avoir un sens, tenir debout. **2** *vt* sentir (intuitivement) (**that** que).
senseless *a* (*stupid*) insensé.
sensible ['sensəb(ə)l] *a* (*wise*) raisonnable.
sensitive ['sensɪtɪv] *a* sensible (**to** à); (*skin*) délicat; (*touchy*) susceptible (**about** à propos de).
sentence ['sentəns] **1** *n Grammar* phrase *f*; (*punishment, in prison*) peine *f*. **2** *vt* **to s. s.o. to 3 years (in prison)** condamner qn à 3 ans de prison.
separate 1 *a* ['sepərət] (*distinct*) séparé; (*independent*) indépendant; (*different*) différent. **2** *vt* ['sepəreɪt] séparer (**from** de). **3** *vi* se séparer (**from** de).
'separately *adv* séparément.
September [sep'tembər] septembre *m*.
sequence ['siːkwəns] (*order*) ordre *m*; (*series*) succession *f*.
sequin ['siːkwɪn] paillette *f*.

sergeant ['sɑːdʒənt] sergent *m*; (*in police force*) brigadier *m*.

serial ['sɪərɪəl] (*story*, *film*) feuilleton *m*.

series ['sɪəriːz] *n inv* série *f*.

serious ['sɪərɪəs] *a* sérieux; (*illness*, *mistake*) grave.

seriously *adv* sérieusement; (*ill*) gravement; **to take s.** prendre au sérieux.

servant ['sɜːvənt] (*in house etc*) domestique *mf*.

serve [sɜːv] *vt* servir (**to s.o.** à qn, **s.o. with sth** qch à qn); (*of train*, *bus etc*) desservir (*un village etc*); **(it) serves you right!** ça t'apprendra!

serve out *or* **up** (*meal etc*) servir.

service ['sɜːvɪs] **1** *n* service *m*; (*machine or vehicle repair*) révision *f*; **s. (charge)** (*in restaurant*) service *m*. **2** *vt* (*machine*, *vehicle*) réviser.

service area (*on motorway*) aire *f* de service.

service station station-service *f*.

serviette [sɜːvɪ'et] serviette *f* (de table).

session ['seʃ(ə)n] séance *f*.

set [set] **1** *n* (*of keys*, *tools etc*) jeu *m*; (*of stamps*, *numbers*) série *f*; (*of people*) groupe *m*; (*in mathematics*) ensemble *m*; (*of books*) collection *f*; (*scenery*) décor *m*; (*hairstyle*) mise *f* en plis; *Tennis* set *m*; **chess s.** jeu *m* d'échecs. **2** *a* (*time*, *price etc*) fixe; (*book at school*) au programme; **the s. menu** le plat du jour; **s. on doing** résolu à faire; **to be s. on sth** vouloir qch à tout prix; **all s.** (*ready*) prêt (**to do** pour faire). **3** *vt** (*put*) mettre; (*date*, *limit etc*) fixer; (*record*) établir; (*mechanism*, *clock*) régler; (*alarm clock*) mettre (**for** pour); (*arm etc in plaster*) plâtrer; (*task*) donner (**for s.o.** à qn); (*trap*) tendre; **to have one's hair s.** se faire faire une mise en plis. **4** *vi* (*of sun*) se coucher; (*of jelly*, *Am jello*) prendre.

set (off) *vt* **to s. s.o. (off) crying**/*etc* faire pleurer/*etc* qn.

set about sth/doing (*begin*) se mettre à qch/à faire.

setback revers *m*.

set down (*object*) déposer.

set off 1 *vt* (*bomb*) faire exploser; (*mechanism*) **déclencher**. **2** *vi* (*leave*) partir.

set out 1 *vt* (*display*, *explain*) exposer (**to** à); (*arrange*) disposer. **2** *vi* (*leave*) partir; **to s. out to do** entreprendre de faire.

setsquare équerre *f*.

settee [se'tiː] canapé *m*.

setting (*surroundings*) cadre *m*.

settle ['set(ə)l] **1** *vt* (*decide*, *arrange*, *pay*) régler; (*date*) fixer; **that's (all) settled** c'est décidé. **2** *vi* (*live*) s'installer.

settle down (*in chair or house*) s'installer; (*calm down*) se calmer; (*in one's lifestyle*) se ranger.
settlement (*agreement*) accord *m*.
settler colon *m*.
settle (up) with s.o. (*pay*) régler qn.
set up 1 *vt* (*tent*) dresser; (*business*) créer. **2** *vi* **to s. up in business** monter une affaire.
seven ['sev(ə)n] *a & n* sept (*m*).
seven'teen *a & n* dix-sept (*m*).
seventh *a & n* septième (*mf*).
seventieth *a & n* soixante-dixième (*mf*).
seventy *a & n* soixante-dix (*m*); **s.-one** soixante et onze.
several ['sev(ə)rəl] *a & pron* plusieurs (**of** d'entre).
severe [sə'vɪər] *a* (*tone etc*) sévère; (*winter*) rigoureux; (*test*) dur.
sew* [səʊ] *vti* coudre.
sewer ['suːər] égout *m*.
sewing couture *f*.
sewing machine machine *f* à coudre.
sew on (*button*) (re)coudre.
sew up (*tear*) (re)coudre.
sex [seks] **1** *n* sexe *m*; (*activity*) relations *fpl* sexuelles; **to have s. with s.o.** coucher avec qn. **2** *a* (*education*, *life etc*) sexuel.
sexual *a* sexuel.
sexy *a* sexy *inv*.
sh! [ʃ] *int* chut! [ʃyt].
shabby ['ʃæbɪ] *a* (*room etc*) minable.
shade [ʃeɪd] ombre *f*; (*of colour*) ton *m*; (*of lamp*) abat-jour *m inv*; *Am* **(window) s.** store *m*; **in the s.** à l'ombre.
shadow ['ʃædəʊ] ombre *f*.
shady *a* (*place*) ombragé.
shake* [ʃeɪk] **1** *vt* secouer; (*bottle*) agiter; (*upset*) bouleverser; **to s. one's head** (*say no*) secouer la tête; **to s. hands with s.o.** serrer la main à qn; **we shook hands** nous nous sommes serré la main. **2** *vi* trembler (**with** de).
shall [ʃæl, *unstressed* ʃəl] *v aux* (*future*) **I s. come, I'll come** je viendrai; **we s. not come, we shan't come** nous ne viendrons pas. **■** (*question*) **s. I leave?** veux-tu que je parte?; **s. we leave?** on part?
shallow ['ʃæləʊ] *a* (*water*, *river etc*) peu profond.
shame [ʃeɪm] (*feeling*, *disgrace*) honte *f*; **it's a s.** c'est dommage (**to do** de faire); **it's a s. (that)** c'est dommage que (+ *subjunctive*); **what a s.!** (quel) dommage!
shameful *a* honteux.

shampoo [ʃæm'puː] **1** *n* shampooing *m*. **2** *vt* **to s. s.o.'s hair** faire un shampooing à qn.

shandy ['ʃændɪ] (*beer*) panaché *m*.

shan't [ʃɑːnt] = **shall not.**

shape [ʃeɪp] forme *f*; **in (good) s.** (*fit*) en (pleine) forme; **to be in good/bad s.** (*of vehicle etc*) être en bon/mauvais état; (*of business*) marcher bien/mal; **to take s.** (*of plan, book etc*) prendre forme; (*progress well*) avancer.

-shaped [ʃeɪpt] *suffix* **pear-s.**/*etc* en forme de poire/*etc*.

share [ʃeər] **1** *n* part *f* (**of, in** de); (*in company*) action *f*. **2** *vt* (*meal, opinion etc*) partager (**with** avec); (*characteristic*) avoir en commun.

shareholder actionnaire *mf*.

share in sth avoir sa part de qch.

share sth out partager *or* répartir qch (**among** entre).

shark [ʃɑːk] requin *m*.

sharp [ʃɑːp] **1** *a* (*knife etc*) tranchant; (*pointed*) pointu; (*point, pain*) aigu (*f* -uë); (*bend*) brusque. **2** *adv* **five o'clock**/*etc* **s.** cinq heures/*etc* pile.

sharpen *vt* (*knife*) aiguiser; (*pencil*) tailler.

sharply *adv* (*suddenly*) brusquement.

shatter ['ʃætər] **1** *vt* (*door, arm etc*) fracasser; (*glass*) faire voler en éclats. **2** *vi* se fracasser; (*of glass*) voler en éclats.

shave [ʃeɪv] **1** *vt* (*person, head*) raser; **to s. off one's beard** se raser la barbe. **2** *vi* se raser. **3** *n* **to have a s.** se raser.

shaver rasoir *m* électrique.

shaving cream crème *f* à raser.

shawl [ʃɔːl] châle *m*.

she [ʃiː] *pron* elle; **she's a happy woman** c'est une femme heureuse.

shed[1] [ʃed] (*in garden*) abri *m* (de jardin); (*for goods or machines*) hangar *m*.

shed[2]* *vt* (*lose*) perdre; (*tears*) répandre.

sheep [ʃiːp] *n inv* mouton *m*.

sheepskin peau *f* de mouton.

sheet [ʃiːt] (*on bed*) drap *m*; (*of paper*) feuille *f*; (*of glass, ice*) plaque *f*.

shelf [ʃelf] (*pl* **shelves**) étagère *f*; (*in shop*) rayon *m*.

shell [ʃel] **1** *n* (*of egg etc*) coquille *f*; (*of tortoise*) carapace *f*; (*seashell*) coquillage *m*; (*explosive*) obus *m*. **2** *vt* (*peas*) écosser.

shellfish (*oysters etc*) fruits *mpl* de mer.

shelter ['ʃeltər] **1** *n* abri *m*; **to take s.** se mettre à l'abri (**from** de). **2** *vt* abriter (**from** de). **3** *vi* s'abriter.

shelving rayonnage(s) *m(pl)*.
shepherd ['ʃepəd] berger *m*.
sheriff ['ʃerɪf] *Am* shérif *m*.
sherry ['ʃerɪ] sherry *m*.
shield [ʃiːld] **1** *n* bouclier *m*; (*screen*) écran *m*. **2** *vt* protéger (**from** de).
shift [ʃɪft] **1** *n* (*change*) changement *m* (**of, in** de); (*period of work*) poste *m*; (*workers*) équipe *f*; **gear s.** *Am* levier *m* de vitesse. **2** *vt* (*move*) bouger; **to s. gear(s)** *Am* changer de vitesse. **3** *vi* bouger.
shin [ʃɪn] tibia *m*.
shine [ʃaɪn] **1** *vi** briller. **2** *vt* (*polish*) faire briller; **to s. a light** *or* **a torch on sth** éclairer qch. **3** *n* (*on shoes, cloth*) brillant *m*.
shiny *a* brillant.
ship [ʃɪp] navire *m*, bateau *m*; **by s.** en bateau.
shipping (*traffic*) navigation *f*.
shipwreck naufrage *m*.
shipwrecked [-rekt] *a* naufragé; **to be s.** faire naufrage.
shipyard chantier *m* naval.
shirt [ʃɜːt] chemise *f*; (*of woman*) chemisier *m*; (*of sportsman*) maillot *m*.
shiver ['ʃɪvər] **1** *vi* frissonner (**with** de). **2** *n* frisson *m*.
shock [ʃɒk] **1** *n* (*emotional, physical*) choc *m*; **(electric) s.** décharge *f* (électrique); **suffering from s.** en état de choc. **2** *vt* (*offend*) choquer; (*surprise*) stupéfier.
shock absorber amortisseur *m*.
shocking *a* affreux; (*outrageous*) scandaleux.
shoe [ʃuː] chaussure *f*, soulier *m*.
shoelace lacet *m*.
shoe polish cirage *m*.
shoot* [ʃuːt] **1** *vt* (*kill*) tuer (d'un coup de feu); (*wound*) blesser (d'un coup de feu); (*execute*) fusiller; (*gun*) tirer un coup de; (*film*) tourner. **2** *vi* (*with gun*) tirer (**at** sur).
shoot ahead/off (*rush*) avancer/partir à toute vitesse.
shooting (*shots*) coups *mpl* de feu; (*murder*) meurtre *m*.
shoot up (*of price*) monter en flèche.
shop [ʃɒp] **1** *n* magasin *m*; (*small*) boutique *f*; **at the baker's s.** à la boulangerie, chez le boulanger. **2** *vi* faire ses courses (**at** chez).
shop assistant vendeur, -euse *mf*.
shopkeeper commerçant, -ante *mf*.
shopping (*goods*) achats *mpl*; **to go s.** faire des courses.
shopping bag sac *m* à provisions.
shopping centre (*purpose-built*) centre *m* commercial; (*district*)

quartier *m* commerçant.
shop window vitrine *f*.
shore [ʃɔːr] (*of sea, lake*) rivage *m*; (*coast*) côte *f*.
short [ʃɔːt] **1** *a* court; (*person, distance*) petit; **a s. time** *or* **while (ago)** (il y a) peu de temps; **to be s. of money/time** être à court d'argent/de temps; **we're s. of ten men** il nous manque dix hommes; **to be s. for sth** (*of name*) être l'abréviation de qch. **2** *adv* **to cut s.** (*hair*) couper court; (*visit etc*) raccourcir; (*person*) couper la parole à; **to get** *or* **run s.** manquer (**of** de).
shortage manque *m*.
short cut raccourci *m*.
shorten *vt* (*dress, text etc*) raccourcir.
shorthand typist sténodactylo *f*.
shortly *adv* (*soon*) bientôt; **s. after** peu après.
shorts *npl* **(a pair of) s.** un short.
short'sighted *a* myope.
short-'term *a* à court terme.
shot [ʃɒt] (*from gun*) coup *m*; (*with camera*) prise *f* de vues.
shotgun fusil *m* (de chasse).
should [ʃʊd, *unstressed* ʃəd] *v aux* (= *ought to*) **you s. do it** vous devriez le faire; **I s. have stayed** j'aurais dû rester; **that s. be Paul** ça doit être Paul. ▮ (= *would*) **I s. like to** j'aimerais bien; **it's strange she s. say no** il est étrange qu'elle dise non. ▮ (*possibility*) **if he s. come** s'il vient.
shoulder ['ʃəʊldər] épaule *f*; **(hard) s.** (*of motorway*) bas-côté *m*.
shoulder bag sac *m* à bandoulière.
shout [ʃaʊt] **1** *n* cri *m*. **2** *vti* crier; **to s. to s.o. to do** crier à qn de faire.
shout at s.o. (*scold*) crier après qn.
shouting (*shouts*) cris *mpl*.
shout out *vti* crier.
shove [ʃʌv] **1** *n* poussée *f*; **to give a s. (to)** pousser. **2** *vt* pousser; (*put*) *Fam* fourrer. **3** *vi* pousser.
shovel ['ʃʌv(ə)l] **1** *n* pelle *f*. **2** *vt* (*snow etc*) enlever à la pelle.
show [ʃəʊ] **1** *n* (*in theatre*) spectacle *m*; (*in cinema*) séance *f*; **Motor S.**, *Am* **Auto S.** le Salon de l'Automobile; **on s.** (*painting etc*) exposé. **2** *vt** montrer (**to** à, **that** que); (*in exhibition*) exposer; (*film*) passer; (*indicate*) indiquer; **to s. s.o. to the door** reconduire qn. **3** *vi* (*be visible*) se voir; (*of film*) passer.
shower ['ʃaʊər] (*bath*) douche *f*; (*of rain*) averse *f*.
show in (*visitor*) faire entrer.
showing (*cinema performance*) séance *f*.

show off *vi* crâner.
show-off crâneur, -euse *mf*.
show out (*visitor*) reconduire.
show s.o. (a)round faire visiter qn; **to s. s.o. (a)round the house** faire visiter la maison à qn.
show up 1 *vi* (*of person*) arriver. **2** *vt* (*embarrass*) mettre (*qn*) dans l'embarras.
shrimp [ʃrɪmp] crevette *f* (grise).
shrink* [ʃrɪŋk] *vi* (*of clothes*) rétrécir.
shrub [ʃrʌb] arbuste *m*.
shrug [ʃrʌg] *vt* **to s. one's shoulders** hausser les épaules.
shudder ['ʃʌdər] *vi* frémir (**with** de).
shuffle ['ʃʌf(ə)l] *vt* (*cards*) battre.
shush! [ʃʊʃ] *int* chut! [ʃyt].
shut* [ʃʌt] **1** *vt* fermer. **2** *vi* (*of door etc*) se fermer; (*of shop etc*) fermer.
shut down *vti* fermer.
shut in enfermer.
shut off (*gas etc*) fermer; (*engine*) arrêter; (*isolate*) isoler.
shut out (*light*) empêcher d'entrer; **to s. s.o. out** (*accidentally*) enfermer qn dehors.
shutter ['ʃʌtər] (*on window*) volet *m*; (*of shop*) rideau *m* (métallique).
shuttle ['ʃʌt(ə)l] **s. (service)** navette *f*; **space s.** navette spatiale.
shut up 1 *vt* (*house etc*) fermer; (*lock up*) enfermer (*personne*, *objet précieux*). **2** *vi* (*be quiet*) se taire.
shy [ʃaɪ] *a* timide.
shyness timidité *f*.
sick [sɪk] **1** *a* malade; **to be s.** (*vomit*) vomir; **off s.** en congé de maladie; **to feel s.** avoir mal au cœur; **to be s. (and tired) of sth/s.o.** *Fam* en avoir marre de qch/qn. **2** *n* **the s.** les malades *mpl*.
sickness maladie *f*.
sick up *vti* vomir.
side [saɪd] côté *m*; (*of hill*, *animal*) flanc *m*; (*of road*, *river*) bord *m*; (*team*) équipe *f*; **at** *or* **by the s. of** à côté de; **at** *or* **by my s.** à côté de moi, à mes côtés; **s. by s.** l'un à côté de l'autre; **to move to one s.** s'écarter; **on this s.** de ce côté; **on the other s.** de l'autre côté; **to take sides with s.o.** se ranger du côté de qn; **on our s.** de notre côté.
sideboard buffet *m*.
sidelight (*of vehicle*) veilleuse *f*.
sidewalk *Am* trottoir *m*.

sideways *adv* & *a* de côté.
sieve [sɪv] tamis *m*; (*for liquids*) passoire *f*.
sift *vt* (*flour etc*) tamiser.
sigh [saɪ] **1** *n* soupir *m*. **2** *vi* soupirer.
sight [saɪt] vue *f*; (*thing seen*) spectacle *m*; **to lose s. of** perdre de vue; **to catch s. of** apercevoir; **by s.** de vue; **in s.** (*target etc*) en vue; **out of s.** caché; **the (tourist) sights** les attractions *fpl* touristiques.
sightseeing to go s. faire du tourisme.
sign [saɪn] **1** *n* signe *m*; (*notice*) panneau *m*; (*over shop*, *inn*) enseigne *f*; **no s. of** aucune trace de. **2** *vti* (*with signature*) signer.
signal ['sɪgnəl] signal *m*; **traffic signals** feux *mpl* de circulation.
signature ['sɪgnətʃər] signature *f*.
significant [sɪg'nɪfɪkənt] *a* (*important*, *large*) important.
significantly *adv* sensiblement.
sign in (*in hotel etc*) signer le registre.
sign on *or* **up** (*of soldier*, *worker*) s'engager; (*for course*) s'inscrire (**for** à).
signpost poteau *m* indicateur.
silence ['saɪləns] **1** *n* silence *m*; **in s.** en silence. **2** *vt* faire taire.
silent *a* silencieux; (*film*) muet (*f* muette); **to keep s.** garder le silence (**about** sur).
silently *adv* silencieusement.
silk [sɪlk] soie *f*.
sill [sɪl] (*of window*) rebord *m*.
silly ['sɪlɪ] *a* bête; **to do something s.** faire une bêtise.
silver ['sɪlvər] **1** *n* argent *m*; (*plates etc*) argenterie *f*. **2** *a* (*spoon etc*) en argent; **s. paper** papier *m* d'argent.
silver 'plated *a* plaqué argent.
silverware ['sɪlvəweər] *n inv* argenterie *f*.
similar ['sɪmɪlər] *a* semblable (**to** à).
simi'larity ressemblance *f* (**to** avec).
simple ['sɪmp(ə)l] *a* simple.
simplify *vt* simplifier.
simply *adv* (*plainly*, *merely*) simplement; (*absolutely*) absolument.
simultaneous [sɪməl'teɪnɪəs, *Am* saɪməl'teɪnɪəs] *a* simultané.
simultaneously *adv* simultanément.
sin [sɪn] péché *m*.
since [sɪns] **1** *prep* depuis. **2** *conj* depuis que; (*because*) puisque; **s. she's been here** depuis qu'elle est ici; **it's a year s. I saw him** ça fait un an que je ne l'ai pas vu. **3** *adv* **(ever) s.** depuis.
sincere [sɪn'sɪər] *a* sincère.
sincerely *adv* sincèrement; **yours s.** (*in letter*) veuillez croire à mes

sentiments dévoués.
sin'cerity sincérité *f*.
sing* [sɪŋ] *vti* chanter.
singer chanteur, -euse *mf*.
single ['sɪŋg(ə)l] **1** *a* seul; (*room*, *bed*) pour une personne; (*unmarried*) célibataire; **not a s. book**/*etc* pas un seul livre/*etc*; **s. ticket** billet *m* simple; **every s. day** tous les jours sans exception. **2** *n* (*ticket*) aller *m* (simple); (*record*) 45 tours *m inv*.
single out choisir.
singular ['sɪŋgjʊlər] **1** *a* (*form*) singulier; (*noun*) au singulier. **2** *n* singulier *m*; **in the s.** au singulier.
sinister ['sɪnɪstər] *a* sinistre.
sink[1] [sɪŋk] (*in kitchen*) évier *m*; (*washbasin*) lavabo *m*.
sink[2]* *vi* (*of ship*, *person etc*) couler.
sink (down) into (*mud*) s'enfoncer dans; (*armchair*) s'affaler dans.
sip [sɪp] *vi* boire à petites gorgées.
sir [sɜːr] monsieur *m*; **S.** (*title*) sir.
siren ['saɪərən] (*of factory etc*) sirène *f*.
sister ['sɪstər] sœur *f*.
sister-in-law (*pl* **sisters-in-law**) belle-sœur *f*.
sit* [sɪt] **1** *vi* s'asseoir; **to be sitting** être assis; **she was sitting reading** elle était assise à lire. **2** *vt* (*child on chair etc*) asseoir.
sit (for) (*exam*) se présenter à.
sit around traîner; (*do nothing*) ne rien faire.
sit down 1 *vi* s'asseoir; **to be sitting down** être assis. **2** *vt* asseoir (*qn*).
site [saɪt] (*position*) emplacement *m*; **(building) s.** chantier *m*.
sitting room salon *m*.
situate ['sɪtʃʊeɪt] *vt* situer; **to be situated** être situé, se situer.
situ'ation situation *f*.
sit up (straight) *vi* s'asseoir (bien droit).
six [sɪks] *a* & *n* six (*m*).
six'teen *a* & *n* seize (*m*).
sixth *a* & *n* sixième (*mf*); **(lower) s. form** = classe *f* de première; **(upper) s. form** = classe *f* terminale.
sixtieth *a* & *n* soixantième (*mf*).
sixty *a* & *n* soixante (*m*).
size [saɪz] (*of person*, *clothes*, *packet etc*) taille *f*; (*measurements*) dimensions *fpl*; (*of town*, *sum*) importance *f*; (*of shoes*, *gloves*) pointure *f*; (*of shirt*) encolure *f*; **hip/chest s.** tour *m* de hanches/de poitrine.
skate [skeɪt] **1** *n* patin *m*. **2** *vi* patiner.

skateboard planche *f* (à roulettes).
skater patineur, -euse *mf*.
skating patinage *m*; **to go s.** faire du patinage.
skating rink (*ice-skating*) patinoire *f*.
skeleton ['skelɪt(ə)n] squelette *m*.
sketch [sketʃ] **1** *n* (*drawing*) croquis *m*; (*comic play*) sketch *m*. **2** *vi* faire un *or* des croquis.
skewer ['skjʊər] (*for meat etc*) broche *f*; (*for kebab*) brochette *f*.
ski [skiː] **1** *n* ski *m*. **2** *vi* (*pt* **skied** [skiːd]) faire du ski.
skid [skɪd] **1** *vi* déraper; **to s. into sth** déraper et heurter qch. **2** *n* dérapage *m*.
skier skieur, -euse *mf*.
skiing 1 *n* ski *m*. **2** *a* (*school, clothes, etc*) de ski.
skilful, *Am* **skillful** *a* habile (**at doing** à faire, **at sth** à qch).
ski lift remonte-pente *m*.
skill [skɪl] habileté *f* (**at** à); (*technique*) technique *f*.
skilled worker ouvrier, -ière qualifié(e).
skimmed milk [skɪmd] lait *m* écrémé.
skin [skɪn] peau *f*.
skin diving plongée *f* sous-marine.
skinny ['skɪnɪ] *a* maigre.
skip[1] [skɪp] **1** *vi* (*hop about*) sautiller; (*with rope*) sauter à la corde. **2** *vt* (*miss*) sauter (*repas, classe etc*).
skip[2] (*container for rubbish*) benne *f*.
skipping rope corde *f* à sauter.
skirt [skɜːt] jupe *f*.
skittle ['skɪt(ə)l] quille *f*; **to play skittles** jouer aux quilles.
skull [skʌl] crâne *m*.
sky [skaɪ] ciel *m*.
skyscraper gratte-ciel *m inv*.
slack [slæk] *a* (*knot, spring*) lâche; **to be s.** (*of rope*) avoir du mou; (*in office etc*) être calme.
slacken *vt* (*rope*) relâcher.
slacks *npl* pantalon *m*.
slam [slæm] **1** *vt* (*door, lid*) claquer. **2** *vi* (*of door*) claquer. **3** *n* claquement *m*.
slang [slæŋ] argot *m*.
slant [slɑːnt] **1** *n* inclinaison *f*. **2** *vi* (*of roof*) être en pente.
slap [slæp] **1** *n* tape *f*; (*on face*) gifle *f*. **2** *vt* (*person*) donner une tape à; **to s. s.o.'s face** gifler qn; **to s. s.o.'s bottom** donner une fessée à qn.
slate [sleɪt] ardoise *f*.

slaughter ['slɔːtər] **1** *vt* massacrer; (*animal*) abattre. **2** *n* massacre *m*; abattage *m*.
slave [sleɪv] esclave *mf*.
slave away se crever (au travail).
slavery esclavage *m*.
sledge [sledʒ] (*Am* **sled** [sled]) luge *f*; (*horse-drawn*) traîneau *m*.
sleep [sliːp] **1** *n* sommeil *m*; **to have a s., get some s.** dormir. **2** *vi** dormir; (*spend the night*) coucher; **to go** *or* **get to s.** s'endormir.
sleeper (*bed in train*) couchette *f*; (*train*) train *m* couchettes.
sleeping *a* (*asleep*) endormi.
sleeping bag sac *m* de couchage.
sleeping car wagon-lit *m*.
sleeping pill somnifère *m*.
sleepy *a* **to be s.** (*of person*) avoir sommeil.
sleet [sliːt] **1** *n* neige *f* fondue. **2** *vi* **it's sleeting** il tombe de la neige fondue.
sleeve [sliːv] (*of shirt etc*) manche *f*; (*of record*) pochette *f*; **long-/short-sleeved** à manches longues/courtes.
sleigh [sleɪ] traîneau *m*.
slept [slept] *pt & pp de* **sleep.**
slice [slaɪs] tranche *f*.
slice (up) *vt* couper (en tranches).
slide [slaɪd] **1** *n* (*in playground*) toboggan *m*; (*for hair*) barrette *f*; (*film*) diapositive *f*. **2** *vi** glisser. **3** *vt* (*letter etc*) glisser (**into** dans); (*table, chair etc*) faire glisser.
sliding door porte *f* à glissière *or* coulissante.
slight [slaɪt] *a* (*noise, mistake etc*) léger, petit; (*chance*) faible; **the slightest thing** la moindre chose; **not in the slightest** pas le moins du monde.
slightly *adv* légèrement.
slim [slɪm] **1** *a* mince. **2** *vi* maigrir.
sling [slɪŋ] **1** *n* (*for arm*) écharpe *f*; **in a s.** en écharpe. **2** *vt** *Fam* = **chuck**.
slip [slɪp] **1** *n* (*mistake*) erreur *f*; (*woman's undergarment*) combinaison *f*; **a s. of paper** un bout de papier. **2** *vi* glisser. **3** *vt* (*slide*) glisser (*qch*) (**to** à, **into** dans).
slip away *vi* s'esquiver.
slip in *vi* entrer furtivement.
slip into (*room etc*) se glisser dans; (*bathrobe etc*) mettre, passer.
slip off (*garment*) enlever.
slip on (*garment*) mettre.
slip out *vi* sortir furtivement; (*for a moment*) sortir (un instant).

slipper ['slɪpər] pantoufle *f*.
slippery *a* glissant.
slip up (*make a mistake*) gaffer.
slit [slɪt] (*opening*) fente *f*; (*cut*) coupure *f*.
slogan ['sləʊgən] slogan *m*.
slope [sləʊp] **1** *n* pente *f*; (*of mountain*) versant *m*; (*for skiing*) piste *f*. **2** *vi* (*of ground, roof etc*) être en pente.
sloping *a* en pente.
slot [slɒt] (*slit*) fente *f*; (*groove*) rainure *f*.
slot machine distributeur *m* automatique; (*gambling*) *Am* machine *f* à sous.
slow [sləʊ] **1** *a* lent; **to be s.** (*of clock, watch*) retarder; **to be five minutes s.** retarder de cinq minutes; **in s. motion** au ralenti. **2** *adv* lentement.
slowcoach *Fam* tortue *f*.
slow down *or* **up** *vti* ralentir.
slowly *adv* lentement; (*bit by bit*) peu à peu.
slowpoke *Am Fam* tortue *f*.
slug [slʌg] limace *f*.
slum [slʌm] (*house*) taudis *m*; **the slums** les quartiers *mpl* pauvres.
sly [slaɪ] *a* (*cunning*) rusé.
smack [smæk] **1** *n* claque *f*; gifle *f*; fessée *f*. **2** *vt* (*person*) donner une claque à; **to s. s.o.'s face** gifler qn; **to s. s.o.('s bottom)** donner une fessée à qn.
small [smɔːl] **1** *a* petit. **2** *adv* (*to cut, chop*) menu.
smallpox ['smɔːlpɒks] petite vérole *f*.
smart [smɑːt] *a* (*in appearance*) élégant; (*clever*) intelligent.
smash [smæʃ] **1** *vt* (*break*) briser; (*shatter*) fracasser. **2** *vi* se briser.
smashing *a Fam* formidable.
smash into sth (*of vehicle*) (r)entrer dans qch.
smash-up collision *f*.
smell [smel] **1** *n* odeur *f*; **(sense of) s.** odorat *m*. **2** *vt** sentir. **3** *vi* (*stink*) sentir (mauvais), (*have a smell*) avoir une odeur; **to s. of smoke/***etc* sentir la fumée/*etc*.
smile [smaɪl] **1** *n* sourire *m*. **2** *vi* sourire (**at s.o.** à qn).
smock [smɒk] blouse *f*.
smoke [sməʊk] **1** *n* fumée *f*; **to have a s.** fumer une cigarette *etc*. **2** *vti* fumer; **'no smoking'** 'défense de fumer'; **smoking compartment** compartiment *m* fumeurs.
smoker fumeur, -euse *mf*; (*train compartment*) compartiment *m* fumeurs.
smooth [smuːð] *a* (*surface, skin etc*) lisse; (*flight*) agréable.

smooth down *or* **out** (*dress, hair etc*) lisser.
smuggle ['smʌg(ə)l] *vt* passer (en fraude).
smuggler contrebandier, -ière *mf*.
smuggling contrebande *f*.
snack [snæk] (*meal*) casse-croûte *m inv*; **snacks** (*things to eat*) petites choses *fpl* à grignoter; (*sweets, Am candies*) friandises *fpl*; **to eat a s.** *or* **snacks** grignoter.
snack bar snack(-bar) *m*.
snail [sneɪl] escargot *m*.
snake [sneɪk] serpent *m*.
snap [snæp] **1** *vt* (*break*) casser (avec un bruit sec). **2** *vi* se casser net.
snap (fastener) bouton-pression *m*.
snap(shot) photo *f*.
snatch [snætʃ] *vt* saisir (*d'un geste vif*); **to s. sth from s.o.** arracher qch à qn.
sneaker ['sniːkər] (chaussure *f* de) tennis *m*.
sneer [snɪər] *vi* ricaner.
sneeze [sniːz] **1** *vi* éternuer. **2** *n* éternuement *m*.
sniff [snɪf] *vti* **to s. (at)** renifler.
snip (off) [snɪp] *vt* couper.
snooker ['snuːkər] snooker *m* (*sorte de jeu de billard*).
snore [snɔːr] *vi* ronfler.
snoring ronflements *mpl*.
snout [snaʊt] museau *m*.
snow [snəʊ] **1** *n* neige *f*. **2** *vi* neiger; **it's snowing** il neige.
snowball boule *f* de neige.
snowdrift congère *f*.
snowflake flocon *m* de neige.
snowman bonhomme *m* de neige.
snowplough, *Am* **snowplow** chasse-neige *m inv*.
snowstorm tempête *f* de neige.
so [səʊ] **1** *adv* (*to such a degree*) si, tellement (**that** que); (*thus*) ainsi; **so that** (*purpose*) pour que (+ *subjunctive*); (*result*) si bien que (+ *indicative*); **so as to do** pour faire; **I think so** je le pense; **if so** si oui; **is that so?** c'est vrai?; **so am I, so do I** *etc* moi aussi; **so much** (*to work etc*) tant (**that** que); **so much courage**/*etc* tant de courage/*etc*; **so many** tant; **so many books**/*etc* tant de livres/*etc*; **ten or so** environ dix; **and so on** et ainsi de suite. **2** *conj* (*therefore*) donc; **so what?** et alors?
soak [səʊk] **1** *vt* (*drench*) tremper (*qn*); (*washing, food*) faire tremper. **2** *vi* (*of washing etc*) tremper.

soaked through [səʊkt] *a (person)* trempé jusqu'aux os.
soaking *a & adv* **s. (wet)** trempé.
soak sth up absorber qch.
soap [səʊp] savon *m*.
soapflakes *npl* savon *m* en paillettes.
soap powder lessive *f*.
soapy *a* savonneux.
sob [sɒb] **1** *n* sanglot *m*. **2** *vi* sangloter.
sober ['səʊbər] *a* **he's s.** (*not drunk*) il n'est pas ivre.
soccer ['sɒkər] football *m*.
social ['səʊʃəl] *a* social; **s. club** club *m*; **s. evening** soireé *f*; **to have a good s. life** sortir beaucoup; **s. security** aide *f* sociale; (*pension*) *Am* pension *f* de retraite; **s. services, S. Security** = Sécurité *f* sociale; **s. worker** assistant, -ante *mf* social(e).
socialist *a & n* socialiste (*mf*).
society [sə'saɪətɪ] société *f*.
sock [sɒk] chaussette *f*.
socket ['sɒkɪt] (*for electric plug*) prise *f* de courant.
soda (pop) ['səʊdə] *Am* soda *m*.
soda (water) eau *f* gazeuse.
sofa ['səʊfə] canapé *m*; **s. bed** canapé-lit *m*.
soft [sɒft] *a (gentle, not stiff)* doux (*f* douce); (*butter, ground*) mou (*f* molle); **s. drink** boisson *f* non alcoolisée.
softly *adv* doucement.
software ['sɒftweər] *n inv* logiciel *m*.
soil [sɔɪl] sol *m*, terre *f*.
soldier ['səʊldʒər] soldat *m*.
sole [səʊl] (*of shoe*) semelle *f*; (*of foot*) plante *f*; (*fish*) sole *f*, **lemon s.** limande *f*.
solemn ['sɒləm] *a (formal)* solennel; (*serious*) grave.
solicitor [sə'lɪsɪtər] notaire *m*.
solid ['sɒlɪd] **1** *a (car, meal etc)* solide; (*wall, line*) plein; (*gold*) massif; **s. line** ligne *f* continue. **2** *n* solide *m*.
solution [sə'luːʃ(ə)n] solution *f* (**to** de).
solve [sɒlv] *vt (problem)* résoudre.
some [sʌm] **1** *a (amount, number)* du, de la, des; **s. wine** du vin; **s water** de l'eau; **s. dogs** des chiens; **s. pretty flowers** de jolies fleurs. ∎ (*unspecified*) un, une; **s. man (or other)** un homme (quelconque). ∎ (*a few*) quelques; (*a little*) un peu de. **2** *pron (number)* quelques-un(e)s (**of** de). ∎ (*a certain quantity*) en; **I want s.** j'en veux.
somebody *pron* = **someone.**
someday *adv* un jour.

somehow *adv* d'une manière ou d'une autre; (*for some reason*) on ne sait pourquoi.
someone *pron* quelqu'un; **s. small**/*etc* quelqu'un de petit/*etc*.
someplace *adv Am* quelque part.
somersault ['sʌməsɔːlt] culbute *f*.
something *pron* quelque chose; **s. awful**/*etc* quelque chose d'affreux/*etc*; **s. of a liar**/*etc* un peu menteur/*etc*.
sometime *adv* un jour.
sometimes *adv* quelquefois.
somewhat *adv* quelque peu.
somewhere *adv* quelque part.
son [sʌn] fils *m*.
song [sɒŋ] chanson *f*.
son-in-law (*pl* **sons-in-law**) gendre *m*.
soon [suːn] *adv* bientôt; (*quickly*) vite; (*early*) tôt; **s. after** peu après; **as s. as she leaves** aussitôt qu'elle partira; **no sooner had he spoken than** à peine avait-il parlé que; **I'd sooner leave** je préférerais partir; **I'd just as s. leave** j'aimerais autant partir; **sooner or later** tôt ou tard.
soot [sʊt] suie *f*.
soothe [suːð] *vt* (*pain*, *nerves*) calmer.
sore [sɔːr] **1** *a* (*painful*) douloureux; (*angry*) *Am* fâché (**at** contre); **she has a s. throat** elle a mal à la gorge. **2** *n* plaie *f*.
sorrow ['sɒrəʊ] chagrin *m*.
sorry ['sɒrɪ] *a* **to be s.** (*regret*) être désolé (**to do** de faire); **I'm s. she can't come** je regrette qu'elle ne puisse pas venir; **I'm s. about the delay** je m'excuse pour ce retard; **s.!** pardon!; **to feel** *or* **be s. for s.o.** plaindre qn.
sort[1] [sɔːt] sorte *f*, espèce *f* (**of** de); **all sorts of** toutes sortes de; **what s. of drink**/*etc* **is it?** qu'est-ce que c'est comme boisson/*etc*?
sort[2] *vt* (*papers etc*) trier.
sort out (*classify*, *select*) trier; (*separate*) séparer (**from** de); (*tidy*) ranger; (*problem*) régler.
soul [səʊl] âme *f*.
sound[1] [saʊnd] **1** *n* son *m*; (*noise*) bruit *m*; **I don't like the s. of it** ça ne me plaît pas du tout. **2** *vt* (*bell*, *alarm etc*) sonner; **to s. one's horn** klaxonner. **3** *vi* (*of bell etc*) sonner; (*seem*) sembler; **to s. like** sembler être; (*resemble*) ressembler à.
sound[2] **1** *a* (*healthy*) sain; (*good*, *reliable*) solide. **2** *adv* **s. asleep** profondément endormi.
soundproof *vt* insonoriser.
soup [suːp] soupe *f*, potage *m*.

sour ['sauər] *a* aigre.
source [sɔːs] source *f*.
south [sauθ] **1** *n* sud *m*; **(to the) s. of** au sud de. **2** *a* (*coast*) sud *inv*. **3** *adv* au sud.
southbound *a* en direction du sud.
south-'east *n* & *a* sud-est *m* & *a inv*.
southern ['sʌðən] *a* (*town*) du sud; (*coast*) sud *inv*.
southerner habitant, -ante *mf* du Sud.
southward(s) [-wəd(z)] *a* & *adv* vers le sud.
south-'west *n* & *a* sud-ouest *m* & *a inv*.
souvenir [suːvə'nɪər] (*object*) souvenir *m*.
sow* [səu] *vt* (*seeds*) semer.
space [speɪs] (*gap, emptiness, atmosphere*) espace *m*; (*period*) période *f*; (*for parking*) place *f*; **to take up s.** (*room*) prendre de la place.
space out *vt* espacer.
spaceship engin *m* spatial.
spacesuit combinaison *f* spatiale.
spacious ['speɪʃəs] *a* spacieux.
spade [speɪd] bêche *f*; (*of child*) pelle *f*; **spade(s)** *Cards* pique *m*
spaghetti [spə'getɪ] spaghetti(s) *mpl*.
Spaniard ['spænjəd] Espagnol, -ole *mf*.
Spanish **1** *a* espagnol. **2** *n* (*language*) espagnol *m*.
spank [spæŋk] *vt* donner une fessée à.
spanking fessée *f*.
spanner ['spænər] (*tool*) clef *f* (à écrous).
spare [speər] **1** *a* (*extra*) de trop; (*clothes*) de rechange; (*wheel*) de secours; (*bed, room*) d'ami; **s. time** loisirs *mpl*. **2** *n* **s. (part)** pièce *f* détachée. **3** *vt* (*do without*) se passer de (*qn, qch*); **to s. s.o.** (*details etc*) épargner à qn; (*time*) accorder à qn; (*money*) donner à qn.
spark [spɑːk] étincelle *f*.
sparkle ['spɑːk(ə)l] *vi* (*of diamond, star*) étinceler.
sparkling *a* (*wine, water*) pétillant.
spark(ing) plug bougie *f*.
sparrow ['spærəu] moineau *m*.
speak* [spiːk] **1** *vi* parler (**about, of** de); **English-/French-speaking** qui parle anglais/français. **2** *vt* (*language*) parler; (*say*) dire.
speaker (*public*) orateur *m*; (*loudspeaker*) haut-parleur *m*; (*of stereo system*) enceinte *f*.
speak up parler plus fort.
spear [spɪər] lance *f*.
special ['speʃ(ə)l] **1** *a* spécial; (*care, attention*) (tout) particulier. **2**

n **today's s.** (*in restaurant*) le plat du jour.
specialist spécialiste *mf* (**in** de).
speci'ality spécialité *f*.
specialize *vi* se spécialiser (**in** dans).
specially *adv* spécialement.
specialty *Am* spécialité *f*.
species ['spiːʃiːz] *n inv* espèce *f*.
specific [spə'sɪfɪk] *a* précis.
specimen ['spesɪmɪn] (*example, person*) spécimen *m*.
spectacular [spek'tækjʊlər] *a* spectaculaire.
spectator [spek'teɪtər] spectateur, -trice *mf*.
speech [spiːtʃ] (*talk, lecture*) discours *m* (**on, about** sur); (*power of language*) parole *f*; (*spoken language*) langage *m*.
speed [spiːd] **1** *n* (*rate*) vitesse *f*; (*quickness*) rapidité *f*; **s. limit** limitation *f* de vitesse. **2** *vi* (*drive too fast*) aller trop vite.
speedboat vedette *f*.
spee'dometer compteur *m* (de vitesse).
speed* up 1 *vt* accélérer. **2** *vi* (*of person*) aller plus vite.
spell[1] [spel] (*period*) (courte) période *f*; (*magic*) charme *m*; **cold s.** vague *f* de froid.
spell[2]* *vt* (*write*) écrire; (*say aloud*) épeler; (*of letters*) former (*mot*); **how is it spelt** *or* **spelled?** comment cela s'écrit-il?
spelling orthographe *f*.
spend* [spend] **1** *vt* (*money*) dépenser (**on** pour); (*time etc*) passer (**on sth** sur qch, **doing** à faire). **2** *vi* dépenser.
sphere [sfɪər] sphère *f*.
spice [spaɪs] **1** *n* épice *f*. **2** *vt* épicer.
spicy *a* (*food*) épicé.
spider ['spaɪdər] araignée *f*; **s.'s web** toile *f* d'araignée.
spike [spaɪk] pointe *f*.
spill* [spɪl] **1** *vt* répandre, renverser. **2** *vi* se répandre, se renverser (**on, over** sur).
spill out 1 *vt* (*empty*) vider (*café, verre etc*). **2** *vi* (*of coffee etc*) se renverser.
spill over déborder.
spin* [spɪn] *vt* (*wheel etc*) faire tourner; (*washing*) essorer.
spin (round) (*of dancer, wheel etc*) tourner.
spinach ['spɪnɪdʒ, *Am* -ɪʃ] (*food*) épinards *mpl*.
spine [spaɪn] (*of back*) colonne *f* vertébrale.
spiral ['spaɪərəl] spirale *f*.
spire ['spaɪər] flèche *f*.
spirits ['spɪrɪts] *npl* (*drinks*) alcool *m*.

spit [spɪt] **1** *vti** cracher. **2** *n* (*for meat*) broche *f*.
spite [spaɪt] **in s. of** malgré.
spiteful *a* méchant.
splash [splæʃ] **1** *vt* éclabousser (**with** de, **over** sur). **2** *n* (*mark*) éclaboussure *f*.
splash (about) *vi* (*in river, mud*) patauger; (*in bath*) barboter.
splendid ['splendɪd] *a* splendide.
splinter ['splɪntər] (*in finger*) écharde *f*.
split [splɪt] **1** *n* fente *f*; (*tear*) déchirure *f*. **2** *vt** (*break apart*) fendre; (*tear*) déchirer.
split (up) **1** *vt* (*group*) diviser; (*money, work*) partager (**between** entre). **2** *vi* (*of group*) se diviser (**into** en); (*because of disagreement*) se séparer.
spoil* [spɔɪl] *vt* gâter; (*damage, ruin*) abîmer; (*child, dog etc*) gâter.
spoke [spəʊk] (*of wheel*) rayon *m*.
spoke, spoken *pt & pp de* **speak**.
spokesman (*pl* **-men**) porte-parole *m inv* (**for, of** de).
sponge [spʌndʒ] éponge *f*.
sponge bag trousse *f* de toilette.
sponge cake gâteau *m* de Savoie.
sponge oneself down se laver à l'éponge.
spontaneous [spɒn'teɪnɪəs] *a* spontané.
spool [spuːl] bobine *f*.
spoon [spuːn] cuillère *f*.
spoonful cuillerée *f*.
sport [spɔːt] sport *m*; **to play s.** *or Am* **sports** faire du sport; **sports club** club *m* sportif; **sports car/jacket/ground** voiture *f*/veste *f*/terrain *m* de sport.
sportsman (*pl* **-men**) sportif *m*.
sportswoman (*pl* **-women**) sportive *f*.
spot¹ [spɒt] (*stain, mark*) tache *f*; (*dot*) point *m*; (*pimple*) bouton *m*; (*place*) endroit *m*; **on the s.** sur place.
spot² *vt* (*notice*) apercevoir.
spotless *a* (*clean*) impeccable.
spotlight (*in theatre etc*) projecteur *m*; (*for photography*) spot *m*.
spotted *a* (*animal*) tacheté.
spout [spaʊt] (*of teapot etc*) bec *m*.
sprain [spreɪn] **1** *n* foulure *f*. **2** *vt* **to s. one's ankle/wrist** se fouler la cheville/le poignet.
spray [spreɪ] **1** *n* (*can*) bombe *f*; **hair s.** laque *f* à cheveux. **2** *vt* (*liquid, surface*) vaporiser; (*plant*) arroser; (*car*) peindre à la bombe.
spread [spred] **1** *vt** (*stretch, open out*) étendre; (*legs, fingers*)

écarter; (*distribute*) répandre (**over** sur); (*paint*, *payment*, *visits*) étaler; (*news*, *germs*) propager. **2** *vi* (*of fire*) s'étendre; (*of news*, *epidemic*) se propager. **3** *n* (*paste*) pâte *f* (à tartiner); **cheese s.** fromage *m* à tartiner.

spread out 1 *vt* étendre; écarter; répandre; étaler. **2** *vi* (*of people*) se disperser.

spring[1] [sprɪŋ] **1** *n* (*metal device*) ressort *m*. **2** *vi** (*leap*) bondir.

spring[2] (*season*) printemps *m*; **in (the) s.** au printemps.

spring[3] (*of water*) source *f*.

springboard tremplin *m*.

spring onion oignon *m* vert.

springtime printemps *m*.

sprinkle ['sprɪŋk(ə)l] *vt* (*sand etc*) répandre (**on, over** sur); **to s. with water, s. water on** asperger d'eau; **to s. with** (*sugar*, *salt*, *flour*) saupoudrer de.

sprinkler (*in garden*) arroseur *m*.

sprout [spraʊt] **(Brussels) s.** chou *m* (*pl* choux) de Bruxelles.

spur [spɜːr] (*of horse rider*) éperon *m*.

spurt (out) [spɜːt] *vi* (*of liquid*) jaillir.

spy [spaɪ] espion, -onne *mf*.

spying espionnage *m*.

spy on s.o. espionner qn.

square [skweər] **1** *n* carré *m*; (*in town*) place *f*. **2** *a* carré; (*meal*) solide.

squash [skwɒʃ] **1** *vt* (*crush*) écraser; (*squeeze*) serrer. **2** *n* (*game*) squash *m*; **lemon/orange s.** sirop *m* de citron/d'orange; (*diluted*) citronnade *f*/orangeade *f*.

squat (down) [skwɒt] s'accroupir.

squatting *a* accroupi.

squeak [skwiːk] *vi* (*of door*) grincer; (*of shoe*) craquer.

squeal [skwiːl] **1** *vi* pousser des cris aigus. **2** *n* cri *m* aigu.

squeeze [skwiːz] **1** *vt* (*press*) presser; (*hand*, *arm*) serrer. **2** *vi* (*force oneself*) se glisser (**through/into/***etc* par/dans/*etc*).

squeeze (out) (*juice etc*) faire sortir (**from** de).

squeeze in *vi* (*of person*) trouver un peu de place.

squeeze sth into sth faire rentrer qch dans qch.

squeeze up *vi* se serrer (**against** contre).

squint [skwɪnt] **1** *n* **to have a s.** loucher. **2** *vi* loucher; (*in the sunlight etc*) plisser les yeux.

squirrel ['skwɪrəl, *Am* 'skwɜːrəl] écureuil *m*.

squirt [skwɜːt] **1** *vt* (*liquid*) faire gicler. **2** *vi* gicler.

stab [stæb] *vt* (*with knife*) poignarder.

stable[1] ['steɪb(ə)l] *a* stable.
stable[2] écurie *f*.
stack [stæk] (*heap*) tas *m*; **stacks of** *Fam* un *or* des tas de.
stack (up) *vt* entasser.
stadium ['steɪdɪəm] stade *m*.
staff [stɑːf] personnel *m*; (*of school*) professeurs *mpl*; (*of army*) état-major *m*; **s. room** (*of school*) salle *f* des professeurs.
stag [stæg] cerf *m*.
stage[1] [steɪdʒ] **1** *n* (*platform*) scène *f*. **2** *vt* (*play*) monter.
stage[2] (*phase, of journey*) étape *f*.
stagecoach diligence *f*.
stagger ['stægər] *vi* chanceler.
stain [steɪn] **1** *vt* (*to mark*) tacher (**with** de). **2** *n* tache *f*.
stained glass window vitrail *m* (*pl* vitraux).
stainless steel *a* (*knife etc*) en inox.
stain remover détachant *m*.
staircase escalier *m*.
stairs [steəz] *npl* escalier *m*.
stake [steɪk] (*post*) pieu *m*.
stale [steɪl] *a* (*bread etc*) rassis (*f* rassie).
stalk [stɔːk] (*of plant*) tige *f*.
stall [stɔːl] **1** *n* (*in market*) étal *m* (*pl* étals); (*for newspapers, flowers*) kiosque *m*. **2** *vti* (*of car engine*) caler.
stammer ['stæmər] **1** *vti* bégayer. **2** *n* **to have a s.** être bègue.
stamp [stæmp] **1** *n* (*for postage, instrument*) timbre *m*; (*mark*) cachet *m*. **2** *vt* (*document*) tamponner; (*letter*) timbrer; **stamped addressed envelope**, *Am* **stamped self-addressed envelope** enveloppe *f* timbrée à votre adresse. **3** *vti* **to s. (one's feet)** taper des pieds.
stamp collecting philatélie *f*.
stand [stænd] **1** *n* (*support*) support *m*; (*at exhibition*) stand *m*; (*for spectators*) tribune *f*; **news/flower s.** kiosque *m* à journaux/à fleurs. **2** *vt** (*pain, person etc*) supporter; (*put*) mettre (debout); **to s. a chance** avoir une chance. **3** *vi* être *or* se tenir (debout); (*get up*) se lever; (*remain*) rester (debout); (*be situated*) se trouver.
stand about *or* **around** traîner.
standard ['stændəd] **1** *n* norme *f*; (*level*) niveau *m*; **standards (of behaviour)** principes *mpl*; **s. of living** niveau *m* de vie; **up to s.** (*of work etc*) au niveau. **2** *a* (*model, size*) standard *inv*.
standard lamp lampadaire *m*.
stand aside s'écarter.
stand back reculer.
stand by **1** *vi* rester là (sans rien faire); (*be ready*) être prêt. **2** *vt*

(*friend*) rester fidèle à.
standby *a* (*ticket*) sans garantie.
stand for (*mean*) signifier, représenter; (*put up with*) supporter.
stand in for remplacer.
standing *a* debout *inv*.
stand out ressortir (**against** sur).
standpoint point *m* de vue.
standstill to bring to a s. immobiliser; **to come to a s.** s'immobiliser.
stand up 1 *vt* mettre debout. **2** *vi* se lever.
stand up for défendre.
stand up to résister à (*qch*); (*defend oneself*) tenir tête à (*qn*).
staple ['steɪp(ə)l] **1** *n* (*for paper etc*) agrafe *f*. **2** *vt* agrafer.
stapler agrafeuse *f*.
star [stɑːr] **1** *n* étoile *f*; (*person*) vedette *f*; **four-s. (petrol)** du super. **2** *vi* (*of actor*) être la vedette (**in** de). **3** *vt* (*of film*) avoir pour vedette.
stare [steər] **1** *n* regard *m* (fixe). **2** *vi* **to s. at** fixer (du regard).
start[1] [stɑːt] **1** *n* commencement *m*, début *m*; (*of race*) départ *m*; (*lead*) avance *f* (**on** sur); **to make a s.** commencer. **2** *vt* commencer; **to s. doing** *or* **to do** commencer à faire. **3** *vi* commencer (**with sth** par qch, **by doing** par faire); **starting from** (*price etc*) à partir de.
start[2] *vi* (*jump*) sursauter.
start (off *or* **out)** partir (**for** pour).
start (up) 1 *vt* (*engine, vehicle*) mettre en marche; (*business*) fonder. **2** *vi* (of engine, *vehicle*) démarrer.
starter (*in vehicle*) démarreur *m*; (*course of meal*) hors-d'œuvre *m inv*, entrée *f*; (*soup*) potage *m*.
startle ['stɑːt(ə)l] *vt* (*make jump*) faire sursauter.
start on sth commencer qch.
star'vation faim *f*.
starve [stɑːv] *vi* souffrir de la faim; (*die*) mourir de faim; **I'm starving!** (*hungry*) je meurs de faim!
state[1] [steɪt] (*condition*) état *m*; **S.** (*nation etc*) État *m*; **the States** *Fam* les États-Unis *mpl*.
state[2] *vt* déclarer (**that** que); (*time, date*) fixer.
statement déclaration *f*; **(bank) s.** relevé *m* de compte.
statesman (*pl* **-men**) homme *m* d'État.
station ['steɪʃ(ə)n] (*for trains*) gare *f*; (*underground*) station *f*; **(police) s.** commissariat *m* (de police); **bus** *or* **coach s.** gare *f* routière; **radio s.** station *f* de radio; **service** *or* **petrol** *or* *Am* **gas s.** station-service *f*.
stationary ['steɪʃən(ə)rɪ] *a* (*vehicle*) à l'arrêt.

stationer's (shop) papeterie *f*.
stationery articles *mpl* de bureau.
stationmaster chef *m* de gare.
station wagon *Am* break *m*, commerciale *f*.
statistic [stə'tɪstɪk] (*fact*) statistique *f*.
statue ['stætʃu:] statue *f*.
stay [steɪ] **1** *n* (*visit*) séjour *m*. **2** *vi* rester; (*reside*) loger; (*visit*) séjourner; **to s. put** ne pas bouger.
stay away ne pas s'approcher (**from** de); **to s. away from** (*school etc*) ne pas aller à.
stay in rester à la maison; (*of nail, screw*) tenir.
stay out rester dehors; (*not come home*) ne pas rentrer.
stay out of sth (*not interfere in*) ne pas se mêler de qch.
stay up ne pas se coucher; (*of fence etc*) tenir; **to s. up late** se coucher tard.
steadily *adv* (*gradually*) progressivement; (*regularly*) régulièrement; (*without stopping*) sans arrêt.
steady ['stedɪ] *a* stable; (*hand*) sûr; (*progress, speed*) régulier; **s. (on one's feet)** solide sur ses jambes.
steak [steɪk] steak *m*, bifteck *m*.
steal* [sti:l] *vti* voler (**from s.o.** à qn).
steam [sti:m] **1** *n* vapeur *f*; (*on glass*) buée *f*. **2** *vt* (*food*) cuire à la vapeur.
steamroller rouleau *m* compresseur.
steel [sti:l] acier *m*.
steep [sti:p] *a* (*stairs, slope etc*) raide; (*hill, path*) escarpé; (*price*) excessif.
steeple ['sti:p(ə)l] clocher *m*.
steer [stɪər] *vt* (*vehicle, ship, person*) diriger (**towards** vers).
steering wheel volant *m*.
stem [stem] (*of plant*) tige *f*.
stenographer [stə'nɒgrəfər] *Am* sténodactylo *f*.
step [step] **1** *n* pas *m*; (*of stairs*) marche *f*; (*on train, bus*) marchepied *m*; (*doorstep*) pas *m* de la porte; (*action*) mesure *f*; **(flight of) steps** escalier *m*; (*outdoors*) perron *m*; **(pair of) steps** (*ladder*) escabeau *m*. **2** *vi* (*walk*) marcher (**on** sur).
step aside s'écarter.
step back reculer.
stepbrother demi-frère *m*.
stepdaughter belle-fille *f*.
stepfather beau-père *m*.
step forward faire un pas en avant.

step into/out of (*car etc*) monter dans/descendre de.
stepladder escabeau *m*.
stepmother belle-mère *f*.
step over (*obstacle*) enjamber.
stepsister demi-sœur *f*.
stepson beau-fils *m*.
stereo ['sterɪəʊ] **1** *n* (*pl* **-os**) (*record player*) chaîne *f* (stéréo *inv*). **2** *a* stéréo *inv*.
sterilize ['sterəlaɪz] *vt* stériliser.
stew [stjuː] ragoût *m*.
steward ['stjuːəd] (*on plane, ship*) steward *m*.
stewar'dess hôtesse *f*.
stewed fruit compote *f*.
stick[1] [stɪk] bâton *m*; (*for walking*) canne *f*.
stick[2]* **1** *vt* (*glue*) coller; (*put*) *Fam* mettre, fourrer; **to s. sth into sth** fourrer qch dans qch. **2** *vi* coller (**to** à); (*of food in pan*) attacher (**to** dans); (*of drawer etc*) se coincer, être coincé.
stick down (*envelope*) coller.
sticker autocollant *m*.
sticking plaster sparadrap *m*.
stick on (*stamp*) coller.
stick out 1 *vt* (*tongue*) tirer. **2** *vi* (*of petticoat etc*) dépasser.
stick up (*notice*) afficher.
stick up for défendre.
sticky *a* collant; (*label*) adhésif.
stiff [stɪf] *a* raide; (*leg etc*) ankylosé; (*brush*) dur; **to have a s. neck** avoir le torticolis; **to feel s.** être courbaturé.
stifle ['staɪf(ə)l] *vi* **it's stifling** on étouffe.
still[1] [stɪl] *adv* encore, toujours; (*even*) encore; (*nevertheless*) tout de même.
still[2] *a* (*not moving*) immobile; (*calm*) calme; **to keep** *or* **stand s.** rester tranquille.
sting [stɪŋ] **1** *vti** (*of insect, ointment etc*) piquer. **2** *n* piqûre *f*.
stink* [stɪŋk] *vi* puer; **to s. of smoke**/*etc* empester la fumée/*etc*.
stink out (*room*) empester.
stir [stɜːr] *vt* (*coffee, leaves etc*) remuer.
stirrup ['stɪrəp] étrier *m*.
stitch [stɪtʃ] point *m*; (*in knitting*) maille *f*; (*in wound*) point *m* de suture.
stitch (up) (*sew*) coudre; (*repair*) recoudre.
stock [stɒk] **1** *n* (*supply*) provision *f*; (*soup*) bouillon *m*; **stocks and shares** valeurs *fpl* (boursières); **in s.** en magasin, en stock; **out of s.**

épuisé; **the S. Exchange** *or* **Market** la Bourse. **2** *vt* (*sell*) vendre.
stock (up) (*shop*, *larder*) approvisionner.
stocking bas *m*.
stock up *vi* s'approvisionner (**with** de, en).
stomach ['stʌmək] (*for digestion*) estomac *m*; (*front of body*) ventre *m*.
stomachache mal *m* de ventre; **to have a s.** avoir mal au ventre.
stone [stəʊn] pierre *f*; (*pebble*) caillou *m* (*pl* cailloux); (*in fruit*) noyau *m*; (*weight*) = 6,348 kg.
stood [stʊd] *pt & pp de* **stand.**
stool [stuːl] tabouret *m*.
stop [stɒp] **1** *n* (*place*, *halt*) arrêt *m*; (*for plane*, *ship*) escale *f*; **bus s.** arrêt *m* d'autobus; **to put a s. to sth** mettre fin à qch; **s. sign** (*on road*) stop *m*. **2** *vt* arrêter; (*end*) mettre fin à; (*prevent*) empêcher (**from doing** de faire). **3** *vi* s'arrêter; (*of pain*, *conversation etc*) cesser; (*stay*) rester; **to s. eating**/*etc* s'arrêter de manger/*etc*; **to s. snowing**/*etc* cesser de neiger/*etc*.
stop by passer (**s.o.'s** chez qn).
stoplight (*on vehicle*) stop *m*.
stop off *or* **over** (*on journey*) s'arrêter.
stopoff, stopover halte *f*.
stopper bouchon *m*.
stop up (*sink*, *pipe etc*) boucher.
stopwatch chronomètre *m*.
store [stɔːr] (*supply*) provision *f*; (*warehouse*) entrepôt *m*; (*shop*) grand magasin *m*, *Am* magasin *m*.
store (away) (*furniture*) entreposer.
store (up) (*in warehouse etc*) stocker; (*for future use*) mettre en réserve.
storekeeper *Am* commerçant, -ante *mf*.
storeroom (*in house*) débarras *m*; (*in office*, *shop*) réserve *f*.
storey ['stɔːrɪ] étage *m*.
stork [stɔːk] cigogne *f*.
storm [stɔːm] tempête *f*; (*thunderstorm*) orage *m*.
stormy *a* orageux.
story[1] ['stɔːrɪ] histoire *f*; (*newspaper article*) article *m*; (*plot*) intrigue *f*; **short s.** nouvelle *f*.
story[2] (*of building*) *Am* étage *m*.
stove [stəʊv] (*for cooking*) cuisinière *f*; (*portable*) réchaud *m*; (*for heating*) poêle *m*.
straight [streɪt] **1** *a* droit; (*hair*) raide; (*route*) direct; (*tidy*) en ordre; (*frank*) franc (*f* franche). **2** *adv* (*to walk etc*) droit; (*directly*)

tout droit; (*to drink whisky etc*) sec; **s. away** tout de suite; **s. ahead** *or* **on** tout droit.
straighten (up) (*tie*, *hair*, *room*) arranger.
straight'forward *a* (*easy*, *clear*) simple.
strain [streɪn] **1** *n* (*tiredness*) fatigue *f*; (*mental*) tension *f* nerveuse. **2** *vt* (*eyes*) fatiguer; (*voice*) forcer; **to s. one's back** se faire mal au dos.
strainer passoire *f*.
strange [streɪndʒ] *a* (*odd*) étrange; (*unknown*) inconnu.
stranger (*unknown*) inconnu, -ue *mf*; (*person from outside*) étranger, -ère *mf*.
strangle ['stræŋg(ə)l] *vt* étrangler.
strap [stræp] sangle *f*, courroie *f*; (*on dress*) bretelle *f*; (*on watch*) bracelet *m*; (*on sandal*) lanière *f*.
strap (down *or* **in)** attacher (avec une courroie).
straw [strɔː] paille *f*; **a (drinking) s.** une paille.
strawberry ['strɔːbərɪ, *Am* -berɪ] **1** *n* fraise *f*. **2** *a* (*ice cream*) à la fraise; (*jam*) de fraises; (*tart*) aux fraises.
streak [striːk] (*line*) raie *f*; (*of colour*) strie *f*; (*of paint*) traînée *f*.
stream [striːm] (*brook*) ruisseau *m*; (*flow*) flot *m*.
street [striːt] rue *f*; **s. door** porte *f* d'entrée.
streetcar (*tram*) *Am* tramway *m*.
street lamp *or* **light** réverbère *m*.
street map *or* **plan** plan *m* des rues.
strength [streŋθ] force *f*; (*health*, *energy*) forces *fpl*; (*of wood etc*) solidité *f*.
strengthen *vt* renforcer.
stress [stres] **1** *n* (*mental*) stress *m*; (*emphasis*) & *Grammar* accent *m*; **under s.** stressé. **2** *vt* insister sur; (*word*) accentuer; **to s. that** souligner que.
stretch [stretʃ] **1** *vt* (*rope*, *neck*) tendre; (*shoe*, *rubber*) étirer; **to s. one's legs** se dégourdir les jambes. **2** *vi* (*of person*, *elastic*) s'étirer. **3** *n* (*area*) étendue *f*.
stretch (out) **1** *vt* (*arm*, *leg*) étendre; **to s. (out) one's arm** (*reach out*) tendre le bras (**to take** pour prendre). **2** *vi* (*of plain etc*) s'étendre.
stretcher brancard *m*.
strict [strɪkt] *a* strict.
strictly *adv* strictement; **s. forbidden** formellement interdit.
strictness sévérité *f*.
stride [straɪd] (grand) pas *m*, enjambée *f*.
stride* along/out/*etc* avancer/sortir/*etc* à grands pas.

strike¹* [straɪk] *vt* (*hit, impress*) frapper; (*collide with*) heurter; (*a match*) frotter; (*of clock*) sonner (*l'heure*); **it strikes me that** il me semble que (+ *indicative*).
strike² (*of workers*) grève *f*; **to go (out) on s.** se mettre en grève (**for** pour obtenir).
striker (*worker*) gréviste *mf*.
striking *a* (*impressive*) frappant.
string [strɪŋ] ficelle *f*; (*of anorak, apron*) cordon *m*; (*of violin, racket etc*) corde *f*; (*of pearls*) collier *m*.
strip [strɪp] (*piece*) bande *f*; **(thin) s.** (*of metal etc*) lamelle *f*.
strip (off) *vi* se déshabiller.
stripe [straɪp] rayure *f*.
striped [straɪpt] *a* rayé.
stroke [strəʊk] **1** *n* (*movement*) coup *m*; (*illness*) coup *m* de sang; (**swimming**) **s.** nage *f*; **a s. of luck** un coup de chance. **2** *vt* (*beard, cat etc*) caresser.
stroll [strəʊl] **1** *n* promenade *f*. **2** *vi* se promener.
stroller (*for baby*) *Am* poussette *f*.
strong [strɒŋ] *a* fort; (*shoes, chair etc*) solide.
structure ['strʌktʃər] structure *f*; (*building*) construction *f*.
struggle ['strʌg(ə)l] **1** *n* (*fight*) lutte *f* (**to do** pour faire); **to have a s. doing** *or* **to do** avoir du mal à faire. **2** *vi* (*fight*) lutter, se battre (**with** avec); (*move about wildly*) se débattre; **to s. to do** s'efforcer de faire.
stub [stʌb] (*of cigarette etc*) bout *m*; (*of ticket, cheque, Am check*) talon *m*.
stubborn ['stʌbən] *a* (*person*) entêté.
stubbornness entêtement *m*.
stub out (*cigarette*) écraser.
stuck [stʌk] (*pt & pp de* **stick**) *a* (*caught, jammed*) coincé; **I'm s.** (*unable to carry on*) je ne sais pas quoi faire *or* dire *etc*.
stud [stʌd] (*for collar*) bouton *m* de col; (*of football boot etc*) crampon *m*.
student ['stjuːdənt] **1** *n* étudiant, -ante *mf*; (*at school*) *Am* élève *mf*; **music**/*etc* **s.** étudiant, -ante en musique/*etc*. **2** *a* (*life, protest*) étudiant; (*restaurant, residence*) universitaire.
studio ['stjuːdɪəʊ] (*pl* **-os**) (*of cinema etc*) studio *m*; **s. flat** *or Am* **apartment** studio *m*.
study ['stʌdɪ] **1** *n* étude *f*; (*office*) bureau *m*. **2** *vt* (*learn, observe*) étudier. **3** *vi* étudier; **to s. to be a doctor**/*etc* faire des études pour devenir médecin/*etc*; **to s. for an exam** préparer un examen.
stuff [stʌf] **1** *n* (*thing*) truc *m*; (*things*) trucs *mpl*; (*possessions*)

affaires *fpl*; **it's good s.** c'est bon. **2** *vt* (*fill*) bourrer (**with** de); (*cushion etc*) rembourrer (**with** avec); (*put*) fourrer (**into** dans); (*chicken etc*) farcir.
stuffed (up) [stʌft] *a* (*nose*) bouché.
stuffing (*for chicken etc*) farce *f*.
stuffy ['stʌfɪ] *a* (*room etc*) mal aéré; **it smells s.** ça sent le renfermé.
stumble ['stʌmb(ə)l] *vi* trébucher (**over** sur).
stump [stʌmp] (*of tree*) souche *f*.
stun [stʌn] *vt* (*with punch etc*) étourdir.
stunned *a* (*amazed*) stupéfait (**by** par).
stupid ['stjuːpɪd, *Am* 'stuːpɪd] *a* stupide; **a s. thing** une stupidité; **s. fool** idiot, -ote *mf*.
stu'pidity stupidité *f*.
sturdy ['stɜːdɪ] *a* robuste.
stutter ['stʌtər] **1** *vi* bégayer. **2** *n* **to have a s.** être bègue.
sty [staɪ] (*for pigs*) porcherie *f*.
style [staɪl] style *m*; (*fashion*) mode *f*; (*design of dress etc*) modèle *m*; (*of hair*) coiffure *f*.
stylish *a* chic *inv*.
subject ['sʌbdʒɪkt] (*matter*) & *Grammar* sujet *m*; (*at school*, *university*) matière *f*; (*citizen*) ressortissant, -ante *mf*.
subjunctive [səb'dʒʌŋktɪv] *Grammar* subjonctif *m*.
submarine ['sʌbməriːn] sous-marin *m*.
subscriber abonné, -ée *mf*.
subscribe to [səb'skraɪb] (*take out subscription*) s'abonner à (*journal etc*); (*be a subscriber*) être abonné à (*journal etc*).
subscription (*to newspaper etc*) abonnement *m*.
subside [səb'saɪd] *vi* (*of ground*) s'affaisser.
substance ['sʌbstəns] substance *f*.
substantial [səb'stænʃ(ə)l] *a* important; (*meal*) copieux.
substitute ['sʌbstɪtjuːt] produit *m* de remplacement; (*person*) remplaçant, -ante *mf* (**for** de).
subtitle ['sʌbtaɪt(ə)l] sous-titre *m*.
subtle ['sʌt(ə)l] *a* subtil.
subtract [səb'trækt] *vt* soustraire (**from** de).
subtraction soustraction *f*.
suburb ['sʌbɜːb] banlieue *f*; **the suburbs** la banlieue.
su'burban *a* (*train etc*) de banlieue.
subway ['sʌbweɪ] passage *m* souterrain; (*railroad*) *Am* métro *m*.
succeed [sək'siːd] *vi* réussir (**in doing** à faire, **in sth** dans qch).
success [sək'ses] succès *m*, réussite *f*; **he was a s.** il a eu du succès; **it was a s.** c'était réussi.

successful *a* (*effort etc*) couronné de succès; (*firm*) prospère; (*candidate in exam*) admis; (*writer, film etc*) à succès; **to be s.** réussir (**in** dans, **in an exam** à un examen, **in doing** à faire).
successfully *adv* avec succès.
such [sʌtʃ] **1** *a* tel, telle; **s. a car**/*etc* une telle voiture/*etc*; **s. happiness**/*etc* tant de bonheur/*etc*; **s. as** comme, tel que. **2** *adv* (*so very*) si; (*in comparisons*) aussi; **s. a large helping** une si grosse portion; **s. a kind woman as you** une femme aussi gentille que vous.
suck [sʌk] **1** *vt* sucer; (*of baby*) téter. **2** *vi* (*of baby*) téter.
suck (up) (*with straw*) aspirer.
sudden ['sʌd(ə)n] *a* soudain; **all of a s.** tout à coup.
suddenly *adv* subitement.
suds [sʌdz] *npl* **(soap) s.** mousse *f* de savon.
suede [sweɪd] **1** *n* daim *m*. **2** *a* de daim.
suffer ['sʌfər] **1** *vi* souffrir (**from** de). **2** *vt* (*loss*) subir; (*pain*) ressentir.
suffering souffrance(s) *f*(*pl*).
sufficient [sə'fɪʃ(ə)nt] *a* (*quantity*) suffisant; **s. money**/*etc* suffisamment d'argent/*etc*.
sufficiently *adv* suffisamment.
suffix ['sʌfɪks] suffixe *m*.
suffocate ['sʌfəkeɪt] *vti* étouffer.
sugar ['ʃʊgər] **1** *n* sucre *m*; **granulated/lump s.** sucre cristallisé/en morceaux. **2** *vt* sucrer.
sugar bowl sucrier *m*.
suggest [sə'dʒest] *vt* (*propose*) suggérer, proposer (**to** à, **doing** de faire, **that** que (+ *subjunctive*)); (*imply*) suggérer.
suggestion suggestion *f*.
suicide ['suːɪsaɪd] suicide *m*; **to commit s.** se suicider.
suit[1] [suːt] (*man's*) costume *m*; (*woman's*) tailleur *m*; *Cards* couleur *f*; **flying/diving/ski s.** combinaison *f* de vol/plongée/ski.
suit[2] *vt* (*please, be acceptable to*) convenir à; (*of dress, colour etc*) aller (bien) à; **it suits me to stay** ça m'arrange de rester; **suited to** (*job, activity*) fait pour.
suitable *a* qui convient (**for** à), convenable (**for** pour); (*dress, colour*) qui va (bien).
suitcase valise *f*.
suite [swiːt] (*rooms*) suite *f*; (*furniture*) mobilier *m*.
sulk [sʌlk] *vi* bouder.
sultana [sʌl'tɑːnə] raisin *m* sec.
sum [sʌm] (*amount of money, total*) somme *f*; (*calculation*) calcul *m*; **sums** le calcul.

summarize ['sʌməraɪz] *vt* résumer.
summary résumé *m*.
summer ['sʌmər] **1** *n* été *m*; **in (the) s.** en été. **2** *a* d'été; **s. holidays** *or Am* **vacation** grandes vacances *fpl*.
summertime été *m*.
sum up *vti* (*facts etc*) résumer.
sun [sʌn] soleil *m*; **in the s.** au soleil; **the sun is shining** il fait (du) soleil; **s. lotion/oil** crème *f*/huile *f* solaire.
sunbathe *vi* prendre un bain de soleil, se faire bronzer.
sunburn coup *m* de soleil.
sunburnt *a* (*tanned*) bronzé; (*burnt*) brûlé par le soleil.
sundae ['sʌndeɪ] glace *f* aux fruits.
Sunday ['sʌndɪ, -deɪ] dimanche *m*.
sunglasses *npl* lunettes *fpl* de soleil.
sunlamp lampe *f* à bronzer.
sunlight (lumière *f* du) soleil *m*.
sunny ['sʌnɪ] *a* (*day etc*) ensoleillé; **it's s.** il fait (du) soleil; **s. periods** *or* **intervals** éclaircies *fpl*.
sunrise lever *m* du soleil.
sunroof toit *m* ouvrant.
sunset coucher *m* du soleil.
sunshade (*over table, on beach*) parasol *m*.
sunshine soleil *m*.
sunstroke insolation *f*.
suntan bronzage *m*; **s. lotion/oil** crème *f*/huile *f* solaire.
suntanned *a* bronzé.
super ['su:pər] *a Fam* sensationnel.
superb [su:'pɜ:b] *a* superbe.
superficial [su:pə'fɪʃ(ə)l] *a* superficiel.
superglue colle *f* extra-forte.
superior [su'pɪərɪər] *a* supérieur **(to** à**)**.
superi'ority supériorité *f*.
supermarket supermarché *m*.
superstition [su:pə'stɪʃ(ə)n] superstition *f*.
superstitious *a* superstitieux.
supervise ['su:pəvaɪz] *vt* (*person, work*) surveiller; (*office, research*) diriger.
supervisor surveillant, -ante *mf*; (*in office*) chef *m* de service; (*in store*) chef *m* de rayon.
supper ['sʌpər] dîner *m*, souper *m*; (*late-night*) souper *m*; **to have s.** dîner, souper.
supple ['sʌp(ə)l] *a* souple.

supply [sə'plaɪ] **1** *vt* fournir; (*with electricity, gas, water*) alimenter (**with** en); (*equip*) équiper (**with** de); **to s. s.o. with sth, s. sth to s.o.** fournir qch à qn. **2** *n* (*stock*) provision *f*; **(food) supplies** vivres *mpl*.
support [sə'pɔːt] **1** *vt* (*bear weight of, help, encourage*) soutenir; (*be in favour of*) être en faveur de; (*family etc*) subvenir aux besoins de. **2** *n* (*help*) soutien *m*; (*object*) support *m*.
supporter partisan *m*; (*in sport*) supporter *m*.
suppose [sə'pəʊz] *vti* supposer (**that** que); **I'm supposed to work** *or* **be working** je suis censé travailler; **he's supposed to be rich** on le dit riche; **I s. (so)** je pense; **you're tired, I s.** vous êtes fatigué, je suppose; **s. we go** (*suggestion*) si nous partions; **s.** *or* **supposing you're right** supposons que tu aies raison.
sure [ʃʊər] *a* sûr (**of** de, **that** que); **she's s. to accept** il est sûr qu'elle acceptera; **to make s. of sth** s'assurer de qch; **be s. to do it!** ne manquez pas de le faire!
surely *adv* sûrement; **s. he didn't refuse?** (*I hope*) il n'a tout de même pas refusé.
surface ['sɜːfɪs] surface *f*; **s. area** superficie *f*; **s. mail** courrier *m* par voie(s) de surface.
surfboard planche *f* (de surf).
surfing ['sɜːfɪŋ] surf *m*; **to go s.** faire du surf.
surgeon ['sɜːdʒ(ə)n] chirurgien *m*.
surgery (*doctor's office*) cabinet *m*; **to have s.** avoir une opération (**for** pour).
surname ['sɜːneɪm] nom *m* de famille.
surprise [sə'praɪz] **1** *n* surprise *f*; **to take s.o. by s.** prendre qn au dépourvu. **2** *a* (*visit etc*) inattendu. **3** *vt* (*astonish*) étonner, surprendre.
surprised *a* surpris (**that** que (+ *subjunctive*), **at sth** de qch); **I'm s. to see you** je suis surpris de te voir.
surprising *a* surprenant.
surrender [sə'rendər] *vi* se rendre (**to** à).
surround [sə'raʊnd] *vt* entourer (**with** de); (*of army, police*) encercler; **surrounded by** entouré de.
surrounding *a* environnant.
surroundings *npl* environs *mpl*; (*setting*) cadre *m*.
survey ['sɜːveɪ] enquête *f*; (*of opinion*) sondage *m*.
sur'veyor (*of land*) géomètre *m*.
survive [sə'vaɪv] **1** *vi* survivre. **2** *vt* survivre à.
survivor survivant, -ante *mf*.
suspect **1** *n* ['sʌspekt] suspect, -ecte *mf*. **2** *vt* [sə'spekt] soupçonner (**that** que, **of sth** de qch, **of doing** d'avoir fait).

suspend [sə'spend] *vt* (*postpone, dismiss*) suspendre; (*pupil*) renvoyer.
suspenders *npl* (*for trousers, Am pants*) *Am* bretelles *fpl*.
suspense [sə'spens] (*in book etc*) suspense *m*.
suspension (*of vehicle*) suspension *f*.
suspicion [sə'spɪʃ(ə)n] soupçon *m*.
suspicious *a* (*person*) méfiant; (*behaviour*) suspect; **s.(-looking)** suspect; **to be s. of** se méfier de.
swallow ['swɒləʊ] **1** *vti* avaler. **2** *n* (*bird*) hirondelle *f*.
swallow sth down avaler qch.
swamp [swɒmp] marécage *m*.
swan [swɒn] cygne *m*.
swap [swɒp] **1** *n* échange *m*. **2** *vt* échanger (**for** contre); **to s. seats** changer de place. **3** *vi* échanger.
swarm [swɔːm] (*of bees etc*) essaim *m*.
sway [sweɪ] *vi* se balancer.
swear* [sweər] **1** *vt* (*promise*) jurer (**to do** de faire, **that** que). **2** *vi* (*curse*) jurer (**at** contre).
swearword gros mot *m*.
sweat [swet] **1** *n* sueur *f*. **2** *vi* transpirer, suer; **I'm sweating** je suis en sueur.
sweater pull *m*.
sweat shirt sweat-shirt *m*.
Swede [swiːd] Suédois, -oise *mf*.
Swedish **1** *a* suédois. **2** *n* (*language*) suédois *m*.
sweep* [swiːp] **1** *vt* (*with broom*) balayer; (*chimney*) ramoner. **2** *vi* balayer.
sweep away (*leaves etc*) balayer; (*carry off*) emporter.
sweep out (*room etc*) balayer.
sweep up balayer.
sweet [swiːt] **1** *a* (*not sour*) doux (*f* douce); (*tea, coffee etc*) sucré; (*child, house, cat*) mignon (*f* mignonne); (*kind*) aimable. **2** *n* (*candy*) bonbon *m*; (*dessert*) dessert *m*.
sweet corn maïs *m*.
sweeten *vt* (*tea etc*) sucrer.
sweetly *adv* (*kindly*) aimablement; (*agreeably*) agréablement.
sweet shop confiserie *f*.
swell* (up) *vi* (*of hand, leg etc*) enfler; (*of wood, dough*) gonfler.
swelling enflure *f*.
swerve [swɜːv] *vi* (*of vehicle*) faire une embardée.
swim [swɪm] **1** *n* **to go for a s.** se baigner. **2** *vi** nager; (*as sport*) faire de la natation; **to go swimming** aller nager. **3** *vt* (*crawl etc*)

nager.

swimmer nageur, -euse *mf.*

swimming natation *f.*

swimming costume maillot *m* de bain.

swimming pool piscine *f.*

swimming trunks slip *m* de bain.

swimsuit maillot *m* de bain

swing [swɪŋ] **1** *n* (*in playground etc*) balançoire *f.* **2** *vi** (*sway*) se balancer. **3** *vt* (*arms etc*) balancer.

swing round *vi* (*turn*) virer; (*of person*) se retourner (vivement).

Swiss [swɪs] **1** *a* suisse. **2** *n inv* Suisse *m*, Suissesse *f*; **the S.** les Suisses *mpl.*

switch [swɪtʃ] **1** *n* (*electric*) bouton *m* (électrique). **2** *vt* (*money, employee*) transférer (**to** à); (*exchange*) échanger (**for** contre); **to s. places** *or* **seats** changer de place.

switch off (*lamp, gas etc*) éteindre; (*engine*) arrêter.

switch on (*lamp, gas etc*) mettre, allumer; (*engine*) mettre en marche.

switch over (*change TV channels*) changer de chaîne.

swollen ['swəʊl(ə)n] (*pp de* **swell**) *a* (*leg etc*) enflé; (*stomach*) gonflé.

swop [swɒp] *n, vt & vi* = **swap.**

sword [sɔːd] épée *f.*

syllable ['sɪləb(ə)l] syllabe *f.*

syllabus ['sɪləbəs] programme *m* (scolaire).

symbol ['sɪmb(ə)l] symbole *m.*

sym'bolic *a* symbolique.

sympa'thetic *a* (*showing pity*) compatissant; (*understanding*) compréhensif.

sympathize *vi* **I s. (with you)** (*pity*) je suis désolé (pour vous); (*understanding*) je vous comprends.

sympathy ['sɪmpəθɪ] (*pity*) compassion *f*; (*understanding*) compréhension *f*; (*when s.o. dies*) condoléances *fpl.*

symphony ['sɪmfənɪ] symphonie *f.*

symptom ['sɪmptəm] symptôme *m.*

synagogue ['sɪnəgɒg] synagogue *f.*

synonym ['sɪnənɪm] synonyme *m.*

syringe [sɪ'rɪndʒ] seringue *f.*

syrup ['sɪrəp] sirop *m.*

system ['sɪstəm] système *m*; (*human body*) organisme *m*; (*order*) méthode *f.*

T

ta! [tɑː] *int Slang* merci!
tab [tæb] (*cloth etc flap*) patte *f*.
table ['teɪb(ə)l] (*furniture*, *list*) table *f*; **bedside t.** table *f* de nuit; **to lay** *or* **set/clear the t.** mettre/débarrasser la table.
tablecloth nappe *f*.
tablemat (*of cloth*) napperon *m*; (*hard*) dessous-de-plat *m inv*.
tablespoon = cuillère *f* à soupe.
tablespoonful = cuillerée *f* à soupe.
tablet ['tæblɪt] (*pill*) comprimé *m*.
tack [tæk] (*nail*) petit clou *m*; (*thumbtack*) *Am* punaise *f*.
tackle ['tæk(ə)l] *vt* (*problem etc*) s'attaquer à; *Rugby* plaquer; *Football* tacler.
tacky ['tækɪ] *a* (*in appearance*) moche; (*remark etc*) de mauvais goût.
tact [tækt] tact *m*.
tactful *a* **to be t.** (*of person*) avoir du tact.
tactic ['tæktɪk] **a t.** une tactique; **tactics** la tactique.
taffy ['tæfɪ] *Am* caramel *n* (*dur*).
tag [tæg] (*label*) étiquette *f*.
tail [teɪl] (*of animal etc*) queue *f*.
tailor ['teɪlər] tailleur *m*.
take* [teɪk] *vt* prendre; (*prize*) remporter; (*exam*) passer; (*subtract*) soustraire (**from** de); (*tolerate*) supporter; (*bring*) amener (*qn*) (**to** à); (*by car*) conduire (*qn*) (**to** à); **to t. sth to s.o.** (ap)porter qch à qn; **to t. s.o. (out) to the theatre/***etc* emmener qn au théâtre/*etc*; **to t. sth with one** emporter qch; **to t. s.o. home** ramener qn; **it takes courage/***etc* il faut du courage/*etc* (**to do** pour faire); **I took an hour to do it** j'ai mis une heure à le faire.
take after s.o. ressembler à qn.
take along (*object*) emporter; (*person*) emmener.
take apart (*machine*) démonter.
take away (*thing*) emporter; (*person*) emmener; (*remove*) enlever; (*subtract*) soustraire (**from** de).
take-away 1 *a* (*meal*) à emporter. **2** *n* (*shop*) restaurant *m* qui fait des plats à emporter; (*meal*) plat *m* à emporter.
take back reprendre; (*return*) rapporter; (*accompany*) ramener (*qn*) (**to** à).
take down (*object*) descendre; (*notes*) prendre.
take in (*chair*, *car etc*) rentrer; (*include*) inclure; (*understand*) comprendre; (*deceive*) *Fam* rouler.

taken *a* (*seat*) pris; **to be t. ill** tomber malade.
take off 1 *vt* (*remove*) enlever; (*lead away*) emmener; (*subtract*) déduire (**from** de). **2** *vi* (*of aircraft*) décoller.
takeoff (*of aircraft*) décollage *m*.
take on *vt* (*work, staff, passenger*) prendre.
take out (*from pocket etc*) sortir; (*stain*) enlever; (*tooth*) arracher; (*insurance*) prendre.
take-out *a* & *n Am* = **take-away.**
take over 1 *vt* (*company etc*) prendre la direction de; **to t. over s.o.'s job** remplacer qn. **2** *vi* prendre la relève (**from** de); (*permanently*) prendre la succession (**from** de).
take round (*bring*) apporter (*qch*) (**to** à); amener (*qn*) (**to** à); (*distribute*) distribuer; (*visitor*) faire visiter.
take up (*carry up*) monter; (*space, time*) prendre; (*hobby*) se mettre à.
takings *npl* recette *f*.
tale [teɪl] (*story*) conte *m*; **to tell tales** *Fam* rapporter.
talent ['tælənt] talent *m*; **to have a t. for** avoir du talent pour.
talented *a* doué.
talk [tɔːk] **1** *n* propos *mpl*; (*gossip*) bavardage(s) *m(pl)*; (*conversation*) conversation *f*; (*lecture*) exposé *m* (**on** sur); **talks** pourparlers *mpl*; **to have a t. with s.o.** parler avec qn; **there's t. of** on parle de. **2** *vi* parler (**to** à; **with** avec; **about, of** de). **3** *vt* (*nonsense*) dire; **to t. s.o. into doing/out of doing** persuader qn de faire/de ne pas faire.
talkative *a* bavard.
talk sth over discuter (de) qch.
tall [tɔːl] *a* (*person*) grand; (*tree, house*) haut; **how t. are you?** combien mesures-tu?
tambourine [tæmbə'riːn] tambourin *m*.
tame [teɪm] **1** *a* (*animal*) apprivoisé. **2** *vt* apprivoiser.
tampon ['tæmpɒn] tampon *m* hygiénique.
tan [tæn] **1** *n* (*suntan*) bronzage *m*. **2** *vti* bronzer.
tangerine [tændʒə'riːn] mandarine *f*.
tangled ['tæŋg(ə)ld] *a* enchevêtré.
tank [tæŋk] (*storing liquid or gas*) réservoir *m*; (*vehicle*) char *m*; (**fish**) **t.** aquarium *m*.
tanker (**oil**) **t.** (*ship*) pétrolier *m*.
tap [tæp] **1** *n* (*for water*) robinet *m*; (*blow*) petit coup *m*. **2** *vti* (*hit*) frapper légèrement.
tape[1] [teɪp] **1** *n* (*of cloth, paper*) ruban *m*; (**sticky** *or* **adhesive**) **t.** ruban *m* adhésif. **2** *vt* (*stick*) coller (*avec du ruban adhésif*).
tape[2] **1** *n* (*for sound/video recording*) bande *f* (magnétique/vidéo).

2 *vt* (*a film etc*) enregistrer, magnétoscoper; (*music*, *voice*) enregistrer; (*event*) faire une cassette de. **3** *vi* enregistrer.
tape measure mètre *m* (à) ruban.
tape recorder magnétophone *m*.
tar [tɑːr] goudron *m*.
target ['tɑːgɪt] cible *f*; (*objective*) objectif *m*.
tarpaulin [tɑː'pɔːlɪn] bâche *f*.
tart [tɑːt] (*pie*) (*open*) tarte *f*; (*with pastry on top*) tourte *f*.
tartan ['tɑːt(ə)n] *a* (*skirt etc*) écossais.
task [tɑːsk] travail *m*.
taste [teɪst] **1** *n* goût *m*. **2** *vt* (*eat*, *drink*) goûter; (*try*) goûter à; (*make out the taste of*) sentir (le goût de). **3** *vi* **to t. of** *or* **like sth** avoir un goût de qch; **to t. delicious**/*etc* avoir un goût délicieux/*etc*.
tasty *a* savoureux.
tattered ['tætəd] *a* (*clothes*) en lambeaux.
tattoo [tæ'tuː] **1** *n* (*pl* **-oos**) (*on body*) tatouage *m*. **2** *vt* tatouer.
tax [tæks] **1** *n* taxe *f*, impôt *m*; (*on income*) impôts *mpl*. **2** *vt* (*person*) imposer; (*goods*) taxer.
taxable *a* imposable.
taxi ['tæksɪ] taxi *m*; **t. rank,** *Am* **t. stand** station *f* de taxis.
taxpayer contribuable *mf*.
TB [tiː'bi] tuberculose *f*.
tea [tiː] thé *m*; (*snack*) goûter *m*; **to have t.** prendre le thé; (*snack*) goûter; **t. break** pause-thé *f*; **t. party** thé *m*; **t. set** service *m* à thé.
teabag sachet *m* de thé.
teach* [tiːtʃ] **1** *vt* apprendre (**s.o. sth** qch à qn, **that** que); (*in school etc*) enseigner (**s.o. sth** qch à qn); **to t. s.o. (how) to do** apprendre à qn à faire. **2** *vi* enseigner.
teacher professeur *m*; (*in primary school*) instituteur, -trice *mf*.
teaching enseignement *m*; **t. staff** = **teachers**.
teacup tasse *f* à thé.
team [tiːm] équipe *f*.
team up faire équipe (**with** avec).
teapot théière *f*.
tear[1] [teər] **1** *n* (*rip*) déchirure *f*. **2** *vt** déchirer.
tear[2] [tɪər] (*in eye*) larme *f*; **in tears** en larmes.
tear off *or* **out** [teər] (*with force*) arracher; (*receipt*, *stamp etc*) détacher.
tear up (*letter etc*) déchirer.
tease [tiːz] *vt* taquiner.
teaspoon petite cuillère *f*, cuillère *f* à café.
teaspoonful cuillerée *f* à café.

teat [tiːt] (*of bottle*) tétine *f*.
teatime l'heure *f* du thé.
tea towel torchon *m*.
technical ['teknɪk(ə)l] *a* technique.
tech'nician technicien, -ienne *mf*.
tech'nique technique *f*.
tech'nology technologie *f*.
teddy (bear) ['tedɪ] ours *m* (en peluche).
teenager ['tiːneɪdʒər] adolescent, -ente *mf*.
tee-shirt ['tiːʃɜːt] tee-shirt *m*.
teeth [tiːθ] *see* **tooth**.
tele- ['telɪ] *prefix* télé-.
telegram télégramme *m*.
telegraph pole poteau *m* télégraphique.
telephone 1 *n* téléphone *m*; **on the t.** (*speaking*) au téléphone. **2** *a* (*call, line etc*) téléphonique; (*number*) de téléphone; **t. booth, t. box** cabine *f* téléphonique; **t. directory** annuaire *m* du téléphone. **3** *vi* téléphoner. **4** *vt* **to t. s.o.** téléphoner à qn.
telescope télescope *m*.
televise ['telɪvaɪz] *vt* retransmettre à la télévision.
tele'vision télévision *f*; **on (the) t.** à la télévision; **t. set** téléviseur *m*.
tell* [tel] **1** *vt* dire (**s.o. sth** qch à qn, **that** que); (*story*) raconter; (*distinguish*) distinguer (**from** de); (*know*) savoir; **to t. s.o. to do** dire à qn de faire; **to t. the difference** voir la différence. **2** *vi* (*know*) savoir; **to t. of** *or* **about sth/s.o.** parler de qch/qn.
teller (bank) t. guichetier, -ière *mf* (*de banque*).
tell s.o. off disputer qn.
telltale *Fam* rapporteur, -euse *mf*.
telly ['telɪ] *Fam* télé *f*.
temper ['tempər] **to lose one's t.** se mettre en colère; **in a bad t.** de mauvaise humeur.
temperature ['temp(ə)rətʃər] température *f*; **to have a t.** avoir de la température.
temple ['temp(ə)l] (*building*) temple *m*.
temporary ['temp(ə)rərɪ] *a* provisoire; (*job*) temporaire; (*secretary*) intérimaire.
tempt [tempt] *vt* tenter; **tempted to do** tenté de faire.
temp'tation tentation *f*.
tempting *a* tentant.
ten [ten] *a* & *n* dix (*m*).
tenant ['tenənt] locataire *mf*.

tend [tend] *vi* **to t. to do** avoir tendance à faire.
tendency tendance *f* (**to do** à faire).
tender ['tendər] *a* (*soft*, *loving*) tendre; (*painful*) sensible.
tennis ['tenɪs] tennis *m*; **table t.** tennis *m* de table; **t. court** court *m* (de tennis).
tenpin bowling bowling *m*.
tense [tens] **1** *a* (*person*, *muscle*, *situation*) tendu. **2** *n* (*of verb*) temps *m*.
tension tension *f*.
tent [tent] tente *f*.
tenth [tenθ] *a* & *n* dixième (*mf*).
term [tɜːm] (*word*) terme *m*; (*period*) période *f*; (*of school year*) trimestre *m*; (*semester*) semestre *m*; **terms** (*conditions*) conditions *fpl*; (*prices*) prix *mpl*; **on good/bad terms** en bons/mauvais termes (**with** avec).
terminal ['tɜːmɪn(ə)l] **(air) t.** aérogare *f*; **(computer) t.** terminal *m* (d'ordinateur).
terrace ['terɪs] (*next to house etc*) terrasse *f*; (*houses*) maisons *fpl* en bande.
terrace house maison *f* attenante aux maisons voisines.
terrible ['terəb(ə)l] *a* affreux.
terribly *adv* (*badly*, *very*) affreusement.
terrific [tə'rɪfɪk] *a Fam* (*excellent*, *very great*) formidable.
terrify ['terɪfaɪ] *vt* terrifier; **to be terrified of** avoir très peur de.
terrifying *a* terrifiant.
territory ['terɪtərɪ] territoire *m*.
terror ['terər] terreur *f*.
terrorist *n* & *a* terroriste (*mf*).
terrorize *vt* terroriser.
Terylene® ['terəliːn] tergal® *m*.
test [test] **1** *vt* (*try*) essayer; (*product*, *machine*) tester; (*pupil*) interroger; (*of doctor*) examiner (*les yeux etc*); (*analyse*) analyser (*le sang etc*). **2** *n* essai *m*; (*of product*) test *m*; (*in school*) interrogation *f*, test *m*; (*by doctor*) examen *m*; (*of blood etc*) analyse *f*; **eye t.** examen *m* de la vue.
test tube éprouvette *f*.
text [tekst] texte *m*.
textbook manuel *m* (scolaire).
textile ['tekstaɪl] *a* & *n* textile (*m*).
than [ðən, *stressed* ðæn] *conj* que; **happier t.** plus heureux que. **▮** (*with numbers*) de; **more t. six** plus de six.
thank [θæŋk] **1** *vt* remercier (**for sth** de qch, **for doing** d'avoir fait);

t. you! merci!; **no, t. you!** (non) merci! **2** *n* **thanks** remerciements *mpl*; **(many) thanks!** merci (beaucoup)!; **thanks to** (*because of*) grâce à.

thankful *a* reconnaissant (**for** de).

Thanks'giving (day) *Am* jour *m* d'action de grâce(s).

that [ðət, *stressed* ðæt] **1** *conj* que; **to say t.** dire que. **2** *rel pron* (*subject*) qui; (*object*) que; (*after prep*) lequel, laquelle, *pl* lesquel(le)s; **the boy t. left** le garçon qui est parti; **the book t. I read** le livre que j'ai lu; **the carpet t. I put it on** le tapis sur lequel je l'ai mis; **the house t. she told me about** la maison dont elle m'a parlé; **the day/moment t.** le jour/moment où. **3** *dem a* (*pl see* **those**) ce, cet (*before vowel or mute h*), cette; (*opposed to 'this'*) ... + -là; **t. day** ce jour; ce jour-là; **t. girl** cette fille; cette fille-là. **4** *dem pron* (*pl see* **those**) ça, cela; **t. (one)** celui-là *m*, celle-là *f*; **give me t.** donne-moi ça *or* cela; **t.'s right** c'est juste; **who's t.?** qui est-ce?; **t.'s the house** c'est la maison; (*pointing*) voilà la maison; **t. is (to say)** c'est-à dire. **5** *adv* (*so*) si; **not t. good** pas si bon; **t. much** (*to cost etc*) (au)tant que ça.

thaw [θɔː] **1** *n* dégel *m*. **2** *vi* dégeler; (*of snow*) fondre; (*of food*) décongeler; **it's thawing** ça dégèle. **3** *vt* (*food*) (faire) décongeler.

the [ðə, *before vowel* ðɪ, *stressed* ðiː] *def art* le, l', la, *pl* les; **t. roof** le toit; **t. man** l'homme; **t. moon** la lune; **t. boxes** les boîtes; **of t., from t.** du, de l', de la, *pl* des; **to t., at t.** au, à l', à la, *pl* aux.

theatre ['θɪətər] (*Am* **theater**) théâtre *m*.

theft [θeft] vol *m*.

their [ðeər] *poss a* leur, *pl* leurs.

theirs [ðeəz] *poss pron* le leur, la leur, *pl* les leurs; **this book is t.** ce livre est à eux *or* est le leur.

them [ðəm, *stressed* ðem] *pron* les, (*after prep*, *'than'*, *'it is'*) eux *mpl*, elles *fpl*; **(to) t.** leur; **I see t.** je les vois; **I give (to) t.** je leur donne; **ten of t.** dix d'entre eux *or* elles; **all of t. came** tous sont venus, toutes sont venues; **I like all of t.** je les aime tous *or* toutes.

them'selves *pron* eux-mêmes *mpl*, elles-mêmes *fpl*; (*reflexive*) se, s'; (*after prep etc*) eux *mpl*, elles *fpl*.

then [ðen] **1** *adv* (*at that time*) à cette époque-là; (*just a moment ago*) à ce moment-là; (*next*) ensuite; **from t. on** dès lors; **before t.** avant cela; **until t.** jusque-là. **2** *conj* (*therefore*) donc.

theory ['θɪərɪ] théorie *f*.

there [ðeər] *adv* là; **(down** *or* **over) t.** là-bas; **on t.** là-dessus; **t. is, t. are** il y a; (*pointing*) voilà; **t. he is** le voilà; **that man t.** cet homme-là.

therefore *adv* donc.

thermometer [θə'mɒmɪtər] thermomètre *m*.
Thermos® (flask) ['θɜːməs] thermos® *m or f*.
thermostat ['θɜːməstæt] thermostat *m*.
these [ðiːz] **1** *dem a* (*sing see* **this**) ces; (*opposed to 'those'*) ... + -ci; **t. men** ces hommes; ces hommes-ci. **2** *dem pron* (*sing see* **this**) **t. (ones)** ceux-ci *mpl*, celles-ci *fpl*; **t. are my friends** ce sont mes amis.
they [ðeɪ] *pron* ils *mpl*, elles *fpl*; (*stressed*) eux *mpl*, elles *fpl*; **t. are doctors** ce sont des médecins. ▮ (*people in general*) on; **t. say** on dit.
thick [θɪk] **1** *a* épais (*f* épaisse). **2** *adv* (*to spread*) en couche épaisse.
thicken **1** *vt* épaissir. **2** *vi* (*of fog etc*) s'épaissir; (*of cream etc*) épaissir.
thickly *adv* (*to spread*) en couche épaisse.
thickness épaisseur *f*.
thief [θiːf] (*pl* **thieves**) voleur, -euse *mf*.
thigh [θaɪ] cuisse *f*.
thimble ['θɪmb(ə)l] dé *m* (à coudre).
thin [θɪn] **1** *a* (*slice, paper etc*) mince; (*person, leg*) maigre; (*soup*) peu épais (*f* épaisse). **2** *adv* (*to spread*) en couche mince.
thin (down) (*paint etc*) diluer.
thing [θɪŋ] chose *f*; **one's things** (*belongings*) ses affaires *fpl*.
think* [θɪŋk] **1** *vi* penser (**about, of** à); **to t. (carefully)** réfléchir (**about, of** à); **to t. of doing** penser à faire; **she doesn't t. much of it** ça ne lui dit pas grand-chose. **2** *vt* penser (**that** que); **I t. so** je pense que oui; **what do you t. of him?** que penses-tu de lui?
think sth over réfléchir à qch.
think up inventer.
thinly *adv* (*to spread*) en couche mince.
third [θɜːd] **1** *a* troisième. **2** *n* troisième *mf*; **a t.** (*fraction*) un tiers. **3** *adv* **to come t.** se classer troisième.
thirdly *adv* troisièmement.
thirst [θɜːst] soif *f*.
thirsty *a* **to be** *or* **feel t.** avoir soif; **to make s.o. t.** donner soif à qn.
thirteen [θɜː'tiːn] *a* & *n* treize (*m*).
thirteenth *a* & *n* treizième (*mf*).
thirtieth *a* & *n* trentième (*mf*).
'thirty *a* & *n* trente (*m*).
this [ðɪs] **1** *dem a* (*pl see* **these**) ce, cet (*before vowel or mute h*), cette; (*opposed to 'that'*) ... + -ci; **t. book** ce livre; ce livre-ci; **t. photo** cette photo; cette photo-ci. **2** *dem pron* (*pl see* **these**) ceci; **t. (one)** celui-ci *m*, celle-ci *f*; **give me t.** donne-moi ceci; **t. is Paul** c'est

Paul; (*pointing*) voici Paul. **3** *adv* **t. high** (*pointing*) haut comme ceci; **t. far** jusqu'ici.

thorn [θɔːn] épine *f*.

thorough ['θʌrə] *a* (*careful*) minutieux; (*knowledge*, *examination*) approfondi; **to give sth a t. washing**/*etc* laver/*etc* qch à fond.

thoroughly *adv* (*completely*) tout à fait; (*carefully*) avec minutie; (*to know*, *clean etc*) à fond.

those [ðəʊz] **1** *dem a* (*sing see* **that**) ces; (*opposed to 'these'*) ... + -là; **t. men** ces hommes; ces hommes-là. **2** *dem pron* (*sing see* **that**) **t. (ones)** ceux-là *mpl*, celles-là *fpl*; **t. are my friends** ce sont mes amis.

though [ðəʊ] **1** *conj* **(even) t.** bien que (+ *subjunctive*); **as t.** comme si. **2** *adv* (*however*) cependant.

thought [θɔːt] (*pt & pp de* **think**) *n* pensée *f*; **(careful) t.** réflexion *f*.

thoughtful *a* (*considerate*) gentil, attentionné.

thoughtless *a* (*towards others*) pas très gentil; (*absent-minded*) étourdi.

thousand ['θaʊzənd] *a & n* mille *a & m inv*; **a t. pages** mille pages; **two t. pages** deux mille pages; **thousands of** des milliers de.

thread [θred] **1** *n* (*yarn*) fil *m*. **2** *vt* (*needle*, *beads*) enfiler.

threat [θret] menace *f*.

threaten *vt* menacer (**to do** de faire, **with sth** de qch).

threatening *a* menaçant.

three [θriː] *a & n* trois (*m*).

threw [θruː] *pt de* **throw**.

thrill [θrɪl] frisson *m*.

thrilled *a* ravi (**with sth** de qch, **to do** de faire).

thriller film *m or* roman *m* à suspense.

thrilling *a* passionnant.

thriving ['θraɪvɪŋ] *a* prospère.

throat [θrəʊt] gorge *f*.

throne [θrəʊn] trône *m*.

through [θruː] **1** *prep* (*place*) à travers; (*window*, *door*) par; (*time*) pendant; (*means*) par; **to go** *or* **get t.** (*forest etc*) traverser; (*hole etc*) passer par; (*wall etc*) passer à travers. **2** *adv* à travers; **to let t.** laisser passer; **to be t.** (*finished*) *Am* avoir fini; **t. to** *or* **till** jusqu'à; **I'll put you t. (to him)** (*on phone*) je vous le passe.

through'out **1** *prep* **t. the neighbourhood**/*etc* dans tout le quartier/*etc*; **t. the day**/*etc* pendant toute la journée/*etc*. **2** *adv* (*everywhere*) partout; (*all the time*) tout le temps.

throw* [θrəʊ] *vt* jeter (**to, at** à); (*party*) donner.

throw away (*unwanted object*) jeter.

throw out (*unwanted object*) jeter; (*expel*) mettre (*qn*) à la porte.
throw up *vti* (*vomit*) *Fam* rendre.
thud [θʌd] bruit *m* sourd.
thug [θʌg] voyou *m*.
thumb [θʌm] pouce *m*.
thumbtack *Am* punaise *f*.
thunder ['θʌndər] **1** *n* tonnerre *m*. **2** *vi* tonner; **it's thundering** il tonne.
thunderstorm orage *m*.
Thursday ['θɜːzdɪ, -deɪ] jeudi *m*.
tick [tɪk] (*mark*) = croix *f*.
tick (off) (*on list etc*) cocher.
ticket ['tɪkɪt] billet *m*; (*for bus*, *underground*, *cloakroom*) ticket *m*; (**price**) **t.** étiquette *f*.
ticket collector contrôleur, -euse *mf*.
ticket office guichet *m*.
tickle ['tɪk(ə)l] *vt* chatouiller.
ticklish *a* chatouilleux.
tide [taɪd] marée *f*.
tidily *adv* (*to put away*) soigneusement.
tidy ['taɪdɪ] *a* (*place*, *toys etc*) bien rangé; (*clothes*, *hair*) soigné; (*person*) ordonné; (*in appearance*) soigné.
tidy sth (up *or* **away)** ranger qch.
tie [taɪ] **1** *n* (*around neck*) cravate *f*; (*drawn match*) match *m* nul. **2** *vt* (*fasten*) attacher (**to** à); (*a knot*) faire (**in** à); (*shoe*) lacer.
tie up attacher (*qch*) (**to** à); (*person*) ligoter.
tiger ['taɪgər] tigre *m*.
tight [taɪt] **1** *a* (*clothes fitting too closely*) (trop) étroit; (*drawer*, *lid*) dur; (*knot*, *screw*) serré; (*rope*, *wire*) raide. **2** *adv* (*to hold*, *shut*) bien; (*to squeeze*) fort.
tighten (up) (*bolt etc*) (res)serrer.
tightly *adv* (*to hold*) bien; (*to squeeze*) fort.
tights [taɪts] *npl* collant(s) *m*(*pl*).
tile [taɪl] **1** *n* (*on roof*) tuile *f*; (*on wall or floor*) carreau *m*. **2** *vt* (*wall*, *floor*) carreler.
till [tɪl] **1** *prep & conj* = **until. 2** *n* (*for money*) caisse *f* (enregistreuse).
tilt [tɪlt] *vti* pencher.
timber ['tɪmbər] bois *m* (de construction).
time [taɪm] **1** *n* temps *m*; (*point in time*) moment *m*; (*period in history*) époque *f*; (*on clock*) heure *f*; (*occasion*) fois *f*; **some/most of the t.** une partie/la plupart du temps; **all of the t.** tout le temps; **in a**

year's t. dans un an; **it's t. (to do)** il est temps (de faire); **to have a good t.** s'amuser; **in t.** (*to arrive*) à temps; **from t. to t.** de temps en temps; **what t. is it?** quelle heure est-il?; **on t.** à l'heure; **at the same t.** en même temps (**as** que); (*simultaneously*) à la fois; **for the t. being** pour le moment; **one at a t.** un à un. **2** *vt* (*sportsman etc*) chronométrer; (*activity*) minuter; (*choose the time of*) choisir le moment de.

timer (*device*) minuteur *m*; (*built into appliance*) programmateur *m*; (*plugged into socket*) prise *f* programmable.

timetable horaire *m*; (*in school*) emploi *m* du temps.

timid ['tɪmɪd] *a* (*afraid*) craintif; (*shy*) timide.

timing **what good t.!** quelle synchronisation!

tin [tɪn] (*metal*) étain *m*; (*coated steel or iron*) fer-blanc *m*; (*can*) boîte *f*.

tinfoil papier *m* (d')alu.

tinned *a* en boîte.

tin opener ouvre-boîtes *m inv*.

tiny ['taɪnɪ] *a* tout petit.

tip [tɪp] **1** *n* (*end*) bout *m*; (*pointed*) pointe *f*; (*money*) pourboire *m*; (*advice*) conseil *m*; (*for rubbish, Am garbage*) décharge *f*. **2** *vt* (*waiter etc*) donner un pourboire à.

tip (out) (*liquid, load*) déverser (**into** dans).

tip (up *or* **over) 1** *vt* (*tilt*) pencher; (*overturn*) faire basculer. **2** *vi* pencher; basculer.

tipped cigarette [tɪpt] cigarette *f* (à bout) filtre.

tiptoe **on t.** sur la pointe des pieds.

tire[1] ['taɪər] **1** *vt* fatiguer. **2** *vi* se fatiguer.

tire[2] *Am* pneu *m* (*pl* pneus).

tired *a* fatigué; **to be t. of sth/s.o./doing** en avoir assez de qch/de qn/de faire.

tiredness fatigue *f*.

tire s.o. out épuiser qn.

tiring *a* fatigant.

tissue ['tɪʃuː] (*handkerchief etc*) mouchoir *m* en papier.

title ['taɪt(ə)l] titre *m*.

to [tə, *stressed* tuː] *prep* à; (*towards*) vers; (*of attitude*) envers; (*right up to*) jusqu'à; **give it to him** *or* **her** donne-le-lui; **to France** en France; **to Portugal** au Portugal; **to the butcher('s)**/*etc* chez le boucher/*etc*; **the road to London** la route de Londres; **the train to Paris** le train pour Paris; **kind/cruel to s.o.** gentil/cruel envers qn; **it's ten (minutes) to one** il est une heure moins dix. ■ (*with infinitive*) **to say/do**/*etc* dire/faire/*etc*; **(in order) to** pour. ■ (*with adjective*) de; à; **happy**/*etc* **to do** heureux/*etc* de faire; **it's easy/difficult to do** c'est facile/difficile à faire.

toad [təʊd] crapaud *m*.

toadstool champignon *m* (vénéneux).

toast [təʊst] **1** *n* pain *m* grillé; **piece** *or* **slice of t.** tranche *f* de pain grillé, toast *m*. **2** *vt* (faire) griller.

toaster grille-pain *m inv*.

tobacco [tə'bækəʊ] tabac *m*.

tobacconist's (shop), *Am* **tobacco store** (bureau *m* de) tabac *m*.

toboggan [tə'bɒgən] luge *f*.

today [tə'deɪ] *adv* aujourd'hui.

toddler ['tɒdlər] enfant *mf* (en bas âge).

toe [təʊ] orteil *m*.

toenail ongle *m* du pied.

toffee ['tɒfɪ] caramel *m* (*dur*).

together [tə'geðər] *adv* ensemble; (*at the same time*) en même temps; **t. with** avec.

toilet ['tɔɪlɪt] (*room*) toilettes *fpl*; (*bowl*, *seat*) cuvette *f or* siège *m* des cabinets; **to go to the t.** aller aux toilettes.

toilet flush chasse *f* d'eau.

toilet paper papier *m* hygiénique.

toiletries *npl* articles *mpl* de toilette.

toilet roll rouleau *m* de papier hygiénique.

toilet water (*perfume*) eau *f* de toilette.

token ['təʊkən] (*disc*, *Am disk*) jeton *m*; **book t.** chèque-livre *m*; **record t.** chèque-disque *m*.

told [təʊld] *pt & pp de* **tell**.

tolerant ['tɒlərənt] *a* tolérant (**of** à l'égard de).

tolerate *vt* tolérer.

toll [təʊl] (*fee*) péage *m*; **t. road/bridge** route *f*/pont *m* à péage.

tollfree number = *Am* numéro *m* vert.

tomato [tə'mɑːtəʊ, *Am* tə'meɪtəʊ] (*pl* **-oes**) tomate *f*.

tomb [tuːm] tombeau *m*.

tomorrow [tə'mɒrəʊ] *adv* demain; **t. morning** demain matin; **the day after t.** après-demain.

ton [tʌn] tonne *f* (*Br = 1016 kg*, *Am = 907 kg*); **tons of** (*lots of*) *Fam* des tonnes de.

tone [təʊn] ton *m*; (*of telephone*) tonalité *f*; **engaged t.** sonnerie *f* 'occupé'.

tongs [tɒŋz] *npl* **sugar t.** pince *f* à sucre.

tongue langue *f*.

tonic ['tɒnɪk] **t. (water)** eau *f* gazeuse (tonique); **gin and t.** gin-tonic *m.*

tonight [tə'naɪt] *adv* (*this evening*) ce soir; (*during the night*) cette nuit.

tonsil ['tɒns(ə)l] amygdale *f*.

tonsillitis [tɒnsə'laɪtəs] **to have t.** avoir une angine.

too [tuː] *adv* trop; (*also*) aussi; (*moreover*) en plus; **t. tired to play** trop fatigué pour jouer; **t. hard to solve** trop difficile à résoudre; **t. much, t. many** trop; **t. much salt/t. many people/***etc* trop de sel/gens/*etc*; **one t. many** un de trop.

took [tʊk] *pt de* **take.**

tool [tuːl] outil *m*.

tooth, *pl* **teeth** [tuːθ, tiːθ] dent *f*.

toothache mal *m* de dents; **to have a t.** avoir mal aux dents.

toothbrush brosse *f* à dents.

toothpaste dentifrice *m*.

toothpick cure-dent *m*.

top¹ [tɒp] **1** *n* (*of mountain, tower, tree*) sommet *m*; (*of wall, ladder, page, garment*) haut *m*; (*of table*) dessus *m*; (*of list*) tête *f*; (*of bottle, tube*) bouchon *m*; (*bottle cap*) capsule *f*; (*of saucepan*) couvercle *m*; (*of pen*) capuchon *m*; **at the t. of the class** le premier de la classe; **on t. of** sur. **2** *a* (*drawer, shelf*) du haut; (*step, layer*) dernier; (*in exam*) premier; (*maximum*) maximum; **on the t. floor** au dernier étage; **at t. speed** à toute vitesse.

top² **(spinning) t.** toupie *f*.

topic ['tɒpɪk] sujet *m*.

top up (*glass*) remplir; (*coffee, tea*) remettre.

torch [tɔːtʃ] (*electric*) lampe *f* électrique; (*flame*) torche *f*.

torment [tɔː'ment] *vt* (*annoy*) agacer.

tornado [tɔː'neɪdəʊ] (*pl* **-oes**) tornade *f*.

tortoise ['tɔːtəs] tortue *f*.

tortoiseshell écaille *f*.

torture ['tɔːtʃər] **1** *n* torture *f*. **2** *vt* torturer.

toss [tɒs] **1** *vt* (*throw*) jeter (**to** à); **to t. a coin** jouer à pile ou face. **2** *vi* **let's t. up** jouons à pile ou face.

total ['təʊt(ə)l] *a* & *n* total (*m*).

totally *adv* totalement.

touch [tʌtʃ] **1** *n* (*contact*) contact *m*; (*sense*) toucher *m*; **in t. with s.o.** en contact avec qn; **to get in t.** se mettre en contact. **2** *vt* toucher; (*interfere with*) toucher à. **3** *vi* (*of lines, hands etc*) se toucher; **don't t.!** n'y *or* ne touche pas!

touch down (*of aircraft*) atterrir.

touchy *a* susceptible.

tough [tʌf] *a* (*meat*) dur; (*sturdy*) solide; (*strong*) fort; (*difficult, harsh*) dur.
tour [tʊər] **1** *n* (*journey*) voyage *m*; (*visit*) visite *f*; (*by artist etc*) tournée *f*. **2** *vt* visiter.
tourism tourisme *m*.
tourist 1 touriste *mf*. **2** *a* touristique.
tourist office syndicat *m* d'initiative.
tournament ['tʊənəmənt] tournoi *m*.
tow [təʊ] *vt* (*car, boat*) remorquer; (*caravan, trailer*) tracter.
toward(s) [tə'wɔːd(z), *Am* tɔːd(z)] *prep* vers; (*of feelings*) envers; **cruel/***etc* **t. s.o.** cruel/*etc* envers qn.
towel ['taʊəl] serviette *f* (de toilette); (*for dishes*) torchon *m*.
towelling, *Am* **toweling** tissu-éponge *m*; **(kitchen) t.** *Am* essuie-tout *m inv*.
tower ['taʊər] tour *f*.
tower block tour *f*.
town [taʊn] ville *f*; **in t., (in)to t.** en ville; **t. centre** centre-ville *m*.
town council conseil *m* municipal.
town hall mairie *f*.
tow truck *Am* dépanneuse *f*.
toy [tɔɪ] **1** *n* jouet *m*. **2** *a* (*gun*) d'enfant; (*house, car*) miniature.
toyshop magasin *m* de jouets.
trace [treɪs] **1** *n* trace *f* (**of** de). **2** *vt* (*with tracing paper*) (dé)calquer; (*find*) retrouver.
tracing paper papier-calque *m inv*.
track [træk] (*of animal, sports stadium etc*) piste *f*; (*of record*) plage *f*; (*for train*) voie *f*; (*path*) chemin *m*; (*racetrack*) *Am* champ *m* de courses; **tracks** (*of wheels*) traces *fpl*; **on the right t.** sur la bonne voie.
track shoe *Am* (*running shoe*) jogging *m*.
tracksuit survêtement *m*.
tractor ['træktər] tracteur *m*.
trade [treɪd] **1** *n* commerce *m*; (*job*) métier *m*. **2** *vi* faire du commerce (**with** avec); (*swap*) échanger; **to t. places** changer de place. **3** *vt* échanger (**for** contre).
trade in reprise *f*.
trademark ['treɪdmɑːk] marque *f* de fabrique; **(registered) t.** marque déposée.
trade union syndicat *m*.
trading commerce *m*.
tradition [trə'dɪʃ(ə)n] tradition *f*.
traditional *a* traditionnel.

traffic ['træfɪk] circulation *f*; (*air*, *sea*, *rail*) trafic *m*.
traffic island refuge *m*.
traffic jam embouteillage *m*.
traffic lights *npl* feux *mpl* (de signalisation); (*when red*) feu *m* rouge.
traffic sign panneau *m* de signalisation.
tragedy ['trædʒədɪ] tragédie *f*.
tragic *a* tragique.
trail [treɪl] **1** *n* (*of smoke*, *blood etc*) traînée *f*. **2** *vti* (*on the ground etc*) traîner.
trailer (*for car*) remorque *f*; *Am* caravane *f*; (*camper*) *Am* camping-car *m*.
train[1] [treɪn] train *m*; (*underground*) rame *f*; **to go** *or* **come by t.** prendre le train; **t. set** petit train *m*.
train[2] **1** *vt* (*teach*) former (**to do** à faire); (*in sport*) entraîner; (*animal*, *child*) dresser (**to do** à faire). **2** *vi* recevoir une formation (**as a doctor**/*etc* de médecin/*etc*); (*of sportsman*) s'entraîner.
trained *a* (*skilled*) qualifié; (*nurse*, *engineer*) diplômé.
trainer (*running shoe*) jogging *m*.
training formation *f*; (*in sport*) entraînement *m*.
traitor ['treɪtər] traître *m*.
tram [træm] tramway *m*.
tramp [træmp] clochard, -arde *mf*.
tranquillizer ['træŋkwɪlaɪzər] tranquillisant *m*.
transfer 1 *vt* [træns'fɜːr] (*person*, *goods etc*) transférer (**to** à); **to t. the charges** téléphoner en PCV. **2** *n* ['trænsfɜːr] transfert *m* (**to** à); (*image*) décalcomanie *f*.
transfusion [træns'fjuːʒ(ə)n] (**blood**) **t.** transfusion *f* (sanguine).
transistor [træn'zɪstər] **t. (radio)** transistor *m*.
transitive ['trænsɪtɪv] *a Grammar* transitif.
translate [træns'leɪt] *vt* traduire (**from** de, **into** en).
translation traduction *f*.
translator traducteur, -trice *mf*.
transparent [træns'pærənt] *a* transparent.
transplant ['trænsplɑːnt] greffe *f*.
transport 1 *vt* [træn'spɔːt] transporter. **2** *n* ['trænspɔːt] transport *m* (**of** de); **means of t.** moyen *m* de transport; **public t.** les transports en commun.
trap [træp] **1** *n* piège *m*. **2** *vt* (*animal*) prendre (au piège); (*jam*) coincer; (*cut off by snow etc*) bloquer (**by** par).
trap door trappe *f*.
trash [træʃ] (*nonsense*) sottises *fpl*; (*junk*) bric-à-brac *m inv*; (*waste*)

Am ordures *fpl*.
trashcan *Am* poubelle *f*.
travel ['træv(ə)l] **1** *vi* voyager. **2** *vt* (*country*, *distance*) parcourir. **3** *n* **travel(s)** voyages *mpl*; **t. agent** agent *m* de voyages.
traveller voyageur, -euse *mf*.
traveller's cheque, *Am* **traveler's check** chèque *m* de voyage.
travelling voyages *mpl*.
travelsickness (*in car*) mal *m* de la route; (*in aircraft*) mal *m* de l'air.
tray [treɪ] plateau *m*.
treacherous ['tretʃ(ə)rəs] *a* (*road*, *conditions*) très dangereux.
tread* [tred] *vi* marcher (**on** sur).
treasure ['treʒər] trésor *m*.
treat [triːt] **1** *vt* traiter; (*consider*) considérer (**as** comme); **to t. s.o. to sth** offrir qch à qn. **2** *n* **(special) t.** petit extra *m*; **to give s.o. a (special) t.** donner une surprise à qn.
treatment traitement *m*.
treble ['treb(ə)l] *vti* tripler.
tree [triː] arbre *m*.
tremble ['tremb(ə)l] *vi* trembler (**with** de).
trench [trentʃ] tranchée *f*.
trial ['traɪəl] (*in court*) procès *m*; **to go** *or* **be on t.** être jugé, passer en jugement.
triangle ['traɪæŋg(ə)l] triangle *m*; (*setsquare*) *Am* équerre *f*.
tri'angular *a* triangulaire.
tribe [traɪb] tribu *f*.
trick [trɪk] **1** *n* (*joke*, *of conjurer etc*) tour *m*; (*clever method*) astuce *f*; **to play a t. on s.o.** jouer un tour à qn. **2** *vt* tromper.
trickle ['trɪk(ə)l] **1** *n* (*of liquid*) filet *m*. **2** *vi* dégouliner.
tricky *a* (*problem etc*) difficile.
tricycle ['traɪsɪk(ə)l] tricycle *m*.
trigger ['trɪgər] (*of gun*) gâchette *f*.
trim [trɪm] *vt* couper (un peu).
trip [trɪp] (*journey*) voyage *m*; (*outing*) excursion *f*.
trip (over *or* **up)** *vi* trébucher; **to t. over sth** trébucher contre qch.
triple ['trɪp(ə)l] *vti* tripler.
trip s.o. up faire trébucher qn.
triumph ['traɪʌmf] **1** *n* triomphe *m* (**over** sur). **2** *vi* triompher (**over** de).
trivial ['trɪvɪəl] *a* (*unimportant*) insignifiant.
trolley ['trɒlɪ] (*for luggage*) chariot *m*; (*in supermarket*) caddie® *m*; **(tea) t.** table *f* roulante.

trombone [trɒm'bəʊn] trombone *m*.
troops [tru:ps] *npl* troupes *fpl*.
trophy ['trəʊfɪ] coupe *f*, trophée *m*.
tropical ['trɒpɪk(ə)l] *a* tropical.
trot [trɒt] **1** *n* trot *m*. **2** *vi* trotter.
trouble ['trʌb(ə)l] **1** *n* (*difficulty*) ennui(s) *m*(*pl*); (*effort*) peine *f*; **trouble(s)** (*social unrest*, *illness*) troubles *mpl*; **to be in t.** avoir des ennuis; **to get into t.** s'attirer des ennuis (**with** avec), **to go to the t. of doing, take the t. to do** se donner la peine de faire. **2** *vt* (*inconvenience*) déranger; (*worry*, *annoy*) ennuyer.
trousers ['traʊzəz] *npl* pantalon *m*; **a pair of t., some t.** un pantalon.
trout [traʊt] truite *f*.
truant ['tru:ənt] **to play t.** sécher (la classe).
truck [trʌk] (*lorry*) camion *m*.
true [tru:] *a* vrai; (*accurate*) exact; **t. to** (*one's promise etc*) fidèle à; **to come t.** se réaliser.
trump (card) [trʌmp] atout *m*.
trumpet ['trʌmpɪt] trompette *f*.
trunk [trʌŋk] (*of tree*, *body*) tronc *m*; (*of elephant*) trompe *f*; (*case*) malle *f*; (*of vehicle*) *Am* coffre *m*; **trunks** (*for swimming*) slip *m* de bain.
trust [trʌst] **1** *n* (*faith*) confiance *f* (**in** en). **2** *vt* (*person*, *judgment*) avoir confiance en; **to t. s.o. with sth, t. sth to s.o.** confier qch à qn.
truth [tru:θ] vérité *f*.
try [traɪ] **1** *vt* essayer (**to do, doing** de faire); **to t. one's luck** tenter sa chance. **2** *vi* essayer; **to t. hard** faire un gros effort. **3** *n* (*attempt*) & *Rugby* essai *m*; **to have a t.** essayer.
try (out) (*car*, *method etc*) essayer; (*person*) mettre à l'essai.
try on (*clothes*, *shoes*) essayer.
T-shirt ['ti:ʃɜ:t] tee-shirt *m*.
tub [tʌb] (*basin*) baquet *m*; (*bath*) baignoire *f*.
tube [tju:b] tube *m*; (*underground railway*) métro *m*.
tuck in [tʌk] (*shirt*, *blanket*) rentrer; (*person in bed*) border.
Tuesday ['tju:zdɪ, -deɪ] mardi *m*.
tuft [tʌft] touffe *f*.
tug [tʌg] *vti* tirer (**at** sur).
tug(boat) remorqueur *m*.
tuition [tju:'ɪʃ(ə)n] enseignement *m*; (*lessons*) leçons *fpl*.
tulip ['tju:lɪp] tulipe *f*.
tumble ['tʌmb(ə)l] dégringolade *f*.
tumble (down) *vi* dégringoler.

tumble drier *or* **dryer** sèche-linge *m inv*.
tumbler (*glass*) gobelet *m*.
tummy ['tʌmɪ] *Fam* ventre *m*.
tuna (fish) ['tjuːnə] thon *m*.
tune [tjuːn] **1** *n* air *m*; **in t./out of t.** (*instrument*) accordé/désaccordé; **to sing in t./out of t.** chanter juste/faux. **2** *vt* (*instrument*) accorder; (*engine*) régler.
tuning (*of engine*) réglage *m*.
tunnel ['tʌn(ə)l] tunnel *m*.
turban ['tɜːbən] turban *m*.
turkey ['tɜːkɪ] dindon *m*, dinde *f*; (*as food*) dinde *f*.
turn [tɜːn] **1** *n* (*movement*, *in game*) tour *m*; (*in road*) tournant *m*; **to take turns** se relayer; **it's your t. (to play)** c'est à toi *or* (à) ton tour (de jouer). **2** *vt* tourner; (*mattress*, *pancake*) retourner; **to t. sth red**/*etc* rendre qch rouge/*etc*, rougir/*etc* qch; **she's turned twenty** elle a vingt ans passés. **3** *vi* (*of wheel etc*) tourner; (*turn head or body*) se (re)tourner; (*become*) devenir; **to t. red**/*etc* rougir/*etc*.
turn around (*of person*) se retourner.
turn away 1 *vt* (*eyes*) détourner; (*person*) renvoyer. **2** *vi* se détourner.
turn back *vi* retourner.
turn down (*gas*, *radio etc*) baisser; (*offer*, *person*) refuser.
turning petite rue *f*; (*bend in road*) tournant *m*.
turn into sth/s.o. 1 *vt* (*change*) changer en qch/qn. **2** *vi* se changer en qch/qn.
turnip ['tɜːnɪp] navet *m* (*plante*).
turn off (*light*, *radio etc*) éteindre; (*tap*, *Am faucet*) fermer; (*machine*) arrêter.
turn on (*light*, *radio etc*) mettre; (*tap*, *Am faucet*) ouvrir; (*machine*) mettre en marche.
turn out 1 *vt* (*light*) éteindre. **2** *vi* (*happen*) se passer.
turn over 1 *vt* (*page*) tourner. **2** *vi* (*of vehicle*, *person*) se retourner.
turn round 1 *vt* (*head*, *object*) tourner; (*vehicle*) faire faire demi-tour à. **2** *vi* (*of person*) se retourner.
turn up 1 *vt* (*radio*, *light etc*) mettre plus fort; (*collar*) remonter. **2** *vi* (*arrive*) arriver.
turnup (*on trousers*) revers *m*.
turtle ['tɜːt(ə)l] tortue *f* de mer; (*tortoise*) *Am* tortue *f*.
turtleneck (*sweater*) col *m* roulé.
tusk [tʌsk] défense *f*.
tutor ['tjuːtər] **1** *n* précepteur, -trice *mf*; (*at university*) directeur,

-trice *mf* d'études. **2** *vt* donner des cours particuliers à.

TV [tiː'viː] télé *f*.

tweezers ['twiːzəz] *npl* pince *f* (à épiler).

twelfth *a* & *n* douzième (*mf*).

twelve [twelv] *a* & *n* douze (*m*).

twentieth *a* & *n* vingtième (*mf*).

twenty ['twentɪ] *a* & *n* vingt (*m*).

twice [twaɪs] *adv* deux fois; **t. as heavy**/*etc* deux fois plus lourd/*etc*.

twig [twɪg] brindille *f*.

twilight ['twaɪlaɪt] crépuscule *m*.

twin [twɪn] jumeau *m*, jumelle *f*; **t. brother** frère *m* jumeau; **t. sister** sœur *f* jumelle; **t. beds** lits *mpl* jumeaux.

twine [twaɪn] (grosse) ficelle *f*.

twinkle ['twɪŋk(ə)l] *vi* (*of star*) scintiller.

twist [twɪst] **1** *vt* (*wire, arm etc*) tordre; (*roll*) enrouler (**round** autour de); (*knob*) tourner; **to t. one's ankle** se tordre la cheville. **2** *n* (*turn*) tour *m*; (*in road*) zigzag *m*.

twist off (*lid*) dévisser.

two [tuː] *a* & *n* deux (*m*); **t.-way traffic** circulation *f* dans les deux sens.

type¹ [taɪp] (*sort*) genre *m*, type *m*; (*print*) caractères *mpl*.

type² *vti* (*write*) taper (à la machine).

typewriter machine *f* à écrire.

typewritten *a* dactylographié.

typical ['tɪpɪk(ə)l] *a* typique (**of** de); **that's t. (of him)!** c'est bien lui!

typing dactylo *f*; **t. error** faute *f* de frappe.

typist dactylo *f*.

tyre ['taɪər] pneu *m* (*pl* pneus).

U

UFO [juːef'əʊ] *abbr* (*unidentified flying object*) OVNI *m*.
ugliness laideur *f*.
ugly ['ʌglɪ] *a* laid.
ulcer ['ʌlsər] ulcère *m*.
umbrella [ʌm'brelə] parapluie *m*.
umpire ['ʌmpaɪər] arbitre *m*.
un- [ʌn] *prefix* in-, peu, non, sans.
unable *a* **to be u. to do** être incapable de faire; **he's u. to swim** il ne sait pas nager.
unacceptable *a* inacceptable.
unaccustomed to be u. to sth/to doing ne pas être habitué à qch/à faire.
unanimous [juː'nænɪməs] *a* unanime.
unanimously *adv* à l'unanimité.
unattractive *a* (*idea*, *appearance*) peu attrayant; (*ugly*) laid.
unavailable *a* (*person*) qui n'est pas disponible; (*product*) épuisé.
unavoidable *a* inévitable.
unavoidably *adv* inévitablement; (*delayed*) pour une raison indépendante de sa volonté.
unaware *a* **to be u. of sth** ignorer qch; **to be u. that** ignorer que.
unawares *adv* **to catch s.o. u.** prendre qn au dépourvu.
unbearable *a* insupportable.
unbelievable *a* incroyable.
unbreakable *a* incassable.
unbutton *vt* déboutonner.
uncertain *a* incertain (**about, of** de); **it's u. whether** il n'est pas certain que (+ *subjunctive*); **I'm u. whether to stay** je ne sais pas très bien si je dois rester.
uncertainty incertitude *f*.
unchanged *a* inchangé.
uncle ['ʌŋk(ə)l] oncle *m*.
unclear *a* (*meaning*) qui n'est pas clair; (*result*) incertain; **it's u. whether** on ne sait pas très bien si.
uncomfortable *a* (*chair etc*) inconfortable; (*uneasy*) mal à l'aise.
uncommon *a* rare.
unconnected *a* (*facts etc*) sans rapport (**with** avec).
unconscious *a* (*person*) sans connaissance.
unconvincing *a* peu convaincant.
uncooperative *a* peu coopératif.
uncork *vt* (*bottle*) déboucher.

uncover *vt* découvrir.
undamaged *a* (*goods*) en bon état.
undecided *a* (*person*) indécis (**about** sur).
undeniable *a* incontestable.
under ['ʌndər] **1** *prep* sous; (*less than*) moins de; (*according to*) selon; **children u. nine** les enfants de moins de neuf ans; **u. the circumstances** dans les circonstances; **u. there** là-dessous; **u. it** dessous. **2** *adv* au-dessous.
under- *prefix* sous-.
under'charge *vt* **I undercharged him (for it)** je ne (le) lui ai pas fait payer assez.
'underclothes *npl* sous-vêtements *mpl.*
under'done *a* (*steak*) saignant.
under'estimate *vt* sous-estimer.
under'go* *vt* subir.
under'graduate étudiant, -ante *mf* (qui prépare la licence).
'underground **1** *a* souterrain. **2** *n* (*railway*) métro *m.*
under'line *vt* (*word etc*) souligner.
underneath [ʌndə'niːθ] **1** *prep* sous. **2** *adv* (en) dessous; **the book u.** le livre d'en dessous. **3** *n* dessous *m.*
'underpants *npl* slip *m*; (*loose, long*) caleçon *m.*
'underpass passage *m* souterrain.
'undershirt *Am* tricot *m* de corps.
understand* [ʌndə'stænd] *vti* comprendre.
understandable *a* compréhensible.
understanding **1** *n* compréhension *f*; (*agreement*) accord *m*; (*sympathy*) entente *f.* **2** *a* (*person*) compréhensif.
understood *a* (*agreed*) entendu.
under'take* *vt* entreprendre (**to do** de faire).
'undertaker entrepreneur *m* de pompes funèbres.
under'taking (*task*) entreprise *f.*
under'water **1** *a* sous-marin. **2** *adv* sous l'eau.
'underwear sous-vêtements *mpl.*
undo* [ʌn'duː] *vt* défaire.
undone *a* **to come u.** (*of knot etc*) se défaire.
undoubtedly *adv* sans aucun doute.
undress **1** *vi* se déshabiller. **2** *vt* déshabiller; **to get undressed** se déshabiller.
uneasy *a* (*ill at ease*) mal à l'aise.
unemployed **1** *a* au chômage. **2** *n* **the u.** les chômeurs *mpl.*
unemployment chômage *m.*
uneven *a* inégal.

uneventful *a* (*trip etc*) sans histoires.
unexpected *a* inattendu.
unexpectedly *adv* à l'improviste; (*suddenly*) subitement.
unfair *a* injuste (**to s.o.** envers qn).
unfairly *adv* injustement.
unfairness injustice *f*.
unfaithful *a* infidèle (**to** à).
unfamiliar *a* inconnu; **to be u. with sth** ne pas connaître qch.
unfashionable *a* (*subject etc*) démodé; (*restaurant etc*) peu chic *inv*.
unfasten *vt* défaire.
unfavourable *a* défavorable.
unfinished *a* inachevé.
unfit *a* en mauvaise santé; (*in bad shape*) pas en forme; (*unsuitable*) impropre; (**for** à, **to do** à faire); (*unworthy*) indigne (**for** de, **to do** de faire); (*unable*) inapte (**for** à, **to do** à faire).
unfold *vt* déplier.
unforgettable *a* inoubliable.
unforgivable *a* impardonnable.
unfortunate *a* malheureux; **you were u.** tu n'as pas eu de chance.
unfortunately *adv* malheureusement.
unfriendly *a* froid, peu aimable (**to** avec).
unfurnished *a* non meublé.
ungrateful *a* ingrat.
unhappiness tristesse *f*.
unhappy *a* (*sad*) malheureux; **u. with** *or* **about sth** mécontent de qch.
unharmed *a* (*person*) indemne.
unhealthy *a* (*climate etc*) malsain; (*person*) en mauvaise santé.
unhelpful *a* (*person*) peu serviable.
unhook *vt* (*picture*, *curtain*) décrocher; (*dress*) dégrafer.
unhurt *a* indemne.
unhygienic *a* pas très hygiénique.
uniform uniforme *m*.
unimportant *a* peu important.
uninhabited *a* inhabité.
uninjured *a* indemne.
unintentional *a* involontaire.
uninteresting *a* (*book etc*) peu intéressant.
union ['juːnɪən] **1** *n* union *f*; (*trade or Am labor union*) syndicat *m*. **2** *a* syndical; **u. member** syndiqué, -ée *mf*; **U. Jack** drapeau *m* britannique.
unique [juː'niːk] *a* unique.

unit ['ju:nɪt] unité *f*; (*of furniture etc*) élément *m*; (*team*) groupe *m*.
unite [ju:'naɪt] **1** *vt* unir; (*country, party*) unifier. **2** *vi* (*of students etc*) s'unir.
universal [ju:nɪ'vɜ:s(ə)l] *a* universel.
universe ['ju:nɪvɜ:s] univers *m*.
university [ju:nɪ'vɜ:sɪtɪ] **1** *n* université *f*; **at u.** à l'université. **2** *a* universitaire; (*student*) d'université.
unjust *a* injuste.
unkind *a* peu gentil (**to s.o.** avec qn).
unknown *a* inconnu.
unleaded [ʌn'ledɪd] *a* (*petrol, Am gasoline*) sans plomb.
unless *conj* à moins que + *subjunctive*; **u. she comes** à moins qu'elle ne vienne.
unlike *prep* **u. me, she...** à la différence de moi, elle...; **that's u. him** ça ne lui ressemble pas.
unlikely *a* peu probable; (*unbelievable*) incroyable; **she's u. to win** il est peu probable qu'elle gagne.
unlimited *a* illimité.
unlisted *a* (*phone number*) *Am* sur la liste rouge.
unload *vt* décharger.
unlock *vt* ouvrir (*avec une clef*).
unluckily *adv* malheureusement.
unlucky *a* (*person*) malchanceux; (*number etc*) qui porte malheur; **you're u.** tu n'as pas de chance.
unmade *a* (*bed*) défait.
unmarried *a* célibataire.
unnecessary *a* inutile.
unnoticed *a* **to go u.** passer inaperçu.
unoccupied *a* (*house*) inoccupé; (*seat*) libre.
unpack **1** *vt* (*suitcase*) défaire; (*goods, belongings*) déballer. **2** *vi* défaire sa valise.
unpaid *a* (*bill, sum*) impayé; (*work, worker*) bénévole.
unpleasant *a* désagréable (**to s.o.** avec qn).
unplug *vt* (*appliance*) débrancher.
unpopular *a* peu populaire; **to be u. with s.o.** ne pas plaire à qn.
unpredictable *a* imprévisible; (*weather*) indécis.
unprepared *a* **to be u. for sth** (*not expect*) ne pas s'attendre à qch.
unreasonable *a* qui n'est pas raisonnable.
unrecognizable *a* méconnaissable.
unrelated *a* (*facts etc*) sans rapport (**to** avec).
unreliable *a* (*person*) peu sûr; (*machine*) peu fiable.
unrest agitation *f*.

unroll **1** *vt* dérouler. **2** *vi* se dérouler.
unsafe *a* (*place, machine etc*) dangereux; (*person*) en danger.
unsatisfactory *a* peu satisfaisant.
unscrew *vt* dévisser.
unskilled worker ouvrier, -ière *mf* non qualifié(e).
unstable *a* instable.
unsteadily *adv* (*to walk*) d'un pas mal assuré.
unsteady *a* (*hand, step*) mal assuré; (*table, ladder etc*) instable.
unsuccessful *a* (*attempt etc*) vain; (*candidate*) malheureux; **to be u.** ne pas réussir (**in doing** à faire).
unsuccessfully *adv* en vain.
unsuitable *a* qui ne convient pas (**for** à).
unsuited *a* **u. to** (*job, activity*) peu fait pour.
unsure *a* incertain (**of, about** de).
untangle *vt* démêler.
untidy *a* (*clothes, hair*) peu soigné; (*room*) en désordre; (*person*) désordonné; (*in appearance*) peu soigné.
untie *vt* (*person, hands*) détacher; (*knot, parcel*) défaire.
until [ʌn'tɪl] **1** *prep* jusqu'à; **u. then** jusque-là; **I didn't come u. yesterday** je ne suis venu qu'hier; **not u. tomorrow** pas avant demain. **2** *conj* jusqu'à ce que + *subjunctive*; **do nothing u. I come** ne fais rien avant que j'arrive.
untrue *a* faux (*f* fausse).
unused [ʌn'juːzd] *a* (*new*) neuf (*f* neuve).
unusual *a* exceptionnel; (*strange*) étrange.
unusually *adv* exceptionnellement.
unwell *a* indisposé.
unwilling *a* **he's u. to do** il ne veut pas faire.
unwillingly *adv* à contrecœur.
unworthy *a* indigne (**of** de).
unwrap *vt* ouvrir.
unzip *vt* ouvrir (la fermeture éclair® de).
up [ʌp] **1** *adv* en haut; (*in the air*) en l'air; (*out of bed*) levé, debout; **to come** *or* **go up** monter; **prices are up** les prix ont augmenté; **up there** là-haut; **further** *or* **higher up** plus haut; **up to** (*as far as*) jusqu'à; **it's up to you to do it** c'est à toi de le faire; **that's up to you** ça dépend de toi; **what are you up to?** que fais-tu?; **to walk up and down** marcher de long en large. **2** *prep* (*a hill*) en haut de; (*a tree*) dans; (*a ladder*) sur; **to go up** (*hill, stairs*) monter.
up'hill *adv* **to go u.** monter.
upon [ə'pɒn] *prep* sur.
upper ['ʌpər] *a* supérieur.

upright *a* & *adv* (*straight*) droit.
uproar vacarme *m*, tapage *m*.
upset 1 *vt** [ʌp'set] (*stomach*, *routine etc*) déranger; **to u. s.o.** (*make sad*) peiner qn; (*offend*) vexer qn. **2** *a* peiné; vexé; (*stomach*) dérangé. **3** *n* ['ʌpset] **to have a stomach u.** avoir l'estomac dérangé.
upside 'down *adv* à l'envers.
up'stairs 1 *adv* en haut; **to go u.** monter (l'escalier). **2** *a* ['ʌpsteəz] (*people*, *room*) du dessus.
up-to-'date *a* moderne; (*information*) à jour; (*well-informed*) au courant (**on** de).
upward(s) ['ʌpwəd(z)] *adv* vers le haut; **from five francs u.** à partir de cinq francs.
urge [ɜːdʒ] *vt* **to u. s.o. to do** conseiller vivement à qn de faire.
urgency urgence *f*.
urgent ['ɜːdʒənt] *a* urgent.
urgently *adv* d'urgence.
us [əs, *stressed* ʌs] *pron* nous; **(to) us** nous; **she sees us** elle nous voit; **he gives (to) us** il nous donne; **all of us** nous tous; **let's** *or* **let us eat!** mangeons!
use 1 *n* [juːs] usage *m*, emploi *m*; **to make u. of sth** se servir de qch; **not in u.** hors d'usage; **to be of u.** être utile; **it's no u. crying/*etc*** ça ne sert à rien de pleurer/*etc*; **what's the u. of worrying/*etc*?** à quoi bon s'inquiéter/*etc*? **2** *vt* [juːz] se servir de, utiliser (**as** comme; **to do, for doing** pour faire); **it's used to do** *or* **for doing** ça sert à faire; **it's used as** ça sert de.
use (up) (*fuel*) consommer; (*supplies*) épuiser; (*money*) dépenser.
used 1 *a* [juːzd] (*secondhand*) d'occasion. **2** *v aux* [juːst] **I u. to sing/*etc*** avant, je chantais/*etc*. **3** *a* **u. to sth/to doing** habitué à qch/à faire; **to get u. to** s'habituer à.
useful ['juːsfəl] *a* utile (**to** à); **to come in u.** être utile.
usefulness utilité *f*.
useless ['juːsləs] *a* inutile; (*person*) nul.
user ['juːzər] (*of road*) usager *m*; (*of machine*, *dictionary*) utilisateur, -trice *mf*.
usual ['juːʒʊəl] *a* habituel; **as u.** comme d'habitude.
usually *adv* d'habitude.
utensil [juː'tens(ə)l] ustensile *m*.
utter ['ʌtər] **1** *a* complet; (*idiot*) parfait. **2** *vt* (*a cry*) pousser; (*a word*) dire.
utterly *adv* complètement.
U-turn ['juːtɜːn] (*in vehicle*) demi-tour *m*.

V

vacancy (*post*) poste *m* vacant; (*room*) chambre *f* libre.
vacant ['veɪkənt] *a* (*room*, *seat*) libre.
vacation [veɪ'keɪʃ(ə)n] *Am* vacances *fpl*; **on v.** en vacances.
vacationer *Am* vacancier, -ière *mf*.
vaccinate ['væksɪneɪt] *vt* vacciner.
vacci'nation vaccination *f*.
vaccine [-iːn] vaccin *m*.
vacuum ['vækjʊ(ə)m] *vt* (*carpet etc*) passer à l'aspirateur.
vacuum cleaner aspirateur *m*.
vacuum flask thermos® *m or f*.
vague [veɪg] *a* vague; (*outline*) flou.
vaguely *adv* vaguement.
vain [veɪn] *a* **in v.** en vain.
valid ['vælɪd] *a* (*ticket etc*) valable.
valley ['vælɪ] vallée *f*.
valuable ['væljʊəb(ə)l] **1** *a* (*object*) de (grande) valeur. **2** *npl* **valuables** objets *mpl* de valeur.
value ['væljuː] valeur *f*; **it's good v. (for money**) ça a un bon rapport qualité/prix.
van [væn] camionnette *f*, fourgonnette *f*; (*large*) camion *m*.
vandal ['vænd(ə)l] vandale *mf*.
vandalize *vt* saccager.
vanilla [və'nɪlə] **1** *n* vanille *f*. **2** *a* (*ice cream*) à la vanille.
vanish ['vænɪʃ] *vi* disparaître.
varied *a* varié.
variety [və'raɪətɪ] variété *f*; **a v. of reasons**/*etc* diverses raisons/*etc*; **v. show** spectacle *m* de variétés.
various ['veərɪəs] *a* divers.
varnish ['vɑːnɪʃ] **1** *vt* vernir. **2** *n* vernis *m*.
vary ['veərɪ] *vti* varier.
vase [vɑːz, *Am* veɪs] vase *m*.
Vaseline® ['væsəliːn] vaseline *f*.
vast [vɑːst] *a* vaste.
VAT [viːeɪ'tiː, væt] *abbr* (*value added tax*) TVA *f*.
VCR [viːsiː'ɑːr] magnétoscope *m*.
VDU [viːdiː'juː] *abbr* (*visual display unit*) écran *m* d'ordinateur.
veal [viːl] (*meat*) veau *m*.
vegetable ['vedʒtəb(ə)l] légume *m*.
vege'tarian *a* & *n* végétarien, -ienne (*mf*).
vege'tation végétation *f*.

vehicle ['viːɪk(ə)l] véhicule *m*.
veil [veɪl] voile *m*.
vein [veɪn] (*in body*) veine *f*.
velvet ['velvɪt] **1** *n* velours *m*. **2** *a* de velours.
vending machine ['vendɪŋ] distributeur *m* automatique.
venetian blind [və'niːʃ(ə)n] store *m* vénitien.
ventilation [ventɪ'leɪʃ(ə)n] (*in room*) aération *f*.
verb [vɜːb] verbe *m*.
verdict ['vɜːdɪkt] verdict *m*.
verge [vɜːdʒ] (*of road*) accotement *m*.
verse [vɜːs] (*part of song*) couplet *m*; (*poetry*) poésie *f*; **in v.** en vers.
version ['vɜːʃ(ə)n] version *f*.
vertical ['vɜːtɪk(ə)l] *a* vertical.
very ['verɪ] **1** *adv* très; **v. much** beaucoup; **at the v. latest** au plus tard. **2** *a* (*actual*) même; **his** *or* **her v. brother** son frère même.
vest [vest] tricot *m* de corps; (*woman's*) chemise *f* (américaine); (*waistcoat*) *Am* gilet *m*.
vet [vet] vétérinaire *mf*.
via ['vaɪə] *prep* par.
vibrate [vaɪ'breɪt] *vi* vibrer.
vibration vibration *f*.
vicar ['vɪkər] pasteur *m*.
vice [vaɪs] vice *m*; (*tool*) étau *m*.
vicious ['vɪʃəs] *a* (*spiteful*) méchant; (*violent*) brutal.
victim ['vɪktɪm] victime *f*; **to be the v. of** être victime de.
victory ['vɪktərɪ] victoire *f*.
video ['vɪdɪəʊ] **1** *n* (*cassette*) cassette *f*; **v. cassette** vidéocassette *f*; **v. (recorder)** magnétoscope *m*; **on v.** sur cassette. **2** *a* (*game*, *camera etc*) vidéo *inv*. **3** *vt* (*event*) faire une (vidéo)cassette de.
videotape bande *f* vidéo.
view [vjuː] vue *f*; **to come into v.** apparaître; **in my v.** à mon avis; **in v. of** compte tenu de.
viewer (*person*) téléspectateur, -trice *mf*.
viewpoint point *m* de vue.
villa ['vɪlə] grande maison *f*; (*holiday or Am vacation home*) maison *f* de vacances.
village ['vɪlɪdʒ] village *m*.
villager villageois, -oise *mf*.
vinegar ['vɪnɪgər] vinaigre *m*.
vineyard ['vɪnjəd] vignoble *m*.
violence ['vaɪələns] violence *f*.

violent *a* violent.
violently *adv* violemment.
violin [vaɪə'lɪn] violon *m*.
virus ['vaɪ(ə)rəs] virus *m*.
visa ['viːzə] visa *m*.
vise [vaɪs] *Am* étau *m*.
visible ['vɪzəb(ə)l] *a* visible.
visit ['vɪzɪt] **1** *n* visite *f*; (*stay*) séjour *m*. **2** *vt* (*place*) visiter; **to visit s.o.** rendre visite à qn; (*stay with*) faire un séjour chez qn. **3** *vi* être en visite.
visiting hours heures *fpl* de visite.
visitor visiteur, -euse *mf*; (*guest*) invité, -ée *mf*.
vital ['vaɪt(ə)l] *a* essentiel; **it's v. that** il est essentiel que (+ *subjunctive*).
vitamin ['vɪtəmɪn, *Am* 'vaɪtəmɪn] vitamine *f*.
vivid ['vɪvɪd] *a* vif; (*description*) vivant.
vocabulary [və'kæbjʊlərɪ] vocabulaire *m*.
vodka ['vɒdkə] vodka *f*.
voice [vɔɪs] voix *f*; **at the top of one's v.** à tue-tête.
volcano [vɒl'keɪnəʊ] (*pl* **-oes**) volcan *m*.
volume ['vɒljuːm] (*book*, *capacity*, *loudness*) volume *m*.
voluntary ['vɒlənt(ə)rɪ] *a* volontaire; (*unpaid*) bénévole.
volun'teer **1** *n* volontaire *mf*. **2** *vi* se proposer (**for sth** pour qch, **to do** pour faire).
vomit ['vɒmɪt] *vti* vomir.
vote [vəʊt] **1** *n* vote *m*. **2** *vi* voter; **to v. Labour** voter travailliste.
voter électeur, -trice *mf*.
voucher ['vaʊtʃər] (*for meal*, *gift etc*) chèque *m*.
vowel ['vaʊəl] voyelle *f*.
voyage ['vɔɪɪdʒ] voyage *m* (par mer).
vulgar ['vʌlgər] *a* vulgaire.

W

wad [wɒd] (*of banknotes etc*) liasse *f*; (*of cotton wool*, *Am absorbent cotton*) tampon *m*.
waddle ['wɒd(ə)l] *vi* se dandiner.
wade through [weɪd] (*mud*, *water etc*) patauger dans.
wading pool *Am* (*small*, *inflatable*) piscine *f* gonflable.
wafer (biscuit) ['weɪfər] gaufrette *f*.
wag [wæg] *vti* (*tail*) remuer.
wage(s) [weɪdʒ(ɪz)] *n*(*pl*) salaire *m*.
wage earner salarié, -ée *mf*.
wag(g)on ['wægən] (*of train*) wagon *m* (de marchandises).
waist [weɪst] taille *f*; **stripped to the w.** torse nu.
waistcoat ['weɪskəʊt] gilet *m*.
wait [weɪt] **1** *n* attente *f*. **2** *vi* attendre; **to w. for s.o./sth** attendre qn/qch; **w. until I've gone, w. for me to go** attends que je sois parti; **to keep s.o. waiting** faire attendre qn.
wait behind *vi* rester.
waiter garçon *m* (de café); **w.!** garçon!
waiting attente *f*; **'no w.'** (*street sign*) 'arrêt interdit'.
waiting room salle *f* d'attente.
waitress serveuse *f*; **w.!** mademoiselle!
wait up *vi* veiller; **to w. up for s.o.** attendre le retour de qn avant de se coucher.
wake* (up) [weɪk] **1** *vi* se réveiller. **2** *vt* réveiller.
walk [wɔːk] **1** *n* promenade *f*; (*shorter*) (petit) tour *m*; (*path*) allée *f*; **to go for a w.** faire une promenade; (*shorter*) faire un (petit) tour; **to take for a w.** (*child*) emmener se promener; (*baby*, *dog*) promener; **five minutes' w. (away)** à cinq minutes à pied. **2** *vi* marcher; (*stroll*) se promener; (*go on foot*) aller à pied. **3** *vt* (*distance*) faire à pied; (*take for a walk*) promener (*chien*).
walk away *or* **off** *vi* s'éloigner (**from** de)
walker (*for pleasure*) promeneur, -euse *mf*.
walk in *vi* entrer.
walking stick canne *f*.
Walkman® ['wɔːkmən] (*pl* **Walkmans**) baladeur *m*.
walk out (*leave*) partir.
wall [wɔːl] mur *m*; (*of cabin*, *tunnel*) paroi *f*.
wallet ['wɒlɪt] portefeuille *m*.
wallpaper 1 *n* papier *m* peint. **2** *vt* tapisser.
wall-to-wall 'carpet(ing) moquette *f*.
walnut ['wɔːlnʌt] (*nut*) noix *f*.

walrus ['wɔːlrəs] (*animal*) morse *m*.
wander (about *or* **around)** ['wɒndər] errer; (*stroll*) flâner.
want [wɒnt] *vt* vouloir (**to do** faire); (*ask for*) demander (*qn*); (*need*) avoir besoin de; **I w. him to go** je veux qu'il parte; **you're wanted** on vous demande.
war [wɔːr] guerre *f*; **at w.** en guerre (**with** avec).
ward [wɔːd] (*in hospital*) salle *f*.
warden ['wɔːd(ə)n] (**traffic**) **w.** contractuel, -elle *mf*.
wardrobe ['wɔːdrəʊb] (*cupboard*, *Am closet*) penderie *f*.
warehouse, *pl* **-ses** ['weəhaʊs, -zɪz] entrepôt *m*.
warm [wɔːm] **1** *a* chaud; **to be** *or* **feel w.** avoir chaud; **it's (nice and) w.** (*of weather*) il fait (agréablement) chaud. **2** *vt* (*person*, *food etc*) réchauffer.
warmth chaleur *f*.
warm up 1 *vt* (*person*, *food etc*) réchauffer. **2** *vi* (*of person*, *room*, *engine*) se réchauffer; (*of food*, *water*) chauffer.
warn [wɔːn] *vt* avertir (**that** que); **to w. s.o. against sth** mettre qn en garde contre qch; **to w. s.o. against doing** conseiller à qn de ne pas faire.
warning avertissement *m*; (*advance notice*) (pré)avis *m*; **(hazard) w. lights** (*of vehicle*) feux *mpl* de détresse.
warship navire *m* de guerre.
wart [wɔːt] verrue *f*.
was [wəz, *stressed* wɒz] *pt de* **be.**
wash [wɒʃ] **1** *n* **to have a w.** se laver; **to give sth a w.** laver qch. **2** *vt* laver; **to w. one's hands** se laver les mains. **3** *vi* (*have a wash*) se laver.
washable *a* lavable.
wash away *or* **off** *or* **out 1** *vt* (*stain*) faire partir (en lavant). **2** *vi* partir (au lavage).
washbasin lavabo *m*.
washcloth *Am* gant *m* de toilette.
washing (*act*) lavage *m*; (*clothes*) lessive *f*; **to do the w.** faire la lessive.
washing machine machine *f* à laver.
washing powder lessive *f*.
washing-'up vaisselle *f*; **to do the w.-up** faire la vaisselle; **w.-up liquid** produit *m* pour la vaisselle.
wash out (*bowl etc*) laver.
washroom *Am* toilettes *fpl*.
wash up (*do the dishes*) faire la vaisselle; (*have a wash*) *Am* se laver.

wasp [wɒsp] guêpe *f*.
waste [weɪst] **1** *n* gaspillage *m*; (*of time*) perte *f*; (*rubbish*, *Am garbage*) déchets *mpl*. **2** *vt* (*money*, *food etc*) gaspiller; (*time*, *opportunity*) perdre.
wastebin (*in kitchen*) poubelle *f*.
waste ground (*in town*) terrain *m* vague.
waste paper vieux papiers *mpl*.
wastepaper basket corbeille *f* (à papier).
watch [wɒtʃ] **1** *n* (*small clock*) montre *f*. **2** *vt* regarder; (*be careful of*) faire attention à. **3** *vi* regarder.
watch (out) for sth/s.o. (*wait for*) guetter qch/qn.
watch (over) (*suspect*, *baby etc*) surveiller.
watch out (*take care*) faire attention (**for** à); **w. out!** attention!
watchstrap, *Am* **watchband** bracelet *m* de montre.
water ['wɔːtər] **1** *n* eau *f*; **w. pistol** pistolet *m* à eau. **2** *vt* (*plant etc*) arroser.
watercolour (*picture*) aquarelle *f*; (*paint*) couleur *f* pour aquarelle.
watercress cresson *m* (de fontaine).
water down (*wine etc*) couper (d'eau).
waterfall chute *f* d'eau.
watering can arrosoir *m*.
watermelon pastèque *f*.
waterproof *a* (*material*) imperméable.
water skiing ski *m* nautique.
watertight *a* étanche.
wave [weɪv] **1** *n* (*of sea*) vague *f*; (*in hair*) ondulation *f*; **medium/short w.** (*on radio*) ondes *fpl* moyennes/courtes; **long w.** grandes ondes, ondes longues. **2** *vi* (*with hand*) faire signe (de la main); **to w. to s.o.** (*greet*) saluer qn de la main. **3** *vt* (*arm*, *flag etc*) agiter.
wavelength longueur *f* d'ondes.
wavy ['weɪvɪ] *a* (*hair*) ondulé.
wax [wæks] **1** *n* cire *f*. **2** *vt* cirer.
way[1] [weɪ] **1** *n* (*path*) chemin *m* (**to** de); (*direction*) sens *m*; (*distance*) distance *f*; **all the w., the whole w.** (*to talk etc*) pendant tout le chemin; **this w.** par ici; **that way** par là; **which w.?** par où?; **to lose one's w.** se perdre; **the w. there** l'aller *m*; **the w. back** le retour; **the w. in** l'entrée *f*; **the w. out** la sortie; **on the w.** en route (**to** pour); **to be** *or* **stand in s.o.'s w.** être sur le chemin de qn; **to get out of the w.** s'écarter; **a long w. (away** *or* **off)** très loin. **2** *adv* (*behind etc*) très loin; **w. ahead** très en avance (**of** sur).
way[2] (*manner*) façon *f*; (*means*) moyen *m*; **(in) this w.** de cette façon; **no w.!** *Fam* pas question!

WC [dʌb(ə)ljuːˈsiː] w-c *mpl.*
we [wiː] *pron* nous; **we teachers** nous autres professeurs.
weak [wiːk] *a* faible; (*tea*, *coffee*) léger.
weaken 1 *vt* affaiblir. **2** *vi* faiblir.
weakness faiblesse *f*; (*fault*) point *m* faible.
wealth [welθ] richesse(s) *f*(*pl*).
wealthy *a* riche.
weapon [ˈwepən] arme *f*.
wear* [weər] **1** *vt* (*have on body*) porter; (*put on*) mettre. **2** *n* **w. (and tear)** usure *f*.
wear off (*of colour*, *pain etc*) disparaître.
wear out 1 *vt* (*clothes etc*) user; (*person*) épuiser. **2** *vi* s'user.
weary [ˈwɪərɪ] *a* fatigué.
weasel [ˈwiːz(ə)l] belette *f*.
weather [ˈweðər] temps *m*; **what's the w. like?** quel temps fait-il?; **it's nice w.** il fait beau; **under the w.** (*ill*) patraque.
weather forecast *or* **report** météo *f*.
weave* [wiːv] *vt* (*cloth*) tisser.
web [web] (*of spider*) toile *f*.
wedding [ˈwedɪŋ] mariage *m*.
wedding ring, *Am* **wedding band** alliance *f*.
wedge [wedʒ] **1** *n* (*under wheel etc*) cale *f*. **2** *vt* (*table etc*) caler.
Wednesday [ˈwenzdɪ, -deɪ] mercredi *m*.
weed [wiːd] mauvaise herbe *f*.
week [wiːk] semaine *f*; **a w. from tomorrow**, **tomorrow w.** demain en huit.
weekday jour *m* de semaine.
weekend [wiːkˈend, *Am* ˈwiːkend] week-end *m*; **at** *or* **on** *or* **over the w.** ce week-end.
weekly 1 *a* hebdomadaire. **2** *adv* toutes les semaines. **3** *n* (*magazine*) hebdomadaire *m*.
weep* [wiːp] *vi* pleurer.
weigh [weɪ] *vti* peser.
weight [weɪt] poids *m*; **by w.** au poids; **to put on w.** grossir; **to lose w.** maigrir.
weird [wɪəd] *a* (*odd*) bizarre.
welcome [ˈwelkəm] **1** *a* **to be w.** (*warmly received*, *of person*) être bien reçu; **w.!** bienvenue!; **to make s.o. (feel) w.** faire bon accueil à qn; **you're w.!** (*after 'thank you'*) il n'y a pas de quoi!; **a coffee/a break would be w.** un café/une pause ne ferait pas de mal. **2** *n* accueil *m*. **3** *vt* accueillir; (*warmly*) faire bon accueil à; **I w. you!** (*I say welcome to you*) je vous souhaite la bienvenue!

weld [weld] *vt* souder.
welfare ['welfeər] **to be on w.** *Am* vivre d'allocations.
well[1] [wel] (*for water*) puits *m*; **(oil) w.** puits *m* de pétrole.
well[2] **1** *adv* bien; **w. done!** bravo!; **as w.** (*also*) aussi; **as w. as** aussi bien que; **as w. as two cats, he has...** en plus de deux chats, il a.... **2** *a* bien *inv*; **she's w.** (*healthy*) elle va bien; **to get w.** se remettre. **3** *int* eh bien!; **huge, w., quite big** énorme, enfin, assez grand.
well-be'haved *a* sage.
well-in'formed *a* bien informé.
wellington (boot) ['welıŋtən] botte *f* de caoutchouc.
well-'known *a* (bien) connu.
well-'mannered *a* bien élevé.
well-'off *a* riche.
Welsh [welʃ] **1** *a* gallois; **the W.** les Gallois *mpl*. **2** *n* (*language*) gallois *m*.
Welshman (*pl* **-men**) Gallois *m*.
Welshwoman (*pl* **-women**) Galloise *f*.
went [went] *pt de* **go**[1].
were [wər, *stressed* wɜːr] *pt de* **be.**
west [west] **1** *n* ouest *m*; **(to the) w. of** à l'ouest de. **2** *a* (*coast*) ouest *inv*. **3** *adv* à l'ouest.
westbound *a* en direction de l'ouest.
western **1** *a* (*coast*) ouest *inv*; (*culture etc*) occidental. **2** *n* (*film*) western *m*.
westward(s) [-wəd(z)] *a & adv* vers l'ouest.
wet [wet] **1** *a* mouillé; (*damp*, *rainy*) humide; (*day*, *month*) de pluie; **'w. paint'** 'peinture fraîche'; **to get w.** se mouiller; **to make w.** mouiller; **it's w.** (*raining*) il pleut. **2** *vt* mouiller.
whale [weıl] baleine *f*.
wharf [wɔːf] quai *m*, débarcadère *m*.
what [wɒt] **1** *a* quel, quelle, *pl* quel(le)s; **w. book?** quel livre?; **w. a fool!** quel idiot! **2** *pron* (*in questions*) qu'est-ce qui; (*object*) (qu'est-ce) que; (*after prep*) quoi; **w.'s happening?** qu'est-ce qui se passe?; **w. does he do?** qu'est-ce qu'il fait?, que fait-il?; **w. is it?** qu'est-ce que c'est?; **w.'s that book?** c'est quoi, ce livre?; **w.!** (*surprise*) quoi!; **w.'s it called?** comment ça s'appelle?; **w. for?** pourquoi?; **w. about me?** et moi?; **w. about leaving?** si on partait? **3** *pron* (*indirect*, *relative*) ce qui; (*object*) ce que; **I know w. will happen/w. she'll do** je sais ce qui arrivera/ce qu'elle fera; **w. I need** ce dont j'ai besoin.
what'ever **1** *a* **w. (the) mistake/***etc* quelle que soit l'erreur/*etc*; **no chance w.** pas la moindre chance; **nothing w.** rien du tout. **2** *pron*

(*no matter what*) quoi que (+ *subjunctive*); **w. you do** quoi que tu fasses; **w. is important** tout ce qui est important; **do w. you want** fais tout ce que tu veux.

wheat [wiːt] blé *m*.

wheel [wiːl] **1** *n* roue *f*; **at the w.** (*driving*) au volant. **2** *vt* pousser.

wheelbarrow brouette *f*.

wheelchair fauteuil *m* roulant.

when [wen] **1** *adv* quand. **2** *conj* quand; **w. I finish, w. I've finished** quand j'aurai fini; **w. I saw him** *or* **w. I'd seen him, I left** après l'avoir vu, je suis parti; **the day/moment w.** le jour/moment où.

when'ever *conj* quand; (*each time that*) chaque fois que.

where [weər] **1** *adv* où; **w. are you from?** d'où êtes-vous? **2** *conj* (là) où; **I found it w. she'd left it** je l'ai trouvé là où elle l'avait laissé; **the place/house w.** l'endroit/la maison où.

whereabouts 1 *adv* où (donc). **2** *n* **his w.** l'endroit *m* où il est.

where'as *conj* alors que.

wher'ever *conj* **w. you go** partout où tu iras; **I'll go w. you like** j'irai (là) où vous voudrez.

whether ['weðər] *conj* si; **I don't know w. to leave** je ne sais pas si je dois partir; **w. she does it or not** qu'elle le fasse ou non.

which [wɪtʃ] **1** *a* (*in questions etc*) quel, quelle, *pl* quel(le)s; **w. hat?** quel chapeau?; **in w. case** auquel cas. **2** *rel pron* (*subject*) qui; (*object*) que; (*after prep*) lequel, laquelle, *pl* lesquel(le)s; (*after clause*) ce qui; ce que; **the house w. is old** la maison qui est vieille; **the book w. I like** le livre que j'aime; **the table which I put it on** la table sur laquelle je l'ai mis; **the film of w.** le film dont; **she's ill, w. is sad** elle est malade, ce qui est triste; **he lies, w. I don't like** il ment, ce que je n'aime pas. **3** *pron* **w. (one)** (*in questions*) lequel, laquelle, *pl* lesquel(le)s; **w. (one) of us?** lequel *or* laquelle d'entre nous *or* de nous? ▮ **w. (one)** (*the one that*) celui qui, celle qui, *pl* ceux qui, celles qui; (*object*) celui *etc* que; **show me w. (one) is red** montrez-moi celui *or* celle qui est rouge; **I know w. (ones) you want** je sais ceux *or* celles que vous désirez.

which'ever *a & pron* **w. book/***etc* *or* **w. of the books/***etc* **you buy** quel que soit le livre/*etc* que tu achètes; **take w. books interest you** prenez les livres qui vous intéressent; **take w. (one) you like** prends celui *or* celle que tu veux; **w. (ones) remain** ceux *or* celles qui restent.

while [waɪl] **1** *conj* (*when*) pendant que; (*although*) bien que (+ *subjunctive*); (*as long as*) tant que; (*whereas*) tandis que; **while eating/***etc* en mangeant/*etc*. **2** *n* **a w.** un moment; **all the w.** tout le temps.

whim [wɪm] caprice *m*.
whine [waɪn] *vi* gémir.
whip [wɪp] **1** *n* fouet *m*. **2** *vt* fouetter.
whirl (round) [wɜːl] *vi* tourbillonner.
whisk [wɪsk] **1** *n* (*for eggs etc*) fouet *m*. **2** *vt* fouetter.
whiskers ['wɪskəz] *npl* (*of cat*) moustaches *fpl*.
whisky, *Am* **whiskey** ['wɪskɪ] whisky *m*.
whisper ['wɪspər] **1** *vti* chuchoter. **2** *n* chuchotement *m*.
whistle ['wɪs(ə)l] **1** *n* sifflement *m*; (*object*) sifflet *m*; **to blow the** *or* **one's w.** siffler. **2** *vti* siffler.
white [waɪt] **1** *a* blanc (*f* blanche); **to go** *or* **turn w.** blanchir; **w. coffee** café *m* au lait; **w. man** blanc *m*, **w. woman** blanche *f*. **2** *n* (*colour, of egg*) blanc *m*.
whitewash *vt* (*wall*) badigeonner.
Whitsun ['wɪts(ə)n] la Pentecôte.
whizz past [wɪz] passer à toute vitesse.
who [huː] *pron* qui; **w. did it?** qui (est-ce qui) a fait ça?
who'ever *pron* qui que ce soit qui; (*object*) qui que ce soit que; **this man, w. he is** cet homme, quel qu'il soit.
whole [həul] **1** *a* entier; (*intact*) intact; **the w. time** tout le temps; **the w. lot** le tout. **2** *n* **the w. of the village**/*etc* tout le village/*etc*; **on the w.** dans l'ensemble.
wholemeal, *Am* **wholewheat** *a* (*bread*) complet.
wholesale **1** *a* (*price*) de gros. **2** *adv* (*to sell*) au prix de gros; (*in bulk*) en gros.
wholesaler grossiste *mf*.
whom [huːm] *pron* (*object*) que; (*in questions and after prep*) qui; **of w.** dont.
whooping cough ['huːpɪŋkɒf] coqueluche *f*.
whose [huːz] *poss pron & a* à qui, de qui; **w. book is this?** à qui est ce livre?; **w. daughter are you?** de qui es-tu la fille?; **the woman w. book I have** la femme de qui j'ai le livre.
why [waɪ] **1** *adv* pourquoi; **w. not?** pourquoi pas? **2** *conj* **the reason w. they...** la raison pour laquelle ils....
wick [wɪk] mèche *f* (*de bougie*).
wicked ['wɪkɪd] *a* (*evil*) méchant; (*mischievous*) malicieux.
wicker ['wɪkər] **1** *n* osier *m*. **2** *a* (*basket etc*) en osier.
wide [waɪd] **1** *a* large; (*choice, variety*) grand; **to be three metres w.** avoir trois mètres de large. **2** *adv* (*to open*) tout grand.
wide-a'wake *a* éveillé.
widely *adv* (*to travel*) beaucoup.
widen **1** *vt* élargir. **2** *vi* s'élargir.

widespread *a* (très) répandu.
widow ['wɪdəʊ] veuve *f*.
widower veuf *m*.
width [wɪdθ] largeur *f*.
wife [waɪf] (*pl* **wives**) femme *f*.
wig [wɪg] perruque *f*.
wild [waɪld] *a* (*animal*, *flower etc*) sauvage.
wilderness ['wɪldənəs] désert *m*.
will[1] [wɪl] *v aux* **he will come, he'll come** (*future tense*) il viendra (**won't he?** n'est-ce pas?); **you will not come, you won't come** tu ne viendras pas (**will you?** n'est-ce pas?); **w. you have a tea?** veux-tu prendre un thé?; **w. you be quiet!** veux-tu te taire!; **I w.!** (*yes*) oui!
will[2] volonté *f*; (*legal document*) testament *m*; **ill w.** mauvaise volonté *f*; **against one's w.** à contrecœur.
willing ['wɪlɪŋ] *a* (*helper*, *worker*) de bonne volonté; **to be w. to do** vouloir bien faire.
willingly *adv* (*with pleasure*) volontiers; (*voluntarily*) volontairement.
willingness bonne volonté *f*; **his** *or* **her w. to do** son empressement *m* à faire.
willow ['wɪləʊ] saule *m*.
win [wɪn] **1** *n* victoire *f*. **2** *vi** gagner. **3** *vt* (*money*, *prize*, *race*) gagner.
wind[1] [wɪnd] vent *m*; **to have w.** (*in stomach*) avoir des gaz.
wind[2]* [waɪnd] **1** *vt* (*roll*) enrouler (**round** autour de). **2** *vi* (*of river*, *road*) serpenter.
wind (up) (*clock*) remonter.
windcheater, *Am* **windbreaker** ['wɪnd-] blouson *m*.
windmill ['wɪnd-] moulin *m* à vent.
window ['wɪndəʊ] fenêtre *f*; (*pane & in vehicle or train*) vitre *f*; (*in shop*) vitrine *f*; (*counter*) guichet *m*; **to go w. shopping** faire du lèche-vitrines.
window box jardinière *f*.
windowpane vitre *f*.
windowsill (*inside*) appui *m* de (la) fenêtre; (*outside*) rebord *m* de (la) fenêtre.
windscreen, *Am* **windshield** ['wɪnd-] pare-brise *m inv*; **w. wiper** essuie-glace *m*.
windsurfing ['wɪnd-] **to go w.** faire de la planche (à voile).
windy ['wɪndɪ] *a* **it's w.** (*of weather*) il y a du vent.
wine [waɪn] vin *m*; **w. bottle** bouteille *f* à vin; **w. list** carte *f* des vins.

wineglass verre *m* à vin.
wing [wɪŋ] aile *f*.
wink [wɪŋk] **1** *vi* faire un clin d'œil (**at, to** à). **2** *n* clin *m* d'œil.
winner ['wɪnər] gagnant, -ante *mf*; (*of argument*, *fight*) vainqueur *m*.
winning 1 *a* (*number*, *horse etc*) gagnant; (*team*) victorieux. **2** *n* **winnings** gains *mpl*.
winter ['wɪntər] **1** *n* hiver *m*; **in (the) w.** en hiver. **2** *a* d'hiver.
wintertime hiver *m*.
wipe [waɪp] *vt* essuyer; **to w. one's feet/hands** s'essuyer les pieds/les mains.
wipe away *or* **off** *or* **up** (*liquid*) essuyer.
wipe out (*clean*) essuyer.
wiper (*in vehicle*) essuie-glace *m*
wipe up (*dry the dishes*) essuyer la vaisselle.
wire ['waɪər] fil *m*.
wire mesh *or* **netting** grillage *m*.
wiring (*electrical*) installation *f* électrique.
wise [waɪz] *a* (*in knowledge*) sage; (*advisable*) prudent.
wish [wɪʃ] **1** *vt* souhaiter, vouloir (**to do** faire); **I w. (that) you could help me/could have helped me** je voudrais que/j'aurais voulu que vous m'aidiez; **I w. I hadn't done that** je regrette d'avoir fait ça; **if you w.** si tu veux; **I w. you a happy birthday** je vous souhaite un bon anniversaire; **I w. I could** si seulement je pouvais. **2** *vi* **to w. for sth** souhaiter qch. **3** *n* (*specific*) souhait *m*; (*general*) désir *m*; **best wishes** (*on greeting card*) meilleurs vœux *mpl*; (*in letter*) amitiés *fpl*; **send him** *or* **her my best wishes** fais-lui mes amitiés.
witch [wɪtʃ] sorcière *f*.
with [wɪð] *prep* avec; **come w. me** viens avec moi; **w. no hat**/*etc* sans chapeau/*etc*. ▮ (*at the house etc of*) chez; **she's staying w. me** elle loge chez moi. ▮ (*cause*) de; **to jump w. joy** sauter de joie. ▮ (*instrument*, *means*) avec, de; **to write w. a pen** écrire avec un stylo; **to fill w.** remplir de. ▮ (*description*) à; **w. blue eyes** aux yeux bleus.
with'draw* **1** *vt* retirer. **2** *vi* se retirer (**from** de).
wither ['wɪðər] *vi* (*of plant etc*) se flétrir.
within [wɪ'ðɪn] *prep* (*place*, *box etc*) à l'intérieur de; **w. 10 km (of)** (*less than*) à moins de 10 km (de); (*inside an area of*) dans un rayon de 10 km (de); **w. a month** (*to return etc*) avant un mois; (*to finish sth*) en moins d'un mois.
without [wɪ'ðaʊt] *prep* sans; **w. a tie**/*etc* sans cravate/*etc*; **w. doing** sans faire.
witness ['wɪtnɪs] **1** *n* (*person*) témoin *m*. **2** *vt* (*accident etc*) être

(le) témoin de.

wobbly *a* (*table*, *tooth*) branlant.

wolf [wʊlf] (*pl* **wolves**) loup *m*.

woman, *pl* **women** ['wʊmən, 'wɪmɪn] femme *f*; **w. doctor** femme *f* médecin; **w. teacher** professeur *m* femme; **women's** (*clothes etc*) féminin.

wonder ['wʌndər] **1** *n* **(it's) no w.** ce n'est pas étonnant (**that** que (+ *subjunctive*)). **2** *vt* se demander (**if** si, **why** pourquoi). **3** *vi* (*think*) réfléchir; **I was just wondering** je réfléchissais.

wonderful *a* merveilleux.

won't [wəʊnt] = **will not.**

wood [wʊd] (*material*, *forest*) bois *m*.

wooden *a* de *or* en bois.

woodwork (*school subject*) menuiserie *f*.

wool [wʊl] laine *f*.

woollen, *Am* **woolen 1** *a* en laine. **2** *n* **woollens,** *Am* **woolens** lainages *mpl*.

word [wɜːd] mot *m*; (*spoken & promise*) parole *f*; **words** (*of song etc*) paroles *fpl*; **to have a w. with s.o.** parler à qn; (*advise*, *criticize*) avoir un mot avec qn; **in other words** autrement dit.

wording termes *mpl*.

word processing traitement *m* de texte.

word processor machine *f* de traitement de texte.

wore [wɔːr] *pt de* **wear**.

work [wɜːk] **1** *n* travail *m*; (*product*, *book etc*) œuvre *f*; (*building or repair work*) travaux *mpl*; **out of w.** au chômage; **a day off w.** un jour de congé; **he's off w.** il n'est pas allé travailler; **the works** (*of clock etc*) le mécanisme; **gas works** usine *f* à gaz. **2** *vi* travailler; (*of machine etc*) marcher; (*of drug*) agir. **3** *vt* (*machine*) faire marcher; **to get worked up** s'exciter.

work at *or* **on sth** (*improve*) travailler qch.

workbench établi *m*.

worker travailleur, -euse *mf*; (*manual*) ouvrier, -ière *mf*; **(office) w.** employé, -ée *mf* (de bureau).

working *a* **w. class** classe *f* ouvrière; **in w. order** en état de marche.

workman (*pl* **-men**) ouvrier *m*.

work on (*book*, *problem etc*) travailler à.

work out 1 *vi* (*succeed*) marcher; (*do exercises*) s'entraîner; **it works out at 50 francs** ça fait 50 francs. **2** *vt* calculer; (*problem*) résoudre; (*scheme*) préparer; (*understand*) comprendre.

workout séance *f* d'entraînement.

workshop atelier *m*.

world [wɜːld] **1** *n* monde *m*; **all over the w.** dans le monde entier. **2** *a* (*war etc*) mondial; (*champion*, *cup*, *record*) du monde.
worm [wɜːm] ver *m*.
worn [wɔːn] (*pp de* **wear**) *a* (*clothes etc*) usé.
worn-'out *a* (*object*) complètement usé; (*person*) épuisé.
worry ['wʌrɪ] **1** *n* souci *m*. **2** *vi* s'inquiéter (**about sth** de qch, **about s.o.** pour qn). **3** *vt* inquiéter; **to be worried** être inquiet.
worrying *a* inquiétant.
worse [wɜːs] **1** *a* pire, plus mauvais (**than** que); **to get w.** se détériorer; **he's getting w.** (*in health*) il va de plus en plus mal. **2** *adv* plus mal (**than** que); **to be w. off** aller moins bien financièrement.
worsen *vti* empirer.
worship ['wɜːʃɪp] *vt* (*person*, *god*) adorer.
worst [wɜːst] **1** *a* pire, plus mauvais. **2** *adv* **(the) w.** le plus mal. **3** *n* **the w. (one)** le *or* la pire, le *or* la plus mauvais(e); **at w.** au pire.
worth [wɜːθ] **1** *n* valeur *f*; **to buy 50 pence w. of chocolates** acheter pour cinquante pence de chocolats. **2** *a* **to be w. sth** valoir qch; **how much** *or* **what is it w.?** ça vaut combien?; **the film's w. seeing** le film vaut la peine d'être vu; **it's w. (one's) while** ça (en) vaut la peine; **it's w. (while) waiting** ça vaut la peine d'attendre.
worthy ['wɜːðɪ] *a* **w. of sth/s.o.** digne de qch/qn.
would [wʊd, *unstressed* wəd] *v aux* **I w. stay, I'd stay** (*conditional tense*) je resterais; **he w. have done it** il l'aurait fait; **w. you help me, please?** voulez-vous m'aider, s'il vous plaît?; **w. you like some tea?** voudriez vous (prendre) du thé?; **I w. see her every day** (*in the past*) je la voyais chaque jour.
wound [wuːnd] **1** *vt* blesser; **the wounded** les blessés *mpl*. **2** *n* blessure *f*.
wrap (up) [ræp] **1** *vt* envelopper; (*parcel*) emballer. **2** *vti* **to w. (oneself) up** (*dress warmly*) se couvrir. **3** *n* **plastic w.** *Am* film *m* plastique.
wrapper (*of sweet*, *Am candy*) papier *m*.
wrapping (*action*, *material*) emballage *m*; **w. paper** papier *m* d'emballage.
wreath [riːθ] (*pl* **-s** [riːðz]) couronne *f*.
wreck [rek] **1** *n* (*ship*) épave *f*; (*sinking*) naufrage *m*; (*train etc*) train *m etc* accidenté. **2** *vt* détruire.
wrench [rentʃ] (*tool*) clef *f* (à écrous), *Am* clef *f* à molette.
wrestle ['res(ə)l] *vi* lutter (**with s.o.** avec qn).
wrestler lutteur, -euse *mf*; catcheur, -euse *mf*.
wrestling (*sport*) lutte *f*; **(all-in) w.** catch *m*.
wring* (out) [rɪŋ] (*clothes by hand*) tordre.

wrinkle ['rɪŋk(ə)l] (*on skin*) ride *f*.
wrist [rɪst] poignet *m*.
wristwatch montre *f*.
write* [raɪt] *vti* écrire.
write away *or* **off** *or* **up for** (*details etc*) écrire pour demander.
write back *vi* répondre.
write sth down noter qch.
write sth out écrire qch; (*copy*) recopier qch.
writer auteur *m* (**of** de); (*literary*) écrivain *m*.
writing (*handwriting*) écriture *f*; **to put sth (down) in w.** mettre qch par écrit; **some w.** (*on page*) quelque chose d'écrit.
writing desk secrétaire *m*.
writing pad bloc *m* de papier à lettres; (*for notes*) bloc-notes *m*.
writing paper papier *m* à lettres.
wrong [rɒŋ] **1** *a* (*sum, idea etc*) faux (*f* fausse); (*direction, time etc*) mauvais; (*unfair*) injuste; **to be w.** (*of person*) avoir tort (**to do** de faire); (*mistaken*) se tromper; **it's w. to swear**/*etc* c'est mal de jurer/*etc*; **the clock's w.** la pendule n'est pas à l'heure; **something's w.** quelque chose ne va pas; **something's w. with the phone** le téléphone ne marche pas bien; **something's w. with her arm** elle a quelque chose au bras; **what's w. with you?** qu'est-ce que tu as?; **the w. way round** *or* **up** à l'envers. **2** *adv* mal; **to go w.** (*of plan*) mal tourner; (*of machine*) tomber en panne. **3** *n* **to be in the w.** être dans son tort.
wrongly *adv* (*incorrectly*) mal.

X

Xmas ['krɪsməs] *Fam* Noël *m*.
X-ray ['eksreɪ] **1** *n* (*photo*) radio(graphie) *f*; **to have an X-ray** passer une radio. **2** *vt* radiographier.

Y

yacht [jɒt] yacht *m*.
yard [jɑːd] (*of farm, school etc*) cour *f*; (*for storage*) dépôt *m*; (*measure*) yard *m* (*= 91,44 cm*).
yarn [jɑːn] (*thread*) fil *m*.
yawn [jɔːn] **1** *vi* bâiller. **2** *n* bâillement *m*.
year [jɪər] an *m*, année *f*; **school/tax y.** année *f* scolaire/fiscale; **this y.** cette année; **in the y. 1992** en (l'an) 1992; **he's ten years old** il a dix ans; **New Y.** Nouvel An; **New Year's Day** le jour de l'An; **New Year's Eve** la Saint-Sylvestre.
yearly *a* annuel.
yeast [jiːst] levure *f*.
yell [jel] hurlement *m*.
yell (out) *vti* hurler.
yell at s.o. (*scold*) crier après qn.
yellow ['jeləʊ] *a & n* (*colour*) jaune (*m*).
yes [jes] *adv* oui; (*contradicting negative question*) si.
yesterday ['jestədɪ] *adv* hier; **y. morning** hier matin; **the day before y.** avant-hier.
yet [jet] **1** *adv* encore; (*already*) déjà; **she hasn't come (as) y.** elle n'est pas encore venue; **has he come y.?** est-il déjà arrivé? **2** *conj* (*nevertheless*) pourtant.
yield [jiːld] *vi* **'y.'** (*road sign*) *Am* 'cédez la priorité'.
yog(h)urt ['jɒgət, *Am* 'jəʊgɜːt] yaourt *m*.
yolk [jəʊk] jaune *m* (d'œuf).
you [juː] *pron* (*polite form singular*) vous; (*familiar form singular*) tu; (*polite and familar form plural*) vous; (*object*) vous; te, t'; *pl* vous; (*after prep, 'than', 'it is'*) vous; toi; *pl* vous; **(to) y.** vous; te, t'; *pl* vous; **y. are** vous êtes; tu es; **I see y.** je vous vois; je te vois; **y. teachers** vous autres professeurs; **y. idiot!** espèce d'imbécile! ■ (*indefinite*) on; (*object*) vous; te, t'; *pl* vous; **y. never know** on ne sait jamais.
young [jʌŋ] **1** *a* jeune; **my young(er) brother** mon (frère) cadet; **his**

or **her youngest brother** le cadet de ses frères; **the youngest son** le cadet. **2** *n* (*of animals*) petits *mpl*; **the y.** (*people*) les jeunes *mpl*.

youngster jeune *mf*.

your [jɔːr] *poss a* (*polite form singular, polite and familiar form plural*) votre, *pl* vos; (*familiar form singular*) ton, ta, *pl* tes; (*one's*) son, sa, *pl* ses.

yours *poss pron* le vôtre, la vôtre, *pl* les vôtres; (*familiar form singular*) le tien, la tienne, *pl* les tien(ne)s; **this book is y.** ce livre est à vous *or* est le vôtre; ce livre est à toi *or* est le tien.

your'self *pron* (*polite form*) vous-même; (*familiar form*) toi-même; (*reflexive*) vous; te, t'; (*after prep*) vous; toi.

your'selves *pron pl* vous-mêmes; (*reflexive & after prep*) vous.

youth [juːθ] jeunesse *f*; (*young man*) jeune *m*; **y. club** maison *f* des jeunes.

Z

zebra ['ziːbrə, 'zebrə] zèbre *m*.

zebra crossing passage *m* pour piétons.

zero ['zɪərəʊ] (*pl* **-os**) zéro *m*.

zigzag ['zɪgzæg] **1** *n* zigzag *m*. **2** *a* en zigzag. **3** *vi* zigzaguer.

zip (fastener) [zɪp] fermeture *f* éclair®.

zip (up) fermer (avec une fermeture éclair®).

zip code *Am* code *m* postal.

zipper *Am* fermeture *f* éclair®.

zit [zɪt] (*pimple*) *Fam* bouton *m*.

zone [zəʊn] zone *f*.

zoo [zuː] (*pl* **zoos**) zoo *m*.

zucchini [zuː'kiːnɪ] (*pl* **-ni** *or* **-nis**) *Am* courgette *f*.

French verb conjugations

REGULAR VERBS

	-ER Verbs	-IR Verbs	-RE Verbs
Infinitive	*donn/er*	*fin/ir*	*vend/re*
1 Present	je donne	je finis	je vends
	tu donnes	tu finis	tu vends
	il donne	il finit	il vend
	nous donnons	nous finissons	nous vendons
	vous donnez	vous finissez	vous vendez
	ils donnent	ils finissent	ils vendent
2 Imperfect	je donnais	je finissais	je vendais
	tu donnais	tu finissais	tu vendais
	il donnait	il finissait	il vendait
	nous donnions	nous finissions	nous vendions
	vous donniez	vous finissiez	vous vendiez
	ils donnaient	ils finissaient	ils vendaient
3 Past historic	je donnai	je finis	je vendis
	tu donnas	tu finis	tu vendis
	il donna	il finit	il vendit
	nous donnâmes	nous finîmes	nous vendîmes
	vous donnâtes	vous finîtes	vous vendîtes
	ils donnèrent	ils finirent	ils vendirent
4 Future	je donnerai	je finirai	je vendrai
	tu donneras	tu finiras	tu vendras
	il donnera	il finira	il vendra
	nous donnerons	nous finirons	nous vendrons
	vous donnerez	vous finirez	vous vendrez
	ils donneront	ils finiront	ils vendront
5 Subjunctive	je donne	je finisse	je vende
	tu donnes	tu finisses	tu vendes
	il donne	il finisse	il vende
	nous donnions	nous finissions	nous vendions
	vous donniez	vous finissiez	vous vendiez
	ils donnent	ils finissent	ils vendent
6 Imperative	donne	finis	vends
	donnons	finissons	vendons
	donnez	finissez	vendez
7 Present participle	donnant	finissant	vendant
8 Past participle	donné	fini	vendu

Note The conditional is formed by adding the following endings to the infinitive: -ais, -ais, -ait, -ions, -iez, -aient. Final 'e' is dropped in infinitives ending '-re'.

SPELLING ANOMALIES OF -ER VERBS

Verbs in **-ger** (e.g. **manger**) take an extra **e** before endings beginning with **o** or **a**: *Present* je mange, nous mangeons; *Imperfect* je mangeais, nous mangions; *Past historic* je mangeai, nous mangeâmes; *Present participle* mangeant. Verbs in **-cer** (e.g. **commencer**) change **c** to **ç** before endings beginning with **o** or **a**: *Present* je commence, nous commençons; *Imperfect* je commençais, nous commencions; *Past historic* je commençai, nous commençâmes; *Present participle* commençant. Verbs containing mute **e** in their penultimate syllable fall into two groups. In the first (e.g. **mener**, **peser**, **lever**), **e** becomes **è** before an unpronounced syllable in the present and subjunctive, and in the future and conditional tenses (e.g. je mène, ils mèneront). The second group contains most verbs ending in **-eler** and **-eter** (e.g. **appeler**, **jeter**). These verbs change **l** to **ll** and **t** to **tt** before an unpronounced syllable (e.g. j'appelle, ils appelleront; je jette, ils jetteront). However, the following four verbs in **-eler** and **-eter** fall into the first group in which **e** changes to **è** before mute **e** (e.g. je pèle, ils pèleront; j'achète, ils achèteront): **geler**, **peler**; **acheter**, **haleter**. Derived verbs (e.g. **dégeler**, **racheter**) are conjugated in the same way. Verbs containing **e** acute in their penultimate syllable change **é** to **è** before the unpronounced endings of the present and subjunctive only (e.g. je cède but je céderai). Verbs in **-yer** (e.g. **essuyer**) change **y** to **i** before an unpronounced syllable in the present and subjunctive, and in the future and conditional tenses (e.g. j'essuie, ils essuieront). In verbs in **-ayer** (e.g. **balayer**), **y** may be retained before mute **e** (e.g. je balaie or balaye, ils balaieront or balayeront).

IRREGULAR VERBS

Listed below are those verbs considered to be the most useful. Forms and tenses not given are fully derivable, such as the third person singular of the present tense which is normally formed by substituting 't' for the final 's' of the first person singular, e.g. 'crois' becomes 'croit', 'dis' becomes 'dit'. Note that the endings of the past historic fall into three categories, the 'a' and 'i' categories shown at *donner*, and at *finir* and *vendre*, and the 'u' category which has the following endings: -us, -ut, -ûmes, -ûtes, -urent. Most of the verbs listed below form their past historic with 'u'. The imperfect may usually be formed by adding -ais, -ait, -ions, -iez, -aient to the stem of the first person plural of the present tense, e.g. 'je buvais' etc may be derived from 'nous buvons' (stem 'buv-' and ending '-ons'); similarly, the present participle may generally be formed by substituting -ant for -ons (e.g. buvant). The future may usually be formed by adding -ai, -as, -a, -ons, -ez, -ont to the infinitive or to an infinitive without final 'e' where the ending is -re (e.g. conduire). The imperative usually has the same forms as the second persons singular and plural and first person plural of the present tense.

1 = Present   2 = Imperfect   3 = Past historic   4 = Future
5 = Subjunctive   6 = Imperative   7 = Present participle
8 = Past participle   n = nous   v = vous   † verbs conjugated with **être** only.

Irregular French Verbs

abattre *like* **battre**
†s'abstenir *like* **tenir**
accourir *like* **courir**
accueillir *like* **cueillir**
acquérir 1 j'acquiers, n acquérons 2 j'acquérais 3 j'acquis 4 j'acquerrai 5 j'acquière 7 acquérant 8 acquis
admettre *like* **mettre**
†aller 1 je vais, tu vas, il va, n allons, v allez, ils vont 4 j'irai 5 j'aille, nous allions, ils aillent 6 va, allons, allez (*but note* vas-y)
apercevoir *like* **recevoir**
apparaître *like* **connaître**
appartenir *like* **tenir**
apprendre *like* **prendre**
asseoir 1 j'assieds, il assied, n asseyons, ils asseyent 2 j'asseyais 3 j'assis 4 j'assiérai 5 j'asseye 7 asseyant 8 assis
atteindre 1 j'atteins, n atteignons, ils atteignent 2 j'atteignais 3 j'atteignis 4 j'atteindrai 5 j'atteigne 7 atteignant 8 atteint
avoir 1 j'ai, tu as, il a, n avons, v avez, ils ont 2 j'avais 3 j'eus 4 j'aurai 5 j'aie, il ait, n ayons, ils aient 6 aie, ayons, ayez 7 ayant 8 eu
battre 1 je bats, il bat, n battons 5 je batte
boire 1 je bois, n buvons, ils boivent 2 je buvais 3 je bus 5 je boive, n buvions 7 buvant 8 bu
bouillir 1 je bous, n bouillons, ils bouillent 2 je bouillais 3 *not used* 5 je bouille 7 bouillant
combattre *like* **battre**
commettre *like* **mettre**
comprendre *like* **prendre**
conclure 1 je conclus, n concluons, ils concluent 5 je conclue
conduire 1 je conduis, n conduisons 3 je conduisis 5 je conduise 8 conduit
connaître 1 je connais, il connaît, n connaissons 3 je connus 5 je connaisse 7 connaissant 8 connu
conquérir *like* **acquérir**
consentir *like* **conduire**
contenir *like* **tenir**
contraindre *like* **atteindre**
contredire *like* **dire** *except* 1 v contredisez
convaincre *like* **vaincre**
convenir *like* **tenir**
coudre 1 je couds, il coud, n cousons, ils cousent 3 je cousis 5 je couse 7 cousant 8 cousu
courir 1 je cours, n courons 3 je courus 4 je courrai 5 je coure 8 couru

Irregular French Verbs

couvrir 1 je couvre, n couvrons 2 je couvrais 5 je couvre 8 couvert

craindre *like* **atteindre**

croire 1 je crois, n croyons, ils croient 2 je croyais 3 je crus 5 je croie, n croyions 7 croyant 8 cru

cueillir 1 je cueille, n cueillons 2 je cueillais 4 je cueillerai 5 je cueille 7 cueillant

cuire 1 je cuis, n cuisons 2 je cuisais 3 je cuisis 5 je cuise 7 cuisant 8 cuit

débattre *like* **battre**

décevoir *like* **recevoir**

découvrir *like* **couvrir**

décrire *like* **écrire**

déduire *like* **conduire**

défaire *like* **faire**

déplaire *like* **plaire**

déteindre *like* **atteindre**

détruire *like* **conduire**

†devenir *like* **tenir**

devoir 1 je dois, n devons, ils doivent 2 je devais 3 je dus 4 je devrai 5 je doive, n devions 6 *not used* 7 devant 8 dû, due, *pl* dus, dues

dire 1 je dis, n disons, v dites 2 je disais 3 je dis 5 je dise 7 disant 8 dit

disparaître *like* **connaître**

dissoudre 1 je dissous, n dissolvons 2 je dissolvais 5 je dissolve 7 dissolvant 8 dissous, dissoute

distraire 1 je distrais, n distrayons 2 je distrayais 3 *none* 5 je distraie 7 distrayant 8 distrait

dormir *like* **mentir**

éclore 1 il éclôt, ils éclosent 8 éclos

écrire 1 j'écris, n écrivons 2 j'écrivais 3 j'écrivis 5 j'écrive 7 écrivant 8 écrit

élire *like* **lire**

émettre *like* **mettre**

émouvoir 1 j'émeus, n émouvons, ils émeuvent 2 j'émouvais 3 j'émus (*rare*) 4 j'émouvrai 5 j'émeuve, n émouvions 8 ému

endormir *like* **mentir**

enfreindre *like* **atteindre**

†s'enfuir *like* **fuir**

entreprendre *like* **prendre**

entretenir *like* **tenir**

envoyer 4 j'enverrai

éteindre *like* **atteindre**

être 1 je suis, tu es, il est, n sommes, v êtes, ils sont 2 j'étais 3 je fus 4 je serai 5 je sois, n soyons, ils soient 6 sois, soyons, soyez 7 étant 8 été

Irregular French Verbs

exclure *like* **conclure**
extraire *like* **distraire**
faillir (*defective*) 3 je faillis 4 je faillirai 8 failli
faire 1 je fais, n faisons, v faites, ils font 2 je faisais 3 je fis 4 je ferai 5 je fasse 7 faisant 8 fait
falloir (*impersonal*) 1 il faut 2 il fallait 3 il fallut 4 il faudra 5 il faille 6 *none* 7 *none* 8 fallu
frire (*defective*) 1 je fris, tu fris, il frit 4 je frirai (*rare*) 6 fris (*rare*) 8 frit (*for other persons and tenses use* faire frire)
fuir 1 je fuis, n fuyons, ils fuient 2 je fuyais 3 je fuis 5 je fuie 7 fuyant 8 fui
haïr 1 je hais, il hait, n haïssons
inscrire *like* **écrire**
instruire *like* **conduire**
interdire *like* **dire** *except* 1 v interdisez
interrompre *like* **rompre**
intervenir *like* **tenir**
introduire *like* **conduire**
joindre *like* **atteindre**
lire 1 je lis, n lisons 2 je lisais 3 je lus 5 je lise 7 lisant 8 lu
maintenir *like* **tenir**
mentir 1 je mens, n mentons 2 je mentais 5 je mente 7 mentant
mettre 1 je mets, n mettons 2 je mettais 3 je mis 5 je mette 7 mettant 8 mis
moudre je mouds, il moud, n moulons 2 je moulais 3 je moulus 5 je moule 7 moulant 8 moulu
†mourir 1 je meurs, n mourons, ils meurent 2 je mourais 3 je mourus 4 je mourrai 5 je meure, n mourions
†naître 1 je nais, il naît, n naissons 2 je naissais 3 je naquis 4 je naîtrai 5 je naisse 7 naissant 8 né
nuire 1 je nuis, n nuisons 2 je nuisais 3 je nuisis 5 je nuise 7 nuisant 8 nui
obtenir *like* **tenir**
offrir *like* **couvrir**
ouvrir *like* **couvrir**
paître (*defective*) 1 il paît 2 il paissait 3 *none* 4 il paîtra 5 il paisse 7 paissant 8 *none*
paraître *like* **connaître**
parcourir *like* **courir**
†partir *like* **mentir**
†parvenir *like* **tenir**
peindre *like* **atteindre**
permettre *like* **mettre**
plaindre *like* **atteindre**
plaire 1 je plais, il plaît, n plaisons 2 je plaisais 3 je plus 5 je plaise 7 plaisant 8 plu

Irregular French Verbs

pleuvoir (*impersonal*) 1 il pleut 2 il pleuvait 3 il plut 4 il pleuvra 5 il pleuve 6 *none* 7 pleuvant 8 plu

poursuivre *like* **suivre**

pouvoir 1 je peux *or* je puis, tu peux, il peut, n pouvons, ils peuvent 2 je pouvais 3 je pus 4 je pourrai 5 je puisse 6 *not used* 7 pouvant 8 pu

prédire *like* **dire** *except* 1 v prédisez

prendre 1 je prends, il prend, n prenons, ils prennent 2 je prenais 3 je pris 5 je prenne 7 prenant 8 pris

prescrire *like* **écrire**

pressentir *like* **mentir**

prévenir *like* **tenir**

prévoir *like* **voir** *except* 4 je prévoirai

produire *like* **conduire**

promettre *like* **mettre**

†provenir *like* **tenir**

rabattre *like* **battre**

recevoir 1 je reçois, n recevons, ils reçoivent 2 je recevais 3 je reçus 4 je recevrai 5 je reçoive, n recevions, ils reçoivent 7 recevant 8 reçu

reconduire *like* **conduire**

reconnaître *like* **connaître**

reconstruire *like* **conduire**

recoudre *like* **coudre**

recouvrir *like* **couvrir**

recueillir *like* **cueillir**

redire *like* **dire**

réduire *like* **conduire**

refaire *like* **faire**

rejoindre *like* **atteindre**

relire *like* **lire**

reluire *like* **nuire**

rendormir *like* **mentir**

renvoyer *like* **envoyer**

†repartir *like* **mentir**

repentir *like* **mentir**

reprendre *like* **prendre**

reproduire *like* **conduire**

résoudre 1 je résous, n résolvons 2 je résolvais 3 je résolus 5 je résolve 7 résolvant 8 résolu

ressentir *like* **mentir**

resservir *like* **mentir**

ressortir *like* **mentir**

restreindre *like* **atteindre**

Irregular French Verbs

retenir	*like* **tenir**
†revenir	*like* **tenir**
revivre	*like* **vivre**
revoir	*like* **voir**
rire	1 je ris, n rions 2 je riais 3 je ris 5 je rie, n riions 7 riant 8 ri
rompre	*regular except* 1 il rompt
satisfaire	*like* **faire**
savoir	1 je sais, n savons, il savent 2 je savais 3 je sus 4 je saurai 5 je sache 6 sache, sachons, sachez 7 sachant 8 su
sentir	*like* **mentir**
servir	*like* **mentir**
sortir	*like* **mentir**
souffrir	*like* **couvrir**
sourire	*like* **rire**
soustraire	*like* **distraire**
soutenir	*like* **tenir**
†se souvenir	*like* **tenir**
suffire	1 je suffis, n suffisons 2 je suffisais 3 je suffis 5 je suffise 7 suffisant 8 suffi
suivre	1 je suis, n suivons 2 je suivais 3 je suivis 5 je suive 7 suivant 8 suivi
surprendre	*like* **prendre**
survivre	*like* **vivre**
taire	1 je tais, n taisons 2 je taisais 3 je tus 5 je taise 7 taisant 8 tu
teindre	*like* **atteindre**
tenir	1 je tiens, n tenons, ils tiennent 2 je tenais 3 je tins, tu tins, il tint, n tînmes, v tîntes, ils tinrent 4 je tiendrai 5 je tienne 7 tenant 8 tenu
traduire	*like* **conduire**
traire	*like* **distraire**
transmettre	*like* **mettre**
vaincre	1 je vaincs, il vainc, n vainquons 2 je vainquais 3 je vainquis 5 je vainque 7 vainquant 8 vaincu
valoir	1 je vaux, il vaut, n valons 2 je valais 3 je valus 4 je vaudrai 5 je vaille 6 *not used* 7 valant 8 valu
†venir	*like* **tenir**
vivre	1 je vis, n vivons 2 je vivais 3 je vécus 5 je vive 7 vivant 8 vécu
voir	1 je vois, n voyons 2 je voyais 3 je vis 4 je verrai 5 je voie, n voyions 7 voyant 8 vu
vouloir	1 je veux, il veut, n voulons, ils veulent 2 je voulais 3 je voulus 4 je voudrai 5 je veuille 6 veuille, veuillons, veuillez 7 voulant 8 voulu

Verbes anglais irréguliers

Infinitif	Prétérit	Participe passé
arise	arose	arisen
awake	awoke	awoken
be	was, were	been
bear	bore	borne
beat	beat	beaten
become	became	become
begin	began	begun
bend	bent	bent
bet	bet, betted	bet, betted
bid	bid	bid
bind	bound	bound
bite	bit	bitten
bleed	bled	bled
blow	blew	blown
break	broke	broken
breed	bred	bred
bring	brought [brɔːt]	brought
broadcast	broadcast	broadcast
build	built	built
burn	burnt, burned	burnt, burned
burst	burst	burst
buy	bought [bɔːt]	bought
cast	cast	cast
catch	caught [kɔːt]	caught
choose	chose	chosen
cling	clung	clung
come	came	come
cost	cost	cost
creep	crept	crept
cut	cut	cut
deal	dealt [delt]	dealt
dig	dug	dug
dive	dived, *Am* dove [dəʊv]	dived
do	did	done
draw	drew	drawn
dream	dreamed, dreamt [dremt]	dreamed, dreamt
drink	drank	drunk
drive	drove	driven
eat	ate [et, *Am* eɪt]	eaten
fall	fell	fallen
feed	fed	fed
feel	felt	felt
fight	fought [fɔːt]	fought
find	found	found

Infinitif	Prétérit	Participe passé
flee	fled	fled
fling	flung	flung
fly	flew	flown
forbid	forbad(e)	forbidden
forecast	forecast	forecast
foresee	foresaw	foreseen
forget	forgot	forgotten
forgive	forgave	forgiven
freeze	froze	frozen
get	got	got, *Am* gotten
give	gave	given
go	went	gone
grind	ground	ground
grow	grew	grown
hang	hung, hanged	hung, hanged
have	had	had
hear	heard [hɜːd]	heard
hide	hid	hidden
hit	hit	hit
hold	held	held
hurt	hurt	hurt
keep	kept	kept
kneel	knelt, kneeled	knelt, kneeled
know	knew	known
lay	laid	laid
lead	led	led
lean	leant [lent], leaned	leant, leaned
leap	leapt [lept], leaped	leapt, leaped
learn	learnt, learned	learnt, learned
leave	left	left
lend	lent	lent
let	let	let
lie	lay	lain
light	lit, lighted	lit, lighted
lose	lost	lost
make	made	made
mean	meant [ment]	meant
meet	met	met
mislay	mislaid	mislaid
mislead	misled	misled
misunderstand	misunderstood	misunderstood
mistake	mistook	mistaken
outdo	outdid	outdone
overcome	overcame	overcome
overdo	overdid	overdone
overtake	overtook	overtaken
put	put	put

Infinitif	**Prétérit**	**Participe passé**
quit	quit, quitted	quit, quitted
read	read [red]	read
redo	redid	redone
rewind	rewound	rewound
ride	rode	ridden
ring	rang	rung
rise	rose	risen
run	ran	run
saw	sawed	sawn, sawed
say	said [sed]	said
see	saw	seen
seek	sought [sɔːt]	sought
sell	sold	sold
send	sent	sent
set	set	set
sew	sewed	sewn, sewed
shake	shook [ʃʊk]	shaken
shed	shed	shed
shine	shone ([ʃɒn, *Am* ʃəʊn])	shone ([ʃɒn, *Am* ʃəʊn])
shoot	shot	shot
show	showed	shown, showed
shrink	shrank	shrunk, shrunken
shut	shut	shut
sing	sang	sung
sink	sank	sunk
sit	sat	sat
sleep	slept	slept
slide	slid	slid
sling	slung	slung
smell	smelt, smelled	smelt, smelled
sow	sowed	sown, sowed
speak	spoke	spoken
speed	sped, speeded	sped, speeded
spell	spelt, spelled	spelt, spelled
spend	spent	spent
spill	spilt, spilled	spilt, spilled
spin	spun	spun
spit	spat, spit	spat, spit
split	split	split
spoil	spoilt, spoiled	spoilt, spoiled
spread	spread	spread
spring	sprang	sprung
stand	stood [stʊd]	stood
steal	stole	stolen
stick	stuck	stuck
sting	stung	stung
stink	stank, stunk	stunk

Infinitif	**Prétérit**	**Participe passé**
stride	strode	stridden (*rare*)
strike	struck	struck
swear	swore	sworn
sweep	swept	swept
swell	swelled	swollen, swelled
swim	swam	swum
swing	swung	swung
take	took [tʊk]	taken
teach	taught [tɔːt]	taught
tear	tore	torn
tell	told	told
think	thought [θɔːt]	thought
throw	threw	thrown
tread	trod	trodden
undergo	underwent	undergone
understand	understood	understood
undertake	undertook	undertaken
undo	undid	undone
upset	upset	upset
wake	woke	woken
wear	wore	worn
weave	wove	woven
weep	wept	wept
win	won [wʌn]	won
wind	wound [waʊnd]	wound
withdraw	withdrew	withdrawn
wring	wrung	wrung
write	wrote	written

Pays et régions	Countries and regions
Afrique *f* (*africain*)	Africa (*African*)
A. du Sud/Nord (*sud-/nord-africain*)	South/North Africa (*South/North African*)
Algérie *f* (*algérien*)	Algeria (*Algerian*)
Allemagne *f* (*allemand*)	Germany (*German*)
Amérique *f* (*américain*)	America (*American*)
A. du Sud/Nord (*sud-nord-américain*)	South/North America (*South/North American*)
Angleterre *f* (*anglais*)	England (*English*)
Antilles *fpl* (*antillais*)	West Indies (*West Indian*)
Arabie *f* Séoudite (*saoudien*)	Saudi Arabia (*Saudi*)
Argentine *f* (*argentin*)	Argentina (*Argentinian*)
Asie *f* (*asiatique*)	Asia (*Asian*)
Australie *f* (*australien*)	Australia (*Australian*)
Autriche *f* (*autrichien*)	Austria (*Austrian*)
Belgique *f* (*belge*)	Belgium (*Belgian*)
Brésil *m* (*brésilien*)	Brazil (*Brazilian*)
Canada *m* (*canadien*)	Canada (*Canadian*)
Antilles *fpl* (les)	Caribbean (the)
CEI *f* (*abrév* Communauté des États Indépendants)	CIS (*abbr* Commonwealth of Independent States)
Chine *f* (*chinois*)	China (*Chinese*)
Chypre *f* (*c(h)ypriote*)	Cyprus (*Cypriot*)
Corée *f* (*coréen*)	Korea (*Korean*)
C. du Sud/Nord	North/South Korea
Cuba *m* (*cubain*)	Cuba (*Cuban*)
Tchéchoslovaquie *f* (*tchèque*)	Czechoslovakia (*Czech*)
Danemark *m* (*danois*)	Denmark (*Danish*)
Écosse *f* (*écossais*)	Scotland (*Scottish*)
Égypte *f* (*égyptien*)	Egypt (*Egyptian*)
Angleterre *f* (*anglais*)	England (*English*)
Espagne *f* (*espagnol*)	Spain (*Spanish*)
États-Unis *mpl* (*américain*)	United States (*American*)
Europe *f* (*européen*)	Europe (*European*)
Finlande *f* (*finlandais*)	Finland (*Finnish*)
France *f* (*français*)	France (*French*)
Allemagne *f* (*allemand*)	Germany (*German*)
Grande-Bretagne *f* (*britannique*)	Great Britain (*British*)
Grèce *f* (*grec*)	Greece (*Greek*)
Pays-Bas *mpl* (*hollandais*)	Holland (*Dutch*)
Hongrie *f* (*hongrois*)	Hungary (*Hungarian*)
Inde *f* (*indien*)	India (*Indian*)
Indonésie *f* (*indonésien*)	Indonesia (*Indonesian*)
Irak *m* (*irakien*)	Iraq (*Iraqi*)

Pays et régions	Countries and regions
Iran *m* (*iranien*)	Iran (*Iranian*)
Irlande *f* (*irlandais*)	Ireland (*Irish*)
Israël *m* (*israélien*)	Israel (*Israeli*)
Italie *f* (*italien*)	Italy (*Italian*)
Jamaïque *f* (*jamaïcain*)	Jamaica (*Jamaican*)
Japon *m* (*japonais*)	Japan (*Japanese*)
Kenya *m* (*kényan*)	Kenya (*Kenyan*)
Corée *f* (*coréen*)	Korea (*Korean*)
Liban *m* (*libanais*)	Lebanon (*Lebanese*)
Libye *f* (*libyen*)	Libya (*Libyan*)
Luxembourg *m* (*luxembourgeois*)	Luxembourg
Malaisie (*malais*)	Malaysia (*Malaysian*)
Maroc *m* (*marocain*)	Morocco (*Moroccan*)
Mexique *m* (*mexicain*)	Mexico (*Mexican*)
Nigéria *m* (*nigérian*)	Nigeria (*Nigerian*)
Norvège *f* (*norvégien*)	Norway (*Norwegian*)
Nouvelle-Zélande *f* (*néo-zélandais*)	New Zealand
Pakistan *m* (*pakistanais*)	Pakistan (*Pakistani*)
Pays-Bas *mpl* (*hollandais*)	Holland (*Dutch*)
Philippines *fpl* (*philippin*)	Philippines (*Filipino*)
Pologne *f* (*polonais*)	Poland (*Polish*)
Portugal *m* (*portugais*)	Portugal (*Portuguese*)
Roumanie *f* (*roumain*)	Romania (*Romanian*)
Royaume Uni *m* (*britannique*)	United Kingdom (*British*)
Russie *f* (*russe*)	Russia (*Russian*)
Arabie *f* Séoudite (*saoudien*)	Saudi Arabia (*Saudi*)
Écosse *f* (*écossais*)	Scotland (*Scottish*)
Espagne *f* (*espagnol*)	Spain (*Spanish*)
Suède *f* (*suédois*)	Sweden (*Swedish*)
Suisse *f* (*suisse*)	Switzerland (*Swiss*)
Syrie *f* (*syrien*)	Syria (*Syrian*)
Tchécoslovaquie *f* (*tchèque*)	Czechoslovakia (*Czech*)
Thaïlande *f* (*thaïlandais*)	Thailand (*Thai*)
Tunisie *f* (*tunisien*)	Tunisia (*Tunisian*)
Turquie *f* (*turc*)	Turkey (*Turkish*)
Royaume-Uni *m* (*britannique*)	United Kingdom (*British*)
États-Unis *mpl* (*américain*)	United States (*American*)
Viêt-nam *m* (*vietnamien*)	Vietnam (*Vietnamese*)
Pays *m* de Galles (*gallois*)	Wales (*Welsh*)
Antilles *fpl* (*antillais*)	West Indies (*West Indian*)

Les nombres | Numerals

Les nombres		Numerals
zéro	0	nought
un	1	one
deux	2	two
trois	3	three
quatre	4	four
cinq	5	five
six	6	six
sept	7	seven
huit	8	eight
neuf	9	nine
dix	10	ten
onze	11	eleven
douze	12	twelve
treize	13	thirteen
quatorze	14	fourteen
quinze	15	fifteen
seize	16	sixteen
dix-sept	17	seventeen
dix-huit	18	eighteen
dix-neuf	19	nineteen
vingt	20	twenty
vingt et un	21	twenty-one
vingt-deux	22	twenty-two
trente	30	thirty
quarante	40	forty
cinquante	50	fifty
soixante	60	sixty
soixante-dix	70	seventy
quatre-vingts	80	eighty
quatre-vingt-un	81	eighty-one
quatre-vingt-dix	90	ninety
cent	100	a *or* one hundred
cent un	101	a hundred and one
cent cinquante	150	a hundred and fifty
deux cents	200	two hundred
deux cent un	201	two hundred and one
mille	1 000 (1,000)	a *or* one thousand
un million	1 000 000 (1,000,000)	a *or* one million

A

a *voir* **avoir.**

à *prép* (**à+le = au** [o], **à+les = aux** [o]) (*direction: lieu*) to; (*temps*) till, to; **aller à Paris** to go to Paris; **de 3 à 4 h** from 3 till *ou* to 4 (o'clock). ▮ (*position: lieu*) at, in; (*surface*) on; (*temps*) at; **être au bureau/à la ferme/au jardin/à Paris** to be at *ou* in the office/on *ou* at the farm/in the garden/in Paris; **à 8 h** at 8 (o'clock); **à mon arrivée** on (my) arrival; **à lundi!** see you (on) Monday! ▮ (*description*) **l'homme à la barbe** the man with the beard; **verre à liqueur** liqueur glass. ▮ (*attribution*) **donner qch à qn** to give sth to s.o., give s.o. sth. ▮ (*devant infinitif*) **apprendre à lire** to learn to read; **travail à faire** work to do; **maison à vendre** house for sale. ▮ (*appartenance*) **c'est (son livre) à lui** it's his (book); **c'est à vous de** (*décider, protester etc*) it's up to you to; (*lire, jouer etc*) it's your turn to. ▮ (*prix*) for; **pain à 2F** loaf for 2F. ▮ (*poids*) by; **vendre au kilo** to sell by the kilo. ▮ (*moyen, manière*) **à bicyclette** by bicycle; **à la main** by hand; **à pied** on foot; **au crayon** with a pencil, in pencil; **au galop** at a gallop; **deux à deux** two by two. ▮ (*appel*) **au voleur!** (stop) thief!

abaisser *vt* to lower.

abaisser (s') *vpr* (*barrière*) to lower; (*température*) to drop.

abandon *m* (*de sportif*) withdrawal; **à l'a.** in a neglected state.

abandonner 1 *vt* (*travail*) to give up; (*endroit*) to desert. **2** *vi* to give up; (*sportif*) to withdraw.

abat-jour *m inv* lampshade.

abattoir *m* slaughterhouse.

abattre* *vt* (*mur*) to knock down; (*arbre*) to cut down; (*animal*) to slaughter; (*avion*) to shoot down; (*personne*) to shoot.

abattre (s') *vpr* **s'a. sur** (*pluie*) to come down on; (*tempête*) to hit.

abbaye [abei] *f* abbey.

abbé *m* (*prêtre*) priest.

abcès *m* abscess.

abdomen [abdɔmɛn] *m* stomach, abdomen.

abeille *f* bee.

abîmer *vt* to spoil.

abîmer (s') *vpr* to get spoilt.

aboiement *m* bark; **aboiements** barking.

abominable *a* terrible.

abondance *f* **une a. de** plenty of.

abondant, -ante *a* plentiful.

abonné, -ée *mf* (*à un journal, au téléphone*) subscriber.

abonnement *m* subscription; **(carte d')a.** (*de train*) season ticket.

abonner (s') *vpr* to subscribe, take out a subscription (**à** to).
abord (d') *adv* first.
abordable *a* (*prix*, *marchandises*) affordable.
abordage *m* (*assaut*) boarding.
aborder 1 *vi* to land. **2** *vt* (*personne*) to approach; (*problème*) to tackle; (*attaquer*) to board (*ship*).
aboutir *vi* to succeed; **a. à** lead to; **n'a. à rien** to come to nothing.
aboyer *vi* to bark.
abréger *vt* (*récit*) to shorten.
abreuvoir *m* watering place; (*récipient*) drinking trough.
abréviation *f* abbreviation.
abri *m* shelter; **a. (de jardin)** (garden) shed; **à l'a. de** (*vent*) sheltered from; (*besoin*) safe from; **sans a.** homeless.
abricot *m* apricot.
abricotier *m* apricot tree.
abriter *vt* to shelter.
abriter (s') *vpr* to (take) shelter.
abrupt, -e [abrypt] *a* (*pente etc*) steep.
abrutir *vt* **a. qn** (*travail*, *télévision*) to turn s.o. into a vegetable.
absence *f* absence.
absent, -ente 1 *a* absent, away. **2** *mf* absentee.
absenter (s') *vpr* to go away (**de** from).
absolu, -ue *a* absolute.
absolument *adv* absolutely.
absorbant, -ante *a* (*papier*) absorbent; (*travail*, *lecture*) absorbing.
absorber *vt* to absorb; (*manger*) to eat.
abstenir* (s') *vpr* to refrain (**de faire** from doing).
absurde *a* absurd.
abus *m* abuse; (*de nourriture*) over-indulgence (**de** in).
abuser *vi* to go too far; **a. de** (*situation*, *personne*) to take unfair advantage of; (*friandises*) to over-indulge in.
acajou *m* mahogany.
accabler *vt* to overwhelm (**de** with).
accéder *vi* **a. à** (*lieu*) to reach.
accélérateur *m* accelerator.
accélérer *vi* to accelerate.
accélérer (s') *vpr* to speed up.
accent *m* accent; (*sur une syllabe*) stress.
accepter *vt* to accept; **a. de faire** to agree to do.
accès *m* access (**à** to); (*de folie*, *colère*, *toux*) fit; (*de fièvre*) bout; **'a. interdit'** 'no entry'.
accessoires *mpl* (*de voiture etc*) accessories; (*de théâtre*) props.

accident *m* accident; **a. d'avion/de train** plane/train crash.
accidentel, -elle *a* accidental.
acclamations *fpl* cheers.
acclamer *vt* to cheer.
accommoder *vt* (*assaisonner*) to prepare.
accompagnateur, -trice *mf* (*musical*) accompanist; (*de touristes*) guide.
accompagnement *m* (*musical*) accompaniment.
accompagner *vt* (*personne*) to go *ou* come with; (*chose, musique*) to accompany.
accomplir *vt* to carry out.
accord *m* agreement; (*musical*) chord; **être d'a.** to agree (**avec** with); **d'a.!** all right!
accordéon *m* accordion.
accorder *vt* (*donner*) to grant; (*instrument*) to tune; (*verbe*) to make agree.
accorder (s') *vpr* (*s'entendre*) to get along.
accotement *m* verge (*of road*), shoulder.
accouchement *m* delivery.
accoucher *vi* to give birth (**de** to).
accouder (s') *vpr* **s'a. à** *ou* **sur** to lean on (*with one's elbows*).
accourir* *vi* to come running.
accroc [akro] *m* tear (**à** in).
accrochage *m* (*de voitures*) minor collision.
accrocher *vt* (*déchirer*) to catch; (*fixer*) to hook; (*suspendre*) to hang up (*on a hook*); (*heurter*) to hit.
accrocher (s') *vpr* (*se cramponner*) to cling (**à** to); (*ne pas céder*) to persevere.
accroupi, -ie *a* squatting
accroupir (s') *vpr* to squat (down).
accueil *m* welcome.
accueillant, -ante *a* welcoming
accueillir* *vt* to welcome.
accumuler *vt*, **s'accumuler** *vpr* to pile up
accusation *f* accusation; (*au tribunal*) charge.
accusé, -ée *mf* accused; (*cour d'assises*) defendant.
accuser *vt* to accuse (**de** of); (*rendre responsable*) to blame (**de** for).
acharnement *m* (stubborn) determination.
acharner (s') *vpr* **s'a. sur** (*attaquer*) to lay into; **s'a. à faire** to struggle to do.
achat *m* purchase; **achats** shopping.
acheter *vti* to buy; **a. à qn** to buy from s.o.; (*pour qn*) to buy for

s.o.

acheteur, -euse *mf* buyer; (*dans un magasin*) shopper.

achever *vt* to finish (off); **a. de faire qch** (*personne*) to finish doing sth; **a. qn** (*tuer*) to finish s.o. off.

acide 1 *a* sour. **2** *m* acid.

acier *m* steel.

acompte *m* deposit.

acquérir* *vt* (*acheter*) to purchase; (*obtenir*) to acquire.

acquisition *f* (*achat*) purchase.

acquittement *m* (*d'un accusé*) acquittal.

acquitter *vt* (*dette*) to pay; (*accusé*) to acquit; **s'a. envers qn** to repay s.o.

acrobate *mf* acrobat.

acrobatie(s) [-asi] *f(pl)* acrobatics.

acrobatique *a* acrobatic.

acte *m* (*action, de pièce de théâtre*) act.

acteur, -trice *mf* actor, actress.

actif, -ive 1 *a* active. **2** *m Grammaire* active.

action *f* action; (*en Bourse*) share.

actionnaire *mf* shareholder.

activer *vt* (*feu*) to boost.

activer (s') *vpr* (*se dépêcher*) *Fam* to get a move on.

activité *f* activity.

actualité *f* (*événements*) current events; **actualités** (*à la télévision etc*) news.

actuel, -elle *a* (*présent*) present; (*contemporain*) topical.

actuellement *adv* at the present time.

adaptation *f* adjustment; (*de roman*) adaptation.

adapter *vt* to adapt; (*ajuster*) to fit (**à** to); **s'a. à** (*s'habituer*) to adapt to, adjust to; (*tuyau etc*) to fit.

additif *m* additive.

addition *f* addition; (*au restaurant*) bill, *Am* check.

additionner *vt* to add (**à** to); (*nombres*) to add up.

adhérent, -ente *mf* member.

adhérer *vi* **a. à** (*coller*) to stick to; (*s'inscrire*) to join.

adhésif, -ive *a* & *m* adhesive.

adieu, -x *int* & *m* farewell.

adjectif *m* adjective.

adjoint, -ointe *mf* assistant; **a. au maire** deputy mayor.

admettre* *vt* (*laisser entrer, accueillir, reconnaître*) to admit; (*autoriser, tolérer*) to allow; (*candidat*) to pass; **être admis à** (*examen*) to have passed.

administratif, -ive *a* administrative.
administration *f* administration; **l'A.** (*service public*) the Civil Service.
administrer *vt* (*gérer*, *donner*) to administer.
admirable *a* admirable.
admirateur, -trice *mf* admirer.
admiratif, -ive *a* admiring.
admiration *f* admiration.
admirer *vt* to admire.
adolescent, -ente *mf* adolescent, teenager.
adopter *vt* to adopt.
adoptif, -ive *a* (*fils*, *patrie*) adopted.
adoption *f* adoption.
adorable *a* adorable.
adoration *f* worship.
adorer *vt* to love, adore (**faire** doing); (*dieu*) to worship.
adosser (s') *vpr* to lean back (**à** against).
adoucir *vt* (*voix*, *traits*) to tone down.
adoucir (s') *vpr* (*temps*) to turn milder.
adresse *f* (*domicile*) address; (*habileté*) skill.
adresser *vt* (*lettre*) to send; (*compliment*, *remarque*) to address; **a. la parole à** to speak to; **s'a. à** to speak to; (*aller trouver*) to go and see; (*bureau*) to inquire at; (*être destiné à*) to be aimed at.
adroit, -oite *a* skilful.
adulte *mf* adult, grown-up.
adverbe *m* adverb.
adversaire *mf* opponent.
aération *f* ventilation.
aérer *vt* to air (out).
aérien, -ienne *a* (*photo*) aerial; **attaque/transport aérien(ne)** air attack/transport.
aérobic *f* aerobics.
aérogare *f* air terminal.
aéroglisseur *m* hovercraft.
aéroport *m* airport.
aérosol *m* aerosol.
affaiblir *vt*, **s'affaiblir** *vpr* to weaken.
affaire *f* (*question*) matter; **affaires** business; (*effets*) things; **avoir a. à** to have to deal with; **c'est mon a.** that's my business; **faire une bonne a.** to get a bargain.
affamé, -ée *a* starving.
affection *f* (*attachement*) affection.

affectueux, -euse *a* affectionate, loving.
affichage *m* **panneau d'a.** hoarding, *Am* billboard.
affiche *f* poster.
afficher *vt* (*affiche*) to stick up.
affirmatif, -ive *a* (*ton*, *réponse*) positive, affirmative.
affirmation *f* assertion.
affirmer *vt* to assert.
affliger *vt* to distress.
affluence *f* crowd; **heure(s) d'a.** rush hour(s).
affluent *m* tributary.
affolement *m* panic.
affoler *vt* to drive crazy.
affoler (s') *vpr* to panic.
affranchir *vt* (lettre) to stamp.
affreux, -euse *a* horrible.
affront *m* insult; **faire un a. à** to insult.
affronter *vt* to confront; (*mauvais temps*, *difficultés etc*) to brave.
affûter *vt* to sharpen.
afin 1 *prép* **a. de** (+ *infinitif*) in order to. **2** *conj* **a. que** (+ *subjonctif*) so that.
africain, -aine *a* & *mf* African.
agacer *vt* to irritate.
âge *m* age; **quel â. as-tu?** how old are you?; **d'un certain â.** middle-aged; **le moyen â.** the Middle Ages.
âgé, -ée *a* elderly; **â. de six ans** six years old; **enfant â. de six ans** six-year-old child.
agence *f* agency; (*succursale*) branch office; **a. immobilière** estate agent's office, *Am* real estate office.
agenda [aʒɛ̃da] *m* diary, *Am* datebook.
agenouiller (s') *vpr* to kneel (down); **être agenouillé** to be kneeling (down).
agent *m* agent; **a. (de police)** policeman; **a. immobilier** estate agent, *Am* real estate agent.
agglomération *f* built-up area; (*ville*) town.
aggloméré *m* chipboard.
aggraver *vt*, **s'aggraver** *vpr* to worsen.
agile *a* agile.
agilité *f* agility.
agir *vi* to act.
agir (s') *vi* **il s'agit d'argent**/*etc* it's a question *ou* matter of money/*etc*; **de quoi s'agit-il?** what is it?, what's it about?
agitation *f* (*de la mer*) roughness; (*d'une personne*) restlessness.

agité, -ée *a* (*mer*) rough; (*personne*) restless.
agiter *vt* (*remuer*) to stir; (*secouer*) to shake; (*brandir*) to wave.
agiter (s') *vpr* (*enfant*) to fidget.
agneau, -x *m* lamb.
agrafe *f* hook; (*pour papiers*) staple.
agrafer *vt* (*robe*) to do up; (*papiers*) to staple.
agrafeuse *f* stapler.
agrandir *vt* to enlarge.
agrandir (s') *vpr* to expand.
agrandissement *m* (*de ville*) expansion; (*de maison*) extension; (*de photo*) enlargement.
agréable *a* pleasant.
agréer *vt* **veuillez a. (l'expression de) mes salutations distinguées** (*dans une lettre*) yours faithfully, *Am* sincerely yours.
agrès *mpl* (*de gymnastique*) apparatus, *Am* equipment.
agresser *vt* to attack.
agresseur *m* attacker; (*dans la rue*) mugger.
agressif, -ive *a* aggressive.
agression *f* (*dans la rue*) mugging.
agressivité *f* aggressiveness.
agricole *a* **ouvrier/machine a.** farm worker/machine; **travaux agricoles** farm work.
agriculteur *m* farmer.
agriculture *f* farming.
aguets (aux) [ozagɛ] *adv* on the look-out.
ah! *int* ah!, oh!
ai *voir* **avoir.**
aide 1 *f* help, **à l'a. de** with the aid of. **2** *mf* (*personne*) assistant.
aider *vt* to help (**à faire** to do); **s'a. de** to make use of.
aïe! *int* ouch!
aie(s), aient *voir* **avoir.**
aigle *m* eagle.
aigre *a* sour.
aigu, -uë *a* (*douleur*) acute; (*dents*) sharp; (*voix*) shrill.
aiguillage *m* (*pour train*) points, *Am* switches.
aiguille *f* (*à coudre, de pin*) needle; (*de montre*) hand.
aiguiller *vt* (*train*) to shunt, *Am* switch.
aiguilleur *m* signalman; **a. du ciel** air traffic controller.
aiguiser *vt* to sharpen.
ail *m* garlic.
aile *f* wing; (*de moulin à vent*) sail; (*d'automobile*) wing, *Am* fender.
ailier *m* *Football* wing(er).

aille(s), aillent *voir* **aller**[1].
ailleurs *adv* somewhere else; **d'a.** (*du reste*) anyway.
aimable *a* (*gentil*) kind; (*sympathique*) likeable.
aimant *m* magnet.
aimanter *vt* to magnetize.
aimer *vt* to love; **a. (bien)** (*apprécier*) to like, be fond of; **a. faire** to like doing *ou* to do; **a. mieux** to prefer; **ils s'aiment** they're in love.
aîné, -ée 1 *a* (*de deux frères etc*) elder, older; (*de plus de deux*) eldest, oldest. **2** *mf* elder *ou* older (child); eldest *ou* oldest (child).
ainsi *adv* (*comme ça*) (in) this *ou* that way; **a. que** as well as; **et a. de suite** and so on.
air[1] *m* air; (*mélodie*) tune; **en plein a.** in the open (air), outdoors; **ficher en l'a.** *Fam* (*jeter*) to chuck away; (*gâcher*) to mess up; **en l'a.** (*jeter*) (up) in the air; (*paroles*) empty.
air[2] *m* (*expression*) look; **avoir l'a.** to look, seem; **avoir l'a. de** to look like.
aire *f* area; **a. de stationnement** parking area.
aise *f* **à l'a.** (*dans un vêtement etc*) comfortable; (*dans une situation*) at ease; **mal à l'a.** uncomfortable.
aisé, -ée *a* (*riche*) comfortably off; (*facile*) easy.
ait *voir* **avoir**.
ajouter *vti* to add (**à** to).
ajuster *vt* (*pièce, salaires*) to adjust; **a. à** (*adapter*) to fit to.
alaise *f* (waterproof) undersheet.
alarme *f* (*signal*) alarm; **a. antivol/d'incendie** burglar/fire alarm.
alarmer *vt* to alarm.
album [albɔm] *m* (*de timbres etc*) album.
alcool *m* alcohol; (*spiritueux*) spirits; **a. à 90°** surgical spirit, *Am* rubbing alcohol.
alcoolique *a* & *mf* alcoholic.
alcoolisé, -ée *a* alcoholic.
alcootest® *m* breath test; (*appareil*) breathalyzer.
alentours *mpl* surroundings.
alerte *f* alarm; **en état d'a.** on the alert.
alerter *vt* to warn.
algèbre *f* algebra.
algérien, -ienne *a* & *mf* Algerian.
algue(s) *f(pl)* seaweed.
alibi *m* alibi.
aliéné, -ée *mf* insane person.
alignement *m* alignment.
aligner *vt*, **s'aligner** *vpr* to line up.

aliment *m* food.
alimentaire *a* **ration**/*etc* **a.** food rations/*etc*; **produits alimentaires** foods.
alimentation *f* (*action*) feeding; (*régime*) diet; (*nourriture*) food; **magasin d'a.** grocer's shop, *Am* grocery store.
alimenter *vt* (*nourrir*) to feed.
allaiter *vti* to breastfeed.
allécher *vt* to tempt.
allée *f* (*de parc etc*) path; (*de cinéma, supermarché etc*) aisle.
allégé, -ée *a* (*fromage etc*) low-fat.
alléger *vt* to make lighter.
allemand, -ande 1 *a* & *mf* German. **2** *m* (*langue*) German.
aller[1]* *vi* (*aux* **être**) to go; **a. à** (*convenir à*) to suit; **a. avec** (*vêtement*) to go with; **a. bien/mieux** (*personne*) to be well/better; **il va savoir**/*etc* he'll know/*etc*, he's going to know/*etc*; **il va partir** he's about to leave, he's going to leave; **va voir!** go and see!; **comment vas-tu?, (comment) ça va?** how are you?; **ça va!** all right!, fine!; **allez-y!** go on!, go ahead!; **allez! au lit!** come on *ou* go on, (to) bed!
aller[2] *m* outward journey; **a. (simple)** single (ticket), *Am* one-way (ticket); **a. (et) retour** return (ticket), *Am* round-trip (ticket).
aller (s'en) [sãnale] *vpr* to go away; (*tache*) to come out.
allergie *f* allergy.
allergique *a* allergic (**à** to).
alliance *f* (*anneau*) wedding ring; (*de pays*) alliance.
allié, -ée *mf* ally.
allier *vt* to combine (**à** with); (*pays*) to ally (**à** with).
allier (s') *vpr* (*pays*) to become allied (**à** with, to).
allô! *int* hello!
allocation *f* allowance, benefit; **a. (de) chômage** unemployment benefit; **allocations familiales** child benefit.
allongé, -ée *a* (*étiré*) elongated.
allonger 1 *vt* (*bras*) to stretch out; (*jupe*) to lengthen. **2** *vi* (*jours*) to get longer.
allonger (s') *vpr* to stretch out.
allumage *m* (*de voiture*) ignition.
allumer *vt* (*feu, cigarette, gaz*) to light; (*électricité*) to turn *ou* switch on.
allumer (s') *vpr* (*lumière*) to come on.
allumette *f* match.
allure *f* (*vitesse*) pace; (*de véhicule*) speed; (*air*) look.
allusion *f* allusion; **faire a. à** to refer to.
alors *adv* (*en ce cas-là*) so; **a. que** (*tandis que*) whereas.

alouette *f* (sky)lark.
alourdir *vt* to weigh down.
alourdir (s') *vpr* to become heavy *ou* heavier.
Alpes (les) *fpl* the Alps.
alphabet *m* alphabet.
alphabétique *a* alphabetical.
alpinisme *m* mountaineering.
alpiniste *mf* mountaineer.
alterner *vti* to alternate.
altitude *f* height.
alu *m* **papier (d')a.** tinfoil.
aluminium [-jɔm] *m* aluminium, *Am* aluminum; **papier a.** tinfoil.
amabilité *f* kindness.
amaigri, -ie *a* thin(ner).
amaigrissant *a* **régime a.** slimming diet.
amande *f* almond.
amarrer *vt* to moor.
amarres *fpl* moorings.
amas *m* heap, pile.
amasser *vt*, **s'amasser** *vpr* to pile up.
amateur *m* (*d'art etc*) lover; (*sportif*) amateur; **une équipe a.** an amateur team.
ambassade *f* embassy.
ambassadeur, -drice *mf* ambassador.
ambiance *f* atmosphere.
ambitieux, -euse *a* ambitious.
ambition *f* ambition.
ambulance *f* ambulance.
ambulant, -ante *a* travelling.
âme *f* soul.
amélioration *f* improvement.
améliorer *vt*, **s'améliorer** *vpr* to improve.
aménagement *m* fitting out; conversion.
aménager *vt* (*arranger*) to fit out (**en** as); (*transformer*) to convert (**en** into).
amende *f* fine.
amener *vt* to bring.
amer, -ère *a* bitter.
américain, -aine *a* & *mf* American.
amertume *f* bitterness.
ameublement *m* furniture.
ami, -ie *mf* friend; (*de la nature etc*) lover (**de** of); **petit a.** boy-

friend; **petite amie** girlfriend.
amical, -e, -aux *a* friendly.
amiral, -aux *m* admiral.
amitié *f* friendship.
amonceler (s') *vpr* to pile up.
amont (en) *adv* upstream.
amorce *f* (*de pêcheur*) bait; (*de pistolet d'enfant*) cap.
amortir *vt* (*coup*) to cushion; (*bruit*) to deaden.
amortisseur *m* shock absorber.
amour *m* love; **pour l'a. de** for the sake of.
amoureux, -euse 1 *mf* lover. **2** *a* **a. de qn** in love with s.o.
amour-propre *m* self-respect.
amovible *a* removable.
amphithéâtre *m* (*romain*) amphitheatre; (*à l'université*) lecture hall.
ample *a* (*vêtement*) full, ample.
ampleur *f* (*de robe*) fullness.
amplificateur *m* amplifier.
amplifier *vt* (*son*, *courant*) to amplify.
ampoule *f* (*électrique*) (light) bulb; (*aux pieds etc*) blister; (*de médicament*) phial.
amputer *vt* to amputate.
amusant, -ante *a* amusing.
amusement *m* amusement.
amuser *vt* to entertain.
amuser (s') *vpr* to enjoy oneself, have fun; **s'a. avec** to play with; **s'a. à faire** to amuse oneself doing.
amygdales *fpl* tonsils.
an *m* year; **il a dix ans** he's ten (years old); **Nouvel A.** New Year.
analogue *a* similar.
analyse *f* analysis.
analyser *vt* to analyse.
ananas *m* pineapple.
anarchie *f* anarchy.
anatomie *f* anatomy.
ancêtre *m* ancestor.
anchois *m* anchovy.
ancien, -ienne *a* old; (*meuble*) antique; (*qui n'est plus*) former; (*antique*) ancient; (*dans une fonction*) senior.
ancre *f* anchor.
ancrer *vt* to anchor.
andouille *f* **espèce d'a.!** *Fam* (you) nitwit!
âne *m* (*animal*) donkey; (*personne*) ass.

anéantir *vt* to wipe out.
anecdote *f* anecdote.
ânesse *f* she-ass.
anesthésie *f* an(a)esthesia; **a. générale** general an(a)esthetic.
anesthésier *vt* to an(a)esthetize.
ange *m* angel.
angine *f* sore throat.
anglais, -aise 1 *a* English. **2** *mf* Englishman, Englishwoman; **les A.** the English. **3** *m* (*langue*) English.
angle *m* angle; (*de rue*) corner.
angoissant, -ante *a* distressing.
angoisse *f* (great) anxiety, anguish.
anguille *f* eel.
animal, -e, -aux *m* & *a* animal.
animateur, -trice *mf* (*de télévision*) compere, *Am* emcee; (*de club*) leader, organizer.
animation *f* (*des rues*) activity; (*de réunion*) liveliness.
animé, -ée *a* lively.
animer *vt* (*débat*) to lead; (*soirée*) to liven up; (*mécanisme*) to drive.
animer (s') *vpr* (*rue etc*) to come to life.
ankylosé, -ée *a* stiff.
anneau, -x *m* ring.
année *f* year; **bonne a.**! Happy New Year!
annexe *f* (*bâtiment*) annex(e).
anniversaire *m* (*d'événement*) anniversary; (*de naissance*) birthday.
annonce *f* (*publicitaire*) advertisement; **petites annonces** classified advertisements.
annoncer *vt* to announce; (*vente*) to advertise; **s'a. pluvieux/difficile**/*etc* to look (like being) rainy/difficult/*etc*.
annuaire *m* (*téléphonique*) directory, phone book.
annuel, -elle *a* yearly.
annulaire *m* ring finger.
annuler *vt* to cancel.
ânonner *vt* to stumble through.
anonyme *a* & *mf* anonymous (person).
anorak *m* anorak.
anormal, -e, -aux *a* abnormal.
anse *f* (*de tasse etc*) handle.
Antarctique (l') *m* the Antarctic.
antenne *f* (*de radio etc*) aerial, *Am* antenna; (*d'insecte*) antenna.
antérieur, -eure *a* (*précédent*) former; (*placé devant*) front.
antibiotique *m* antibiotic.

antibrouillard *a & m* **(phare) a.** fog lamp.
antichoc *a inv* shockproof.
anticorps *m* antibody.
antilope *f* antelope.
antipathique *a* disagreeable.
antiquaire *mf* antique dealer.
antique *a* ancient.
antiquité *f* (*temps, ancienneté*) antiquity; (*objet ancien*) antique.
antivol *m* anti-theft device.
anxiété *f* anxiety.
anxieux, -euse *a* anxious.
août [u(t)] *m* August.
apaiser *vt* to calm.
apercevoir* *vt* to see; (*brièvement*) to catch a glimpse of; **s'a. de** to realize.
apéritif *m* aperitif.
aplanir *vt* (*terrain*) to level; (*difficulté*) to iron out, smooth out.
aplati, -ie *a* flat.
aplatir *vt* to flatten (out).
aplomb (d') *adv* (*meuble etc*) level, straight.
apostrophe *f* (*signe*) apostrophe.
apparaître* *vi* to appear.
appareil *m* (*électrique*) appliance; (*téléphonique*) telephone; (*avion*) aircraft; (*dentaire*) brace, (*digestif*) system; **a. (photo)** camera.
apparemment *adv* apparently.
apparence *f* appearance.
apparent, -ente *a* apparent; (*visible*) conspicuous, noticeable.
apparition *f* appearance; (*spectre*) apparition.
appartement *m* flat, *Am* apartment.
appartenir* *vi* to belong (**à** to).
appât *m* bait.
appâter *vt* to lure.
appauvrir (s') *vpr* to become impoverished.
appel *m* (*cri*) call, (*en justice*) appeal; **faire l'a.** to take the register; **faire a. à** to call upon.
appeler *vt* (*personne, nom etc*) to call; (*en criant*) to call out to (*s.o*); **a. à l'aide** to call for help.
appeler (s') *vpr* to be called; **il s'appelle Paul** his name is Paul.
appendicite [apɛ̃disit] *f* appendicitis.
appétissant, -ante *a* appetizing.
appétit *m* appetite (**de** for); **bon a.!** enjoy your meal!
applaudir *vti* to applaud.

applaudissements *mpl* applause.
application *f* application.
applique *f* wall lamp.
appliqué, -ée *a* painstaking.
appliquer (s') *vpr* **s'a. à** (*un travail*) to apply oneself to; (*concerner*) to apply to; **s'a. à faire** to take pains to do.
apporter *vt* to bring.
appréciation *f* (*de professeur*) comment (**sur** on).
apprécier *vt* (*aimer, percevoir*) to appreciate.
appréhender *vt* (*craindre*) to dread (**de faire** doing).
apprendre* *vti* (*étudier*) to learn; (*événement, fait*) to hear of; (*nouvelle*) to hear; **a. à faire** to learn to do; **a. qch à qn** to teach s.o. sth; (*informer*) to tell s.o. sth; **a. à qn à faire** to teach s.o. to do; **a. que** to learn that; (*être informé*) to hear that.
apprenti, -ie *mf* apprentice.
apprentissage *m* apprenticeship; (*d'une langue*) learning (**de** of).
apprêter (s') *vpr* to get ready (**à faire** to do).
apprivoisé, -ée *a* tame.
apprivoiser *vt* to tame.
approcher 1 *vt* (*chaise etc*) to draw up (**de** to); (*personne*) to come *ou* get close to, approach. **2** *vi* to draw near(er), get close(r) (**de** to).
approcher (s') *vpr* to come *ou* get near(er) (**de** to); **il s'est approché de moi** he came up to me.
approfondir *vt* (*trou*) to dig deeper; (*question*) to go into thoroughly.
approprier (s') *vpr* to take, help oneself to.
approuver *vt* to approve.
approvisionner (s') *vpr* to get one's supplies (**de** of).
appui *m* support; (*pour coude etc*) rest.
appuyer 1 *vt* (*soutenir*) to support; **a. qch sur** (*poser*) to rest sth on; **s'a. sur** to lean on, rest on. **2** *vi* **a. sur** to rest on; (*bouton*) to press.
après 1 *prép* (*temps*) after; (*espace*) beyond; **a. un an** after a year; **a. le pont** beyond the bridge; **a. avoir mangé** after eating. **2** *adv* after(wards); **l'année d'a.** the following year.
après (d') *prép* according to.
après-demain *adv* the day after tomorrow.
après-midi *m ou f inv* afternoon.
apte *a* capable (**à** of).
aptitudes *fpl* aptitude (**pour** for).
aquarelle *f* watercolour.

aquarium [akwarjɔm] *m* aquarium.
aquatique *a* aquatic.
arabe 1 *a* & *mf* Arab. **2** *a* & *m* (*langue*) Arabic; **chiffres arabes** Arabic numerals.
arachide *f* peanut.
araignée *f* spider.
arbitre *m Football, Boxe* referee; *Tennis* umpire.
arbitrer *vt* to referee; to umpire.
arbre *m* tree.
arbuste *m* (small) shrub.
arc *m* (*arme*) bow; (*voûte*) arch; (*de cercle*) arc.
arcades *fpl* arcade, arches.
arc-en-ciel *m* (*pl* **arcs-en-ciel**) rainbow.
arche *f* (*voûte*) arch.
archer *m* archer.
archiplein, -pleine *a* chock-a-block.
architecte *m* architect.
architecture *f* architecture.
archives *fpl* records.
Arctique (l') *m* the Arctic.
ardent, -ente *a* (*passionné*) ardent.
ardeur *f* (*énergie*) enthusiasm.
ardoise *f* slate.
are *m* – 100 square metres.
arène *f* (*pour taureaux*) bullring; **arènes** (*romaines*) amphitheatre.
arête *f* (*de poisson*) bone; (*de cube*) edge, ridge.
argent *m* (*métal*) silver; (*monnaie*) money; **a. comptant** cash.
argenterie *f* silverware.
argile *f* clay.
argot *m* slang.
argument *m* argument.
arithmétique *f* arithmetic.
armature *f* (*de lunettes, tente*) frame.
arme *f* arm, weapon; **a. à feu** firearm.
armée *f* army; **a. de l'air** air force.
armement(s) *m(pl)* arms.
armer *vt* (*personne*) to arm (**de** with); (*fusil*) to cock; **s'a.** to arm oneself (**de** with).
armoire *f* (*penderie*) wardrobe, *Am* closet; **a. à pharmacie** medicine chest *ou* cabinet.
armure *f* armour.
arôme *m* (*goût*) flavour; (*odeur*) (pleasant) smell.

arracher *vt* (*clou*, *dent*, *cheveux*, *page*) to pull out; (*plante*) to pull up; **a. qch à qn** to snatch sth from s.o.
arranger *vt* (*chambre*, *visite etc*) to fix up; (*voiture*, *texte*) to put right; **ça m'arrange** that suits me.
arranger (s') *vpr* to come to an agreement; (*finir bien*) to turn out fine; **s'a. pour faire** to manage to do.
arrestation *f* arrest.
arrêt *m* (*halte*, *endroit*) stop; (*action*) stopping; **temps d'a.** pause; **sans a.** constantly.
arrêté *m* order.
arrêter 1 *vt* to stop; (*voleur etc*) to arrest. **2** *vi* to stop; **il n'arrête pas de critiquer**/*etc* he's always criticizing/*etc*.
arrêter (s') *vpr* to stop (**de faire** doing).
arrière 1 *adv* **en a.** (*marcher*) backwards; (*rester*) behind. **2** *m* & *a inv* rear, back; **faire marche a.** to reverse, back. **3** *m Football* (full) back.
arrière-boutique *m* back room (*of a shop*).
arrière-goût *m* aftertaste.
arrière-grand-mère *f* great-grandmother.
arrière-grand-père *m* great-grandfather.
arrivage *m* consignment.
arrivée *f* arrival; (*ligne, poteau*) (winning) post.
arriver *vi* (*aux* **être**) to arrive; (*survenir*) to happen; **a. à** to reach; **a. à faire** to manage to do; **a. à qn** to happen to s.o.; **il m'arrive d'oublier**/*etc* I (sometimes) forget/*etc*.
arrondir *vt* (*chiffre*, *angle*) to round off.
arrondissement *m* (*d'une ville*) district.
arrosage *m* watering.
arroser *vt* (*terre*) to water.
arrosoir *m* watering can.
art *m* art.
artère *f* artery; (*rue*) main road.
artichaut *m* artichoke.
article *m* (*de presse*, *de commerce*, *en grammaire*) article; **articles de toilette** toiletries.
articulation *f* (*de membre*) joint; **a. (du doigt)** knuckle.
articuler *vt* (*mot etc*) to articulate.
artifice *m* **feu d'a.** firework display.
artificiel, -elle *a* artificial.
artisan *m* craftsman.
artiste *mf* artist.
artistique *a* artistic.

as[1] [a] *voir* **avoir.**
as[2] [ɑs] *m* (*carte*, *champion*) ace.
ascenseur *m* lift, *Am* elevator.
ascension *f* ascent; **l'A.** Ascension Day.
asiatique *a* & *mf* Asian.
asile *m* (*abri*) shelter.
aspect [aspɛ] *m* (*air*) appearance.
asperge *f* asparagus.
asperger *vt* to spray (**de** with).
asphyxie *f* suffocation.
asphyxier *vt* to suffocate.
aspirateur *m* vacuum cleaner, hoover®; **passer (à) l'a.** to vacuum, hoover.
aspirer *vt* (*liquide*) to suck up.
aspirine *f* aspirin.
assaisonnement *m* seasoning.
assaisonner *vt* to season.
assassin *m* murderer.
assassinat *m* murder.
assassiner *vt* to murder.
assaut *m* onslaught; **prendre d'a.** to (take by) storm.
assemblée *f* (*personnes réunies*) gathering; (*parlement*) assembly.
assembler *vt* to put together.
assembler (s') *vpr* to gather.
asseoir* (s') *vpr* to sit (down).
assez *adv* enough; **a. de pain/gens** enough bread/people; **j'en ai a.** I've had enough; **a. grand**/*etc* (*suffisamment*) big/*etc* enough (**pour faire** to do); **a. fatigué**/*etc* (*plutôt*) fairly *ou* quite tired/*etc*.
assiéger *vt* (*magasin*, *vedette*) to mob.
assiette *f* plate; **a. anglaise** (assorted) cold meats, *Am* cold cuts.
assis, -ise (*pp of* **asseoir**) *a* sitting (down).
assises *fpl* **(cour d')a.** court of assizes.
assistance *f* (*assemblée*) audience; (*aide*) assistance.
assistant, -ante *mf* assistant; **assistant(e) social(e)** social worker; **assistante maternelle** child minder.
assister 1 *vt* (*aider*) to help. **2** *vi* **a. à** (*réunion*, *cours etc*) to attend; (*accident*) to witness.
association *f* association.
associé, -ée *mf* partner.
associer (s') *vpr* to associate (**à** with).
assoiffé, -ée *a* thirsty.
assombrir (s') *vpr* (*ciel*) to cloud over.

assommer *vt* (*personne*) to knock unconscious.
assortiment *m* assortment.
assortir *vt*, **s'assortir** *vpr* to match.
assoupir (s') *vpr* to doze off.
assouplir *vt* (*corps*) to limber up.
assouplissement *m* **exercices d'a.** limbering up exercises.
assourdir *vt* to deafen.
assourdissant, -ante *a* deafening.
assurance *f* (*aplomb*) self-assurance; (*contrat*) insurance.
assurer *vt* (*par un contrat*) to insure; (*travail*) to carry out; **s'a.** to insure oneself (**contre** against); **a. à qn que** to assure s.o. that; **a. qn de qch,** to assure s.o. of sth; **s'a. que/de** to make sure that/of.
astérisque *m* asterisk.
asthmatique *a* & *mf* asthmatic.
asthme [asm] *m* asthma.
asticot *m* maggot, *Am* worm.
astiquer *vt* to polish.
astre *m* star.
astrologie *f* astrology.
astronaute *mf* astronaut.
astronomie *f* astronomy.
astuce *f* (*pour faire qch*) knack, trick.
astucieux, -euse *a* clever.
atelier *m* (*d'ouvrier etc*) workshop; (*de peintre*) studio.
athlète *mf* athlete.
athlétique *a* athletic.
athlétisme *m* athletics.
atlantique 1 *a* Atlantic. **2** *m* **l'A.** the Atlantic.
atlas [atlɑs] *m* atlas.
atmosphère *f* atmosphere.
atome *m* atom.
atomique *a* (*bombe etc*) atomic.
atout *m* trump (card).
atroce *a* atrocious.
atrocités *fpl* atrocities.
attabler (s') *vpr* to sit down at the table.
attachant, -ante *a* (*enfant etc*) likeable.
attaché-case [-kɛz] *m* attaché case.
attacher *vt* (*lier*) to tie (up) (**à** to); (*boucler, fixer*) to fasten; **s'a. à qn** to become attached to s.o.
attaquant, -ante *mf* attacker.
attaque *f* attack.

attaquer *vti* to attack; **s'a. à** to attack.
attarder (s') *vpr* (*en chemin*) to dawdle.
atteindre* *vt* to reach; **être atteint de** (*maladie*) to be suffering from.
attelage *m* (*crochet*) hook (*for towing*).
atteler *vt* (*bêtes*) to harness; (*remorque*) to hook up.
attendre 1 *vt* to wait for; **elle attend un bébé** she's expecting a baby. **2** *vi* to wait; **s'a. à** to expect; **a. que qn vienne** to wait for s.o. to come; **faire a. qn** to keep s.o. waiting; **en attendant** meanwhile; **en attendant que** (+ *subjonctif*) until.
attendrir (s') *vpr* to be moved (**sur** by).
attentat *m* attempt on s.o.'s life; **a. (à la bombe)** (bomb) attack.
attente *f* wait(ing); **salle d'a.** waiting room.
attentif, -ive *a* (*personne*) attentive; (*travail, examen*) careful.
attention *f* attention; **faire a. à** to pay attention to; **a.!** watch out!, be careful!; **a. à la voiture!** watch out for the car!
attentivement *adv* attentively.
atterrir *vi* to land.
atterrissage *m* landing.
attirer *vt* to attract; (*attention*) to draw (**sur** on).
attitude *f* attitude.
attraction *f* attraction.
attraper *vt* (*ballon, maladie, voleur, train etc*) to catch; (*accent, contravention etc*) to pick up; **se laisser a.** (*duper*) to get taken in.
attrayant, -ante *a* attractive.
attribuer *vt* (*donner*) to assign (**à** to); (*décerner*) to award (**à** to).
attribut *m* attribute.
attrister *vt* to sadden.
attroupement *m* (disorderly) crowd.
attrouper *vt*, **s'attrouper** *vpr* to gather.
au *voir* **à, le**.
aube *f* dawn.
auberge *f* inn; **a. de jeunesse** youth hostel.
aubergine *f* aubergine, *Am* eggplant.
aucun, -une 1 *a* no, not any; **il n'a a. talent** he has no talent, he doesn't have any talent; **a. professeur n'est venu** no teacher has come. **2** *pron* none, not any; **il n'en a a.** he has none (at all), he doesn't have any (at all).
audace *f* (*courage*) daring.
audacieux, -euse *a* daring.
au-dessous de *prép* under, below.
au-dessus 1 *adv* above; over; (*à l'étage supérieur*) upstairs. **2** *prép*

au-d. de above; (*âge*, *température*, *prix*) over.
audio *a inv* audio.
auditeur, -trice *mf* listener; **les auditeurs** the audience.
auditoire *m* audience.
auge *f* (feeding) trough.
augmentation *f* increase (**de** in, of); **a. de salaire** (pay) rise, *Am* raise.
augmenter *vti* to increase (**de** by).
aujourd'hui *adv* today.
auprès de *prép* by, close to.
auquel *voir* **lequel**.
aura, aurai(t) *etc voir* **avoir**.
aurore *f* dawn.
ausculter *vt* to examine (*with a stethoscope*).
aussi *adv* (*comparaison*) as; **a. sage que** as wise as. ▮ (*également*) too, also, as well; **moi a.** so do, can, am *etc* I. ▮ (*tellement*) so; **un repas a. délicieux** so delicious a meal, such a delicious meal.
aussitôt *adv* immediately; **a. que** as soon as; **a. levé, il partit** as soon as he was up, he left.
australien, -ienne *a* & *mf* Australian.
autant *adv* **a. de...que** (*quantité*) as much...as; (*nombre*) as many...as. ▮ **a. de** (*tant de*) so much; (*nombre*) so many. ▮ **a. (que)** (*souffrir*, *lire etc*) as much (as); **en faire a.** to do the same; **j'aimerais a. aller au cinéma** I'd just as soon go to the cinema.
autel *m* altar.
auteur *m* (*de livre*) author; (*de chanson*) composer.
authentique *a* genuine.
auto *f* car; **autos tamponneuses** bumper cars.
autobus *m* bus.
autocar *m* bus, coach.
autocollant *m* sticker.
auto-école *f* driving school.
autographe *m* autograph.
automatique *a* automatic.
automatiquement *adv* automatically.
automne *m* autumn, *Am* fall.
automobile *f* & *a* car, *Am* automobile.
automobiliste *mf* motorist, driver.
autoradio *m* car radio.
autorisation *f* permission.
autoriser *vt* to permit (**à faire** to do).
autoritaire *a* authoritarian.

autorité *f* authority.
autoroute *f* motorway, *Am* highway.
auto-stop *m* hitchhiking; **faire de l'a.** to hitchhike.
auto-stoppeur, -euse *mf* hitchhiker.
autour 1 *adv* around. **2** *prép* **a. de** around.
autre *a* & *pron* other; **un a. livre** another book; **un a.** another (one); **d'autres** others; **d'autres médecins** other doctors; **d'autres questions?** any other questions?; **qn/personne/rien d'a.** s.o./no one/ nothing else; **a. chose/part** something/somewhere else; **qui/quoi d'a.?** who/what else?; **l'un l'a., les uns les autres** each other; **l'un et l'a.** both (of them); **l'un ou l'a.** either (of them); **ni l'un ni l'a.** neither (of them); **les uns...les autres** some...others; **d'un moment à l'a.** any moment.
autrefois *adv* in the past.
autrement *adv* differently; (*sinon*) otherwise.
autrichien, -ienne *a* & *mf* Austrian.
autruche *f* ostrich.
aux *voir* **à, le.**
auxiliaire *a* & *m* **(verbe) a.** auxiliary (verb).
auxquel(le)s *voir* **lequel.**
aval (en) *adv* downstream.
avalanche *f* avalanche.
avaler *vti* to swallow.
avance *f* **à l'a., d'a.** in advance; **en a.** (*arriver, partir*) early; (*avant l'horaire prévu*) ahead (of time); **en a. sur** ahead of; **avoir une heure d'a.** (*train etc*) to be an hour early.
avancement *m* (*de personne*) promotion.
avancer 1 *vt* (*date*) to bring forward; (*main, chaise*) to move forward; (*travail*) to speed up. **2** *vi* to advance, move forward; (*montre*) to be fast.
avancer (s') *vpr* to move forward.
avant 1 *prép* before; **a. de voir** before seeing; **a. qu'il (ne) parte** before he leaves; **a. tout** above all. **2** *adv* before; **en a.** (*mouvement*) forward; (*en tête*) ahead; **la nuit d'a.** the night before. **3** *m* & *a inv* front. **4** *m* (*joueur*) forward.
avantage *m* advantage.
avantager *vt* to favour.
avant-bras *m inv* forearm.
avant-dernier, -ière *a* & *mf* last but one.
avant-hier [avɑ̃tjɛr] *adv* the day before yesterday.
avant-veille *f* **l'a.-veille (de)** two days before.
avare 1 *a* miserly. **2** *mf* miser.

avarice *f* miserliness, avarice.
avarié, -ée *a* (*aliment*) rotting, rotten.
avec *prép* with; (*envers*) to(wards); **et a. ça?** (*dans un magasin*) anything else?
avenir *m* future; **à l'a.** in future.
aventure *f* adventure.
aventurer (s') *vpr* to venture.
aventurier, -ière *mf* adventurer.
avenue *f* avenue.
averse *f* shower.
avertir *vt* (*mettre en garde*) to warn; (*informer*) to notify.
avertissement *m* warning; notification.
avertisseur *m* (*klaxon*®) horn; **a. d'incendie** fire alarm.
aveu, -x *m* confession.
aveugle 1 *a* blind. **2** *mf* blind man, blind woman; **les aveugles** the blind.
aveugler *vt* to blind.
aveuglette (à l') *adv* **chercher qch à l'a.** to grope for sth.
aviateur, -trice *mf* airman, airwoman.
aviation *f* (*armée de l'air*) air force; (*avions*) aircraft *inv*; **l'a.** (*activité*) flying; **base d'a.** air base.
avion *m* aircraft *inv*, (aero)plane, *Am* airplane; **a. à réaction** jet; **a. de ligne** airliner; **par a.** (*lettre*) airmail; **en a., par a.** (*voyager*) by plane, by air.
aviron *m* oar; **l'a.** (*sport*) rowing.
avis *m* opinion; (*communiqué*) notice; **à mon a.** in my opinion; **changer d'a.** to change one's mind.
avocat, -ate 1 *mf* barrister, *Am* attorney. **2** *m* (*fruit*) avocado (pear).
avoine *f* oats.
avoir* 1 *v aux* to have; **je l'ai vu** I've seen him. **2** *vt* (*posséder*) to have; (*obtenir*) to get; **qu'est-ce que tu as?** what's the matter with you?; **il n'a qu'à essayer** he only has to try; **a. faim/chaud/***etc* to be *ou* feel hungry/hot/*etc*; **a. cinq ans** to be five (years old); **j'en ai pour dix minutes** this will take me ten minutes. **3** (*locution*) **il y a** there is, *pl* there are; **il y a six ans** six years ago; (*voir* **il**).
avouer *vti* to confess (**que** that).
avril *m* April.
axe *m* (*ligne*) axis; (*essieu*) axle; **grands axes** (*routes*) main roads.
ayant, ayez, ayons *voir* **avoir**.
azote *m* nitrogen.
azur *m* (sky) blue; **la Côte d'A.** the (French) Riviera.

B

baby-foot *m inv* table football.
bac 1 *m* (*bateau*) ferry(boat); (*cuve*) tank. **2** *abrév* = **baccalauréat.**
baccalauréat *m* school leaving certificate.
bâche *f* tarpaulin.
bachelier, -ière *mf* holder of the *baccalauréat*.
bâcher *vt* to cover over (*with a tarpaulin*).
badaud, -aude *mf* onlooker.
badigeonner *vt* (*mur*) to whitewash; (*écorchure*) to coat, paint.
bafouiller *vti* to stammer.
bagage *m* piece of luggage *ou* baggage; **bagages** luggage, baggage.
bagarre *f* fight(ing).
bagarrer (se) *vpr* to fight.
bagnole *f Fam* car.
bague *f* (*anneau*) ring.
baguette *f* stick; (*de chef d'orchestre*) baton; (*pain*) (long thin) loaf; **baguettes** (*de tambour*) drumsticks; (*pour manger*) chopsticks; **b. (magique)** (magic) wand.
baie *f* (*de côte*) bay.
baignade *f* (*bain*) bathe, bathing; (*endroit*) bathing place.
baigner 1 *vt* to bathe; (*enfant*) to bath, *Am* bathe. **2** *vi* **b. dans** (*aliment*) to be steeped in.
baigner (se) *vpr* to go swimming *ou* bathing.
baigneur, -euse 1 *mf* bather. **2** *m* (*poupée*) baby doll.
baignoire *f* bath (tub).
bâillement *m* yawn.
bâiller *vi* to yawn.
bâillon *m* gag.
bâillonner *vt* to gag.
bain *m* bath; **prendre un b. de soleil** to sunbathe; **salle de bain(s)** bathroom; **être dans le b.** *Fam* to have got into the swing of things; **b. de bouche** mouthwash.
baiser *m* kiss.
baisse *f* fall, drop (**de** in); **en b.** falling.
baisser 1 *vt* to lower, drop; (*tête*) to bend; (*radio*, *chauffage*) to turn down. **2** *vi* to go down, drop.
baisser (se) *vpr* to bend down.
bal, *pl* **bals** *m* ball; (*populaire*) dance.
balade *f Fam* walk; (*en auto*) drive.
balader (se) *vpr Fam* (*à pied*) to (go for a) walk; **se b. (en voiture)** to go for a drive.

baladeur *m* Walkman®.
balai *m* broom; **manche à b.** broomstick.
balance *f* (pair of) scales.
balancer *vt* to sway; (*lancer*) *Fam* to chuck; (*se débarrasser de*) *Fam* to chuck out.
balancer (se) *vpr* to swing (from side to side).
balançoire *f* (*suspendue*) swing.
balayer *vt* to sweep (up); (*enlever*) to sweep away.
balayette *f* (hand) brush.
balayeur, -euse 1 *mf* roadsweeper. **2** *f* (*véhicule*) roadsweeper.
balbutier *vti* to stammer.
balcon *m* balcony.
baleine *f* whale.
balisage *m* beacons.
balise *f* (*pour naviguer*) beacon.
baliser *vt* to mark with beacons.
ballast *m* ballast.
balle *f* (*de tennis, golf etc*) ball; (*projectile*) bullet.
ballerine *f* ballerina.
ballet *m* ballet.
ballon *m* (*jouet d'enfant, appareil*) balloon; (*sport*) ball; **b. de football** football.
ballot *m* bundle.
ballottage *m* (*scrutin*) second ballot.
balnéaire *a* **station b.** seaside resort, *Am* beach resort.
balustrade *f* (hand)rail.
bambin *m* tiny tot.
bambou *m* bamboo.
ban *m* (*applaudissements*) round of applause; **un (triple) b. pour...** three cheers for....
banane *f* banana.
banc *m* (*siège*) bench; **b. de sable** sandbank.
bancaire *a* **compte b.** bank account.
bandage *m* bandage.
bande[1] *f* (*de terrain, papier etc*) strip; (*de film*) reel; (*rayure*) stripe; (*pansement*) bandage; (*sur la chaussée*) line; **b. (magnétique)** tape; **b. vidéo** videotape; **b. dessinée** comic strip.
bande[2] *f* (*groupe*) gang.
bandeau, -x *m* (*sur les yeux*) blindfold; (*pour la tête*) headband.
bander *vt* (*blessure*) to bandage; (*yeux*) to blindfold.
banderole *f* (*sur montants*) banner.
bandit *m* robber.

banlieue *f* **la b.** the suburbs; **une b.** a suburb; **maison**/*etc* **de b.** suburban house/*etc*.
banque *f* bank; (*activité*) banking.
banquette *f* (*de véhicule, train*) seat.
banquier *m* banker.
banquise *f* ice floe.
baptême [batεm] *m* christening, baptism.
baptiser *vt* (*enfant*) to christen, baptize.
baquet *m* tub, basin.
bar *m* (*lieu, comptoir*) bar.
baraque *f* hut, shack.
baraquement *m* (makeshift) huts.
barbare *a* (*cruel*) barbaric.
barbe *f* beard; **se faire la b.** to shave.
barbecue *m* barbecue.
barbelé *a* **fil de fer b.** barbed wire.
barboter *vi* to splash about.
barbouillage *m* smear(ing); (*gribouillage*) scribble, scribbling.
barbouiller *vt* (*salir*) to smear; (*gribouiller*) to scribble.
barbu, -ue *a* bearded.
baril *m* barrel; **b. de poudre** powder keg.
barman, *pl* **-men** *ou* **-mans** *m* barman, *Am* bartender.
baromètre *m* barometer.
baron *m* baron.
baronne *f* baroness.
barque *f* (small) boat.
barrage *m* (*sur une route*) roadblock; (*sur un fleuve*) dam
barre *f* bar; (*de bateau*) helm; (*trait*) stroke.
barreau, -x *m* (*de fenêtre*) bar; (*d'échelle*) rung.
barrer *vt* (*route etc*) to block; (*mot, phrase*) to cross out.
barrette *f* (hair)slide, *Am* barrette.
barricade *f* barricade
barricader *vt* to barricade; **se b.** to barricade oneself (in).
barrière *f* (*porte*) gate; (*clôture*) fence; (*obstacle*) barrier.
barrique *f* (large) barrel.
bas, basse 1 *a* low. **2** *adv* low; (*parler*) in a whisper; **plus b.** further *ou* lower down. **3** *m* (*de côte, page, mur etc*) bottom; **tiroir**/*etc* **du b.** bottom drawer/*etc*; **en b.** down (below); (*par l'escalier*) downstairs; **en** *ou* **au b. de** at the bottom of.
bas *m* (*chaussette*) stocking.
bas-côté *m* roadside, verge, shoulder.
bascule *f* weighing machine; (*jeu d'enfant*) seesaw.

basculer *vti* to topple over.
base *f* base; **bases** (*d'un argument, accord etc*) basis; **salaire de b.** basic pay; **à b. de lait/citron** milk-/lemon-based.
baser *vt* to base (**sur**, on).
basket(-ball) [baskɛt(bol)] *m* basketball.
basque *a* & *mf* Basque.
basse *voir* **bas.**
basse-cour *f* (*pl* **basses-cours**) farmyard.
bassin *m* pond; (*rade*) dock; (*du corps*) pelvis; **b. houiller** coalfield.
bassine *f* bowl.
bataille *f* battle.
batailleur, -euse 1 *mf* fighter. **2** *a* fond of fighting, belligerent.
bateau, -x *m* boat; (*grand*) ship.
bâtiment *m* building; (*navire*) vessel; **le b.** (*industrie*) the building trade.
bâtir *vt* to build; **bien bâti** well-built.
bâton *m* stick; (*d'agent*) baton; **b. de rouge** lipstick; **donner des coups de b. à qn** to beat s.o. (with a stick).
battante *af* **pluie b.** driving rain.
battement *m* beat(ing); (*de paupières*) blink(ing); (*délai*) interval; **b. de cœur** heartbeat.
batterie *f* battery; **la b.** (*d'un orchestre*) the drums.
batteur *m* (*d'orchestre*) drummer.
battre* 1 *vt* to beat. **2** *vi* to beat; **b. des mains** to clap (one's hands); **b. des paupières** to blink; **b. des ailes** (*oiseau*) to flap its wings.
battre (se) *vpr* to fight.
bavard, -arde *a* talkative.
bavardage *m* chatting.
bavarder *vi* to chat.
bave *f* dribble; (*de limace*) slime.
baver *vi* to dribble; **en b.** *Fam* to have a rough time of it.
bavoir *m* bib.
bavure *f* (*tache*) smudge.
bazar *m* (*magasin*) bazaar; (*désordre*) mess.
beau (*or* **bel** *before vowel or mute h*), **belle,** *pl* **beaux, belles** *a* beautiful, attractive; (*voyage, temps etc*) fine, lovely; **au b. milieu** right in the middle; **j'ai b. crier**/*etc* it's no use (my) shouting/*etc*.
beaucoup *adv* (*lire etc*) a lot; **aimer b.** to like very much *ou* a lot; **b. de** (*livres etc*) many, a lot of; (*courage etc*) a lot of; **pas b. d'argent**/*etc* not much money/*etc*; **j'en ai b.** (*quantité*) I have a lot; (*nombre*) I have lots; **b. plus** much more; many more (**que** than).

beau-frère *m* (*pl* **beaux-frères**) brother-in-law.
beau-père *m* (*pl* **beaux-pères**) father-in-law.
beauté *f* beauty.
beaux-parents *mpl* parents-in-law.
bébé *m* baby.
bec *m* (*d'oiseau*) beak; (*de cruche*) spout; **coup de b.** peck.
bécane *f* *Fam* bike
bêche *f* spade.
bêcher *vt* (*cultiver*) to dig.
becquée *f* **donner la b. à** (*oiseau*) to feed.
bedonnant, -ante *a* potbellied.
bégayer *vi* to stutter.
bègue 1 *mf* stutterer. **2** *a* **être b.** to stutter.
beige *a* & *m* beige.
beignet *m* (*pâtisserie*) fritter.
bel *voir* **beau.**
bêler *vi* to bleat.
belette *f* weasel.
belge *a* & *mf* Belgian.
belle *voir* **beau.**
belle-fille *f* (*pl* **belles-filles**) (*épouse d'un fils*) daughter-in-law.
belle-mère *f* (*pl* **belles-mères**) mother-in-law.
belle-sœur *f* (*pl* **belles-sœurs**) sister-in-law.
belliqueux, -euse *a* (*agressif*) aggressive.
bénédiction *f* blessing.
bénéfice *m* (*gain*) profit; (*avantage*) benefit.
bénéficier *vi* to benefit (**de** from).
bénéfique *a* beneficial.
bénévole *a* & *mf* voluntary (worker).
bénir *vt* to bless; (*remercier*) to give thanks to.
bénit, -ite *a* (*pain*) consecrated; **eau bénite** holy water.
bénitier [benitje] *m* (holy water) stoup
benjamin, -ine [bɛ̃-] *mf* youngest child; (*sportif*) young junior.
benne *f* (*de camion*) (movable) container; **camion à b. basculante** dump truck.
béquille *f* (*canne*) crutch; (*de moto*) stand.
berceau, -x *m* cradle.
bercer *vt* (*balancer*) to rock; (*apaiser*) to soothe, lull.
berceuse *f* lullaby
béret *m* beret.
berge *m* (*rive*) (raised) bank.
berger *m* shepherd; **b. allemand** Alsatian (dog), *Am* German shep-

herd.
bergère *f* shepherdess.
bergerie *f* sheepfold.
besogne *f* job, task.
besoin *m* need; **avoir b. de** to need.
bestiole *f* (*insecte*) bug.
bétail *m* livestock.
bête[1] *f* animal; (*insecte*) bug; **b. noire** pet hate.
bête[2] *a* stupid.
bêtement *adv* stupidly; **tout b.** quite simply.
bêtise *f* stupidity; (*action*, *parole*) stupid thing.
béton *m* concrete; **mur**/*etc* **en b.** concrete wall/*etc*.
betterave *f* beetroot, *Am* beet.
beurre *m* butter.
beurrer *vt* to butter.
beurrier *m* butter dish.
bibelot *m* (small) ornament, trinket.
biberon *m* (feeding) bottle.
bible *f* bible; **la B.** the Bible.
bibliothécaire *mf* librarian.
bibliothèque *f* library; (*meuble*) bookcase.
bic® *m* biro®, ballpoint.
biceps [bisɛps] *m* (*muscle*) biceps.
biche *f* doe.
bicyclette *f* bicycle.
bidon 1 *m* can. **2** *a inv Fam* phoney.
bidonville *f* shantytown.
bidule *m* (*chose*) *Fam* whatsit.
bien 1 *adv* well; **b. fatigué/souvent**/*etc* (*très*) very tired/often/*etc*; **merci b.!** thanks very much!; **b.!** fine!, right!; **b. des fois/des gens**/*etc* lots of *ou* many times/people/*etc*; **je l'ai b. dit** (*intensif*) I *did* say so; **tu as b. fait** you did right; **c'est b. fait (pour lui)** it serves him right. **2** *a inv* (*convenable*, *compétent etc*) fine. **3** *m* (*avantage*) good; (*chose*) possession; **ça te fera du b.** it will do you good; **pour ton b.** for your own good; **le b. et le mal** good and evil.
bien-être *m* wellbeing.
bienfaisant, -ante *a* beneficial.
bien que *conj* (+ *subjonctif*) although.
bientôt *adv* soon; **à b.!** see you soon!; **il est b. midi**/*etc* it's nearly twelve/*etc*.
bienvenu, -ue 1 *a* welcome. **2** *f* welcome; **souhaiter la bienvenue à** to welcome.

bière *f* beer; **b. pression** draught beer.
bifteck *m* steak.
bifurcation *f* (*de route etc*) fork.
bifurquer *vi* to fork.
bigoudi *m* (hair) roller.
bijou, -x *m* jewel.
bijouterie *f* (*commerce*) jeweller's shop, *Am* jewelry shop.
bijoutier, -ière *mf* jeweller, *Am* jeweler.
bilan *m* (*financier*) balance sheet; (*résultat*) outcome; (*d'un accident*) (casualty) toll; **b. de santé** checkup.
bile *f* bile; **se faire de la b.** *Fam* to worry.
bilingue *a* bilingual.
billard *m* (*jeu*) billiards; (*table*) billiard table.
bille *f* (*d'enfant*) marble; **stylo à b.** ballpoint (pen).
billet *m* ticket; **b. (de banque)** (bank)note, *Am* bill; **b. aller, b. simple** single ticket, *Am* one-way ticket; **b. (d')aller et retour** return ticket, *Am* round trip ticket.
biologique *a* biological; (*légumes etc*) organic.
bip(-bip) *m* bleeper.
biscotte *f* Melba toast.
biscuit *m* biscuit, *Am* cookie.
bison *m* (American) buffalo.
bissextile *af* **année b.** leap year.
bistouri *m* scalpel.
bitume *m* (*revêtement*) asphalt.
bizarre *a* peculiar, odd.
blague *f* (*plaisanterie, farce*) joke; **blagues** (*absurdités*) *Fam* nonsense.
blaguer *vi* to be joking.
blâmer *vt* to criticize, blame.
blanc, blanche 1 *a* white; (*page*) blank. **2** *mf* (*personne*) white man *ou* woman. **3** *m* (*couleur*) white; (*de poulet*) breast; (*espace*) blank; **b. (d'œuf)** (egg) white; **laisser en b.** to leave blank; **chèque en b.** blank cheque *ou Am* check.
blancheur *f* whiteness.
blanchir *vi* to turn white.
blanchisserie *f* (*lieu*) laundry.
blanchisseur, -euse *mf* laundryman, laundrywoman.
blé *m* wheat.
blessant, -ante *a* hurtful.
blessé, -ée *mf* casualty.
blesser *vt* to injure, hurt; (*avec un couteau, une balle etc*) to wound;

(*offenser*) to hurt; **se b. le** *ou* **au bras**/*etc* to hurt one's arm/*etc*.
blessure *f* injury; wound.
bleu, -e 1 *a* (*mpl* **bleus**) blue. **2** *m* (*pl* **-s**) (*couleur*) blue; (*contusion*) bruise; (*vêtement*) overalls.
blindé, -ée *a* (*voiture etc*) armoured; **porte blindée** reinforced steel door; **une vitre blindée** bulletproof glass.
bloc *m* block; (*de papier*) pad; **à b.** (*visser etc*) tight.
bloc-notes *m* (*pl* **blocs-notes**) writing pad.
blond, -onde 1 *a* fair(-haired). **2** *mf* fair-haired man *ou* woman; **(bière) blonde** lager.
bloquer *vt* (*obstruer*) to block; (*coincer*) to jam; (*roue*) to lock; (*prix*) to freeze.
bloquer (se) *vpr* to jam; (*roue*) to lock.
blottir (se) *vpr* to crouch; (*dans son lit*) to snuggle down; **se b. contre** to snuggle up to.
blouse *f* (*tablier*) smock.
blouson *m* windcheater, *Am* windbreaker.
blue-jean [bludʒin] *m* jeans.
bobine *f* reel, spool.
bocal, -aux *m* glass jar; (*à poissons*) bowl.
bœuf, *pl* **-fs** [bœf, bø] *m* ox (*pl* oxen); (*viande*) beef.
boire* *vti* to drink; **offrir à b. à qn** to offer s.o. a drink.
bois *m* wood; (*de construction*) timber; **en** *ou* **de b.** wooden; **b. de chauffage** firewood.
boisé, -ée *a* wooded.
boisson *f* drink.
boîte *f* box; (*de conserve*) tin, *Am* can; **b. aux** *ou* **à lettres** letterbox.
boiter *vi* to limp.
boîtier *m* (*de montre*) case.
bol *m* bowl; **un b. d'air** a breath of fresh air.
bombardement *m* bombing; shelling.
bombarder *vt* to bomb; (*avec des obus*) to shell.
bombe *f* bomb; (*de laque etc*) spray.
bon, bonne *a* good; (*qui convient*) right; (*apte*) fit; **b. anniversaire!** happy birthday!; **le b. choix/moment** the right choice/time; **b. à manger** fit to eat; **c'est b. à savoir** it's worth knowing; **croire b. de** to think it wise to; **b. en français**/*etc* good at French/*etc*; **un b. moment** (*intensif*) a good while; **pour de b.** really (and truly); **ah b.?** is that so?
bon *m* (*billet*) coupon, voucher.
bonbon *m* sweet, *Am* candy.
bond *m* leap.

bondé, -ée *a* packed.
bondir *vi* to leap.
bonheur *m* happiness; (*chance*) good luck; **par b.** luckily.
bonhomme, *pl* **bonshommes** [bɔnɔm, bɔ̃zɔm] *m* fellow; **b. de neige** snowman.
bonjour *m & int* good morning; (*après-midi*) good afternoon; **donner le b. à, dire b. à** to say hello to.
bonne[1] *voir* **bon.**
bonne[2] *f* maid.
bonnet *m* (*de ski etc*) cap; (*de femme, d'enfant*) bonnet, hat.
bonsoir *m & int* (*en rencontrant qn*) good evening; (*en quittant qn*) goodbye; (*au coucher*) good night.
bonté *f* kindness.
bord *m* (*rebord*) edge; (*rive*) bank; **au b. de la mer/route** at *ou* by the seaside/roadside; **b. du trottoir** kerb, *Am* curb; **à bord (de)** (*avion, bateau*) on board.
border *vt* (*vêtement*) to edge; (*lit, personne*) to tuck in; **b. la rue**/*etc* (*maisons, arbres*) to line the street/*etc.*
bordure *f* border.
borne *f* boundary mark; **b. kilométrique** = milestone.
bosse *f* (*dans le dos*) hump; (*enflure, de terrain*) bump.
bosser *vi Fam* to work (hard).
bossu, -ue 1 *a* hunchbacked. **2** *mf* hunchback.
botte *f* (*chaussure*) boot; (*de fleurs etc*) bunch.
bottine *f* (ankle) boot.
bouc *m* billy goat; (*barbe*) goatee.
bouche *f* mouth; **b. de métro** métro entrance; **b. d'égout** drain opening.
bouchée *f* mouthful.
boucher[1] *vt* (*évier, nez etc*) to stop up; (*bouteille*) to cork; (*vue, rue etc*) to block; **se b. le nez** to hold one's nose.
boucher[2] *m* butcher.
boucherie *f* butcher's (shop).
bouchon *m* stopper; (*de liège*) cork; (*de tube, bidon*) cap; (*embouteillage*) traffic jam.
boucle *f* (*de ceinture*) buckle; **b. d'oreille** earring; **b. (de cheveux)** curl.
bouclé, -ée *a* (*cheveux*) curly.
boucler 1 *vt* (*attacher*) to fasten; (*cheveux*) to curl. **2** *vi* to be curly.
bouclier *m* shield.
bouder *vi* to sulk.
boudin *m* black pudding, *Am* blood sausage.

boue *f* mud.
bouée *f* buoy; **b. de sauvetage** lifebuoy.
boueux, -euse *a* muddy.
bouffée *f* (*de fumée*) puff.
bougeoir *m* candlestick.
bouger *vti* to move.
bougie *f* candle; (*d'automobile*) spark(ing) plug.
bouillie *f* porridge.
bouillir* *vi* to boil.
bouilloire *f* kettle.
bouillon *m* (*aliment*) broth; (*bulles*) bubbles.
bouillonner *vi* to bubble.
boulanger, -ère *mf* baker.
boulangerie *f* baker's (shop).
boule *f* ball; **boules** (*jeu*) bowls; **b. de neige** snowball.
bouleau, -x *m* (silver) birch.
bouledogue *m* bulldog.
boulet *m* **b. de canon** cannonball.
boulette *f* (*de papier*) ball; (*de viande*) meatball.
boulevard *m* boulevard.
bouleversement *m* upheaval.
bouleverser *vt* (*déranger*) to turn upside down; (*émouvoir*) to upset (greatly).
boulon *m* bolt.
bouquet *m* (*de fleurs*) bunch.
bouquin *m* *Fam* book.
bourdon *m* (*insecte*) bumblebee.
bourdonnement *m* buzzing.
bourdonner *vi* to buzz.
bourg *m* (small) market town.
bourgeois, -oise *a* & *mf* middle-class (person).
bourgeon *m* bud.
bourgeonner *vi* to bud.
bourrasque *f* squall, gust of wind.
bourrer *vt* to stuff, cram (**de** with); (*pipe*) to fill.
bourse *f* (*sac*) purse; (*d'études*) grant; **la B.** the Stock Exchange.
bousculade *f* jostling.
bousculer *vt* (*heurter*, *pousser*) to jostle.
boussole *f* compass.
bout *m* end; (*de langue*, *canne*, *doigt*) tip; (*de papier*, *pain*, *ficelle*) bit; **un b. de temps** a little while; **au b. d'un moment** after a moment; **à b.** exhausted; **à b. de souffle** out of breath.

bouteille *f* bottle; (*de gaz*) cylinder.
boutique *f* shop.
bouton *m* (*bourgeon*) bud; (*au visage etc*) pimple; (*de vêtement*) button; (*poussoir*) (push-)button; (*de porte, télévision*) knob.
bouton-d'or *m* (*pl* **boutons-d'or**) buttercup.
boutonner *vt*, **se boutonner** *vpr* to button (up).
boutonnière *f* buttonhole.
bouton-pression *m* (*pl* **boutons-pression**) snap (fastener), press-stud.
box, *pl* **boxes** *m* (*garage*) (lockup) garage.
boxe *f* boxing.
boxer *vi* to box.
boxeur *m* boxer.
boycotter [bɔjkɔte] *vt* to boycott.
bracelet *m* bracelet; (*de montre*) strap, *Am* band.
braconner *vi* to poach.
braconnier *m* poacher.
braguette *f* (*de pantalon*) fly, flies.
brailler *vti* to bawl.
braise(s) *f(pl)* embers.
brancard *m* (*civière*) stretcher.
branchages *mpl* (cut) branches.
branche *f* (*d'arbre*) branch; (*de compas*) arm, leg.
branchement *m* connection
brancher *vt* to plug in.
brandir *vt* to flourish.
branlant, -ante *a* (*table etc*) wobbly, shaky.
braquer 1 *vt* (*arme etc*) to point (**sur** at). **2** *vi* to turn the steering wheel, steer.
bras *m* arm; **b. dessus b. dessous** arm in arm; **à b. ouverts** with open arms.
brasier *m* blaze.
brassard *m* armband.
brasse *f* (*nage*) breaststroke.
brasserie *f* (*usine*) brewery; (*café*) brasserie.
brassière *f* (*de bébé*) vest, *Am* undershirt.
brave *a* & *m* brave (man).
bravement *adv* bravely.
bravo 1 *int* well done. **2** *m* cheer.
bravoure *f* bravery.
brebis *f* ewe.
brèche *f* gap.

bredouille *a* **rentrer b.** to come back empty-handed.
bref, brève 1 *a* brief, short. **2** *adv* **(enfin) b.** in a word.
bretelle *f* strap; (*d'accès*) access road; **bretelles** (*pour pantalon*) braces, *Am* suspenders.
breton, -onne *a* & *mf* Breton.
brevet *m* diploma; **b. (des collèges)** = GCSE (*examination for 16-year-olds*); **b. (d'invention)** patent.
bricolage *m* (*passe-temps*) do-it-yourself.
bricoler 1 *vi* to do odd jobs. **2** *vt* (*fabriquer*) to put together.
bricoleur, -euse *mf* handyman, handywoman.
bride *f* bridle.
bridés *a* **avoir les yeux bridés** to have slit eyes.
brièvement *adv* briefly.
brièveté *f* shortness, brevity.
brigand *m* robber; (*enfant*) rascal.
brillamment *adv* brilliantly.
brillant, -ante 1 *a* (*luisant*) shining; (*astiqué*) shiny; (*couleur*) bright; (*doué*) brilliant. **2** *m* shine; (*de couleur*) brightness.
briller *vi* to shine; **faire b.** (*meuble*) to polish (up).
brin *m* (*d'herbe*) blade; (*de corde, fil*) strand; (*de muguet*) spray.
brindille *f* twig.
brioche *f* brioche (*light sweet bun*).
brique *f* brick; (*de lait, jus de fruit*) carton.
briquet *m* (cigarette) lighter.
brise *f* breeze.
briser *vt*, **se briser** *vpr* to break.
britannique 1 *a* British. **2** *mf* Briton; **les Britanniques** the British.
broc [bro] *m* pitcher, jug.
brocanteur, -euse *mf* secondhand dealer (*in furniture etc*).
broche *f* (*pour rôtir*) spit; (*bijou*) brooch.
brochet *m* pike.
brochette *f* (*tige*) skewer; (*plat*) kebab.
brochure *f* brochure, booklet.
broder *vt* to embroider (**de** with).
broderie *f* embroidery.
bronchite *f* bronchitis.
bronzage *m* (sun)tan.
bronze *m* bronze.
bronzer 1 *vt* to tan; **se (faire) b.** to sunbathe, get a (sun)tan. **2** *vi* to get (sun)tanned.
brosse *f* brush; **b. à dents** toothbrush.
brosser *vt* to brush; **se b. les dents/cheveux** to brush one's teeth/

hair.
brouette *f* wheelbarrow.
brouhaha *m* hubbub.
brouillard *m* fog; **il y a du b.** it's foggy.
brouiller *vt* (*œufs*) to scramble; **b. la vue à qn** to blur s.o.'s vision.
brouiller (se) *vpr* (*temps*) to cloud over; (*vue*) to get blurred; (*amis*) to fall out (**avec** with).
brouillon *m* rough draft.
broussailles *fpl* bushes.
brousse *f* **la b.** the bush.
brouter *vti* to graze.
broyer *vt* to grind.
bruit *m* noise, sound; (*nouvelle*) rumour; **faire du b.** to make a noise.
brûlant, -ante *a* (*objet*, *soleil*) burning (hot).
brûlé *m* **odeur de b.** smell of burning.
brûler *vti* to burn; **se b.** to burn oneself; **b. un feu (rouge)** to go through the lights.
brûlure *f* burn.
brume *f* mist, haze.
brumeux, -euse *a* misty, hazy.
brun, brune 1 *a* brown; (*cheveux*) dark, brown; (*personne*) dark-haired. **2** *m* (*couleur*) brown. **3** *mf* dark-haired person.
brunir *vi* to turn brown; (*cheveux*) to go darker.
brushing [brœʃiŋ] *m* blow-dry.
brusque *a* (*manière*, *personne*) abrupt; (*subit*) sudden.
brusquement *adv* suddenly.
brusquerie *f* abruptness.
brut *a* (*pétrole*) crude; (*poids*) gross.
brutal, -e, -aux *a* (*violent*) brutal; (*enfant*) rough.
brutaliser *vt* to ill-treat.
brutalité *f* brutality.
brute *f* brute.
bruyamment *adv* noisily.
bruyant, -ante *a* noisy.
bu, bue *pp of* **boire**.
bûche *f* log.
bûcheron *m* lumberjack.
budget [bydʒɛ] *m* budget.
buée *f* mist.
buffet *m* (*armoire*) sideboard; (*table*, *repas*) buffet.
buisson *m* bush.

bulldozer [byldozœr] *m* bulldozer.
bulle *f* bubble; (*de bande dessinée*) balloon.
bulletin *m* (*météo*) report; (*scolaire*) report, *Am report card*; **b. de paie** pay slip *ou Am* stub; **b. de vote** ballot paper.
bureau, -x *m* (*table*) desk; (*lieu*) office; **b. de change** foreign exchange office, bureau de change; **b. de tabac** tobacconist's (shop), *Am* tobacco store.
burette *f* oilcan.
bus [bys] *m Fam* bus.
but [by(t)] *m* (*objectif*) aim, goal; *Football* goal.
buter *vi* **b. contre** to stumble over.
butoir *m* (*de porte*) stop(per).
butte *f* mound.
buvard *m* blotting paper.
buvette *f* refreshment bar.
buveur, -euse *mf* drinker.

C

ça *pron dém* (*abrév de* **cela**) (*pour désigner*) that; (*plus près*) this; (*sujet indéfini*) it, that; **ça m'amuse que...** it amuses me that...; **où/quand/comment/***etc* **ça?** where?/when?/how?/*etc*; **ça va (bien)?** how's it going?; **ça va!** fine!, OK!; **ça alors!** (*surprise, indignation*) never!, how about that!; **c'est ça** that's right.

cabane *f* hut, cabin; (*à outils*) shed; (*à lapins*) hutch.

cabine *f* (*de bateau*) cabin; (*téléphonique*) phone booth *ou* box; (*à la piscine*) cubicle; **c. (de pilotage)** cockpit; (*d'un grand avion*) flight deck; **c. d'essayage** fitting room.

cabinet *m* (*de médecin*) surgery, *Am* office; (*de ministre*) department; **cabinets** (*toilettes*) toilet, lavatory; **c. de toilette** (small) bathroom; **c. de travail** study.

câble *m* cable; (*cordage*) rope; **la télévision par c.** cable television.

cabosser *vt* to dent.

cabrer (se) *vpr* (*cheval*) to rear (up).

cacah(o)uète *f* peanut.

cacao *m* cocoa.

cachalot *m* sperm whale.

cache-cache *m inv* hide-and-seek.

cache-nez *m inv* scarf, muffler.

cacher *vt* to hide (**à** from); **je ne cache pas que...** I don't hide the fact that...

cacher (se) *vpr* to hide.

cachet *m* (*de la poste*) postmark; (*comprimé*) tablet.

cacheter *vt* to seal.

cachette *f* hiding place; **en c.** in secret.

cachot *m* dungeon.

cactus [kaktys] *m* cactus.

cadavre *m* corpse.

caddie® *m* (supermarket) trolley *ou Am* cart.

cadeau, -x *m* present, gift.

cadenas *m* padlock.

cadence *f* (*vitesse*) rate; **en c.** in time.

cadet, -ette 1 *a* (*de deux frères etc*) younger; (*de plus de deux*) youngest. **2** *mf* younger (child); youngest (child); (*sportif*) junior.

cadran *m* (*de téléphone*) dial; (*de montre*) face.

cadre *m* (*de photo, vélo etc*) frame; (*décor*) setting; (*sur un imprimé*) box; (*chef*) executive, manager.

cafard *m* **avoir le c.** to be in the dumps; **ça me donne le c.** it depresses me.

café *m* coffee; (*bar*) café; **c. au lait, c. crème** white coffee, coffee with milk; **c. noir, c. nature** black coffee; **c. soluble** *ou* **instantané** instant coffee; **tasse de c.** cup of black coffee.
cafétéria *f* cafeteria.
cafetière *f* coffeepot; (*électrique*) percolator.
cage *f* cage; (*d'escalier*) well; *Football* goal (area).
cageot *m* crate, box.
cagoule *f* (*de bandit, moine*) hood; (*d'enfant*) balaclava.
cahier *m* exercise book; **c. de brouillon** rough book, *Am* = scratch pad; **c. d'appel** register (*in school*).
cahot *m* jolt, bump.
cailler *vti* (*sang*) to clot; (*lait*) to curdle; **faire c.** (*lait*) to curdle.
caillot *m* (blood) clot.
caillou, -x *m* stone.
caisse *f* case, box; (*guichet*) cash desk; (*de supermarché*) checkout; (*tambour*) drum; **c. (enregistreuse)** till, cash register; **c. d'épargne** savings bank.
caissier, -ière *mf* cashier; (*de supermarché*) checkout assistant.
cake *m* fruit cake.
calcaire *a* (*eau*) hard.
calciné, -ée *a* charred.
calcul [kalkyl] *m* calculation; (*discipline*) arithmetic.
calculatrice *f* calculator.
calculer *vt* to calculate.
cale *f* (*pour maintenir*) wedge; (*de bateau*) hold.
caleçon *m* underpants; **c. de bain** bathing trunks.
calendrier *m* calendar.
caler 1 *vt* (*meuble etc*) to wedge; (*appuyer*) to prop (up). **2** *vti* (*moteur*) to stall.
calfeutrer *vt* to draughtproof; **se c. (chez soi)** to shut oneself away.
calibre *m* (*diamètre*) calibre; (*d'œuf*) grade.
califourchon (à) *adv* astride; **se mettre à c. sur** to straddle.
câlin, -ine 1 *a* affectionate. **2** *m* cuddle.
calmant *m* (*pour la nervosité*) sedative; (*la douleur*) painkiller; **sous calmants** under sedation; on painkillers.
calme 1 *a* calm. **2** *m* calm(ness); **du c.!** keep quiet!; (*pas de panique*) keep calm!; **dans le c.** (*travailler, étudier*) in peace and quiet.
calmer *vt* (*douleur*) to soothe; (*inquiétude*) to calm; **c. qn** to calm s.o. (down).
calmer (se) *vpr* to calm down.
calorie *f* calorie.
calque *m* (*dessin*) tracing; **(papier-)c.** tracing paper.

camarade *mf* friend; **c. de jeu** playmate.
camaraderie *f* friendship.
cambouis *m* (dirty) oil.
cambriolage *m* burglary.
cambrioler *vt* to burgle, *Am* burglarize.
cambrioleur, -euse *mf* burglar.
camelote *f* junk.
camembert *m* Camembert (cheese).
caméra *f* (TV *ou* film) camera.
caméscope *m* camcorder.
camion *m* lorry, *Am* truck.
camion-benne *m* (*pl* **camions-bennes**) dustcart, *Am* garbage truck.
camionnette *f* van.
camp *m* camp; **feu de c.** campfire; **lit de c.** camp bed; **dans mon c.** (*jeu*) on my side.
campagnard, -arde *mf* countryman, countrywoman.
campagne *f* country(side); (*électorale, militaire etc*) campaign; **à la c.** in the country.
camper *vi* to camp.
campeur, -euse *mf* camper.
camping *m* camping; (*terrain*) camp(ing) site.
camping-car *m* camper.
canadien, -ienne *a* & *mf* Canadian.
canal, -aux *m* (*pour bateaux*) canal.
canalisation *f* (*de gaz etc*) mains.
canaliser *vt* (*foule*) to channel.
canapé *m* (*siège*) sofa, couch, settee.
canard *m* duck.
canari *m* canary.
cancer *m* cancer.
cancéreux, -euse *mf* cancer patient.
candidat, -ate *mf* candidate; **être** *ou* **se porter c. à** to apply for.
candidature *f* application; (*aux élections*) candidacy; **poser sa c.** to apply (**à** for).
cane *f* (female) duck.
caneton *m* duckling.
canette *f* (*de bière*) (small) bottle.
caniche *m* poodle.
canif *m* penknife.
canine *f* canine (tooth).
caniveau, -x *m* gutter (*in street*).
canne *f* (walking) stick; **c. à pêche** fishing rod.

cannibale *mf* cannibal.
canoë *m* canoe; (*sport*) canoeing.
canon *m* (big) gun; (*de fusil etc*) barrel.
canot *m* boat; **c. de sauvetage** lifeboat; **c. pneumatique** rubber dinghy.
canoter *vi* to go boating.
cantine *f* canteen; **manger à la c.** (*écolier*) to have school dinners *ou Am* school lunch.
cantique *m* hymn.
cantonnier *m* road mender.
caoutchouc [kautʃu] *m* rubber; **balle**/*etc* **en c.** rubber ball/*etc*.
CAP [seɑpe] *m abrév* (*certificat d'aptitude professionnelle*) technical and vocational diploma.
cap *m* (*pointe de terre*) cape; (*direction*) course; **mettre le c. sur** to steer a course for.
capable *a* capable, able; **c. de faire** able to do, capable of doing.
capacité *f* ability; (*contenance*) capacity.
cape *f* cape; (*grande*) cloak.
capitaine *m* captain.
capital *m* (*argent*) capital.
capitale *f* (*lettre*, *ville*) capital.
capitulation *f* surrender.
capituler *vi* to surrender.
capot *m* (*de véhicule*) bonnet, *Am* hood.
capote *f* (*de véhicule*) hood, *Am* (convertible) top.
caprice *m* (passing) whim.
capricieux, -euse *a* temperamental.
capsule *f* (*spatiale*) capsule; (*de bouteille*) cap.
capter *vt* (*signal*, *radio*) to pick up.
captiver *vt* to fascinate.
capture *f* capture.
capturer *vt* to capture.
capuche *f* hood.
capuchon *m* hood; (*de stylo*) cap.
car 1 *conj* because, for. **2** *m* bus, coach; **c. de police** police van.
carabine *f* rifle; **c. à air comprimé** airgun.
caractère[1] *m* (*lettre*) character; **petits caractères** small letters; **caractères d'imprimerie** capitals.
caractere[2] *m* (*tempérament*, *nature*) character; **avoir bon c.** to be good-natured.
caractéristique *a* & *f* characteristic.
carafe *f* decanter.

carambolage *m* pileup (*of vehicles*).
caramel *m* caramel; (*bonbon dur*) toffee, *Am* taffy.
carapace *f* shell.
caravane *f* (*pour camper*) caravan, *Am* trailer.
carbone *m* **(papier) c.** carbon (paper).
carboniser *vt* to burn (to ashes).
carburant *m* fuel.
carburateur *m* carburettor, *Am* carburetor.
carcasse *f* carcass; (*d'immeuble etc*) frame, shell.
cardiaque *a* **être c.** to have a weak heart; **crise/problème c.** heart attack/trouble.
cardinal, -aux 1 *a* (*nombre, point*) cardinal. **2** *m* cardinal.
caressant, -ante *a* loving.
caresse *f* caress.
caresser *vt* to stroke.
cargaison *f* cargo.
cargo *m* cargo boat.
carie *f* **la c. (dentaire)** tooth decay; **une c.** a cavity.
cariée *af* **dent c.** decayed *ou* bad tooth.
carillon *m* (*cloches*) chimes; (*horloge*) chiming clock.
carlingue *f* (*d'avion*) cabin.
carnaval, *pl* **-als** *m* carnival.
carnet *m* notebook; (*de timbres, chèques, adresses*) book; **c. de notes** school report, *Am* report card.
carotte *f* carrot.
carpe *f* carp.
carpette *f* rug.
carré, -ée *a* & *m* square.
carreau, -x *m* (*vitre*) (window) pane; (*pavé*) tile; *Cartes* (*couleur*) diamonds; **à carreaux** (*nappe etc*) check.
carrefour *m* crossroads.
carrelage *m* (*sol*) tiled floor.
carrément *adv* (*dire etc*) bluntly; (*complètement*) downright.
carrière *f* (*terrain*) quarry; (*métier*) career.
carrosse *m* (horse-drawn) carriage.
carrosserie *f* body(work).
carrure *f* build.
cartable *m* satchel.
carte *f* card; (*routière*) map; (*menu*) menu; **c. (postale)** (post)card; **c. à jouer** playing card; **jouer aux cartes** to play cards; **c. de visite** visiting card; (*professionnelle*) business card; **c. de crédit** credit card; **c. des vins** wine list; **c. grise** vehicle registration document.

carton *m* cardboard; (*boîte*) cardboard box.
cartonné *a* **livre c.** hardback.
cartouche *f* cartridge; (*de cigarettes*) carton.
cas *m* case; **en tout c.** in any case; **en aucun c.** on no account; **en c. de besoin** if need be; **en c. d'accident** in the event of an accident; **en c. d'urgence** in an emergency; **au c. où elle tomberait** if she should fall; **pour le c. où il pleuvrait** in case it rains.
cascade *f* waterfall; (*de cinéma*) stunt.
cascadeur, -euse *mf* stunt man, stunt woman.
case *f* pigeonhole; (*de tiroir*) compartment; (*d'échiquier etc*) square; (*de formulaire*) box; (*hutte*) hut, cabin.
caserne *f* barracks; **c. de pompiers** fire station.
casier *m* pigeonhole; (*fermant à clef*) locker; **c. à bouteilles/à disques** bottle/record rack; **c. judiciaire** criminal record.
casino *m* casino.
casque *m* helmet; (*de coiffeur*) (hair) dryer; **c. (à écouteurs)** headphones.
casqué, -ée *a* helmeted.
casquette *f* (*coiffure*) cap.
casse-croûte *m inv* snack.
casse-noisettes *m inv*, **casse-noix** *m inv* nut-cracker(s).
casse-pieds *mf inv* (*personne*) *Fam* pain in the neck.
casser 1 *vt* to break; (*noix*) to crack; **elle me casse les pieds** *Fam* she's getting on my nerves. **2** *vi*, **se casser** *vpr* to break; **se c. la figure** (*tomber*) *Fam* to come a cropper, *Am* take a spill.
casserole *f* (sauce)pan.
cassette *f* (*audio*) cassette *f*; (*vidéo*) video, cassette; **sur c.** (*film*) on video.
cassis *m* [kasis] (*fruit*) blackcurrant; [kasi] (*obstacle*) dip (*across road*).
castor *m* beaver.
catalogue *m* catalogue, *Am* catalog.
catastrophe *f* disaster; **atterrir en c.** to make an emergency landing.
catastrophique *a* disastrous.
catch *m* (all-in) wrestling.
catcheur, -euse *mf* wrestler.
catéchisme [kateʃism] *m* catechism.
catégorie *f* category.
cathédrale *f* cathedral.
catholique *a* & *mf* Catholic.
cauchemar *m* nightmare.

cause *f* cause; **à c. de** because of, on account of.
causer 1 *vt* (*provoquer*) to cause. **2** *vi* (*bavarder*) to chat (**de** about).
cavalier, -ière *mf* rider; (*pour danser*) partner.
cave *f* cellar.
caveau, -x *m* (burial) vault.
caverne *f* cave.
cavité *f* hollow.
CCP [sesepe] *m abrév* (*compte chèque postal*) PO Giro account, *Am* Post Office checking account.
ce[1] (c' *before e and é*) *pron dém* it, that; **c'est toi/bon/***etc* it's *ou* that's you/good/*etc*; **c'est mon médecin** he's my doctor; **ce sont eux qui...** they are the ones who...; **c'est à elle de jouer** it's her turn to play; **est-ce que tu viens?** are you coming? ▮ **ce que, ce qui** what; **je sais ce qui est bon/ce que tu veux** I know what is good/what you want; **ce que c'est beau!** how beautiful it is!, it's so beautiful!
ce[2]**, cette,** *pl* **ces** (**ce** *becomes* **cet** *before a vowel or mute h*) *a dém* this, that, *pl* these, those; (+ *-ci*) this, *pl* these; (+ *-là*) that, *pl* those; **cet homme** this *ou* that man; **cet homme-ci** this man; **cet homme-là** that man.
ceci *pron dém* this.
céder 1 *vt* to give up (**à** to). **2** *vi* (*personne*) to give in (**à** to); (*branche, chaise etc*) to give way.
cédille *f Grammaire* cedilla.
CEE [seøø] *f abrév* (*Communauté économique européenne*) EEC.
ceinture *f* belt; (*taille*) waist; **c. de sécurité** seatbelt; **c. de sauvetage** lifebelt, *Am* life preserver.
cela *pron dém* (*pour désigner*) that; (*sujet indéfini*) it, that; **c. m'attriste que...** it saddens me that...; **quand/comment/***etc* **c.?** when?/how?/*etc*.
célèbre *a* famous.
célébrer *vt* to celebrate.
célébrité *f* fame.
céleri *m* (*en branches*) celery.
célibataire 1 *a* single, unmarried. **2** *m* bachelor. **3** *f* unmarried woman.
cellophane® *f* cellophane®.
cellule *f* cell.
celui, celle, *pl* **ceux, celles** *pron dém* the one, *pl* those, the ones; **c. de Jean** John's (one); **ceux de Jean** John's (ones). ▮ (+ *-ci*) this one, *pl* these (*ones*); (*dont on vient de parler*) the latter; (+ *-là*) that one, *pl* those (ones); the former; **ceux-ci sont gros** these (ones)

are big.

cendre *f* ash.

cendrier *m* ashtray.

cent [sɑ̃] ([sɑ̃t] *pl* [sɑ̃z] *before vowel and mute h except* **un** *and* **onze**) *a* & *m* hundred; **c. pages** a *ou* one hundred pages; **cinq pour c.** five per cent.

centaine *f* **une c.** a hundred (or so); **des centaines de** hundreds of.

centième *a* & *mf* hundredth.

centigrade *a* centigrade.

centime *m* centime.

centimètre *m* centimetre; (*ruban*) tape measure.

central, -e, -aux 1 *a* central. **2** *m* **c. (téléphonique)** (telephone) exchange.

centrale *f* (*usine*) power station, *Am* power plant.

centre *m* centre; **c. commercial** shopping centre *ou* mall.

centre-ville *m inv* city *ou* town centre, *Am* downtown area.

cependant *conj* however, yet.

céramique *f* (*matière*) ceramic; **de c.** ceramic.

cerceau, -x *m* hoop.

cercle *m* circle.

cercueil *m* coffin.

céréale *f* cereal.

cérémonie *f* ceremony.

cerf *m* deer *inv*.

cerf-volant *m* (*pl* **cerfs-volants**) kite.

cerise *f* cherry.

cerisier *m* cherry tree.

cerner *vt* to surround; **avoir les yeux cernés** to have rings under one's eyes.

certain[1], -aine *a* (*sûr*) certain, sure; **c'est c. que tu réussiras** you're certain *ou* sure to succeed; **je suis c. de réussir** I'm certain *ou* sure I'll succeed; **être c. de qch** to be certain *ou* sure of sth.

certain[2], -aine *a* (*difficile à fixer*) certain; **un c. temps** a certain (amount of) time.

certainement *adv* certainly.

certains *pron pl* some (people).

certificat *m* certificate.

certifier *vt* to certify.

certitude *f* certainty; **avoir la c. que** to be certain that.

cerveau, -x *m* brain; **rhume de c.** head cold.

cervelle *f* brain; (*plat*) brains.

ces [se] *voir* **ce[2]**.

CES [seəεs] *m abrév* (*collège d'enseignement secondaire*) comprehensive school, *Am* high school.
cesse *f* **sans c.** constantly.
cesser *vti* to stop; **faire c.** to put a stop to; **il ne cesse (pas) de parler** he doesn't stop talking.
cessez-le-feu *m inv* ceasefire.
c'est-à-dire *conj* that is (to say).
cet, cette [sεt] *voir* **ce²**.
ceux *voir* **celui**.
chacun, -une *pron* each (one), every one; (*tout le monde*) everyone.
chagrin *m* grief; **avoir du c.** to be very upset.
chahut *m* racket.
chahuter *vi* to create a racket.
chahuteur, -euse *mf* rowdy.
chaîne *f* chain; (*de télévision*) channel; (*de montagnes*) chain, range; **travail à la c.** production-line work; **c. hi-fi** hi-fi system.
chaînette *f* (small) chain.
chair *f* flesh; **(couleur) c.** flesh-coloured; **en c. et en os** in the flesh; **la c. de poule** goose pimples *or* bumps; **c. à saucisses** sausage meat.
chaise *f* chair; **c. longue** deckchair; **c. haute** high-chair.
châle *m* shawl.
chalet *m* chalet.
chaleur *f* heat; (*douce*) warmth.
chaleureux, -euse *a* warm.
chaloupe *f* (*bateau*) launch.
chalumeau, -x *m* blowlamp, *Am* blowtorch.
chalutier *m* trawler.
chamailler (se) *vpr* to squabble.
chambouler *vt Fam* to make topsy-turvy.
chambre *f* (bed)room; **c. à coucher** bedroom; (*mobilier*) bedroom suite *or* set; **c. à air** (*de pneu*) inner tube; **c. de commerce** chamber of commerce; **c. d'ami** spare room; **garder la c.** to stay indoors.
chameau, -x *m* camel.
chamois *m* **peau de c.** wash leather, shammy, chamois.
champ *m* field; **c. de bataille** battlefield; **c. de courses** racecourse, *Am* racetrack.
champagne *m* champagne.
champignon *m* mushroom.
champion, -onne *mf* champion.
championnat *m* championship.
chance *f* luck; (*probabilité, occasion*) chance; **avoir de la c.** to be

lucky; **c'est une c. que** it's lucky that.
chanceler *vi* to stagger.
chandail *m* (thick) sweater.
chandelier *m* candlestick.
chandelle *f* candle; **en c.** (*tir*) straight into the air.
change *m* (*de devises*) exchange.
changement *m* change.
changer *vti* to change; **c. qn en** to change s.o. into; **ça la changera de ne pas travailler** it'll be a change for her not to be working; **c. de train/voiture/***etc* to change trains/one's car/*etc*; **c. de vitesse/sujet** to change gear/change the subject.
changer (se) *vpr* to change (one's clothes).
chanson *f* song.
chant *m* singing; (*chanson*) song; **c. de Noël** Christmas carol.
chantage *m* blackmail.
chanter 1 *vi* to sing; (*coq*) to crow; **si ça te chante** *Fam* if you feel like it. **2** *vt* to sing.
chanteur, -euse *mf* singer.
chantier *m* (building) site; **c. naval** shipyard, dockyard.
chantonner *vti* to hum.
chaos [kao] *m* chaos.
chapeau, -x *m* hat.
chapelet *m* rosary; **un c. de** (*saucisses etc*) a string of.
chapelle *f* chapel.
chapelure *f* breadcrumbs.
chapiteau, -x *m* (*de cirque*) big top; (*pour expositions etc*) marquee, tent.
chapitre *m* chapter.
chaque *a* each, every.
char *m* (*romain*) chariot; (*de carnaval*) float; **c. (d'assaut)** tank.
charade *f* (*énigme*) riddle.
charbon *m* coal; **c. de bois** charcoal.
charcuterie *f* pork butcher's shop; (*aliments*) cooked pork meats.
charcutier, -ière *mf* pork butcher.
chardon *m* thistle.
charge *f* (*poids*) load; (*fardeau*) burden; **à la c. de qn** (*personne*) dependent on s.o.; (*frais*) payable by s.o.; **prendre en c.** to take charge of.
chargé, -ée *a* (*véhicule, arme etc*) loaded; (*journée*) busy.
chargement *m* loading; (*objet*) load.
charger *vt* to load; (*soldats, batterie*) to charge; **se c. de** (*enfant, travail etc*) to take charge of; **c. qn de** (*travail etc*) to entrust s.o. with;

c. qn de faire to instruct s.o. to do.
chariot *m* (*à bagages etc*) trolley, *Am* cart.
charité *f* (*secours*) charity.
charmant, -ante *a* charming.
charme *m* charm; (*magie*) spell.
charmer *vt* to charm.
charnière *f* hinge
charpente *f* frame(work).
charpentier *m* carpenter.
charrette *f* cart.
charrier *vt* (*transporter*) to cart; (*rivière*) to carry along (*sand etc*).
charrue *f* plough, *Am* plow.
charter [ʃartɛr] *m* charter (flight).
chasse[1] *f* hunting, hunt; **c. à courre** hunting; **avion de c.** fighter plane; **faire la c. à** to hunt for.
chasse[2] *f* **c. d'eau** toilet flush; **tirer la c.** to flush the toilet.
chasse-neige *m inv* snowplough, *Am* snowplow.
chasser 1 *vt* (*animal*) to hunt; (*faire partir*) to chase (*s.o.*, *smell etc*) away; (*mouche*) to brush away. **2** *vi* to hunt.
chasseur, -euse *mf* hunter.
châssis *m* frame; (*d'automobile*) chassis.
chat *m* cat; **pas un c.** not a soul; **c. perché** (*jeu*) tag.
châtaigne *f* chestnut.
châtaignier *m* chestnut tree.
châtain *a inv* (chestnut) brown.
château, -x *m* castle; (*palais*) palace; **c. fort** fortified castle; **c. d'eau** water tower.
châtiment *m* punishment.
chaton *m* kitten.
chatouiller *vt* to tickle.
chatouilleux, -euse *a* ticklish.
chatte *f* (she-)cat.
chatterton [ʃatɛrtɔn] *m* (adhesive) insulating tape.
chaud, chaude 1 *a* hot; (*doux*) warm. **2** *m* **avoir c.** to be hot; to be warm; **il fait c.** it's hot; it's warm; **être au c.** to be in the warm.
chaudement *adv* warmly.
chaudière *f* boiler.
chauffage *m* heating.
chauffant, -ante *a* (*couverture*) electric; **plaque chauffante** hot plate.
chauffé, -ée *a* (*piscine etc*) heated.
chauffe-eau *m inv* water heater.

chauffer 1 *vt* to heat (up). **2** *vi* to heat (up); (*moteur*) to overheat.
chauffeur *m* driver; (*employé*) chauffeur.
chaume *m* (*pour toiture*) thatch; **toit de c.** thatched roof.
chaumière *f* thatched cottage.
chaussée *f* road(way).
chausse-pied *m* shoehorn.
chausser *vt* **c. qn** to put shoes on (to) s.o.; **se c.** to put on one's shoes; **c. du 40** to take a size 40 shoe.
chaussette *f* sock.
chausson *m* slipper; (*de danse*) shoe.
chaussure *f* shoe.
chauve *a* & *mf* bald (person).
chauve-souris *f* (*pl* **chauves-souris**) (*animal*) bat.
chaux *f* lime.
chavirer *vti* to capsize.
chef *m* leader, head; **c. d'entreprise** company head; **c. de gare** stationmaster; **c. d'orchestre** conductor; **en c.** (*commandant, rédacteur*) in chief.
chef-d'œuvre [ʃɛdœvr] *m* (*pl* **chefs-d'œuvre**) masterpiece.
chef-lieu *m* (*pl* **chefs-lieux**) chief town (*of a département*).
chemin *m* road, path; (*trajet, direction*) way; **beaucoup de c. à faire** a long way to go; **se mettre en c.** to set out.
chemin de fer *m* railway, *Am* railroad.
cheminée *f* fireplace; (*encadrement*) mantelpiece; (*sur le toit*) chimney; (*de navire*) funnel.
cheminot *m* railway *ou Am* railroad employee.
chemise *f* shirt; (*cartonnée*) folder; **c. de nuit** nightdress.
chemisette *f* short-sleeved shirt.
chemisier *m* blouse.
chêne *m* oak.
chenil *m* kennels, *Am* kennel.
chenille *f* caterpillar.
chèque *m* cheque, *Am* check; **c. de voyage** traveller's cheque, *Am* traveler's check.
chèque-repas *m* (*pl* **chèques-repas**) luncheon voucher, *Am* meal ticket.
chéquier *m* cheque book, *Am* checkbook.
cher, chère *a* (*aimé*) dear (**à** to); (*coûteux*) expensive; **payer c.** (*objet*) to pay a lot for; (*erreur etc*) to pay dearly for.
chercher *vt* to look for; (*dans un dictionnaire*) to look up; **aller c.** to (go and) fetch *ou* get; **c. à faire** to attempt to do.
chercheur, -euse *mf* research worker.

chéri, -ie 1 *a* dearly loved. **2** *mf* darling.
chétif, -ive *a* puny.
cheval, -aux *m* horse; **à c.** on horseback; **faire du c.** to go horse riding *ou Am* horseback riding; **chevaux de bois** merry-go-round.
chevalier *m* knight.
chevaline *af* **boucherie c.** horse butcher's (shop).
chevelure *f* (head of) hair.
chevet *m* **table/livre de c.** bedside table/book; **au c. de** at the bedside of.
cheveu, -x *m* **un c.** a hair; **cheveux** hair; **tiré par les cheveux** far-fetched.
cheville *f* ankle; (*pour vis*) (wall) plug.
chèvre *f* goat.
chevreau, -x *m* (*petit de la chèvre*) kid.
chez *prép* **c. qn** at s.o.'s house, flat *etc*; **il est c. Jean/c. l'épicier** he's at John's (place)/at the grocer's, **il va c. Jean/c. l'épicier** he's going to John's (place)/to the grocer's; **c. moi, c. nous** at home; **je vais c. moi** I'm going home; **une habitude c. elle** a habit with her; **c. Mme Dupont** (*adresse*) care of Mme Dupont.
chic 1 *a inv* smart; (*gentil*) *Fam* nice. **2** *int* **c. (alors)!** great! **3** *m* style.
chicorée *f* (*à café*) chicory; (*pour salade*) endive.
chien *m* dog; **un mal de c.** an awful lot of trouble; **temps de c.** rotten *ou* filthy weather.
chien-loup *m* (*pl* **chiens-loups**) wolfhound.
chienne *f* dog, bitch.
chiffon *m* rag; **c. (à poussière)** duster.
chiffonner *vt* to crumple.
chiffre *m* figure, number; (*romain, arabe*) numeral; **c. d'affaires** (sales) turnover.
chimie *f* chemistry.
chimique *a* chemical.
chimpanzé *m* chimpanzee.
chinois, -oise 1 *a* Chinese. **2** *mf* Chinese man *ou* woman, Chinese *inv*; **les C.** the Chinese. **3** *m* (*langue*) Chinese.
chiot *m* pup(py).
chips [ʃips] *mpl* (potato) crisps, *Am* chips.
chirurgical, -e, -aux *a* surgical.
chirurgie *f* surgery.
chirurgien *m* surgeon.
choc *m* (*d'objets, émotion*) shock.
chocolat *m* chocolate; **c. à croquer** plain *ou Am* bittersweet choco-

late; **c. au lait** milk chocolate.
chocolaté, -ée *a* chocolate-flavoured.
chœur [kœr] *m* (*chanteurs*, *nef*) choir; **en c.** (all) together.
choisir *vt* to choose, pick.
choix *m* choice; (*assortiment*) selection.
cholestérol [kɔl-] *m* cholesterol.
chômage *m* unemployment; **au c.** unemployed.
chômer *vi* to be unemployed.
chômeur, -euse *mf* unemployed person; **les chômeurs** the unemployed.
choquant, -ante *a* shocking.
choquer *vt* to shock.
chorale [kɔral] *f* choral society.
chose *f* thing; **monsieur C.** Mr What's-his-name.
chou, -x *m* cabbage; **choux de Bruxelles** Brussels sprouts.
choucroute *f* sauerkraut.
chouette 1 *f* owl. **2** *a Fam* super, great.
chou-fleur *m* (*pl* **choux-fleurs**) cauliflower.
choyer *vt* to pamper.
chrétien, -ienne *a* & *mf* Christian.
chrome *m* chrome.
chromé, -ée *a* chrome-plated.
chronique *f* (*à la radio*) report; (*dans le journal*) column.
chronomètre *m* stopwatch.
chronométrer *vt* to time.
chrysanthème *m* chrysanthemum.
chuchotement *m* whisper(ing).
chuchoter *vti* to whisper.
chut! [ʃyt] *int* sh!, shush!
chute *f* fall; **c. d'eau** waterfall; **c. de neige** snowfall; **c. de pluie** rainfall.
ci 1 *adv* **par-ci par-là** here and there. **2** *pron dém* **comme ci comme ça** so so.
cible *f* target.
cicatrice *f* scar.
cicatrisation *f* healing (up).
cicatriser *vt*, **se cicatriser** *vpr* to heal up (*leaving a scar*).
cidre *m* cider.
Cie *abrév* (*compagnie*) Co.
ciel *m* (*pl* **ciels**) sky; (*pl* **cieux**) (*paradis*) heaven.
cierge *m* candle.
cigale *f* (*insecte*) cicada.

cigare *m* cigar.
cigarette *f* cigarette.
cigogne *f* stork.
cil [sil] *m* (eye)lash.
cime *f* (*d'un arbre*) top; (*d'une montagne*) peak.
ciment *m* cement.
cimenter *vt* to cement.
cimetière *m* cemetery.
ciné *m Fam* cinema.
ciné-club [sineklœb] *m* film society.
cinéma *m* cinema; **faire du c.** to make films.
cinglé, -ée *a Fam* crazy.
cinq 1 *m* [sɛ̃k] five. **2** *a* ([sɛ̃] *before consonant*) five.
cinquantaine *f* about fifty.
cinquante *a* & *m* fifty.
cinquantième *a* & *mf* fiftieth.
cinquième *a* & *mf* fifth.
cintre *m* coathanger.
cirage *m* (shoe) polish.
circonférence *f* circumference.
circonflexe *a Grammaire* circumflex.
circonstance *f* circumstance; **pour la c.** for this occasion.
circonstanciel, -ielle *a Grammaire* adverbial.
circuit *m* (*électrique*, *sportif etc*) circuit; (*voyage*) tour.
circulaire 1 *a* circular. **2** *f* (*lettre*) circular.
circulation *f* circulation; (*automobile*) traffic.
circuler *vi* to circulate; (*véhicule*, *train*) to travel; (*passant*) to walk about; (*rumeur*) to go round, **faire c.** (*piétons etc*) to move on.
cire *f* wax.
cirer *vt* to polish.
cirque *m* circus.
ciseau, -x *m* chisel; **(une paire de) ciseaux** (a pair of) scissors.
citadin, -ine *mf* city dweller.
citation *f* quotation.
cité *f* city; **c. universitaire** (students') halls of residence, *Am* university dormitory complex.
citer *vt* to quote.
citerne *f* (*réservoir*) tank.
citoyen, -enne *mf* citizen.
citron *m* lemon; **c. pressé** (fresh) lemon juice.
citronnade *f* lemon drink.
citrouille *f* pumpkin.

civière *f* stretcher.
civil, -e [sivil] **1** *a* civil; (*non militaire*) civilian; **année civile** calendar year. **2** *m* civilian; **en c.** (*policier*) in plain clothes.
civilisation *f* civilization.
civilisé, -ée *a* civilized.
civique *a* civic; **instruction c.** civics.
clair, -e 1 *a* (*distinct, limpide, évident*) clear; (*éclairé*) light; (*pâle*) light(-coloured); **bleu/vert c.** light blue/green. **2** *adv* (*voir*) clearly. **3** *m* **c. de lune** moonlight.
clairement *adv* clearly.
clairière *f* clearing.
clairon *m* bugle.
clairsemé, -ée *a* sparse.
clandestin, -ine *a* (*journal, mouvement*) underground; **passager c.** stowaway.
claque *f* smack, slap.
claquement *m* (*de porte*) slam(ming).
claquer 1 *vt* (*porte*) to slam, bang; **se c. un muscle** to tear a muscle. **2** *vi* (*porte*) to slam, bang; (*coup de feu*) to ring out; **c. des mains** to clap one's hands; **elle claque des dents** her teeth are chattering.
clarinette *f* clarinet.
clarté *f* light; (*précision*) clarity.
classe *f* class; **aller en c.** to go to school.
classement *m* classification; filing; grading; (*rang*) place; (*en sport*) placing.
classer *vt* to classify; (*papiers*) to file; (*candidats*) to grade; **se c. premier** to come first.
classeur *m* (*meuble*) filing cabinet; (*portefeuille*) (loose leaf) file.
classique *a* classical.
clavicule *f* collarbone.
clavier *m* keyboard.
clé, clef *f* key; (*outil*) spanner, wrench; **fermer à c.** to lock; **sous c.** under lock and key; **c. de contact,** ignition key.
clémentine *f* clementine.
clergé *m* clergy.
cliché *m* (*de photo*) negative.
client, -ente *mf* customer; (*d'un avocat*) client; (*d'un médecin*) patient; (*d'hôtel*) guest.
clientèle *f* customers; (*d'un avocat, d'un médecin*) practice.
cligner *vi* **c. des yeux** to blink; (*fermer à demi*) to screw up one's eyes; **c. de l'œil** to wink.
clignotant *m* indicator, *Am* directional signal.

clignoter *vi* to blink; (*lumière*) to flicker.
climat *m* climate.
climatisation *f* air-conditioning.
climatiser *vt* to air-condition.
clin d'œil *m* wink; **en un c. d'œil** in no time (at all).
clinique *f* (private) clinic.
clochard, -arde *mf* down-and-out, tramp.
cloche *f* bell.
cloche-pied (à) *adv* **sauter à c.-pied** to hop on one foot.
clocher *m* bell tower; (*en pointe*) steeple.
clochette *f* (small) bell.
cloison *f* partition.
clope *m ou f Fam* fag, smoke, cigarette.
clopin-clopant *adv* **aller c.-clopant** to hobble.
cloque *f* blister.
clos, close *a* closed.
clôture *f* (*barrière*) fence.
clôturer *vt* to enclose.
clou *m* nail; **les clous** (*passage*) pedestrian crossing, *Am* crosswalk.
clouer *vt* to nail; **cloué au lit** confined to bed.
clouté, ée *a* (*pneus*) studded; **passage c.** pedestrian crossing, *Am* crosswalk.
clown [klun] *m* clown.
club [klœb] *m* (*association*) club.
cm *abrév* (*centimètre*) cm.
coaguler *vti*, **se coaguler** *vpr* to clot.
coalition *f* coalition.
cobaye *m* guinea pig.
coca *m* (*Coca-Cola*®) coke.
cocaïne *f* cocain.
coccinelle *f* ladybird, *Am* ladybug
cocher[1] *vt* to tick (off), *Am* to check (off).
cocher[2] *m* coachman
cochon, -onne 1 *m* pig; **c. d'Inde** guinea pig. **2** *mf* (*personne sale*) (dirty) pig.
cocorico *int & m* cock-a-doodle-doo.
cocotier *m* coconut palm.
cocotte *f* casserole; **c. minute**® pressure cooker.
code *m* code; **codes, phares c.** dipped headlights, *Am* low beams; **C. de la route** Highway Code, *Am* traffic regulations.
cœur *m* heart; (*couleur*) *Cartes* hearts; **au c. de** (*ville*, *hiver etc*) in the middle *ou* heart of; **par c.** (off) by heart; **avoir mal au c.** to feel

sick; **avoir le c. gros** to have a heavy heart; **avoir bon c.** to be kind-hearted; **de bon c.** (*offrir*) willingly; (*rire*) heartily.
coffre *m* chest; (*de banque*) safe; (*de voiture*) boot, *Am* trunk.
coffre-fort *m* (*pl* **coffres-forts**) safe.
coffret *m* (*à bijoux etc*) box.
cogner *vti* to knock, bang; **se c. la tête**/*etc* to knock *ou* bang one's head/*etc*; **se c. à qch** to knock *ou* bang into sth.
cohue *f* crowd.
coiffer *vt* **c. qn** to do s.o.'s hair; **se c.** to do one's hair.
coiffeur, -euse *mf* hairdresser.
coiffure *f* hat; (*arrangement*) hairstyle.
coin *m* (*angle*) corner; (*endroit*) spot; **du c.** (*magasin etc*) local; **dans le c.** in the (local) area.
coincé, -ée *a* stuck.
coincer *vt* (*mécanisme etc*) to jam; **se c.** to get stuck *ou* jammed; **se c. le doigt** to get one's finger stuck.
coïncidence *f* coincidence.
coing *m* quince.
col *m* collar; (*de montagne*) pass; **c. roulé** polo neck, *Am* turtleneck.
colère *f* anger; **une c.** a fit of anger; **en c.** angry (**contre** with); **se mettre en c.** to lose one's temper.
coléreux, -euse *a* quick-tempered.
colique *f* diarrh(o)ea.
colis *m* parcel.
collaboration *f* collaboration.
collaborer *vi* collaborate (**à** on).
collant, -ante 1 *a* (*papier*) sticky; (*vêtement*) skin-tight. **2** *m* (pair of) tights; (*de danse*) leotard.
colle *f* glue; (*blanche*) paste.
collecte *f* (*quête*) collection.
collectif, -ive *a* collective; **billet c.** group ticket.
collection *f* collection.
collectionner *vt* to collect.
collectionneur, -euse *mf* collector.
collège *m* (secondary) school, *Am* (high) school.
collégien *m* schoolboy.
collégienne *f* schoolgirl.
collègue *mf* colleague.
coller *vt* to stick; (*à la colle transparente*) to glue; (*à la colle blanche*) to paste; (*affiche*) to stick up; (*papier peint*) to hang; (*mettre*) *Fam* to stick; **c. contre** (*nez, oreille etc*) to press against.
collier *m* (*bijou*) necklace; (*de chien*) collar.

colline *f* hill.

collision *f* collision; **entrer en c. avec** to collide with.

colombe *f* dove.

colonel *m* colonel.

colonie *f* colony; **c. de vacances** (children's) holiday camp *ou Am* vacation *ou* summer camp.

colonne *f* column; **c. vertébrale** spine.

coloré, -ée *a* colourful; (*verre*, *liquide*) coloured.

colorer *vt* to colour.

coloriage *m* **album de coloriages** colouring book.

colorier *vt* (*dessin*) to colour (in).

coloris *m* (*nuance*) shade.

colosse *m* giant.

coma *m* coma; **dans le c.** in a coma.

combat *m* fight.

combatif, -ive *a* eager to fight; (*instinct*, *esprit*) fighting.

combattant *m* fighter, brawler.

combattre* *vti* to fight.

combien 1 *adv* (*quantité*) how much; (*nombre*) how many; **c. de** (*temps*, *argent etc*) how much; (*gens*, *livres etc*) how many. ▮ (*à quel point*) how; **c. y a-t-il d'ici à...?** how far is it to...? **2** *m inv* **le c. sommes-nous?** *Fam* what date is it?; **tous les c.?** *Fam* how often?

combinaison *f* combination; (*vêtement de femme*) slip; (*de mécanicien*) boiler suit, *Am* overalls; **c. de vol/plongée/ski** flying/diving/ski suit; **c. spatiale** spacesuit.

combiné *m* (*de téléphone*) receiver.

combiner *vt* (*assembler*) to combine.

comble 1 *m* **le c. de** (*la joie etc*) the height of; **c'est un** *ou* **le c.!** that's the limit! **2** *a* (*bondé*) packed.

combler *vt* (*trou etc*) to fill; **c. son retard** to make up lost time.

combustible *m* fuel.

comédie *f* comedy; **c. musicale** musical; **jouer la c.** to put on an act, pretend.

comédien *m* actor.

comédienne *f* actress.

comestible *a* edible.

comique *a* (*amusant*) funny; (*acteur etc*) comic.

comité *m* committee.

commandant *m* (*d'un navire*) captain; **c. de bord** (*d'un avion*) captain.

commande *f* (*achat*) order; **sur c.** to order; **les commandes** (*d'un avion etc*) the controls.

commandement *m* (*autorité*) command.
commander 1 *vt* to command; (*acheter*) to order. **2** *vi* **c. à qn de faire** to command s.o. to do.
comme 1 *adv & conj* like; **c. moi** like me; **c. cela** like that; **qu'as-tu c. diplômes?** what do you have in the way of certificates? ▮ as; **blanc c. neige** (as) white as snow; **c. si** as if; **c. pour faire** as if to do; **c. par hasard** as if by chance. **2** *adv* (*exclamatif*) **regarde c. il pleut!** look how it's raining!; **c. c'est petit!** isn't it small! **3** *conj* (*temps, cause*) as; **c. elle entrait** as she was coming in.
commencement *m* beginning, start.
commencer *vti* to begin, start (**à faire** to do, doing; **par** with; **par faire** by doing); **pour c.** to begin with.
comment *adv* how; **c. le sais-tu?** how do you know?; **c.?** (*répétition, surprise*) what?; **c. est-il?** what is he like?; **c. faire?** what's to be done?; **c. t'appelles-tu?** what's your name?; **c. allez-vous?** how are you?
commerçant, -ante *mf* shopkeeper; **rue commerçante** shopping street.
commerce *m* trade, commerce; (*magasin*) shop, business; **dans le c.** (*objet*) (on sale) in the shops.
commercial, -e, -aux *a* commercial.
commettre* *vt* (*délit etc*) to commit; (*erreur*) to make.
commissaire *m* **c. (de police)** police superintendent *ou Am* chief.
commissariat *m* **c. (de police)** (central) police station.
commission *f* (*course*) errand; (*pourcentage*) commission (**sur** on); **faire les commissions** to do the shopping.
commode 1 *a* (*pratique*) handy. **2** *f* chest of drawers, *Am* dresser.
commun, -une *a* (*collectif, habituel etc*) common; (*frais, cuisine*) shared; **ami c.** mutual friend; **en c.** in common; **avoir** *ou* **mettre en c.** to share.
commune *f* commune.
communication *f* communication; **c. (téléphonique)** (telephone) call.
communier *vi* to receive Holy Communion.
communion *f* (Holy) Communion.
communiqué *m* (official) statement; (*publicitaire*) message; **c. de presse** press release.
communiquer *vti* to communicate.
communiste *a & mf* communist.
compact, -e *a* dense.
compagne *f* friend; (*épouse*) companion.
compagnie *f* (*présence, société*) company; **tenir c. à qn** to keep s.o.

company.

compagnon *m* companion; **c. de jeu** playmate; **c. de travail** fellow worker, workmate.

comparable *a* comparable.

comparaison *f* comparison (**avec** with).

comparer *vt* to compare (**à**, to, with).

compartiment *m* compartment.

compas *m* (pair of) compasses, *Am* compass; (*boussole*) compass.

compatriote *mf* compatriot.

compenser 1 *vt* to compensate for. **2** *vi* to compensate.

compétence *f* competence.

compétent, -ente *a* competent.

compétition *f* competition; (*épreuve sportive*) event; **de c.** (*esprit*, *sport*) competitive.

complaisance *f* kindness.

complaisant, -ante *a* kind.

complément *m* *Grammaire* complement.

complet, -ète 1 *a* complete; (*train*, *hôtel etc*) full; (*aliment*) whole. **2** *m* suit.

complètement *adv* completely.

compléter *vt* to complete; (*somme*) to make up.

complexe 1 *a* complex. **2** *m* (*sentiment*, *construction*) complex.

complication *f* complication.

complice *m* accomplice.

compliment *m* compliment; **mes compliments!** congratulations!

complimenter *vt* to compliment (**sur, pour** on).

compliqué, -ée *a* complicated.

compliquer *vt* to complicate; **se c.** to get complicated.

complot *m* plot.

comploter *vti* to plot (**de faire** to do).

comporter (se) *vpr* to behave; (*joueur*, *voiture*) to perform.

composé, -ée *a & m* (*mot*, *en chimie etc*) compound; **temps c.** compound tense; **passé c.** perfect (tense).

composer *vt* to make up, compose; (*numéro*) to dial; **se c. de, être composé de** to be made up *ou* composed of.

compositeur, -trice *mf* composer.

composter *vt* (*billet*) to cancel.

compote *f* stewed fruit, *Am* sauce; **c. de pommes** stewed apples, *Am* applesauce.

compréhensible *a* understandable.

compréhensif, -ive *a* (*personne*) understanding.

comprendre* *vt* to understand; (*comporter*) to include; **je n'y**

comprends rien I don't understand anything about it; **ça se comprend** that's understandable.
comprimé *m* tablet.
comprimer *vt* to compress.
compris, -ise *a* (*inclus*) included (**dans** in); **tout c.** (all) inclusive; **y c.** including.
comptable *mf* bookkeeper; (*expert*) accountant.
comptant 1 *a* **argent c.** (hard) cash. **2** *adv* **payer c.** to pay (in) cash.
compte *m* account; (*calcul*) count; (*nombre*) (right) number; **avoir un c. en banque** to have a bank(ing) account; **c. chèque** cheque account, *Am* checking account; **c. à rebours** countdown; **tenir c. de** to take into account; **c. tenu de** considering; **se rendre c. de** to realize; **à son c.** (*travailler*) for oneself; (*s'installer*) on one's own; **en fin de c.** all things considered.
compte-gouttes *m inv* dropper.
compter 1 *vt* (*calculer*) to count; **c. faire** to expect to do; (*avoir l'intention de*) to intend to do; **c. qch à qn** (*facturer*) to charge s.o. for sth. **2** *vi* (*calculer, avoir de l'importance*) to count; **c. sur** to rely on.
compte rendu *m* report; (*de livre, film*) review.
compteur *m* meter; **c. (de vitesse)** speedometer; **c. (kilométrique)** milometer, clock, *Am* odometer.
comptoir *m* (*de magasin*) counter; (*de café*) bar; (*de bureau*) (reception) desk.
comte *m* count; *Br* earl.
comtesse *f* countess.
concentré, -ée 1 *a* (*lait*) condensed; (*attentif*) concentrating (hard). **2** *m* **c. de tomates** tomato purée.
concentrer *vt*, **se concentrer** *vpr* to concentrate.
concerner *vt* to concern.
concert *m* concert.
concessionnaire *mf* (authorized) dealer.
concierge *mf* caretaker, *Am* janitor.
concitoyen, -enne *mf* fellow citizen.
conclure* *vti* to conclude (**que** that).
conclusion *f* conclusion.
concombre *m* cucumber.
concordant, -ante *a* in agreement.
concorder *vi* to agree; **c. avec** to match.
concours *m* (*examen*) competitive examination; (*jeu*) competition; **c. hippique** horse show.

concret, -ète *a* concrete.
conçu, -ue *a* **c. pour faire/pour qn** designed to do/for s.o.; **bien c.** (*maison etc*) well designed.
concurrence *f* competition; **faire c. à** to compete with.
concurrencer *vt* to compete with.
concurrent, -ente *mf* competitor.
condamnation *f* sentence; (*censure*) condemnation.
condamné, -ée *mf* condemned man *ou* woman.
condamner *vt* to condemn; (*accusé*) to sentence (**à** to); (*porte*) to block up; **c. à une amende** to fine.
condition *f* condition; **conditions** (*clauses, tarifs*) terms; **à c. de faire, à c. que l'on fasse** providing *ou* provided (that) one does.
conditionné *a* **à air c.** (*pièce etc*) air-conditioned.
conditionnel *m Grammaire* conditional.
condoléances *fpl* sympathy.
conducteur, -trice *mf* driver.
conduire* *vt* to lead; (*voiture*) to drive; (*eau*) to carry; **c. qn à** (*accompagner*) to take s.o. to.
conduire (se) *vpr* to behave.
conduite *f* behaviour; (*de voiture*) driving (**de** of); (*d'eau, de gaz*) main; **c. à gauche** (*volant*) left-hand drive.
cône *m* cone.
confection *f* making (**de** of); **vêtements de c.** ready-made clothes.
confectionner *vt* to make.
conférence *f* conference.
confesser *vt*, **se confesser** *vpr* to confess.
confession *f* confession.
confettis *mpl* confetti.
confiance *f* trust, **faire c. à qn, avoir c. en qn** to trust s.o.; **c. en soi** (self-)confidence.
confiant, -ante *a* trusting; (*sûr de soi*) confident.
confidence *f* (*secret*) confidence; **faire une c. à qn** to confide in s.o.
confidentiel, -ielle *a* confidential.
confier *vt* **c. à qn** (*enfant, objet*) to give s.o. to look after; **c. un secret/***etc* **à qn** to confide a secret/*etc* to s.o.; **se c. à qn** to confide in s.o.
confirmation *f* confirmation.
confirmer *vt* to confirm (**que** that).
confiserie *f* sweet shop, *Am* candy store; **confiseries** (*produits*) sweets, *Am* candy.
confiseur, -euse *mf* confectioner.
confisquer *vt* to confiscate (**à qn** from s.o.).

confit *a* **fruits confits** candied fruit.
confiture *f* jam.
conflit *m* conflict.
confondre *vt* (*choses, personnes*) to mix up, confuse; **c. avec** to mistake for.
confort *m* comfort.
confortable *a* comfortable.
confrère *m* colleague.
confus, -fuse *a* confused; (*gêné*) embarrassed; **je suis c.!** (*désolé*) I'm terribly sorry!
confusion *f* confusion; (*gêne, honte*) embarrassment.
congé *m* (*vacances*) holiday, *Am* vacation; **c. de maladie** sick leave; **congés payés** paid holidays, *ou Am* vacation.
congélateur *m* freezer, deep-freeze.
congeler *vt* to freeze.
congère *f* snowdrift.
congrès *m* congress.
conjoint *m* spouse.
conjonction *f Grammaire* conjunction.
conjugaison *f* conjugation.
conjuguer *vt* (*verbe*) to conjugate.
connaissance *f* knowledge; (*personne*) acquaintance; **connaissances** knowledge (**en** of); **faire la c. de qn, faire c. avec qn** to meet s.o.; **perdre c.** to lose consciousness; **sans c.** unconscious.
connaître* *vt* to know; (*rencontrer*) to meet; **nous nous connaissons déjà** we've met before; **s'y c. à** *ou* **en qch** to know (all) about sth.
connu, -ue (*pp of* **connaître**) *a* (*célèbre*) well-known.
conquérant, -ante *mf* conqueror.
conquérir* *vt* to conquer.
conquête *f* conquest; **faire la c. de** to conquer.
consacrer *vt* (*temps, vie etc*) to devote (**à** to); **se c. à** to devote oneself to.
conscience *f* (*psychologique*) consciousness; (*morale*) conscience; **avoir/prendre c. de** to be/become conscious *ou* aware of; **c. professionnelle** conscientiousness.
consciencieux, -euse *a* conscientious.
conscient, -ente *a* **c. de** aware of.
conseil[1] *m* **un c.** a piece of advice; **des conseils** advice.
conseil[2] *m* (*assemblée*) council; **c. d'administration** board of directors; **c. des ministres** (*réunion*) cabinet meeting.
conseiller *vt* to advise; **c. qch à qn** to recommend sth to s.o.; **c. à qn de faire** to advise s.o. to do.

conseiller, -ère *mf* (*expert*) consultant, adviser; (*d'un conseil*) councillor, *Am* councilor; **c. municipal** town councillor *Am* councilman *ou* -woman.
consentement *m* consent.
consentir* *vi* **c. à** to consent to.
conséquence *f* consequence.
conservation *f* preservation.
conservatoire *m* school (*of music, drama*).
conserve *f* **conserves** tinned *ou* canned food; **de** *ou* **en c.** tinned, canned; **mettre en c.** to tin, can.
conserver *vt* to keep; (*fruits, vie, tradition etc*) to preserve; **(se) c.** (*aliment*) to keep.
considérable *a* considerable.
considérer *vt* to consider (**que** that, **comme** to be).
consigne *f* (*instruction*) orders; (*de gare*) left-luggage office, *Am* baggage checkroom; (*somme*) deposit; **c. automatique** luggage lockers, *Am* baggage lockers.
consigner *vt* (*bouteille etc*) to charge a deposit on.
consistant, -ante *a* (*sauce etc*) thick; (*repas*) solid.
consister *vi* **c. en/dans** to consist of/in; **c. à faire** to consist in doing.
consolation *f* comfort.
console *f* console.
consoler *vt* to comfort, console (**de** for); **se c. de** (*la mort de qn etc*) to get over.
consolider *vt* to strengthen.
consommateur, -trice *mf* consumer; (*au café*) customer.
consommation *f* consumption; (*boisson*) drink.
consommer 1 *vt* (*aliment etc*) to consume. **2** *vi* (*au café*) to drink; **c. beaucoup/peu** (*véhicule*) to be heavy/light on petrol *ou Am* gas.
consonne *f* consonant.
conspirateur, -trice *mf* plotter.
conspiration *f* plot.
conspirer *vi* to plot (**contre** against).
constamment *adv* constantly.
constat *m* (official) report.
constatation *f* observation.
constater *vt* to note, observe (**que** that); (*enregistrer*) to record.
consternation *f* distress.
consterner *vt* to distress.
constipé, -ée *a* constipated.
constituer *vt* (*composer*) to make up; (*représenter*) to represent; **constitué de** made up of; **se c. prisonnier** to give oneself up.

constitution *f* constitution; (*composition*) composition.
construction *f* building; **matériaux/jeu de c.** building materials/set.
construire* *vt* to build.
consul *m* consul.
consulat *m* consulate.
consultation *f* consultation; **cabinet de c.** surgery, *Am* office.
consulter *vt*, **se consulter** *vpr* to consult.
contact *m* contact; (*toucher*) touch; (*de voiture*) ignition; **être en c. avec** to be in touch *ou* contact with; **entrer en c. avec** to come into contact with; **mettre/couper le c.** (*dans une voiture*) to switch on/off the ignition; **lentilles** *ou* **verres de c.** contact lenses.
contacter *vt* to contact.
contagieux, -euse *a* contagious, infectious.
contagion *f* infection.
conte *m* tale; **c. de fée** fairy tale.
contempler *vt* to gaze at.
contemporain, -aine *a* & *mf* contemporary.
contenance *f* (*d'un récipient*) capacity.
contenir* *vt* to contain; (*avoir comme capacité*) to hold.
content, -ente *a* pleased, happy (**de faire** to do, **de qn/qch** with s.o./sth); **c. de soi** self-satisfied.
contenter *vt* to satisfy, please; **se c. de** to be content *or* happy with.
contenu *m* (*de récipient*) contents.
conter *vt* (*histoire etc*) to tell.
contestataire *mf* protester.
contestation *f* protest.
contester 1 *vi* (*étudiants etc*) to protest. **2** *vt* to protest against.
conteur, -euse *mf* storyteller.
contexte *m* context.
continent *m* continent; (*opposé à une île*) mainland.
continu, -ue *a* continuous.
continuel, -elle *a* continual.
continuellement *adv* continually.
continuer 1 *vt* to continue, carry on (**à** *ou* **de faire** doing). **2** *vi* to continue, go on.
contour *m* outline.
contourner *vt* (*colline etc*) to go round.
contraceptif, -ive *a* & *m* contraceptive.
contracter *vt*, **se contracter** *vpr* to contract.
contractuel, -elle *mf* traffic warden, *Am* meter man *ou* maid.
contradiction *f* contradiction.
contradictoire *a* contradictory; (*théories*) conflicting.

contraindre* *vt* to compel (**à faire** to do).
contrainte *f* compulsion.
contraire 1 *a* opposite; **c. à** contrary to. **2** *m* opposite; **au c.** on the contrary.
contrairement *adv* **c. à** contrary to.
contrariant, -ante *a* (*action etc*) annoying; (*personne*) difficult.
contrarier *vt* (*projet etc*) to spoil; (*personne*) to annoy.
contrariété *f* annoyance.
contraste *m* contrast.
contrat *m* contract.
contravention *f* (*pour stationnement interdit*) (parking) ticket.
contre *prép & adv* against; (*en échange de*) (in exchange) for; **échanger c.** to exchange for; **fâché c.** angry with; **six voix c. deux** six votes to two; **Nîmes c. Arras** (*match*) Nîmes versus Arras; **un médicament c.** (*toux etc*) a medicine for; **par c.** on the other hand; **tout c. qch/qn** close to sth/s.o.
contre- *préfixe* counter-.
contre-attaque *f* counterattack.
contrebande *f* (*fraude*) smuggling; **de c.** (*tabac etc*) smuggled; **passer qch en c.** to smuggle sth.
contrebandier, -ière *mf* smuggler.
contrecœur (à) *adv* reluctantly.
contredire* *vt* to contradict; **(se) c.** to contradict oneself.
contre-jour (à) *adv* against the (sun)light.
contremaître *m* foreman.
contre-plaqué *m* plywood.
contretemps *m* hitch.
contribuable *mf* taxpayer.
contribuer *vi* to contribute (**à** to).
contribution *f* contribution; (*impôt*) tax.
contrôle *m* inspection, check(ing) (**de** of); (*des prix, de la qualité*) control; (*maîtrise*) control; **un c.** (*examen*) a check (**sur** on).
contrôler *vt* (*examiner*) to inspect, check; (*maîtriser, surveiller*) to control.
contrôleur, -euse *mf* (*de train*) (ticket) inspector, *Am* conductor; (*au quai*) ticket collector; (*de bus*) conductor, conductress.
contrordre *m* change of orders.
contusion *f* bruise.
convaincant, -ante *a* convincing.
convaincre* *vt* to convince (**de** of); **c. qn de faire** to persuade s.o. to do.
convaincu, -ue *a* (*certain*) convinced (**de** of).

convalescence *f* convalescence; **être en c.** to convalesce.
convalescent, -ente 1 *mf* convalescent. **2** *a* **être c.** to convalesce.
convenable *a* suitable; (*correct*) decent.
convenablement *adv* suitably; decently.
convenir* *vi* **c. à** (*être fait pour*) to be suitable for; (*plaire à*, *aller à*) to suit; **ça convient** (*date etc*) that's suitable.
convenu, -ue *a* (*prix etc*) agreed.
conversation *f* conversation.
convertir *vt* to convert (**à** to, **en** into).
conviction *f* (*certitude*) conviction.
convive *mf* guest (*at table*).
convocation *f* (*lettre*) (written) notice to attend.
convoi *m* (*véhicules*) convoy.
convoquer *vt* to summon (**à** to).
coopération *f* co-operation.
coopérer *vi* to co-operate (**à** in, **avec** with).
coordonnées *fpl* (*adresse*, *téléphone*) *Fam* contact address and phone number, particulars.
copain *m Fam* (*camarade*) pal; (*petit ami*) boyfriend; **être c. avec** to be pals with.
copeau, -x *m* (*de bois*) shaving.
copie *f* copy; (*devoir*, *examen*) paper.
copier *vti* to copy (**sur** from).
copieux, -euse *a* plentiful.
copine *f Fam* (*camarade*) pal; (*petite amie*) girlfriend; **être c. avec** to be pals with.
copropriété *f* **(immeuble en) c.** block of flats in joint ownership, *Am* condominium.
coq *m* rooster, cock.
coque *f* (*de navire*) hull; (*de noix*) shell; (*fruit de mer*) cockle; **œuf à la c.** boiled egg.
coquelicot *m* poppy.
coqueluche *f* whooping cough.
coquet, -ette *a* (*chic*) smart.
coquetier *m* egg cup.
coquetterie *f* (*élégance*) smartness.
coquillage *m* (*mollusque*) shellfish; (*coquille*) shell.
coquille *f* shell; **c. Saint-Jacques** scallop.
coquin, -ine *a* mischievous.
cor *m* (*instrument*) horn; **c. (au pied)** corn.
corail, -aux *m* coral.
Coran *m* **le C.** the Koran.

corbeau, -x *m* crow.
corbeille *f* basket; **c. à papier** waste paper basket.
corbillard *m* hearse.
corde *f* rope; (*plus mince*) cord; (*de raquette*, *violon etc*) string; **c. à linge** (washing- *ou* clothes-)line; **c. à sauter** skipping rope, *Am* jump rope.
cordial, -e, -aux *a* warm.
cordon *m* (*de tablier*, *sac etc*) string; (*de rideau*) cord.
cordon-bleu *m* (*pl* **cordons-bleus**) first-class cook.
cordonnerie *f* shoe repair *ou* repairer's shop.
cordonnier *m* shoe repairer.
coriace *a* tough.
corne *f* (*de chèvre etc*) horn; (*de cerf*) antler; (*matière*, *instrument*) horn.
corneille *f* crow.
cornet *m* (*de glace*) cornet, cone; **c. (de papier)** (paper) cone.
cornichon *m* (*concombre*) gherkin.
corps *m* body; **lutter c. à c.** to fight hand-to-hand; **prendre c.** (*projet*) to take shape.
correct, -e *a* (*exact*, *décent*) correct.
correctement *adv* correctly.
correction *f* correction; (*punition*) thrashing; (*exactitude*, *décence*) correctness; **la c. de** (*devoirs*, *examen*) the marking of.
correspondance *f* correspondence; (*de train*, *d'autocar*) connection, *Am* transfer.
correspondant, -ante 1 *a* corresponding. **2** *mf* (*d'un adolescent etc*) pen friend, *Am* pen pal; (*au téléphone*) caller.
correspondre *vi* to correspond (**à** to, with); (*écrire*) to correspond (**avec** with).
corrida *f* bullfight.
corriger *vt* to correct; (*devoir*) to mark; **c. qn de** (*défaut*) to cure s.o. of.
corrompu, -ue *a* corrupt.
corsage *m* (*chemisier*) blouse.
cortège *m* procession; **c. officiel** (*automobiles*) motorcade.
corvée *f* chore.
cosmonaute *mf* cosmonaut.
cosmos [kɔsmos] *m* (*univers*) cosmos; (*espace*) outer space.
cosse *f* (*de pois etc*) pod.
costaud, -aude *a Fam* brawny.
costume *m* (*déguisement*) costume; (*complet*) suit.
costumé *a* **bal c.** fancy-dress *ou* costume ball.

côte *f* rib; (*de mouton*) chop; (*de veau*) cutlet; (*montée*) hill; (*littoral*) coast; **c. à c.** side by side.

côté *m* side; (*direction*) way; **de l'autre c.** on the other side (**de** of); (*direction*) the other way; **du c. de** (*vers*, *près de*) towards; **de c.** (*mettre de l'argent etc*) to one side; (*regarder*) sideways; **à c.** nearby; (*pièce*) in the other room; (*maison*) next door; **à c. de** next to, beside; (*comparaison*) compared to; **à mes côtés** by my side.

coteau, -x *m* (small) hill.

côtelette *f* (*d'agneau*, *de porc*) chop; (*de veau*) cutlet.

côtier, -ière *a* coastal.

cotisation *f* (*de club*) dues.

cotiser (se) *vpr* to club together (**pour acheter** to buy).

coton *m* cotton; **c. (hydrophile)** cotton wool, *Am* (absorbent) cotton.

cou *m* neck.

couchage *m* **sac de c.** sleeping bag.

couchant *a* (*soleil*) setting.

couche *f* (*épaisseur*) layer; (*de peinture*) coat; (*linge de bébé*) nappy, *Am* diaper.

couché, -ée *a* **être c.** to be in bed; (*étendu*) to be lying (down).

coucher 1 *vt* to put to bed; (*héberger*) to put up; (*allonger*) to lay (down *ou* out). **2** *vi* to sleep (**avec** with).

coucher (se) *vpr* to go to bed; (*s'allonger*) to lie flat *ou* down; (*soleil*) to set.

couchette *f* (*de train*) sleeper, sleeping berth; (*de bateau*) bunk.

coucou *m* (*oiseau*) cuckoo; (*fleur*) cowslip.

coude *m* elbow; **se serrer les coudes** to help one another; **c. à c.** side by side; **coup de c.** nudge; **pousser du c.** to nudge.

coudre* *vti* to sew.

couette *f* duvet, continental quilt.

couler[1] *vi* (*eau etc*) to flow; (*robinet*, *nez*, *sueur*) to run; (*fuir*) to leak.

couler[2] *vti* (*bateau*, *nageur*) to sink.

couleur *f* colour; *Cartes* suit; **couleurs** (*teint*) colour; **de c.** coloured; **photo**/*etc* **en couleurs** colour photo/*etc*; **téléviseur c.** *ou* **en couleurs** colour TV set.

couleuvre *f* (grass) snake.

coulisses *fpl* **dans les c.** in the wings, backstage.

couloir *m* corridor; (*de circulation*, *d'une piste*) lane.

coup *m* blow, knock; (*léger*) tap; (*choc moral*) blow; (*de fusil etc*) shot; (*de crayon*, *d'horloge*) stroke; (*aux échecs etc*) move; (*fois*) *Fam* time; **donner des coups à** to hit; **c. de brosse** brush(-up); **c. de**

chiffon wipe (with a rag); **c. de sonnette** ring (on a bell); **c. de dents** bite; **c. de chance** stroke of luck; **tenter le c.** *Fam* to have a go; **tenir le c.** to hold out; **sous le c. de** (*émotion*) under the influence of; **après c.** afterwards; **tué sur le c.** killed outright; **à c. sûr** for sure; **tout à c., tout d'un c.** suddenly; **d'un seul c.** in one go; **du c.** (*de ce fait*) as a result.

coupable 1 *a* guilty (**de** of). **2** *mf* guilty person, culprit.

coupant, -ante *a* sharp.

coupe *f* (*trophée*) cup; (*à boire*) goblet; (*de vêtement etc*) cut; **c. de cheveux** haircut.

coupe-ongles *m inv* (finger nail) clippers.

coupe-papier *m inv* paper knife.

couper 1 *vt* to cut; (*arbre*) to cut down; (*téléphone*) to cut off; (*courant etc*) to switch off; (*morceler*) to cut up; (*croiser*) to cut across; **c. la parole à qn** to cut s.o. short. **2** *vi* to cut; **ne coupez pas!** (*au téléphone*) hold the line!

couper (se) *vpr* (*routes*) to intersect; **se c. au doigt** to cut one's finger.

couple *m* pair, couple.

couplet *m* verse.

coupure *f* cut; (*de journal*) cutting, *Am* clipping; **c. d'électricité** blackout, power cut.

cour *f* court(yard); (*de roi*) court; **c. (de récréation)** playground, *Am* school yard.

courage *m* courage; **bon c.!** good luck!

courageux, -euse *a* courageous.

couramment *adv* (*parler*) fluently; (*souvent*) frequently.

courant, -ante 1 *a* (*fréquent*) common; (*eau*) running; (*modèle, taille*) standard. **2** *m* (*de l'eau, électrique*) current; **c. d'air** draught; **coupure de c.** blackout, power cut; **être/mettre au c.** to know/tell (**de** about).

courbaturé, -ée *a* aching (all over).

courbe 1 *a* curved. **2** *f* curve.

courber *vti* to bend.

coureur *m* runner; (*cycliste*) cyclist; (*automobile*) racing driver.

courgette *f* courgette, *Am* zucchini.

courir* 1 *vi* to run; (*se hâter*) to rush; (*à bicyclette, en auto*) to race; **le bruit court que...** there's a rumour going around that... **2** *vt* (*risque*) to run; (*épreuve sportive*) to run (in); (*danger*) to face.

couronne *f* crown; (*pour enterrement*) wreath.

couronnement *m* (*de roi etc*) coronation.

couronner *vt* to crown.

courrier *m* post, mail.
courroie *f* strap; (*de transmission*) belt.
cours *m* course; (*d'une monnaie etc*) rate; (*leçon*) class; (*série de leçons*) course; **c. d'eau** river, stream; **en c.** (*travail*) in progress; (*année*) current; **en c. de route** on the way; **au c. de** during.
course[1] *f* (*action*) run(ning); (*épreuve de vitesse*) race; **courses** (*de chevaux*) races; **cheval de c.** racehorse; **voiture de c.** racing car.
course[2] *f* (*commission*) errand; **courses** (*achats*) shopping; **faire une c.** to run an errand; **faire les courses** to do the shopping.
coursier, -ière *mf* messenger.
court, courte 1 *a* short. **2** *adv* (*couper*, *s'arrêter*) short; **à c. de** (*argent etc*) short of. **3** *m Tennis* court.
couscous [kuskus] *m* couscous.
cousin, -ine *mf* cousin.
coussin *m* cushion.
couteau, -x *m* knife.
coûter *vti* to cost; **ça coûte combien?** how much does it cost?; **coûte que coûte** at all costs.
coûteux, -euse *a* costly, expensive.
coutume *f* custom; **avoir c. de faire** to be accustomed to doing.
couture *f* sewing; (*métier*) dressmaking; (*raccord*) seam.
couturier *m* fashion designer.
couturière *f* dressmaker.
couvée *f* (*oiseaux*) brood.
couvent *m* convent.
couver 1 *vt* (*œufs*) to sit on. **2** *vi* (*poule*) to brood.
couvercle *m* lid, cover.
couvert *m* (set of) cutlery; **mettre le c.** to set *ou* lay the table.
couvert, -erte *a* covered (**de** with, in); (*ciel*) overcast.
couverture *f* (*de lit*) blanket; (*de livre etc*) cover.
couveuse *f* incubator.
couvrir* *vt* to cover (**de** with).
couvrir (se) *vpr* (*s'habiller*) to wrap up; (*ciel*) to cloud over.
cow-boy [kɔbɔj] *m* cowboy.
crabe *m* crab.
crachat *m* spit, spittle.
cracher 1 *vi* to spit. **2** *vt* to spit (out).
craie *f* chalk.
craindre* *vt* to be afraid of, fear; (*chaleur*, *froid*) to be sensitive to; **c. de faire** to be afraid of doing; **ne craignez rien** don't be afraid.
crainte *f* fear.
craintif, -ive *a* timid.

crampe *f* cramp.
cramponner (se) *vpr* **se c. à** to hold on to, cling to.
crampons *mpl* (*de chaussures*) studs.
cran *m* (*entaille*) notch; (*de ceinture*) hole; **couteau à c. d'arrêt** flick-knife, *Am* switchblade; **c. de sûreté** safety catch.
crâne *m* skull.
crapaud *m* toad.
craquement *m* snapping *ou* cracking (sound).
craquer *vi* (*branche*) to snap; (*bois sec*) to crack; (*sous la dent*) to crunch; (*se déchirer*) to split, rip; (*personne*) to break down.
crasse *f* filth.
crasseux, -euse *a* filthy.
cratère *m* crater.
cravate *f* tie.
crawl [krol] *m* (*nage*) crawl.
crayon *m* pencil; **c. de couleur** coloured pencil; (*en cire*) crayon; **c. à bille** ballpoint (pen).
crayonner *vt* to pencil.
création *f* creation.
créature *f* creature.
crèche *f* (*de Noël*) manger; (*pour bébé*) (day) nursery, crèche.
crédit *m* credit; **à c.** on credit; **faire c.** (*prêter*) to give credit (**à** to).
créditeur *a* **compte c.** account in credit.
créer *vt* to create.
crémaillère *f* **pendre la c.** to have a house-warming (party).
crématorium *m* crematorium, *Am* crematory.
crème *f* cream; (*dessert*) cream dessert; **c. Chantilly** whipped cream; **c. glacée** ice cream; **c. à raser** shaving cream; **c. anglaise** custard.
créneau, -x *m* **faire un c.** to park between two vehicles.
crêpe *f* pancake.
crépiter *vi* to crackle.
crépu, -ue *a* frizzy.
crépuscule *m* twilight, dusk.
cresson *m* (water)cress.
crête *f* (*de montagne etc*) crest.
creuser *vt* to dig; **se c. la tête** to rack one's brains.
creux, -euse 1 *a* hollow; (*estomac*) empty; **assiette creuse** soup plate. **2** *m* hollow; (*de l'estomac*) pit.
crevaison *f* (*de pneu*) puncture, flat.
crevasse *f* (*trou*) crevice.
crevé, -ée *a* (*fatigué*) *Fam* worn out; (*mort*) *Fam* dead.
crever 1 *vi* (*bulle etc*) to burst; (*pneu*) to puncture, burst; (*mourir*)

Fam to die. **2** *vt* to burst; (*œil*) to put out.
crevette *f* (*grise*) shrimp; (*rose*) prawn.
cri *m* (*de joie*, *surprise*) cry, shout; (*de peur*) scream; (*de douleur*) cry; (*appel*) call, cry.
cric *m* (*de voiture*) jack.
crier 1 *vi* to shout (out), cry (out); (*de peur*) to scream; **c. après qn** *Fam* to shout at s.o. **2** *vt* (*injure*, *ordre*) to shout (out).
crime *m* crime; (*assassinat*) murder.
criminel, -elle 1 *a* criminal. **2** *mf* criminal; (*assassin*) murderer.
crinière *f* mane.
crise *f* crisis; (*accès*) attack; (*de colère etc*) fit.
crisper *vt* (*visage*) to make tense; (*poing*) to clench.
cristal, -aux *m* crystal.
critique 1 *a* critical. **2** *f* (*reproche*) criticism.
critiquer *vt* to criticize.
croc [kro] *m* (*dent*) fang.
croche-pied *m* **faire un c.-pied à qn** to trip s.o. up.
crochet *m* hook; (*aiguille*) crochet hook; (*travail*) crochet; **faire qch au c.** to crochet sth; **faire un c.** (*personne*) to make a detour.
crochu, -ue *a* (*nez*) hooked.
crocodile *m* crocodile.
croire* 1 *vt* to believe; (*estimer*) to think, believe (**que** that); **j'ai cru la voir** I thought I saw her. **2** *vi* to believe (**à, en** in).
croisement *m* (*de routes*) crossroads.
croiser *vt* (*jambes*, *ligne etc*) to cross; **c. qn** to pass *ou* meet s.o.
croiser (se) *vpr* (*voitures etc*) to pass (each other); (*routes*) to cross.
croisière *f* cruise.
croissant *m* crescent; (*pâtisserie*) croissant.
croix *f* cross.
croque-monsieur *m inv* toasted cheese and ham sandwich.
croquer *vti* to crunch.
croquis *m* sketch.
crosse *f* (*de fusil*) butt.
crotte *f* (*de lapin etc*) droppings, mess.
crottin *m* (horse) dung.
croustillant, -ante *a* (*pain*) crusty.
croustiller *vi* to be crusty.
croûte *f* (*de pain etc*) crust; (*de fromage*) rind; (*de plaie*) scab.
croûton *m* crust (*at end of loaf*).
croyant, -ante 1 *a* **être c.** to be a believer. **2** *mf* believer.
CRS [seɛrɛs] *mpl abrév* (*Compagnies républicaines de sécurité*) riot police.

cru[1], crue *pp of* **croire.**
cru[2], crue *a* (*aliment etc*) raw.
cruauté *f* cruelty (**envers** to).
cruche *f* pitcher, jug.
crudités *fpl* assorted raw vegetables.
cruel, -elle *a* cruel (**envers, avec** to).
cube 1 *m* cube; **cubes** (*jeu*) building blocks. **2** *a* (*mètre etc*) cubic.
cueillette *f* picking; (*fruits cueillis*) harvest.
cueillir* *vt* to pick.
cuiller, cuillère *f* spoon; **petite c., c. à café** teaspoon; **c. à soupe** soup spoon, tablespoon.
cuillerée *f* spoonful; **c. à café** teaspoonful; **c. à soupe** tablespoonful.
cuir *m* leather.
cuire* 1 *vt* to cook; (*à l'eau*) to boil; **c. (au four)** to bake; (*viande*) to roast. **2** *vi* to cook; to boil; to bake; to roast; **faire c.** to cook.
cuisine *f* (*pièce*) kitchen; (*art, aliments*) cooking; **faire la c.** to cook, do the cooking; **livre de c.** cook(ery) book.
cuisiner *vti* to cook.
cuisinier, -ière 1 *mf* cook. **2** *f* (*appareil*) cooker, stove, *Am* range.
cuisse *f* thigh; (*de poulet*) leg.
cuisson *m* cooking.
cuit, cuite (*pp of* **cuire**) *a* cooked; **bien c.** well done.
cuivre *m* (*rouge*) copper; (*jaune*) brass.
culbute *f* (*saut*) sommersault; (*chute*) (backward) tumble.
culbuter *vi* to tumble over (backwards).
culotte *f* (*de sportif*) (pair of) shorts; (*de femme*) (pair of) knickers *ou Am* panties; **culottes (courtes)** short trousers *ou Am* pants.
culte *m* (*de dieu*) worship; (*religion*) form of worship.
cultivateur, -trice *mf* farmer.
cultivé, -ée *a* (*personne*) cultivated.
cultiver *vt* (*terre*) to farm; (*plantes*) to grow.
cultiver (se) *vpr* to improve one's mind.
culture *f* culture; (*agriculture*) farming; (*de légumes*) growing.
culturel, -elle *a* cultural.
cure *f* (course of) treatment, cure.
curé *m* (parish) priest.
cure-dent *m* toothpick.
curer *vt* (*fossé etc*) to clean out.
curieux, -euse 1 *a* (*bizarre*) curious; (*indiscret*) inquisitive, curious (**de** about). **2** *mf* inquisitive person; (*badaud*) onlooker.
curiosité *f* curiosity.
curriculum (vitæ) [kyrikylɔm(vite)] *m inv* cv, *Am* résumé.

curseur *m* (*d'ordinateur*) cursor.
cuve *f* (*réservoir*) tank.
cuvette *f* (*récipient*) basin, bowl; (*des toilettes*) bowl.
cycle *m* (*série*) cycle.
cyclisme *m* cycling.
cycliste *mf* cyclist; **course c.** cycle *ou* bicycle race; **champion c.** cycling champion.
cyclomoteur *m* moped.
cyclone *m* cyclone.
cygne *m* swan.
cylindre *m* cylinder.
cylindrée *f* (engine) capacity.
cylindrique *a* cylindrical.
cymbale *f* cymbal.
cyprès *m* (*arbre*) cypress.

D

d'abord *adv* first.
dactylo *f* (*personne*) typist; (*action*) typing.
dactylographier *vt* to type.
daim *m* fallow deer; (*cuir*) suede.
dallage *m* paving.
dalle *f* paving stone.
dallé, -ée *a* paved.
dame *f* lady; (*mariée*) married lady; *Échecs Cartes* queen; (*au jeu de dames*) king; **(jeu de) dames** draughts, *Am* checkers.
damier *m* draughtboard, *Am* checkerboard.
dandiner (se) *vpr* to waddle.
danger *m* danger; **en d.** in danger; **mettre en d.** to endanger; **en cas de d.** in an emergency; **en d. de mort** in peril of death; **'d. de mort'** (*panneau*) 'danger'; **être sans d.** to be safe.
dangereusement *adv* dangerously.
dangereux, -euse *a* dangerous (**pour** to).
danois, -oise 1 *a* Danish. **2** *mf* Dane. **3** *m* (*langue*) Danish.
dans *prép* in; (*changement de lieu*) into; (*à l'intérieur de*) inside; **entrer d.** to go in(to); **boire/prendre**/*etc* **d.** to drink/take/*etc* from *ou* out of; **d. deux jours**/*etc* (*temps futur*) in two days/*etc*; **d. les dix francs**/*etc* about ten francs/*etc*.
danse *f* dance; (*art*) dancing.
danser *vti* to dance.
danseur, -euse *mf* dancer.
date *f* date; **en d. du...** dated the...; **d. d'expiration** expiry date; **d. limite** deadline.
dater 1 *vt* (*lettre etc*) to date. **2** *vi* **d. de** to date from; **à d. de** as from.
datte *f* (*fruit*) date.
dauphin *m* dolphin.
davantage *adv* (*quantité*) more; (*temps*) longer; **d. de temps**/*etc* more time/*etc*; **d. que** more than; longer than.
de[1] (**d'** *before a vowel or mute h*; **de + le = du, de + les = des**) *prép* (*complément d'un nom*) of; **les rayons du soleil** the rays of the sun; **le livre de Paul** Paul's book; **un pont de fer** an iron bridge; **une augmentation d'impôts**/*etc* an increase in taxes/*etc*. ▮ (*complément d'un adjectif*) **digne de** worthy of; **heureux de** happy to; **content de qch/qn** pleased with sth/s.o. ▮ (*complément d'un verbe*) **parler de** to speak of *ou* about; **décider de faire** to decide to do. ▮ (*provenance: lieu & temps*) from; **mes amis du village** my

friends from the village. ▮ (*agent*) **accompagné de** accompanied by. ▮ (*moyen*) **armé de** armed with; **se nourrir de** to live on. ▮ (*manière*) **d'une voix douce** in *ou* with a gentle voice. ▮ (*cause*) **mourir de faim** to die of hunger. ▮ (*temps*) **travailler de nuit** to work by night; **six heures du matin** six o'clock in the morning. ▮ (*mesure*) **avoir** *ou* **faire six mètres de haut** to be six metres high; **homme de trente ans** thirty-year-old man; **gagner cent francs de l'heure** to earn a hundred francs an hour.

de² *art partitif* some; **elle boit du vin** she drinks (some) wine; **il ne boit pas de vin** (*négation*) he doesn't drink (any) wine; **des fleurs** (some) flowers; **de jolies fleurs** (some) pretty flowers; **il y en a six de tués** (*avec un nombre*) there are six killed.

dé *m* (*à jouer*) dice; (*à coudre*) thimble; **jouer aux dés** to play dice.

déballer *vt* to unpack.

débarbouiller (se) *vpr* to wash one's face.

débarcadère *m* quay, wharf.

débarquement *m* landing; unloading.

débarquer 1 *vt* (*passagers*) to land; (*marchandises*) to unload. **2** *vi* (*passagers*) to land.

débarras *m* lumber room, *Am* storeroom; **bon d.!** *Fam* good riddance!

débarrasser *vt* (*table etc*) to clear (**de** of); **d. qn de** (*ennemi*, *soucis etc*) to rid s.o. of; (*manteau etc*) to relieve s.o. of; **se d. de** to get rid of.

débat *m* discussion, debate.

débattre* *vt* to discuss, debate.

débattre (se) *vpr* to struggle (to get free).

débile 1 *a* (*esprit*, *enfant etc*) weak; *Fam* idiotic. **2** *mf Fam* idiot.

débit *m* (*vente*) turnover; (*compte*) debit; (*de fleuve*) flow; **d. de boissons** bar, café.

débiter *vt* (*découper*) to cut up (**en** into); (*vendre*) to sell; (*compte*) to debit.

débiteur, -trice 1 *mf* debtor. **2** *a* **compte d.** account in debit.

déblayer *vt* (*terrain*, *décombres*) to clear.

débloquer *vt* (*mécanisme*) to unjam; (*crédits*) to release.

déboîter 1 *vt* (*tuyau*) to disconnect; (*os*) to dislocate. **2** *vi* (*véhicule*) to pull out, change lanes.

déborder 1 *vi* (*fleuve*, *liquide*) to overflow; **l'eau déborde du vase** the water is overflowing the vase. **2** *vt* (*dépasser*) to go beyond; **débordé de travail** snowed under with work.

débouché *m* (*carrière*) opening; (*marché pour produit*) outlet.

déboucher *vt* (*bouteille*) to open, uncork; (*lavabo*, *tuyau*) to unblock.

débourser *vti* to pay out.

debout *adv* standing (up); **mettre d.** (*planche etc*) to stand up, put upright; **se mettre d.** to stand *ou* get up; **rester d.** to remain standing; **être d.** (*levé*) to be up; **d.!** get up!

déboutonner *vt* to unbutton, undo.

débraillé, -ée *a* (*tenue etc*) slovenly, sloppy.

débrancher *vt* to unplug, disconnect.

débrayer *vi* (*conducteur*) to press the clutch.

débris *mpl* fragments; (*restes*) remains; (*détritus*) rubbish *Am* garbage.

débrouillard, -arde *a* smart, resourceful.

débrouiller (se) *vpr* to manage (**pour faire** to do).

début *m* start, beginning; **au d.** at the beginning.

débutant, -ante *mf* beginner.

débuter *vi* to start, begin.

décaféiné, -ée *a* decaffeinated.

décalage *m* (*écart*) gap; **d. horaire** time difference.

décalcomanie *f* (*image*) transfer, *Am* decal.

décaler *vt* to shift.

décalquer *vt* (*dessin*) to trace.

décapant *m* cleaning agent; (*pour enlever la peinture*) paint stripper.

décaper *vt* (*métal*) to clean; (*surface peinte*) to strip.

décapiter *vt* to behead.

décapotable *a* (*voiture*) convertible.

décapsuler *vt* **d. une bouteille** to take the top off a bottle.

décapsuleur *m* bottle-opener.

décéder *vi* to die.

déceler *vt* (*trouver*) to detect.

décembre *m* December.

décemment [desamɑ̃] *adv* decently.

décent, -ente *a* (*convenable*) decent.

déception *f* disappointment.

décerner *vt* (*prix*) to award.

décès *m* death.

décevant, -ante *a* disappointing.

décevoir* *vt* to disappoint.

déchaîné, -ée *a* (*foule*) wild.

déchaîner *vt* **d. l'enthousiasme/les rires** to set off wild enthusiasm/a storm of laughter.

déchaîner (se) *vpr* (*tempête*, *rires*) to break out; (*foule*) to run riot;

(*personne*) to fly into a rage.
décharge *f* **d. (publique)** (rubbish) dump, *Am* (garbage) dump; **d. (électrique)** (electric) shock.
déchargement *m* unloading.
décharger *vt* to unload; (*batterie*) to discharge.
décharger (se) *vpr* (*batterie*) to go flat.
déchausser (se) *vpr* to take one's shoes off.
déchet *m* **déchets** (*restes*) waste; **il y a du d.** there's some waste.
déchiffrer *vt* to decipher.
déchiqueter *vt* to tear to shreds.
déchirer *vt* (*page etc*) to tear (up); (*vêtement*) to tear; (*ouvrir*) to tear open.
déchirer (se) *vpr* (*robe etc*) to tear.
déchirure *f* tear.
décidé, -ée *a* (*air*, *ton*) determined; **d. à faire** determined to do.
décidément *adv* undoubtedly.
décider 1 *vt* (*opération*) to decide on; **d. que** to decide that. **2** *vi* **d. de faire** to decide to do.
décider (se) *vpr* **se d. à faire** to make up one's mind to do.
décimal, -e, -aux *a* decimal.
décimètre *m* decimetre; **double d.** ruler.
décisif, -ive *a* decisive.
décision *f* decision; (*fermeté*) determination.
déclaration *f* declaration; (*de vol etc*) notification; (*commentaire*) statement; **d. de revenus** tax return.
déclarer *vt* to declare (**que** that); (*vol etc*) to notify.
déclarer (se) *vpr* (*incendie*) to break out.
déclencher *vt* (*mécanisme*, *réaction*) to trigger off, start (off); (*attaque*) to launch.
déclencher (se) *vpr* (*alarme etc*) to go off.
déclic *m* (*bruit*) click.
décoiffer *vt* **d. qn** to mess up s.o.'s hair.
décollage *m* (*d'avion*) takeoff.
décoller 1 *vi* (*avion*) to take off. **2** *vt* (*timbre*) to unstick; **se d.** to come unstuck.
décolorer (se) *vpr* to fade.
décombres *mpl* rubble.
décongeler 1 *vt* **(faire) d.** (*aliment*) to thaw. **2** *vi* to thaw.
déconseiller *vt* **d. qch à qn** to advise s.o. against sth; **d. à qn de faire** to advise s.o. against doing.
décontracter (se) *vpr* to relax.
décor *m* (*théâtre*, *paysage*) scenery; (*d'intérieur*) decoration.

décorateur, -trice *mf* (interior) decorator.
décoratif, -ive *a* decorative.
décoration *f* decoration.
décorer *vt* (*maison, soldat*) to decorate (**de** with).
découdre *vt* to unstitch; **se d.** to come unstitched.
découpage *m* (*image*) cutout.
découper *vt* (*viande*) to carve; (*article*) to cut out.
découragement *m* discouragement.
décourager *vt* to discourage; **se d.** to get discouraged.
découvert *m* (*d'un compte*) overdraft.
découverte *f* discovery.
découvrir* *vt* to discover (**que** that).
découvrir (se) *vpr* (*dans son lit*) to push to bedcovers off; (*ciel*) to clear (up).
décrasser *vt* (*nettoyer*) to clean.
décrire* *vt* to describe.
décroché *a* (*téléphone*) off the hook.
décrocher *vt* (*détacher*) to unhook; (*tableau*) to take down; **se d.** (*tableau*) to fall down; **d. (le téléphone)** to pick up the phone.
décrotter *vt* to clean (the mud off).
déçu, -ue (*pp of* **décevoir**) *a* disappointed.
déculotter (se) *vpr* to take off one's trousers *ou Am* pants.
dédaigner *vt* to scorn, despise.
dédaigneux, -euse *a* scornful.
dédain *m* scorn.
dedans 1 *adv* inside; **en d.** on the inside; **tomber d.** (*trou*) to fall in (it); **je me suis fait rentrer d.** (*accident de voiture*) someone crashed into me. **2** *m* **le d.** the inside.
dédommagement *m* compensation.
dédommager *vt* to compensate (**de** for).
déduction *f* deduction.
déduire* *vt* (*soustraire*) to deduct (**de** from).
déesse *f* goddess.
défaire* *vt* (*nœud etc*) to undo; **se d.** to come undone.
défait *a* (*lit*) unmade.
défaite *f* defeat.
défaut *m* (*faiblesse*) fault; (*de fabrication*) defect.
défavorable *a* unfavourable (**à** to).
défavoriser *vt* to put at a disadvantage.
défectueux, -euse *a* faulty, defective.
défendre[1] *vt* (*protéger*) to defend; **se d.** to defend oneself.
défendre[2] *vt* (*interdire*) **d. à qn de faire** to forbid s.o. to do; **d. qch**

à qn to forbid s.o. sth.

défense[1] *f* (*protection*) defence, *Am* defense; (*d'éléphant*) tusk.

défense[2] *f* (*interdiction*) **'d. de fumer'** 'no smoking'; **'d. (absolue) d'entrer'** '(strictly) no entry'.

défenseur *m* defender.

défi *m* challenge; **lancer un d. à qn** to challenge s.o.

défier *vt* to challenge (**à** to); **d. qn de faire** to challenge s.o. to do.

défiguré, -ée *a* disfigured.

défilé *m* (*militaire*) parade; (*gorge*) pass.

défiler *vi* (*soldats*) to march.

définir *vt* to define; **article défini** *Grammaire* definite article.

définitif, -ive *a* final, definitive.

définition *f* definition; (*de mots croisés*) clue.

défoncé, -ée *a* (*route*) bumpy; (*drogué*) *Fam* high.

défoncer *vt* (*porte, mur*) to smash in *ou* down; (*trottoir, route*) to dig up.

déformé, -ée *a* misshapen; **chaussée déformée** uneven road surface, bumpy road.

déformer *vt* to put out of shape; **se d.** to lose its shape.

défouler (se) *vpr* to let off steam.

défricher *vt* (*terrain*) to clear.

défroisser *vt* to smooth out.

dégagé, -ée *a* (*ciel*) clear.

dégagement *m* (*action*) clearing; *Football* kick (down the pitch); **itinéraire de d.** relief road, alternative road (*to ease traffic congestion*).

dégager 1 *vt* (*table etc*) to clear (**de** of); (*odeur*) to give off; **d. qn de** (*décombres etc*) to pull s.o. out of. **2** *vi Football* to clear the ball (down the pitch); **dégagez!** clear the way!

dégager (se) *vpr* (*ciel*) to clear; **se d. de** (*personne*) to pull oneself free from (*rubble*); (*odeur*) to come out of (*kitchen*).

dégainer *vti* (*arme*) to draw.

dégarni, -ie *a* bare; **front d.** receding hairline.

dégarnir *vt* (*arbre de Noël*) to take down the decorations from.

dégarnir (se) *vpr* (*crâne*) to go bald.

dégâts *mpl* damage.

dégel *m* thaw.

dégeler *vti* to thaw (out).

dégivrer *vt* (*réfrigérateur*) to defrost.

déglingué, -ée *a* falling to bits.

dégonflé, -ée 1 *a* (*pneu*) flat; (*lâche*) *Fam* yellow. **2** *mf Fam* yellow belly.

dégonfler *vt* (*pneu*) to let down.
dégonfler (se) *vpr* (*pneu*) to go down; (*se montrer lâche*) *Fam* to chicken out.
dégouliner *vi* to trickle.
dégourdi, -ie 1 *a* (*malin*) smart. **2** *mf* smart boy *ou* girl.
dégourdir (se) *vpr* **se d. les jambes** to stretch one's legs.
dégoût *m* disgust; **avoir du d. pour qch** to have a (strong) dislike for sth.
dégoûtant, -ante *a* disgusting.
dégoûté, -ée *a* disgusted (**de**, with, by); **il n'est pas d.** (*difficile*) he's not fussy.
dégoûter *vt* to disgust; **d. qn de qch** to put s.o. off sth, *Am* (be enough to) make s.o,. sick of sth.
degré *m* (*angle*, *température*) degree.
dégringolade *f* tumble.
dégringoler *vi* to tumble (down).
déguerpir *vi* to clear off *ou* out, make tracks.
dégueulasse *a Fam* disgusting.
déguisement *m* disguise; (*de bal costumé*) fancy dress, costume.
déguiser *vt* to disguise; **d. qn (en)** (*costumer*) to dress s.o. up (as); **se d. (en)** to dress oneself up (as).
déguster *vt* (*goûter*) to taste.
dehors 1 *adv* out(side); **en d.** on the outside; **en d. de la maison** outside the house; **en d. de la ville** out of town; **au-d. (de), au d. (de)** outside. **2** *m* (*extérieur*) outside.
déjà *adv* already; **elle l'a d. vu** she's seen it before, she's already seen it; **quand partez-vous, d.?** when did you say you are leaving?
déjeuner 1 *vi* (*à midi*) to have lunch; (*le matin*) to have breakfast. **2** *m* lunch; **petit d.** breakfast.
delà *adv* **au-d. (de), au d. (de)**, beyond.
délabré, -ée *a* dilapidated.
délacer *vt* (*chaussures*) to undo.
délai *m* time limit; **sans d.** without delay; **dernier d.** final date.
délasser (se) *vpr* to relax.
délayer *vt* (*mélanger*) to mix (with liquid).
délégation *f* delegation.
délégué, -ée *mf* delegate.
délibérer *vi* (*se consulter*) to deliberate (**de** about).
délicat, -ate *a* (*santé*, *travail*) delicate; (*geste*) tactful; (*exigeant*) particular.
délicatement *adv* (*doucement*) delicately.
délice *m* delight.

délicieux, -euse *a* (*plat*) delicious.
délier *vt* to undo; **se d.** (*paquet*) to come undone.
délimiter *vt* (*terrain*) to mark off.
délinquant, -ante *mf* delinquent.
délirer *vi* (*dire n'importe quoi*) to rave.
délit *m* offence, *Am* offense.
délivrer *vt* (*prisonnier*) to release, (set) free; (*billet*) to issue.
déloger *vt* to drive out.
deltaplane® *m* hang-glider.
déluge *m* flood; (*de pluie*) downpour.
demain *adv* tomorrow; **à d.**! see you tomorrow!
demande *f* request (**de qch** for sth); **demandes d'emploi** situations *ou* jobs wanted.
demander *vt* to ask for; (*nécessiter*) to require; **d. le chemin/l'heure** to ask the way/the time; **d. qch à qn** to ask s.o. for sth; **d. à qn de faire** to ask s.o. to do; **ça demande du temps** it takes time; **être très demandé** to be in great demand.
demander (se) *vpr* to wonder (**pourquoi** why, **si** if).
démangeaison *f* itch; **avoir des démangeaisons** to be itching.
démanger *vti* to itch; **son bras le démange** his arm itches.
démaquiller (se) *vpr* to take off one's make-up.
démarche *f* walk; **faire des démarches** to go through the process (**pour faire** of doing).
démarrage *m* start.
démarrer *vi* (*moteur*) to start (up); (*voiture*) to move off.
démarreur *m* starter.
démasquer *vt* to expose.
démêler *vt* (*cheveux*) to untangle.
déménagement *m* move, moving (house); **camion de d.** removal van, *Am* moving van.
déménager *vi* to move (house).
déménageur *m* removal man, *Am* (furniture) mover.
démettre *vt* **se d. le pied**/*etc* to dislocate one's foot/*etc*.
demeure *f* (*belle maison*) mansion.
demeurer *vi* (*aux* **être**) (*rester*) to remain; (*aux* **avoir**) (*habiter*) to live.
demi, -ie **1** *a* half; **d.-journée** half-day; **une heure et demie** an hour and a half; (*horloge*) half past one. **2** *adv* **(à) d. plein**/*etc* half-full/*etc*. **3** *m* (*verre*) (half-pint) glass of beer.
demi-cercle *m* semicircle.
demi-douzaine *f* **une d.-douzaine (de)** half a dozen.
demi-finale *f* semifinal.

demi-frère *m* stepbrother.
demi-heure *f* **une d.-heure** a half-hour, half an hour.
demi-pension *f* half-board, *Am* breakfast and one meal.
demi-pensionnaire *mf* day boarder, *Am* day student.
démission *f* resignation.
démissionner *vi* to resign.
demi-sœur *f* stepsister.
demi-tarif *a inv* (*billet*) half-price.
demi-tour *m* (*en voiture*) U-turn; **faire d.-tour** (*à pied*) to turn back; (*en voiture*) to make a U-turn.
démocratie [-asi] *f* democracy.
démocratique *a* democratic.
démodé, -ée *a* old-fashioned.
demoiselle *f* (*célibataire*) single woman; **d. d'honneur** (*à un mariage*) bridesmaid.
démolir *vt* (*maison*) to demolish, knock *ou* pull down.
démolition *f* demolition.
démonstratif, -ive *a & m Grammaire* demonstrative.
démonstration *f* demonstration.
démonter *vt* (*mécanisme*) to take apart; (*tente*) to take down; **se d.** to come apart; to come down.
démontrer *vt* to show.
démoraliser *vt* to demoralize; **se d.** to become demoralized.
déneiger *vt* to clear of snow.
dénicher *vt* (*trouver*) to dig up.
dénoncer *vt* **d. qn** (*au professeur*) to tell on s.o. (**à** to); **se d.** to own up (**à** to).
dénouer *vt* (*corde*) to undo, untie; **se d.** (*nœud*) to come undone *ou* untied.
denrées *fpl* **d. alimentaires** foods.
dense *a* dense.
dent *f* tooth (*pl* teeth); (*de fourchette*) prong; **faire ses dents** (*enfant*) to be teething; **coup de d.** bite.
dentaire *a* dental.
dentelle *f* lace.
dentier *m* (set of) false teeth.
dentifrice *m* toothpaste.
dentiste *mf* dentist.
déodorant *m* deodorant.
dépannage *m* (emergency) repair.
dépanner *vt* (*voiture*) to repair.
dépanneur *m* (*de télévision*) repairman; (*de voiture*) breakdown

mechanic, emergency car mechanic.
dépanneuse *f* (*voiture*) breakdown lorry, *Am* tow truck.
départ *m* departure; (*d'une course*) start; **ligne de d.** starting post; **au d.** at the start.
département *m* department.
départementale *af* **route d.** secondary road.
dépasser 1 *vt* (*véhicule*) to overtake; **d. qn** (*en hauteur*) to be taller than s.o.; (*surclasser*) to be ahead of s.o. **2** *vi* (*clou etc*) to stick out.
dépêcher (se) *vpr* to hurry (up).
dépeigné, -ée *a* **être d.** to have untidy hair.
dépendre *vi* to depend (**de** on, upon).
dépense *f* (*frais*) expense.
dépenser *vt* (*argent*) to spend.
dépenser (se) *vpr* to exert oneself.
dépensier, -ière *a* wasteful.
dépister *vt* (*criminel*) to track down; (*maladie*) to detect.
dépit *m* **en d. de** in spite of; **en d. du bon sens** (*mal*) atrociously.
déplacement *m* (*voyage*) (business) trip.
déplacer *vt* to shift, move.
déplacer (se) *vpr* (*voyager*) to travel (about).
déplaire* *vi* **ça me déplaît** I don't like it.
dépliant *m* (*prospectus*) leaflet.
déplier *vt*, **se déplier** *vpr* to unfold.
déplorable *a* regrettable, deplorable.
déplorer *vt* (*regretter*) to deplore; **d. que** (+ *subjonctif*) to regret that.
déployer *vt* (*ailes*) to spread.
déporter *vt* (*dévier*) to carry (off course).
déposer *vt* (*poser*) to put down; (*laisser*) to leave; (*plainte*) to lodge; (*ordures*) to dump; **d. qn** (*en voiture*) to drop s.o. (off).
déposer (se) *vpr* (*poussière*) to settle.
dépôt *m* (*d'ordures*) dump; (*dans une bouteille*) deposit.
dépotoir *m* rubbish dump, *Am* garbage dump.
dépouillé, -ée *a* (*arbre*) bare.
dépression *f* depression; **d. nerveuse** nervous breakdown.
déprimé, -ée *a* depressed.
déprimer *vt* to depress.
depuis 1 *prép* since; **d. lundi** since Monday; **d. qu'elle est partie** since she left; **j'habite ici d. un mois** I've been living here for a month; **d. quand êtes-vous là?** how long have you been here?; **d. Paris** from Paris. **2** *adv* since (then).

député *m* (*au Parlement*) deputy, = *Br* MP, = *Am* congressman, congresswoman.

déraciner *vt* (*arbre*) to uproot.

déraillement *m* derailment.

dérailler *vi* (*train*) to jump the rails.

dérangement *m* **en d.** (*téléphone*) out of order.

déranger *vt* (*affaires*) to disturb, upset; **d. qn** to disturb *ou* bother s.o.; **ça vous dérange si je fume?** do you mind if I smoke?

déranger (se) *vpr* (*se déplacer*) to bother to come *ou* go; **ne te dérange pas!** don't bother!

dérapage *m* skid.

déraper *vi* to skid.

déréglé, -ée *a* out of order.

dérégler *vt* (*télévision etc*) to put out of order; **se d.** (*montre etc*) to go wrong.

dériver *vi* (*bateau*) to drift.

dernier, -ière 1 *a* last; (*mode*) latest; (*étage*) top; **en d.** last. **2** *mf* last (person *ou* one); **ce d.** the latter; **être le d. de la classe** to be (at the) bottom of the class.

dernièrement *adv* recently.

dérober *vt* (*voler*) to steal (**à** from).

dérouiller *vt* **se d. les jambes** to stretch one's legs.

dérouler *vt* (*tapis*) to unroll; (*fil*) to unwind.

dérouler (se) *vpr* (*événement*) to take place.

derrick *m* oil rig.

derrière 1 *prép & adv* behind; **assis d.** (*dans une voiture*) sitting in the back; **par d.** (*attaquer*) from behind. **2** *m* back; (*fesses*) behind; **pattes de d.** hind legs..

des [de] *voir* **de**[1,2], **le**.

dès *prep* from; **d. le début** (right) from the start; **d. qu'elle viendra** as soon as she comes.

désaccord *m* disagreement.

désaccordé, -ée *a* (*violon etc*) out of tune.

désaffecté, -ée *a* (*gare etc*) disused.

désagréable *a* unpleasant.

désaltérer *vt* **d. qn** to quench s.o.'s thirst; **se d.** to quench one's thirst.

désapprouver *vt* to disapprove of.

désarmer *vt* to disarm.

désastre *m* disaster.

désastreux, -euse *a* disastrous.

désavantage *m* disadvantage.

désavantager *vt* to handicap.
desceller (se) *vpr* to come loose.
descendre 1 *vi* (*aux* **être**) to come *ou* go down; (*d'un train*) to get off; (*d'un arbre*) to climb down (**de** from); (*thermomètre*) to fall; (*marée*) to go out; **d. de cheval** to dismount; **d. en courant** to run down. **2** *vt* (*aux* **avoir**) (*escalier*) to come *ou* go down; (*objet*) to bring *ou* take down.
descente *f* (*d'avion etc*) descent; (*pente*) slope; **d. de lit** (*tapis*) bed-side rug.
description *f* description.
désenfler *vi* to go down.
déséquilibre (en) *adv* (*meuble*) unsteady.
déséquilibrer *vt* to throw off balance.
désert -erte *a* deserted; **île déserte** desert island.
désert *m* desert.
désespérant, -ante *a* (*enfant*) hopeless.
désespéré, -ée *a* (*personne*) in despair; (*situation*) hopeless; (*efforts*) desperate.
désespérer *vt* to drive to despair.
désespoir *m* despair.
déshabiller *vt*, **se déshabiller** *vpr* to undress.
désherbant *m* weed killer.
désherber *vti* to weed.
désigner *vt* (*montrer*) to point to; (*élire*) to appoint; (*signifier*) to indicate.
désinfectant *m* disinfectant.
désinfecter *vt* to disinfect.
désirer *vt* to want; **je désire que tu viennes** I want you to come.
désobéir *vi* to disobey; **d. à qn** to disobey s.o.
désobéissant, -ante *a* disobedient.
désodorisant *m* air freshener.
désolé, -ée *a* **être d.** (*navré*) to be sorry (**que** (+ *subjonctif*) that, **de faire** to do).
désoler *vt* to upset (very much).
désordonné, -ée *a* (*personne*) messy, untidy.
désordre *m* (*dans une chambre*) mess; (*dans une classe*) disturbance; **en d.** messy, untidy.
désorganisé, -ée *a* disorganized.
désormais *adv* from now on.
desquel(le)s *voir* **lequel**.
dessécher *vt* (*bouche*) to parch.
dessécher (se) *vpr* (*plante*) to wither; (*peau*) to get dry.

desserrer *vt* (*ceinture*) to loosen; (*poing*) to open; (*frein*) to release; **se d.** to come loose.
dessert *m* dessert, sweet.
desservir *vt* (*table*) to clear (away); **le car dessert ce village** the bus stops at this village.
dessin *m* drawing; **d. (humoristique)** cartoon; **d. animé** (*film*) cartoon; **école de d.** art school.
dessinateur, -trice *mf* drawer; **d. humoristique** cartoonist.
dessiner *vt* to draw.
dessous 1 *adv* under(neath), below; **en d.** under(neath); **par-d.** (*passer*) under(neath). **2** *m* underside, underneath; **drap de d.** bottom sheet; **les gens du d.** the people downstairs.
dessous-de-plat *m inv* tablemat.
dessus 1 *adv* (*marcher, monter*) on it; (*passer*) over it; **par-d.** (*sauter*) over (it). **2** *m* top; **drap de d.** top sheet; **les gens du d.** the people upstairs.
dessus-de-lit *m inv* bedspread.
destin *m* fate.
destination *f* (*lieu*) destination; **à d. de** (*train*) to, for.
destiner *vt* **d. qch à qn** to intend sth for s.o.
destruction *f* destruction.
détachant *m* stain remover.
détacher[1] *vt* (*ceinture*) to undo; (*personne*) to untie; (*ôter*) to take off; **se d.** (*chien*) to break loose; (*se dénouer*) to come undone; **se d. (de qch)** (*fragment*) to come off (sth).
détacher[2] *vt* (*linge*) to remove the stains from.
détail[1] *m* detail; **en d.** in detail.
détail[2] *m* **de d.** (*magasin, prix*) retail; **vendre au d.** to sell retail.
détaillant, -ante *mf* retailer.
détaillé, -ée *a* (*récit etc*) detailed.
détaler *vi* to run off.
détecteur *m* detector.
détective *m* **d. (privé)** (private) detective.
déteindre* *vi* (*couleur*) to run; **ton tablier bleu a déteint sur ma chemise** the blue of your apron has come off on my shirt.
détendre *vt* **d. qn** to relax s.o.
détendre (se) *vpr* (*se reposer*) to relax; (*corde etc*) to slacken.
détendu, -ue *a* relaxed; (*ressort etc*) slack.
détente *f* (*repos*) relaxation.
détenu, -ue *mf* prisoner.
détergent *m* detergent.
détérioration *f* deterioration (**de** in).

détériorer (se) *vpr* to deteriorate.
déterminer *vt* (*préciser*) to determine.
déterrer *vt* to dig up.
détester *vt* to hate (**faire** doing, to do).
détonation *f* explosion.
détour *m* (*crochet*) detour.
détourné, -ée *a* (*chemin*) roundabout.
detournement *m* (*d'avion*) hijack(ing).
détourner *vt* (*dévier*) to divert; (*tête*) to turn (away); (*avion*) to hijack; **d. les yeux** to look away.
détourner (se) *vpr* to turn away; **se d. de** (*chemin*) to stray from.
détraqué, -ée *a* out of order.
détraquer *vt* (*mécanisme*) to put out of order.
détraquer (se) *vpr* (*machine*) to go wrong.
détresse *f* distress; **en d.** (*navire*) in distress.
détritus [detritys] *mpl* rubbish, *Am* garbage.
détroit *m* strait(s).
détruire* *vt* to destroy.
dette *f* debt; **avoir des dettes** to be in debt.
deuil *m* (*vêtements*) mourning; **en d.** in mourning.
deux *a* & *m* two; **d. fois** twice; **tous (les) d.** both.
deuxième *a* & *mf* second.
deuxièmement *adv* secondly.
deux-pièces *m inv* (*maillot de bain*) bikini.
deux-points *m inv Grammaire* colon.
deux-roues *m inv* two-wheeled vehicle.
dévaler 1 *vt* (*escalier*) to race down. **2** *vi* (*tomber*) to tumble down.
dévaliser *vt* to rob.
devancer *vt* to get *ou* be ahead of.
devant 1 *prép* & *adv* in front (of); **d. (l'hôtel/***etc***)** in front (of the hotel/*etc*); **passer d. (l'église/***etc***)** to go past (the church/*etc*); **assis d.** (*dans une voiture*) sitting in the front. **2** *m* front; **roue de d.** front wheel; **patte de d.** foreleg.
devanture *f* (*vitrine*) shop window.
dévaster *vt* to ruin, devastate.
développer *vt* (*muscles, photos etc*) to develop; **se d.** to develop.
devenir* *vi* (*aux* **être**) to become; **qu'est-il devenu?** what's become of him?
déverser *vt*, **se déverser** *vpr* (*liquide*) to pour out (**dans** into).
déviation *f* (*itinéraire provisoire*) diversion.
dévier 1 *vt* (*circulation*) to divert. **2** *vi* (*de sa route*) to veer (off

course).
deviner *vt* to guess.
devinette *f* riddle.
devis *m* estimate (*of cost of work to be done*).
devise *f* (*légende*) motto; **devises** (*argent*) (foreign) currency.
dévisser *vt* to unscrew.
dévisser (se) *vpr* (*bouchon*) to unscrew; (*se desserrer*) to come loose.
dévoiler *vt* (*secret*) to disclose.
devoir*¹ *v aux* (*nécessité*) **je dois refuser** I must refuse, I have (got) to refuse; **j'ai dû refuser** I had to refuse. ▮ (*probabilité*) **il doit être tard** it must be late; **elle a dû oublier** she must have forgotten; **il ne doit pas être bête** he can't be stupid. ▮ (*obligation*) **tu dois apprendre tes leçons**, you must learn your lessons; **il aurait dû venir** he should have come; **vous devriez rester** you should stay. ▮ (*événement prévu*) **elle doit venir** she's supposed to be coming, she's due to come.
devoir*² **1** *vt* (*argent etc*) to owe (**à** to). **2** *m* (*obligation*) duty; (*exercice*) exercise; **devoirs** (*à faire à la maison*) homework; **d. sur table** class exam(ination).
dévorer *vt* (*manger*) to eat up.
dévoué, -ée *a* (*soldat etc*) dedicated.
dévouement *m* dedication.
dévouer (se) *vpr* **se d. (pour qn)** to sacrifice oneself (for s.o.)
diabète *m* diabetes.
diabétique *mf* diabetic.
diable *m* devil; **habiter au d.** to live miles from anywhere.
diagnostic [djagnɔstik] *m* diagnosis.
diagonale *f* diagonal (line); **en d.** diagonally.
dialecte *m* dialect.
dialogue *m* conversation; (*de film*) dialogue.
diamant *m* diamond.
diamètre *m* diameter.
diapositive, *Fam* **diapo** *f* (colour) slide.
diarrhée *f* diarrh(o)ea.
dictée *f* dictation.
dicter *vt* to dictate (**à** to).
dictionnaire *m* dictionary.
dicton *m* saying.
diesel [djezel] *a* & *m* **(moteur) d.** diesel (engine).
diète *f* (*jeûne*) **à la d.** on a starvation diet.
diététique *a* **produit d.** health food.

dieu, -x *m* god; **D.** God.
différence *f* difference (**de** in).
différent, -ente *a* different (**de** from, to).
difficile *a* difficult; (*exigeant*) fussy; **d. à faire** difficult to do; **il nous est d. de** it's difficult for us to.
difficulté *f* difficulty; **en d.** in a difficult situation.
diffuser *vt* (*émission*) to broadcast.
digérer *vti* to digest.
digestif, -ive 1 *a* digestive. **2** *m* after-dinner liqueur.
digestion *f* digestion.
digne *a* **d. de** worthy of.
digue *f* dike; (*en bord de mer*) sea wall.
dilater *vt*, **se dilater** *vpr* to expand.
diligence *f* (*véhicule*) stagecoach.
dimanche *m* Sunday.
dimension *f* dimension.
diminuer 1 *vt* to reduce. **2** *vi* (*réserves*) to decrease; (*jours*) to get shorter; (*prix*) to drop.
diminutif *m* (*prénom*) nickname.
dinde *f* turkey.
dindon *m* turkey (cock).
dîner 1 *vi* to have dinner; (*au Canada*, *en Belgique*) to have lunch. **2** *m* dinner.
dînette *f* (*jouet*) doll's dinner service *ou* set.
dinosaure *m* dinosaur.
diphtongue [dif-] *f* diphthong.
diplôme *m* certificate, diploma.
dire* *vt* (*mot*) to say; (*vérité*, *secret*, *heure*) to tell; **d. des bêtises** to talk nonsense; **d. qch à qn** to tell s.o. sth, say sth to s.o.; **d. à qn que** to tell s.o. that, say to s.o. that; **d. à qn de faire** to tell s.o. to do; **on dirait un château/du Mozart** it looks like a castle/sounds like Mozart; **ça ne me dit rien** (*envie*) I don't feel like it; (*souvenir*) it doesn't ring a bell; **ça ne se dit pas** that's not said.
direct, -e 1 *a* direct; **train d.** fast train. **2** *m* **en d.** (*émission*) live.
directement *adv* directly.
directeur, -trice *mf* director; (*d'école*) headmaster, headmistress, *Am* principal.
direction *f* (*sens*) direction; **en d. de** (*train*) to, for; **sous la d. de** (*orchestre*) conducted by; **la d.** (*équipe dirigeante*) the management.
dirigeable *a* & *m* **(ballon) d.** airship, dirigible.
dirigeant *m* (*de parti etc*) leader; (*d'entreprise*, *club*) manager.
diriger *vt* (*société*) to run; (*parti*, *groupe*) to lead; (*véhicule*) to

steer; (*orchestre*) to conduct; (*arme etc*) to point (**vers** towards); **se d. vers** (*lieu*) to make one's way towards.

dis, disant *voir* **dire.**

discipline *f* (*règle*) discipline.

discipliné, -ée *a* well-disciplined.

discipliner (se) *vpr* to discipline oneself.

disco *f* disco.

discothèque *f* (*club*) discothèque.

discours *m* speech.

discret, -ète *a* (*personne*) discreet.

discrètement *adv* discreetly.

discrétion *f* discretion.

discrimination *f* discrimination.

discussion *f* discussion; (*conversation*) talk; **pas de d.!** no argument!

discuter *vi* (*parler*) to talk (**de** about); (*répliquer*) to argue; **d. sur qch** to discuss sth.

dise(nt) *etc voir* **dire.**

disloquer (se) *vpr* (*meuble*) to fall apart.

disparaître* *vi* to disappear; (*être porté manquant*) to go missing.

disparition *f* disappearance.

disparu, -ue *a* (*soldat*) missing.

dispense *f* exemption.

dispenser *vt* **d. qn de** (*obligation*) to exempt s.o. from.

disperser *vt* (*objets*) to scatter.

disperser (se) *vpr* (*foule*) to disperse.

disponible *a* (*article, place etc*) available.

disposé, -ée *a* **bien d.** in a good mood; **d. à faire** prepared to do.

disposer 1 *vt* (*objets*) to arrange; **se d. à faire** to prepare to do. **2** *vi* **d. de qch** to make use of sth.

dispositif *m* (*mécanisme*) device.

disposition *f* arrangement; **à la d. de qn** at s.o.'s disposal; **prendre ses dispositions** to make arrangements.

dispute *f* quarrel.

disputer *vt* (*match*) to play; (*rallye*) to compete in; **d. qn** (*gronder*) to tell s.o. off.

disputer (se) *vpr* to quarrel (**avec** with).

disqualifier *vt* (*équipe*) to disqualify.

disque *m* (*de musique*) record; (*cercle*) disc, *Am* disk; (*d'ordinateur*) disk; **d. compact** compact disc *ou Am* disk.

disquette *f* (*d'ordinateur*) floppy (disk).

dissertation *f* (*au lycée etc*) essay.

dissimuler *vt* (*cacher*) to hide (**à** from); **se d.** to hide (oneself).
dissipé, -ée *a* (*élève*) unruly.
dissiper *vt* (*brouillard*) to dispel; **d. qn** to distract s.o.
dissiper (se) *vpr* (*brume*) to lift; (*élève*) to misbehave.
dissoudre* *vt*, **se dissoudre** *vpr* to dissolve.
distance *f* distance; **à deux mètres de d.** two metres apart.
distancer *vt* to leave behind.
distinct, -incte *a* distinct.
distinctement *adv* clearly.
distinguer *vt* to distinguish; (*voir*) to make out; **d. le blé de l'orge** to tell wheat from barley; **se d. de** to be distinguishable from.
distraction *f* amusement; (*étourderie*) absent-mindedness.
distraire* *vt* (*divertir*) to entertain; **se d.** to amuse oneself.
distrait, -aite *a* absent-minded.
distribuer *vt* (*donner*) to hand out; (*courrier*) to deliver; (*cartes*) to deal.
distributeur *m* **d. (automatique)** vending machine; **d. de billets** ticket machine; (*de banque*) cash dispenser *ou* machine.
distribution *f* distribution; (*du courrier*) delivery.
dit, dite, dites *voir* **dire**.
divan *m* couch.
divers, -erses *apl* (*distincts*) varied; (*plusieurs*) various.
divertir *vt* to entertain.
divertir (se) *vpr* to enjoy oneself.
divertissement *m* entertainment.
diviser *vt*, **se diviser** *vpr* to divide (**en** into).
division *f* division.
divorce *m* divorce.
divorcé, -ée *a* divorced.
divorcer *vi* to get divorced.
dix [dis] ([di] *before consonant*, [diz] *before vowel*) *a* & *m* ten.
dix-huit *a* & *m* eighteen.
dixième *a* & *mf* tenth.
dix-neuf [diznœf] *a* & *m* nineteen.
dix-sept *a* & *m* seventeen.
dizaine *f* **une d. (de)** about ten.
docile *a* docile.
docker *m* docker.
docteur *m* doctor.
doctorat *m* doctorate, = PhD.
document *m* document.
documentaire *m* (*film*) documentary.

documentaliste *mf* (*à l'école*) (school) librarian.
documentation *f* (*documents*) documentation.
documenter (se) *vpr* to collect information.
dodo *m* (*langage enfantin*) **faire d.** to sleep.
doigt *m* finger; **d. de pied** toe; **petit d.** little finger, *Am* pinkie.
dois, doit, doive(nt) *voir* **devoir**[1,2].
dollar *m* dollar.
domaine *m* (*terres*) estate.
dôme *m* dome.
domestique **1** *a* (*animal*) domestic; **travaux domestiques** housework. **2** *mf* servant.
domicile *m* home; **livrer à d.** to deliver (to the house).
domination *f* domination.
dominer **1** *vt* to dominate. **2** *vi* (*être le plus fort*) to dominate.
domino *m* domino; **dominos** (*jeu*) dominoes.
dommage *m* **(c'est) d.!** it's a pity *ou* a shame! (**que** + *subjonctif* that); **dommages** (*dégâts*) damage.
dompter *vt* (*animal*) to tame.
dompteur, -euse *mf* (*de lions*) lion tamer.
don *m* (*cadeau, uptitude*) gift; (*charité*) donation.
donc [dɔ̃(k)] *conj* (*par conséquent*) so; **asseyez-vous d.!** will you sit down!
données *fpl* (*information*) data.
donner **1** *vt* to give; (*récolte*) to produce; (*sa place*) to give up; (*cartes*) to deal; **d. un coup à** to hit; **d. à réparer** to take (in) to be repaired; **ça donne soif/faim** it makes you thirsty/hungry; **se d. du mal** to go to a lot of trouble (**pour faire** to do). **2** *vi* **d. sur** (*fenêtre*) to overlook; (*porte*) to open onto.
dont *pron rel* (= **de qui, duquel, de quoi** *etc*) (*personne*) of whom; (*chose*) of which; (*appartenance*: *personne, chose*) whose; **une mère d. le fils est malade** a mother whose son is ill; **la fille d. il est fier** the daughter he is proud of *ou* of whom he is proud; **la façon d.** the way in which.
doré, -ée *a* (*objet*) gilt, gold; (*couleur*) golden.
dorer *vt* (*objet*) to gild; **se d. au soleil** to sunbathe.
dormir* *vi* to sleep.
dortoir *m* dormitory.
dos *m* (*de personne, d'animal*) back; **à d. d'âne** (riding) on a donkey; **'voir au d.'** (*verso*) 'see over'.
dose *f* dose.
dossier *m* (*de siège*) back; (*papiers*) file.
douane *f* customs.

douanier *m* customs officer.

double 1 *a & adv* double. **2** *m* **le d. (de)** (*quantité*) twice as much (as), double; **je l'ai en d.** I have two of them.

doubler 1 *vt* (*vêtement*) to line; (*film*) to dub. **2** *vti* (*augmenter*) to double; (*en voiture*) to overtake.

doublure *f* (*étoffe*) lining.

douce *voir* **doux**.

doucement *adv* (*délicatement*) gently; (*à voix basse*) softly; (*lentement*) slowly.

douceur *f* (*de miel*) sweetness; (*de peau*) softness; (*de temps*) mildness.

douche *f* shower.

doucher *vt* **d. qn** to give s.o. a shower; **se d.** to take *ou* have a shower.

doué, -ée *a* gifted (**en** at); (*intelligent*) clever.

douillet, -ette *a* (*lit*) soft, cosy, *Am* cozy; **tu es d.** (*délicat*) you're such baby.

douleur *f* (*mal*) pain; (*chagrin*) sorrow.

douloureux, -euse *a* painful.

doute *m* doubt; **sans d.** probably, no doubt.

douter *vi* to doubt; **se d. de qch** to suspect sth; **je m'en doute** I would think so.

doux, douce *a* (*miel etc*) sweet; (*peau*) soft; (*temps*) mild.

douzaine *f* dozen; (*environ*) about twelve; **une d. d'œufs**/*etc* a dozen eggs/*etc*.

douze *a & m* twelve.

douzième *a & mf* twelfth.

dragée *f* sugared almond.

dragon *m* (*animal*) dragon.

draguer *vt* (*rivière*) to dredge; (*personne*) *Fam* to chat up, *Am* smooth-talk.

dramatique *a* dramatic; **film d.** drama.

drame *m* drama; (*catastrophe*) tragedy.

drap *m* (*de lit*) sheet; **d. housse** fitted sheet; **d. de bain** bath towel.

drapeau, -x *m* flag.

dressage *m* training.

dresser *vt* (*échelle*) to put up; (*animal*) to train.

dresser (se) *vpr* (*personne*) to stand up; (*montagne*) to stand.

dribbler *vti Football* to dribble.

drogue *f* **une d.** (*stupéfiant*) a drug; **la d.** drugs.

drogué, -ée *mf* drug addict.

droguer (se) *vpr* to take drugs.

droguerie *f* hardware shop *ou Am* store.
droit[1] *m* (*privilège*) right (**de faire** to do); (*d'inscription etc*) fee(s); **le d.** (*science*) law; **avoir d. à** to be entitled to.
droit[2], **droite 1** *a* (*route etc*) straight; (*vertical*) upright; (*angle*) right. **2** *adv* straight; **tout d.** straight ahead.
droit[3], **droite** *a* (*côté etc*) right.
droite *f* **la d.** (*côté*) the right (side); **à d.** (*tourner*) (to the) right; (*rouler etc*) on the right; **de d.** (*fenêtre etc*) right-hand; **à d. de** on *ou* to the right of.
droitier, -ière *a* & *mf* right-handed (person).
drôle *a* funny; **d. d'air/de type** funny look/fellow.
drôlement *adv* (*extrêmement*) terribly.
du *voir* **de**[1,2], **le.**
dû, due (*pp of* **devoir**[1,2]) *a* **d. à** due to.
duc *m* duke.
duchesse *f* duchess.
duel *m* duel.
dune *f* (sand) dune.
duplex *m* split-level flat, *Am* duplex.
duquel *voir* **lequel**.
dur, -e 1 *a* (*substance*) hard; (*difficile*) hard, tough; (*hiver, personne, ton*) harsh; (*œuf*) hard-boiled. **2** *adv* (*travailler*) hard.
durant *prép* during.
durcir *vti*, **se durcir** *vpr* to harden.
durée *f* (*de film etc*) length.
durer *vi* to last; **ça dure depuis** it's been going on for.
dureté *f* hardness; (*de ton etc*) harshness.
duvet *m* (*d'oiseau*) down; (*sac*) sleeping bag.
dynamique *a* dynamic.
dynamite *f* dynamite.
dynamo *f* dynamo.
dyslexique *a* & *mf* dyslexic.

E

eau, -x *f* water; **e. douce/salée** fresh/salt water; **e. de Cologne** eau de Cologne; **tomber à l'e.** (*projet*) to fall through.
eau-de-vie *f* (*pl* **eaux-de-vie**) brandy.
ébattre (s') *vpr* to run about, play about.
ébéniste *m* cabinet-maker.
éblouir *vt* to dazzle.
éboueur *m* dustman, *Am* garbage collector.
ébouillanter (s') *vpr* to scald oneself.
éboulement *m* landslide.
ébouler (s') *vpr* (*falaise*) to crumble; (*roches*) to fall.
ébouriffé, -ée *a* (*cheveux*) dishevelled.
ébranler *vt* to shake; (*santé*) to weaken.
ébranler (s') *vpr* (*train etc*) to move off.
ébrécher *vt* (*assiette*) to chip.
ébullition *f* **être en é.** (*eau*) to be boiling.
écaille *f* (*de poisson*) scale; (*de tortue*) shell; (*pour lunettes*) tortoise-shell; (*de peinture*) flake.
écailler *vt* (*poisson*) to scale; (*huître*) to shell.
écailler (s') *vpr* (*peinture*) to flake (off), peel.
écarlate *a* scarlet.
écarquiller *vt* **é. les yeux** to open one's eyes wide.
écart *m* (*intervalle*) gap; (*embardée*) swerve; (*différence*) difference (**de** in, **entre** between); **à l'é.** out of the way; **à l'é. de** away from.
écarté, -ée *a* (*endroit*) remote; **les jambes écartées** with legs apart.
écarter *vt* (*objets*) to move apart; (*jambes*, *rideaux*) to open; **é. qch de qch** to move sth away from sth; **é. qn de** (*exclure*) to keep s.o. out of.
écarter (s') *vpr* (*s'éloigner*) to move away (**de** from).
échafaud *m* scaffold.
échafaudage *m* (*de peintre etc*) scaffold(ing).
échalote *f* shallot.
échange *m* exchange; **en é.** in exchange (**de** for).
échanger *vt* to exchange (**contre** for).
échangeur *m* (*intersection*) interchange.
échantillon *m* sample.
échapper *vi* **é. à qn** to escape from s.o.; **é. à la mort** to escape death; **ce nom m'échappe** that name escapes me.
échapper (s') *vpr* (*s'enfuir*) to escape (**de** from); (*gaz*, *eau*) to escape.
écharde *f* splinter.

écharpe *f* scarf; (*de maire*) sash; **en é.** (*bras*) in a sling.
échauffer (s') *vpr* (*sportif*) to warm up.
échec *m* failure; **les échecs** (*jeu*) chess; **é.!** check!; **é. et mat!** checkmate!
échelle *f* (*marches*) ladder; (*dimension*) scale; **faire la courte é. à qn** to give s.o. a leg up *ou Am* a boost.
échelon *m* (*d'échelle*) rung; (*de fonctionnaire*) grade.
échiquier *m* chessboard.
écho *m* (*d'un son*) echo.
échouer *vi* to fail; **é. à** (*examen*) to fail.
échouer (s') *vpr* (*navire*) to run aground.
éclabousser *vt* to splash (**de** with).
éclaboussure *f* splash.
éclair *m* (*lumière*) flash; (*d'orage*) flash of lightning.
éclairage *m* (*de pièce etc*) lighting.
éclaircie *f* (*durée*) sunny spell.
éclaircir *vt* (*couleur etc*) to make lighter; (*mystère*) to clear up.
éclaircir (s') *vpr* (*ciel*) to clear (up); (*situation*) to become clear.
éclaircissement *m* explanation.
éclairé, -ée *a* **bien/mal é.** well/badly lit.
éclairer *vt* (*pièce etc*) to light (up); **é. qn** (*avec une lampe*) to give s.o. some light.
éclairer (s') *vpr* (*visage*) to brighten up; (*situation*) to become clear; **s'é. à la bougie** to use candlelight.
éclaireur, -euse *mf* (boy) scout, (girl) guide.
éclat[1] *m* (*de la lumière*) brightness; (*de phare*) glare.
éclat[2] *m* (*de verre ou de bois*) splinter; (*de rire*) (out)burst.
éclatant, -ante *a* (*lumière, succès*) brilliant.
éclatement *m* (*de pneu etc*) bursting; (*de bombe*) explosion.
éclater *vi* (*pneu etc*) to burst; (*bombe*) to go off; (*verre*) to shatter; (*guerre, incendie*) to break out; (*orage*) to break; **é. de rire** to burst out laughing; **é. en sanglots** to burst into tears.
éclore* *vi* (*œuf*) to hatch.
éclosion *f* hatching.
écluse *f* (*de canal*) lock.
écœurer *vt* to make (*s.o.*) feel sick.
école *f* school; **à l'é.** in *ou* at school; **aller à l'é.** to go to school.
écolier, -ière *mf* schoolboy, schoolgirl.
écologiste *mf* environmentalist.
économe *a* thrifty.
économie *f* economy; **économies** (*argent*) savings; **une é. de** a saving of; **faire des économies** to save (up).

économique *a* (*bon marché*) economical.
économiser *vti* to economize (**sur** on).
écorce *f* (*d'arbre*) bark; (*de fruit*) peel, skin.
écorcher *vt* (*érafler*) to graze; **s'é.** to graze oneself; **é. les oreilles** to grate on one's ears.
écorchure *f* graze.
écossais, -aise 1 *a* Scottish; (*tissu*) tartan; (*whisky*) Scotch. **2** *mf* Scot.
écosser *vt* (*pois*) to shell.
écoulement *m* (*de liquide*) flow; (*de temps*) passage.
écouler (s') *vpr* (*eau*) to flow out; (*temps*) to pass.
écouter 1 *vt* to listen to. **2** *vi* to listen.
écouteur *m* (*de téléphone*) earpiece; **écouteurs** (*casque*) earphones.
écran *m* screen; **le petit é.** television.
écrasant, -ante *a* overwhelming.
écraser *vt* to crush; (*cigarette*) to put *ou* stub out; (*piéton*) to run over; **se faire é.** to get run over.
écraser (s') *vpr* to crash (**contre** into).
écrémé *a* (*lait*) skimmed.
écrier (s') *vpr* to exclaim (**que** that).
écrire* 1 *vt* to write; (*en toutes lettres*) to spell; **é. à la machine** to type. **2** *vi* to write.
écrire (s') *vpr* (*mot*) to be spelled *ou* spelt.
écrit *m* **par é.** in writing.
écriteau, -x *m* notice, sign.
écriture *f* writing.
écrivain *m* author, writer.
écrou *m* (*de boulon*) nut.
écrouler (s') *vpr* to collapse.
écueil *m* reef; (*obstacle*) pitfall.
écuelle *f* bowl.
écume *f* (*de mer etc*) foam.
écureuil *m* squirrel.
écurie *f* stable.
écusson *m* (*en étoffe*) badge.
édifice *m* building.
édifier *vt* to erect.
éditer *vt* to publish.
éditeur, -trice *mf* publisher.
édition *f* (*livre, journal*) edition; (*métier*) publishing.
édredon *m* eiderdown.
éducatif, -ive *a* educational.

éducation *f* education; **avoir de l'é.** to have good manners.
éduquer *vt* to educate.
effacer *vt* to rub out, erase; (*en lavant*) to wash out; (*avec un chiffon*) to wipe away.
effectif *m* (*de classe etc*) total number.
effectivement *adv* actually.
effectuer *vt* (*expérience etc*) to carry out; (*trajet etc*) to make.
effet *m* effect (**sur** on); **faire de l'e.** (*remède*) to be effective; **en e.** indeed, in fact; **sous l'e. de la colère** in anger.
efficace *a* (*mesure etc*) effective; (*personne*) efficient.
efficacité *f* effectiveness; efficiency.
effilocher (s') *vpr* to fray.
effleurer *vt* to skim, touch (lightly).
effondrer (s') *vpr* to collapse.
efforcer (s') *vpr* **s'e. de faire** to try (hard) to do.
effort *m* effort; **sans e.** (*réussir etc*) effortlessly.
effrayant, -ante *a* frightening.
effrayer *vt* to frighten, scare.
effroyable *a* dreadful.
égal, -e, -aux 1 *a* equal (**à** to); (*uniforme, régulier*) even; **ça m'est é.** I don't care. **2** *mf* (*personne*) equal.
également *adv* (*aussi*) also, as well.
égaler *vt* to equal.
égaliser *vi* to equalize.
égalité *f* equality; (*regularité*) evenness; **à é. (de score)** even, equal (in points).
égard *m* **à l'é. de** (*envers*) towards.
égarer *vt* (*objet*) to mislay.
égarer (s') *vpr* to lose one's way.
égayer *vt* (*pièce*) to brighten up; **é. qn** to cheer s.o. up.
église *f* church.
égoïste *a* & *mf* selfish (person).
égorger *vt* to cut the throat of.
égout *m* sewer; **eaux d'é.** sewage.
égoutter 1 *vt* to drain. **2** *vi*, **s'égoutter** *vpr* to drain; (*linge*) to drip.
égouttoir *m* (dish) drainer.
égratigner *vt* to scratch.
égratignure *f* scratch.
eh! *int* hey!; **eh bien!** well!
élan *m* (*vitesse*) momentum; (*impulsion*) impulse; **prendre son é.** to take a run (up).

élancer (s') *vpr* (*bondir*) to leap *ou* rush (forward).
élargir *vt*, **s'élargir** *vpr* (*route etc*) to widen.
élastique 1 *a* (*objet*) elastic. **2** *m* (*lien*) elastic *ou* rubber band.
électeur, -trice *mf* voter.
élection *f* election.
électoral, -e, -aux *a* **campagne électorale** election campaign.
électricien *m* electrician.
électricité *f* electricity.
électrique *a* electric.
électrocuter *vt* to electrocute.
électronique *a* electronic.
électrophone *m* record player.
élégance *f* elegance; **avec é.** elegantly; (*s'habiller*) smartly.
élégant, -ante *a* elegant; (*bien habillé*) smart.
élément *m* element; (*de meuble*) unit; **éléments** (*notions*) rudiments.
élémentaire *a* basic; (*cours, école etc*) elementary.
éléphant *m* elephant.
élevage *m* breeding, rearing.
élève *mf* pupil.
élevé, -ée *a* (*haut*) high; **bien/mal é.** well-/bad-mannered.
élever *vt* (*prix, voix etc*) to raise; (*enfant*) to bring up, raise; (*animal*) to breed, rear.
élever (s') *vpr* (*prix, ton etc*) to rise; **s'é. à** (*prix*) to amount to.
éleveur, -euse *mf* breeder.
éliminatoire *a* & *f* **(épreuve) é.** heat.
éliminer *vt* to eliminate.
élire* *vt* to elect (**à** to).
elle *pron* (*sujet*) she; (*chose, animal*) it; **elles** they. ▮ (*complément*) her; (*chose, animal*) it; **elles** them.
elle-même *pron* herself; (*chose, animal*) itself; **elles-mêmes** themselves.
éloigné, -ée *a* (*lieu*) far away; (*date*) distant; **é. de** (*village etc*) far (away) from.
éloigner *vt* (*chose, personne*) to move *ou* take away (**de** from).
éloigner (s') *vpr* (*partir*) to move *ou* go away (**de** from).
émail, -aux *m* enamel.
emballage *m* (*action*) packing; wrapping; (*caisse*) packaging; (*papier*) wrapping (paper).
emballer *vt* (*dans une caisse etc*) to pack; (*dans du papier*) to wrap (up); **e. qn** (*passionner*) to thrill s.o.
emballer (s') *vpr* (*personne*) to get carried away; (*cheval*) to bolt.
embarcadère *m* quay, wharf.

embarcation *f* (small) boat.
embardée *f* (sudden) swerve.
embarquement *m* (*de passagers*) boarding.
embarquer 1 *vt* (*passagers*) to take on board; (*marchandises*) to load (up). **2** *vi*, **s'embarquer** *vpr* to (go on) board.
embarras *m* (*gêne*) embarrassment.
embarrassant, -ante *a* (*paquet*) cumbersome; (*question*) embarrassing.
embarrasser *vt* **e. qn** to be in s.o.'s way; (*question etc*) to embarrass s.o.; **s'e. de** to burden oneself with.
embaucher *vt* (*ouvrier*) to hire.
embêtant, -ante *a* annoying; boring.
embêtement *m* trouble.
embêter *vt* (*agacer*) to bother; (*ennuyer*) to bore.
embêter (s') *vpr* to get bored.
emboîter *vt*, **s'emboîter** *vpr* (*tuyau*(*x*))to fit together.
embouchure *f* (*de fleuve*) mouth.
embourber (s') *vpr* to get bogged down.
embouteillage *m* traffic jam.
embouteillé, -ée *a* (*rue*) congested.
emboutir *vt* (*voiture*) to crash into.
embranchement *m* (*de voie*) junction.
embrasser *vt* (*donner un baiser à*) to kiss; **s'e.** to kiss (each other).
embrayage *m* (*de véhicule*) clutch.
embrocher *vt* to skewer.
embrouiller *vt* (*fils*) to tangle (up); (*papiers etc*) to mix up; **e. qn** to confuse s.o.
embrouiller (s') *vpr* to get confused (**dans** in, with).
embuscade *f* ambush.
émerger *vi* to emerge (**de** from).
émerveiller *vt* to amaze, fill with wonder.
émetteur *m* (**poste**) **é.** transmitter.
émettre* *vt* (*lumière, son etc*) to give out; (*message radio*) to broadcast; (*timbre, monnaie*) to issue.
émeute *f* riot.
émietter *vt*, **s'émietter** *vpr* to crumble.
émigrer *vi* to emigrate.
émission *f* (*de radio etc*) broadcast; (*diffusion*) transmission; (*de timbre, monnaie*) issue.
emmanchure *f* arm hole.
emmêler *vt* to tangle (up).
emménager *vi* (*dans un logement*) to move in; **e. dans** to move

into.

emmener *vt* to take (**à** to); **e. qn en promenade** to take s.o. for a walk.

emmitoufler (s') *vpr* to wrap (oneself) up.

émotion *f* emotion; (*trouble*) excitement; **une é.** (*peur*) a scare.

émouvant, -ante *a* moving.

émouvoir* *vt* to move, touch.

empailler *vt* to stuff.

emparer (s') *vpr* **s'e. de** to take, grab.

empêchement *m* **avoir un e.** to have soomething come up at the last minute (*to prevent or delay an action*).

empêcher *vt* to prevent, stop (**de faire** (from) doing); **elle ne peut pas s'e. de rire** she can't help laughing.

empereur *m* emperor.

empester 1 *vt* (*tabac etc*) to stink of; **e. qn** to stink s.o. out. **2** *vi* to stink.

empiler *vt*, **s'empiler** *vpr* to pile up (**sur** on).

empire *m* empire.

emplacement *m* site; (*de stationnement*) place.

emplir *vt*, **s'emplir** *vpr* to fill (**de** with).

emploi *m* (*usage*) use; (*travail*) job, employment; **e. du temps** timetable; **sans e.** (*au chômage*) unemployed.

employé, -ée *mf* employee; (*de bureau*, *banque*) clerk, employee.

employer *vt* (*utiliser*) to use; **e. qn** to employ s.o.

employer (s') *vpr* (*expression*) to be used.

employeur, -euse *mf* employer.

empoigner *vt* to grab.

empoisonner *vt* to poison; **s'e.** to poison oneself; (*par accident*) to be poisoned.

emporter *vt* (*prendre*) to take (away) (**avec soi** with one); (*entraîner*) to carry away; (*par le vent*) to blow off *ou* away.

emporter (s') *vpr* to lose one's temper (**contre** with).

empreinte *f* mark; **e. (digitale)** fingerprint; **e. (de pas)** footprint.

empresser (s') *vpr* **s'e. de faire** to hasten to do.

emprisonner *vt* to jail.

emprunt *m* (*argent etc*) loan.

emprunter *vt* (*argent*) to borrow (**à** from); (*route*) to use.

ému, -ue *a* moved; (*attristé*) upset.

en[1] *prép* (*lieu*) in; (*direction*) to; **être/aller en France** to be in/go to France. ∎ (*temps*) in; **en février** in February; **d'heure en heure** from hour to hour. ∎ (*moyen*, *état etc*) by; in; on; **en avion** by plane; **en groupe** in a group; **en congé** on leave. ∎ (*matière*) in; **en bois** in wood; **chemise en nylon** nylon shirt; **c'est en or** it's (made of) gold. ▮ (*comme*) **en cadeau** as a present. ▮ (+ *participe présent*) **en mangeant**/*etc* while eating/*etc*; **en apprenant que** on hearing that; **en souriant** smiling, with a smile. ▮ (*transformation*) into; **traduire en** to translate into.

en[2] *pron & adv* (= *de là*) from there; **j'en viens** I've just come from there. ▮ (= *de ça, lui etc*) **il en est content** he's pleased with it *ou* him *ou* them; **en parler** to talk about it; **en mourir** to die of *ou* from it. ▮ (*partitif*) some; **j'en ai** I have some.

encadrer *vt* (*tableau*) to frame; (*entourer d'un trait*) to circle (*word*).

encaisser *vt* (*argent, loyer etc*) to collect.

enceinte *a* (*femme*) pregnant; **e. de six mois** six months pregnant.

encens [ɑ̃sɑ̃] *m* incense.

encercler *vt* to surround.

enchaîner *vt* to chain (up); (*idées etc*) to link (up).

enchaîner (s') *vpr* (*idées etc*) to be linked (up).

enchanté, -ée *a* (*ravi*) delighted (**de** with, **que** (+ *subjonctif*) that); **e. de faire votre connaissance!** pleased to meet you!

enchantement *m* delight; **comme par e.** as if by magic.

enchanter *vt* (*ravir*) to delight.

enchanteur *m* magician.

enclos *m* enclosure.

encoche *f* nick (**à** in).

encolure *f* neck; (*tour du cou*) collar (size).

encombrant, -ante *a* (*paquet*) bulky.

encombrement *m* (*d'objets*) clutter; (*de rue*) traffic jam.

encombrer *vt* (*pièce etc*) to clutter up (**de** with); (*rue*) to congest (**de** with); **e. qn** to hamper s.o.

encore *adv* (*toujours*) still; **e. là** still here. ▮ (*avec négation*) yet; **pas e.** not yet. ▮ (*de nouveau*) again; **essaie e.** try again. ▮ (*de plus*) **e. un café** another coffee, one more coffee; **e. une fois** (once) again, once more; **e. un** another (one), one more; **e. du pain** (some) more bread; **e. quelque chose** something else; **qui/quoi e.?** who/what else? ▮ (*avec comparatif*) even, still; **e. mieux** even better, better still.

encourageant, -ante *a* encouraging.

encouragement *m* encouragement.

encourager *vt* to encourage (**à faire** to do).

encrasser *vt* to clog up (with dirt).

encre *f* ink; **e. de Chine** Indian *ou Am* India ink.

encrier *m* inkpot.

encyclopédie *f* encyclop(a)edia.

endetter (s') *vpr* to get into debt.

endive *f* chicory, endive.
endommager *vt* to damage.
endormi, -ie *a* asleep, sleeping.
endormir* *vt* to put to sleep.
endormir (s') *vpr* to fall asleep, go to sleep.
endroit *m* (*lieu*) place; **à l'e.** (*vêtement*) right side out.
endurant, -ante *a* tough.
endurcir *vt* **e. qn** to harden s.o.; **s'e. à** to become hardened to (*pain etc*).
endurer *vt* to endure.
énergie *f* energy.
énergique *a* energetic; (*remède*) powerful; (*mesure*, *ton*) forceful.
énergiquement *adv* energetically.
énervé, -ée *a* on edge.
énerver *vt* **é. qn** (*irriter*) to get on s.o.'s nerves; (*rendre énervé*) to make s.o. nervous.
énerver (s') *vpr* to get worked up.
enfance *f* childhood.
enfant *mf* child (*pl* children); **e. en bas âge** infant; **e. de chœur** altar boy.
enfantin, -ine *a* (*voix*, *joie*) childlike; (*simple*) easy.
enfer *m* hell; **d'e.** (*bruit etc*) infernal; **à un train d'e.** at breakneck speed.
enfermer *vt* to lock up; **s'e. dans** (*chambre etc*) to lock oneself (up) in.
enfiler *vt* (*aiguille*) to thread; (*perles etc*) to string; (*vêtement*) to pull on.
enfin *adv* (*à la fin*) finally, at last; (*en dernier lieu*) lastly; **e. bref** in a word; **(mais) e.!** for heaven's sake!
enflammer *vt* to set fire to; (*allumette*) to light; (*irriter*) to inflame (*throat etc*).
enflammer (s') *vpr* to catch fire.
enfler *vti* to swell.
enflure *f* swelling.
enfoncer 1 *vt* (*clou*) to knock in, bang in; (*porte*, *voiture*) to smash in; **e. dans qch** (*couteau*, *mains etc*) to plunge into sth. **2** *vi*, **s'enfoncer** *vpr* (*s'enliser*) to sink (**dans** into).
enfouir *vt* to bury.
enfuir* (s') *vpr* to run away *ou* off (**de** from).
enfumer *vt* (*pièce*) to fill with smoke.
engagement *m* (*promesse*) commitment; (*dans une compétition*) entry; **prendre l'e. de** to undertake to.

engager *vt* (*discussion, combat*) to start; **e. qn** (*embaucher*) to hire s.o.
engager (s') *vpr* (*dans l'armée*) to enlist; (*sportif*) to enter (**pour** for); (*action, jeu*) to start; **s'e. à faire** to undertake to do.
engelure *f* chilblain.
engin *m* machine; **e. spatial** spaceship.
engloutir *vt* (*nourriture*) to wolf down; (*faire disparaître*) to swallow up.
engouffrer (s') *vpr* **s'e. dans** to sweep *ou* rush into.
engourdir (s') *vpr* to go numb.
engrais *m* fertilizer; (*naturel*) manure.
engraisser 1 *vt* (*animal*) to fatten (up). **2** *vi* to get fat.
engrenage *m* gears.
engueuler *vt* **e. qn** *Fam* to give s.o. hell, bawl s.o. out.
énigme *f* riddle.
enivrer (s') *vpr* to get drunk (**de** on).
enjambée *f* stride.
enjamber *vt* to step over; (*pont etc*) to span (*river etc*).
enjoliveur *m* hubcap.
enlèvement *m* (*d'enfant*) kidnapping.
enlever *vt* to take away (**à qn** from s.o.); (*vêtement*) to take off; (*tache*) to take out; (*enfant etc*) to kidnap.
enlever (s') *vpr* (*tache*) to come out.
enliser (s') *vpr* to get bogged down (**dans** in).
enneigé, -ée *a* snow-covered.
enneigement *m* **bulletin d'e.** snow report.
ennemi, -ie 1 *mf* enemy. **2** *a* **pays/soldat e.** enemy country/soldier.
ennui *m* boredom; **un e.** (*tracas*) trouble; **l'e., c'est que** the annoying thing is that.
ennuyé, -ée *a* (*air*) bored; **je suis e.** that bothers me.
ennuyer *vt* (*agacer, préoccuper*) to bother; (*fatiguer*) to bore.
ennuyer (s') *vpr* to get bored.
ennuyeux, -euse *a* boring; (*contrariant*) annoying
énorme *a* enormous, huge.
énormément *adv* enormously; **e. de** an enormous amount of.
enquête *f* (*de police*) investigation; (*judiciaire*) inquiry; (*sondage*) survey.
enquêter *vi* to investigate; **e. sur** to investigate.
enquêteur, -euse *mf* investigator.
enragé, -ée *a* (*chien*) rabid; (*furieux*) furious.
enregistrement *m* (*des bagages*) registration, *Am* checking; (*sur bande etc*) recording.

enregistrer 1 *vt* (*par écrit, sur bande etc*) to record; **(faire) e.** (*bagages*) to register, *Am* check. **2** *vi* to record; **ça enregistre** it's recording.
enrhumer (s') *vpr* to catch a cold.
enrichir (s') *vpr* to get rich.
enrobé, -ée *a* **e. de chocolat** chocolate-coated.
enroué, -ée *a* hoarse.
enrouler *vt* to wind; (*tapis*) to roll up; **s'e. dans** (*couvertures*) to wrap oneself up in.
enseignant, -ante *mf* teacher.
enseigne *f* sign; **e. lumineuse** neon sign.
enseignement *m* education; (*action, métier*) teaching.
enseigner 1 *vt* to teach; **e. qch à qn** to teach s.o. sth. **2** *vi* to teach.
ensemble 1 *adv* together. **2** *m* (*d'objets*) set; (*vêtement féminin*) outfit; **l'e. du personnel** the whole of the staff; **l'e. des enseignants** all of the teachers; **dans l'e.** on the whole; **d'e.** (*vue etc*) general.
ensevelir *vt* to bury.
ensoleillé, -ée *a* sunny.
ensuite *adv* (*puis*) next; (*plus tard*) afterwards.
entaille *f* (*fente*) notch; (*blessure*) gash.
entailler *vt* to notch; to gash.
entamer *vt* (*pain, peau etc*) to cut (into); (*bouteille etc*) to start (on).
entasser *vt*, **s'entasser** *vpr* (*objets*) to pile up; **(s')e. dans** (*passagers etc*) to crowd *ou* pile into.
entendre *vt* to hear; **e. parler de** to hear of; **e. dire que** to hear (it said) that.
entendre (s') *vpr* (*être d'accord*) to agree (**sur** on); **s'e. (avec qn)** to get on (with s.o.).
entendu, -ue *a* (*convenu*) agreed; **e.!** all right!; **bien e.** of course.
entente *f* (*accord*) agreement; **(bonne) e.** (*amitié*) good relationship.
enterrement *m* burial; (*funérailles*) funeral.
enterrer *vt* to bury.
entêtement *m* stubbornness; (*à faire qch*) persistence.
entêter (s') *vpr* to persist (**à faire** in doing).
enthousiasme *m* enthusiasm.
enthousiasmer *vt* to fill with enthusiasm; **s'e. pour** to be *ou* get enthusiastic about.
enthousiaste *a* enthusiastic.
entier, -ière 1 *a* (*total*) whole; (*intact*) intact; **le pays tout e.** the whole country. **2** *m* **en e.** completely.
entièrement *adv* entirely.

entonnoir *m* (*ustensile*) funnel.
entorse *f* sprain.
entortiller *vt* **e. qch autour de qch** to wrap sth around sth.
entourage *m* circle of family and friends.
entourer *vt* to surround (**de** with); **entouré de** surrounded by.
entracte *m* (*au théâtre*) interval, *Am* intermission.
entraider (s') *vpr* to help each other.
entrain *m* **plein d'e.** lively.
entraînant, -ante *a* (*musique*) lively.
entraînement *m* (*sportif*) training.
entraîner *vt* to carry away; (*causer*) to bring about; (*emmener de force*) to drag (*s.o.*) (away); (*athlète etc*) to train (**à** for).
entraîner (s') *vpr* (*sportif*) to train.
entraîneur *m* (*d'athlète*) coach.
entre *prép* between; **l'un d'e. vous** one of you.
entrebâillé, -ée *a* slightly open.
entrebâiller *vt* to open slightly.
entrechoquer (s') *vpr* to chink.
entrecôte *f* (boned *ou Am* filleted) rib steak.
entrée *f* (*action*) entry; (*porte*) entrance; (*accès*) admission (**de** to); (*vestibule*) entrance hall; (*billet*) ticket (for admission); (*plat*) first course; (*en informatique*) input; **à son e.** as he *ou* she came in; **'e. interdite'** 'no entry'; **'e. libre'** 'admission free'.
entreposer *vt* to store.
entrepôt *m* warehouse.
entreprendre* *vt* to undertake (**de faire** to do).
entrepreneur *m* (*en bâtiment*) contractor.
entreprise *f* company, firm.
entrer *vi* (*aux* **être**) to go in; (*venir*) to come in; **e. dans** (*pièce*) to come *ou* go into; (*arbre etc*) to crash into; **faire/laisser e. qn** to show/let s.o. in.
entre-temps *adv* meanwhile.
entretenir* *vt* to maintain; **e. sa forme** to keep fit.
entretenir (s') *vpr* **s'e. de** to talk about (**avec** with).
entretien *m* maintenance; (*dialogue*) conversation; (*entrevue*) interview.
entrevue *f* interview.
entrouvert, -erte *a* half-open.
énumération *f* list(ing).
énumérer *vt* to list.
envahir *vt* to invade; (*herbe etc*) to overrun (*garden*).
envahisseur *m* invader.

enveloppe *f* (*pour lettre*) envelope; **e. timbrée à votre adresse** stamped addressed envelope, *Am* stamped self-addressed envelope.
envelopper *vt* to wrap (up) (**dans** in).
envers 1 *prép* toward(s), to. **2** *m* **à l'e.** (*chaussette*) inside out; (*pantalon*) back to front; (*la tête en bas*) upside down.
envie *f* (*jalousie*) envy; (*désir*) desire; **avoir e. de qch** to want sth; **j'ai e. de faire** I feel like doing.
envier *vt* to envy (**qch à qn** s.o. sth).
environ *adv* (*à peu près*) about.
environnant, -ante *a* surrounding.
environnement *m* environment.
environner *vt* to surround.
environs *mpl* surroundings; **aux environs de** around.
envisager *vt* to consider (**de faire** doing).
envoi *m* sending; (*paquet*) package; **coup d'e.** *Football* kick-off.
envoler (s') *vpr* (*oiseau*) to fly away; (*avion*) to take off; (*chapeau etc*) to blow away.
envoyé, -ée *mf* (*reporter*) correspondent.
envoyer* *vt* to send; (*lancer*) to throw.
épais, -aisse *a* thick.
épaisseur *f* thickness.
épaissir *vti*, **s'épaissir** *vpr* to thicken.
épanoui, -ie *a* in full bloom; (*visage*) beaming.
épanouir (s') *vpr* to blossom; (*visage*) to beam.
épargner *vt* (*argent*) to save; (*ennemi etc*) to spare; **e. qch à qn** (*ennuis etc*) to spare s.o. sth.
éparpiller *vt*, **s'éparpiller** *vpr* to scatter.
épatant, -ante *a* marvellous.
épaule *f* shoulder.
épave *f* wreck.
épée *f* sword.
épeler *vt* (*mot*) to spell.
éperon *m* spur.
épi *m* (*de blé etc*) ear.
épice *f* spice.
épicé, -ée *a* spicy.
épicer *vt* to spice.
épicerie *f* grocer's (shop), *Am* grocery (store); (*produits*) groceries.
épicier, -ière *mf* grocer.
épidémie *f* epidemic.
épinards *mpl* spinach.
épine *f* (*de plante*) thorn.

épineux, -euse *a* thorny.
épingle *f* pin; **é. de nourrice** safety pin; **é. à linge** clothes peg, *Am* clothes pin; **é. à cheveux** hairpin.
épisode *m* episode.
épithète *f* (*adjectif*) attribute.
éplucher *vt* (*carotte, pomme etc*) to peel; (*salade*) to clean.
épluchure *f* peeling.
éponge *f* sponge.
éponger *vt* to sponge up.
époque *f* (*date*) time; (*historique*) age.
épouse *f* wife.
épouser *vt* **é. qn** to marry s.o.
épousseter *vt* to dust.
épouvantable *a* terrifying; (*mauvais*) appalling.
épouvantail *m* scarecrow.
épouvante *f* terror; **film d'é.** horror film.
épouvanter *vt* to terrify.
époux *m* husband.
épreuve *f* (*examen*) test; (*sportive*) event; (*malheur*) ordeal.
éprouver *vt* to test; (*sentiment etc*) to feel.
éprouvette *f* test tube.
épuisant, -ante *a* exhausting.
épuisé, -ée *a* exhausted; (*marchandise*) out of stock.
épuiser *vt* to exhaust; **s'é. à faire** to exhaust oneself doing.
épuiser (s') *vpr* (*réserves*) to run out.
équateur *m* equator.
équation *f* equation.
équerre *f* setsquare, *Am* triangle.
équilibre *m* balance; **tenir** *ou* **mettre en é.** to balance (**sur** on); **perdre l'é.** to lose one's balance.
équilibrer *vt* (*budget*) to balance.
équipage *m* crew
équipe *f* team; (*d'ouvriers*) gang; **é. de secours** search party
équipement *m* equipment; (*de camping, ski*) gear.
équiper *vt* to equip (**de** with).
équipier, -ière *mf* team member.
équitable *a* fair.
équitation *f* (horse) riding, *Am* (horseback) riding.
équivalent, -ente *a* & *m* equivalent.
érafler *vt* to graze.
éraflure *f* graze.
errer *vi* to wander.

erreur *f* mistake.
éruption *f* (*de boutons*) rash.
es *voir* **être.**
escabeau, -x *m* stepladder.
escadrille *f* (*groupe d'avions*) flight.
escalade *f* climbing.
escalader *vt* to climb.
escale *f* **faire e. à** (*avion*) to stop (over) at; (*navire*) to put in at.
escalier *m* stairs; **e. roulant** escalator.
escalope *f* escalope (*thin slice of veal*).
escargot *m* snail.
escarpé, -ée *a* steep.
esclave *mf* slave.
escorte *f* escort.
escorter *vt* to escort.
escrime *f* fencing.
escrimeur, -euse *mf* fencer.
escroc [ɛskro] *m* crook.
espace *m* space; **e. vert** garden, park.
espacer *vt* to space out.
espagnol, -ole 1 *a* Spanish. **2** *mf* Spaniard. **3** *m* (*langue*) Spanish.
espèce *f* (*race*) species; (*genre*) kind, sort; **e. d'idiot!** (you) silly fool!
espérance *f* hope.
espérer 1 *vt* to hope for; **e. que** to hope that; **e. faire** to hope to do. **2** *vi* to hope.
espiègle *a* mischievous.
espion, -onne *mf* spy.
espionnage *m* spying.
espionner *vt* to spy on.
espoir *m* hope; **sans e.** (*cas etc*) hopeless.
esprit *m* spirit; (*intellect*) mind; (*humour*) wit; **venir à l'e. de qn** to cross s.o.'s mind.
Esquimau, -de, -aux *mf* Eskimo.
esquiver *vt* to dodge.
essai *m* (*épreuve*) test; (*tentative*) try, attempt; *Rugby* try.
essaim *m* swarm (*of bees etc*).
essayage *m* (*de costume*) fitting.
essayer *vt* to try (**de faire** to do); (*vêtement*) to try on.
essence *f* petrol, *Am* gas.
essentiel, -ielle 1 *a* essential. **2** *m* **l'e.** the main thing.

essentiellement *adv* essentially.
essieu, -x *m* axle.
essoufflé, -ée *a* out of breath.
essuie-glace *m* windscreen wiper, *Am* windshield wiper.
essuie-mains *m inv* (hand) towel.
essuyer *vt* to wipe.
est[1] [ɛ] *voir* **être.**
est[2] [ɛst] *m & a inv* east; **d'e.** (*vent*) east(erly); **de l'e.** eastern.
estime *f* regard.
estimer *vt* (*objet*) to value; (*juger*) to consider (**que** that); **e. qn** to have a high regard for s.o.; **s'e. heureux**/*etc* to consider oneself happy/*etc*.
estomac [ɛstɔma] *m* stomach.
estrade *f* platform.
estropier *vt* to cripple.
estuaire *m* estuary.
et *conj* and; **vingt et un**/*etc* twenty-one/*etc*.
étable *f* cowshed.
établi *m* (work)bench.
établir *vt* (*installer*) to set up; (*plan, liste*) to draw up.
établir (s') *vpr* (*habiter*) to settle.
établissement *m* establishment; **é. scolaire** school.
étage *m* (*d'immeuble*) floor; **à l'é.** upstairs; **au premier é.** on the first *ou Am* second floor.
étagère *f* shelf.
étais, était *etc voir* **être.**
étalage *m* (*vitrine*) display window.
étaler *vt* to lay out; (*en vitrine*) to display; (*beurre etc*) to spread.
étanche *a* watertight; (*montre*) waterproof.
étang *m* pond.
étant *voir* **être.**
étape *f* stage; (*lieu*) stop(over).
Etat *m* (*nation*) State; **homme d'É.** statesman.
état *m* (*condition*) state; **en bon é.** in good condition; **en é. de faire** in a position to do.
étau, -x *m* vice, *Am* vise.
été[1] *pp of* **être.**
été[2] *m* summer; **en é.** in (the) summer.
éteindre* 1 *vt* (*feu etc*) to put out; (*lampe etc*) to turn *ou* switch off. **2** *vi* to switch off.
éteindre (s') *vpr* (*feu*) to go out.
éteint, -einte *a* (*feu, bougie*) out; (*lampe*) off.

étendre *vt* (*nappe*) to spread (out); (*linge*) to hang out; **é. le bras/** *etc* to stretch out one's arm/*etc*.
étendre (s') *vpr* (*personne*) to stretch out; (*plaine*) to stretch; (*feu*) to spread.
étendu, -ue *a* (*forêt etc*) extensive; (*personne*) stretched out.
étendue *f* (*importance*) extent; (*surface*) area.
éternité *f* eternity.
éternuement *m* sneeze.
éternuer *vi* to sneeze.
êtes *voir* **être.**
étinceler *vi* to sparkle.
étincelle *f* spark.
étiqueter *vt* to label.
étiquette *f* label.
étirer (s') *vpr* to stretch (oneself).
étoffe *f* material.
étoile *f* star; **à la belle é.** in the open.
étoilé, -ée *a* (*ciel*) starry.
étonnant, -ante *a* surprising.
étonnement *m* surprise.
étonner *vt* to surprise.
étonner (s') *vpr* to be surprised (**de qch** at sth, **que** (+ *subjonctif*) that).
étouffant, -ante *a* (*air*) stifling.
étouffer 1 *vt* (*tuer*) to suffocate, smother; (*bruit*) to muffle; (*feu*) to smother; **é. qn** (*chaleur*) to stifle s.o. **2** *vi* **on étouffe!** it's stifling!
étouffer (s') *vpr* (*en mangeant*) to choke (**sur, avec** on).
étourderie *f* thoughtlessness; **une é.** a thoughtless blunder.
étourdi, -ie *a* thoughtless.
étourdir *vt* to stun; (*vertige*) to make dizzy.
étourdissant, -ante *a* (*bruit*) deafening.
étourdissement *m* (*malaise*) dizzy spell.
étrange *a* strange, odd.
étranger, -ère 1 *a* (*d'un autre pays*) foreign; (*non familier*) strange (**à** to). **2** *mf* foreigner; (*inconnu*) stranger; **à l'é.** abroad; **de l'é.** from abroad.
étrangler *vt* (*tuer*) to strangle.
étrangler (s') *vpr* to choke.
être* 1 *vi* to be; **il est tailleur** he's a tailor; **est-ce qu'elle vient?** is she coming?; **il vient, n'est-ce pas?** he's coming, isn't he?; **est-ce qu'il aime le thé?** does he like tea?; **nous sommes dix** there are ten of us; **nous sommes le dix** today is the tenth (of the month); **il a été**

à **Paris** he has been to Paris. **2** *v aux* (*avec venir*, *partir etc*) to have; **elle est arrivée** she has arrived. **3** *m* **ê. humain** human being.
étrennes *fpl* New Year gift.
étrier *m* stirrup.
étroit, -oite *a* narrow; (*vêtement*) tight; **être à l'é.** to be cramped.
étroitement *adv* (*surveiller etc*) closely.
étude *f* study; (*salle*) study room; **à l'é.** (*projet*) under consideration; **faire des études de** (*médecine etc*) to study.
étudiant, -ante *mf* & *a* student.
étudier *vti* to study.
étui *m* (*à lunettes etc*) case.
eu, eue [y] *pp of* **avoir.**
euh! [ø] *int* hem!, er!
euro- *préfixe* Euro-.
européen, -enne *a* & *mf* European.
eux *pron* (*sujet*) they; (*complément*) them; (*réfléchi*, *emphase*) themselves.
eux-mêmes *pron* themselves.
évacuer *vt* to evacuate.
évadé, -ée *mf* escaped prisoner.
évader (s') *vpr* to escape (**de** from).
évaluer *vt* to estimate.
Évangile *m* Gospel.
évanouir (s') *vpr* to faint, pass *ou* black out.
évanouissement *m* blackout.
évasion *f* escape (**de** from).
éveiller *vt* (*susciter*) to arouse.
événement *m* event.
éventail *m* fan; (*choix*) range.
éventrer *vt* (*sac*, *oreiller*) to rip open; (*animal*) to open up.
éventuellement *adv* possibly.
évêque *m* bishop.
évidemment [-amɑ̃] *adv* obviously.
évident *a* obvious (**que** that); (*facile*) *Fam* easy.
évier *m* (kitchen) sink.
éviter *vt* to avoid (**de faire** doing); **é. qch à qn** to spare s.o. sth.
ex- *préfixe* ex-; **ex-mari** ex-husband.
exact, -e *a* (*précis*) exact, accurate; (*juste*, *vrai*) correct.
exactement *adv* exactly.
exactitude *f* accuracy; correctness.
ex aequo [ɛgzeko] *adv* **être classés ex ae.** to tie.
exagération *f* exaggeration.

exagéré, -ée *a* excessive.
exagérer *vti* to exaggerate.
examen [ɛgzamɛ̃] *m* examination; (*bac etc*) exam(ination).
examinateur, -trice *mf* examiner.
examiner *vt* to examine.
excédent *m* **e. de bagages** excess luggage *ou Am* baggage.
excellent, -ente *a* excellent.
excepté *prép* except.
exception *f* exception; **à l'e. de** except (for).
exceptionnel, -elle *a* exceptional.
exceptionnellement *adv* exceptionally.
excès *m* excess; **e. de vitesse** speeding.
excessif, -ive *a* excessive.
excitant, -ante *a Fam* exciting.
excitation *f* excitement.
excité, -ée *a* excited.
exciter *vt* **e. qn** (*mettre en colère*) to provoke s.o.
exclamation *f* exclamation.
exclamer (s') *vpr* to exclaim.
exclure* *vt* to exclude (**de** from).
excursion *f* trip, outing; (*à pied*) hike.
excuse *f* (*prétexte*) excuse; **excuses** (*regrets*) apology; **faire des excuses** to apologize (**à** to).
excuser *vt* to excuse (**qn d'avoir fait, qn de faire** s.o. for doing).
excuser (s') *vpr* to apologize (**de** for, **auprès de** to).
exécuter *vt* (*travail etc*) to carry out; (*jouer*) to perform; **e. qn** (*tuer*) to execute s.o.
exécution *f* (*mise à mort*) execution.
exemplaire *m* copy.
exemple *m* example; **par e.** for example; **donner l'e.** to set an example (**à** to).
exercer *vt* (*muscles*, *droits*) to exercise.
exercer (s') *vpr* to practise (**à qch** sth, **à faire** doing).
exercice *m* exercise; **faire de l'e.** to (take) exercise.
exigeant, -eante *a* demanding.
exigence *f* demand.
exiger *vt* to demand (**de** from, **que** (+ *subjonctif*) that).
existence *f* existence.
exister *vi* to exist; **il existe** there is; (*plural*) there are.
exorbitant, -ante *a* exorbitant.
expédier *vt* (*envoyer*) to send off.
expéditeur, -trice *mf* sender.

expédition *f* (*envoi*) dispatch; (*voyage*) expedition.
expérience *f* (*connaissance*) experience; (*scientifique*) experiment; **faire l'e. de qch** to experience sth.
expérimenté, -ée *a* experienced.
expert *m* expert (**en** on, in).
expirer *vi* to breathe out; (*mourir*) to pass away.
explication *f* explanation; (*mise au point*) discussion.
expliquer *vt* to explain (**à** to, **que** that).
expliquer (s') *vpr* (*discuter*) to talk things over (**avec** with).
exploit *m* feat, exploit.
exploitation *f* (*agricole*) farm.
exploiter *vt* (*champs*) to farm; (*profiter de*) to exploit.
explorateur, -trice *mf* explorer.
exploration *f* exploration.
explorer *vt* to explore.
exploser *vi* to explode.
explosif *m* explosive.
explosion *f* explosion.
exportation *f* export.
exporter *vt* to export (**vers** to, **de** from).
exposé, -ée *a* **e. au sud**/*etc* facing south/*etc*.
exposer *vt* to expose (**à** to); (*tableau etc*) to exhibit; (*vie*) to risk; **s'e. à** to expose oneself to.
exposition *f* (*salon*) exhibition.
exprès *adv* on purpose; (*spécialement*) specially.
express *m inv* (*train*) express; (*café*) espresso.
expression *f* (*phrase*, *mine*) expression.
exprimer *vt* to express; **s'e.** to express oneself.
exquis, -ise *a* (*nourriture*) delicious.
exténué, -ée *a* exhausted.
extérieur, -e 1 *a* outside; (*surface*) outer, external; (*signe*) outward. **2** *m* outside; **à l'e. (de)** outside.
externe *mf* (*élève*) day pupil
extincteur *m* fire extinguisher.
extra- *préfixe* extra-.
extraire* *vt* to extract (**de** from).
extrait *m* extract.
extraordinaire *a* extraordinary.
extrême *a* & *m* extreme.
extrêmement *adv* extremely.
extrémité *f* end.

F

fable *f* fable.
fabricant, -ante *mf* manufacturer.
fabrication *f* manufacture.
fabriquer *vt* to make; (*en usine*) to manufacture; **qu'est-ce qu'il fabrique?** *Fam* what's he up to?
fabuleux, -euse *a* fabulous.
fac *f* university.
façade *f* (*de bâtiment*) front.
face *f* face; (*de cube etc*) side; **en f.** opposite; **en f. de** opposite, facing; (*en présence de*) in front of, face to face with; **f. à un problème** faced with a problem; **regarder qn en f.** to look s.o. in the face; **f. à f.** face to face.
fâché, -ée *a* (*air*) angry; (*amis*) on bad terms.
fâcher *vt* to anger.
fâcher (se) *vpr* to get angry (**contre** with); **se f. avec qn** to fall out with s.o.
facile *a* easy; **c'est f. à faire** it's easy to do; **il nous est f. de** it's easy for us to.
facilement *adv* easily.
facilité *f* easiness; (*à faire qch*) ease.
faciliter *vt* to make easier.
façon *f* way; **la f. dont elle parle** the way (in which) she talks; **f. (d'agir)** behaviour; **façons** (*manières*) manners; **de toute f.** anyway; **à ma f.** my way.
facteur *m* postman, *Am* mailman.
factrice *f* postwoman, *Am* mail woman.
facture *f* bill, invoice.
facultatif, -ive *a* optional.
faculté *f* university; **à la f.** at university, *Am* at school.
fade *a* (*nourriture*) bland.
faible 1 *a* weak; (*bruit*) faint; (*vent*) slight; **f. en anglais**/*etc* poor at English/*etc*. **2** *m* **avoir un f. pour** to have a soft spot for.
faiblement *adv* weakly; (*légèrement*) slightly; (*éclairer*) faintly.
faiblesse *f* weakness; faintness; slightness.
faiblir *vi* (*forces*) to weaken.
faillir* *vi* **il a failli tomber** he almost fell.
faillite *f* **faire f.** to go bankrupt.
faim *f* hunger; **avoir f.** to be hungry; **donner f. à qn** to make s.o. hungry.
fainéant, -ante *mf* idler.

faire* 1 *vt* (*bruit*, *faute*, *gâteau etc*) to make; (*devoir*, *ménage etc*) to do; (*rêve*, *chute*) to have; (*sourire*) to give; (*promenade*) to have, take; **ça fait dix mètres/francs** (*mesure*, *prix*) it's *ou* that's ten metres/francs; **qu'a-t-il fait (de)?** what's he done (with)?; **que f.?** what's to be done?; **f. du tennis**/*etc* to play tennis/*etc*; **f. l'idiot** to play the fool; **ça ne fait rien** that doesn't matter. **2** *vi* (*agir*) to do; (*paraître*) to look; **il fait vieux** he looks old; **elle ferait bien de partir** she'd do well to leave; **il fait beau/froid**/*etc* it's fine/cold/*etc*; **ça fait deux ans que je ne l'ai pas vu** I haven't seen him for two years; **ça fait un an que je suis là** I've been here for a year. **3** *v aux* (+ *infinitif*); **f. construire une maison** to have *ou* get a house built; **f. crier/***etc* **qn** to make s.o. shout/*etc*; **se f. obéir**/*etc* to make oneself obeyed/*etc*; **se f. tuer**/*etc* to get *ou* be killed/*etc*.

faire (se) *vpr* **se f. des amis** to make friends; **se f. vieux**/*etc* to get old/*etc*; **il se fait tard** it's getting late; **se f. à** to get used to; **ne t'en fais pas!** don't worry!

faire-part *m inv* announcement.

fais, fait, faites *voir* **faire**.

faisan [fəzɑ̃] *m* pheasant.

faisceau, -x *m* (*rayons*) beam.

fait, faite (*pp of* **faire**) **1** *a* (*fromage*) ripe; (*yeux*) made up; **tout f.** ready made; **c'est bien f.!** it serves you right! **2** *m* event; (*réalité*) fact; **prendre sur le f.** to catch red-handed; **f. divers** news item; **au f.** by the way; **en f.** [ɑ̃fɛt] in fact.

falaise *f* cliff.

falloir* *vi* **il faut qch/qn** I, you, we *etc* need sth/s.o.; **il lui faut un stylo** he *ou* she needs a pen; **il faut partir** I, you, we *etc* have to go; **il faut que je parte** I have to go; **il faudrait qu'elle reste** she ought to stay; **il faut un jour** it takes a day (**pour faire** to do).

fameux, -euse *a* famous; (*excellent*) first-class.

familiarité *f* familiarity (**avec** with).

familier, -ière *a* familiar (**à** to); **f. avec qn** (over)familiar with s.o.; **animal f.** pet.

familièrement *adv* (*parler*) informally.

famille *f* family; **en f.** with one's family.

fan [fan] *m* fan.

fana *mf* **être f. de** to be crazy about.

fané, -ée *a* faded.

faner (se) *vpr* to fade.

fantaisie *f* (*caprice*) whim; **(de) f.** (*bouton etc*) novelty, fancy.

fantastique *a* fantastic.

fantôme *m* ghost.

farce[1] *f* practical joke.
farce[2] *f* (*viande*) stuffing.
farceur, -euse *mf* practical joker.
farcir *vt* to stuff.
fardeau, -x *m* burden.
farine *f* flour.
farouche *a* (*animal*) easily scared; (*violent*) fierce.
fascination *f* fascination.
fasciner *vt* to fascinate.
fasse(s), fassent *etc voir* **faire.**
fatal, -e, *mpl* **-als** *a* fatal; (*inévitable*) inevitable.
fatalement *adv* inevitably.
fatigant, -ante *a* tiring; (*ennuyeux*) tiresome.
fatigue *f* tiredness.
fatigué, -ée *a* tired (**de** of).
fatiguer *vt* to tire.
fatiguer (se) *vpr* to get tired (**de** of).
faucher *vt* (*herbe*) to mow; (*blé*) to reap.
faucon *m* hawk.
faufiler (se) *vpr* to edge one's way (**dans** through, into).
fausse *voir* **faux.**
faut *voir* **falloir.**
faute *f* mistake; (*responsabilité*) fault; (*péché*) sin; **c'est ta f.** it's your fault.
fauteuil *m* armchair; **f. roulant** wheelchair.
fauve *m* wild animal, big cat.
faux, fausse 1 *a* false; (*pas exact*) wrong; (*monnaie*) forged. **2** *adv* (*chanter*) out of tune.
faux *f* scythe.
faux-filet *m* sirloin.
faveur *f* **en f. de** in aid *ou* favour of.
favorable *a* favourable (**à** to).
favori, -ite *a* & *mf* favourite.
favoriser *vt* to favour.
fax *m* (*appareil*, *message*) fax.
faxer *vt* (*message*) to fax.
fée *f* fairy.
féerique *a* fairy(-like).
fêler *vt*, **se fêler** *vpr* to crack.
félicitations *fpl* congratulations (**pour** on).
féliciter *vt* to congratulate (**qn de** *ou* **sur** s.o. on).
fêlure *f* crack.

femelle *a & f* (*animal*) female.
féminin, -ine *a* (*prénom etc*) female; (*trait, pronom etc*) feminine; (*mode, revue etc*) women's.
femme *f* woman (*pl* women); (*épouse*) wife; **f. médecin** woman doctor; **f. de ménage** cleaning woman.
fendre *vt* (*bois etc*) to split.
fendre (se) *vpr* to crack.
fenêtre *f* window.
fente *f* slit.
fer *m* iron; **barre de f.** iron bar; **f. forgé** wrought iron; **f. à cheval** horseshoe; **santé de f.** cast-iron health.
fer (à repasser) *m* iron (*for clothes*).
fera, ferai(t) *etc voir* **faire.**
fer-blanc *m* (*pl* **fers-blancs**) tin.
férié *a* **jour f.** (public) holiday.
ferme[1] *f* farm.
ferme[2] **1** *a* firm; (*pas, voix*) steady. **2** *adv* (*travailler, boire*) hard.
fermé, -ée *a* (*porte etc*) closed, shut; (*route etc*) closed; (*gaz etc*) off.
fermement *adv* firmly.
fermer 1 *vt* to close, shut; (*gaz etc*) to turn *ou* switch off; (*vêtement*) to do up; **f. (à clef)** to lock. **2** *vi*, **se fermer** *vpr* to close, shut.
fermeture *f* closing; (*heure*) closing time; **f. éclair®** zip (fastener), *Am* zipper.
fermier, -ière *mf* farmer.
féroce *a* fierce, savage.
feront *voir* **faire.**
ferraille *f* scrap metal, old iron; **mettre à la f.** to scrap.
ferrée *af* **voie ferrée** railway, *Am* railroad; (*rails*) track.
ferroviaire *a* **compagnie f.** railway company, *Am* railroad company.
fertile *a* fertile.
fesse *f* buttock; **les fesses** one's behind.
fessée *f* spanking.
festin *m* (*banquet*) feast.
festival, *pl* **-als** *m* festival.
fête *f* (*civile*) holiday; (*religieuse*) festival; (*entre amis*) party; **f. foraine** (fun)fair, *Am* carnival; **f. de famille** family celebration; **c'est sa f.** it's his *ou* her saint's day; **f. des Mères** Mother's Day; **jour de f.** (public) holiday; **faire la f.** to have a good time.
fêter *vt* to celebrate.
feu, -x *m* fire; (*de réchaud*) burner; **feux (tricolores)** traffic lights; **feux de détresse** (hazard) warning lights; **f. rouge** red light; (*objet*)

traffic lights; **mettre le f. à** to set fire to; **en f.** on fire; **faire du f.** to light *ou* make a fire; **avez-vous du f.?** have you got a light?; **à f. doux** on a low light; **au f.!** fire!; **coup de f.** (*bruit*) gunshot.
feuillage *m* leaves.
feuille *f* leaf; (*de papier etc*) sheet; **f. d'impôt** tax form; **f. de paye** pay slip *ou Am* stub.
feuilleter *vt* to flip through; **pâte feuilletée** puff pastry *ou Am* paste.
feuilleton *m* serial.
feutre *m* **crayon f.** felt-tip (pen).
février *m* February.
fiançailles *fpl* engagement.
fiancé *m* fiancé.
fiancée *f* fiancée.
fiancer (se) *vpr* to become engaged (**avec** to).
ficeler *vt* to tie up.
ficelle *f* string.
fiche *f* (*carte*) index card; (*papier*) form.
fiche(r) *vt* (*pp* **fichu**) *Fam* **f. le camp** to shove off; **fiche-moi la paix!** leave me alone!; **se f. de qn** to make fun of s.o.; **je m'en fiche!** I don't give a damn!
fichier *m* card index.
fichu, -ue *a* **c'est f.** (*abîmé*) *Fam* it's had it.
fidèle *a* faithful (**à** to); (*client*) regular.
fier (se) *vpr* **se f. à** to trust.
fier, fière [fjɛr] *a* proud (**de** of).
fièrement *adv* proudly.
fierté *f* pride.
fièvre *f* fever; **avoir de la f.** to have a temperature *ou* a fever.
fiévreux, -euse *a* feverish.
figer *vti*, **se figer** *vpr* to congeal.
figue *f* fig.
figure *f* (*visage*) face; (*géométrique*) figure.
figurer *vi* to appear.
figurer (se) *vpr* to imagine.
fil[1] [fil] *m* thread; **f. dentaire** dental floss.
fil[2] *m* (*métallique*) wire; **f. de fer** wire; **passer un coup de f. à qn** to give s.o. a ring, call s.o. up.
file *f* line; (*couloir*) lane; **f. d'attente** queue, *Am* line; **en f. (indienne)** in single file.
filer 1 *vt* **f. qn** (*suivre*) to shadow s.o. **2** *vi* (*partir*) to rush off; (*aller vite*) to speed along.
filet *m* (*à bagages*) rack; (*d'eau*) trickle; (*de poisson*) fillet; **f. (à pro-**

visions) net bag.
fille *f* girl; (*parenté*) daughter; **petite f.** (little *ou* young) girl; **jeune f.** girl, young lady.
fillette *f* little girl.
filleul *m* godson.
filleule *f* goddaughter.
film *m* film, movie; (*pellicule*) film; **f. plastique** clingfilm, *Am* plastic wrap.
filmer *vt* to film.
fils [fis] *m* son.
filtre *m* filter; **(à bout) f.** (*cigarette*) (filter-)tipped; **(bout) f.** filter tip.
filtrer *vt* to filter.
fin *f* end; **mettre f. à** to put an end to; **prendre f.** to come to an end; **sans f.** endless; **à la f.** in the end; **f. mai** at the end of May.
fin, fine 1 *a* (*pointe etc*) fine; (*peu épais*) thin; (*esprit*, *oreille*) sharp. **2** *adv* (*couper etc*) finely.
final, -e, -aux *ou* **-als** *a* final.
finale *f* final.
finalement *adv* finally.
finance *f* finance.
financer *vt* to finance.
financier, -ière *a* financial.
finir *vti* to finish; **f. de faire** to finish doing; (*cesser*) to stop doing; **f. par faire** to end up doing; **c'est fini** it's over.
finlandais, -aise 1 *a* Finnish. **2** *mf* Finn.
fissure *f* crack.
fissurer (se) *vpr* to crack.
fixe *a* fixed; **idée f.** obsession; **regard f.** stare.
fixement *adv* **regarder f.** to stare at.
fixer *vt* (*attacher*) to fix (**à** to); (*date etc*) to fix; **f. (du regard)** to stare at; **être fixé** (*décidé*) to be decided.
flacon *m* (small) bottle.
flair *m* (*d'un chien etc*) (sense of) smell; (*intuition*) insight.
flairer *vt* to smell.
flamand, -ande 1 *a* Flemish. **2** *m* (*langue*) Flemish.
flamber *vi* to burn.
flamme *f* flame; **en flammes** on fire.
flan *m* (*dessert*) custard tart, baked custard.
flanc *m* side.
flâner *vi* to stroll.
flaque *f* puddle.
flash, *pl* **flashes** *m* (*de photographie*) flash(light); (*dispositif*)

flash(gun); (*d'informations*) (news) flash.
flatter *vt* to flatter.
flatterie *f* flattery.
fléau, -x *m* (*catastrophe*) scourge.
flèche *f* arrow; (*d'église*) spire; **monter en f.** (*prix*) to shoot up.
flécher *vt* to signpost (with arrows).
fléchette *f* dart; **fléchettes** (*jeu*) darts.
fléchir 1 *vt* (*membre*) to flex. **2** *vi* (*poutre*) to sag.
flétrir *vt*, **se flétrir** *vpr* to wither.
fleur *f* flower; (*d'arbre*) blossom; **en fleur(s)** in flower; **à fleurs** (*tissu*) flowered, flowery.
fleuri, -ie *a* in bloom; (*tissu*) flowered, flowery.
fleurir *vi* to flower; (*arbre*) to blossom.
fleuriste *mf* florist.
fleuve *m* river.
flexible *a* pliable.
flic *m Fam* cop.
flipper [flipœr] *m* (*jeu*) pinball; (*appareil*) pinball machine.
flocon *m* (*de neige*) flake.
flot *m* (*de souvenirs etc*) flood; **à f.** afloat.
flotte *f* (*de bateaux*) fleet; (*pluie*) *Fam* rain; (*eau*) *Fam* water.
flotter *vi* to float; (*drapeau*) to fly.
flotteur *m Pêche* float.
flou, -e *a* fuzzy, blurred.
fluide *a* & *m* fluid.
fluo *a inv* (*couleur etc*) luminous, fluorescent.
fluorescent, -ente *a* fluorescent.
flûte 1 *f* flute; (*verre*) champagne glass. **2** *int* heck!
foi *f* faith; **être de bonne/mauvaise f.** to be/not to be (completely) sincere.
foie *m* liver.
foin *m* hay.
foire *f* fair.
fois *f* time; **une f.** once; **deux f.** twice; **chaque f. que** whenever; **une f. qu'il sera arrivé** once he has arrived; **à la f.** at the same time; **des f.** sometimes; **une f. pour toutes** once and for all.
fol *voir* **fou.**
folie *f* madness.
folklore *m* folklore.
folklorique *a* **musique f.** folk music.
folle *voir* **fou.**
foncé, -ée *a* (*couleur*) dark.

foncer *vi* (*aller vite*) to tear along; **f. sur qn** to charge at s.o.
fonction *f* function; **la f. publique** the public *ou* civil service.
fonctionnaire *mf* civil servant.
fonctionnement *m* working.
fonctionner *vi* (*machine etc*) to work; **faire f.** to operate.
fond *m* (*de boîte, jardin etc*) bottom; (*de salle etc*) back; (*arrière-plan*) background; **au f. de** at the bottom of, at the back of; **f. de teint** foundation cream; **à f.** (*connaître etc*) thoroughly.
fonder *vt* (*ville etc*) to found.
fondre 1 *vt* to melt; (*métal*) to melt down; **faire f.** (*sucre etc*) to dissolve. **2** *vi* to melt; (*sucre etc*) to dissolve; **f. en larmes** to burst into tears.
fonds *mpl* (*argent*) funds.
font *voir* **faire**.
fontaine *f* fountain.
fonte *f* (*des neiges*) melting; (*fer*) cast iron.
football *m* football, soccer.
footballeur, -euse *mf* footballer.
footing *m* jogging.
force *f* force; (*physique, morale*) strength; **ses forces** one's strength; **de f.** by force; **à f. de lire**/*etc* through reading/*etc*, after much reading/*etc*.
forcément *adv* obviously; **pas f.** not necessarily.
forcer *vt* (*porte etc*) to force; **f. qn à faire** to force s.o. to do; **se f.** to force oneself (**à faire** to do).
forêt *f* forest.
forfait *m* **déclarer f.** to withdraw from the game.
formalité *f* formality.
format *m* size.
formation *f* education, training.
forme *f* (*contour*) shape, form; **en f. de poire**/*etc* pear/*etc*-shaped; **en (pleine) f.** in good shape *ou* form.
formel, -elle *a* (*absolu*) formal.
former *vt* to form; (*apprenti etc*) to train.
former (se) *vpr* (*apparaître*) to form.
formidable *a* terrific, tremendous.
formulaire *m* (*feuille*) form.
formule *f* formula; (*phrase*) (set) expression; **f. de politesse** polite form of address.
fort, forte 1 *a* strong; (*pluie, mer*) heavy; (*voix, radio*) loud; (*fièvre*) high; (*élève*) bright; **f. en** (*maths etc*) good at; **c'est plus f. qu'elle** she can't help it. **2** *adv* (*frapper, pleuvoir*) hard; (*parler*)

loud(ly); (*serrer*) tight; **sentir f.** to have a strong smell.
fort *m* fort.
forteresse *f* fortress.
fortifiant *m* tonic.
fortune *f* fortune; **faire f.** to make one's fortune.
fosse *f* (*trou*) pit; (*tombe*) grave.
fossé *m* ditch.
fou (*or* **fol** *before vowel or mute h*), **folle 1** *a* mad; (*succès*, *temps*) tremendous; **f. de** (*musique etc*) mad about; **f. de joie** wildly happy. **2** *mf* madman, madwoman. **3** *m Échecs* bishop; **faire le f.** to play the fool.
foudre *f* **la f.** lightning.
foudroyant, -ante *a* (*succès etc*) staggering.
foudroyer *vt* (*tuer*) to electrocute.
fouet *m* whip; (*de cuisine*) (egg) whisk.
fouetter *vt* to whip; (*œufs*) to whisk.
fougère *f* fern.
fouiller 1 *vt* (*personne*, *maison etc*) to search. **2** *vi* **f. dans** (*tiroir etc*) to search through.
fouillis *m* jumble, mess.
foulard *m* (head) scarf.
foule *f* crowd; **une f. de** (*objets etc*) a mass of.
fouler *vt* **se f. la cheville**/*etc* to sprain one's ankle/*etc*.
foulure *f* sprain.
four *m* oven.
fourche *f* fork.
fourchette *f* fork (*used for eating or cooking*).
fourgon *m* van; (*mortuaire*) hearse.
fourgonnette *f* (small) van.
fourmi *f* ant; **avoir des fourmis** to have pins and needles (**dans** in).
fourneau, -x *m* (*poêle*) stove.
fournée *f* batch.
fournir *vt* to supply; (*effort*) to make; **f. qch à qn** to supply s.o. with sth.
fourré, -ée *a* (*gant etc*) fur-lined.
fourrer *vt Fam* (*mettre*) to stick.
fourre-tout *m inv* (*sac*) holdall, *Am* carryall.
fourrière *f* (*lieu*) pound.
fourrure *f* fur.
foyer *m* (*maison*, *famille*) home; (*résidence de jeunes etc*) hostel.
fracas *m* din.
fracasser *vt*, **se fracasser** *vpr* to smash.

fraction *f* fraction.
fracture *f* fracture; **se faire une f. au bras**/*etc* to fracture one's arm/*etc*.
fracturer *vt* (*porte etc*) to break (open); **se f. la jambe**/*etc* to fracture one's leg/*etc*.
fragile *a* fragile.
fragment *m* fragment.
fraîcheur *f* freshness; coolness.
frais, fraîche 1 *a* fresh; (*temps*) cool; (*boisson*) cold; **servir f.** (*vin etc*) to serve chilled. **2** *m* **il fait f.** it's cool; **mettre au f.** to put in a cool place; (*au frigo*) to refrigerate.
frais *mpl* expenses; **à mes f.** at my (own) expense.
fraise *f* strawberry.
framboise *f* raspberry.
franc, franche *a* (*personne etc*) frank; **coup f.** *Football* free kick.
franc *m* (*monnaie*) franc.
français, -aise 1 *a* French. **2** *mf* Frenchman, Frenchwoman; **les F.** the French. **3** *m* (*langue*) French.
franchement *adv* frankly; (*vraiment*) really.
franchir *vt* (*fossé*) to jump (over), clear; (*frontière etc*) to cross; (*porte*) to go through; (*distance*) to cover.
franchise *f* frankness.
francophone *mf* French speaker.
frange *f* (*de cheveux*) fringe, *Am* bangs.
frappant, -ante *a* striking.
frapper 1 *vt* to hit, strike; **f. qn** (*surprendre*) to strike s.o. **2** *vi* (*à la porte etc*) to knock (**à** at); **f. du pied** to stamp (one's foot).
fraude *f* (*à un examen*) cheating; (*crime*) fraud; **passer qch en f.** to smuggle sth.
frauder *vi* (*à un examen*) to cheat (**à** in).
frayer *vt* **se f. un passage** to clear a way (**à travers, dans** through).
frayeur *f* fright.
fredonner *vt* to hum.
freezer [frizœr] *m* freezer.
frein *m* brake; **donner un coup de f.** to brake.
freinage *m* braking.
freiner *vi* to brake.
frémir *vi* (*trembler*) to shudder (**de** with).
fréquemment [-amɑ̃] *adv* frequently.
fréquent, -ente *a* frequent.
fréquenter *vt* (*école, église*) to attend; **f. qn** to see s.o.; **se f.** to see each other.

frère *m* brother.
friandises *fpl* sweets, *Am* candies.
fric *m* (*argent*) *Fam* cash.
frictionner *vt* to rub (down).
frigo *m* fridge.
frileux, -euse *a* sensitive to cold.
frire* *vti* to fry; **faire f.** to fry.
frisé, -ée *a* curly.
friser *vti* (*cheveux*) to curl.
frisson *m* shiver; shudder.
frissonner *vi* (*de froid*) to shiver; (*de peur etc*) to shudder (**de** with).
frit, frite (*pp of* **frire**) *a* fried.
frites *fpl* chips, *Am* French fries.
friteuse *f* (deep) fryer.
froid, froide 1 *a* cold. **2** *m* cold; **avoir/prendre f.** to be/catch cold; **il fait f.** it's cold.
froisser *vt* (*tissu*) to crumple; (*personne*) to offend.
froisser (se) *vpr* (*tissu*) to crumple; (*personne*) to take offence *ou Am* offense (**de** at).
frôler *vt* (*toucher*) to brush against.
fromage *m* cheese; **f. blanc** soft white cheese.
fromagerie *f* (*magasin*) cheese shop.
froncer *vt* **f. les sourcils** to frown.
front *m* forehead, brow; (*de bataille*) front.
frontière *f* border.
frotter *vti* to rub; (*pour nettoyer*) to scrub.
frousse *f Fam* fear; **avoir la f.** to be scared.
fruit *m* fruit; **des fruits, les fruits** fruit; **fruits de mer** seafood.
fruitier *a* **arbre f.** fruit tree.
fuel [fjul] *m* (fuel) oil.
fugitif, -ive *mf* fugitive.
fuir* *vi* to run away; (*gaz, robinet etc*) to leak.
fuite *f* flight (**de** from); (*de gaz etc*) leak; **en f.** on the run; **prendre la f.** to run away *ou* off.
fumé, -ée *a* smoked.
fumée *f* smoke; (*vapeur*) fumes.
fumer 1 *vi* to smoke; (*liquide brûlant*) to steam. **2** *vt* to smoke.
fumeur, -euse *mf* smoker; **compartiment fumeurs** smoking compartment.
fumier *m* manure.
funérailles *fpl* funeral.

fur et à mesure (au) *adv* as one goes along; **au f. et à m. que** as.
fureur *f* fury; **faire f.** (*mode etc*) to be all the rage.
furie *f* fury.
furieux, -euse *a* furious (**contre** with, at); (*vent*) raging.
furoncle *m* boil.
fuseau, -x *m* (*pantalon*) ski pants; **f. horaire** time zone.
fusée *f* rocket.
fusible *m* fuse.
fusil *m* rifle, gun; (*de chasse*) shotgun; **coup de f.** gunshot.
fusillade *f* (*tirs*) gunfire.
fusiller *vt* (*exécuter*) to shoot; **f. qn du regard** to glare at s.o.
fût *m* (*tonneau*) barrel, cask.
futé, -ée *a* cunning.
futur, -ure *a* & *m* future.

G

gâcher *vt* to spoil; (*argent etc*) to waste.
gâchette *f* trigger.
gâchis *m* (*gaspillage*) waste.
gadget [gadʒɛt] *m* gadget.
gag *m* gag.
gage *m* (*garantie*) security; **mettre en g.** to pawn.
gagnant, -ante 1 *a* winning. **2** *mf* winner.
gagner 1 *vt* to earn; (*par le jeu*) to win; (*atteindre*) to reach; **g. une heure**/*etc* to save an hour/*etc*. **2** *vi* to win.
gai, -e *a* cheerful.
gaiement *adv* cheerfully.
gaieté *f* cheerfulness.
gain *m* **un g. de temps** a saving of time; **gains** (*salaire*) earnings; (*au jeu*) winnings.
gaine *f* (*sous-vêtement*) girdle; (*étui*) sheath.
gala *m* gala.
galant, -ante *a* gallant.
galerie *f* gallery; (*porte-bagages*) roof rack.
galet *m* pebble.
gallois, -oise 1 *a* Welsh. **2** *m* (*langue*) Welsh. **3** *mf* Welshman, Welshwoman.
galon *m* (*ruban*) braid; (*de soldat*) stripe.
galop *m* gallop; **aller au g.** to gallop.
galoper *vi* to gallop.
gambade *f* leap.
gambader *vi* to leap about.
gamelle *f Fam* pan; (*de chien*) bowl; (*d'ouvrier*) lunch tin *ou* box.
gamin, -ine *mf* (*enfant*) kid.
gamme *f* (*de notes*) scale; (*série*) range.
gangster *m* gangster.
gant *m* glove; **g. de toilette** facecloth; **boîte à gants** glove compartment.
ganté, -ée *a* (*main*) gloved; (*personne*) wearing gloves.
garage *m* garage.
garagiste *mf* garage mechanic.
garantie *f* guarantee; **garantie(s)** (*d'assurance*) cover.
garantir *vt* to guarantee (**contre** against); **g. à qn que** to assure *ou* guarantee s.o. that.
garçon *m* boy; (*jeune homme*) young man; **g. (de café)** waiter.
garde 1 *m* guard; **g. du corps** bodyguard. **2** *f* (*d'enfants*, *de bagages*

etc) care (**de** of); **avoir la g. de** to be in charge of; **prendre g.** to pay attention (**à qch** to sth); **prendre g. de ne pas faire** to be careful not to do; **mettre en g.** to warn (**contre** against); **mise en g.** warning; **de g.** on duty; **monter la g.** to stand guard; **sur ses gardes** on one's guard; **chien de g.** watchdog.

garde-chasse *m* (*pl* **gardes-chasses**) gamekeeper.

garder *vt* to keep; (*vêtement*) to keep on; (*surveiller*) to watch (over); (*enfant*) to look after; **g. la chambre** to stay in one's room.

garder (se) *vpr* (*aliment*) to keep.

garderie *f* crèche, nursery.

gardien, -ienne *mf* (*d'immeuble etc*) caretaker, *Am* janitor; (*de prison*) (prison) guard; (*de zoo, parc*) keeper; (*de musée*) attendant, *Am* guard; **g. de but** goalkeeper.

gare *f* station; **g. routière** bus *ou* coach station.

garer *vt* to park; (*au garage*) to put in the garage.

garer (se) *vpr* to park.

garnement *m* rascal.

garnir *vt* (*équiper*) to fit out (**de** with); (*magasin*) to stock; (*orner*) to trim (**de** with).

garniture *f* (*de légumes*) garnish.

gars [gɑ] *m* fellow, guy.

gas-oil [gɑzwal] *m* diesel (oil).

gaspillage *m* waste.

gaspiller *vt* to waste.

gâté, -ée *a* (*dent etc*) bad.

gâteau, -x *m* cake; **g. de riz** rice pudding; **g. sec** (sweet) biscuit, *Am* cookie.

gâter *vt* to spoil.

gâter (se) *vpr* (*aliment, dent*) to go bad; (*temps, situation*) to get worse.

gauche 1 *a* left. **2** *f* **la g.** (*côté*) the left (side); **à g.** (*tourner*) (to the) left; (*marcher etc*) on the left; **de g.** (*fenêtre etc*) left-hand; **à g. de** on *ou* to the left of.

gaucher, -ère *a & mf* left-handed (person).

gaufre *f* waffle.

gaufrette *f* wafer (biscuit).

Gaulois *mpl* **les G.** the Gauls.

gaver (se) *vpr* to stuff oneself (**de** with).

gaz *m inv* gas; **réchaud à g.** gas stove.

gaze *f* gauze.

gazeux, -euse *a* (*boisson, eau*) fizzy, carbonated.

gazinière *f* gas cooker *ou Am* stove.

gazole *m* diesel (oil).
gazon *m* grass, lawn.
géant, -ante *a* & *mf* giant.
gel *m* frost; (*pour cheveux etc*) gel.
gelé, -ée *a* frozen.
gelée *f* frost; (*de fruits*) jelly.
geler *vti* to freeze; **il gèle** it's freezing.
gémir *vi* to groan.
gémissement *m* groan.
gênant, -ante *a* (*objet*) cumbersome; (*situation*) awkward; (*bruit*) annoying.
gencive *f* gum.
gendarme *m* gendarme.
gendarmerie *f* (*local*) police headquarters.
gendre *m* son-in-law.
gêne *f* (*trouble physique*) discomfort; (*confusion*) embarrassment.
gêné, -ée *a* (*mal à l'aise*) awkward.
gêner *vt* to bother; (*troubler*) to embarrass; (*mouvement*) to hamper; (*circulation*) to hold up; **g. qn** (*par sa présence*) to be in s.o.'s way.
général, -e, -aux 1 *a* general; **en g.** in general. **2** *m* (*officier*) general.
généralement *adv* generally.
génération *f* generation.
généreusement *adv* generously.
généreux, -euse *a* generous (**de** with).
générosité *f* generosity.
génial, -e, -aux *a* brilliant.
génie *m* genius.
genou, -x *m* knee; **à genoux** kneeling (down); **se mettre à genoux** to kneel (down); **sur ses genoux** on one's lap.
genre *m* (*espèce*) kind, sort; (*d'un nom*) gender.
gens *mpl* people; **jeunes g.** young people; (*hommes*) young men.
gentil, -ille *a* nice; **g. avec qn** nice *ou* kind to s.o.; **sois g.** (*sage*) be good.
gentillesse *f* kindness.
gentiment *adv* kindly; (*sagement*) nicely.
géographie *f* geography.
géographique *a* geographical.
géomètre *m* surveyor.
géométrie *f* geometry.
géométrique *a* geometric(al).

gerbe *f* (*de blé*) sheaf; (*de fleurs*) bunch.
gercer *vti*, **se gercer** *vpr* to chap.
gerçure *f* **avoir des gerçures aux mains/lèvres** to have chapped hands/lips.
germe *m* (*microbe*) germ; (*de plante*) shoot.
germer *vi* (*graine*) to start to grow; (*pomme de terre*) to sprout.
geste *m* gesture; **ne pas faire un g.** not to make a move.
gesticuler *vi* to gesticulate.
gibier *m* (*animaux etc*) game.
giboulée *f* shower.
gicler *vi* (*liquide*) to spurt; **faire g.** to spurt.
gifle *f* slap (in the face).
gifler *vt* **g. qn** to slap s.o.
gigantesque *a* gigantic.
gigot *m* leg of mutton *ou* lamb.
gigoter *vi* to wriggle, fidget.
gilet *m* cardigan; (*de costume*) waistcoat, *Am* vest; **g. de sauvetage** life jacket.
girafe *f* giraffe.
giratoire *a* **sens g.** roundabout, *Am* traffic circle.
girouette *f* weathercock, *Am* weather vane.
gitan, -ane *mf* (Spanish) gipsy.
givre *m* frost.
givré, -ée *a* frost-covered.
glace *f* (*eau gelée*) ice; (*crème glacée*) ice cream; (*vitre*) window; (*miroir*) mirror.
glacé, -ée *a* (*eau, main etc*) icy.
glacer *vt* to chill.
glacial, -e, -aux *a* icy.
glacier *m* (*vendeur*) ice-cream man.
glacière *f* icebox.
glaçon *m* ice cube.
gland *m* acorn.
glande *f* gland.
glissant, -ante *a* slippery.
glisser 1 *vi* (*involontairement*) to slip; (*volontairement*) (*sur la glace etc*) to slide; (*coulisser*) (*tiroir etc*) to slide; **ça glisse** it's slippery. **2** *vt* to slip (*sth*) (**dans** into).
glissière *f* **porte à g.** sliding door.
globe *m* globe.
gloire *f* glory.
glorieux, -euse *a* glorious.

gloussement *m* cluck(ing).
glousser *vi* to cluck.
glouton, -onne 1 *a* greedy. **2** *mf* glutton.
gluant, -ante *a* sticky.
goal [gol] *m* goalkeeper.
gobelet *m* (*de plastique*, *papier*) cup.
godet *m* pot.
golf *m* golf; (*terrain*) golf course.
golfe *m* gulf, bay.
golfeur, -euse *mf* golfer.
gomme *f* (*à effacer*) rubber, *Am* eraser.
gommer *vt* (*effacer*) to rub out, erase.
gond *m* hinge.
gonflable *a* inflatable.
gonflé, -ée *a* swollen.
gonfler 1 *vt* (*pneu*) to pump up; (*en soufflant*) to blow up. **2** *vi*, **se gonfler** *vpr* to swell.
gonfleur *m* (air) pump.
gorge *f* throat; (*vallée*) gorge.
gorgée *f* mouthful (*of wine etc*); **petite g.** sip.
gorille *m* gorilla.
gosier *m* throat.
gosse *mf* (*enfant*) *Fam* kid.
gouache *f* gouache.
goudron *m* tar.
goudronner *vt* to tar.
goulot *m* (*de bouteille*) neck; **boire au g.** to drink from the bottle.
gourde *f* water bottle.
gourdin *m* club, cudgel.
gourmand, -ande 1 *a* (over)fond of food; **g. de** fond of. **2** *mf* hearty eater.
gourmandise *f* (over)fondness for food.
gourmet *m* gourmet.
gourmette *f* identity bracelet.
gousse *f* **g. d'ail** clove of garlic.
goût *m* taste; **de bon g.** in good taste; **sans g.** tasteless.
goûter 1 *vt* to taste; **g. à qch** to taste (a little of) sth. **2** *vi* to have an afternoon snack, have tea. **3** *m* afternoon snack, tea.
goutte *f* drop.
gouttelette *f* droplet.
goutter *vi* to drip (**de** from).
gouttière *f* (*d'un toit*) gutter.

gouvernail *m* rudder; (*barre*) helm.
gouvernement *m* government.
gouverner *vti* to govern.
grâce 1 *f* grace; (*avantage*) favour. **2** *prép* **g. à** thanks to.
gracieux, -euse *a* (*élégant*) graceful.
grade *m* rank.
gradin *m* tier (of seats).
graffiti *mpl* graffiti.
grain *m* grain; (*de café*) bean; (*de poussière*) speck; **g. de beauté** mole; (*sur le visage*) beauty spot.
graine *f* seed.
graisse *f* fat; (*pour machine*) grease.
graisser *vt* to grease.
graisseux, -euse *a* (*vêtement etc*) greasy.
grammaire *f* grammar; **livre de g.** grammar (book).
gramme *m* gram(me).
grand, grande 1 *a* big, large; (*en hauteur*) tall; (*chaleur, découverte etc*) great; (*bruit*) loud; (*différence*) big, great; **g. frère**/*etc* (*plus âgé*) big brother/*etc*; **il est g. temps** it's high time (**que** that). **2** *adv* **g. ouvert** wide-open; **ouvrir g.** to open wide.
grand-chose *pron* **pas g.-chose** not much.
grandeur *f* (*importance*) greatness; (*dimension*) size; **g. nature** life-size.
grandir *vi* to grow.
grand-mère *f* (*pl* **grands-mères**) grandmother.
grand-père *m* (*pl* **grands-pères**) grandfather.
grand-route *f* main road.
grands-parents *mpl* grandparents.
grange *f* barn.
graphique *m* graph.
grappe *f* cluster; **g. de raisin** bunch of grapes.
gras, grasse 1 *a* fat; (*aliment*) fatty; (*graisseux*) greasy; **matières grasses** fat. **2** *m* (*de viande*) fat.
gratin *m* **macaronis/chou-fleur au g.** macaroni/cauliflower cheese.
gratitude *f* gratitude.
gratte-ciel *m inv* skyscraper.
gratter *vt* to scrape; (*avec les ongles etc*) to scratch; **se g.** to scratch oneself; **ça me gratte** it itches.
gratuit, -uite *a* free.
gratuitement *adv* free (of charge).
gravats *mpl* rubble.
grave *a* serious; (*voix*) deep; **ce n'est pas g.!** it's not important!;

accent g. grave [grɑːv] accent.
gravement *adv* seriously.
graver *vt* (*sur métal etc*) to engrave; (*sur bois*) to carve.
graveur *m* engraver.
gravier *m* gravel.
gravillons *mpl* gravel, (loose) chippings.
gravir *vt* to climb (*with effort*).
gravité *f* (*de situation etc*) seriousness.
gravure *f* (*image*) print.
grec, grecque 1 *a & mf* Greek. **2** *m* (*langue*) Greek.
greffe *f* (*de peau, d'arbre*) graft; (*d'organe*) transplant.
greffer *vt* (*peau etc*) to graft (**à** on to); (*organe*) to transplant.
grêle *f* hail.
grêler *vi* to hail.
grêlon *m* hailstone.
grelot *m* (small round) bell (*that jingles*).
grelotter *vi* to shiver (**de** with).
grenade *f* (*fruit*) pomegranate; (*projectile*) grenade.
grenadine *f* pomegranate syrup, grenadine.
grenier *m* attic.
grenouille *f* frog.
grève *f* strike; **g. de la faim** hunger strike; **se mettre en g.** to go (out) on strike.
gréviste *mf* striker.
gribouiller *vti* to scribble.
gribouillis *m* scribble.
grièvement *adv* **g. blessé** seriously injured.
griffe *f* (*ongle*) claw; (*de couturier*) (designer) label.
griffer *vt* to scratch.
griffonner *vt* to scribble.
grignoter *vti* to nibble.
gril [gril] *m* grill.
grillade *f* (*viande*) grill.
grillage *m* wire mesh *ou* netting.
grille *f* (*clôture*) railings.
grille-pain *m inv* toaster.
griller 1 *vt* (*viande*) to grill; (*pain*) to toast; **g. un feu rouge** to jump a red light. **2** *vi* **mettre à g.** to put on the grill.
grillon *m* (*insecte*) cricket.
grimace *f* **faire des grimaces/la g.** to make faces/a face.
grimacer *vi* to make faces *ou* a face.
grimpant, -ante *a* climbing.

grimper 1 *vi* to climb (**à qch** up sth). **2** *vt* to climb.
grincement *m* creaking; grinding.
grincer *vi* to creak; **g. des dents** to grind one's teeth.
grincheux, -euse *a* grumpy.
grippe *f* flu.
grippé, -ée *a* **être g.** to have (the) flu.
gris, grise 1 *a* grey, *Am* gray. **2** *m* grey, *Am* gray.
grisaille *f* greyness, *Am* grayness.
grisâtre *a* greyish, *Am* grayish.
grognement *m* growl; grunt.
grogner *vi* to growl (**contre** at); (*cochon*) to grunt.
grognon, -onne *a* grumpy.
grondement *m* growl; rumble.
gronder 1 *vi* to growl; (*tonnerre*) to rumble. **2** *vt* to scold, tell off.
groom *m* page (boy), *Am* bellboy.
gros, grosse 1 *a* big; (*gras*) fat; (*épais*) thick; (*effort, progrès*) great; (*somme*) large; (*averse, rhume*) heavy; **g. mot** swear word. **2** *adv* **en g.** roughly; (*écrire*) in big letters; (*vendre*) wholesale.
groseille *f* (white *ou* red) currant.
grossesse *f* pregnancy.
grosseur *f* size; (*tumeur*) lump.
grossier, -ière *a* rough; (*personne*) rude (**envers** to).
grossièrement *adv* roughly; (*répondre*) rudely.
grossièreté *f* roughness; (*insolence*) rudeness; (*mot*) rude word.
grossir *vi* to put on weight.
grossiste *mf* wholesaler.
grotte *f* cave, grotto.
grouiller *vi* to be swarming (**de** with).
groupe *m* group.
grouper *vt*, **se grouper** *vpr* to group (together).
grue *f* crane.
grumeau, -x *m* lump.
gruyère *m* gruyère (cheese).
guenilles *fpl* rags (and tatters).
guêpe *f* wasp.
guère *adv* **(ne)... g.** hardly; **il ne sort g.** he hardly goes out.
guéri, -ie *a* cured, better.
guérir 1 *vt* to cure (**de** of). **2** *vi* to recover (**de** from).
guérison *f* recovery.
guerre *f* war; **en g.** at war (**avec** with).
guerrier, -ière *mf* warrior.
guet *m* **faire le g.** to be on the lookout.

guetter *vt* to be on the lookout for.
gueule *f* mouth.
guichet *m* ticket office; (*de banque etc*) window.
guichetier, -ière *mf* (*de banque etc*) counter clerk, *Am* teller; (*à la gare*) ticket office clerk.
guide *m* (*personne*, *livre*) guide.
guider *vt* to guide; **se g. sur un manuel**/*etc* to use a handbook/*etc* as a guide.
guidon *m* handlebar(s).
guignol *m* (*spectacle*) = Punch and Judy show.
guillemets *mpl* inverted commas; **entre g.** in inverted commas.
guirlande *f* garland.
guitare *f* guitar.
guitariste *mf* guitarist.
gymnase *m* gymnasium.
gymnastique *f* gymnastics.
gynécologue *mf* gynaecologist, *Am* gynecologist.

H

habile *a* skilful (**à qch** at sth, **à faire** at doing).
habileté *f* skill.
habillé, -ée *a* dressed (**de** in, **en** as a).
habiller *vt* to dress (**de** in).
habiller (s') *vpr* to dress, get dressed; (*avec élégance*) to dress up.
habitable *a* (*maison*) fit to live in.
habitant, -ante *mf* (*de pays etc*) inhabitant; (*de maison*) occupant.
habitation *f* house.
habité, -ée *a* (*région*) inhabited; (*maison*) occupied.
habiter 1 *vi* to live (**à, en, dans** in). **2** *vt* (*maison etc*) to live in.
habits *mpl* (*vêtements*) clothes.
habitude *f* habit; **avoir l'h. de qch/faire** to be used to sth/doing; **d'h.** usually; **comme d'h.** as usual.
habituel, -elle *a* usual.
habituellement *adv* usually.
habituer *vt* **h. qn à** to accustom s.o. to.
habituer (s') *vpr* to get accustomed (**à** to).
'hache *f* axe, *Am* ax.
'hacher *vt* to chop (up); (*avec un appareil*) to mince, *Am* grind.
'hachis *m* mince(meat), *Am* ground meat.
'haie *f* (*clôture*) hedge; **course de haies** (*coureurs*) hurdle race.
'haine *f* hatred.
'haïr* *vt* to hate.
haleine *f* breath; **hors d'h.** out of breath.
'haleter *vi* to pant.
'hall [ol] *m* (*de gare*) main hall; (*de maison*) hall(way).
'halte 1 *f* (*arrêt*) stop. **2** *int* stop!
haltères *mpl* weights.
'hamac *m* hammock.
hameçon *m* (fish) hook.
'hamster *m* hamster.
'hanche *f* hip.
'handicapé, -ée *a & mf* handicapped (person).
'hangar *m* shed; (*pour avions*) hangar.
'hanté, -ée *a* haunted.
'harassé, -ée *a* (*fatigué*) exhausted.

words marked **'h** *(see pronunciation table on page x) indicate no liaison or elision.*

'hardi, -ie *a* bold.
'hareng [arɑ̃] *m* herring.
'hargneux, -euse *a* bad-tempered.
'haricot *m* (*blanc*) (haricot) bean; (*vert*) French bean, green bean.
harmonica *m* harmonica.
harmonie *f* harmony.
harmonieux, -euse *a* harmonious.
'harnais *m* harness.
'harpe *f* harp.
'hasard *m* **le h.** chance; **un h.** a coincidence; **par h.** by chance; **au h.** at random; **à tout h.** just in case.
'hasardeux, -euse *a* risky.
'hâte *f* haste; **à la h.** in a hurry; **avoir h. de faire** to be eager to do.
'hâter (se) *vpr* to hurry (**de faire** to do).
'hausse *f* rise (**de** in); **en h.** rising.
'haut, haute 1 *a* high; (*de taille*) tall; **à haute voix** aloud; **h. de 5 mètres** 5 metres high *ou* tall. **2** *adv* (*voler etc*) high (up); (*parler*) loud; **tout h.** (*lire etc*) aloud; **h. placé** (*personne*) in a high position. **3** *m* top; **en h. de** at the top of; **en h.** (*loger*) upstairs; (*regarder*) up; (*mettre*) on (the) top; **avoir 5 mètres de h.** to be 5 metres high *ou* tall.
'hauteur *f* height.
'haut-parleur *m* loudspeaker.
'hayon *m* (*porte*) hatchback.
hé! *int* (*appel*) hey!
hebdomadaire *a* & *m* weekly.
héberger *vt* to put up.
hectare *m* hectare (= *2.47 acres*).
hein! [ɛ̃] *int Fam* eh!
'hélas! [elɑs] *int* unfortunately.
hélice *f* propeller.
hélicoptère *m* helicopter.
hémorragie *f* h(a)emorrhage; **h. cérébrale** stroke.
'hennir *vi* to neigh.
hépatite *f* hepatitis.
herbe *f* grass; (*pour soigner etc*) herb; **mauvaise h.** weed; **fines herbes** herbs.
'hérisser (se) *vpr* (*poils*) to bristle (up).
'hérisson *m* hedgehog.

héritage *m* (*biens*) inheritance.
hériter *vti* to inherit (**qch de qn** sth from s.o.); **h. de qch** to inherit sth.
héritier *m* heir.
héritière *f* heiress.
hermétique *a* airtight.
héroïne *f* (*femme*) heroine; (*drogue*) heroin.
héroïque *a* heroic.
'héros *m* hero.
hésitant, -ante *a* hesitant; (*pas*, *voix*) unsteady.
hésitation *f* hesitation; **avec h.** hesitantly.
hésiter *vi* to hesitate (**sur** over, about; **à faire** to do).
hêtre *m* (*arbre*, *bois*) beech.
heu! [ø] *int* er!
heure *f* hour; (*moment*) time; **quelle h. est il?** what time is it?; **il est six heures** it's six (o'clock); **six heures moins cinq** five to six; **six heures cinq** five past *ou Am* after six; **à l'h.** (*arriver*) on time; **dix kilomètres à l'h.** ten kilometres an hour; **de bonne h.** early; **tout à l'h.** (*futur*) later; (*passé*) a moment ago; **heures supplémentaires** overtime; **l'h. de pointe** (*circulation etc*) rush hour.
heureusement *adv* (*par chance*) fortunately (**pour** for).
heureux, -euse 1 *a* happy; (*chanceux*) lucky; **h. de qch/de voir qn** happy *ou* glad about sth/to see s.o. **2** *adv* (*vivre etc*) happily.
'heurter *vt* to hit; **se h. à** to bump into, hit.
'hibou, -x *m* owl.
hier [(i)jɛr] *adv* & *m* yesterday; **h. soir** last *ou* yesterday night.
'hi-fi [ifi] *a inv* & *f inv Fam* hi-fi.
hippopotame *m* hippopotamus.
hirondelle *f* swallow.
histoire *f* history; (*récit*, *mensonge*) story; **des histoires** (*ennuis*) trouble; **sans histoires** (*voyage etc*) uneventful.
historique *a* historical; (*lieu*, *événement*) historic.
hiver *m* winter.
'HLM [aʃɛlɛm] *m ou f abrév* (*habitation à loyer modéré*) = council flats, *Am* = low-rent apartment building.
'hocher *vt* **h. la tête** (*pour dire oui*) to nod one's head; (*pour dire non*) to shake one's head.
'hochet *m* (*jouet*) rattle.
'hockey *m* hockey; **h. sur glace** ice hockey.

'hold-up *m inv* (*attaque*) holdup.
'hollandais, -aise 1 *a* Dutch. **2** *mf* Dutchman, Dutchwoman; **les H.** the Dutch. **3** *m* (*langue*) Dutch.
'homard *m* lobster.
homme *m* man (*pl* men); **l'h.** (*espèce*) man(kind); **des vêtements d'h.** men's clothes; **h. d'affaires** businessman.
homosexuel, -elle *a* & *mf* homosexual.
honnête *a* honest; (*satisfaisant*) decent.
honnêtement *adv* honestly; decently.
honnêteté *f* honesty.
honneur *m* honour; **en l'h. de** in honour of; **faire h. à** (*sa famille etc*) to be a credit to; (*repas*) to do justice to.
honorable *a* honourable; (*convenable*) respectable.
'honte *f* shame; **avoir h.** to be *ou* feel ashamed (**de qch/de faire** of sth/to do, of doing).
'honteux, -euse *a* ashamed; (*scandaleux*) shameful.
hôpital, -aux *m* hospital; **à l'h.** in hospital, *Am* in the hospital.
'hoquet *m* **avoir le h.** to have (the) hiccups.
horaire *m* timetable.
horizon *m* horizon; **à l'h.** on the horizon.
horizontal, -e, -aux *a* horizontal.
horloge *f* clock.
horreur *f* horror; **faire h. à** to disgust; **avoir h. de** to hate.
horrible *a* horrible.
horriblement *adv* horribly.
horrifiant, -ante *a* horrifying.
horrifié, -ée *a* horrified.
'hors *prép* **h. de** out of.
'hors-bord *m inv* speedboat.
'hors-d'œuvre *m inv* (*à table*) hors d'oeuvre, starter.
'hors-taxe *a inv* duty-free.
hospitaliser *vt* to hospitalize.
hospitalité *f* hospitality.
hostile *a* hostile (**à** to, towards).
hostilité *f* hostility (**envers** to, towards).
hôte 1 *m* (*qui reçoit*) host. **2** *mf* (*invité*) guest.
hôtel *m* hotel; **h. de ville** town hall, *Am* city hall.
hôtesse *f* hostess; **h. (de l'air)** (air) hostess.
'hotte *f* basket (*carried on back*).

'hourra! *int* hurray!
'housse *f* (protective) cover.
'hublot *m* porthole.
huile *f* oil.
'huit [ɥit] *a & m* ([ɥi] *before consonant*) eight; **h. jours** a week.
'huitième *a & mf* eighth.
huître *f* oyster.
humain, -aine *a* human.
humanité *f* humanity.
humble *a* humble.
humblement *adv* humbly.
humecter *vt* to moisten.
humeur *f* mood; (*caractère*) temperament; **bonne h.** (*gaieté*) good humour; **de bonne/mauvaise h.** in a good/bad mood.
humide *a* damp.
humidité *f* humidity; (*plutôt froide*) damp(ness).
humiliation *f* humiliation.
humilier *vt* to humiliate.
humoristique *a* humorous.
humour *m* humour; **avoir de l'h.** to have a sense of humour.
'hurlement *m* howl; scream.
'hurler 1 *vi* (*loup, vent*) to howl; (*personne*) to scream. **2** *vt* to scream.
hygiène *f* hygiene.
hygiénique *a* hygienic; **papier h.** toilet paper.
hymne *m* **h. national** national anthem.
hypermarché *m* hypermarket.
hypocrisie *f* hypocrisy.
hypocrite 1 *a* hypocritical. **2** *mf* hypocrite.
hypothèse *f* (*supposition*) assumption.

words marked **'h** *(see pronunciation table on page x) indicate no liaison or elision.*

I

iceberg [isbɛrg] *m* iceberg.
ici *adv* here; **par i.** (*passer*) this way; (*habiter*) around here; **jusqu'i.** (*temps*) up to now; (*lieu*) as far as this *ou* here; **d'i. peu** before long.
idéal, -e, -aux *ou* **-als** *a* & *m* ideal.
idée *f* idea; **changer d'i.** to change one's mind.
identifier *vt* to identify; **s'i. à** *ou* **avec** to identify (oneself) with.
identique *a* identical (**à** to, with).
identité *f* identity; **carte d'i.** identity card.
idiot, -ote 1 *a* silly. **2** *mf* idiot.
idiotie [idjɔsi] *f* **une i.** a silly thing.
idole *m* idol.
igloo [iglu] *m* igloo.
ignifugé, -ée *a* fireproof(ed).
ignorance *f* ignorance.
ignorant, -ante *a* ignorant (**de** of).
ignorer *vt* not to know; **i. qn** to ignore s.o.
il *pron* (*personne*) he; (*chose*, *animal*) it; **il pleut** it's raining; **il y a** there is; *pl* there are; **il y a six ans** six years ago; **il y a une heure qu'il travaille** he's been working for an hour; **qu'est-ce qu'il y a?** what's the matter?
île *f* island.
illégal, -e, -aux *a* illegal.
illettré, -ée *a* illiterate.
illisible *a* (*écriture*) illegible.
illuminer *vt*, **s'illuminer** *vpr* to light up.
illusion *f* illusion; **se faire des illusions** to delude oneself (**sur** about).
illustration *f* illustration.
illustré *m* comic.
illustrer *vt* to illustrate (**de** with).
ils *pron* they.
image *f* picture; (*dans une glace*) reflection.
imaginaire *a* imaginary.
imagination *f* imagination.
imaginer *vt*, **s'imaginer** *vpr* to imagine (**que** that).
imbattable *a* unbeatable.
imbécile *mf* idiot.
imitateur, -trice *mf* (*artiste*) impersonator.
imitation *f* imitation.

imiter *vt* to imitate; **i. qn** (*pour rire*) to mimic s.o.; (*faire comme*) to do the same as s.o.
immangeable *a* inedible.
immatriculation *f* registration.
immédiat, -ate *a* immediate.
immédiatement *adv* immediately.
immense *a* immense.
immeuble *m* building; (*d'habitation*) block of flats, *Am* apartment building; (*de bureaux*) office building *ou* block.
immigration *f* immigration.
immigré, -ée *a* & *mf* immigrant.
immobile *a* still.
immobiliser *vt* to bring to a stop.
immobiliser (s') *vpr* to come to a stop.
immortel, -elle *a* immortal.
impair, -e *a* (*nombre*) odd.
impardonnable *a* unforgivable.
imparfait *m* (*temps*) *Grammaire* imperfect.
impartial, -e, -aux *a* fair, unbiased.
impasse *f* dead end.
impatience *f* impatience.
impatient, -ente *a* impatient (**de faire** to do).
impatienter (s') *vpr* to get impatient.
impeccable *a* (*propre*) immaculate.
impératif *m Grammaire* imperative.
imperméable 1 *a* (*tissu*) waterproof. **2** *m* raincoat.
impitoyable *a* ruthless.
impoli, -ie *a* rude.
impolitesse *f* rudeness.
importance *f* importance; **ça n'a pas d'i.** it doesn't matter.
important, -ante 1 *a* important; (*quantité etc*) big. **2** *m* **l'i., c'est de** the important thing is to.
importation *f* import; **d'i.** (*article*) imported.
importer 1 *vi* **n'importe qui/quoi/où/quand/comment** anyone/anything/anywhere/any time/anyhow. **2** *vt* to import (**de** from).
imposer *vt* to impose (**à** on).
impossibilité *f* impossibility.
impossible *a* impossible (**à faire** to do); **il (nous) est i. de le faire** it is impossible (for us) to do it.
impôt *m* tax; **i. sur le revenu** income tax; **(service des) impôts** tax authorities.
impression *f* impression.

impressionnant, -ante *a* impressive.
impressionner *vt* (*émouvoir*) to make a strong impression on.
imprévisible *a* unforeseeable.
imprévu, -ue *a* unexpected.
imprimante *f* (*d'ordinateur*) printer.
imprimé *m* printed form.
imprimer *vt* (*livre etc*) to print.
imprimerie *f* printing works, *Am* print shop.
improviser *vti* to improvise.
improviste (à l') *adv* unexpectedly.
imprudence *f* carelessness, foolishness; **commettre une i.** to do something foolish.
imprudent, -ente *a* careless, foolish.
impuissant, -ante *a* helpless.
impulsif, -ive *a* impulsive.
inabordable *a* (*prix*) prohibitive.
inacceptable *a* unacceptable.
inachevé, -ée *a* unfinished.
inadmissible *a* unacceptable, inadmissible.
inanimé, -ée *a* (*mort*) lifeless; (*évanoui*) unconscious.
inaperçu, -ue *a* **passer i.** to go unnoticed.
inattendu, -ue *a* unexpected.
inattention *f* lack of attention; **un moment d'i.** a moment of distraction.
inauguration *f* inauguration.
inaugurer *vt* to inaugurate.
incapable *a* **i. de faire** unable to do.
incassable *a* unbreakable.
incendie *m* fire.
incendier *vt* to set fire to.
incertain, -aine *a* uncertain; (*temps*) unsettled.
incertitude *f* uncertainty.
incessant, -ante *a* continual.
inchangé, -ée *a* unchanged.
incident *m* incident.
incisive *f* incisor (tooth).
incliner *vt* (*courber*) to bend; (*pencher*) to tilt.
incliner (s') *vpr* (*se courber*) to bow (down).
inclus, -use *a* inclusive; **jusqu'à lundi i.** up to and including Monday.
incolore *a* colourless; (*vernis*) clear.
incommoder *vt* to bother.

incompatible *a* incompatible.
incompétent, -ente *a* incompetent.
incomplet, -ète *a* incomplete.
incompréhensible *a* incomprehensible.
inconnu, -ue 1 *a* unknown (**à** to). **2** *mf* (*étranger*) stranger.
inconscient, -ente *a* unconscious (**de** of); (*imprudent*) thoughtless.
inconsolable *a* heartbroken, cut up.
incontestable *a* undeniable.
inconvénient *m* drawback.
incorrect, -e *a* (*grossier*) impolite.
incroyable *a* incredible.
inculpé, -ée *mf* **l'i.** the accused.
inculper *vt* to charge (**de** with).
incurable *a* incurable.
indécis, -ise *a* (*hésitant*) undecided.
indéfini, -ie *a* indefinite.
indéfiniment *adv* indefinitely.
indemne [ɛ̃dɛmn] *a* unhurt.
indemnité *f* compensation; (*allocation*) allowance.
indépendance *f* independence.
indépendant, -ante *a* independent (**de** of).
indescriptible *a* indescribable.
index *m* (*doigt*) index finger, forefinger.
indicatif *m* (*à la radio*) signature tune; (*téléphonique*) dialling code, *Am* area code; *Grammaire* indicative.
indication *f* (piece of) information; **indications** (*pour aller quelque part*) directions.
indice *m* (*dans une enquête*) clue.
indien, -ienne *a* & *mf* Indian.
indifférence *f* indifference (**à** to).
indifférent, -ente *a* indifferent (**à** to).
indigestion *f* (attack of) indigestion.
indignation *f* indignation.
indigner (s') *vpr* to be *ou* become indignant (**de** at).
indiquer *vt* (*montrer*) to show; (*dire*) to tell; **i. du doigt** to point to *ou* at.
indirect, -e *a* indirect.
indirectement *adv* indirectly.
indiscipliné, -ée *a* unruly.
indiscret, -ète *a* inquisitive.
indiscrétion *f* indiscretion.
indispensable *a* essential.

indistinct, -incte *a* unclear.
individu *m* individual.
individuel, -elle *a* individual.
indolore *a* painless.
indulgent, -ente *a* indulgent (**envers** to).
industrialisé, -ée *a* industrialized.
industrie *f* industry.
industriel, -elle *a* industrial.
inefficace *a* (*mesure etc*) ineffective; (*personne*) inefficient.
inépuisable *a* inexhaustible.
inestimable *a* priceless.
inévitable *a* inevitable, unavoidable.
inexact, -e *a* inaccurate.
inexcusable *a* inexcusable.
inexplicable *a* inexplicable.
inexpliqué, -ée *a* unexplained.
infaillible *a* infallible.
infarctus [ɛ̃farktys] *m* **un i.** a coronary.
infatigable *a* tireless.
infect, -e *a* (*odeur*) foul; (*café etc*) vile.
infecter (s') *vpr* to get infected.
infection *f* infection; (*odeur*) stench.
inférieur, -e *a* lower; (*qualité etc*) inferior (**à** to); **l'étage i.** the floor below.
infériorité *f* inferiority.
infernal, -e, -aux *a* infernal.
infesté, -ée *a* **i. de requins**/*etc* shark/*etc*-infested.
infiltrer (s') *vpr* (*liquide*) to seep (through) (**dans** into).
infini, -ie 1 *a* infinite. **2** *m* infinity.
infiniment *adv* (*regretter*, *remercier*) very much.
infinitif *m Grammaire* infinitive.
infirme *a* & *mf* disabled (person).
infirmerie *f* sick room, sickbay.
infirmier *m* male nurse.
infirmière *f* nurse.
inflammable *a* (in)flammable.
inflammation *f* inflammation.
inflation *f* inflation.
inflexible *a* inflexible.
influence *f* influence.
influencer *vt* to influence.
information *f* information; (*nouvelle*) piece of news; **les informa-**

tions the news.
informatique *f* (*science*) computer science; (*technique*) data processing.
informatisé, -ée *a* computerized.
informer *vt* to inform (**de** of, about; **que** that).
informer (s') *vpr* to inquire (**de** about; **si** if, whether).
infraction *f* offence, *Am* offense.
infusion *f* herbal *ou* herb tea.
ingénieur *m* engineer; **femme i.** woman engineer.
ingénieux, -euse *a* ingenious.
ingrat, -ate *a* ungrateful (**envers** to).
ingratitude *f* ingratitude.
ingrédient *m* ingredient.
inhabité, -ée *a* uninhabited.
inhabituel, -elle *a* unusual.
inhumain, -aine *a* inhuman.
inimaginable *a* unimaginable.
ininflammable *a* non-flammable.
ininterrompu, -ue *a* continuous.
initiale *f* (*lettre*) initial.
injecter *vt* to inject.
injection *f* injection.
injure *f* insult.
injurier *vt* to insult.
injuste *a* (*contraire à la justice*) unjust; (*non équitable*) unfair.
injustice *f* injustice.
innocence *f* innocence.
innocent, -ente 1 *a* innocent (**de** of). **2** *mf* innocent person.
innombrable *a* countless.
inoccupé, -ée *a* unoccupied.
inoffensif, -ive *a* harmless.
inondation *f* flood.
inonder *vt* to flood.
inoubliable *a* unforgettable.
inox *m* stainless steel.
inoxydable *a* **acier i.** stainless steel.
inquiet, -iète *a* worried (**de** about).
inquiétant, -ante *a* worrying.
inquiéter *vt* to worry; **s'i. (de)** to worry (about).
inquiétude *f* worry.
inscription *f* enrolment (*Am* enrollment), registration; (*sur écriteau etc*) inscription; **frais d'i.** (*à l'université*) tuition fees.

inscrire* *vt* to write *ou* put down; **i. qn** to enrol *ou Am* enroll s.o.
inscrire (s') *vpr* to put one's name down; **s'i. à** (*club*) to join; (*examen*) to enrol *ou Am* enroll for, register for.
insecte *m* insect.
insecticide *m* insecticide.
insensible *a* insensitive (**à** to).
inséparable *a* inseparable (**de** from).
insigne *m* badge.
insignifiant, -ante *a* insignificant.
insistance *f* insistence.
insister *vi* to insist (**pour faire** on doing); **i. sur** (*détail etc*) to stress.
insolation *f* sunstroke.
insolence *f* insolence.
insolent, -ente *a* insolent.
insomnie *f* insomnia.
insonoriser *vt* to soundproof.
insouciant, -ante *a* carefree.
inspecter *vt* to inspect.
inspecteur, -trice *mf* inspector.
inspection *f* inspection.
inspiration *f* inspiration.
inspirer *vt* to inspire (**qch à qn** s.o. with sth).
instable *a* (*meuble*) shaky.
installation *f* putting in; moving in. .
installer *vt* (*appareil etc*) to install, put in; (*étagère*) to put up.
installer (s') *vpr* (*s'asseoir*, *s'établir*) to settle (down); **s'i. dans** (*maison*) to move into.
instant *m* moment; **à l'i.** a moment ago; **pour l'i.** for the moment.
instinct *m* instinct.
instinctif, -ive *a* instinctive.
instituteur, -trice *mf* primary school teacher.
institution *f* (*organisation*, *structure*) institution.
instructif, -ive *a* instructive.
instruction *f* education; **instructions** (*ordres*) instructions.
instruire* *vt* to teach, educate; **s'i.** to educate oneself.
instrument *m* instrument; (*outil*) implement.
insuffisant, -ante *a* inadequate.
insulte *f* insult (**à** to).
insulter *vt* to insult.
insupportable *a* unbearable.
intact, -e *a* intact.
intégralement *adv* in full.

intellectuel, -elle *a & mf* intellectual.
intelligemment [-amã] *adv* intelligently.
intelligence *f* intelligence.
intelligent, -ente *a* intelligent.
intempéries *fpl* **les i.** bad weather.
intense *a* intense; (*circulation*) heavy.
intensifier *vt*, **s'intensifier** *vpr* to intensify.
intensité *f* intensity.
intention *f* intention; **avoir l'i. de faire** to intend to do.
interchangeable *a* interchangeable.
interdiction *f* ban (**de** on); **'i. de fumer'** 'no smoking'.
interdire* *vt* to forbid, not to allow (**qch à qn** s.o. sth); **i. à qn de faire** not to allow s.o. to do.
interdit, -ite *a* forbidden; **'stationnement i.'** 'no parking'.
intéressant, -ante *a* interesting; (*prix etc*) attractive.
intéresser *vt* to interest; **s'i. à** to take an interest in.
intérêt *m* interest; **intérêts** (*argent*) interest; **tu as i. à faire** you'd do well to do.
intérieur, -e 1 *a* inner; (*poche*) inside; (*politique*) domestic. **2** *m* inside (**de** of); **à l'i. (de)** inside.
interlocuteur, -trice *mf* **mon i.** the person I am, was *etc* speaking to.
intermédiaire *mf* **par l'i. de** through (the medium of).
interminable *a* endless.
international, -e, -aux *a* international.
interne *mf* (*élève*) boarder.
interpeller *vt* (*appeler*) to shout at.
interphone *m* intercom.
interposer (s') *vpr* to intervene (**dans** in).
interprète *mf* interpreter; (*chanteur*) singer.
interpréter *vt* (*expliquer*) to interpret; (*chanter*) to sing.
interrogatif, -ive *a & m Grammaire* interrogative.
interrogation *f* question; (*à l'école*) test.
interrogatoire *m* interrogation.
interroger *vt* to question.
interrompre* *vt* to interrupt.
interrupteur *m* (*électrique*) switch.
interruption *f* interruption.
intersection *f* intersection.
intervalle *m* (*écart*) gap; (*temps*) interval.
intervenir* *vi* to intervene; (*survenir*) to occur.
intervention *f* intervention; **i. (chirurgicale)** operation.

interview [ɛ̃tɛrvju] *f* interview.
interviewer [-vjuve] *vt* to interview.
intestin *m* bowel.
intime *a* intimate; (*journal, mariage*) private.
intimider *vt* to intimidate.
intituler (s') *vpr* to be entitled.
intolérable *a* intolerable (**que** (+ *subjonctif*) that).
intraduisible *a* difficult to translate.
intransitif, -ive *a Grammaire* intransitive.
intrépide *a* fearless.
introduction *f* introduction.
introduire* *vt* (*insérer*) to put in (**dans** to); (*faire entrer*) to show (*s.o.*) in; **s'i. dans** to get into.
introuvable *a* nowhere to be found.
inusable *a* hardwearing, durable.
inutile *a* useless.
inutilement *adv* needlessly.
inutilisable *a* unusable.
invariable *a* invariable.
invasion *f* invasion.
inventer *vt* to invent; (*imaginer*) to make up.
inventeur, -trice *mf* inventor.
invention *f* invention.
inverse *a* (*sens*) opposite; (*ordre*) reverse.
inverser *vt* (*ordre*) to reverse.
investir *vti* to invest (**dans** in).
investissement *m* investment.
invisible *a* invisible.
invitation *f* invitation.
invité, -ée *mf* guest.
inviter *vt* to invite; **s'i. (chez qn)** to gatecrash.
involontaire *a* (*geste etc*) unintentional.
ira, irai(t) *voir* **aller**[1].
irlandais, -aise 1 *a* Irish. **2** *mf* Irishman, Irishwoman; **les I.** the Irish. **3** *m* (*langue*) Irish.
ironie *f* irony.
ironique *a* ironic(al).
iront *voir* **aller**[1].
irrégulier, -ière *a* irregular.
irremplaçable *a* irreplaceable.
irréparable *a* (*véhicule etc*) beyond repair.
irrésistible *a* irresistible.

irriguer *vt* to irrigate.
irritable *a* irritable.
irritation *f* irritation.
irriter *vt* to irritate.
islamique *a* Islamic.
isolant *m* insulation (material).
isolé, -ée *a* isolated (**de** from).
isoler *vt* to isolate (**de** from); (*du froid etc*) to insulate.
issue *f* way out; **rue** *etc* **sans i.** dead end.
italien, -ienne 1 *a* & *mf* Italian. **2** *m* (*langue*) Italian.
italique *m* italics.
itinéraire *m* route.
ivoire *m* ivory.
ivre *a* drunk.
ivresse *f* drunkenness.
ivrogne *mf* drunk(ard).

J

jaillir *vi* (*liquide*) to spurt (out); (*lumière*) to beam out, shine (forth).
jalousie *f* jealousy.
jaloux, -ouse *a* jealous (**de** of).
jamais *adv* never; **elle ne sort j.** she never goes out; **j. de la vie!** (absolutely) never!; **si j.** if ever.
jambe *f* leg.
jambon *m* ham.
janvier *m* January.
japonais, -aise 1 *a* Japanese. **2** *mf* Japanese man *ou* woman, Japanese *inv*; **les J.** the Japanese. **3** *m* (*langue*) Japanese.
jardin *m* garden; **j. public** park.
jardinage *m* gardening.
jardinier *m* gardener.
jardinière *f* (*caisse à fleurs*) window box.
jaune 1 *a* yellow. **2** *m* yellow; **j. d'œuf** (egg) yolk.
jaunir *vti* to turn yellow.
jaunisse *f* jaundice.
Javel (eau de) *f* bleach.
jazz *m* jazz.
je *pron* (**j'** *before vowel or mute h*) I.
jean [dʒin] *m* (pair of) jeans.
jeep® *f* jeep®.
jerrycan [-kan] *m* petrol *ou Am* gasoline can; (*pour l'eau*) water can.
jet *m* (*de vapeur*) burst; (*de tuyau d'arrosage*) nozzle; **j. d'eau** fountain.
jetable *a* disposable.
jetée *f* pier.
jeter *vt* to throw (**à** to, **dans** into); (*à la poubelle*) to throw away; **se j. sur** to pounce on; **le fleuve se jette dans** the river flows into.
jeton *m* (*pièce*) token; (*de jeu*) chip.
jeu, -x *m* game; (*amusement*) play; (*d'argent*) gambling; (*série complète*) set; (*de cartes*) deck; **j. de mots** play on words; **jeux de société** parlour *ou* indoor games; **j. télévisé** television quiz.
jeudi *m* Thursday.
jeun (à) *adv* **être à j.** to have eaten no food.
jeune 1 *a* young. **2** *mf* young person; **les jeunes** young people.
jeunesse *f* youth; **la j.** (*jeunes*) the young.
jockey *m* jockey.

jogging *m* jogging; **faire du j.** to jog.
joie *f* joy.
joindre* *vt* to join; (*envoyer avec*) to enclose (**à** with); **j. qn** to get in touch with s.o.; **se j. à** (*un groupe etc*) to join.
joker [ʒɔkɛr] *m Cartes* joker.
joli, -ie *a* nice; (*femme*, *enfant*) pretty.
jongler *vi* to juggle (**avec** with).
jongleur, -euse *mf* juggler.
jonquille *f* daffodil.
joue *f* cheek.
jouer 1 *vi* to play; (*acteur*) to act; (*au tiercé etc*) to gamble, bet; **j. au tennis/aux cartes**/*etc* to play tennis/cards/*etc*; **j. du piano**/*etc* to play the piano/*etc*. **2** *vt* to play; (*risquer*) to bet (**sur** on); (*pièce*, *film*) to put on.
jouet *m* toy.
joueur, -euse *mf* player; (*au tiercé etc*) gambler; **bon j.**, good loser.
jour *m* day; (*lumière*) (day)light; **il fait j.** it's light; **en plein j.** in broad daylight; **de nos jours** nowadays; **du j. au lendemain** overnight; **le j. de l'An** New Year's Day.
journal, -aux *m* (news)paper; (*intime*) diary; **j. (parlé)** news bulletin.
journaliste *mf* journalist.
journée *f* day; **toute la j.** all day (long).
joyeux, -euse *a* merry, happy; **j. Noël!** merry *ou* happy Christmas!; **j. anniversaire!** happy birthday!
judo *m* judo.
juge *m* judge.
jugement *m* judg(e)ment; (*verdict*) sentence; **passer en j.** to stand trial.
juger *vt* to judge; (*au tribunal*) to try; (*estimer*) to consider (**que** that).
juif, juive 1 *a* Jewish. **2** *mf* Jew.
juillet *m* July.
juin *m* June.
jumeau, -elle, *pl* **-eaux, -elles** *mf & a* twin; **frère j.** twin brother; **sœur jumelle** twin sister; **lits jumeaux** twin beds.
jumelles *fpl* (*pour regarder*) binoculars.
jument *f* mare.
jungle *f* jungle.
jupe *f* skirt.
jupon *m* petticoat.
jurer 1 *vi* (*dire un gros mot*) to swear (**contre** at). **2** *vt* (*promettre*)

to swear (**que** that, **de faire** to do).
juron *m* swearword.
jury *m* jury.
jus *m* juice; (*de viande*) gravy.
jusque 1 *prép* **jusqu'à** (*espace*) as far as; (*temps*) until; **jusqu'à dix francs** (*limite*) up to ten francs; **jusqu'en mai** until May; **jusqu'où?** how far?; **jusqu'ici** (*temps*) up till now. **2** *conj* **jusqu'à ce qu'il vienne** until he comes.
juste 1 *a* (*équitable*) fair; (*légitime*) just; (*exact*) right; (*étroit*) tight. **2** *adv* (*deviner etc*) right; (*chanter*) in tune; (*seulement*) just.
justement *adv* exactly.
justice *f* justice; (*autorités*) law.
justifier *vt* to justify.
juteux, -euse *a* juicy.

K

kangourou *m* kangaroo.
karaté *m* karate.
képi *m* cap, kepi.
kidnapper *vt* to kidnap.
kilo *m* kilo.
kilogramme *m* kilogram(me).
kilométrage *m* = mileage.
kilomètre *m* kilometre.
kiosque *m* (*à journaux*) kiosk.
kit [kit] *m* **meuble en k.** self-assembly unit.
klaxon® *m* horn.
klaxonner *vi* to hoot, *Am* honk.
k.-o. [kao] *a inv* **mettre k.-o.** to knock out.

L

l', la *voir* **le.**
là 1 *adv* (*lieu*) there; (*chez soi*) in; (*temps*) then, **je reste là** I'll stay here; **c'est là que** that's where; **à cinq mètres de là** five metres away; **jusque-là** (*lieu*) as far as that; (*temps*) up till then. **2** *int* **oh là là!** oh dear!
là-bas *adv* over there.
laboratoire *m* laboratory.
labourer *vt* to plough, *Am* plow.
labyrinthe *m* maze.
lac *m* lake.
lacer *vt* to lace (up).
lacet *m* (shoe-)lace; (*de route*) twist.
lâche 1 *a* cowardly. **2** *mf* coward.
lâcher 1 *vt* to let go of; (*bombe*) to drop. **2** *vi* (*corde*) to give way.
lâcheté *f* cowardice.
là-dedans *adv* in there.
là-dessous *adv* underneath.
là-dessus *adv* on there.
là-haut *adv* up there; (*à l'étage*) upstairs.
laid, laide *a* ugly.
laideur *f* ugliness.
lainage *m* woolly, woollen garment.
laine *f* wool; **en l.** woollen, *Am* woolen.
laisse *f* lead, leash.
laisser *vt* to leave; **l. qn partir**/*etc* to let s.o. go/*etc*; **l. qch à qn** to let s.o. have sth.
lait *m* milk.
laitage *m* milk product.
laitier *a* **produit l.** dairy product.
laitue *f* lettuce.
lambeau, -x *m* shred, bit.
lame *f* (*de couteau etc*) blade; (*vague*) wave.
lamentable *a* (*mauvais*) terrible.
lampadaire *m* standard lamp; (*de rue*) street lamp.
lampe *f* lamp; (*au néon*) light; **l. de poche** torch, *Am* flashlight.
lance *f* spear; (*extrémité de tuyau*) nozzle; **l. d'incendie** fire hose.
lancement *m* (*de fusée etc*) launch(ing).
lance-pierres *m inv* catapult.
lancer *vt* to throw (**à** to); (*avec force*) to hurl; (*fusée, produit etc*) to launch; (*appel etc*) to issue.

lancer (se) *vpr* (*se précipiter*) to rush.
landau *m* (*pl* -s) pram, *Am* baby carriage.
langage *m* language.
langouste *f* (spiny) lobster.
langue *f* tongue; (*langage*) language; **l. maternelle** mother tongue; **langues vivantes** modern languages.
lanière *f* strap.
lanterne *f* lantern; **lanternes** (*de véhicule*) sidelights, *Am* parking lights.
lapin *m* rabbit.
laque *f* lacquer.
lard *m* (*fumé*) bacon; (*gras*) (pig's) fat.
large 1 *a* wide, broad; (*vêtement*) loose; **l. de six mètres** six metres wide. **2** *m* breadth, width; **avoir six mètres de l.** to be six metres wide; **le l.** (*mer*) the open sea; **au l. de Cherbourg** off Cherbourg.
largement *adv* (*ouvrir*) wide; (*au moins*) easily; **avoir l. le temps** to have plenty of time.
largeur *f* width, breadth.
larme *f* tear; **en larmes** in tears.
laser *m* laser.
lasser *vt*, **se lasser** *vpr* to tire (**de** of).
latin *m* (*langue*) Latin.
lavabo *m* washbasin, sink.
lave-auto *m* car wash.
laver *vt* to wash; **se l.** to wash (oneself), *Am* wash up; **se l. les mains** to wash one's hands.
laverie *f* (*automatique*) launderette, *Am* laundromat.
lavette *f* dish cloth.
lave-vaisselle *m* dishwasher.
layette *f* baby clothes.
le, la, *pl* **les** (**le** & **la** *become* **l'** *before a vowel or mute h*) **1** *art déf* (**à + le = au, à + les = aux; de + le = du, de + les = des**) the. ▮ (*généralisation*) **la beauté** beauty; **la France** France; **les hommes** men; **aimer le café** to like coffee. ▮ (*possession*) **il ouvrit la bouche** he opened his mouth; **avoir les cheveux blonds** to have blond hair. ▮ (*mesure*) **dix francs le kilo** ten francs a kilo. ▮ (*temps*) **elle vient le lundi** she comes on Monday(s); **l'an prochain** next year; **une fois l'an** once a year. **2** *pron* (*homme*) him; (*femme*) her; (*chose, animal*) it; *pl* them; **es-tu fatigué? — je le suis** are you tired? — I am; **je le crois** I think so.
lécher *vt* to lick; **se l. les doigts** to lick one's fingers.
leçon *f* lesson.

lecteur, -trice *mf* reader; **l. de cassettes/CD** cassette/CD player.
lecture *f* reading; **lectures** (*livres*) books.
légal, -e, -aux *a* legal.
légende *f* (*histoire*) legend; (*de plan*) key; (*de photo*) caption.
léger, -ère *a* light; (*bruit*, *fièvre etc*) slight; (*café*, *thé*) weak; (*bière*, *tabac*) mild.
légèrement *adv* (*un peu*) slightly.
légèreté *f* lightness.
légitime *a* **être en état de l. défense** to be acting in self-defence.
légume *m* vegetable.
lendemain *m* **le l.** the next day; **le l. de** the day after; **le l. matin** the next morning.
lent, lente *a* slow.
lentement *adv* slowly.
lenteur *f* slowness.
lentille *f* (*graine*) lentil.
léopard *m* leopard.
lequel, laquelle, *pl* **lesquels, lesquelles** (+ **à** = **auquel, à laquelle, auxquel(le)s**; + **de** = **duquel, de laquelle, desquel(le)s**) *pron* (*chose*, *animal*) which; (*personne*) who, (*indirect*) whom; (*interrogatif*) which (one); **dans l.** in which; **parmi lesquels** (*choses*, *animaux*) among which; (*personnes*) among whom.
les [le] *voir* **le.**
lessive *f* washing powder; (*linge*) washing; **faire la l.** to do the wash(ing).
lettre *f* letter; **en toutes lettres** (*mot*) in full.
leur 1 *a poss* their. **2** *pron poss* **le l., la l., les leurs** theirs. **3** *pron inv* (*indirect*) (to) them; **il l. est facile de** it's easy for them to.
levé, -ée *a* **être l.** (*debout*) to be up.
lever 1 *vt* to lift (up); **l. les yeux** to look up. **2** *m* **le l. du soleil** sunrise.
lever (se) *vpr* to get up; (*soleil*, *rideau*) to rise; (*jour*) to break.
levier *m* lever; (*pour soulever*) crowbar.
lèvre *f* lip.
levure *f* yeast.
lézard *m* lizard.
liaison *f* (*routière etc*) link; (*entre mots*) liaison.
liasse *f* bundle.
libération *f* freeing, release.
libérer *vt* to (set) free, release (**de** from); **se l.** to free oneself (**de** from).
liberté *f* freedom; **en l. provisoire** on bail; **mettre en l.** to free.

libraire *mf* bookseller.
librairie *f* bookshop.
libre *a* free (**de qch** from sth, **de faire** to do); (*voie*) clear.
librement *adv* freely.
libre-service *m* (*pl* **libres-services**) self-service.
licence *f* (*diplôme*) (Bachelor's) degree; (*sportive*) licence.
licencié, -ée *a* & *mf* graduate; **l. ès lettres/sciences** Bachelor of Arts/Science.
licenciement *m* dismissal.
licencier *vt* (*ouvrier*) to lay off, dismiss.
liège *m* (*matériau*) cork.
lien *m* (*rapport*) link; (*ficelle*) tie; **l. de parenté** family tie.
lier *vt* (*attacher*) to tie (up); (*relier*) to link (up).
lierre *m* ivy.
lieu, -x *m* place; (*d'un accident*) scene; **les lieux** (*locaux*) the premises; **avoir l.** to take place; **au l. de** instead of.
lièvre *m* hare.
ligne *f* line; (*belle silhouette*) figure; **(se) mettre en l.** to line up; **en l.** (*au téléphone*) connected; **grandes lignes** (*de train*) main line (services); **à la l.** new paragraph.
ligoter *vt* to tie up.
lilas *m* lilac.
limace *f* slug.
limande *f* lemon sole.
lime *f* file.
limer *vt* to file.
limitation *f* (*de vitesse*, *poids*) limit.
limite 1 *f* limit (**à** to); (*frontière*) boundary. **2** *a* (*cas*) extreme; (*vitesse etc*) maximum; **date l.** latest date; **date l. de vente** sell-by date.
limiter *vt* to limit (**à** to).
limonade *f* (fizzy) lemonade.
limpide *a* (crystal) clear.
linge *m* linen; (*à laver*) washing.
lingerie *f* underwear.
lingot *m* **l. d'or** gold bar.
lion *m* lion.
lionne *f* lioness.
liqueur *f* liqueur.
liquide 1 *a* liquid; **argent l.** ready cash. **2** *m* liquid; **du l.** (*argent*) ready cash.
lire* *vti* to read.

lis [lis] *m* lily.
lis, lisant, lise(nt) *etc voir* **lire**.
lisible *a* (*écriture*) legible.
lisse *a* smooth.
lisser *vt* to smooth.
liste *f* list; **sur la l. rouge** (*numéro de téléphone*) ex-directory, *Am* unlisted.
lit[1] *m* bed; **l. d'enfant** cot, *Am* crib; **lits superposés** bunk beds.
lit[2] *voir* **lire**.
literie *f* bedding.
litre *m* litre, *Am* liter.
littéraire *a* literary.
littérature *f* literature.
littoral *m* coast(line).
livraison *f* delivery.
livre[1] *m* book; **l. de poche** paperback (book).
livre[2] *f* (*monnaie, poids*) pound.
livrer *vt* to deliver (**à** to); **l. qn à** (*la police etc*) to give s.o. over to.
livret *m* **l. scolaire** school report book; **l. de famille** family registration book; **l. de caisse d'épargne** bankbook.
livreur, -euse *mf* delivery man, delivery woman.
local, -ale, -aux *a* local.
local, -aux *m* room; **locaux** premises.
locataire *mf* tenant.
location *f* (*de maison etc*) renting; (*de voiture*) hiring; (*par propriétaire*) renting (out), letting; hiring (out); (*loyer*) rental.
locomotive *f* (*de train*) engine.
locution *f* phrase.
loge *f* (*de concierge*) lodge; (*d'acteur*) dressing room; (*de spectateur*) box.
logement *m* accommodation; (*appartement*) flat, *Am* apartment; (*maison*) house; **le l.** housing.
loger 1 *vt* to accommodate; (*héberger*) to put up. **2** *vi* (*à l'hôtel etc*) to put up, (*habiter*) to live.
logiciel *m* software *inv*.
logique *a* logical.
logiquement *adv* logically.
loi *f* law; (*du Parlement*) act; **projet de l.** bill.
loin *adv* far (away *ou* off); **Boston est l. (de Paris)** Boston is a long way away (from Paris); **plus l.** further, farther; **de l.** from a distance.
lointain, -aine *a* distant.

loisirs *mpl* spare time, leisure (time); (*distractions*) leisure activities.

long, longue 1 *a* long; **être l. (à faire)** to be a long time *ou* slow (in doing); **l. de deux mètres** two metres long. **2** *m* **avoir deux mètres de l.** to be two metres long; **(tout) le l. de** (*espace*) (all) along; **de l. en large** (*marcher etc*) up and down; **à la longue** in the long run.

longer *vt* to go along; (*forêt*, *mer*) to skirt; (*mur*) to hug.

longtemps *adv* (for) a long time; **trop l.** too long.

longueur *f* length; **à l. de journée** all day long; **l. d'ondes** wavelength.

lors *adv* **l. de** at the time of.

losange *m* (*forme*) diamond.

lot *m* (*de loterie*) prize; **gros l.** top prize.

loterie *f* lottery.

lotion *f* lotion.

lotissement *m* (*habitations*) housing estate *ou Am* development.

louche *f* ladle.

loucher *vi* to squint.

louer *vt* (*prendre en location*) to rent (*house etc*); (*voiture*) to hire, rent; (*donner en location*) to rent (out), let; to hire (out); **maison à l.** house to let.

loup *m* wolf; **avoir une faim de l.** to be ravenous.

loupe *f* magnifying glass.

lourd, lourde 1 *a* heavy; (*temps*) close; (*faute*) gross. **2** *adv* **peser l.** to be heavy.

loyal, -e, -aux *a* (*honnête*) fair (**envers** to).

loyauté *f* fairness.

loyer *m* rent.

lu, lue *pp of* **lire**.

lucarne *f* (*fenêtre*) skylight.

lueur *f* glimmer.

luge *f* sledge, *Am* sled.

lui 1 *pron mf* (*complément indirect*) (to) him; (*femme*) (to) her; (*chose*, *animal*) (to) it; **il lui est facile de** it's easy for him *ou* her to. **2** *pron m* (*complément direct*) him; (*chose*, *animal*) it; (*sujet emphatique*) he.

lui-même *pron* himself; (*chose*, *animal*) itself.

luisant, -ante *a* shiny.

lumière *f* light.

lumineux, -euse *a* (*idée*, *ciel etc*) bright.

lundi *m* Monday.

lune *f* moon; **l. de miel** honeymoon.

lunettes *fpl* glasses, spectacles; (*de protection*, *de plongée*) goggles; **l. de soleil** sunglasses.
lustre *m* (*éclairage*) chandelier.
lutte *f* fight, struggle; (*sport*) wrestling.
lutter *vi* to fight, struggle.
luxe *m* luxury; **article de l.** luxury article.
luxueux, -euse *a* luxurious.
lycée *m* (secondary) school, *Am* high school.
lycéen, -enne *mf* pupil *ou Am* student (*at lycée*).

M

ma *voir* **mon**.
macaroni(s) *m(pl)* macaroni.
macédoine *f* **m. (de légumes)** mixed vegetables.
mâcher *vt* to chew.
machin *m Fam* (*chose*) what's-it.
machinal, -e, -aux *a* instinctive.
machinalement *adv* instinctively.
machine *f* machine; **m. à coudre** sewing machine; **m. à écrire** typewriter; **m. à laver** washing machine.
mâchoire *f* jaw.
maçon *m* bricklayer.
madame, *pl* **mesdames** *f* madam; **bonjour mesdames** good morning (ladies); **Madame** *ou* **Mme Legras** Mrs Legras; **Madame** (*dans une lettre*) Dear Madam.
madeleine *f* (small) sponge cake.
mademoiselle, *pl* **mesdemoiselles** *f* miss; **bonjour mesdemoiselles** good morning (ladies); **Mademoiselle** *ou* **Mlle Legras** Miss Legras; **Mademoiselle** (*dans une lettre*) Dear Madam.
magasin *m* shop, *Am* store; **grand m.** department store; **en m.** in stock.
magazine *m* magazine.
magicien, -ienne *mf* magician.
magie *f* magic.
magique *a* (*baguette etc*) magic; (*mystérieux*) magical.
magnétophone (*Fam* **magnéto**) *m* tape recorder; **m. à cassettes** cassette recorder.
magnétoscope *m* video (recorder), VCR.
magnétoscoper *vt* (*film etc*) to tape, record (*on a video recorder*).
magnifique *a* magnificent.
mai *m* May.
maigre *a* (*personne*) thin; (*viande*) lean.
maigrir *vi* to get thin(ner).
maille *f* (*de tricot*) stitch; (*de filet*) mesh.
maillon *m* (*de chaîne*) link.
maillot *m* (*de sportif*) jersey, shirt; **m. (de corps)** vest, *Am* undershirt; **m. (de bain)** (*de femme*) swimsuit; (*d'homme*) (swimming) trunks.
main *f* hand; **tenir à la m.** to hold in one's hand; **à la m.** (*faire, coudre etc*) by hand; **haut les mains!** hands up!; **donner un coup de m. à qn** to lend s.o. a (helping) hand; **sous la m.** handy.

maintenant *adv* now; **m. que** now that.
maintenir* *vt* (*conserver*) to keep; (*retenir*) to hold.
maire *m* mayor.
mairie *f* town hall, *Am* city hall.
mais *conj* but; **m. oui, m. si** yes of course; **m. non** definitely not.
maïs [mais] *m* (*céréale*) maize, *Am* corn.
maison *f* (*bâtiment*) house; (*chez-soi*) home; (*entreprise*) firm; **à la m.** at home; **aller à la m.** to go home; **m. de la culture** arts centre; **m. des jeunes** youth club.
maître *m* (*d'un chien etc*) master; **m. d'école** teacher; **m. d'hôtel** (*restaurant*) head waiter; **m. nageur** swimming instructor (and lifeguard).
maîtresse *f* mistress; **m. d'école** teacher.
maîtrise *f* (*diplôme*) Master's degree (**de** in).
maîtriser *vt* (*incendie*) to (bring under) control, **m. qn** to overpower s.o.
majesté *f* **Votre M.** (*titre*) Your Majesty.
majeur, -e 1 *a* **être m.** to be of age. **2** *m* (*doigt*) middle finger.
majorette *f* majorette.
majorité *f* majority (**de** of); (*âge*) coming of age.
majuscule *f* capital letter.
mal, maux 1 *m* (*douleur*) pain; **dire du m. de qn** to say bad things about s.o.; **m. de dents** toothache; **m. de gorge** sore throat; **m. de tête** headache; **m. de ventre** stomachache; **avoir le m. de mer** to be seasick; **avoir m. à la tête/gorge/***etc* to have a headache/sore throat/*etc*; **ça (me) fait m., j'ai m.** it hurts (me); **faire du m. à** to hurt; **avoir du m. à faire** to have trouble doing; **le bien et le m.** good and evil. **2** *adv* (*travailler etc*) badly; (*entendre, comprendre*) not too well; **pas m.!** not bad!; **c'est m. de mentir** it's wrong to lie.
malade 1 *a* ill, sick; **être m. du cœur** to have a bad heart. **2** *mf* sick person; (*d'un médecin*) patient.
maladie *f* illness.
maladresse *f* clumsiness.
maladroit, -droite *a* clumsy.
malaise *m* **avoir un m.** to feel dizzy.
malaria *f* malaria.
malchance *f* bad luck.
mâle *a* & *m* male.
malentendu *m* misunderstanding.
malfaiteur *m* criminal.
malgré *prép* in spite of; **m. tout** after all.
malheur *m* (*événement, malchance*) misfortune.

malheureusement *adv* unfortunately.
malheureux, -euse 1 *a* (*triste*) miserable. **2** *mf* (*pauvre*) poor man *ou* woman.
malhonnête *a* dishonest.
malice *f* mischievousness.
malicieux, -euse *a* mischievous.
malin, -igne *a* (*astucieux*) clever.
malle *f* (*coffre*) trunk; (*de véhicule*) boot, *Am* trunk.
mallette *f* small suitcase; (*pour documents*) attaché case.
malpoli, -ie *a* rude.
malsain, -saine *a* unhealthy.
maltraiter *vt* to ill-treat.
maman *f* mum(my), *Am* mom(my).
mamie *f* *Fam* grandma.
mammifère *m* mammal.
manche[1] *f* (*de vêtement*) sleeve; (*d'un match*) round; **la M.** the Channel.
manche[2] *m* (*d'outil*) handle; **m. à balai** broomstick; (*d'avion etc*) joystick.
manchette *f* (*de chemise*) cuff.
manchot *m* (*oiseau*) penguin.
mandarine *f* tangerine.
mandat *m* (*postal*) money order.
manège *m* (*à la foire*) merry-go-round.
manette *f* lever.
mangeoire *f* (feeding) trough.
manger *vti* to eat; **donner à m. à** to feed.
maniable *a* easy to handle.
maniaque 1 *a* fussy. **2** *mf* fusspot, *Am* fussbudget.
manie *f* craze.
manier *vt* to handle.
manière *f* way; **de toute m.** anyway; **à ma m.** (in) my own way; **la m. dont elle parle** the way (in which) she talks; **faire des manières** (*chichis*) to make a fuss.
manifestant, -ante *mf* demonstrator.
manifestation *f* (*défilé*) demonstration.
manifester 1 *vt* (*sa colère etc*) to show; **se m.** (*maladie*) to show itself. **2** *vi* (*dans la rue*) to demonstrate.
manipuler *vt* (*manier*) to handle.
mannequin *m* (*personne*) (fashion) model; (*statue*) dummy.
manœuvre 1 *m* (*ouvrier*) labourer. **2** *f* (*action*) manoeuvre, *Am* maneuver.

manœuvrer *vti* (*véhicule*) to manoeuvre, *Am* maneuver.
manque *m* lack (**de** of).
manquer 1 *vt* (*cible*, *train etc*) to miss. **2** *vi* (*faire défaut*) to be short; (*être absent*) to be absent (**à** from); **m. de** (*pain*, *argent etc*) to be short of; (*attention*) to lack; **ça manque de sel** there isn't enough salt; **elle/cela lui manque** he misses her/that; **elle a manqué (de) tomber** she nearly fell; **il manque/il nous manque dix tasses** there are/we are ten cups short.
mansarde *f* attic.
manteau, -x *m* coat.
manuel, -elle 1 *a* (*travail*) manual. **2** *m* handbook, manual; (*scolaire*) textbook.
mappemonde *f* map of the world; (*sphère*) globe.
maquereau, -x *m* (*poisson*) mackerel.
maquette *f* (scale) model.
maquillage *m* (*fard*) make-up.
maquiller *vt* (*visage*) to make up; **se m.** to make (oneself) up.
marais *m* marsh.
marathon *m* marathon.
marbre *m* marble.
marchand, -ande *mf* shopkeeper; (*de voitures*, *meubles*) dealer; **m. de journaux** (*dans un magasin*) newsagent, *Am* news dealer; **m. de légumes** greengrocer.
marchander *vi* to haggle.
marchandise(s) *f(pl)* goods.
marche *f* (*d'escalier*) step; (*trajet*) walk; **la m.** (*sport*) walking; **faire m. arrière** (*en voiture*) to reverse; **un train en m.** a moving train; **mettre qch en m.** to start sth (up).
marché *m* (*lieu*) market; **faire son** *ou* **le m.** to do one's shopping (*in the market*); **bon m.** cheap.
marcher *vi* (*à pied*) to walk; (*poser le pied*) to step (**dans** in); (*fonctionner*) to work; **faire m.** (*machine*) to work; **ça marche?** *Fam* how's it going?
mardi *m* Tuesday; **M. gras** Shrove Tuesday.
mare *f* (*étang*) pond.
marécage *m* swamp.
marécageux, -euse *a* swampy.
marée *f* tide; **m. noire** oil slick.
marelle *f* hopscotch.
margarine *f* margarine.
marge *f* (*de cahier etc*) margin.
marguerite *f* daisy.

mari *m* husband.
mariage *m* marriage; (*cérémonie*) wedding.
marié, -ée 1 *a* married. **2** *m* (bride)groom; **les mariés** the bride and (bride)groom. **3** *f* bride.
marier *vt* **m. qn** (*prêtre etc*) to marry s.o.
marier (se) *vpr* to get married (**avec qn** to s.o.).
marin, -ine 1 *a* **air**/*etc* **m.** sea air/*etc.* **2** *m* sailor.
marine 1 *f* **m. (de guerre)** navy. **2** *m* & *a inv* (*couleur*) **(bleu) m.** (*couleur*) navy (blue).
marionnette *f* puppet.
marmelade *f* **m. (de fruits)** stewed fruit.
marmite *f* (cooking) pot.
marmonner *vti* to mutter.
maroquinerie *f* (*magasin*) leather goods shop.
marque *f* (*trace*) mark; (*de produit*) make, brand; (*points*) score; **m. de fabrique** trademark; **m. déposeé** (registered) trademark.
marquer 1 *vt* (*par une marque*) to mark; (*écrire*) to note down; (*but*) to score; **m. les points** to keep (the) score. **2** *vi* (*trace*) to leave a mark; (*joueur*) to score.
marqueur *m* (*crayon*) marker.
marraine *f* godmother.
marrant, -ante *a Fam* funny.
marre *f* **en avoir m.** *Fam* to be fed up (**de** with).
marron 1 *m* chestnut. **2** *m* & *a inv* (*couleur*) brown.
mars *m* March.
marteau, -x *m* hammer; **m. piqueur** pneumatic drill.
martien, -ienne *mf* & *a* Martian.
martyriser *vt* (*enfant*) to batter.
mascara *m* mascara.
mascotte *f* mascot.
masculin, -ine 1 *a* male. **2** *a* & *m Grammaire* masculine.
masque *m* mask.
massacre *m* slaughter.
massacrer *vt* to slaughter.
massage *m* massage.
masse *f* (*volume*) mass; **en m.** in large numbers.
masser *vt* (*frotter*) to massage.
masser (se) *vpr* (*gens*) to (form a) crowd.
masseur *m* masseur.
masseuse *f* masseuse.
massif, -ive 1 *a* (*or*, *bois etc*) solid. **2** *m* (*de fleurs*) clump; (*de montagnes*) massif.

mastic *m* (*pour vitres*) putty.
mastiquer *vt* (*vitre*) to putty; (*mâcher*) to chew.
mat, mate [mat] *a* (*papier*, *couleur*) mat(t).
mât *m* (*de navire*) mast; (*poteau*) pole.
match *m* *Sp* match, *Am* game.
matelas *m* mattress; **m. pneumatique** air bed.
matelot *m* sailor.
matériaux *mpl* (building) materials.
matériel, -ielle 1 *a* (*dégâts*) material. **2** *m* (*de camping etc*) equipment; (*d'ordinateur*) hardware *inv*.
maternel, -elle 1 *a* (*amour*, *femme etc*) maternal. **2** *f* **(école) maternelle** nursery school.
maternité *f* (*hôpital*) maternity hospital.
mathématiques *fpl* mathematics.
maths [mat] *fpl* maths, *Am* math.
matière *f* (*à l'école*) subject; (*substance*) material; **m. première** raw material.
matin *m* morning; **le m.** (*chaque matin*) in the morning; **à sept heures du m.** at seven in the morning.
matinal, -e, -aux *a* **être m.** to be an early riser.
matinée *f* morning; **faire la grasse m.** to sleep late.
matraque *f* (*de policier*) truncheon, *Am* billy (club); (*de malfaiteur*) cosh.
maussade *a* (*personne*) bad-tempered, moody; (*temps*) gloomy.
mauvais, -aise *a* bad; (*méchant*) wicked; (*mal choisi*) wrong; (*mer*) rough; **plus m.** worse; **le plus m.** the worst; **il fait m.** the weather's bad; **m. en** (*anglais etc*) bad at.
mauve *a* & *m* (*couleur*) mauve.
maximal, -e *a* maximum.
maximum [-mɔm] *m* maximum; **le m. de** (*force etc*) the maximum (amount of); **au m.** (*tout au plus*) at most.
mayonnaise *f* mayonnaise.
mazout [mazut] *m* (fuel) oil.
me (**m'** *before vowel or mute h*) *pron* (*complément direct*) me; (*indirect*) (to) me; (*réfléchi*) myself.
mécanicien *m* mechanic; (*de train*) train driver.
mécanique *a* mechanical; **jouet m.** wind-up toy.
mécanisme *m* mechanism.
méchanceté *f* malice; **une m.** (*parole*) a malicious word.
méchant, -ante *a* (*cruel*) wicked; (*enfant*) naughty.
mèche *f* (*de cheveux*) lock; (*de bougie*) wick; (*de pétard*) fuse.
méconnaissable *a* unrecognizable.

mécontent, -ente *a* dissatisfied (**de** with).
mécontentement *m* dissatisfaction.
mécontenter *vt* to displease.
médaille *f* (*décoration*) medal; (*bijou*) medallion; **être m. d'or** to be a gold medallist.
médecin *m* doctor.
médecine *f* medicine; **étudiant en m.** medical student.
médias *mpl* (mass) media.
médical, -e, -aux *a* medical.
médicament *m* medicine.
médiéval, -e, -aux *a* medi(a)eval.
médiocre *a* second-rate.
médisance(s) *f(pl)* malicious gossip.
Méditerranée *f* **la M.** the Mediterranean.
méditerranéen, -enne *a* Mediterranean.
meeting [mitiŋ] *m* meeting.
méfiance *f* distrust.
méfiant, -ante *a* suspicious.
méfier (se) *vpr* **se m. de** to distrust; (*faire attention à*) to watch out for; **méfie-toi!** watch out!; **je me méfie** I'm suspicious.
mégot *m* cigarette butt.
meilleur, -e 1 *a* better (**que** than); **le m. résultat**/*etc* the best result/*etc*. **2** *mf* **le m., la meilleure** the best (one).
mélange *m* mixture.
mélanger *vt*, **se mélanger** *vpr* (*mêler*) to mix.
mêlée *f Rugby* scrum.
mêler *vt* to mix (**à** with).
mêler (se) *vpr* to mix (**à** with); **se m. à** (*la foule*) to join; **mêle-toi de ce qui te regarde!** mind your own business!
mélodie *f* melody.
melon *m* (*fruit*) melon; **(chapeau) m.** bowler (hat).
membre *m* (*bras*, *jambe*) limb; (*d'un groupe*) member.
même 1 *a* same; **en m. temps** at the same time (**que** as). **2** *pron* **le m., la m.** the same (one); **les mêmes** the same (ones). **3** *adv* even; **m. si** even if; **ici m.** in this very place.
mémoire *f* memory; **à la m. de** in memory of.
mémorable *a* memorable.
menaçant, -ante *a* threatening.
menace *f* threat.
menacer *vt* to threaten (**de faire** to do).
ménage *m* housekeeping; (*couple*) couple; **faire le m.** to do the housework.

ménager, -ère *a* (*appareil*) domestic; **travaux ménagers** housework.
ménagère *f* housewife.
mendiant, -ante *mf* beggar.
mendier 1 *vi* to beg. **2** *vt* to beg for.
mener 1 *vt* (*personne*, *vie etc*) to lead; (*enquête etc*) to carry out; **m. qn à** to take s.o. to. **2** *vi* (*en sport*) to lead.
menottes *fpl* handcuffs.
mensonge *m* lie.
mensuel, -elle *a* monthly.
mental, -e, -aux *a* mental.
menteur, -euse *mf* liar.
menthe *f* mint.
mention *f* (*à un examen*) distinction.
mentir* *vi* to lie (**à** to).
menton *m* chin.
menu *m* menu.
menuiserie *f* carpentry.
menuisier *m* carpenter.
mépris *m* contempt (**pour** for).
méprisant, -ante *a* contemptuous.
mépriser *vt* to despise.
mer *f* sea; **en m.** at sea; **aller à la m.** to go to the seaside.
mercerie *f* (*magasin*) haberdasher's, *Am* notions store.
merci *int* & *m* thank you (**de, pour** for).
mercredi *m* Wednesday.
merde! *int Fam* hell!
mère *f* mother; **m. de famille** mother (of a family).
mériter *vt* (*être digne de*) to deserve.
merle *m* blackbird.
merveille *f* wonder.
merveilleux, -euse *a* wonderful.
mes [me] *voir* **mon.**
mésaventure *f* slight mishap.
mesdames *voir* **madame.**
mesdemoiselles *voir* **mademoiselle.**
message *m* message.
messager *m* messenger.
messe *f* mass (*church service*).
messieurs *voir* **monsieur.**
mesure *f* (*dimension*) measurement; (*action*) measure; (*cadence*) time.
mesurer *vt* to measure; **m. 1 mètre 83** (*personne*) to be six feet tall;

(*objet*) to measure six feet.
métal, -aux *m* metal.
métallique *a* **échelle**/*etc* **m.** metal ladder/*etc*.
métallurgie *f* (*industrie*) steel industry.
météo *f* (*bulletin*) weather forecast.
météorologique *a* **bulletin**/*etc* **m.** weather report/*etc*.
méthode *f* (*manière*, *soin*) method.
méthodique *a* methodical.
métier *m* (*travail*) job.
mètre *m* (*mesure*) metre, *Am* meter; (*règle*) (metre) rule; **m. carré** square metre.
métrique *a* metric.
métro *m* underground, *Am* subway.
metteur *m* **m. en scène** (*de cinéma*) director.
mettre* *vt* to put; (*table*) to set, lay; (*vêtement*) to put on; (*chauffage etc*) to put on, switch on; (*réveil*) to set (**à** for); **j'ai mis une heure** it took me an hour; **m. en colère** to make angry.
mettre (se) *vpr* to put oneself; (*debout*) to stand; (*assis*) to sit; (*objet*) to go; **se m. en short**/*etc* to get into one's shorts/*etc*; **se m. à faire** to start doing; **se m. à table** to sit (down) at the table.
meuble *m* piece of furniture; **meubles** furniture.
meubler *vt* to furnish.
meugler *vi* (*vache*) to moo.
meule *f* (*de foin*) haystack.
meurtre *m* murder.
meurtrier, -ière *mf* murderer.
mi- *préfixe* **la mi-mars**/*etc* mid March/*etc*.
miauler *vi* to miaow.
miche *f* round loaf.
mi-chemin (à) [amiʃmɛ̃] *adv* halfway.
mi-côte (à) [amikot] *adv* halfway up *ou* down (the hill).
micro *m* microphone.
microbe *m* germ.
micro-onde *f* **four à micro-ondes** microwave oven.
microscope *m* microscope.
midi *m* (*heure*) twelve o'clock, noon; (*heure du déjeuner*) lunchtime.
mie *f* **la m.** the soft part of the bread; **pain de m.** sandwich loaf.
miel *m* honey.
mien, mienne *pron poss* **le m., la mienne, les miens, les miennes** mine; **les deux miens** my two.
miette *f* (*de pain*) crumb.
mieux *adv* & *a inv* better (**que** than); **le m., la m., les m.** the best;

(*de deux*) the better; **tu ferais m. de partir** you had better leave.
mignon, -onne *a* (*joli*) cute; (*agréable*) nice.
migraine *f* headache.
mil *m inv* (*dans les dates*) **l'an deux m.** the year two thousand.
milieu, -x *m* (*centre*) middle; **au m. de** in the middle of.
militaire 1 *a* military. **2** *m* soldier.
mille *a & m inv* thousand; **m. hommes/***etc* a *ou* one thousand men/*etc*.
mille-pattes *m inv* centipede.
milliard *m* billion, thousand million.
millième *a & mf* thousandth.
millier *m* thousand; **un m. (de)** a thousand or so.
millimètre *m* millimetre.
million *m* million; **un m. de livres/***etc* a million pounds/*etc*; **deux millions** two million.
millionnaire *mf* millionaire.
mime *mf* (*acteur*) mime.
mimer *vti* to mime.
minable *a* shabby.
mince *a* thin; (*élancé*) slim.
mincir *vi* to grow slim.
mine[1] *f* appearance; **avoir bonne m.** to look well.
mine[2] *f* (*de charbon etc*) mine; (*de crayon*) lead; (*engin explosif*) mine.
miner *vt* (*terrain*) to mine.
minerai *m* ore.
minéral, -e, -aux *a & m* mineral.
mineur *m* (*ouvrier*) miner.
miniature *a inv* (*train etc*) miniature.
minimal, -e *a* minimum.
minimum [-mɔm] *m* minimum; **le m. de** (*force etc*) the minimum (amount of); **au (grand) m.** at the very least.
ministère *m* ministry.
ministre *m* minister.
minorité *f* minority.
minou *m* (*chat*) puss.
minuit *m* midnight.
minuscule *a* (*petit*) tiny.
minute *f* minute.
minuterie *f* time switch (*for lighting in a stairway*).
minuteur *m* timer.
minutieux, -euse *a* meticulous.

miracle *m* miracle; **par m.** miraculously.
miraculeux, -euse *a* miraculous.
miroir *m* mirror.
mis, mise *pp of* **mettre.**
mise[1] *f* (*action*) putting; **m. en marche** starting up; **m. en scène** (*de film*) direction.
mise[2] (*argent*) stake.
misérable 1 *a* (*très pauvre*) destitute. **2** *mf* (*personne pauvre*) pauper.
misère *f* (grinding) poverty.
missile *m* (*fusée*) missile.
mission *f* mission.
mite *f* (clothes) moth.
mi-temps *f* (*pause*) (*en sport*) half-time; (*période*) (*en sport*) half; **à mi-t.** (*travailler*) part-time.
mitraillette *f* machinegun (*portable*).
mitrailleuse *f* machinegun (*heavy*).
mixe(u)r *m* (*pour mélanger*) (food) mixer.
mixte *a* (*école*) co-educational, mixed.
mobile *a* (*pièce*) moving; (*personne*) mobile.
mobilier *m* furniture.
mobylette® *f* moped.
moche *a* (*laid*) ugly.
mode 1 *f* fashion; **à la m.** fashionable. **2** *m Grammaire* mood; **m. d'emploi** directions (for use).
modèle *m* model; **m. (réduit)** (scale) model.
modération *f* moderation.
modéré, -ée *a* moderate.
modérer *vt* (*vitesse, chaleur etc*) to reduce.
moderne *a* modern.
moderniser *vt*, **se moderniser** *vpr* to modernize.
modeste *a* modest.
modestie *f* modesty.
modification *f* alteration.
modifier *vt* to alter.
moelle [mwal] *f* (*d'os*) marrow; **m. épinière** spinal cord.
moelleux, -euse *a* (*lit, tissu*) soft.
moi *pron* (*complément direct*) me; (*indirect*) (to) me; (*sujet emphatique*) I.
moi-même *pron* myself.
moindre *a* **la m. erreur**/*etc* the slightest mistake/*etc*; **le m.** (*de mes problèmes etc*) the least (**de** of).

moine *m* monk.
moineau, -x *m* sparrow.
moins [mwɛ̃] **1** *adv* ([mwɛ̃z] *before vowel*) less (**que** than); **m. de** (*temps*, *travail*) less (**que** than); (*gens*, *livres*) fewer (**que** than); (*cent francs*) less than; **m. grand** not as big (**que** as); **de m. en m.** less and less; **le m.** (*travailler*) the least; **le m. grand, la m. grande, les m. grand(e)s** the smallest; **au m., du m.** at least; **de m., en m.** (*qui manque*) missing; **dix ans de m.** ten years less; **en m.** (*personne*, *objet*) less; (*personnes*, *objets*) fewer; **à m. que** (+ *subjonctif*) unless. **2** *prép* (*en calcul*) minus; **deux heures m. cinq** five to two; **il fait m. dix (degrés)** it's minus ten (degrees).
mois *m* month; **au m. de juin** in (the month of) June.
moisi, -ie 1 *a* mouldy, *Am* moldy. **2** *m* mould, *Am* mold; **sentir le m.** to smell musty.
moisir *vi* to go mouldy.
moisson *f* harvest.
moissonner *vt* to harvest.
moite *a* sticky.
moitié *f* half; **la m. de la pomme** half (of) the apple; **à m. fermé** half closed; **à m. prix** (at) half-price; **de m.** by half.
mol *voir* **mou.**
molaire *f* back tooth.
molette *f* **clé à m.** adjustable wrench *ou* spanner.
molle *voir* **mou.**
mollet *m* (*de jambe*) calf.
moment *m* (*instant*) moment; (*période*) time; **en ce m.** at the moment; **par moments** at times; **au m. de partir** when just about to leave; **au m. où** just as; **du m. que** (*puisque*) seeing that.
mon, ma, *pl* **mes** (**ma** *becomes* **mon** [mɔ̃n] *before a vowel or mute h*) *a poss* my; **mon père** my father; **ma mère** my mother; **mon ami(e)** my friend.
monde *m* world; **du m.** (*beaucoup de gens*) a lot of people; **le m. entier** the whole world; **tout le m.** everybody.
mondial, -e, -aux *a* (*crise etc*) worldwide; **guerre mondiale** world war.
moniteur, -trice *mf* instructor; (*de colonie de vacances*) assistant, *Am* camp counselor.
monnaie *f* (*devise*) currency; (*pièces*) change; **faire de la m.** to get change; **faire de la m. à qn** to give s.o. change (**sur un billet** for a note).
monopoliser *vt* to monopolize.
monotone *a* monotonous.

monotonie *f* monotony.
monsieur, *pl* **messieurs** [məsjø, mesjø] *m* (*homme*) man, gentleman; **oui m.** yes sir; **oui messieurs** yes gentlemen; **M. Legras** Mr Legras; **Monsieur** (*dans une lettre*) Dear Sir.
monstre *m* monster.
monstrueux, -euse *a* (*abominable*) hideous.
mont *m* (*montagne*) mount.
montagne *f* mountain; **la m.** (*zone*) the mountains.
montagneux, -euse *a* mountainous.
montant *m* (*somme*) amount; (*de barrière*) post.
montée *f* (*ascension*) climb; (*chemin*) slope.
monter 1 *vi* (*aux* **être**) (*personne*) to go *ou* come up; (*s'élever*) (*ballon*, *prix etc*) to go up; (*grimper*) to climb (up) (**sur** onto); (*marée*) to come in; **m. dans un véhicule** to get in(to) a vehicle; **m. dans un train** to get on(to) a train; **m. sur** *ou* **à** (*échelle*) to climb up; **m. en courant**/*etc* to run/*etc* up; **m. (à cheval)** to ride (a horse). **2** *vt* (*aux* **avoir**) (*côte*) to climb (up); (*objet*) to bring *ou* take up; (*cheval*) to ride; (*tente*) to set up; **m. l'escalier** to go *ou* come up the stairs.
montre *f* (wrist)watch.
montrer *vt* to show (**à** to); **m. du doigt** to point to; **se m.** to show oneself.
monture *f* (*de lunettes*) frame.
monument *m* monument; **m. aux morts** war memorial.
moquer (se) *vpr* **se m. de** to make fun of; **je m'en moque!** I couldn't care less!
moquette *f* fitted carpet(s), *Am* wall-to-wall carpeting.
moral *m* spirits, morale.
morale *f* (*d'histoire*) moral.
morceau, -x *m* piece; (*de sucre*) lump.
mordiller *vt* to nibble.
mordre *vti* to bite.
morse *m* (*animal*) walrus.
morsure *f* bite.
mort *f* death.
mort, morte (*pp of* **mourir**) **1** *a* (*personne*, *plante etc*) dead. **2** *mf* dead man, dead woman; **les morts** the dead; **de nombreux morts** (*victimes*) many casualties *ou* dead.
mortel, -elle *a* (*hommes*, *ennemi etc*) mortal; (*accident*) fatal.
morue *f* cod.
mosquée *f* mosque.
mot *m* word; **envoyer un m. à** to drop a line to; **mots croisés** cross-

word (puzzle); **m. de passe** password.
motard *m* motorcyclist.
moteur *m* (*de véhicule etc*) engine, motor.
motif *m* (*raison*) reason (**de** for).
motivé, -ée *a* motivated.
moto *f* motorcycle, motorbike.
motocycliste *mf* motorcyclist.
motte *f* (*de terre*) lump.
mou (*or* **mol** *before vowel or mute h*), **molle** *a* soft; (*sans énergie*) feeble.
mouche *f* (*insecte*) fly.
moucher (se) *vpr* to blow one's nose.
mouchoir *m* handkerchief; (*en papier*) tissue.
moudre* *vt* (*café*) to grind.
moue *f* long face; **faire la m.** to pull a (long) face.
mouette *f* (sea)gull.
moufle *f* mitten.
mouillé, -ée *a* wet (**de** with).
mouiller *vt* to (make) wet; **se faire m.** to get wet; **se m.** to get (oneself) wet.
moule[1] *m* mould, *Am* mold; **m. à gâteaux** cake tin.
moule[2] *f* (*animal*) mussel.
mouler *vt* to mould, *Am* mold; **m. qn** (*vêtement*) to fit s.o. tightly.
moulin *m* mill; **m. à vent** windmill; **m. à café** coffee-grinder.
moulu (*pp of* **moudre**) *a* (*café*) ground.
mourir* *vi* (*aux* **être**) to die (**de** of, from); **m. de froid** to die of exposure; **je meurs de faim!** I'm starving!
mousse *f* (*plante*) moss; (*écume*) foam; (*de bière*) froth; (*de savon*) lather; (*dessert*) mousse.
mousser *vi* (*bière*) to froth; (*savon*) to lather; (*eau*) to foam.
moustache *f* moustache, *Am* mustache; **moustaches** (*de chat*) whiskers.
moustachu, -ue *a* wearing a moustache.
moustique *m* mosquito.
moutarde *f* mustard.
mouton *m* sheep *inv*; (*viande*) mutton.
mouvement *m* (*geste, groupe etc*) movement; (*de colère*) outburst.
mouvementé, -ée *a* (*vie, voyage etc*) eventful.
moyen, -enne 1 *a* average; (*format etc*) medium(-sized); **classe moyenne** middle class. **2** *f* average; (*dans un examen*) pass mark; (*dans un devoir*) half marks; **en moyenne** on average.
moyen *m* (*procédé, façon*) means, way (**de faire** of doing, to do); **il**

n'y a pas m. de faire it's not possible to do; **je n'ai pas les moyens** (*argent*) I can't afford it.
muer *vi* (*animal*) to moult, *Am* molt; (*voix*) to break.
muet, -ette 1 *a* (*infirme*) dumb; (*film*, *voyelle*) silent. **2** *mf* dumb person.
mufle *m* (*d'animal*) muzzle.
mugir *vi* (*bœuf*) to bellow.
mugissement(s) *m*(*pl*) bellow(ing).
muguet *m* lily of the valley.
mule *f* (*pantoufle*) mule; (*animal*) (she-)mule.
multicolore *a* multicoloured.
multiple *m* (*nombre*) multiple.
multiplication *f* multiplication.
multiplier *vt* to multiply.
municipal, -e, -aux *a* municipal; **conseil m.** town *ou Am* city council.
munir *vt* **m. de** to equip with; **se m. de** to provide oneself with.
munitions *fpl* ammunition.
mur *m* wall; **m. du son** sound barrier.
mûr, mûre *a* (*fruit*) ripe.
muraille *f* (high) wall.
mûre *f* (*baie*) blackberry.
mûrir *vti* (*fruit*) to ripen.
murmure *m* murmur.
murmurer *vti* to murmur.
muscle *m* muscle.
musclé, -ée *a* (*bras*) muscular.
museau, -x *m* (*de chien*, *chat*) nose, muzzle.
musée *m* museum.
muselière *f* (*appareil*) muzzle.
musical, -e, -aux *a* musical.
musicien, -ienne *mf* musician.
musique *f* music.
musulman, -ane *a* & *mf* Muslim.
mutuel, -elle *a* (*réciproque*) mutual.
myope *a* & *mf* shortsighted (person).
mystère *m* mystery.
mystérieux, -euse *a* mysterious.

N

nage *f* (swimming) stroke; **traverser à la n.** to swim across; **en n.** sweating.
nageoire *f* (*de poisson*) fin.
nager 1 *vi* to swim. **2** *vt* (*crawl etc*) to swim.
nageur, -euse *mf* swimmer.
naïf, -ïve *a* naïve.
nain, naine *mf* dwarf.
naissance *f* (*de personne, animal*) birth.
naître* *vi* to be born.
nappe *f* (*sur une table*) table cloth.
napperon *m* (*pour vase etc*) (cloth) mat.
narine *f* nostril.
naseau, -x *m* (*de cheval*) nostril.
natal, -e, *mpl* **-als** *a* (*pays*) native; **sa maison natale** the house where he *ou* she was born.
natation *f* swimming.
nation *f* nation.
national, -e, -aux *a* national; **(route) nationale** trunk road, *Am* highway.
nationalité *f* nationality.
natte *f* (*de cheveux*) plait, *Am* braid; (*tapis*) mat.
nature 1 *f* (*monde naturel, caractère*) nature. **2** *a inv* (*omelette, yaourt etc*) plain; (*café*) black.
naturel, -elle *a* natural.
naufrage *m* (ship)wreck; **faire n.** to be (ship)wrecked.
naufragé, -ée *a* & *mf* shipwrecked (person)
nautique *a* **ski**/*etc* **n.** water skiing/*etc.*
naval, -e, *mpl* **-als** *a* naval.
navet *m* (*plante*) turnip.
navette *f* **faire la n.** to shuttle back and forth (**entre** between); **n. spatiale** space shuttle.
navigation *f* (*trafic de bateaux*) shipping.
naviguer *vi* (*bateau*) to sail.
navire *m* ship.
navré, -ée *a* **je suis n.** I'm (terribly) sorry (**de faire** to do).
ne (**n'** *before vowel or mute h; used to form negative verb with* **pas, jamais, personne, rien, que** *etc*) *adv* (+ *pas*) not; **il ne boit pas** he does not *ou* doesn't drink.
né, -ée *a* (*pp of* **naître**) born; **elle est née** she was born.
nécessaire 1 *a* necessary. **2** *m* **n. de toilette** sponge bag; **faire le n.**

to do what's necessary.
nécessité *f* necessity.
nécessiter *vt* to require.
nectarine *f* nectarine.
négatif, -ive 1 *a* negative. **2** *m* (*de photo*) negative.
négation *f Grammaire* negation; (*mot*) negative.
négligence *f* (*défaut*) carelessness.
négligent, -ente *a* careless.
négliger *vt* (*personne*, *travail etc*) to neglect; **n. de faire** to neglect to do.
négociation *f* negotiation.
négocier *vti* to negotiate.
neige *f* snow; **n. fondue** sleet.
neiger *vi* to snow.
nénuphar *m* water lily.
néon *m* **éclairage au n.** neon lighting.
nerf *m* nerve; **du n.!** buck up!; **ça me tape sur les nerfs** it gets on my nerves.
nerveux, -euse *a* (*agité*) nervous.
nescafé® *m* instant coffee.
n'est-ce pas? *adv* isn't he?, don't you? *etc.*
net, nette [nɛt] **1** *a* (*image*, *refus*) clear; (*coupure*, *linge*) clean; (*soigné*) neat; (*poids*, *prix*) net. **2** *adv* (*s'arrêter*) dead; (*casser*, *couper*) clean.
nettement *adv* (*bien plus*) definitely.
nettoyage *m* cleaning; **n. à sec** dry cleaning.
nettoyer *vt* to clean (up).
neuf, neuve 1 *a* new; **quoi de n.?** what's new(s)? **2** *m* **remettre à n.** to make as good as new.
neuf *a* & *m* ([nœv] *before* **heures & ans**) nine.
neutre *a* (*pays*) neutral.
neuvième *a* & *mf* ninth.
neveu, -x *m* nephew.
nez *m* nose; **n. à n.** face to face (**avec** with).
ni *conj* **ni...ni** (+ *ne*) neither...nor; **il n'a ni faim ni soif** he's neither hungry nor thirsty; **sans manger ni boire** without eating or drinking; **ni l'un(e) ni l'autre** neither (of them).
niche *f* (*de chien*) kennel, *Am* doghouse.
nicher *vi*, **se nicher** *vpr* (*oiseau*) to nest.
nid *m* nest.
nièce *f* niece.
nier *vt* to deny (**que** that).

niveau, -x *m* level; **au n. de qn** (*élève etc*) up to s.o.'s standard.
noble 1 *a* noble. **2** *mf* nobleman, noblewoman.
noce(s) *nf(pl)* wedding.
nocif, -ive *a* harmful.
Noël *m* Christmas; **le père N.** Father Christmas, Santa Claus.
nœud *m* knot; (*ruban*) bow; **n. coulant** slipknot, noose; **n. papillon** bow tie.
noir, noire 1 *a* black; (*nuit, lunettes etc*) dark; **il fait n.** it's dark. **2** *m* (*couleur*) black, (*obscurité*) dark; **N.** (*homme*) black. **3** *f* **Noire** (*femme*) black.
noircir 1 *vt* to make black. **2** *vi*, **se noircir** *vpr* to turn black.
noisetier *m* hazel (tree).
noisette *f* hazelnut.
noix *f* (*du noyer*) walnut; **n. de coco** coconut.
nom *m* name; *Grammaire* noun; **n. de famille** surname; **n. propre** *Grammaire* proper noun.
nombre *m* number.
nombreux, -euse *a* (*amis, livres*) numerous, many; (*famille*) large; **peu n.** few; **venir n.** to come in large numbers.
nombril *m* navel.
nommer *vt* (*appeler*) to name; **n. qn** (*désigner*) to appoint s.o. (**à un poste** to a post).
nommer (se) *vpr* to be called.
non *adv* & *m inv* no; **tu viens ou n.?** are you coming or not?; **n. seulement** not only; **je crois que n.** I don't think so; **(ni) moi n. plus** neither do, am, can *etc* I.
nonante *a* (*en Belgique, en Suisse*) ninety.
non-fumeur, -euse *mf* non-smoker.
nord *m* north; **au n. de** north of; **du n.** (*vent*) northerly; (*ville*) northern.
nord-africain, -aine *a* & *mf* North African.
nord-américain, -aine *a* & *mf* North American.
nord-est *m* & *a inv* north-east.
nord-ouest *m* & *a inv* north-west.
normal, -e, -aux *a* normal.
normale *f* **au-dessus/au-dessous de la n.** above/below normal.
normalement *adv* normally.
norvégien, -ienne *a* & *mf* Norwegian.
nos *voir* **notre.**
notaire *m* solicitor, lawyer.
notamment *adv* particularly.
note *f* (*de musique, remarque*) note; (*à l'école*) mark, *Am* grade;

(*facture*) bill, *Am* check; **prendre n. de** to make a note of.
noter *vt* to note; (*un devoir*) to mark, *Am* grade.
notice *f* (*mode d'emploi*) instructions.
notre, *pl* **nos** *a poss* our.
nôtre *pron poss* **le** *ou* **la n., les nôtres** ours.
nouer *vt* (*chaussure etc*) to tie.
nouilles *fpl* noodles.
nounours [nunurs] *m* teddy bear.
nourrice *f* (*assistante maternelle*) child minder.
nourrir *vt* to feed.
nourrissant, -ante *a* nourishing.
nourrisson *m* infant.
nourriture *f* food.
nous *pron* (*sujet*) we; (*complément direct*) us; (*indirect*) (to) us; (*réfléchi*) ourselves; (*réciproque*) each other.
nous-mêmes *pron* ourselves.
nouveau (*or* **nouvel** *before vowel or mute h*), **nouvelle,** *pl* **nouveaux, nouvelles 1** *a* new. **2** *mf* (*dans une classe*) new boy, new girl. **3** *m* **de n., à n.** again.
nouveau-né, -ée *mf* new-born baby.
nouvelle *f* (*information*) **nouvelle(s)** news; **une n.** a piece of news.
novembre *m* November.
noyade *f* drowning.
noyau, -x *m* (*de fruit*) stone, *Am* pit.
noyé, -ée *mf* drowned man *ou* woman.
noyer[1] *vt*, **se noyer** *vpr* to drown.
noyer[2] *m* (*arbre*) walnut tree.
nu, nue *a* (*personne*) naked; (*mains*) bare; **tout nu** (stark) naked; **tête nue, nu-tête** bare-headed.
nuage *m* cloud.
nuageux, -euse *a* cloudy.
nuance *f* (*de couleurs*) shade.
nucléaire *a* nuclear.
nuire* *vi* **n. à qn** to harm s.o.
nuisible *a* harmful.
nuit *f* night; (*obscurité*) dark(ness); **il fait n.** it's dark; **la n.** (*se promener etc*) at night; **cette n.** (*aujourd'hui*) tonight; (*hier*) last night; **bonne n.** (*au coucher*) good night.
nul, nulle *a* (*médiocre*) hopeless; **faire match n.** to draw; **nulle part** nowhere.
numéro *m* number; (*de journal*) issue; (*au cirque*) act; **un n. de danse** a dance number; **n. vert** (*au téléphone*) = 0-800 number, *Am*

– tollfree number.
numéroter *vt* (*page etc*) to number.
nuque *f* back of the neck.
nylon *m* nylon; **chemise/*etc* en n.** nylon shirt/*etc*.

O

obéir *vi* to obey; **o. à qn** to obey s.o.
obéissance *f* obedience.
obéissant, -ante *a* obedient.
objectif *m* (*but*) objective; (*d'appareil photo*) lens.
objet *m* (*chose*) object; **objets trouvés** (*bureau*) lost property, *Am* lost and found.
obligation *f* obligation.
obligatoire *a* compulsory.
obliger *vt* to force, compel (**à faire** to do); **être obligé de faire** to have to do.
oblique *a* oblique.
obscène *a* obscene.
obscur, -e *a* (*noir*) dark.
obscurcir *vt* (*pièce*) to make dark(er).
obscurcir (s') *vpr* (*ciel*) to get dark(er).
obscurité *f* dark(ness).
obsèques *fpl* funeral.
observation *f* (*étude*) observation; (*reproche*) (critical) remark.
observatoire *m* (*endroit élevé*) lookout (post).
observer *vt* (*regarder*) to watch; (*remarquer*, *respecter*) to observe.
obstacle *m* obstacle.
obstiné, -ée *a* stubborn, obstinate.
obstiner (s') *vpr* **s'o. à faire** to persist in doing.
obtenir* *vt* to get, obtain.
obus *m* (*arme*) shell.
occasion *f* chance (**de faire** to do); (*prix avantageux*) bargain; **d'o.** second-hand, used.
occidental, -e, -aux *a* western.
occupation *f* (*activité etc*) occupation.
occupé, -ée *a* busy (**à faire** doing); (*place*, *maison etc*) occupied; (*téléphone*) engaged, *Am* busy; (*taxi*) hired.
occuper *vt* (*maison*, *pays etc*) to occupy; (*place*, *temps*) to take up; **o. qn** (*travail*, *jeu*) to keep s.o. busy.
occuper (s') *vpr* to keep (oneself) busy (**à faire** doing); **s'o. de** (*affaire*, *problème*) to deal with; **s'o. de qn** (*malade etc*) to take care of s.o.; **occupe-toi de tes affaires!** mind your own business!
océan *m* ocean.
octobre *m* October.
oculiste *mf* eye specialist.
odeur *f* smell.

odieux, -euse *a* horrible.
odorat *m* sense of smell.
œil, *pl* **yeux** *m* eye; **lever/baisser les yeux** to look up/down; **coup d'o.** look; **jeter un coup d'o. sur** to (have a) look at; **o. poché, o. au beurre noir** black eye.
œillet *m* (*fleur*) carnation.
œuf, *pl* **œufs** [œf, ø] *m* egg; **o. sur le plat** fried egg
œuvre *f* (*travail, livre etc*) work.
offenser *vt* to offend.
office *m* (*messe*) service.
officiel, -ielle *a* official.
officier *m* (*dans l'armée etc*) officer.
offre *f* offer; **l'o. et la demande** supply and demand; **offres d'emploi** job vacancies, situations vacant.
offrir* *vt* to offer (**de faire** to do); (*cadeau*) to give; **s'o. qch** to treat oneself to sth.
oh! *int* oh!
oie *f* goose (*pl* geese).
oignon [ɔɲɔ̃] *m* (*légume*) onion; (*de fleur*) bulb.
oiseau, -x *m* bird.
oisif, -ive *a* (*inactif*) idle.
oisiveté *f* idleness.
olive *f* olive; **huile d'o.** olive oil.
olivier *m* olive tree.
olympique *a* (*jeux*) Olympic.
ombragé, -ée *a* shady.
ombre *f* (*d'arbre etc*) shade; (*de personne, objet*) shadow; **à l'o.** in the shade.
omelette *f* omelet(te); **o. au fromage**/*etc* cheese/*etc* omelet(te).
omnibus *a* & *m* **(train) o.** slow *ou* stopping train.
omoplate *f* shoulder blade.
on *pron* (*les gens*) they, people; (*nous*) we; (*vous*) you; **on frappe** someone's knocking; **on m'a dit que** I was told that.
oncle *m* uncle.
onde (*de radio*) wave; **grandes ondes** long wave; **ondes courtes** short wave.
ondulation *f* (*de cheveux*) wave.
onduler *vi* (*cheveux*) to be wavy.
ongle *m* (finger) nail.
ont *voir* **avoir.**
onze *a* & *m* eleven.
onzième *a* & *mf* eleventh.

opaque *a* opaque.
opéra *m* (*musique*) opera; (*édifice*) opera house.
opération *f* operation.
opérer *vt* (*en chirurgie*) to operate on (**de** for); **se faire o.** to have an operation.
opinion *f* opinion (**sur** about, on).
opposé, -ée 1 *a* (*direction*, *opinion etc*) opposite; (*équipe*) opposing; **o. à** opposed to. **2** *m* **l'o.** the opposite (**de** of); **à l'o.** (*côté*) on the opposite side (**de** from, to).
opposer *vt* (*résistance*) to put up (**à** against); (*équipes*) to bring together; **o. qn à qn** to set s.o. against s.o.
opposer (s') *vpr* (*équipes*) to play against each other; **s'o. à** (*mesure*, *personne*) to be opposed to, oppose.
opposition *f* opposition (**à** to).
opticien, -ienne *mf* optician.
optimiste *a* optimistic.
or 1 *m* gold; **montre**/*etc* **en or** gold watch/*etc*; **d'or** (*règle*) golden; **mine d'or** goldmine. **2** *conj* (*cependant*) now, well.
orage *m* (thunder)storm.
orageux, -euse *a* stormy.
oral, -e, -aux 1 *a* oral. **2** *m* (*examen*) oral.
orange 1 *f* (*fruit*) orange. **2** *a & m inv* (*couleur*) orange.
orangeade *f* orangeade.
orbite *f* (*d'astre*) orbit; (*d'œil*) socket.
orchestre *m* (*classique*) orchestra; (*jazz*, *pop*) band; (*places*) stalls, *Am* orchestra.
ordinaire *a* (*habituel*, *normal*) ordinary, *Am* regular; (*médiocre*) ordinary; **d'o.** usually.
ordinateur *m* computer.
ordonnance *f* (*de médecin*) prescription.
ordonné, -ée *a* tidy.
ordonner *vt* to order (**que** (+ *subjonctif*) that); (*médicament etc*) to prescribe; **o. à qn de faire** to order s.o. to do.
ordre *m* (*commandement*, *classement*) order; (*absence de désordre*) tidiness (*of room*, *person etc*); **en o.** (*chambre etc*) tidy; **mettre en o., mettre de l'o. dans** to tidy (up); **jusqu'à nouvel o.** until further notice.
ordures *fpl* (*débris*) rubbish, *Am* garbage.
oreille *f* ear; **faire la sourde o.** to take no notice, refuse to listen.
oreiller *m* pillow.
oreillons *mpl* mumps.
organe *m* (*de corps*) organ.

organisateur, -trice *mf* organiser.
organisation *f* organization.
organiser *vt* to organize; **s'o.** to get organized.
organisme *m* (*corps*) body; (*bureaux etc*) organization.
orge *f* barley.
orgue 1 *m* (*instrument*) organ. **2** *fpl* **grandes orgues** great organ.
orgueil *m* pride.
orgueilleux, -euse *a* proud.
oriental, -e, -aux *a* (*côte, pays etc*) eastern; (*du Japon, de la Chine*) far-eastern, oriental.
orientation *f* direction; (*de maison*) aspect; **o. professionnelle** careers' advice.
orienté, -ée *a* (*appartement etc*) **o. à l'ouest** facing west.
orienter *vt* (*lampe etc*) to position; (*voyageur, élève*) to direct.
orienter (s') *vpr* to find one's bearings *ou* direction.
original, -e, -aux 1 *a* (*idée, artiste etc*) original. **2** *m* (*texte*) original.
originalité *f* originality.
origine *f* origin; **à l'o.** originally; **d'o.** (*pneu etc*) original; **pays d'o.** country of origin.
ornement *m* ornament.
orner *vt* to decorate (**de** with).
orphelin, -ine *mf* orphan.
orphelinat *m* orphanage.
orteil *m* toe; **gros o.** big toe.
orthographe *f* spelling.
ortie *f* nettle.
os [ɔs, *pl* o] *m* bone; **trempé jusqu'aux os** soaked to the skin.
oser *vti* to dare; **o. faire** to dare (to) do.
osier *m* wicker; **panier d'o.** wicker basket.
otage *m* hostage; **prendre qn en o.** to take s.o. hostage.
otarie *f* (*animal*) sea lion.
ôter *vt* to take away (**à qn** from s.o.), (*vêtement*) to take off; (*déduire*) to take (away).
otite *f* ear infection.
ou *conj* or; **ou bien** or else; **ou elle ou moi** either her or me.
où *adv & pron* where; **le jour où** the day when; **la table où** the table on which; **par où?** which way?; **d'où?** where from?; **le pays d'où** the country from which.
oubli *m* **l'o. de qch** forgetting sth; **un o.** (*dans une liste etc*) an oversight.
oublier *vt* to forget (**de faire** to do).

ouest [wɛst] *m & a inv* west; **d'o.** (*vent*) west(erly); **de l'o.** western.
ouf! *int* what a relief!
oui *adv & m inv* yes; **tu viens, o. ou non?** are you coming or aren't you?; **je crois que o.** I think so.
ouïe *f* hearing.
ouïes *fpl* (*de poisson*) gills.
ouille! *int* ouch!
ouragan *m* hurricane.
ourlet *m* hem.
ours [urs] *m* bear; **o. blanc** polar bear.
outil *m* tool.
outillage *m* tools.
outre 1 *prép* besides. **2** *adv* **en o.** besides.
outré, -ée *a* (*révolté*) outraged.
ouvert, -erte (*pp of* **ouvrir**) *a* open; (*robinet*, *gaz*) on.
ouvertement *adv* openly.
ouverture *f* opening; (*trou*) hole.
ouvrage *m* (*travail*, *livre*) work; (*couture*) (needle)work; **un o.** (*travail*) a piece of work.
ouvre-boîtes *m inv* tin opener, *Am* can-opener.
ouvre-bouteilles *m inv* bottle opener.
ouvrier, -ière 1 *mf* worker; **o. qualifié/spécialisé** skilled/unskilled worker. **2** *a* (*quartier*) working-class; **classe ouvrière** working class.
ouvrir* 1 *vt* to open (up); (*gaz*, *radio etc*) to turn on, switch on. **2** *vi* to open; (*ouvrir la porte*) to open (up).
ouvrir (s') *vpr* (*porte*, *boîte etc*) to open (up).
ovale *a & m* oval.
OVNI [ɔvni] *m abrév* (*objet volant non identifié*) UFO.
oxygène *m* oxygen.

P

pacifique 1 *a* (*manifestation etc*) peaceful; (*côte etc*) Pacific. **2** *m* **le P.** the Pacific.
pagaie *f* paddle.
pagaïe, pagaille *f* (*désordre*) mess; **en p.** in a mess.
pagayer *vi* to paddle.
page *f* (*de livre etc*) page.
paie *f* pay, wages.
paiement *m* payment.
paillasson *m* (door)mat.
paille *f* straw; (*pour boire*) (drinking) straw; **tirer à la courte p.** to draw lots.
paillette *f* (*d'habit*) sequin; **paillettes** (*de savon*) flakes.
pain *m* bread; **un p.** a loaf (of bread); **p. grillé** toast; **p. complet** wholemeal bread; **p. d'épice** gingerbread; **p. de seigle** rye bread; **petit p.** roll.
pair, -e *a* (*numéro*) even.
paire *f* pair (**de** of).
paisible *a* (*vie*, *endroit*) peaceful.
paître* *vi* to graze.
paix *f* peace; (*traité*) peace treaty; **en p.** in peace; **avoir la p.** to have (some) peace and quiet.
palais[1] *m* (*château*) palace; **P. de justice** law courts; **p. des sports** sports stadium.
palais[2] (*dans la bouche*) palate.
pâle *a* pale.
paletot *m* (knitted) cardigan.
palette *f* (*de peintre*) palette.
pâleur *f* paleness.
palier *m* (*d'escalier*) landing; **être voisins de p.** to live on the same floor.
pâlir *vi* to turn pale (**de** with).
palissade *f* fence (*of stakes*).
palme *f* palm (leaf); (*de nageur*) flipper.
palmier *m* palm (tree).
palper *vt* to feel.
palpitant, -ante *a* thrilling.
palpiter *vi* (*cœur*) to throb.
pamplemousse *m* grapefruit.
pan! *int* bang!
panaché *a* & *m* **(demi) p.** shandy (*beer and lemonade*).

pancarte *f* sign; (*de manifestant*) placard.
pané, -ée *a* breaded.
panier *m* basket; **p. à salade** (*ustensile*) salad basket.
panique *f* panic.
paniqué, -ée *a* panic-stricken.
paniquer *vi* to panic.
panne *f* breakdown; **tomber en p.** to break down; **être en p.** to have broken down; **p. d'électricité** blackout, power cut.
panneau, -x *m* (*écriteau*) sign; (*de porte etc*) panel; **p. (de signalisation)** road sign; **p. (d'affichage)** hoarding, *Am* billboard.
panoplie *f* (*jouet*) outfit.
panorama *m* view.
pansement *m* dressing, bandage; **p. adhésif** sticking plaster, *Am* Band-Aid®.
panser *vt* (*main etc*) to dress, bandage.
pantalon *m* (pair of) trousers *ou Am* pants; **en p.** in trousers, *Am* in pants.
pantin *m* puppet, jumping jack.
pantoufle *f* slipper.
paon [pɑ̃] *m* peacock.
papa *m* dad(dy).
pape *m* pope.
papeterie *f* (*magasin*) stationer's shop.
papi *m Fam* grand(d)ad.
papier *m* (*matière*) paper; **un p.** (*feuille*) a sheet of paper; (*formulaire*) a form; **sac**/*etc* **en p.** paper bag/*etc*; **papiers (d'identité)** (identity) papers; **p. hygiénique** toilet paper; **p. à lettres** writing paper; **du p. journal** (some) newspaper; **p. peint** wallpaper; **p. de verre** sandpaper.
papillon *m* butterfly; **p. (de nuit)** moth.
paquebot *m* (ocean) liner.
pâquerette *f* daisy.
Pâques *m sing & fpl* Easter.
paquet *m* (*de bonbons etc*) packet; (*colis*) package; (*de cigarettes*) pack(et); (*de cartes*) pack, deck.
par *prép* (*agent*, *manière*, *moyen*) by; **choisi p.** chosen by; **p. le train** by train; **p. le travail** by *ou* through work; **apprendre p. un ami** to learn from *ou* through a friend; **commencer p. qch** to begin with sth. ▮ (*lieu*) through; **p. la porte** through *ou* by the door; **jeter p. la fenêtre** to throw out (of) the window; **p. ici/là** (*aller*) this/that way; (*habiter*) around here/there. ▮ (*motif*) out of, from; **p. pitié** out of *ou* from pity. ▮ (*temps*) on; **p. un jour d'hiver** on a winter's day; **p.**

ce froid in this cold. ▮ (*distributif*) **dix fois p. an** ten times a year; **deux p. deux** two by two.

parachute *m* parachute.

paradis *m* heaven, paradise.

paragraphe *m* paragraph.

paraître* *vi* (*sembler*) to seem; (*livre*) to come out; **il paraît qu'il va partir** it appears *ou* seems he's leaving.

parallèle *a* parallel (**à** with, to).

paralyser *vt* to paralyse, *Am* paralyze.

parapluie *m* umbrella.

parasite *m* parasite; **parasites** (*à la radio*) interference.

parasol *m* sunshade.

paravent *m* (folding) screen.

parc *m* park; (*de château*) grounds; (*de bébé*) (play)pen; **p. (de stationnement)** car park, *Am* parking lot.

parce que [parsk(ə)] *conj* because.

parcelle *f* fragment; (*terrain*) plot.

par-ci par-là *adv* here, there and everywhere.

parcomètre *m* parking meter.

parcourir* *vt* (*région*) to travel all over; (*distance*) to cover; (*texte*) to glance through

parcours *m* (*itinéraire*) route; (*distance*) distance.

par-dessous *prép & adv* under(neath).

pardessus *m* overcoat.

par-dessus *prép & adv* over (the top of); **p.-dessus tout** above all.

pardon *m* **p.!** (*excusez-moi*) sorry!; **demander p.** to apologize (**à** to).

pardonner *vt* to forgive; **p. qch à qn/à qn d'avoir fait qch** to forgive s.o. for sth/for doing sth.

pare-brise *m inv* windscreen, *Am* windshield.

pare-chocs *m inv* bumper.

pareil, -eille 1 *a* similar; **p. à** the same as; **être pareils** to be the same; **un p. désordre**/*etc* such a mess/*etc*. **2** *adv Fam* the same.

parent, -ente 1 *mf* relative. **2** *mpl* (*père et mère*) parents. **3** *a* related (**de** to).

parenthèse *f* (*signe*) bracket.

paresse *f* laziness.

paresseux, -euse *a & mf* lazy (person).

parfait, -aite *a* perfect; **p.!** excellent!

parfaitement *adv* perfectly; (*certainement*) certainly.

parfois *adv* sometimes.

parfum *m* (*odeur*) fragrance; (*goût*) flavour; (*liquide*) perfume.

parfumé, -ée *a* (*savon, fleur*) scented; **p. au café**/*etc* coffee-/*etc*

flavoured.
parfumer *vt* to perfume; (*glace, crème*) to flavour (**à** with).
parfumer (se) *vpr* to put on perfume.
parfumerie *f* perfume shop.
pari *m* bet; **p. mutuel urbain** = the tote, *Am* pari-mutuel.
parier *vti* to bet (**sur** on, **que** that).
parisien, -ienne 1 *a* Parisian; **la banlieue parisienne** the Paris suburbs. **2** *mf* Parisian.
parking *m* car park, *Am* parking lot.
parlement *m* parliament.
parlementaire *mf* member of parliament.
parler 1 *vi* to talk, speak (**de** about, of; **à** to). **2** *vt* (*langue*) to speak.
parler (se) *vpr* (*langue*) to be spoken.
parmi *prép* among(st).
paroi *f* (inside) wall; (*de rocher*) (rock) face.
paroisse *f* parish.
paroissial, -e, -aux *a* **église**/*etc* **paroissiale** parish church/*etc*.
parole *f* (*mot, promesse*) word; **adresser la p. à** to speak to; **prendre la p.** to speak; **demander la p.** to ask to speak.
parquet *m* (parquet) floor.
parrain *m* godfather.
parrainer *vt* (*course etc*) to sponsor.
parsemé, -ée *a* **p. de** (*sol*) strewn (all over) with.
part *f* (*portion*) share; (*de gâteau*) portion; **prendre p. à** (*activité*) to take part in; (*la joie etc de qn*) to share; **de toutes parts** from *ou* on all sides; **de p. et d'autre** on both sides; **d'autre p.** (*d'ailleurs*) moreover; **de la p. de** (*provenance*) from; **quelque p.** somewhere; **nulle p.** nowhere; **autre p.** somewhere else; **à p.** (*mettre*) aside; (*excepté*) apart from; (*personne*) different.
partage *m* (*de gâteau, trésor etc*) sharing.
partager *vt* (*repas, joie etc*) to share (**avec** with).
partenaire *mf* partner.
parterre *m* (*de jardin*) flower bed.
parti *m* (*politique*) party.
participant, -ante *mf* participant.
participation *f* participation; **p. (aux frais)** contribution (*towards expenses*).
participe *m* *Grammaire* participle.
participer *vi* **p. à** (*jeu etc*) to take part in; (*frais, joie*) to share (in).
particularité *f* peculiarity.
particulier, -ière *a* (*spécial*) particular; (*privé*) private; (*bizarre*)

peculiar; **en p.** (*surtout*) in particular.

particulièrement *adv* particularly.

partie *f* part; (*de cartes, tennis etc*) game; **en p.** partly; **faire p. de** to be a part of; (*club etc*) to belong to.

partir* *vi* (*aux* **être**) (*aller*) to go; (*s'en aller*) to go, leave; (*coup de feu*) to go off; (*tache*) to come out; **à p. de** (*date, prix*) from.

partisan *m* supporter; **être p. de qch/de faire** to be in favour of sth/ of doing.

partition *f* (*musique*) score.

partout *adv* everywhere; **p. où tu vas** *ou* **iras** everywhere *ou* wherever you go.

parvenir* *vi* (*aux* **être**) **p. à** (*lieu*) to reach; **p. à faire** to manage to do.

pas[1] *adv* (*négatif*) not; **(ne)... p.** not; **je ne sais p.** I don't know; **p. de pain**/*etc* no bread/*etc*; **p. encore** not yet; **p. du tout** not at all.

pas[2] *m* step; (*allure*) pace; (*bruit*) footstep; (*trace*) footprint; **rouler au p.** (*véhicule*) to go dead slow; **au p. (cadencé)** in step; **faire les cent p.** to walk up and down; **faux p.** (*en marchant*) stumble; **le p. de la porte** the doorstep.

passable *a* (*travail, résultat*) (just) average.

passage *m* passing; (*traversée en bateau*) crossing; (*extrait, couloir*) passage; (*droit*) right of way; (*chemin*) path; **p. clouté** *ou* **pour piétons** (pedestrian) crossing, *Am* crosswalk; **p. souterrain** subway, *Am* underpass; **p. à niveau** level crossing, *Am* grade crossing; **'p. interdit'** 'no through traffic'; **'cédez le p.'** (*au carrefour*) 'give way', *Am* 'yield'.

passager, -ère *mf* passenger.

passant, -ante *mf* passer-by.

passe *f Football etc* pass; **mot de p.** password.

passé, -ée 1 *a* (*temps*) past; (*couleur*) faded; **la semaine passée** last week; **dix heures passées** after ten (o'clock); **être passé** (*personne*) to have been; (*orage*) to be over; **avoir vingt ans passés** to be over twenty. **2** *m* past, *Grammaire* past (tense).

passe-passe *m inv* **tour de p.-passe** conjuring trick.

passeport *m* passport.

passer 1 *vi* (*aux* **être** *ou* **avoir**) to pass (**à** to, **de** from); (*traverser*) to go through *ou* over; (*facteur*) to come; (*temps*) to pass, go by; (*film*) to be shown, be on; (*douleur*) to pass; (*couleur*) to fade; **p. devant** (*maison etc*) to go past, pass (by); **p. à la boulangerie** *ou* **chez le boulanger** to go round to the baker's; **laisser p.** (*personne, lumière*) to let through; **p. prendre** to fetch; **p. voir qn** to drop in on s.o.; **p. pour** (*riche etc*) to be taken for; **p. en** (*seconde etc*) (*à* *l'école*) to pass up into; (*en voiture*) to change up to. **2** *vt* (*aux* **avoir**) (*frontière etc*) to cross; (*donner*) to pass, hand (**à** to); (*temps*) to spend (**à faire** doing); (*disque*, *chemise*, *film*) to put on; (*examen*) to take; (*thé*) to strain; (*café*) to filter; (*limites*) to go beyond; (*visite médicale*) to have; **p. qch à qn** (*caprice etc*) to grant s.o. sth; **p. un coup d'éponge**/*etc* **à qch** to go over sth with a sponge/*etc*.

passer (se) *vpr* to take place, happen; (*douleur*) to go (away); **se p. de** to do *ou* go without; **ça s'est bien passé** it went off well.

passerelle *f* footbridge; (*d'avion*, *de bateau*) gangway.

passe-temps *m inv* pastime.

passif, -ive 1 *a* passive. **2** *m Grammaire* passive.

passion *f* passion; **avoir la p. des voitures/d'écrire** to have a passion for cars/writing.

passionnant, -ante *a* thrilling.

passionné, -ée *a* passionate; **p. de qch** passionately fond of sth.

passionner *vt* to thrill; **se p. pour** to have a passion for.

passoire *f* sieve; (*à thé*) strainer; (*à légumes*) colander.

pasteurisé, -ée pasteurized.

pastille *f* pastille, lozenge.

patauger *vi* to wade (*in the mud etc*); (*barboter*) to splash about.

pâte *f* paste; (*à pain*) dough; (*à tarte*) pastry; **pâtes (alimentaires)** pasta; **p. à modeler** plasticine®.

pâté *m* (*charcuterie*) pâté; **p. (en croûte)** meat pie; **p. (de sable)** sand castle; **p. de maisons** block of houses.

pâtée *f* (*pour chien*, *chat*) dog food, cat food.

paternel, -elle *a* paternal.

patiemment [-amɑ̃] *adv* patiently.

patience *f* patience.

patient, -ente 1 *a* patient. **2** *mf* (*malade*) patient.

patin *m* **p. (à glace)** (ice) skate; **p. à roulettes** roller-skate.

patinage *m* skating.

patiner *vi* (*en sport*) to skate; (*roue*) to spin round.

patinoire *f* skating rink.

pâtisserie *f* pastry; (*magasin*) cake shop.

pâtissier, -ière *mf* pastrycook.

patrie *f* (native) country.

patriote 1 *mf* patriot. **2** *a* patriotic.

patriotique *a* (*chant etc*) patriotic.

patron, -onne 1 *mf* (*chef*) boss. **2** *m* (*modèle de papier*) pattern.

patrouille *f* patrol.

patrouiller *vi* to patrol.

patte *f* leg; (*de chat*, *chien*) paw; **marcher à quatre pattes** to crawl.

pâturage *m* pasture.
paume *f* (*de main*) palm.
paupière *f* eyelid.
pause *f* (*arrêt*) break.
pauvre 1 *a* poor. **2** *mf* poor man *ou* woman; **les pauvres** the poor.
pauvreté *f* (*besoin*) poverty.
pavé *m* (*de rue*) paving stone.
paver *vt* to pave.
pavillon *m* (*maison*) (detached) house; (*drapeau*) flag.
payant, -ante *a* (*hôte*, *spectateur*) paying; (*place*, *entrée*) that one has to pay for.
paye *f* pay, wages.
payer 1 *vt* (*personne*, *somme*) to pay; (*service*, *objet*) to pay for; **p. qn pour faire** to pay s.o. to do *ou* for doing. **2** *vi* (*personne*, *métier*) to pay.
pays *m* country; **du p.** (*vin*, *gens*) local.
paysage *m* landscape.
paysan, -anne *mf* (small) farmer.
PCV [peseve] *abrév* (*paiement contre vérification*) **téléphoner en PCV** to reverse the charges, *Am* call collect.
PDG [pedeʒe] *abrév* = **président directeur général.**
péage *m* (*droit*) toll; (*lieu*) tollbooth.
peau, -x *f* skin; (*de fruit*) peel, skin; (*cuir*) hide.
pêche[1] *f* fishing; (*poissons*) catch; **p. (à la ligne)** angling; **aller à la p.** to go fishing.
pêche[2] *f* (*fruit*) peach.
péché *m* sin.
pêcher[1] 1 *vi* to fish. **2** *vt* (*attraper*) to catch.
pêcher[2] *m* peach tree.
pêcheur *m* fisherman; (*à la ligne*) angler.
pédale *f* pedal; **p. de frein** footbrake (pedal).
pédaler *vi* to pedal.
pédalo *m* pedal boat.
pédiatre *mf* children's doctor.
pédicure *mf* chiropodist.
peigne *m* comb; **se donner un coup de p.** to give one's hair a comb.
peigner *vt* (*cheveux*) to comb; **p. qn** to comb s.o.'s hair.
peigner (se) *vpr* to comb one's hair.
peignoir *m* dressing gown, *Am* bathrobe; **p. (de bain)** bathrobe.
peindre* *vti* to paint; **p. en bleu**/*etc* to paint blue/*etc*.
peine (à) *adv* hardly.
peine *f* (*châtiment*) **la p. de mort** the death penalty; **p. de prison**

prison sentence. ▮ (*chagrin*) sorrow; **avoir de la p.** to be upset; **faire de la p. à** to upset. ▮ (*effort, difficulté*) trouble; **se donner de la p.** to go to a lot of trouble (**pour faire** to do); **avec p.** with difficulty; **ça vaut la p. d'attendre**/*etc* it's worth (while) waiting/*etc*; **ce n'est pas** *ou* **ça ne vaut pas la p.** it's not worth it.

peintre *m* painter; **p. (en bâtiment)** (house) painter.

peinture *f* (*tableau, activité*) painting; (*matière*) paint; **'p. fraîche'** 'wet paint'.

pelage *m* (*d'animal*) coat, fur.

peler 1 *vt* (*fruit*) to peel. **2** *vi* (*peau bronzée*) to peel.

pelle *f* shovel; (*d'enfant*) spade; **p. à poussière** dustpan.

pelleteuse *f* mechanical digger *ou* shovel.

pellicule *f* (*pour photos*) film; (*couche*) layer; **pellicules** (*dans les cheveux*) dandruff.

pelote *f* (*de laine*) ball.

peloton *m* (*cyclistes*) pack.

pelotonner (se) *vpr* to curl up (into a ball).

pelouse *f* lawn.

peluche *f* **peluches** (*flocons*) fluff; **jouet en p.** soft toy; **chien en p.** (*jouet*) furry dog; **ours en p.** teddy bear.

penalty *m Football* penalty.

penché, -ée *a* leaning.

pencher 1 *vt* (*objet*) to tilt; (*tête*) to lean. **2** *vi* (*arbre etc*) to lean (over).

pencher (se) *vpr* to lean (over *ou* forward); **se p. par** (*fenêtre*) to lean out of.

pendant *prép* during; **p. la nuit** during the night; **p. deux mois** for two months; **p. que** while.

penderie *f* wardrobe, *Am* closet.

pendre *vti* to hang (**à** from); **p. qn** to hang s.o. (**pour** for); **se p.** (*se suspendre*) to hang (**à** from).

pendu, -ue *a* (*objet*) hanging (**à** from).

pendule *f* clock.

pénétrer *vi* **p. dans** to enter; (*profondément*) to penetrate (into).

pénible *a* difficult; (*douloureux*) painful.

péniblement *adv* with difficulty.

péniche *f* barge.

pénicilline *f* penicillin.

pensée *f* (*idée*) thought.

penser 1 *vi* to think (**à** of, about); **p. à qch/à faire qch** (*ne pas oublier*) to remember sth/to do sth. **2** *vt* to think (**que** that); **je pensais rester** I was thinking of staying; **je pense réussir** I hope to succeed; **que pensez-vous de?** what do you think of *ou* about?

pension[1] *f* boarding school; (*somme à payer*) board; **être en p.** to board (**chez** with); **p. complète** full board.

pension[2] *f* (*de retraite etc*) pension.

pensionnaire *mf* (*élève*) boarder; (*d'hôtel*) resident; (*de famille*) lodger.

pensionnat *m* boarding school.

pente *f* slope; **en p.** sloping.

Pentecôte *f* Whitsun, *Am* Pentecost.

pépin *m* (*de fruit*) pip, *Am* seed, pit.

perçant, -ante *a* (*cri, froid*) piercing; (*yeux*) sharp.

percepteur *m* tax collector.

percer 1 *vt* to pierce; (*avec une perceuse*) to drill (a hole in); (*ouverture*) to make. **2** *vi* (*avec un outil*) to drill.

perceuse *f* (*outil*) drill.

perche *f* (*bâton*) pole.

percher (se) *vpr* (*oiseau*) to perch.

perchoir *m* perch.

percuter *vt* (*véhicule*) to crash into.

perdant, -ante *mf* loser.

perdre 1 *vt* to lose; (*gaspiller*) to waste; **p. de vue** to lose sight of. **2** *vi* to lose.

perdre (se) *vpr* (*s'égarer*) to get lost; **je m'y perds** I'm lost *ou* confused.

perdrix [perdri] *f* partridge.

perdu, -ue *a* lost; (*gaspillé*) wasted; **c'est du temps p.** it's a waste of time.

père *m* father.

perfection *f* perfection; **à la p.** perfectly.

perfectionné, -ée *a* (*machine*) advanced.

perfectionner *vt* to improve; **se p. en anglais**/*etc* to improve one's English/*etc*.

perforeuse *f* (paper) punch.

performance *f* (*d'athlète etc*) performance.

péril [peril] *m* danger, peril.

périlleux, -euse *a* dangerous.

périmé, -ée *a* (*billet*) expired.

période *f* period.

périphérique *a & m* **(boulevard) p.** (motorway) ring road, *Am* beltway.

perle *f* (*bijou*) pearl; (*de bois, verre*) bead.

permanence *f* (*salle d'étude*) study room; **être de p.** to be on duty;

en p. permanently.

permanent, -ente 1 *a* permanent; (*spectacle*) continuous. **2** *f* (*coiffure*) perm.

permettre* *vt* to allow; **p. à qn de faire** to allow s.o. to do; **vous permettez?** may I?; **je ne peux pas me p. d'acheter** I can't afford to buy.

permis, -ise 1 *a* allowed. **2** *m* licence, *Am* license; **p. de conduire** driving licence, *Am* driver's license; **passer son p. de conduire** to take one's driving test.

permission *f* permission; (*congé de soldat*) leave; **demander la p.** to ask permission (**de faire** to do).

perpendiculaire *a* perpendicular (**à** to).

perpétuel, -elle *a* (*incessant*) continual.

perron *m* (front) steps.

perroquet *m* parrot.

perruche *f* budgerigar, *Am* parakeet.

perruque *f* wig.

persécuter *vt* to persecute.

persécution *f* persecution.

persévérance *f* perseverance.

persévérer *vi* to persevere (**dans** in).

persil *m* parsley.

persister *vi* to persist (**à faire** in doing, **dans qch** in sth).

personnage *m* (important) person; (*de livre, film*) character.

personnalité *f* personality.

personne 1 *f* person; **personnes** people; **grande p.** grown-up; **en p.** in person. **2** *pron* (*négatif*) nobody; **je ne vois p.** I don't see anybody; **mieux que p.** better than anybody.

personnel, -elle 1 *a* personal. **2** *m* staff.

personnellement *adv* personally.

perspective *f* (*idée, possibilité*) prospect (**de** of).

persuader *vt* to persuade (**qn de faire** s.o. to do); **être persuadé que** to be convinced that.

persuasion *f* persuasion.

perte *f* loss; (*gaspillage*) waste (**de temps/d'argent** of time/money).

perturbation *f* disruption.

perturber *vt* (*trafic etc*) to disrupt; (*personne*) to disturb.

pesant, -ante *a* heavy.

pesanteur *f* (*force*) gravity.

pèse-personne *m* (bathroom) scales.

peser *vti* to weigh; **p. lourd** to be heavy.

pessimiste *a* pessimistic.

peste *f* (*maladie*) plague.
pétale *m* petal.
pétanque *f* (*jeu*) bowls.
pétard *m* firecracker.
pétillant, -ante *a* fizzy; (*vin*, *yeux*) sparkling.
pétiller *vi* (*champagne*) to fizz; (*yeux*) to sparkle.
petit, -ite 1 *a* small, little; (*de taille*) short; (*bruit*, *coup*) slight; (*jeune*) little; **tout p.** tiny; **un p. Français** a (little) French boy. **2** *mf* (little) boy *ou* girl; (*personne*) small person; (*à l'école*) junior; **petits** (*d'animal*) young. **3** *adv* **p. à p.** little by little.
petite-fille *f* (*pl* **petites-filles**) granddaughter.
petit-fils *m* (*pl* **petits-fils**) grandson.
petits-enfants *mpl* grandchildren.
petit-suisse *m* soft cheese (*for dessert*).
pétrole *m* oil.
pétrolier *m* (*navire*) (oil) tanker.
peu *adv* (*manger etc*) not much, little; **un p.** a little, a bit; **p. de sel/de temps**/*etc* not much salt/time/*etc*; **un p. de fromage**/*etc* a little cheese/*etc*; **p. de gens**/*etc* few people/*etc*; **un (tout) petit p.** a (tiny) little bit; **p. intéressant**/*etc* not very interesting/*etc*; **p. de chose** not much, **p. à p.** little by little; **à p. près** more or less; **p. après** shortly after.
peuple *m* people.
peuplé, -ée *a* **très/peu**/*etc* **p.** highly/sparsely/*etc* populated; **p. de** populated by.
peur *f* fear; **avoir p.** to be afraid *ou* frightened (**de qch/qn** of sth/s.o.; **de faire** to do, of doing); **faire p. à** to frighten; **de p. que** (+ *subjonctif*) for fear that.
peureux, -euse *a* easily frightened.
peut, peuvent, peux *voir* **pouvoir.**
peut-être *adv* perhaps, maybe; **p.-être qu'il viendra** perhaps *ou* maybe he'll come.
phare *m* (*pour bateaux*) lighthouse; (*de véhicule*) headlight; **faire un appel de phares** to flash one's lights.
pharmacie *f* chemist's shop, *Am* drugstore; (*armoire*) medicine cabinet.
pharmacien, -ienne *mf* chemist, *Am* druggist.
philatélie *f* stamp collecting.
philatéliste *mf* stamp collector.
philosophe 1 *mf* philosopher. **2** *a* (*résigné*) philosophical.
philosophie *f* philosophy.
phonétique *a* phonetic.

phoque *m* (*animal*) seal.
photo *f* photo; (*art*) photography; **prendre une p. de** to take a photo of; **se faire prendre en p.** to have one's photo taken.
photocopie *f* photocopy.
photocopier *vt* to photocopy.
photocopieuse *f* (*machine*) photocopier.
photographe *mf* photographer.
photographier *vt* to photograph.
photographique *a* photographic.
photomaton® *m* photo booth.
phrase *f* sentence.
physique 1 *a* physical. **2** *m* (*corps*, *aspect*) physique; (*science*) physics.
physiquement *adv* physically.
pianiste *mf* pianist.
piano *m* piano.
pic *m* (*cime*) peak.
pic (à) *adv* **couler à p.** to sink to the bottom.
pichet *m* jug.
pickpocket *m* pickpocket.
picorer *vti* to peck.
picoter *vt* (*yeux*) to make smart; **les yeux me picotent** my eyes are smarting.
pièce *f* (*de maison etc*) room; (*de pantalon*) patch; **p. (de monnaie)** coin; **p. (de théâtre)** play; **p. d'identité** identity card; **pièces détachées** (*de véhicule etc*) spare parts; **cinq dollars p.** five dollars each.
pied *m* foot (*pl* feet); (*de meuble*) leg; (*de verre*, *lampe*) base; **à p.** on foot; **au p. de** at the foot of; **coup de p.** kick; **donner un coup de p.** to kick (**à qn** s.o.).
piège *m* trap.
piéger *vt* (*animal*) to trap; (*voiture*) to booby-trap.
pierre *f* stone; (*précieuse*) gem; **p. (à briquet)** flint.
piétiner 1 *vt* to trample (on). **2** *vi* to stamp (one's feet).
piéton *m* pedestrian.
piétonne *a* **rue p.** pedestrian(ized) street.
pieu, -x *m* post, stake.
pieuvre *f* octopus.
pigeon *m* pigeon.
pile 1 *f* (*électrique*) battery; (*tas*) pile; **radio à piles** battery radio; **en p.** in a pile; **p. (ou face)?** heads (or tails)? **2** *adv* **s'arrêter p.** to stop short; **à deux heures p.** on the dot of two.
pilier *m* pillar.

pillage *m* looting.
piller *vti* to loot.
pilotage *m* **poste de p.** cockpit.
pilote *m* (*d'avion*) pilot; (*de voiture*) driver.
piloter *vt* (*avion*) to fly; (*voiture*) to drive.
pilule *f* pill; **prendre la p.** to be on the pill.
piment *m* pepper.
pimenté, -ée *a* spicy.
pin *m* (*arbre*) pine; **pomme de p.** pine cone.
pince *f* (*outil*) pliers; (*de cycliste*) clip; (*de crabe*) pincer; **p. (à linge)** (clothes) peg *ou Am* pin; **p. (à épiler)** tweezers; **p. (à sucre)** sugar tongs; **p. à cheveux** hairgrip, *Am* bobby pin.
pinceau, -x *m* (paint)brush.
pincée *f* (*de sel etc*) pinch (**de** of).
pincer *vt* to pinch; **se p. le doigt** to get one's finger caught (**dans** in).
pingouin *m* penguin.
ping-pong [piŋpɔ̃g] *m* table tennis.
pin's [pinz] *m inv* badge, lapel pin.
pioche *f* pick(axe).
piocher *vti* to dig (with a pick).
pion *m* (*au jeu de dames*) piece; *Échecs* pawn.
pipe *f* pipe; **fumer la p.** to smoke a pipe.
pipi *m* **faire p.** *Fam* to go for a pee.
piquant, -ante *a* (*plante, barbe*) prickly.
pique *m* (*couleur*) *Cartes* spades.
pique-nique *m* picnic.
pique-niquer *vi* to picnic.
piquer 1 *vt* (*percer*) to prick; (*langue, yeux*) to sting; (*coudre*) to (machine-)stitch; **p. qn** (*abeille*) to sting s.o.; **p. qch dans** (*enfoncer*) to stick sth into; **p. une colère** to fly into a rage. **2** *vi* (*avion*) to dive; (*moutarde etc*) to be hot.
piquet *m* (*pieu*) stake; (*de tente*) peg.
piqûre *f* (*d'abeille*) sting; (*avec une seringue*) injection.
pirate *m* pirate; **p. de l'air** hijacker.
pire 1 *a* worse (**que** than); **le p. moment**/*etc* the worst moment/*etc*. **2** *mf* **le** *ou* **la p.** the worst.
piscine *f* swimming pool.
pissenlit *m* dandelion.
pistache *f* pistachio.
piste *f* (*traces*) trail; (*de course*) racetrack; (*de cirque*) ring; (*de patinage*) rink; **p. (d'envol)** runway; **p. cyclable** cycle track, *Am* bicycle path; **p. de danse** dance floor; **p. de ski** ski run *ou* slope.

pistolet *m* gun; **p. à eau** water pistol.
pitié *f* pity; **j'ai p. de lui** I feel sorry for him.
pittoresque *a* picturesque.
pivoter *vi* (*personne*) to swing round; (*fauteuil*) to swivel.
pizza [pidza] *f* pizza.
pizzeria *f* pizzeria.
placard *m* (*armoire*) cupboard, *Am* closet.
place *f* (*endroit*, *rang*) place; (*espace*) room; (*lieu public*) square; (*siège*) seat, place; (*emploi*) job; **p. de parking** parking place *ou* space; **à la p. (de)** instead (of); **à votre p.** in your place; **sur p.** on the spot; **en p.** in place; **mettre en p.** (*installer*) to set up; **changer de p.** to change places; **changer qch de p.** to move sth.
placement *m* (*d'argent*) investment.
placer *vt* to place; (*invité*, *spectateur*) to seat; (*argent*) to invest (**dans** in).
placer (se) *vpr* (*debout*) to (go and) stand; (*s'asseoir*) to (go and) sit; **se p. troisième**/*etc* (*en sport*) to come third/*etc*.
plafond *m* ceiling.
plage *f* beach; **p. arrière** (*de voiture*) (back) window shelf.
plaie *f* wound; (*coupure*) cut.
plaindre* *vt* to feel sorry for.
plaindre (se) *vpr* to complain (**de** about, **que** that); **se p. de** (*douleur*) to complain of.
plaine *f* plain.
plainte *f* complaint; (*cri*) moan.
plaire* *vi* **p. à qn** to please s.o.; **elle lui plaît** he likes her; **ça me plaît** I like it; **s'il vous** *ou* **te plaît** please.
plaire (se) *vpr* (*à Paris etc*) to like *ou* enjoy it.
plaisanter *vi* to joke (**sur** about).
plaisanterie *f* joke; **par p.** for a joke.
plaisir *m* pleasure; **faire p. à** to please; **pour le p.** for fun.
plan *m* (*projet*, *dessin*) plan; (*de ville*) map; **au premier p.** in the foreground.
planche *f* board; **p. à repasser** ironing board; **p. (à roulettes)** skateboard; **p. (à voile)** sailboard; **faire de la p. (à voile)** to go windsurfing.
plancher *m* floor.
planer *vi* (*oiseau*, *avion*) to glide.
planète *f* planet.
plante[1] *f* plant; **p. verte** house plant.
plante[2] *f* **p. des pieds** sole (of the foot).
planter *vt* (*fleur etc*) to plant; (*clou*, *couteau*) to drive in; **se p.**

devant to come *ou* go and stand in front of, plant oneself in front of.

plaque *f* plate; (*de verre*, *métal*, *verglas*) sheet; (*de chocolat*) bar; **p. chauffante** hotplate; **p. d'immatriculation** number *ou Am* license plate.

plaqué, -ée *a* **p. or** gold-plated.

plaquer *vt Rugby* to tackle; (*aplatir*) to flatten (**contre** against).

plastique *a* & *m* **(matière) p.** plastic; **en p.** (*bouteille etc*) plastic.

plat, plate 1 *a* flat; **à p. ventre** flat on one's face; **à p.** (*pneu*, *batterie*) flat; **poser à p.** to put down flat; **assiette plate** dinner plate; **eau plate** still water. **2** *m* (*récipient*, *nourriture*) dish; (*partie du repas*) course; **'p. du jour'** 'today's special'.

platane *m* plane tree.

plateau, -x *m* (*pour servir*) tray; **p. à fromages** cheeseboard.

plate-forme *f* (*pl* **plates-formes**) platform; **p.-forme pétrolière** oil rig.

plâtre *m* (*matière*) plaster; **un p.** a plaster cast; **dans le p.** in plaster.

plâtrer *vt* (*bras*, *jambe*) to put in plaster.

plein, pleine 1 *a* full (**de** of); **en pleine mer** out at sea; **en pleine figure** right in the face. **2** *prép* & *adv* **des billes p. les poches** pockets full of marbles; **du chocolat p. la figure** chocolate all over one's face; **p. de lettres/d'argent**/*etc Fam* lots of letters/money/*etc*. **3** *m* **faire le p. (d'essence)** to fill up (the tank).

pleurer *vi* to cry.

pleuvoir* *vi* to rain; **il pleut** it's raining.

pli *m* (*de papier*) fold; (*de jupe*) pleat; (*de pantalon*) crease; **(faux) p.** crease; **mise en plis** (*coiffure*) set.

pliant, -ante *a* (*chaise etc*) folding.

plier 1 *vt* to fold; (*courber*) to bend. **2** *vi* (*branche*) to bend.

plier (se) *vpr* (*lit*, *chaise etc*) to fold (up).

plissé, -ée *a* (*tissu*, *jupe*) pleated.

plisser *vt* (*front*) to wrinkle; (*yeux*) to screw up.

plomb *m* (*métal*) lead; (*fusible*) fuse; **plombs** (*de chasse*) lead shot

plombage *m* (*de dent*) filling

plomber *vt* (*dent*) to fill.

plomberie *f* plumbing.

plombier *m* plumber.

plongée *f* (*sport*) diving.

plongeoir *m* diving board.

plongeon *m* dive.

plonger 1 *vi* (*personne*) to dive. **2** *vt* (*mettre*) to plunge (**dans** into).

plongeur, -euse *mf* diver.

plu *voir* **plaire, pleuvoir.**

pluie *f* rain; **sous la p.** in the rain.

plume *f* (*d'oiseau*) feather; (*de stylo*) (pen) nib; **stylo à p.** (fountain) pen.

plumer *vt* (*volaille*) to pluck.

plupart (la) *f* most; **la p. des cas** most cases; **la p. du temps** most of the time; **la p. d'entre eux** most of them; **pour la p.** mostly.

pluriel, -ielle *a* & *m* plural; **au p.** in the plural.

plus[1] [ply] ([plyz] *before vowel*, [plys] *in end position*) **1** *adv comparatif* (*travailler etc*) more (**que** than); **p. d'un kilo/de dix** more than a kilo/ten; **p. de thé** more tea; **p. beau** more beautiful (**que** than); **p. tard** later; **p. petit** smaller; **de p. en p.** more and more; **p. ou moins** more or less; **en p.** in addition (**de** to); **de p.** more (**que** than); (*en outre*) moreover; **(âgé) de p. de dix ans** over ten; **j'ai dix ans de p. qu'elle** I'm ten years older than she is; **il est p. de cinq heures** it's after five. **2** *adv superlatif* **le p.** (*travailler etc*) (the) most; **le p. beau** the most beautiful (**de** in); **le p. grand** the biggest (**de** in); **j'ai le p. de livres** I have (the) most books.

plus[2] [ply] *adv de négation* **p. de** (*pain*, *argent*) no more; **il n'a p. de pain** he has no more bread, he doesn't have any more bread; **tu n'es p. jeune** you're not young any more; **je ne la reverrai p.** I won't see her again.

plus[3] [plys] *prép* plus; **deux p. deux** two plus two; **il fait p. deux (degrés)** it's two degrees above freezing.

plusieurs *a* & *pron* several.

plutôt *adv* rather (**que** than).

pluvieux, -euse *a* rainy.

pneu *m* (*pl* **-s**) tyre, *Am* tire.

pneumatique *a* **matelas p.** air-bed; **canot p.** rubber dinghy.

poche *f* pocket; (*de kangourou*) pouch.

pocher *vt* (*œufs*) to poach; **p. l'œil à qn** to give s.o. a black eye.

pochette *f* (*sac*) bag; (*d'allumettes*) book; (*de disque*) sleeve; (*sac à main*) (clutch) bag.

poêle 1 *m* stove. **2** *f* **p. (à frire)** frying pan.

poème *m* poem.

poésie *f* (*art*) poetry; (*poème*) poem.

poète *m* poct.

poétique *a* poetic.

poids *m* weight; **au p.** by weight.

poids lourd (heavy) lorry *ou Am* truck.

poignard *m* dagger.

poignarder *vt* to stab.
poignée *f* (*quantité*) handful (**de** of); (*de porte etc*) handle; **p. de main** handshake; **donner une p. de main à** to shake hands with.
poignet *m* wrist; (*de chemise*) cuff.
poil *m* hair; (*pelage*) fur.
poilu, -ue *a* hairy.
poinçonner *vt* (*billet*) to punch.
poing *m* fist; **coup de p.** punch.
point *m* (*lieu, score etc*) point; (*sur i, à l'horizon*) dot; (*tache*) spot; (*note scolaire*) mark; (*de couture*) stitch; **sur le p. de faire** about to do; **p. (final)** full stop, *Am* period; **p. d'exclamation** exclamation mark *ou Am* point; **p. d'interrogation** question mark; **points de suspension** suspension points; **p. de vue** (*opinion*) point of view; **à p.** (*steak*) medium rare; **au p. mort** (*véhicule*) in neutral; **p. de côté** (*douleur*) stitch (in one's side).
pointe *f* (*extrémité*) tip; (*clou*) nail; **sur la p. des pieds** on tiptoe; **en p.** pointed.
pointer 1 *vt* (*cocher*) to tick (off), *Am* check (off); (*braquer*) to point (**sur** at). **2** *vi* **p. vers** to point upwards towards.
pointillé *m* dotted line.
pointu, -ue *a* (*en pointe*) pointed.
pointure *f* (*de chaussure, gant*) size.
point-virgule *m* (*pl* **points-virgules**) semicolon.
poire *f* pear.
poireau, -x *m* leek.
poirier *m* pear tree.
pois *m* pea; **petits p.** (garden) peas, *Am* peas; **p. chiche** chickpea.
poison *m* poison.
poisseux, -euse *a* sticky.
poisson *m* fish; **p. rouge** goldfish.
poissonnerie *f* fish shop.
poissonnier, -ière *mf* fishmonger.
poitrine *f* chest; (*de femme*) bust.
poivre *m* pepper.
poivré, -ée *a* (*piquant*) peppery.
poivrer *vt* to pepper.
poivrière *f* pepperpot.
poivron *m* (*légume*) pepper.
pôle *m* **p. Nord/Sud** North/South Pole.
poli, -ie *a* (*courtois*) polite (**avec** to, with); (*lisse*) polished.
police[1] *f* police; **p. secours** emergency services.
police[2] *f* **p. (d'assurance)** (insurance) policy.

policier, -ière 1 *a* **enquête**/*etc* **policière** police inquiry/*etc*; **roman p.** detective novel. **2** *m* policeman, detective.
poliment *adv* politely.
polio 1 *f* (*maladie*) polio. **2** *mf* (*personne*) polio victim.
polir *vt* to polish.
politesse *f* politeness.
politique 1 *a* political; **homme p.** politician. **2** *f* (*activité*) politics; **une p.** a policy.
pollen [pɔlɛn] *m* pollen.
polluer *vt* to pollute.
pollution *f* pollution.
polo *m* (*chemise*) sweat shirt.
polochon *m* bolster.
polonais, -aise 1 *a* Polish. **2** *mf* Pole. **3** *m* (*langue*) Polish.
polycopié *m* duplicated course notes.
polyester *m* polyester; **chemise**/*etc* **en p.** polyester shirt/*etc*.
pommade *f* ointment.
pomme *f* apple; **p. de terre** potato; **pommes frites** chips, *Am* French fries; **pommes chips** potato crisps *ou Am* chips.
pommier *m* apple tree.
pompe *f* pump; **p. à essence** petrol *ou Am* gas station; **pompes funèbres** undertaker's; **entrepreneur de pompes funèbres** undertaker.
pomper *vt* (*eau*) to pump out (**de** of).
pompier *m* fireman; **voiture des pompiers** fire engine.
pompiste *mf* petrol *ou Am* gas station attendant.
pompon *m* pompon.
poncer *vt* to rub down, sand.
ponctuation *f* punctuation.
ponctuel, -elle *a* (*à l'heure*) punctual.
pondre 1 *vt* (*œuf*) to lay. **2** *vi* (*poule*) to lay (eggs *ou* an egg).
poney *m* pony.
pont *m* bridge; (*de bateau*) deck.
pop *m & a inv* (*musique*) pop.
populaire *a* (*qui plaît*) popular; (*quartier*) working-class; (*expression*) colloquial.
population *f* population.
porc *m* pig; (*viande*) pork.
porcelaine *f* china.
porche *m* porch.
porcherie *f* (pig)sty.
port *m* port, harbour.
portable *a* (*portatif*) portable.

portail *m* (*de jardin*) gate(way).
portant, -ante *a* **bien p.** in good health.
portatif, -ive *a* portable.
porte *f* door; (*de jardin*) gate; (*de ville*) entrance; **p. (d'embarquement)** (*d'aéroport*) (departure) gate; **p. d'entrée** front door; **p. coulissante** sliding door; **mettre à la p.** to throw out.
porte-avions *m inv* aircraft carrier.
porte-bagages *m inv* luggage rack.
porte-bonheur *m inv* (lucky) charm.
porte-clefs *m inv* key ring.
porte-documents *m inv* briefcase.
portée *f* (*de fusil etc*) range; (*animaux*) litter; **à p. de la main** within (easy) reach; **à p. de voix** within earshot; **hors de p.** out of reach.
porte-fenêtre *f* (*pl* **portes-fenêtres**) French door *ou* window.
portefeuille *m* wallet.
portemanteau, -x *m* hatstand, hallstand; (*crochet*) coat peg.
porte-monnaie *m inv* purse.
porte-parole *m inv* spokesman, (*femme*) spokeswoman.
porter 1 *vt* to carry; (*vêtement, lunettes, barbe etc*) to wear; **p. qch à** (*apporter*) to take sth to; **p. bonheur/malheur** to bring good/bad luck. **2** *vi* (*voix*) to carry.
porter (se) *vpr* (*vêtement*) to be worn; **se p. bien/mal** to be well/ill; **comment te portes-tu?** how are you?
porte-revues *m inv* newspaper rack.
porte-savon *m* soapdish.
porte-serviettes *m inv* towel rail.
porteur *m* (*à la gare*) porter.
porte-voix *m inv* loudspeaker, megaphone.
portier *m* doorkeeper.
portière *f* (*de véhicule, train*) door.
portion *f* (*partie*) portion; (*de nourriture*) helping.
portique *m* (*de balançoire etc*) crossbar.
portrait *m* portrait.
portugais, -aise 1 *a* Portuguese. **2** *mf* Portuguese man *ou* woman, Portuguese *inv*; **les P.** the Portuguese. **3** *m* (*langue*) Portuguese.
pose *f* (*installation*) putting up; putting in; laying; (*attitude de modèle*) pose.
poser 1 *vt* to put (down); (*papier peint, rideaux*) to put up; (*sonnette, chauffage*) to put in; (*moquette*) to lay; (*question*) to ask (**à qn** s.o.). **2** *vi* (*modèle*) to pose (**pour** for).
poser (se) *vpr* (*oiseau, avion*) to land.
positif, -ive *a* positive.

position *f* position.
posséder *vt* to possess; (*maison etc*) to own.
possessif, -ive *a* & *m Grammaire* possessive.
possibilité *f* possibility.
possible 1 *a* possible (**à faire** to do); **il (nous) est p. de le faire** it is possible (for us) to do it; **il est p. que** (+ *subjonctif*) it is possible that; **si p.** if possible; **le plus tôt p.** as soon as possible; **autant que p.** as far as possible; **le plus p.** as much *ou* as many as possible. **2** *m* **faire son p.** to do one's best (**pour faire** to do).
postal, -e -aux *a* postal; **boîte postale** PO Box; **code p.** postcode, *Am* zip code.
poste 1 *f* (*service*) post; **(bureau de) p.** post office; **par la p.** by post; **p. aérienne** airmail. **2** *m* (*lieu*, *emploi*) post; (*radio*, *télévision*) set; **p. de secours** first aid post; **p. de police** police station.
poster *vt* (*lettre*) to post, mail.
postier, -ière *mf* postal worker.
pot *m* pot; (*à confiture*) jar; (*à lait*) jug; (*à bière*) mug; (*de crème*, *yaourt*) carton; (*de bébé*) potty; **p. de fleurs** flower pot.
potable *a* drinkable; **'eau p.'** 'drinking water'.
potage *m* soup.
potager *a* & *m* **(jardin) p.** vegetable garden.
pot-au-feu *m inv* beef stew.
pot-de-vin *m* (*pl* **pots-de-vin**) bribe.
poteau, -x *m* post; **p. indicateur** signpost; **p. d'arrivée** winning post; **p. télégraphique** telegraph pole.
poterie *f* (*art*) pottery; **une p.** a piece of pottery; **des poteries** (*objets*) pottery.
potier *m* potter.
potiron *m* pumpkin.
pou, -x *m* louse; **poux** lice.
poubelle *f* dustbin, *Am* garbage can.
pouce *m* thumb; (*mesure*) inch.
poudre *f* powder; (*explosif*) gunpowder; **en p.** (*lait*) powdered; (*chocolat*) drinking.
poudrer (se) *vpr* (*femme*) to powder one's face.
poudrier *m* (powder) compact.
pouf *m* (*siège*) pouf(fe).
poulailler *m* henhouse.
poulain *m* (*cheval*) foal.
poule *f* hen.
poulet *m* chicken.
poulie *f* pulley.

pouls [pu] *m* pulse.
poumon *m* lung; **à pleins poumons** (*respirer*) deeply; (*crier*) loudly.
poupée *f* doll.
pour 1 *prép* for; **p. toi**/*etc* for you/*etc*; **partir p.** (*Paris, cinq ans*) to leave for; **elle est p.** she's in favour; **p. faire** (in order) to do; **p. que tu saches** so (that) you may know; **p. quoi faire?** what for?; **trop petit**/*etc* **p. faire** too small/*etc* to do; **assez grand**/*etc* **p. faire** big/*etc* enough to do. **2** *m* **le p. et le contre** the pros and cons.
pourboire *m* (*argent*) tip.
pourcentage *m* percentage.
pourquoi *adv* & *conj* why; **p. pas?** why not?
pourra, pourrai(t) *etc voir* **pouvoir.**
pourri, -ie *a* (*fruit, temps etc*) rotten.
pourrir *vi* to rot.
poursuite *f* chase; **se mettre à la p. de** to go after, chase (after).
poursuivant, -ante *mf* pursuer
poursuivre* *vt* to chase, go after; (*lecture, voyage etc*) to carry on (with).
poursuivre (se) *vpr* to continue, go on.
pourtant *adv* yet.
pourvu que *conj* (*condition*) provided *ou* providing (that); (*souhait*) **p. qu'elle soit là!** I only hope (that) she's there!
pousser 1 *vt* to push; (*cri*) to utter; (*soupir*) to heave; **p. qn à faire** to urge s.o. to do. **2** *vi* (*croître*) to grow; **faire p.** (*plante etc*) to grow.
poussette *f* pushchair, *Am* stroller.
poussière *f* dust.
poussiéreux, -euse *a* dusty.
poussin *m* (*poulet*) chick.
poutre *f* (*en bois*) beam; (*en acier*) girder.
pouvoir* 1 *v aux* (*capacité*) can, be able to; (*permission, éventualité*) may, can; **je peux deviner** I can guess; **tu peux entrer** you may *ou* can come in; **il peut être sorti** he may *ou* might be out; **elle pourrait/pouvait venir** she might/could come; **j'ai pu l'obtenir** I managed to get it; **j'aurais pu l'obtenir** I could have got it *ou Am* gotten it; **je n'en peux plus** I'm utterly exhausted. **2** *m* (*capacité, autorité*) power; **les pouvoirs publics** the authorities; **au p.** in power.
pouvoir (se) *vpr* **il se peut qu'elle parte** (it's possible that) she might leave.
prairie *f* meadow.
pratique 1 *a* practical. **2** *f* (*exercice, procédé*) practice; **la p. de la natation/du golf** swimming/golfing.

pratiquement *adv* (*presque*) practically.
pratiquer *vt* (*sport, art etc*) to practise, *Am* practice.
pré *m* meadow.
préau, -x *m* (*d'école*) covered playground.
précaution *f* precaution (**de faire** of doing); (*prudence*) caution.
précédent, -ente 1 *a* previous. **2** *mf* previous one.
précéder *vti* to precede.
précieux, -euse *a* precious.
précipice *m* chasm, precipice.
précipitamment *adv* hastily.
précipitation *f* haste.
précipiter *vt* (*hâter*) to rush.
précipiter (se) *vpr* to throw oneself; (*foncer*) to rush (**à, sur** on to); (*s'accélérer*) to speed up.
précis, -ise *a* precise; **à deux heures précises** at two o'clock sharp.
préciser *vt* to specify (**que** that).
préciser (se) *vpr* to become clear(er).
précision *f* precision; (*explication*) explanation.
précoce *a* (*fruit etc*) early; (*enfant*) precocious.
prédécesseur *m* predecessor.
prédiction *f* prediction.
prédire* *vt* to predict (**que** that).
préfabriqué, -ée *a* prefabricated.
préface *f* preface.
préféré, -ée *a* & *mf* favourite.
préférence *f* preference (**pour** for); **de p.** preferably.
préférer *vt* to prefer (**à** to); **p. faire** to prefer to do.
préfet *m* prefect (*chief administrator in a department*).
préfixe *m* prefix.
préhistorique *a* prehistoric.
préjugé *m* prejudice; **être plein de préjugés** to be full of prejudice.
premier, -ière 1 *a* first; **nombre p.** prime number; **le p. rang** the front row; **P. ministre** Prime Minister. **2** *mf* first (one); **arriver le p.** to arrive first; **être le p. de la classe** to be (at the) top of the class. **3** *m* (*date*) first; (*étage*) first *ou Am* second floor; **le p. de l'an** New Year's Day. **4** *f* (*wagon, billet*) first class; (*au lycée*) = sixth form, *Am* = twelfth grade; (*de véhicule*) first (gear).
premièrement *adv* firstly.
prendre* 1 *vt* to take (**à qn** from s.o.); (*attraper*) to catch; (*voyager par*) to take (*train etc*); (*douche, bain*) to take, have; (*repas*) to have; (*photo*) to take; (*temps*) to take (up); **p. qn pour** (*un autre*) to mistake s.o. for; (*considérer*) to take s.o. for; **p. feu** to catch fire;

p. de la place to take up room; **p. du poids** to put on weight. **2** *vi* (*feu*) to catch; (*ciment*) to set; (*vaccin*) to take.

prendre (se) *vpr* (*objet*) to be taken; (*s'accrocher*) to get caught; **se p. pour un génie** to think one is a genius; **s'y p.** to go about it; **s'en p. à** to attack; (*accuser*) to blame.

prénom *m* first name.

préoccupation *f* worry.

préoccupé, -ée *a* worried.

préoccuper *vt* (*inquiéter*) to worry; **se p. de** to be worried about.

préparatifs *mpl* preparations (**de** for).

préparation *f* preparation.

préparer *vt* to prepare (**qch pour** sth for, **qn à** s.o. for); (*examen*) to prepare for; **se p.** to get (oneself) ready (**à** *ou* **pour qch** for sth); **se p. à faire** to prepare to do.

préposition *f Grammaire* preposition.

près *adv* **p. de** (*qn*, *qch*) near (to); **p. de deux ans**/*etc* nearly two years/*etc*; **tout p.** nearby (**de qn/qch** s.o./sth); **de p.** (*lire*, *suivre*) closely.

prescrire* *vt* (*médicament*) to prescribe.

présence *f* presence; (*à l'école etc*) attendance (**à** at); **feuille de p.** attendance sheet; **en p. de** in the presence of.

présent, -ente 1 *a* (*non absent*) present (**à** at, **dans** in); (*actuel*) present. **2** *m Grammaire* present (tense); **à p.** at present.

présentateur, -trice *mf* announcer.

présentation *f* presentation; (*d'une personne à une autre*) introduction.

présenter *vt* to present; **p. qn à qn** to introduce s.o. to s.o.

présenter (se) *vpr* to introduce oneself (**à** to); **se p. à** (*examen*) to take; (*élections*) to run in.

préservatif *m* condom.

préserver *vt* to protect (**de, contre** from).

présidence *f* (*de nation*) presidency; (*de firme*) chairmanship.

président, -ente *mf* (*de nation*) president; (*de réunion*, *firme*) chairman, chairwoman; **p. directeur général** (chairman and) managing director, *Am* chief executive officer.

présidentiel, -ielle *a* presidential.

presque *adv* almost.

presqu'île *f* peninsula.

presse *f* (*journaux*, *appareil*) press; **conférence**/*etc* **de p.** press conference/*etc*.

presse-citron *m inv* lemon squeezer.

pressé, -ée *a* (*personne*) in a hurry; (*travail*) urgent.

pressentir* *vt* to sense (**que** that).
presser 1 *vt* (*serrer*) to squeeze; (*bouton*) to press; (*fruit*) to squeeze. **2** *vi* (*temps*) to press; **rien ne presse** there's no hurry.
presser (se) *vpr* (*se serrer*) to squeeze (together); (*se hâter*) to hurry (**de faire** to do).
pressing [presiŋ] *m* (*magasin*) dry cleaner's.
pression *f* pressure.
prestidigitateur, -trice *mf* conjurer.
prestidigitation *f* **tour de p.** conjuring trick.
prêt *m* (*emprunt*) loan.
prêt, prête *a* (*préparé*) ready (**à faire** to do, **à qch** for sth).
prêt-à-porter *m inv* ready-to-wear clothes.
prétendre *vt* to claim (**que** that, **être** to be); **elle se prétend riche** she claims to be rich.
prétendu, -ue *a* so-called.
prétentieux, -euse *a & mf* conceited (person).
prêter *vt* (*argent*, *objet*) to lend (**à** to); **p. attention** to pay attention (**à** to).
prétexte *m* excuse; **sous p. de/que** on the pretext of/that.
prêtre *m* priest.
preuve *f* **preuve(s)** proof, evidence; **faire p. de** to show.
prévenir* *vt* (*avertir*) to warn (**que** that); (*aviser*) to inform (**que** that).
prévention *f* prevention; **p. routière** road safety.
prévision *f* forecast.
prévoir* *vt* (*anticiper*) to foresee (**que** that); (*prédire*) to forecast (**que** that); (*temps*) to forecast; (*organiser*) to plan; (*préparer*) to provide, make provision for.
prévu, -ue *a* **un repas est p.** a meal is provided; **au moment p.** at the appointed time; **comme p.** as expected; **p. pour** (*véhicule*, *appareil*) designed for.
prier 1 *vti* to pray (**pour** for). **2** *vt* **p. qn de faire** to ask s.o. to do; **je vous en prie** (*faites donc*) please; (*en réponse à 'merci'*) don't mention it.
prière *f* prayer; **p. de répondre**/*etc* please answer/*etc.*
primaire *a* primary.
prime *f* (*d'employé*) bonus; **en p.** (*cadeau*) as a free gift; **p. (d'assurance)** (insurance) premium.
primevère *f* primrose.
primitif, -ive *a* (*société etc*) primitive.
prince *m* prince.
princesse *f* princess.

principal, -e, -aux 1 *a* main. **2** *m* (*de collège*) principal, headmaster; **le p.** (*essentiel*) the main thing.

principe *m* principle; **en p.** theoretically; (*normalement*) as a rule.

printemps *m* (*saison*) spring.

prioritaire *a* **être p.** to have priority; (*en voiture*) to have the right of way.

priorité *f* priority (**sur** over); **la p.** (*sur la route*) the right of way; **la p. à droite** right of way to traffic coming from the right; **'cédez la p.'** 'give way', *Am* 'yield'.

pris, prise (*pp of* **prendre**) *a* (*place*) taken; (*crème*, *ciment*) set; (*nez*) congested; **être (très) p.** to be (very) busy; **p. de** (*peur*, *panique*) stricken with.

prise *f* (*de judo etc*) hold; (*objet saisi*) catch; **p. (de courant)** (*mâle*) plug; (*femelle*) socket; **p. multiple** (*électrique*) adaptor; **p. de sang** blood test.

prison *f* prison, jail; **en p.** in prison *ou* jail.

prisonnier, -ière *mf* prisoner; **faire qn p.** to take s.o. prisoner.

privé, -ée *a* private.

priver *vt* to deprive (**de** of); **se p. de** to do without.

prix[1] *m* (*d'un objet etc*) price; **à tout p.** at all costs; **à aucun p.** on no account.

prix[2] *m* (*récompense*) prize.

probable *a* likely, probable (**que** that); **peu p.** unlikely.

probablement *adv* probably.

problème *m* problem.

procédé *m* process.

procès *m* (*criminel*) trial; (*civil*) lawsuit; **faire un p. à** to take to court.

procès-verbal, -aux *m* (*contravention*) (traffic) fine.

prochain, -aine *a* next.

prochainement *adv* shortly.

proche *a* (*espace*) near, close; (*temps*) close (at hand); (*parent*, *ami*) close; **p. de** near (to), close to.

procurer *vt* **p. qch à qn** (*personne*) to obtain sth for s.o.; **se p. qch** to obtain sth.

prodigieux, -euse *a* extraordinary.

producteur, -trice 1 *mf* producer. **2** *a* **pays p. de pétrole** oil-producing country.

production *f* production.

produire* *vt* (*fabriquer*, *causer etc*) to produce.

produire (se) *vpr* (*événement etc*) to happen.

produit *m* (*article etc*) product; (*pour la vaisselle*) liquid; **produits**

(*de la terre*) produce; **p. (chimique)** chemical; **p. de beauté** cosmetic.
prof *m Fam* = **professeur.**
professeur *m* teacher; (*à l'université*) lecturer, *Am* professor.
profession *f* occupation; (*de médecin etc*) profession; (*manuelle*) trade.
professionnel, -elle 1 *a* professional; (*école*) vocational. **2** *mf* professional.
profil [prɔfil] *m* **de p.** (viewed) from the side, in profile.
profit *m* profit; **tirer p. de** to benefit from *ou* by.
profitable *a* (*utile*) beneficial (**à** to).
profiter *vi* **p. de** to take advantage of; **p. à qn** to profit s.o.
profond, -onde 1 *a* deep; **p. de deux mètres** two metres deep. **2** *adv* (*pénétrer etc*) deep.
profondément *adv* deeply; (*dormir*) soundly.
profondeur *f* depth; **à six mètres de p.** at a depth of six metres.
progiciel *m* (software) package.
programmateur *m* (*de four etc*) timer.
programme *m* programme, *Am* program; (*scolaire*) syllabus; (*d'ordinateur*) program.
programmer *vt* (*ordinateur*) to program.
progrès *m & mpl* progress; **faire des p.** to make progress.
progresser *vi* to progress.
progressif, -ive *a* gradual.
progressivement *adv* gradually.
proie *f* prey.
projecteur *m* (*de monument*) floodlight; (*de film etc*) projector.
projectile *m* missile.
projection *f* (*de film*) projection; (*séance*) showing.
projet *m* plan.
projeter *vt* (*lancer*) to hurl; (*film*) to project; (*voyage, fête etc*) to plan; **p. de faire** to plan to do.
prolonger *vt* to extend.
prolonger (se) *vpr* (*séance, rue*) to continue.
promenade *f* (*à pied*) walk; (*en voiture*) drive; (*en vélo, à cheval*) ride; **faire une p.** = **se promener.**
promener *vt* to take for a walk *ou* ride.
promener (se) *vpr* to (go for a) walk; (*en voiture*) to (go for a) drive.
promeneur, -euse *mf* stroller.
promesse *f* promise.
promettre* *vt* to promise (**qch à qn** s.o. sth, **que** that); **p. de faire** to promise to do; **c'est promis** it's a promise.

promotion *f* **en p.** (*produit*) on (special) offer.
pronom *m* pronoun.
prononcer *vt* (*articuler*) to pronounce; (*dire*) to utter; (*discours*) to deliver.
prononcer (se) *vpr* (*mot*) to be pronounced.
prononciation *f* pronunciation.
propager *vt*, **se propager** *vpr* to spread.
proportion *f* proportion; (*rapport*) ratio.
propos 1 *mpl* (*paroles*) remarks. **2** *prép* **à p. de** about. **3** *adv* **à p.!** by the way!
proposer *vt* to suggest, propose (**qch à qn** sth to s.o., **que** (+ *subjonctif*) that); (*offrir*) to offer (**qch à qn** s.o. sth, **de faire** to do); **je te propose de rester** I suggest you stay; **se p. pour faire** to offer to do.
proposition *f* suggestion; *Grammaire* clause.
propre[1] 1 *a* clean; (*soigné*) neat. **2** *m* **mettre qch au p.** to make a fair copy of sth.
propre[2] *a* own; **mon p. argent** my own money.
proprement *adv* cleanly; (*avec netteté*) neatly.
propreté *f* cleanliness; (*netteté*) neatness.
propriétaire *mf* owner; (*qui loue*) landlord, landlady.
propriété *f* (*bien*, *maison*) property.
prose *f* prose.
prospectus [prɔspɛktys] *m* leaflet.
prospère *a* thriving
protecteur, -trice 1 *mf* protector. **2** *a* (*geste etc*) protective.
protection *f* protection; **de p.** (*écran etc*) protective.
protège-cahier *m* exercise book cover.
protéger *vt* to protect (**de** from, **contre** against).
protestant, -ante *a & mf* Protestant.
protestation *f* protest (**contre** against).
protester *vi* to protest (**contre** against).
prouver *vt* to prove (**que** that).
provenir* *vi* **p. de** to come from.
proverbe *m* proverb.
province *f* province; **la p.** the provinces; **en p.** in the provinces; **de p.** (*ville etc*) provincial.
provincial, -e, -aux *a & mf* provincial.
proviseur *m* (*de lycée*) headmaster, headmistress; *Am* principal.
provision *f* supply; **provisions** (*achats*) shopping; (*nourriture*) food; **sac à provisions** shopping bag; **chèque sans p.** dud cheque, *Am* bad check.

provisoire *a* temporary.
provisoirement *adv* temporarily.
provoquer *vt* (*causer*) to bring (*sth*) about; (*défier*) to provoke (*s.o.*).
proximité *f* closeness; **à p.** close by; **à p. de** close to.
prudemment [-amɑ̃] *adv* cautiously, carefully.
prudence *f* caution, care.
prudent, -ente *a* cautious, careful.
prune *f* (*fruit*) plum.
pruneau, -x *m* prune.
prunier *m* plum tree.
psychiatre *mf* psychiatrist.
psychologique *a* psychological.
psychologue *mf* psychologist.
PTT [petete] *fpl* (*Postes*, *Télégraphes*, *Téléphones*) Post Office.
pu *voir* **pouvoir.**
puanteur *f* stink.
public, -ique 1 *a* public. **2** *m* public; (*de spectacle*) audience; **en p.** in public.
publication *f* publication.
publicité *f* advertising, publicity; (*annonce*) advertisement; (*filmée*) commercial.
publier *vt* to publish.
puce *f* flea; (*d'ordinateur*) chip; **marché aux puces** flea market.
puer 1 *vi* to stink. **2** *vt* to stink of.
puéricultrice *f* children's nurse.
puis *adv* then.
puiser *vt* to draw (**dans** from).
puisque *conj* since, as.
puissance *f* (*force*, *nation*) power.
puissant, -ante *a* powerful.
puisse(s), puissent *etc voir* **pouvoir**.
puits *m* well; (*de mine*) shaft.
pull(-over) [pyl(ɔvɛr)] *m* sweater.
pulvérisateur *m* spray.
pulvériser *vt* (*liquide*) to spray.
punaise *f* (*insecte*) bug; (*clou*) drawing pin, *Am* thumbtack.
punir *vt* to punish (**de qch** for sth, **pour avoir fait** for doing).
punition *f* punishment.
pupille *f* (*de l'œil*) pupil.
pur, -e *a* pure.
purée *f* purée; **p. (de pommes de terre)** mashed potatoes.

pureté *f* purity.
puzzle [pœzl] *m* (jigsaw) puzzle.
p.-v. [peve] *m inv* (*procès-verbal*) (traffic) fine.
pyjama *m* pyjamas, *Am* pajamas; **un p.** a pair of pyjamas *ou Am* pajamas.
pylône *m* pylon.
pyramide *f* pyramid.

Q

QI *m inv abrév* (*quotient intellectuel*) IQ.
quadrillé, -ée *a* (*papier*) squared.
quai *m* (*de port*) (*pour passagers*) quay; (*pour marchandises*) wharf; (*de fleuve*) embankment; (*de gare*) platform.
qualifié, -ée *a* (*équipe etc*) that has qualified; (*ouvrier*) skilled.
qualifier (se) *vpr* (*en sport*) to qualify (**pour** for).
qualité *f* quality.
quand *conj* & *adv* when; **q. je viendrai** when I come; **q. même** all the same.
quant à [kɑ̃ta] *prép* as for.
quantité *f* quantity; **une q.** (*beaucoup*) a lot (**de** of).
quarantaine *f* **une q.** (**de**) about forty.
quarante *a* & *m* forty.
quarantième *a* & *mf* fortieth.
quart *m* quarter; **q. (de litre)** quarter litre; **q. d'heure** quarter of an hour; **une heure et q.** an hour and a quarter; **il est une heure et q.** it's a quarter past *ou Am* after one; **une heure moins le q.** quarter to one.
quartier[1] *m* (*de ville*) neighbourhood, district; (*chinois etc*) quarter; **de q.** (*cinéma etc*) local.
quartier[2] *m* (*de pomme*) quarter; (*d'orange*) segment.
quartz [kwarts] *m* **montre**/*etc* **à q.** quartz watch/*etc.*
quatorze *a* & *m* fourteen.
quatre *a* & *m* four; **q. heures** (*goûter*) afternoon snack.
quatre-vingt(s) *a* & *m* eighty; **q.-vingts ans** eighty years; **q.-vingt-un** eighty-one; **page quatre-vingt** page eighty.
quatre-vingt-dix *a* & *m* ninety.
quatrième *a* & *mf* fourth.
que (**qu'** *before a vowel or mute h*) **1** *conj* that; **je pense qu'elle restera** I think (that) she'll stay; **qu'elle vienne ou non** whether she comes or not; **qu'il s'en aille!** let him leave! ▮ **(ne)...q.** only; **tu n'as qu'un franc** you only have one franc. ▮ (*comparaison*) than; (*avec aussi*, *même*, *tel*, *autant*) as; **plus âgé q.** older than; **aussi sage q.** as wise as; **le même q.** the same as. **2** *adv* **(ce) qu'il est bête!** how silly he is! **3** *pron rel* (*chose*) that, which; (*personne*) that; (*temps*) when; **le livre q. j'ai** the book (that *ou* which) I have; **l'ami q. j'ai** the friend (that) I have; **un jour q.** one day when. **4** *pron interrogatif* what; **q. fait-il?, qu'est-ce qu'il fait?** what is he doing?; **qu'est-ce qui est dans ta poche?** what's in your pocket?
quel, quelle 1 *a interrogatif* what, which; (*qui*) who; **q. livre/**

acteur? what *ou* which book/actor?; **je sais q. est ton but** I know what your aim is. **2** *pron interrogatif* which (one); **q. est le meilleur?** which (one) is the best? **3** *a exclamatif* **q. idiot!** what a fool!

quelconque *a* any (whatever); **une raison q.** any reason (whatever).

quelque 1 *a* **quelques femmes/livres/***etc* some *ou* a few women/ books/*etc*; **les quelques amies qu'elle a** the few friends she has. **2** *pron* **q. chose** something; (*interrogation*) anything, something; **il a q. chose** (*un problème*) there's something the matter with him; **q. chose d'autre/de grand/***etc* something else/big/*etc*. **3** *adv* **q. part** somewhere; (*interrogation*) anywhere, somewhere.

quelquefois *adv* sometimes.

quelques-uns, -unes *pron pl* some.

quelqu'un *pron* someone; (*interrogation*) anyone, someone; **q. d'intelligent/***etc* someone clever/*etc*.

question *f* question; (*problème*) matter; **il est q. de** there's some talk about (**faire** doing); **il a été q. de vous** we *ou* they talked about you; **il n'en est pas q.** it's out of the question.

questionner *vt* to question (**sur** about).

quête *f* (*collecte*) collection; **faire la q. = quêter.**

quêter *vi* to collect money.

queue¹ *f* (*d'animal etc*) tail; (*de fleur*) stem; (*de fruit*) stalk; (*de poêle*) handle; (*de train*) rear; **q. de cheval** (*coiffure*) ponytail; **à la q. leu leu** in single file.

queue² *f* (*file*) queue, *Am* line; **faire la q.** to queue up, *Am* line up.

qui *pron* (*personne*) who, that; (*interrogatif*) who; (*chose*) which, that; **l'homme q.** the man who *ou* that; **la maison q.** the house which *ou* that; **q. est là?** who's there?; **q. désirez-vous voir?, q. est-ce que vous désirez voir?** who do you want to see?; **la femme de q. je parle** the woman I'm talking about; **l'ami sur l'aide de q. je compte** the friend on whose help I rely; **à q. est ce livre?** whose book is this?

quiche *f* quiche.

quille *f* (*de jeu*) (bowling) pin, skittle; **jouer aux quilles** to bowl, play skittles.

quincaillerie hardware shop.

quincaillier, -ière *mf* ironmonger.

quinzaine *f* **une q. (de)** about fifteen; **q. (de jours)** two weeks.

quinze *a & m* fifteen; **q. jours** two weeks.

quinzième *a & mf* fifteenth.

quitte *a* even (**envers** with).

quitter 1 *vt* to leave; **q. qn des yeux** to take one's eyes off s.o. **2** *vi*

ne quittez pas! (*au téléphone*) hold on!

quitter (se) *vpr* (*se séparer*) to part, say goodbye.

quoi *pron* what; (*après prép*) which; **à q. penses-tu?** what are you thinking about?; **de q. manger** something to eat; **de q. couper/écrire** something to cut/write with; **il n'y a pas de q.!** (*en réponse à 'merci'*) don't mention it!

quotidien, -ienne 1 *a* daily. **2** *m* daily (paper).

R

rabattre* *vt* to pull down; (*refermer*) to close (down).
rabattre (se) *vpr* (*barrière*) to come down; (*après avoir doublé un véhicule*) to cut in.
rabbin *m* rabbi.
rabot *m* (*outil*) plane.
raboter *vt* to plane.
raccommodage *m* mending; darning.
raccommoder *vt* to mend; (*chaussette*) to darn.
raccompagner *vt* to see back (home); **r. à la porte** to see to the door.
raccord *m* (*dispositif*) connection, connector; (*de papier peint*) join.
raccourci *m* (*chemin*) short cut.
raccourcir 1 *vt* to shorten. **2** *vi* to get shorter.
raccrocher 1 *vt* (*objet tombé*) to hang back up; (*téléphone*) to put down. **2** *vi* (*au téléphone*) to hang up.
race *f* (*groupe ethnique*) race; (*animale*) breed.
racheter *vt* **r. un manteau/une voiture**/*etc* to buy another coat/car/*etc*; **r. des chaussettes/du pain**/*etc* to buy some more socks/bread/*etc*.
racial, -e, -aux *a* racial.
racine *f* root; **prendre r.** (*plante*) to take root.
racisme *m* racism.
raciste *a* & *mf* racist.
racler *vt* to scrape; (*enlever*) to scrape off, **se r. la gorge** to clear one's throat.
raconter *vt* (*histoire*) to tell; **r. qch à qn** (*vacances etc*) to tell s.o about sth; **r. à qn que** to tell s.o. that.
radar *m* radar.
radeau, -x *m* raft.
radiateur *m* heater; (*de chauffage central, voiture*) radiator.
radieux, -euse *a* (*personne, visage*) beaming; (*soleil*) brilliant; (*temps*) glorious.
radio¹ *f* radio; (*poste*) radio (set); **à la r.** on the radio.
radio² *f* (*examen, photo*) X-ray; **passer une r.** to have an X-ray.
radioactif, -ive *a* radioactive.
radiodiffuser *vt* to broadcast (on the radio).
radiographier *vt* to X-ray.
radis *m* radish.
radoucir (se) *vpr* (*temps*) to become milder.
radoucissement *m* **r. (du temps)** milder weather.
rafale *f* (*vent*) gust.

raffoler *vi* **r. de** (*aimer*) to be mad about.
rafistoler *vt Fam* to patch up.
rafraîchir *vt* to cool (down).
rafraîchir (se) *vpr* (*boire*) to refresh oneself; (*temps*) to get cooler.
rafraîchissant, -ante *a* refreshing.
rafraîchissement *m* (*de température*) cooling; (*boisson*) cold drink; **rafraîchissements** (*glaces etc*) refreshments.
rage *f* (*colère*) rage; (*maladie*) rabies; **r. de dents** violent toothache.
ragoût *m* stew.
raid [rɛd] *m* raid.
raide *a* (*rigide*) stiff; (*côte*) steep; (*cheveux*) straight; (*corde*) tight.
raidir *vt*, **se raidir** *vpr* to stiffen; (*corde*) to tighten.
raie *f* (*trait*) line; (*de tissu*, *zèbre*) stripe; (*de cheveux*) parting, *Am* part.
rail *m* (*barre*) rail (*for train*).
rainure *f* groove.
raisin *m* **(grain de) r.** grape; **du r., des raisins** grapes; **r. sec** raisin.
raison *f* reason; **la r. de/pour laquelle...** the reason for/why...; **en r. de** on account of; **avoir r.** to be right (**de faire** to do).
raisonnable *a* reasonable.
raisonnement *m* reasoning.
raisonner 1 *vi* (*penser*) to reason. **2** *vt* **r. qn** to reason with s.o.
rajeunir *vt* to make (*s.o.*) (feel *ou* look) younger.
ralenti *m* **au r.** (*filmer*) in slow motion; **tourner au r.** (*moteur*) to tick over, *Am* turn over.
ralentir *vti* to slow down.
rallonge *f* (*de table*) extension; (*électrique*) extension (lead).
rallonger *vti* to lengthen.
rallumer *vt* (*feu*, *pipe*) to light again; (*lampe*) to switch on again.
rallye *m* (*automobile*) rally.
ramassage *m* picking up; collection; gathering; **r. scolaire** school bus service.
ramasser *vt* (*prendre par terre*, *réunir*) to pick up; (*ordures*, *copies*) to collect; (*fruits*, *coquillages*) to gather.
rame *f* (*aviron*) oar; (*de métro*) train.
ramener *vt* to bring *ou* take (*s.o.*) back.
ramer *vi* to row.
ramollir *vt*, **se ramollir** *vpr* to soften.
ramoner *vt* (*cheminée*) to sweep.
rampe *f* (*d'escalier*) banister(s); **r. (d'accès)** ramp; **r. de lancement** (*de fusées*) launch pad.
ramper *vi* to crawl.

ranch [rɑ̃ʃ, rɑ̃tʃ] *m* ranch.
rançon *f* (*argent*) ransom.
rancune *f* grudge; **garder r. à qn** to bear s.o. a grudge.
rancunier, -ière *a* spiteful.
randonnée *f* (*à pied*) hike; (*en voiture*) drive; (*en vélo*) ride.
rang *m* (*rangée*) row, line; (*classement*) rank; **se mettre en rang(s)** to line up (**par trois**/*etc* in threes/*etc*).
rangé, -ée *a* (*chambre etc*) tidy.
rangée *f* row, line.
rangements *mpl* (*placards*) storage space.
ranger *vt* (*papiers etc*) to put away; (*chambre etc*) to tidy (up); (*chiffres, mots*) to arrange; (*voiture*) to park.
ranger (se) *vpr* (*élèves etc*) to line up; (*s'écarter*) to stand aside; (*voiture*) to pull over.
ranimer *vt* (*réanimer*) to revive (*s.o.*); (*feu*) to poke, stir.
rapace *m* bird of prey.
râpe *f* (*à fromage etc*) grater.
râper *vt* (*fromage, carottes*) to grate.
rapetisser *vi* to get smaller.
rapide 1 *a* fast, quick. **2** *m* (*train*) express (train).
rapidement *adv* fast, quickly.
rapidité *f* speed.
rapiécer *vt* to patch (up).
rappeler *vt* to call back; (*souvenir*) to recall; **r. qch à qn** to remind s.o. of sth.
rappeler (se) *vpr* to remember (**que** that).
rapport *m* (*lien*) connection; (*récit*) report; **rapports** (*entre personnes*) relations; **par r. à** compared to; **ça n'a aucun r.!** it has nothing to do with it!
rapporter 1 *vt* to bring *ou* take back; (*profit*) to bring in; **se r. à** to relate to. **2** *vi* (*dénoncer*) *Fam* to tell tales; (*investissement*) to bring in a good return.
rapporteur, -euse 1 *mf* telltale. **2** *m* (*en géométrie*) protractor.
rapprocher *vt* to bring closer (**de** to); (*chaise*) to pull up (**de** to).
rapprocher (se) *vpr* to come *ou* get closer (**de** to).
raquette *f* (*de tennis*) racket; (*de ping-pong*) bat.
rare *a* rare; **il est r. que** (+ *subjonctif*) it's seldom that.
rarement *adv* rarely, seldom.
ras, rase *a* (*cheveux*) close-cropped; (*herbe, poil*) short; **en rase campagne** in the open country; **à r. bord** (*remplir*) to the brim.
rasé, -ée *a* **être bien r.** to have shaved, **mal r.** unshaven.
raser *vt* (*menton, personne*) to shave; (*barbe, moustache*) to shave

off; (*démolir*) to knock down; (*frôler*) to skim.
raser (se) *vpr* to (have a) shave.
rasoir *m* razor; (*électrique*) shaver.
rassemblement *m* gathering.
rassembler *vt* (*gens*, *objets*) to gather (together).
rassembler (se) *vpr* to gather.
rassis, *f* **rassie** *a* (*pain etc*) stale.
rassurant, -ante *a* reassuring.
rassurer *vt* to reassure; **rassure-toi** don't worry.
rat *m* rat.
râteau, -x *m* (*outil*) rake.
rater *vt* (*bus*, *cible etc*) to miss; (*travail*, *gâteau etc*) to ruin; (*examen*) to fail.
ration *f* ration.
rationnement *m* rationing.
rationner *vt* to ration.
ratisser *vt* (*allée etc*) to rake; (*feuilles etc*) to rake up.
rattacher *vt* (*lacets etc*) to tie up again.
rattrapage *m* **cours de r.** remedial class.
rattraper *vt* to catch; (*prisonnier*) to recapture; (*temps perdu*) to make up for; **r. qn** (*rejoindre*) to catch up with s.o.
rature *f* crossing out.
raturer *vt* to cross out.
ravager *vt* to devastate.
ravages *mpl* havoc; **faire des r.** to cause havoc *ou* widespread damage.
ravaler *vt* (*façade etc*) to clean (and restore).
ravi, -ie *a* delighted (**de** with, **de faire** to do).
ravin *m* ravine.
ravioli *mpl* ravioli.
ravir *vt* (*plaire*) to delight.
ravissant, -ante *a* beautiful.
ravisseur, -euse *mf* kidnapper.
ravitaillement *m* supplying; (*denrées*) supplies.
ravitailler *vt* to supply (**en** with).
ravitailler (se) *vpr* to stock up (with supplies).
rayé, -ée *a* scratched; (*tissu*) striped.
rayer *vt* (*érafler*) to scratch; (*mot etc*) to cross out.
rayon *m* (*de lumière*, *soleil*) ray; (*de cercle*) radius; (*de roue*) spoke; (*planche*) shelf; (*de magasin*) department.
rayonnant, -ante *a* (*visage etc*) beaming (**de** with).
rayure *f* scratch; (*bande*) stripe; **à rayures** striped.

raz-de-marée *m inv* tidal wave.
re-, ré- *préfixe* re-.
réacteur *m* (*d'avion*) jet engine; (*nucléaire*) reactor.
réaction *f* reaction; **avion à r.** jet (aircraft).
réagir *vi* to react (**contre** against, **à** to).
réalisateur, -trice *mf* (*de film*) director.
réaliser *vt* (*projet etc*) to carry out; (*rêve*) to fulfil; (*fabriquer*) to make; (*film*) to direct.
réaliser (se) *vpr* (*vœu*) to come true; (*projet*) to materialize.
réaliste *a* realistic.
réalité *f* reality; **en r.** in fact.
réanimation *f* **en r.** in intensive care.
réanimer *vt* to revive.
rebond *m* bounce.
rebondir *vi* to bounce.
rebord *m* **r. de (la) fenêtre** windowsill.
reboucher *vt* (*flacon*) to put the top back on; (*trou*) to fill in again.
rébus [rebys] *m inv* rebus (*word guessing game*).
récemment [-amɑ̃] *adv* recently.
récent, -ente *a* recent.
réception *f* (*réunion, de radio etc*) reception; (*d'hôtel*) reception (desk); **dès r. de** on receipt of.
recette *f* (*de cuisine*) recipe (**de** for); (*argent, bénéfice*) takings.
recevoir* 1 *vt* to receive; (*accueillir*) to welcome; **être reçu (à)** (*examen*) to pass. **2** *vi* to have guests.
rechange (de) *a* (*outil etc*) spare; **vêtements de r.** a change of clothes.
recharge *f* (*de stylo*) refill.
recharger *vt* (*fusil, appareil photo*) to reload; (*briquet, stylo*) to refill; (*batterie*) to recharge.
réchaud *m* (portable) stove.
réchauffement *m* (*de température*) rise (**de** in).
réchauffer *vt* to warm up; **se r.** to warm oneself up; (*temps*) to get warmer.
recherche *f* **la r., des recherches** (*scientifique etc*) research (**sur** on, into); **faire des recherches** to (do) research; (*enquêter*) to make investigations.
recherché, -ée *a* **r. pour meurtre** wanted for murder.
rechercher *vt* (*personne, objet*) to search for.
récif *m* reef.
récipient *m* container.
réciproque *a* mutual.

récit *m* (*histoire*) story.
récitation *f* (*poème*) poem (*learnt by heart and recited aloud*).
réciter *vt* to recite.
réclamation *f* complaint.
réclame *f* advertising; (*annonce*) advertisement; **en r.** on (special) offer.
réclamer 1 *vt* (*demander*) to ask for (*sth*) back. **2** *vi* to complain.
recoin *m* nook.
recoller *vt* (*objet cassé*) to stick back together; (*enveloppe*) to stick back down.
récolte *f* (*action*) harvest; (*produits*) crop.
récolter *vt* to harvest.
recommandation *f* recommendation.
recommander *vt* to recommend (**à** to, **pour** for); **r. à qn de faire** to recommend s.o. to do; **lettre recommandée** registered letter; **en recommandé** (*envoyer*) by registered post.
recommencer *vti* to start again.
récompense *f* reward (**pour** for).
récompenser *vt* to reward (**de, pour** for).
réconciliation *f* reconciliation.
réconcilier (se) *vpr* to settle one's differences, make it up (**avec** with).
reconduire* *vt* **r. qn** to see s.o. back.
réconfortant, -ante *a* comforting.
réconforter *vt* to comfort.
reconnaissance *f* (*gratitude*) gratitude.
reconnaissant, -ante *a* grateful (**à qn de qch** to s.o. for sth).
reconnaître* *vt* to recognize (**à qch** by sth); (*admettre*) to admit (**que** that); **reconnu coupable** found guilty.
reconstruire* *vt* (*ville*) to rebuild.
recopier *vt* to copy out.
record *m* & *a inv* (*en sport etc*) record.
recoudre* *vt* (*bouton*) to sew (back) on; (*vêtement*) to stitch (up).
recourbé, -ée *a* (*clou etc*) bent; (*nez*) hooked.
recouvrir* *vt* (*livre, meuble etc*) to cover.
récréation *f* (*à l'école*) break.
recroquevillé, -ée *a* (*personne, papier etc*) curled up.
recrue *f* recruit.
rectangle *m* rectangle.
rectangulaire *a* rectangular.
rectification *f* correction.
rectifier *vt* to correct.

recto *m* front (of the page).
reçu, reçue 1 *pp of* **recevoir**. **2** *m* (*écrit*) receipt.
recueil *m* anthology, collection (**de** of).
recueillir* *vt* to collect; (*prendre chez soi*) to take (*s.o.*) in.
reculer 1 *vi* to move back; (*véhicule*) to reverse. **2** *vt* to push back.
reculons (à) *adv* backwards.
récupérer 1 *vt* (*objet prêté*) to get back. **2** *vi* to get one's strength back.
récurer *vt* (*casserole etc*) to scrub.
recycler *vt* (*matériaux*) to recycle.
rédacteur, -trice *mf* (*de journal*) editor; **r. en chef** editor(-in-chief).
rédaction *f* (*devoir de français*) essay, composition.
redescendre 1 *vi* (*aux* **être**) to come *ou* go back down. **2** *vt* (*aux* **avoir**) to bring *ou* take back down.
rediffusion *f* (*de film etc*) repeat.
rédiger *vt* to write.
redire* *vt* to repeat.
redonner *vt* (*donner plus*) to give more (*bread etc*); **r. un franc**/*etc* to give another franc/*etc*.
redoublant, -ante *mf* pupil repeating a year *ou Am* a grade.
redoublement *m* repeating a year *ou Am* a grade.
redoubler *vti* **r. (une classe)** to repeat a year *ou Am* a grade.
redoutable *a* formidable.
redouter *vt* to dread (**de faire** doing).
redresser *vt* (*objet tordu etc*) to straighten (out).
redresser (se) *vpr* to sit up; (*debout*) to stand up.
réduction *f* reduction (**de** in); (*prix réduit*) discount; **en r.** (*copie, modèle*) small-scale.
réduire* *vt* to reduce (**à** to, **de** by); **r. en cendres** to reduce to ashes.
réduit, -uite *a* (*prix, vitesse*) reduced; (*modèle*) small scale.
réel, -elle *a* real.
réellement *adv* really.
réexpédier *vt* (*faire suivre*) to forward (*letter*).
refaire* *vt* (*exercice, travail*) to do again, redo; (*chambre etc*) to do up, redo.
réfectoire *m* refectory.
référence *f* reference.
refermer *vt*, **se refermer** *vpr* to close (again).
réfléchir 1 *vt* (*image*) to reflect; **se r.** to be reflected; **verbe réfléchi** reflexive verb. **2** *vi* (*penser*) to think (**à** about).
reflet *m* (*image*) reflection; (*couleur*) tint.
refléter *vt* (*image etc*) to reflect; **se r.** to be reflected.

réflexe *m* reflex.
réflexion *f* (*méditation*) thought; (*remarque*) remark.
réforme *f* (*changement*) reform.
refrain *m* (*de chanson*) chorus.
réfrigérateur *m* refrigerator.
refroidir *vti* to cool (down).
refroidir (se) *vpr* (*prendre froid*) to catch cold; (*temps*) to get cold.
refroidissement *m* (*rhume*) chill; **r. de la température** fall in the temperature.
refuge *m* refuge; (*pour piétons*) (traffic) island; (*de montagne*) (mountain) hut.
réfugié, -ée *mf* refugee.
réfugier (se) *vpr* to take refuge.
refus *m* refusal.
refuser 1 *vt* to refuse (**qch à qn** s.o. sth, **de faire** to do); (*candidat*) to fail. **2** *vi* to refuse.
regagner *vt* to regain, get back; (*revenir à*) to get back to.
régaler (se) *vpr* to have a feast.
regard *m* look; (*fixe*) stare; **jeter un r. sur** to glance at.
regarder[1] 1 *vt* to look at; (*fixement*) to stare at; (*observer*) to watch; **r. qn faire** to watch s.o. do. **2** *vi* to look; to stare; to watch.
regarder[2] *vt* (*concerner*) to concern; **ça ne te regarde pas!** it's none of your business!
régime[1] *m* (*politique*) (form of) government; (*alimentaire*) diet; **se mettre au r.** to go on a diet; **suivre un r.** to be on a diet.
régime[2] *m* (*de bananes, dattes*) bunch.
régiment *m* (*soldats*) regiment.
région *f* region, area.
régional, -e, -aux *a* regional.
registre *m* register.
réglable *a* (*siège*) adjustable.
réglage *m* adjustment; (*de moteur*) tuning.
règle *f* rule; (*instrument*) ruler; **en r. générale** as a rule; **règles** (*de femme*) (monthly) period.
règlement *m* (*règles*) regulations; (*paiement*) payment; **contraire au r.** against the rules *ou Am* the rule.
régler 1 *vt* (*problème etc*) to settle; (*mécanisme*) to adjust; (*moteur*) to tune. **2** *vti* (*payer*) to pay; **r. qn** to settle up with s.o.
réglisse *f* liquorice, *Am* licorice.
règne *m* (*de roi*) reign.
régner *vi* (*roi, silence*) to reign (**sur** over).
regret *m* regret; **à r.** with regret.

regrettable *a* unfortunate, regrettable.
regretter *vt* to regret; **r. qn** to miss s.o.; **r. que** (+ *subjonctif*) to be sorry that; **je (le) regrette** I'm sorry.
regrouper *vt*, **se regrouper** *vpr* to gather together.
régularité *f* regularity; steadiness.
régulier, -ière *a* regular; (*progrès*, *vitesse*) steady.
régulièrement *adv* regularly.
rein *m* kidney; **les reins** (*dos*) the (small of the) back.
reine *f* queen.
rejeter *vt* to throw back; (*refuser*) to reject.
rejoindre* *vt* (*famille, lieu etc*) to get back to; **r. qn** (*se joindre à*) to join s.o.; (*rattraper*) to catch up with s.o.
rejoindre (se) *vpr* (*personnes*, *routes*) to meet.
réjouir (se) *vpr* to be delighted (**de** at, about; **de faire** to do).
réjouissances *fpl* festivities.
relâcher *vt* (*corde etc*) to slacken; **r. qn** to release s.o.
relais *m* **prendre le r.** to take over (**de** from).
relatif, -ive *a* relative.
relation *f* relation(ship); (*ami*) acquaintance; **entrer en relations avec** to come into contact with.
relativement *adv* (*assez*) relatively.
relayer *vt* to take over from (*s.o.*).
relayer (se) *vpr* to take (it in) turns (**pour faire** to do).
relevé *m* (*de compteur*) reading; **r. de compte** (bank) statement.
relever *vt* to raise; (*personne tombée*) to help up; (*col*) to turn up; (*manches*) to roll up; (*compteur*) to read.
relever (se) *vpr* (*personne tombée*) to get up.
relief *m* (*forme*) relief; **en r.** (*cinéma*) three-D.
relier *vt* to connect (**à** to); (*livre*) to bind.
religieux, -euse 1 *a* religious. **2** *f* nun.
religion *f* religion.
relire* *vt* to read again, reread.
reliure *f* (*de livre*) binding.
reluire* *vi* to shine.
remarquable *a* remarkable (**par** for).
remarquablement *adv* remarkably.
remarque *f* remark; (*écrite*) note.
remarquer *vt* to notice (**que** that); **faire r.** to point out (**à** to, **que** that); **se faire r.** to attract attention; **remarque!** mind you!, you know!
rembobiner *vt*, **se rembobiner** *vpr* (*bande*) to rewind.
rembourré, -ée *a* (*fauteuil etc*) padded.

remboursement *m* repayment; refund.
rembourser *vt* to pay back, repay; (*billet*) to refund.
remède *m* cure; (*médicament*) medicine.
remerciements *mpl* thanks.
remercier *vt* to thank (**de qch, pour qch** for sth); **je vous remercie d'être venu** thank you for coming.
remettre* *vt* to put back; (*vêtement*) to put back on; (*donner*) to hand over (**à** to); (*démission, devoir*) to hand in; (*différer*) to postpone (**à** until); **r. en question** to call into question; **r. en état** to repair; **se r. à** (*activité*) to go back to; **se r. à faire** to start to do again; **se r. de** (*chagrin, maladie*) to get over.
remise *f* (*rabais*) discount.
remonte-pente *m* ski lift.
remonter 1 *vi* (*aux* **être**) to come *ou* go back up; **r. dans** (*voiture*) to get back in(to); (*bus, train*) to get back on(to); **r. sur** (*cheval, vélo*) to get back on(to). **2** *vt* (*aux* **avoir**) (*escalier, pente*) to come *ou* go back up; (*porter*) to bring *ou* take back up; (*montre*) to wind up; (*relever*) to raise; (*col*) to turn up; (*objet démonté*) to put back together.
remords *m* & *mpl* remorse; **avoir des r.** to feel remorse.
remorque *f* (*de voiture etc*) trailer; **prendre en r.** to tow; **en r.** on tow.
remorquer *vt* to tow.
remorqueur *m* tug(boat).
remplaçant, -ante *mf* (*personne*) replacement; (*enseignant*) substitute teacher; (*en sport*) reserve.
remplacement *m* replacement; **assurer le r. de qn** to stand in for s.o.
remplacer *vt* to replace (**par** with, by); (*succéder à*) to take over from.
rempli, -ie *a* full (**de** of).
remplir *vt* to fill (up) (**de** with); (*fiche etc*) to fill in *ou* out.
remplir (se) *vpr* to fill (up).
remporter *vt* (*objet*) to take back; (*prix, victoire*) to win.
remuant, -ante *a* (*enfant*) restless.
remuer 1 *vt* to move; (*café etc*) to stir; (*salade*) to toss. **2** *vi* to move; (*gigoter*) to fidget.
renard *m* fox.
rencontre *f* meeting; (*en sport*) match, *Am* game; **aller à la r. de qn** to go to meet s.o.
rencontrer *vt* to meet; (*équipe*) to play.
rencontrer (se) *vpr* to meet.

rendez-vous *m inv* appointment; (*d'amoureux*) date; (*lieu*) meeting place; **donner r.-vous à qn** to make an appointment with s.o.
rendormir* (se) *vpr* to go back to sleep.
rendre 1 *vt* to give back; (*monnaie*) to give; (*vomir*) to bring up; **r. célèbre/plus grand/***etc* to make famous/bigger/*etc*. **2** *vti* (*vomir*) to throw up.
rendre (se) *vpr* to surrender (**à qn** to s.o.); (*aller*) to go (**à** to); **se r. utile/***etc* to make oneself useful/*etc*.
rênes *fpl* reins.
renfermé *m* **sentir le r.** (*chambre etc*) to smell stuffy.
renfermer *vt* to contain.
renflement *m* bulge.
renforcer *vt* to strengthen.
renforts *mpl* (*troupes*) reinforcements.
renifler *vti* to sniff.
renne *m* reindeer.
renommé, -ée *a* famous (**pour** for).
renommée *f* fame.
renoncer *vi* **r. à qch/à faire** to give up sth/doing.
renouveler *vt* to renew; (*erreur*, *question*) to repeat.
renouveler (se) *vpr* (*incident*) to happen again.
renseignement *m* (piece of) information; **des renseignements** information; **les renseignements** (*au téléphone*) directory inquiries, *Am* information.
renseigner *vt* to inform, give some information to (**sur** about).
renseigner (se) *vpr* to find out, inquire (**sur** about).
rentrée *f* return; **r. (des classes)** beginning of term *ou* of the school year.
rentrer 1 *vi* (*aux* **être**) to go *ou* come back; (*chez soi*) to go *ou* come (back) home; (*entrer de nouveau*) to go *ou* come back in; (*élèves*) to go back to school; **r. dans** to go *ou* come back into; (*pays*) to return to; (*heurter*) to crash into; (*s'emboîter dans*) to fit into. **2** *vt* (*aux* **avoir**) to bring *ou* take in; (*voiture*) to put away; (*chemise*) to tuck in; (*griffes*) to draw in.
renverse (à la) *adv* (*tomber*) backwards.
renverser *vt* (*mettre à l'envers*) to turn upside down; (*faire tomber*) to knock over; (*piéton*) to knock down; (*liquide*) to spill.
renverser (se) *vpr* (*vase etc*) to fall over; (*liquide*) to spill.
renvoi *m* (*d'un employé*) dismissal; (*rot*) burp.
renvoyer* *vt* to send back; (*employé*) to dismiss; (*élève*) to expel; (*balle etc*) to throw back.
réorganiser *vt* to reorganize.

repaire *m* den.
répandre *vt* (*liquide*) to spill; (*nouvelle*) to spread; (*odeur*) to give off; (*lumière*, *larmes*) to shed; (*gravillons etc*) to scatter.
répandre (se) *vpr* (*nouvelle*) to spread; (*liquide*) to spill; **se r. dans** (*fumée*, *odeur*) to spread through.
répandu, -ue *a* (*opinion etc*) widespread.
reparaître *vi* to reappear.
réparateur, -trice *mf* repairer.
réparation *f* repair; **en r.** under repair.
réparer *vt* to repair, mend; (*erreur*) to put right.
repartir* *vi* (*aux* **être**) to set off again; (*s'en retourner*) to go back.
répartir *vt* (*partager*) to share (out).
repas *m* meal; **prendre un r.** to have a meal.
repassage *m* ironing.
repasser 1 *vi* to come *ou* go back. **2** *vt* (*traverser*) to go back over; (*leçon*) to go over; (*film*) to show again; (*linge*) to iron.
repêcher *vt* (*objet*) to fish out.
repentir* (se) *vpr* to be sorry (**de** for).
repère *m* (guide) mark; **point de r.** (*espace*, *temps*) landmark.
repérer *vt* to locate.
repérer (se) *vpr* to get one's bearings.
répertoire *m* **r. d'adresses** address book.
répéter *vti* to repeat; (*pièce de théâtre*) to rehearse.
répéter (se) *vpr* (*événement*) to happen again.
répétitif, -ive *a* repetitive.
répétition *f* repetition; (*au théâtre*) rehearsal.
replacer *vt* to put back.
repli *m* fold.
replier *vt* to fold (up); (*couverture*) to fold back; (*ailes*, *jambes*) to tuck in.
replier (se) *vpr* (*siège*) to fold up; (*couverture*) to fold back.
réplique *f* (sharp) reply; (*au théâtre*) lines.
répliquer 1 *vt* to reply (sharply) (**que** that). **2** *vi* to answer back.
répondeur *m* (*téléphonique*) answering machine.
répondre 1 *vi* to answer; (*être impertinent*) to answer back; (*réagir*) to respond (**à** to); **r. à qn** to answer s.o.; (*avec impertinence*) to answer s.o. back; **r. à** (*lettre*, *question*) to answer. **2** *vt* **r. que** to answer that.
réponse *f* answer.
reportage *m* (news) report; (*en direct*) commentary.
reporter[1] *vt* to take back; (*différer*) to put off (**à** until).
reporter[2] [r(ə)pɔrtɛr] *m* reporter.

repos *m* rest; (*tranquillité*) peace (and quiet); **jour de r.** day off.
reposant, -ante *a* restful.
reposer *vt* (*objet*) to put back down; (*délasser*) to relax.
reposer (se) *vpr* to rest.
repousser 1 *vt* to push back; (*écarter*) to push away; (*différer*) to put off. **2** *vi* (*cheveux*, *feuilles*) to grow again.
reprendre* 1 *vt* (*objet*) to take back; (*évadé*) to recapture; (*souffle*, *forces*) to get back; (*activité*) to take up again; (*refrain*) to take up; **r. de la viande/un œuf**/*etc* to take (some) more meat/another egg/ etc. **2** *vi* (*recommencer*) to start (up) (again); (*affaires*) to pick up; (*dire*) to go on.
reprendre (se) *vpr* to correct oneself; **s'y r. à deux fois** to have another go (at it).
représentant, -ante *mf* representative; **r. de commerce** (travelling) salesman *ou* saleswoman.
représentation *f* (*au théâtre*) performance.
représenter *vt* to represent; (*pièce de théâtre*) to perform.
reprise *f* (*d'émission de télévision*) repeat; (*de tissu*) mend; *Boxe* round; (*économique*) recovery; (*pour nouvel achat*) part exchange, trade-in; **à plusieurs reprises** on several occasions.
repriser *vt* (*chaussette etc*) to mend.
reproche *m* criticism; **faire des reproches à qn** to criticize s.o.
reprocher *vt* **r. qch à qn** to criticize s.o. for sth.
reproduction *f* breeding; (*copie*) copy.
reproduire* *vt* (*modèle etc*) to copy.
reproduire (se) *vpr* (*animaux*) to breed; (*incident etc*) to happen again.
reptile *m* reptile.
républicain, -aine *a* & *mf* republican.
république *f* republic.
réputation *f* reputation; **avoir la r. d'être** to have a reputation for being.
requin *m* (*poisson*) shark.
rescapé, -ée *mf* survivor.
réseau, -x *m* network.
réservation *f* reservation, booking.
réserve *f* (*provision*) stock, reserve; (*entrepôt*) storeroom; **en r.** in reserve; **r. naturelle** nature reserve.
réservé, -ée *a* (*personne*, *place*) reserved.
réserver *vt* (*garder*) to save, reserve (**à** for); (*place*, *table*) to book, reserve; **se r. pour** to save oneself for.
réservoir *m* (*citerne*) tank; **r. d'essence** petrol *ou Am* gas tank.

résidence *f* residence; **r. secondaire** second home.
résidentiel, -ielle *a* (*quartier*) residential.
résider *vi* to be resident (**à, en, dans** in).
résigner (se) *vpr* to resign oneself (**à qch** to sth, **à faire** to doing).
résistance *f* resistance (**à** to); (*électrique*) (heating) element; **plat de r.** main dish.
résistant, -ante *a* tough; **r. à la chaleur** heat-resistant; **r. au choc** shockproof.
résister *vi* **r. à** to resist; (*chaleur*, *fatigue*) to withstand.
résolu, -ue *a* determined (**à faire** to do).
résolution *f* (*décision*) decision.
résonner *vi* (*cris etc*) to ring out; (*salle*) to echo (**de** with).
résoudre* *vt* (*problème*) to solve; (*difficulté*) to clear up.
respect *m* respect (**pour, de** for).
respecter *vt* to respect.
respectueux, -euse *a* respectful (**envers** to).
respiration *f* breathing; (*haleine*) breath.
respirer 1 *vi* to breathe; (*reprendre haleine*) to get one's breath back. **2** *vt* to breathe (in).
resplendissant, -ante *a* (*visage*) glowing (**de** with).
responsabilité *f* responsibility.
responsable 1 *a* responsible (**de qch** for sth, **devant qn** to s.o.). **2** *mf* (*chef*) person in charge; (*coupable*) person responsible (**de** for).
ressemblance *f* likeness (**avec** to).
ressembler *vi* **r. à** to look *ou* be like.
ressembler (se) *vpr* to look *ou* be alike.
ressentir* *vt* to feel.
resserrer *vt*, **se resserrer** *vpr* (*nœud etc*) to tighten.
resservir* *vi* (*outil etc*) to come in useful (again); **se r. de** (*plat*) to have another helping of.
ressort *m* (*objet*) spring.
ressortir* *vi* (*aux* **être**) to go *ou* come back out; (*se voir*) to stand out.
ressources *fpl* (*moyens*, *argent*) resources.
restaurant *m* restaurant.
restaurer *vt* (*réparer*) to restore.
reste *m* rest (**de** of); **restes** (*de repas*) leftovers; **un r. de fromage**/*etc* some left-over cheese/*etc*.
rester *vi* (*aux* **être**) to stay; (*calme*, *jeune etc*) to keep, stay; (*subsister*) to be left; **il reste du pain**/*etc* there's some bread/*etc* left (over); **il me reste une minute** I have one minute left; **l'argent qui lui reste** the money he *ou* she has left.

restreindre* *vt* to limit (**à** to).
résultat *m* (*score, d'examen etc*) result; (*conséquence*) outcome, result.
résumé *m* summary.
résumer *vt* to summarize; (*situation*) to sum up.
rétablir *vt* to restore.
rétablir (se) *vpr* (*malade*) to recover.
rétablissement *m* (*de malade*) recovery.
retard *m* (*sur un programme etc*) delay; **en r.** late; **en r. dans qch** behind in sth; **en r. sur qn/qch** behind s.o./sth; **rattraper son r.** to catch up; **avoir du r.** to be late; (*sur un programme*) to be behind; (*montre*) to be slow; **avoir une heure de r.** to be an hour late.
retardataire *mf* latecomer.
retarder 1 *vt* to delay; (*date, montre*) to put back; **r. qn** (*dans une activité*) to put s.o. behind. **2** *vi* (*montre*) to be slow; **r. de cinq minutes** to be five minutes slow.
retenir* *vt* (*empêcher d'agir*) to hold back; (*souffle*) to hold; (*réserver*) to book; (*se souvenir de*) to remember; (*fixer*) to hold (in place); (*chiffre*) to carry; (*chaleur, odeur*) to retain; **r. qn prisonnier** to keep s.o. prisoner.
retenir (se) *vpr* (*se contenir*) to restrain oneself; **se r. de faire** to stop oneself (from) doing; **se r. à** to cling to.
retentir *vi* to ring (out) (**de** with).
retenue *f* (*punition*) detention.
retirer *vt* (*sortir*) to take out; (*ôter*) to take off; (*éloigner*) to take away; **r. qch à qn** (*permis etc*) to take sth away from s.o.
retomber *vi* to fall (again); (*pendre*) to hang (down); (*après un saut etc*) to land.
retouche *f* (*de vêtement*) alteration.
retoucher *vt* (*vêtement*) to alter.
retour *m* return; **être de r.** to be back (**de** from); **à mon retour** when I get *ou* got back.
retourner 1 *vt* (*aux* **avoir**) (*matelas, steak etc*) to turn over; (*terre etc*) to turn; (*vêtement, sac etc*) to turn inside out. **2** *vi* (*aux* **être**) to go back, return.
retourner (se) *vpr* to turn round, look round; (*sur le dos*) to turn over; (*voiture*) to overturn.
retraite *f* (*d'employé*) retirement; (*pension*) (retirement) pension; **prendre sa r.** to retire; **à la r.** retired.
retraité, -ée 1 *a* retired. **2** *mf* senior citizen, pensioner.
retransmettre *vt* to broadcast.
retransmission *f* broadcast.

rétrécir *vi* (*au lavage*) to shrink.
rétrécir (se) *vpr* (*rue etc*) to narrow.
rétro *a inv* (*personne, idée etc*) old-fashioned.
retrousser *vt* (*manches*) to roll up.
retrouver *vt* to find (again); (*rejoindre*) to meet (again); (*forces, santé*) to get back; (*se rappeler*) to recall.
retrouver (se) *vpr* to find oneself (back); (*se rencontrer*) to meet (again); **s'y r.** to find one's way.
rétroviseur *m* (*de véhicule*) mirror.
réunion *f* (*séance*) meeting.
réunir *vt* (*objets*) to gather; (*convoquer*) to call together.
réunir (se) *vpr* to meet, get together.
réussi, -ie *a* successful.
réussir 1 *vi* to succeed (**à faire** in doing); **r. à** (*examen*) to pass; **r. à qn** (*aliment, climat*) to agree with s.o. **2** *vt* to make a success of.
réussite *f* success.
revanche *f* (*en sport*) return game; **en r.** on the other hand.
rêve *m* dream; **faire un r.** to have a dream (**de** about); **maison**/*etc* **de r.** dream house/*etc*.
réveil *m* (*pendule*) alarm (clock); **à son r.** when he wakes (up) *ou* woke (up).
réveillé, -ée *a* awake.
réveiller *vt*, **se réveiller** *vpr* to wake (up).
réveillon *m* midnight supper (*on Christmas Eve or New Year's Eve*).
révéler *vt* to reveal (**que** that).
revenant *m* ghost.
revendication *f* claim; demand.
revendiquer *vt* to claim; (*exiger*) to demand.
revenir* *vi* (*aux* **être**) to come back; (*coûter*) to cost (**à qn** s.o.); **r. à** (*activité, sujet*) to go back to; **r. à qn** (*forces, mémoire*) to come back to s.o.; **r. à soi** to come round; **r. de** (*surprise*) to get over; **r. sur** (*décision, promesse*) to go back on.
revenu *m* income (**de** from).
rêver 1 *vi* to dream (**de** of, **de faire** of doing). **2** *vt* to dream (**que** that).
revers *m* (*de veste*) lapel; (*de pantalon*) turn-up, *Am* cuff.
revêtement *m* (*de route etc*) surface.
rêveur, -euse *mf* dreamer.
revient *m* **prix de r.** cost price.
réviser *vt* (*leçon*) to revise; (*machine, voiture*) to service.
révision *f* revision; service.

revoir* *vt* to see (again); (*texte, leçon*) to revise; **au r.** goodbye.
révoltant, -ante *a* revolting.
révolte *f* rebellion, revolt.
révolté, -ée *mf* rebel.
révolter *vt* to sicken.
révolter (se) *vpr* to rebel (**contre** against).
révolution *f* revolution.
révolutionnaire *a* & *mf* revolutionary.
revolver [revɔlvɛr] *m* gun.
revue *f* (*magazine*) magazine.
rez-de-chaussée *m inv* ground floor, *Am* first floor.
rhabiller (se) *vpr* to get dressed again.
rhinocéros [-ɔs] *m* rhinoceros.
rhubarbe *f* rhubarb.
rhum [rɔm] *m* rum.
rhumatisme *m* rheumatism; **avoir des rhumatismes** to have rheumatism.
rhume *m* cold; **r. des foins** hay fever.
ri, riant *pp* & *pres p of* **rire**.
ricaner *vi* to snigger, *Am* snicker.
riche 1 *a* rich. **2** *mf* rich person; **les riches** the rich.
richesse *f* wealth; **richesses** (*trésor*) riches.
ricocher *vi* to rebound.
ricochet *m* (*de pierre*) rebound.
ride *f* wrinkle.
ridé, -ée *a* wrinkled.
rideau, -x *m* curtain; (*de magasin*) shutter.
ridicule *a* ridiculous.
ridiculiser (se) *vpr* to make a fool of oneself.
rien 1 *pron* nothing; **il ne sait r.** he knows nothing, he doesn't know anything; **r. du tout** nothing at all; **r. d'autre/de bon/***etc* nothing else/good/*etc*; **de r.!** (*je vous en prie*) don't mention it!; **ça ne fait r.** it doesn't matter; **r. que** just. **2** *m* (mere) nothing.
rigide *a* rigid; (*carton, muscle*) stiff.
rigoler *vi Fam* to laugh; (*s'amuser*) to have fun
rigolo, -ote *a Fam* funny.
rime *f* rhyme.
rimer *vi* to rhyme (**avec** with).
rinçage *m* rinsing.
rincer *vt* to rinse; (*verre*) to rinse (out).
ring [riŋ] *m* (boxing) ring.
rire* 1 *vi* to laugh (**de** at); (*s'amuser*) to have a good time;

(*plaisanter*) to joke; **pour r.** for a joke. **2** *m* laugh; **rires** laughter; **le fou r.** the giggles.
risque *m* risk (**de faire** of doing, **à faire** in doing); **assurance tous risques** comprehensive insurance.
risqué, -ée *a* risky.
risquer *vt* to risk; **r. de faire** to stand a good chance of doing.
rivage *m* shore.
rival, -e, -aux *a & mf* rival.
rivaliser *vi* to compete (**avec** with, **de** in).
rive *f* (*de fleuve*) bank; (*de lac*) shore.
rivière *f* river.
riz *m* rice; **r. au lait** rice pudding.
RN [ɛrɛn] *abrév* = **route nationale.**
robe *f* (*de femme*) dress; **r. du soir/de mariée** evening/wedding dress; **r. de chambre** dressing gown, *Am* bathrobe.
robinet *m* tap, *Am* faucet; **eau du r.** tap water.
robot *m* robot.
robuste *a* sturdy.
roche *f*, **rocher** *m* rock.
rocheux, -euse *a* rocky.
rock *m* (*musique*) rock.
roder *vt* (*moteur*, *voiture*) to run in, *Am* break in.
rôder *vi* to prowl (about).
rôdeur, -euse *mf* prowler.
rognon *m* (*d'animal*) kidney.
roi *m* king.
rôle *m* (*au théâtre*) role, part; (*d'un père etc*) job; **à tour de r.** in turn.
romain, -aine *a & mf* Roman.
roman *m* novel; **r. d'aventures** adventure story.
romancier, -ière *mf* novelist.
romantique *a* romantic.
rompre* (se) *vpr* (*corde etc*) to break; (*digue*) to burst.
ronces *fpl* brambles.
ronchonner *vi Fam* to grumble.
rond, ronde 1 *a* round; **dix francs tout r.** ten francs exactly. **2** *m* (*cercle*) circle, ring; **en r.** (*s'asseoir etc*) in a ring *ou* circle; **tourner en r.** to go round and round.
ronde *f* (*de soldat*) round; (*de policier*) beat, round.
rondelle *f* (*tranche*) slice.
rondin *m* log.
rond-point *m* (*pl* **ronds-points**) roundabout, *Am* traffic circle.

ronflement *m* snore; **ronflements** snoring.
ronfler *vi* to snore.
ronger *vt* to gnaw (at); (*ver*, *mer*, *rouille*) to eat into (*sth*); **se r. les ongles** to bite one's nails.
ronronnement *m* purr(ing).
ronronner *vi* to purr.
rosbif *m* **du r.** roast beef; (*à rôtir*) roasting beef; **un r.** a joint of roast beef.
rose 1 *f* (*fleur*) rose. **2** *a* & *m* (*couleur*) pink.
rosé *a* & *m* (*vin*) rosé.
roseau, -x *m* (*plante*) reed.
rosée *f* dew.
rosier *m* rose bush.
rossignol *m* nightingale.
rot *m Fam* burp.
roter *vi Fam* to burp.
rôti *m* **du r.** roasting meat; (*cuit*) roast meat; **un r.** a joint; **r. de porc** (joint of) roast pork.
rotin *m* cane.
rôtir *vti*, **se rôtir** *vpr* to roast; **faire r.** to roast.
roue *f* wheel.
rouge 1 *a* red; (*fer*) red-hot. **2** *m* (*couleur*) red; **r. (à lèvres)** lipstick; **le feu est au r.** the (traffic) lights are red.
rouge-gorge *m* (*pl* **rouges-gorges**) robin.
rougeole *f* measles.
rougir *vi* (*de honte*) to blush; (*de colère*) to flush (**de** with).
rouille *f* rust.
rouillé, -ée *a* rusty.
rouiller *vi*, **se rouiller** *vpr* to rust.
roulant, -ante *a* (*escalier*) moving; (*meuble*) on wheels.
rouleau, -x *m* (*outil*) roller, (*de papier etc*) roll; **r. à pâtisserie** rolling pin; **r. compresseur** steamroller.
rouler 1 *vt* to roll; (*brouette*) to push; (*crêpe*, *ficelle etc*) to roll up. **2** *vi* to roll; (*train*, *voiture*) to go; (*conducteur*) to drive.
rouler (se) *vpr* to roll; **se r. dans** (*couverture etc*) to roll oneself (up) in.
roulette *f* (*de meuble*) castor; (*de dentiste*) drill.
roulotte *f* (*de gitan*) caravan.
round [rawnd, rund] *m Boxe* round.
rouspéter *vi Fam* to complain.
rousse *voir* **roux**.
rousseur *f* **tache de r.** freckle.

roussir *vt* (*brûler*) to scorch.
route *f* road (**de** to); (*itinéraire*) way; **r. nationale/départementale** main/secondary road; **en r.!** let's go!; **par la r.** by road; **mettre en r.** (*voiture etc*) to start (up); **se mettre en r.** to set out (**pour** for); **une heure de r.** an hour's drive *ou* walk *etc*; **bonne r.!** have a good trip!
routier, -ière 1 *a* **carte/sécurité routière** road map/safety. **2** *m* (long-distance) lorry *ou Am* truck driver.
roux, rousse 1 *a* (*cheveux*) red; (*personne*) red-haired. **2** *mf* redhead.
royal, -e, -aux *a* (*famille, palais*) royal.
royaume *m* kingdom.
ruban *m* ribbon; **r. adhésif** sticky tape.
rubéole *f* German measles.
rubis *m* ruby; (*de montre*) jewel.
ruche *f* (bee)hive.
rude *a* (*pénible*) tough; (*hiver, voix*) harsh; (*grossier*) crude; (*rêche*) rough.
rudement *adv* (*parler, traiter*) harshly; (*très*) *Fam* awfully.
rue *f* street; **à la r.** (*sans domicile*) on the streets.
ruelle *f* alley(way).
ruer *vi* (*cheval*) to kick (out).
ruer (se) *vpr* to rush (**sur** at).
rugby *m* rugby.
rugbyman, *pl* **-men** *m* rugby player.
rugir *vi* to roar.
rugissement *m* roar.
rugueux, -euse *a* rough.
ruine *f* ruin; **en r.** in ruins; **tomber en r.** (*bâtiment*) to become a ruin, crumble; (*mur*) to crumble.
ruiner *vt* (*personne, santé etc*) to ruin; **se r.** to be(come) ruined, ruin oneself.
ruisseau, -x *m* stream.
ruisseler *vi* to stream (**de** with).
rural, -e, -aux *a* **vie/école/***etc* **rurale** country life/school/*etc*.
ruse *f* (*subterfuge*) trick; **la r.** (*habileté*) cunning.
rusé, -ée *a* & *mf* cunning (person).
russe 1 *a* & *mf* Russian. **2** *m* (*langue*) Russian.
rythme *m* rhythm; (*de travail*) rate; **au r. de trois par jour** at a rate of three a day.
rythmé, -ée *a* rhythmical.

S

sa *voir* **son.**
sable *m* sand.
sabler *vt* (*rue*) to sand.
sablier *m* (*de cuisine*) egg timer.
sablonneux, -euse *a* sandy.
sabot *m* (*de cheval etc*) hoof; (*chaussure*) clog; **s. (de Denver)** (wheel) clamp.
sac *m* bag; (*grand et en toile*) sack; **s. (à main)** handbag; **s. à dos** rucksack.
saccadé, -ée *a* jerky.
saccager *vt* (*détruire*) to wreck.
sachant, sache(s), sachent *etc voir* **savoir**.
sachet *m* (small) bag; **s. de thé** teabag.
sacoche *f* bag; (*de vélo*) saddlebag.
sacré, -ée *a* (*saint*) sacred; **un s. menteur**/*etc Fam* a damned liar/*etc*.
sacrifice *m* sacrifice.
sacrifier *vt* to sacrifice (**à** to, **pour** for); **se s.** to sacrifice oneself.
sage *a* wise; (*enfant*) good.
sage-femme *f* (*pl* **sages-femmes**) midwife.
sagement *adv* wisely; (*avec calme*) quietly.
saignant, -ante *a* (*viande*) rare.
saignement *m* bleeding; **s. de nez** nosebleed.
saigner *vti* to bleed.
sain, saine *a* healthy; **s. et sauf** safe and sound.
saint, sainte 1 *a* holy, **s. Jean** Saint John; **la Sainte Vierge** the Blessed Virgin. **2** *mf* saint.
Saint-Sylvestre *f* New Year's Eve.
sais, sait *voir* **savoir.**
saisir *vt* to grab (hold of); (*occasion*) to jump at; (*comprendre*) to understand; **se s. de** to grab (hold of).
saison *f* season.
salade *f* (*laitue*) lettuce; **s. (verte)** (green) salad; **s. de fruits**/*etc* fruit/*etc* salad.
saladier *m* salad bowl.
salaire *m* wage(s).
salarié, -ée *mf* wage earner.
sale *a* dirty; (*dégoûtant*) filthy.
salé, -ée *a* (*goût, plat*) salty; (*aliment*) salted.
saler *vt* to salt.
saleté *f* dirtiness; filthiness; (*crasse*) dirt, filth; **saletés** (*détritus*)

rubbish, *Am* garbage.
salière *f* saltcellar, *Am* saltshaker.
salir *vt* to (make) dirty.
salir (se) *vpr* to get dirty.
salissant, -ante *a* dirty; (*étoffe*) that shows the dirt.
salive *f* saliva.
salle *f* room; (*très grande*) hall; (*de théâtre*) theatre, auditorium; (*de cinéma*) cinema; (*d'hôpital*) ward; **s. à manger** dining room; **s. de bain(s)** bathroom; **s. d'opération** operating theatre.
salon *m* sitting room, lounge; (*exposition*) show.
salopette *f* (*d'enfant*, *d'ouvrier*) dungarees, *Am* overalls.
saluer *vt* to greet; (*de la main*) to wave to; (*de la tête*) to nod to.
salut 1 *m* greeting; wave; nod. **2** *int* hello!, hi!; (*au revoir*) bye!
samedi *m* Saturday.
sandale *f* sandal.
sandwich [sɑ̃dwitʃ] *m* sandwich; **s. au fromage/***etc* cheese/*etc* sandwich.
sandwicherie *f* sandwich bar.
sang *m* blood.
sang-froid *m* self-control; **garder son s.-froid** to keep calm; **avec s.-froid** calmly.
sanglant, -ante *a* bloody.
sanglier *m* wild boar.
sanglot *m* sob.
sangloter *vi* to sob.
sanguin *a* **groupe s.** blood group.
sans [sɑ̃] ([sɑ̃z] *before vowel and mute h*) *prép* without; **s. faire** without doing; **s. qu'il le sache** without him *ou* his knowing; **s. cela** otherwise; **s. importance** unimportant.
sans-abri *mf inv* homeless person.
santé *f* health; **(à votre) s.!** your (good) health!, cheers!
sapin *m* (*arbre*, *bois*) fir; **s. de Noël** Christmas tree.
sardine *f* sardine.
satellite *m* satellite.
satin *m* satin.
satisfaction *f* satisfaction.
satisfaire* *vt* to satisfy (*s.o.*); **satisfait (de)** satisfied (with).
satisfaisant, -ante *a* satisfactory.
sauce *f* sauce; (*jus de viande*) gravy; **s. tomate** tomato sauce.
saucisse *f* sausage.
saucisson *m* (cold) sausage.
sauf *prép* except (**que** that).

saule *m* willow.
saumon *m* salmon.
sauna *m* sauna.
saupoudrer *vt* to sprinkle (**de** with).
saura, saurai(t) *etc voir* **savoir**.
saut *m* jump, leap; **faire un s.** to jump, leap; **faire un s. chez qn** to drop in on s.o., pop round to s.o.
sauter 1 *vi* to jump, leap; **faire s.** (*détruire*) to blow up; **s. à la corde** to skip, *Am* jump rope; **ça saute aux yeux** it's obvious. **2** *vt* to jump (over); (*mot*, *repas*) to skip.
sauterelle *f* grasshopper.
sauvage *a* (*animal*, *plante*) wild; (*tribu*, *homme*) primitive.
sauver *vt* to save; (*d'un danger*) to rescue (**de** from); **s. la vie à qn** to save s.o.'s life.
sauver (se) *vpr* to run away *ou* off.
sauvetage *m* rescue.
sauveteur *m* rescuer.
sauveur *m* saviour.
savant *m* scientist.
savate *f* old slipper.
saveur *f* flavour.
savoir* *vt* to know, **s. lire/nager**/*etc* to know how to read/swim/*etc*; **faire s. à qn que** to inform s.o. that; **je n'en sais rien** I have no idea.
savon *m* soap; (*morceau*) (bar of) soap.
savonner *vt* to wash with soap.
savonnette *f* bar of soap.
savonneux, -euse *a* soapy.
savourer *vt* to enjoy
savoureux, -euse *a* tasty.
saxophone *m* saxophone.
scandale *m* scandal; **faire un s.** to make a scene.
scandaleux, -euse *a* shocking.
scandaliser *vt* to shock.
scandinave *a & mf* Scandinavian.
scanner [skaner] *m* (*appareil*) scanner.
scarlatine *f* scarlet fever.
scénario *m* (*dialogues etc*) film script.
scène *f* (*plateau*) stage; (*décors*, *partie de pièce*, *dispute*) scene; **mettre en s.** to direct.
schéma *m* diagram.
scie *f* saw.

science *f* science; **étudier les sciences** to study science.
science-fiction *f* science fiction.
scientifique 1 *a* scientific. **2** *mf* scientist.
scier *vt* to saw.
scintiller *vi* to sparkle; (*étoiles*) to twinkle.
scolaire *a* **année**/*etc* **s.** school year/*etc*.
score *m* (*de match*) score.
scotch® *m* (*ruban*) sellotape®, *Am* scotch (tape)®.
scrutin *m* voting, ballot.
sculpter *vt* to carve, sculpture.
sculpteur *m* sculptor.
sculpture *f* (*art*, *œuvre*) sculpture.
se (**s'** *before vowel or mute h*) *pron* (*complément direct*) himself; (*féminin*) herself; (*non humain*) itself; (*indéfini*) oneself; *pl* themselves. ■ (*indirect*) to himself; to herself; to itself; to oneself. ■ (*réciproque*) each other, one another; (*indirect*) to each other, to one another. ■ (*possessif*) **il se lave les mains** he washes his hands.
séance *f* (*au cinéma*) show(ing).
seau, -x *m* bucket.
sec, sèche 1 *a* dry; (*légumes*) dried; (*ton*) harsh; **coup s.** (sharp) knock, bang; **frapper un coup s.** to knock (sharply), bang; **bruit s.** (*rupture*) snap. **2** *m* **à s.** (*rivière*) dried up; **au s.** in a dry place.
sécateur *m* pruning shears.
sèche-cheveux *m inv* hair drier.
sèche-linge *m inv* tumble drier.
sécher 1 *vti* to dry. **2** *vt* (*cours*) to skip.
sécheresse *f* (*période*) drought.
séchoir *m* **s. à linge** clotheshorse.
second, -onde [sgɔ̃, -ɔ̃d] **1** *a* & *mf* second. **2** *m* (*étage*) second floor, *Am* third floor. **3** *f* (*de lycée*) = fifth form, *Am* = eleventh grade; (*vitesse*) second (gear).
secondaire *a* secondary.
seconde *f* (*instant*) second.
secouer *vt* to shake.
secourir *vt* to assist.
secouriste *mf* first-aid worker.
secours *m* assistance, help; **(premiers) s.** first aid; **au s.!** help!; **sortie de s.** emergency exit; **roue de s.** spare wheel.
secousse *f* jolt.
secret, -ète 1 *a* secret. **2** *m* secret; **en s.** in secret.
secrétaire 1 *mf* secretary; (*de médecin etc*) receptionist. **2** *m* (*meuble*) writing desk.

secrétariat *m* (*bureau*) secretary's office.
secteur *m* (*électricité*) mains.
sécurité *f* safety; **en s.** safe; **S. sociale** = social services *ou* Social security.
séduisant, -ante *a* attractive.
segment *m* segment.
seigneur *m* lord.
sein *m* breast.
seize *a* & *m* sixteen.
seizième *a* & *mf* sixteenth.
séjour *m* stay; **(salle de) s.** living room.
séjourner *vi* to stay.
sel *m* salt; **sels de bain** bath salts.
sélection *f* selection.
sélectionner *vt* to select.
self(-service) *m* self-service restaurant *ou* shop.
selle *f* saddle.
selon *prép* according to (**que** whether).
semaine *f* week; **en s.** in the week.
semblable *a* similar (**à** to).
semblant *m* **faire s.** to pretend (**de faire** to do).
sembler *vi* to seem (**à** to); **il (me) semble vieux** he seems *ou* looks old (to me); **il me semble que** (+ *indicatif*) I think that, it seems to me that.
semelle *f* (*de chaussure*) sole.
semer *vt* (*graines*) to sow.
semestre *m* half-year; (*scolaire*) semester.
semi-remorque *m* articulated lorry, *Am* semi(trailer)
semoule *f* semolina.
sénat *m* senate.
sens[1] [sɑ̃s] *m* (*signification*) meaning, sense; **avoir du bon s.** to have sense, be sensible; **avoir un s.** to make sense; **ça n'a pas de s.** that doesn't make sense.
sens[2] *m* (*direction*) direction; **s. giratoire** roundabout, *Am* traffic circle; **s. interdit** *ou* **unique** (*rue*) one way street; **'s. interdit'** 'no entry'; **s. dessus dessous** [sɑ̃dsydsu] upside down; **dans le s./le s. inverse des aiguilles d'une montre** clockwise/anticlockwise, *Am* counterclockwise.
sensation *f* feeling.
sensationnel, -elle *a* sensational.
sensible *a* sensitive (**à** to); (*douloureux*) tender; (*progrès etc*) noticeable.

sentier *m* path.
sentiment *m* feeling.
sentir* *vt* to feel; (*odeur*) to smell; (*goût*) to taste; **s. le parfum/***etc* to smell of perfume/*etc*; **s. le poisson/***etc* (*avoir le goût de*) to taste of fish/*etc*; **je ne peux pas le s.** (*supporter*) I can't stand him; **se s. fatigué/***etc* to feel tired/*etc*.
séparément *adv* separately.
séparer *vt* to separate (**de** from).
séparer (se) *vpr* (*se quitter*) to part; (*couple*) to separate; **se s. de** (*chien etc*) to part with.
sept [sɛt] *a & m* seven.
septante *a* (*en Belgique*, *Suisse*) seventy.
septembre *m* September.
septième [sɛtjɛm] *a & mf* seventh.
sera, serai(t) *etc voir* **être.**
série *f* series; (*ensemble*) set.
sérieusement *adv* seriously; (*travailler*) conscientiously.
sérieux, -euse 1 *a* serious. **2** *m* **prendre au s.** to take seriously; **garder son s.** to keep a straight face.
seringue *f* syringe.
serment *m* oath; **faire le s. de faire** to promise to do.
serpent *m* snake.
serpillière *f* floor cloth.
serre *f* greenhouse.
serré, -ée *a* (*nœud etc*) tight; (*gens*) packed (together).
serrer 1 *vt* (*tenir*) to grip; (*presser*) to squeeze; (*nœud*, *vis*) to tighten; (*poing*) to clench; (*frein*) to apply; **s. la main à qn** to shake hands with s.o.; **s. qn** (*embrasser*) to hug s.o. **2** *vi* **s. à droite** to keep (to the) right.
serrer (se) *vpr* to squeeze up *ou* together; **se s. contre** to squeeze up against.
serrure *f* lock.
serveur, -euse *mf* waiter, waitress; (*au bar*) barman, barmaid.
serviable *a* helpful.
service *m* service; (*pourboire*) service (charge); (*dans une entreprise*) department; **un s.** (*aide*) a favour; **rendre s.** to be of service (**à qn** to s.o.); **s. (non) compris** service (not) included; **s. après-vente** aftersales service; **être de s.** to be on duty.
serviette *f* towel; (*sac*) briefcase; **s. hygiénique** sanitary towel *ou Am* napkin; **s. (de table)** napkin, serviette.
servir* 1 *vt* to serve (**qch à qn** s.o. with sth, sth to s.o.). **2** *vi* (*être utile*) to be useful; **s. à qch/à faire** (*objet*) to be used for sth/to do;

ça ne sert à rien it's useless (**de faire** doing); **ça me sert à faire/de qch** I use it to do/as sth.

servir (se) *vpr* (*à table*) to help oneself (**de** to); **se s. de** (*utiliser*) to use.

ses [se] *voir* **son.**

set [sɛt] *m Tennis* set; **s. (de table)** place mat.

seuil *m* doorstep.

seul[1], **-e 1** *a* alone; **tout s.** by oneself, on one's own; **se sentir s.** to feel lonely. **2** *adv* **(tout) s.** (*rentrer, vivre etc*) by oneself, on one's own, alone; (*parler*) to oneself.

seul[2], **-e 1** *a* (*unique*) only; **la seule femme**/*etc* the only woman/*etc*; **un s. chat**/*etc* only one cat/*etc*; **pas un s. livre**/*etc* not a single book/*etc*. **2** *mf* **le s., la seule** the only one; **un s., une seule** only one; **pas un s.** not (a single) one.

seulement *adv* only.

sévère *a* severe; (*parents etc*) strict

sévérité *f* (*de parents etc*) strictness.

sexe *m* sex

sexuel, -elle *a* sexual; **éducation/vie sexuelle** sex education/life.

shampooing [ʃɑ̃pwɛ̃] *m* shampoo; **faire un s. à qn** to shampoo s.o.'s hair.

short [ʃɔrt] *m* (pair of) shorts.

si[1] **1** (= **s'** [s] *before* **il, ils**) *conj* if; **je me demande si** I wonder whether *ou* if; **si on restait?** what if we stayed? **2** *adv* (*tellement*) so; **pas si riche que toi** not as rich as you; **un si bon dîner** such a good dinner; **si bien que** (+ *indicatif*) with the result that.

si[2] *adv* (*après négative*) yes; **tu ne viens pas? – si!** you're not coming? – yes (I am)!

SIDA *m* AIDS.

siècle *m* century; (*époque*) age.

siège *m* seat; (*de parti etc*) headquarters; **s. (social)** head office.

sien, sienne *pron poss* **le s., la sienne, les sien(ne)s** his; (*de femme*) hers; (*de chose*) its; **les deux siens** his *ou* her two.

sieste *f* **faire la s.** to take a nap.

sifflement *m* whistling; hiss(ing).

siffler 1 *vi* to whistle; (*avec un sifflet*) to blow one's whistle; (*gaz, serpent*) to hiss. **2** *vt* (*chanson*) to whistle; (*chien*) to whistle to; (*acteur*) to boo.

sifflet *m* whistle; **(coup de) s.** (*son*) whistle; **sifflets** (*des spectateurs*) boos.

signal, -aux *m* signal; **s. d'alarme** (*de train*) alarm, communication cord.

signaler *vt* to point out (**à qn** to s.o., **que** that); (*à la police etc*) to report (**à** to).
signature *f* signature.
signe *m* sign; **faire s. à qn** (*geste*) to motion (to) s.o. (**de faire** to do).
signer *vt* to sign.
signification *f* meaning.
signifier *vt* to mean (**que** that).
silence *m* silence; **en s.** in silence; **garder le s.** to keep silent (**sur** about).
silencieusement *adv* silently.
silencieux, -euse *a* silent.
silhouette *f* outline; (*ligne du corps*) figure.
simple *a* simple.
simplement *adv* simply.
simplifier *vt* to simplify.
simultané, -ée *a* simultaneous.
simultanément *adv* simultaneously.
sincère *a* sincere.
sincèrement *adv* sincerely.
sincérité *f* sincerity.
singe *m* monkey, ape.
singeries *fpl* antics.
singulier, -ière *a* & *m* (*non pluriel*) singular; **au s.** in the singular.
sinistre 1 *a* sinister. **2** *m* disaster.
sinon *conj* (*autrement*) otherwise, or else.
sirène *f* (*d'usine etc*) siren.
sirop *m* syrup; **s. contre la toux** cough medicine *ou* mixture *ou* syrup.
situation *f* situation.
situé, -ée *a* situated.
situer (se) *vpr* to be situated.
six [sis] ([si] *before consonant*, [siz] *before vowel*) *a* & *m* six.
sixième *a* & *mf* sixth.
sketch *m* (*pl* **sketches**) (*de théâtre*) sketch.
ski *m* ski; (*sport*) skiing; **faire du s.** to ski; **s. nautique** water skiing.
skier *vi* to ski.
skieur, -euse *mf* skier.
slip [slip] *m* (*d'homme*) briefs, (under)pants; (*de femme*) panties, knickers; **s. de bain** (swimming) trunks.
slogan *m* slogan.
SNCF [ɛsɛnseɛf] *f abrév* (*Société nationale des chemins de fer*

français) French railways *ou Am* railroad system.
social, -e, -aux *a* social.
socialiste *a* & *mf* socialist.
société *f* society; (*compagnie*) company.
socquette *f* ankle sock.
sœur *f* sister.
soi *pron* oneself; **cela va de soi** it's evident (**que** that).
soie *f* silk.
soient *voir* **être**.
soif *f* thirst; **avoir s.** to be thirsty; **donner s. à qn** to make s.o. thirsty.
soigné, -ée *a* (*vêtement*) neat; (*travail*) careful.
soigner *vt* to look after, take care of; (*maladie*) to treat; **se faire s.** to have (medical) treatment.
soigneusement *adv* carefully.
soigneux, -euse *a* careful (**de** with); (*propre*) neat.
soi-même *pron* oneself.
soin *m* care; **soins** (*à un malade*) treatment, care; **avec s.** carefully; **prendre s. de qch** to take care of sth; **les premiers soins** first aid.
soir *m* evening; **le s.** (*chaque soir*) in the evening; **à neuf heures du s.** at nine in the evening.
soirée *f* evening; (*réunion*) party.
sois, soit *voir* **être.**
soit *conj* **s....s....** either...or....
soixantaine *f* **une s. (de)** about sixty.
soixante [swasɑ̃t] *a* & *m* sixty.
soixante-dix *a* & *m* seventy.
soixante-dixième *a* & *mf* seventieth.
soixantième *a* & *mf* sixtieth.
sol *m* ground; (*plancher*) floor.
solaire *a* solar; **crème/huile s.** sun(tan) lotion/oil.
soldat *m* soldier.
solde *m* (*de compte*) balance; **en s.** (*acheter*) at sale price, *Am* on sale; **soldes** (*marchandises*) sale goods; (*vente*) (clearance) sale(s).
soldé, -ée *a* (*article etc*) reduced.
solder *vt* (*articles*) to clear.
sole *f* (*poisson*) sole.
soleil *m* sun; (*chaleur, lumière*) sunshine; **au s.** in the sun; **il fait (du) s.** it's sunny; **coup de s.** sunburn.
solennel, -elle [sɔlanɛl] *a* solemn.
solidarité *f* (*de personnes*) solidarity.
solide *a* & *m* solid.

solidement *adv* solidly.

solitaire *a* (*tout seul*) all alone.

solitude *f* **aimer la s.** to like being alone.

sombre *a* dark; **il fait s.** it's dark.

somme 1 *f* sum; **faire la s. de** to add up. **2** *m* (*sommeil*) nap; **faire un s.** to take a nap.

sommeil *m* sleep; **avoir s.** to be *ou* feel sleepy.

sommes *voir* **être.**

sommet *m* top.

somnifère *m* sleeping pill.

son *m* (*bruit*) sound.

son, sa, *pl* **ses** (**sa** *becomes* **son** [sɔ̃n] *before a vowel or mute h*) *a poss* his; (*de femme*) her; (*de chose*) its; (*indéfini*) one's; **son père/sa mère** his *ou* her *ou* one's father/mother; **son ami(e)** his *ou* her *ou* one's friend; **sa durée** its duration.

sondage *m* **s. (d'opinion)** opinion poll.

songer *vi* **s. à qch/à faire** to think of sth/of doing.

sonner *vi* to ring; **on a sonné** (*à la porte*) someone has rung the (door)bell.

sonnerie *f* (*son*) ring(ing); (*appareil*) bell; (*au téléphone*) ringing tone, *Am* ring; **s. 'occupé'** engaged tone, *Am* busy signal.

sonnette *f* bell; **coup de s.** ring.

sonore *a* (*rire*) loud; (*salle*) resonant.

sont *voir* **être.**

sorcière *f* witch.

sort *m* (*destin*, *hasard*) fate; (*condition*) lot.

sorte *f* sort, kind (**de** of); **toutes sortes de** all sorts *ou* kinds of; **de (telle) s. que** (+ *subjonctif*) so that; **faire en s. que** (+ *subjonctif*) to see to it that.

sortie *f* (*promenade à pied*) walk; (*en voiture*) drive; (*excursion*) outing; (*porte*) exit, way out; (*de disque*, *film*) release; **à la s. de l'école** when the children come out of school.

sortir* 1 *vi* (*aux* **être**) to go out, leave; (*venir*) to come out; (*pour s'amuser*, *danser etc*) to go out; (*film etc*) to come out; **s. de table** to leave the table; **s'en s.** to pull *ou* come through. **2** *vt* (*aux* **avoir**) to take out (**de** of).

sottise *f* (*action*, *parole*) foolish thing; **faire des sottises** (*enfant*) to be naughty.

sou *m* **sous** (*argent*) money; **elle n'a pas un s.** she doesn't have a penny; **appareil** *ou* **machine à sous** fruit machine, *Am* slot machine.

souche *f* (*d'arbre*) stump.

souci *m* worry; (*préoccupation*) concern (**de** for); **se faire du s.** to worry; **ça lui donne du s.** it worries him *ou* her.

soucier (se) *vpr* **se s. de** to be worried about.

soucieux, -euse *a* worried (**de qch** about sth).

soucoupe *f* saucer; **s. volante** flying saucer.

soudain *adv* suddenly.

souder *vt* to weld.

souffle *m* puff; (*haleine*) breath; (*respiration*) breathing; (*de bombe etc*) blast.

souffler 1 *vi* to blow. **2** *vt* (*bougie*) to blow out; (*chuchoter*) to whisper.

souffrance(s) *f(pl)* suffering.

souffrant, -ante *a* unwell.

souffrir* *vi* to suffer (**de** from); **faire s. qn** to hurt s.o.

souhait *m* wish; **à vos souhaits!** (*après un éternuement*) bless you!

souhaitable *a* desirable.

souhaiter *vt* to wish for; **s. qch à qn** to wish s.o. sth; **s. faire** to hope to do; **s. que** (+ *subjonctif*) to hope that.

soulagement *m* relief.

soulager *vt* to relieve (**de** of).

soulever *vt* to lift (up); (*poussière, question*) to raise.

soulier *m* shoe.

souligner *vt* to underline; (*faire remarquer*) to emphasize.

soupçon *m* suspicion.

soupçonner *vt* to suspect (**de** of, **d'avoir fait** of doing, **que** that).

soupe *f* soup.

souper 1 *m* supper. **2** *vi* to have supper.

soupir *m* sigh.

soupirer *vi* to sigh.

souple *a* supple; (*tolérant*) flexible.

souplesse *f* suppleness; flexibility.

source *f* (*point d'eau*) spring; (*origine*) source; **eau de s.** spring water.

sourcil *m* eyebrow.

sourd, sourde 1 *a* deaf; (*douleur*) dull; **bruit s.** thump. **2** *mf* deaf person.

sourd-muet (*pl* **sourds-muets**), **sourde-muette** (*pl* **sourdes-muettes**) *a & mf* deaf and dumb (person).

sourire* 1 *vi* to smile (**à qn** at s.o.). **2** *m* smile; **faire un s. à qn** to give s.o. a smile.

souris *f* mouse (*pl* mice).

sous *prép* (*position*) under(neath), beneath; **s. la pluie** in the rain; **s. Charles X** under Charles X; **s. peu** (*bientôt*) shortly.

sous-entendre *vt* to imply.
sous-marin *m* submarine.
sous-sol *m* (*d'immeuble*) basement.
sous-titre *m* subtitle.
soustraction *f* subtraction.
soustraire* *vt* (*nombre*) to take away, subtract (**de** from).
sous-vêtements *mpl* underwear.
soutenir* *vt* to support; **s. que** to maintain that.
soutenir (se) *vpr* (*blessé etc*) to hold oneself up straight.
souterrain, -aine 1 *a* underground. **2** *m* underground passage.
soutien *m* support; (*personne*) supporter.
soutien-gorge *m* (*pl* **soutiens-gorge**) bra.
souvenir *m* memory; (*objet*) memento; (*cadeau*) keepsake; (*pour touristes*) souvenir.
souvenir* (se) *vpr* **se s. de** to remember; **se s. que** to remember that.
souvent *adv* often; **peu s.** seldom; **le plus s.** usually.
soyez, soyons *voir* **être.**
spacieux, -euse *a* spacious.
spaghetti(s) *mpl* spaghetti.
sparadrap *m* sticking plaster, *Am* adhesive tape.
speaker [spikœr] *m*, **speakerine** [spikrin] *f* (*à la radio etc*) announcer.
spécial, -e, -aux *a* special.
spécialement *adv* specially.
spécialiste *mf* specialist.
spécialité *f* speciality, *Am* specialty.
spécimen [-mɛn] *m* specimen.
spectacle *m* (*vue*) sight; (*représentation*) show.
spectaculaire *a* spectacular.
spectateur, -trice *mf* spectator; (*témoin*) onlooker; **les spectateurs** (*le public*) the audience.
sphère *f* sphere.
spirale *f* spiral.
spirituel, -elle *a* (*amusant*) witty.
splendide *a* splendid.
spontané, -ée *a* spontaneous.
sport *m* sport; **faire du s.** to play sport *ou Am* sports; **voiture/veste/terrain de s.** sports car/jacket/ground.
sportif, -ive 1 *a* (*personne*) fond of sport *ou Am* sports. **2** *mf* sportsman, sportswoman.
spot [spɔt] *m* (*lampe*) spotlight; **s. (publicitaire)** commercial.

squash *m* (*jeu*) squash.
squelette *m* skeleton.
stable *a* stable.
stade *m* stadium.
stage *m* (*cours*) (training) course.
stand [stɑ̃d] *m* (*d'exposition etc*) stand.
standard 1 *m* (*téléphonique*) switchboard. **2** *a inv* (*modèle etc*) standard.
station *f* station; (*de ski etc*) resort; (*d'autobus*) stop; **s. de taxis** taxi rank, *Am* taxi stand.
stationnement *m* parking.
stationner *vi* (*se garer*) to park; (*être garé*) to be parked.
station-service *f* (*pl* **stations-service**) service station, petrol *ou Am* gas station.
statistique *f* (*donnée*) statistic.
statue *f* statue.
steak *m* steak.
sténodactylo *f* shorthand typist, *Am* stenographer.
stéréo *a inv* stereo.
stériliser *vt* to sterilize.
stock *m* stock (**de** of); **en s.** in stock.
stocker *vt* (*provisions etc*) to store.
stop [stɔp] **1** *int* stop. **2** *m* (*panneau*) stop sign; (*feu arrière*) brake light, stoplight; **faire du s.** to hitchhike.
stopper *vti* to stop.
store *m* blind, *Am* (window) shade.
stress *m inv* stress.
stressé, -ée *a* under stress.
strict, -e *a* strict.
strictement *adv* strictly.
structure *f* structure.
studio *m* (*de cinéma etc*) studio; (*logement*) studio flat *ou Am* apartment.
stupéfaction *f* amazement.
stupéfait, -faite *a* amazed (**de** at, by).
stupide *a* stupid.
stupidité *f* stupidity; (*action, parole*) stupid thing.
style *m* style.
stylo *m* pen; **s. à bille** ballpoint (pen); **s.-plume** fountain pen.
su, sue *pp of* **savoir**.
subir *vt* to undergo; (*conséquences, défaite*) to suffer; (*influence*) to be under.

subit, -ite *a* sudden.
subitement *adv* suddenly.
subjonctif *m Grammaire* subjunctive.
submergé, -ée *a* flooded (**de** with); **s. de travail** overwhelmed with work.
substance *f* substance.
subtil, -e [syptil] *a* subtle.
succéder *vi* **s. à qch** to follow sth; **se s.** to follow one another.
succès *m* success; **avoir du s.** to be successful.
successif, -ive *a* successive.
succession *f* (*série*) sequence (**de** of).
sucer *vt* to suck.
sucette *f* lollipop; (*tétine*) dummy, *Am* pacifier.
sucre *m* sugar; (*morceau*) sugar lump; **s. cristallisé** granulated sugar; **s. en morceaux** lump sugar; **s. en poudre, s. semoule** caster sugar, *Am* finely ground sugar.
sucré, -ée *a* sweet.
sucrer *vt* to sugar.
sucrier *m* sugar bowl.
sud [syd] *m* south; **au s. de** south of; **du s.** (*vent*) southerly; (*ville*) southern.
sud-est *m & a inv* south-east.
sud-ouest *m & a inv* south-west.
suédois, -oise 1 *a* Swedish. **2** *mf* Swede. **3** *m* (*langue*) Swedish.
suer *vi* to sweat; **faire s. qn** *Fam* to get on s.o.'s nerves.
sueur *f* sweat; **en s.** sweating.
suffire* *vi* to be enough (**à** for); **ça suffit!** that's enough!; **il suffit d'une goutte**/*etc* **pour faire** a drop/*etc* is enough to do.
suffisamment *adv* sufficiently; **s. de** enough.
suffisant, -ante *a* sufficient.
suffocant, -ante *a* stifling.
suggérer [sygʒere] *vt* to suggest (**à** to, **de faire** doing, **que** (+ *subjonctif*) that).
suggestion *f* suggestion.
suicide *m* suicide.
suicider (se) *vpr* to commit suicide.
suis *voir* **être, suivre.**
suisse 1 *a* Swiss. **2** *mf* Swiss *inv*; **les Suisses** the Swiss.
Suissesse *f* Swiss woman *ou* girl, Swiss *inv*.
suite *f* (*reste*) rest; (*de film, roman*) sequel; (*série*) series; **faire s. (à)** to follow; **par la s.** afterwards; **à la s.** one after another; **à la s. de** (*événement etc*) as a result of; **de s.** (*deux jours etc*) in a row.

suivant, -ante 1 *a* next, following. **2** *mf* next (one); **au s.!** next!

suivre* 1 *vt* to follow; (*accompagner*) to go with; (*classe*) to attend, go to; **s. (des yeux** *ou* **du regard)** to watch; **se s.** to follow each other. **2** *vi* to follow; **faire s.** (*courrier*) to forward; **'à s.'** 'to be continued'.

sujet *m* (*question*) & *Grammaire* subject; (*d'examen*) question; **au s. de** about; **à quel s.?** about what?

super [syper] **1** *a inv* (*bon*) great. **2** *m* (*essence*) four-star (petrol), *Am* premium gas.

superbe *a* superb.

superficie *f* surface.

superficiel, -ielle *a* superficial.

supérieur, -e *a* upper; (*qualité etc*) superior (**à** to); (*études*) higher; **l'étage s.** the floor above.

supériorité *f* superiority.

supermarché *m* supermarket.

superposer *vt* (*objets*) to put on top of each other.

superstitieux, -euse *a* superstitious.

superstition *f* superstition.

supplément *m* (*argent*) extra charge; **en s.** extra.

supplémentaire *a* extra.

supplier *vt* **s. qn de faire** to beg s.o. to do.

support *m* support; (*d'instrument etc*) stand.

supporter[1] *vt* to bear; (*résister à*) to withstand; (*soutenir*) to support.

supporter[2] [sypɔrtɛr] *m* supporter.

supposer *vti* to suppose (**que** that).

supposition *f* assumption.

suppositoire *m* suppository.

suppression *f* removal; (*de train*) cancellation.

supprimer *vt* to get rid of; (*mot*) to cut out; (*train*) to cancel.

sur *prép* on, upon; (*par-dessus*) over; (*au sujet de*) on, about; **six s. dix** six out of ten; **un jour s. deux** every other day; **six mètres s. dix** six metres by ten.

sûr, sûre *a* sure, certain (**de** of, **que** that); (*digne de confiance*) reliable; (*lieu*) safe; **c'est s. que** (+ *indicatif*) it's certain that; **s. de soi** self-assured; **bien s.!** of course!

sûrement *adv* certainly.

sûreté *f* safety; **être en s.** to be safe; **mettre en s.** to put in a safe place.

surexcité, -ée *a* overexcited.

surf [sœrf] *m* surfing; **faire du s.** to go surfing.

surface *f* surface; (*dimensions*) (surface) area; **(magasin à) grande s.** hypermarket.
surgelé, -ée *a* (*viande etc*) frozen.
surgelés *mpl* frozen foods.
surgir *vi* to appear suddenly (**de** from); (*problème*) to arise.
sur-le-champ *adv* immediately.
surlendemain *m* **le s.** two days later; **le s. de** two days after.
surmener (se) *vpr* to overwork.
surmonter *vt* (*obstacle etc*) to get over.
surnom *m* nickname.
surnommer *vt* to nickname.
surpasser (se) *vpr* to excel oneself.
surprenant, -ante *a* surprising.
surprendre* *vt* (*étonner*) to surprise; (*prendre sur le fait*) to catch; (*conversation*) to overhear.
surpris, -ise *a* surprised (**de** at, **que** (+ *subjonctif*) that); **je suis surpris de te voir** I'm surprised to see you.
surprise *f* surprise.
sursauter *vi* to jump, start.
surtout *adv* especially; (*avant tout*) above all; **s. pas** certainly not; **s. que** especially since.
surveillant, -ante *mf* (*de lycée*) supervisor (in charge of discipline); (*de prison*) (prison) guard, warder.
surveiller *vt* to watch; (*contrôler*) to supervise.
survêtement *m* tracksuit.
survivant, -ante *mf* survivor.
survivre* *vi* to survive (**à qch** sth).
survoler *vt* to fly over.
susceptible *a* touchy.
suspect, -ecte [syspɛ, -ɛkt] **1** *a* suspicious. **2** *mf* suspect.
suspendre *vt* (*accrocher*) to hang (up) (**à** on); **se s. à** to hang from.
suspendu, -ue *a* **s. à** hanging from.
suspense [syspɛns] *m* suspense.
suspension *f* (*de véhicule*) suspension.
suture *f* **point de s.** stitch (*in wound*).
SVP [ɛsvepe] *abrév* (*s'il vous plaît*) please.
syllabe *f* syllable.
symbole *m* symbol.
symbolique *a* symbolic.
sympa *a inv Fam* = **sympathique.**
sympathie *f* liking; **avoir de la s. pour qn** to be fond of s.o.
sympathique *a* nice, pleasant.

symphonie *f* symphony.
symptôme *m* symptom.
synagogue *f* synagogue.
syndicat *m* (*d'ouvriers*) (trade) union, *Am* (*labor*) union; **s. d'initiative** tourist (information) office.
syndiqué, -ée *mf* union member.
synonyme 1 *a* synonymous (**de** with). **2** *m* synonym.
système *m* system.

T

ta *voir* **ton.**

tabac [taba] *m* tobacco; (*magasin*) tobacconist's (shop), *Am* tobacco store.

table *f* table; (*d'école*) desk; **t. de nuit** bedside table; **t. basse** coffee table; **t. à repasser** ironing board; **t. roulante** (tea) trolley, *Am* (serving) cart; **t. des matières** table (of contents); **à t.** sitting at the table; **à t.!** (food's) ready!

tableau, -x *m* (*image*) picture; (*panneau*) board; (*liste*) list; (*graphique*) chart; **t. (noir)** (black)board; **t. d'affichage** notice board, *Am* bulletin board; **t. de bord** dashboard.

tablette *f* (*de chocolat*) bar; (*de lavabo etc*) shelf.

tablier *m* apron; (*d'écolier*) smock.

tabouret *m* stool.

tache *f* spot; (*salissure*) stain.

tacher *vti*, **se tacher** *vpr* to stain.

tâcher *vi* **t. de faire** to try to do.

tact *m* tact; **avoir du t.** to be tactful.

tactique *f* **la t.** tactics; **une t.** a tactic.

tag *m* tag (*spray-painted graffiti*).

taie d'oreiller *f* pillowcase.

taille *f* (*hauteur*) height; (*dimension*, *mesure*) size; (*ceinture*) waist; **tour de t.** waist measurement.

taille-crayon(s) *m inv* pencil sharpener.

tailler *vt* to cut; (*haie*, *barbe*) to trim; (*arbre*) to prune; (*crayon*) to sharpen.

tailleur *m* (*personne*) tailor; (*vêtement*) suit.

taire* (se) *vpr* (*ne rien dire*) to keep quiet (**sur qch** about sth); (*cesser de parler*) to stop talking; **tais-toi!** be quiet!

talent *m* talent; **avoir du t. pour** to have a talent for.

talon *m* heel; (*de chèque*, *carnet*) stub.

talus *m* slope, embankment.

tambour *m* drum; (*personne*) drummer.

tambourin *m* tambourine.

tamiser *vt* (*farine*) to sift.

tampon *m* (*marque*, *instrument*) stamp; (*de coton*) wad; **t. hygiénique** tampon; **t. à récurer** scrubbing pad.

tandis que *conj* while.

tant *adv* (*travailler etc*) so much (**que** that); **t. de** (*temps etc*) so much (**que** that); (*gens etc*) so many (**que** that); **t. que** (*aussi longtemps que*) as long as; **t. mieux!** good!; **t. pis!** too bad!

tante *f* aunt.
tantôt *adv* **t....t.** sometimes...sometimes.
tapage *m* din, uproar.
tape *f* slap.
taper[1] **1** *vt* (*enfant, cuisse*) to slap; (*table*) to bang. **2** *vi* **t. sur qch** to bang on sth; **t. du pied** to stamp one's foot.
taper[2] *vti* **t. (à la machine)** to type.
tapis *m* carpet; **t. roulant** (*pour marchandises*) conveyor belt.
tapisser *vt* (*mur*) to (wall)paper.
tapisserie *f* (*papier peint*) wallpaper; (*broderie*) tapestry.
tapoter *vt* to tap; (*joue*) to pat.
taquiner *vt* to tease.
tard *adv* late; **plus t.** later (on); **au plus t.** at the latest.
tarder *vi* **t. à faire** to take one's time doing; **elle ne va pas t.** she won't be long; **sans t.** without delay.
tarif *m* (*prix*) rate; (*de train*) fare; (*tableau*) price list.
tarte *f* (open) pie, tart.
tartine *f* slice of bread; **t. (de beurre/de confiture)** slice of bread and butter/jam.
tartiner *vt* (*beurre etc*) to spread.
tas *m* pile, heap; **un** *ou* **des t. de** (*beaucoup*) *Fam* lots of; **mettre en t.** to pile *ou* heap up.
tasse *f* cup; **t. à café** coffee cup; **t. à thé** teacup.
tasser *vt* to pack, squeeze (*sth, s.o.*) (**dans** into).
tasser (se) *vpr* (*se serrer*) to squeeze up.
tâter *vt* to feel.
tâtonner *vi* to grope about.
tâtons (à) *adv* **avancer à t.** to feel one's way (along); **chercher à t.** to grope for.
tatouage *m* (*dessin*) tattoo.
tatouer *vt* to tattoo.
taudis *m* slum.
taupe *f* mole
taureau, -x *m* bull.
taux *m* rate; **t. d'alcool**/*etc* alcohol/*etc* level.
taxe *f* (*impôt*) tax; (*de douane*) duty; **t. à la valeur ajoutée** value-added tax.
taxé, -ée *a* taxed.
taxi *m* taxi.
te (**t'** *before vowel or mute h*) *pron* (*complément direct*) you; (*indirect*) (to) you; (*réfléchi*) yourself.
technicien, -ienne *mf* technician.

technique 1 *a* technical. **2** *f* technique.
technologie *f* technology.
tee-shirt [tiʃœrt] *m* tee-shirt.
teindre* *vt* to dye; **t. en rouge** to dye red.
teindre (se) *vpr* to dye one's hair.
teint *m* complexion.
teinte *f* shade.
teinture *f* (*produit*) dye.
teinturerie *f* (*boutique*) (dry) cleaner's.
teinturier, -ière *mf* (dry) cleaner.
tel, telle *a* such; **un t. livre**/*etc* such a book/*etc*; **un t. intérêt**/*etc* such interest/*etc*; **de tels mots**/*etc* such words/*etc*; **rien de t. que** (there's) nothing like.
télé *f* TV; **à la t.** on TV.
télécommande *f* remote control.
télécopie *f* fax.
télécopieur *m* fax (machine).
téléfilm *m* TV film.
télégramme *m* telegram.
téléphérique *m* cable car.
téléphone *m* (tele)phone; **coup de t.** (phone) call; **passer un coup de t. à qn** to give s.o. a ring; **au t.** on the (tele)phone.
téléphoner 1 *vt* (*nouvelle etc*) to (tele)phone (**à** to). **2** *vi* to (tele)phone; **t. à qn** to (tele)phone s.o.
téléphonique *a* **appel**/*etc* **t.** (tele)phone call/*etc*.
télescope *m* telescope.
télésiège *m* chair lift.
téléspectateur, -trice *mf* (television) viewer.
télévisé *a* **journal t.** television news.
téléviseur *m* television (set).
télévision *f* television; **à la t.** on (the) television.
telle *voir* **tel**.
tellement *adv* (*si*) so; (*tant*) so much; **t. de** (*travail etc*) so much; (*soucis etc*) so many; **pas t.!** not much!
témoignage *m* evidence; (*récit*) account.
témoigner *vi* to give evidence (**contre** against).
témoin *m* witness; **être t. de** to witness.
température *f* temperature; **avoir de la t.** to have a temperature.
tempête *f* storm; **t. de neige** snowstorm.
temple [tɑ̃pl] *m* (*romain*, *grec*) temple.
temporaire *a* temporary.
temps[1] *m* time; (*de verbe*) tense; **il est t. (de faire)** it's time (to do);

ces derniers t. lately; **de t. en t.** [dətɑ̃zɑ̃tɑ̃], from time to time; **à t.** (*arriver*) in time; **à plein t.** (*travailler*) full-time; **à t. partiel** (*travailler*) part-time; **dans le t.** (*autrefois*) once.

temps^{2} *m* (*climat*) weather; **quel t. fait-il?** what's the weather like?

tenailles *fpl* (*outil*) pincers.

tendance *f* tendency; **avoir t. à faire** to tend to do.

tendeur *m* (*à bagages*) elastic strap, *Am* bungee.

tendre^{1} *vt* to stretch; (*main*) to hold out (**à qn** to s.o.); (*bras, jambe*) to stretch out; (*piège*) to set, lay; **t. qch à qn** to hold out sth to s.o.; **t. l'oreille** to prick up one's ears.

tendre^{2} *a* (*viande etc*) tender; (*personne*) affectionate (**avec** to).

tendrement *adv* tenderly.

tendresse *f* affection.

tendu, -ue *a* (*corde*) tight; (*personne, situation, muscle*) tense; (*main*) held out.

tenir* **1** *vt* to hold; (*promesse, comptes, hôtel*) to keep; (*rôle*) to play; **t. sa droite** (*conducteur*) to keep to the right. **2** *vi* to hold; (*résister*) to hold out; **t. à** (*personne, jouet etc*) to be attached to; **t. à faire** to be anxious to do; **t. dans qch** (*être contenu*) to fit into sth; **tenez!** (*prenez*) here (you are)!; **tiens!** (*surprise*) well!

tenir (se) *vpr* (*avoir lieu*) to be held; **se t. (debout)** to stand (up); **se t. droit** to stand up *ou* sit up straight; **se t. par la main** to hold hands; **se t. bien** to behave oneself.

tennis *m* tennis; (*terrain*) (tennis) court; (*chaussure*) plimsoll, *Am* sneaker; **t. de table** table tennis.

tension *f* tension; **t. (artérielle)** blood pressure; **avoir de la t.** to have high blood pressure.

tentant, -ante *a* tempting.

tentation *f* temptation.

tentative *f* attempt.

tente *f* tent.

tenter^{1} *vt* to try (**de faire** to do).

tenter^{2} *vt* (*faire envie à*) to tempt.

tenue *f* (*vêtements*) clothes; (*conduite*) (good) behaviour; **t. de soirée** evening dress.

tergal® *m* Terylene®, *Am* Dacron®

terme *m* (*mot*) term; (*fin*) end; **mettre un t. à** to put an end to; **à court/long t.** (*conséquences*) short-/long-term; **en bons/mauvais termes** on good/bad terms (**avec** with).

terminaison *f* (*de mot*) ending.

terminal, -e, -aux **1** *a & f* **(classe) terminale** = sixth form, *Am* = twelfth grade. **2** *m* **t. (d'ordinateur)** (computer) terminal.

terminer *vt* to end.
terminer (se) *vpr* to end (**par** with, **en** in).
terne *a* dull.
terrain *m* ground; (*étendue*) land; (*à bâtir*) plot; *Football etc* pitch; **un t.** a piece of land; **t. de camping** campsite; **t. de jeux** (*pour enfants*) playground; (*stade*) playing field; **t. vague** waste ground, *Am* vacant lot.
terrasse *f* terrace; (*de café*) pavement *ou Am* sidewalk area.
terre *f* (*matière*, *monde*) earth; (*sol*) ground; (*opposé à mer*) land; **par t.** (*poser*, *tomber*) to the ground; (*assis*, *couché*) on the ground; **sous t.** underground.
terrestre *a* **la surface t.** the earth's surface; **globe t.** globe (*model*).
terreur *f* terror.
terrible *a* awful, terrible; (*formidable*) *Fam* terrific.
terrifiant, -ante *a* terrifying.
terrifier *vt* to terrify.
territoire *m* territory.
terroriser *vt* to terrorize.
terroriste *a* & *mf* terrorist.
tes [te] *voir* **ton.**
test *m* test.
testament *m* (*en droit*) will.
tester *vt* to test.
tête *f* head; (*visage*) face; (*d'arbre*) top; **tenir t. à** to stand up to; **faire la t.** to sulk; **à la t. de** (*entreprise*) at the head of; (*classe*) at the top of; **en t.** (*sportif*) in the lead.
tête-à-tête *adv* **(en) t.-à-tête** alone together.
téter 1 *vt* to suck. **2** *vi* **le bébé tète** the baby is feeding; **donner à t. à** to feed.
tétine *f* (*de biberon*) teat, *Am* nipple; (*sucette*) dummy, *Am* pacifier.
têtu, -ue *a* stubborn.
texte *m* text.
textile *a* & *m* textile.
TGV [teʒeve] *abrév* = **train à grande vitesse.**
thé *m* tea.
théâtre *m* theatre; (*œuvres*) drama; **faire du t.** to act.
théière *f* teapot.
théorie *f* theory; **en t.** in theory.
thermomètre *m* thermometer.
thermos® *m ou f* Thermos® (flask).
thermostat *m* thermostat.
thon *m* tuna (fish).

tibia *m* shin (bone).
ticket *m* ticket.
tiède *a* (luke)warm.
tien, tienne *pron poss* **le t., la tienne, les tien(ne)s** yours; **les deux tiens** your two.
tiens, tient *voir* **tenir.**
tiercé *m* **jouer/gagner au t.** = to bet/win on the horses.
tiers *m* (*fraction*) third.
tige *f* (*de plante*) stem; (*barre*) rod.
tigre *m* tiger.
timbre *m* stamp.
timbre-poste *m* (*pl* **timbres-poste**) (postage) stamp.
timbrer *vt* (*lettre*) to stamp.
timide *a* shy.
timidement *adv* shyly.
timidité *f* shyness.
tinter *vi* (*cloche*) to ring; (*clefs*) to jingle.
tir *m* shooting; *Football* shot; **t. à l'arc** archery.
tirage *m* (*de journal*) circulation; (*de loterie*) draw; **t. au sort** drawing of lots.
tire-bouchon *m* corkscrew.
tirelire *f* moneybox, *Am* coin bank.
tirer 1 *vt* to pull; (*langue*) to stick out; (*trait, rideaux*) to draw; (*balle, canon*) to shoot; **t. de** (*sortir*) to pull *ou* draw out of; (*obtenir*) to get from; **t. qn de** (*danger, lit*) to get s.o. out of; **se t. de** (*travail*) to cope with; (*situation*) to get out of; **se t. d'affaire** to get out of trouble. **2** *vi* to pull (**sur** on, at); (*faire feu*) to shoot (**sur** at); *Football* to shoot; **t. au sort** to draw lots; **t. à sa fin** to draw to a close.
tiret *m* (*trait*) dash.
tireur *m* (*au fusil*) gunman.
tiroir *m* drawer.
tisonnier *m* poker.
tisser *vt* to weave.
tissu *m* material, cloth; **du t.-éponge** towelling, *Am* toweling.
titre *m* title; **(gros) t.** (*de journal*) headline; **à t. d'exemple** as an example; **à juste t.** rightly.
toast *m* (*pain grillé*) piece *ou* slice of toast.
toboggan *m* slide; (*pour voitures*) flyover, *Am* overpass.
toc *int* **t. t.!** knock knock!
toi *pron* (*complément, sujet*) you; (*réfléchi*) **assieds-t.** sit (yourself) down; **dépêche-t.** hurry up.

toile *f* cloth; (*à voile*, *sac etc*) canvas; (*tableau*) painting; **t. d'araignée** spider's web.
toilette *f* (*action*) wash(ing); (*vêtements*) clothes; **eau de t.** toilet water; **faire sa t.** to wash (and dress); **les toilettes** the toilet(s), *Am* the men's *ou* ladies' room; **aller aux toilettes** to go to the toilet *ou* *Am* to the men's *ou* ladies' room.
toi-même *pron* yourself.
toit *m* roof; **t. ouvrant** (*de voiture*) sunroof.
toiture *f* roof(ing).
tôle *f* **une t.** a metal sheet; **t. ondulée** corrugated iron.
tolérant, -ante *a* tolerant (**à l'égard de** of).
tolérer *vt* to tolerate.
tomate *f* tomato.
tombe *f* grave.
tombeau, -x *m* tomb.
tombée *f* **t. de la nuit** nightfall.
tomber *vi* (*aux* **être**) to fall; **t. malade** to fall ill; **t. (par terre)** to fall (down); **faire t.** (*personne*) to knock over; **laisser t.** to drop; **tu tombes bien/mal** you've come at the right/wrong time; **t. sur** (*trouver*) to come across.
tombola *f* raffle.
ton, ta, *pl* **tes** (**ta** *becomes* **ton** [tɔ̃n] *before a vowel or mute h*) *a poss* your; **t. père** your father; **ta mère** your mother; **ton ami(e)** your friend.
ton *m* (*de voix etc*) tone.
tonalité *f* (*téléphonique*) dialling tone, *Am* dial tone.
tondeuse *f* **t. (à gazon)** (lawn)mower.
tondre *vt* (*gazon*) to mow.
tonne *f* metric ton, tonne; **des tonnes de** (*beaucoup*) *Fam* tons of.
tonneau, -x *m* barrel.
tonner *vi* **il tonne** it's thundering.
tonnerre *m* thunder; **coup de t.** burst of thunder.
tonton *m Fam* uncle.
torche *f* (*flamme*) torch; **t. électrique** torch, *Am* flashlight.
torchon *m* (*à vaisselle*) tea towel, *Am* dish towel; (*de ménage*) duster.
tordre *vt* to twist; (*linge*) to wring (out); (*barre*) to bend; **se t. la cheville** to twist *ou* sprain one's ankle.
tordre (se) *vpr* to twist; (*barre*) to bend; **se t. de douleur** to be doubled up with pain; **se t. (de rire)** to split one's sides (laughing).
torrent *m* (mountain) stream; **il pleut à torrents** it's pouring (down).
torse *m* chest; **t. nu** stripped to the waist.

tort *m* **avoir t.** to be wrong (**de faire** to do, in doing); **être dans son t.** to be in the wrong; **donner t. à qn** (*accuser*) to blame s.o.; **à t.** wrongly; **parler à t. et à travers** to talk nonsense.
torticolis *m* **avoir le t.** to have a stiff neck.
tortiller *vt* to twist, twirl.
tortue *f* tortoise, *Am* turtle; (*de mer*) turtle.
torture *f* torture.
torturer *vt* to torture.
tôt *adv* early; **le plus t. possible** as soon as possible; **t. ou tard** sooner or later; **je n'étais pas plus t. sorti que** no sooner had I gone out than.
total, -e, -aux *a* & *m* total.
totalement *adv* totally.
totalité *f* **en t.** (*détruit etc*) entirely; (*payé*) fully.
touchant, -ante *a* moving, touching.
touche *f* (*de clavier*) key; (*de téléphone*) (push-)button; **téléphone à touches** push-button phone.
toucher 1 *vt* to touch; (*paie*) to draw; (*chèque*) to cash; (*cible*) to hit; (*émouvoir*) to touch, move. **2** *vi* **t. à** to touch. **3** *m* (*sens*) touch.
toucher (se) *vpr* (*lignes, mains etc*) to touch.
touffe *f* (*de cheveux, d'herbe*) tuft.
toujours *adv* always; (*encore*) still; **pour t.** for ever.
toupie *f* (spinning) top.
tour[1] *f* tower; (*immeuble*) tower block, high-rise; *Échecs* castle.
tour[2] *m* turn; (*de magie etc*) trick; **t. de poitrine**/*etc* chest/*etc* measurement **faire le t. de** to go round; **faire un t.** to go for a walk; (*en voiture*) to go for a drive; (*voyage*) to go on a trip; **jouer un t. à qn** to play a trick on s.o.; **c'est mon t.** it's my turn; **à t. de rôle** in turn.
tourisme *m* tourism; **faire du t.** to go sightseeing.
touriste *mf* tourist.
touristique *a* **guide**/*etc* **t.** tourist guide/*etc*.
tournage *m* (*de film*) shooting.
tournant *m* (*de route*) bend.
tourne-disque *m* record player.
tournée *f* (*de livreur, boissons*) round; (*de spectacle*) tour.
tourner 1 *vt* to turn; (*film*) to shoot. **2** *vi* to turn; (*tête*) to spin; (*moteur*) to run; (*lait*) to go off; **t. autour de** (*objet*) to go round.
tourner (se) *vpr* to turn (**vers** to).
tournevis [turnəvis] *m* screwdriver.
tournoi *m* tournament.
Toussaint *f* All Saints' Day.

tousser *vi* to cough.

tout, toute, *pl* **tous, toutes 1** *a* all; **tous les livres** all the books; **t. l'argent/le temps/le village** all the money/time/village; **toute la nuit** all night; **tous (les) deux** both; **tous (les) trois** all three. ▮ (*chaque*) every; **tous les ans** every *ou* each year; **tous les cinq mois/mètres** every five months/metres. **2** *pron pl* (**tous** = [tus]) all; **ils sont tous là** they're all there. **3** *pron m sing* **tout** everything; **t. ce que** everything that, all that; **en t.** (*au total*) in all. **4** *adv* (*tout à fait*) quite, very; **t. simplement** quite simply; **t. petit** very small; **t. neuf** brand new; **t. seul** all alone; **t. autour** all around; **t. en chantant**/*etc* while singing/*etc*; **t. à coup** suddenly; **t. à fait** completely; **t. de même** all the same; **t. de suite** at once. **5** *m* **le t.** everything, the lot; **pas du t.** not at all; **rien du t.** nothing at all.

toux *f* cough.

toxique *a* poisonous.

trac *m* **avoir le t.** to be *ou* become nervous, have *ou* get nerves.

tracasser *vt*, **se tracasser** *vpr* to worry.

trace *f* trace (**de** of); (*marque*) mark; **traces** (*de bête, pneus*) tracks; **traces de pas** footprints.

tracer *vt* (*dessiner*) to draw.

tracteur *m* tractor.

tradition *f* tradition.

traditionnel, -elle *a* traditional.

traducteur, -trice *mf* translator.

traduction *f* translation.

traduire* *vt* to translate (**de** from, **en** into).

trafic *m* traffic.

tragédie *f* tragedy.

tragique *a* tragic.

trahir *vt* to betray.

trahir (se) *vpr* to give oneself away.

trahison *f* betrayal.

train[1] *m* train; **t. à grande vitesse** high-speed train; **t. couchettes** sleeper.

train[2] *m* **être en t. de faire** to be (busy) doing.

traîneau, -x *m* sledge, *Am* sled.

traînée *f* (*de peinture etc*) streak.

traîner 1 *vt* to drag. **2** *vi* (*jouets etc*) to lie around; (*s'attarder*) to lag behind; **t. (par terre)** (*robe etc*) to trail (on the ground).

traîner (se) *vpr* (*par terre*) to crawl.

train-train *m* routine.

traire* *vt* to milk.

trait *m* line; (*en dessinant*) stroke; (*caractéristique*) feature; **t. d'union** hyphen.

traitement *m* treatment; (*salaire*) salary; **t. de texte** word processing; **machine de t. de texte** word processor.

traiter *vt* **1** to treat; (*problème*) to deal with; **t. qn de lâche**/*etc* to call s.o. a coward/*etc*. **2** *vi* **t. de** (*sujet*) to deal with.

traiteur *m* **chez le t.** at the delicatessen.

traître *m* traitor.

trajectoire *f* path.

trajet *m* trip; (*distance*) distance; (*itinéraire*) route.

tramway [tramwɛ] *m* tram, *Am* streetcar.

tranchant, -ante *a* (*couteau, voix*) sharp.

tranche *f* (*morceau*) slice.

tranchée *f* trench.

trancher *vt* to cut.

tranquille [trɑ̃kil] *a* quiet; (*mer*) calm; (*conscience*) clear; **laisser t.** to leave alone.

tranquillement *adv* calmly.

tranquillisant *m* tranquillizer.

tranquilliser *vt* to reassure.

tranquillité *f* (peace and) quiet.

transférer *vt* to transfer (**à** to).

transfert *m* transfer.

transformation *f* change.

transformer *vt* to change; (*maison*) to carry out alterations to; **t. en** to turn into.

transfusion *f* **t. (sanguine)** (blood) transfusion.

transistor *m* transistor (radio)

transitif, -ive *a Grammaire* transitive.

transmettre* *vt* (*message etc*) to pass on (**à** to).

transparent, -ente *a* clear, transparent.

transpercer *vt* to pierce.

transpirer *vi* to sweat.

transport *m* transport (**de** of); **moyen de t.** means of transport; **les transports en commun** public transport.

transporter *vt* to transport; (*à la main*) to carry; **t. d'urgence à l'hôpital** to rush to hospital *or Am* to the hospital.

trappe *f* trap door.

travail, -aux *m* (*activité, lieu*) work; (*à effectuer*) job, task; (*emploi*) job; **travaux** (*dans la rue*) roadworks, *Am* roadwork; (*aménagement*) alterations; **travaux pratiques** (*à l'école etc*) practical work.

travailler *vi* to work (**à qch** at *ou* on sth).

travailleur, -euse 1 *a* hard-working. **2** *mf* worker.
travers 1 *prép* & *adv* **à t.** through; **en t. (de)** across. **2** *adv* **de t.** (*chapeau etc*) crooked; (*comprendre*) badly; **j'ai avalé de t.** it went down the wrong way.
traversée *f* crossing.
traverser *vt* to cross, go across; (*foule*, *période*) to go through.
traversin *m* bolster.
trébucher *vi* to stumble (**sur** over); **faire t. qn** to trip s.o. (up).
trèfle *m* (*couleur*) *Cartes* clubs.
treize *a* & *m inv* thirteen.
treizième *a* & *mf* thirteenth.
tremblement *m* shaking, trembling; **t. de terre** earthquake.
trembler *vi* to shake, tremble (**de** with).
tremper 1 *vt* to soak; (*plonger*) to dip (**dans** in). **2** *vi* to soak; **faire t. qch** to soak sth.
tremplin *m* springboard.
trentaine *f* **une t. (de)** about thirty.
trente *a* & *m* thirty; **un t.-trois tours** an LP.
trentième *a* & *mf* thirtieth.
très [trɛ] *adv* ([trɛz] *before vowel or mute h*) very; **t. aimé**/*etc* (*with past participle*) much *ou* greatly liked/*etc*.
trésor *m* treasure.
tresse *f* (*cheveux*) plait, *Am* braid.
tresser *vt* to plait, *Am* braid.
tri *m* sorting (out).
triangle *m* triangle.
triangulaire *a* triangular.
tribu *f* tribe.
tribunal, -aux *m* court.
tribune *f* (*de stade*) (grand)stand.
tricher *vi* to cheat.
tricheur, -euse *mf* cheat, *Am* cheater.
tricolore *a* red, white and blue; **feu t.** traffic lights.
tricot *m* (*activité*) knitting; (*chandail*) sweater.
tricoter *vti* to knit.
tricycle *m* tricycle.
trier *vt* to sort (out).
trimestre *m* (*période*) quarter; (*scolaire*) term.
trimestriel, -ielle *a* (*revue*) quarterly; **bulletin t.** end-of-term report *ou Am* report card.
tringle *f* rail, rod.
triomphe *m* triumph (**sur** over).

triompher *vi* to triumph (**de** over).
triple *m* **le t.** three times as much (**de** as).
tripler *vti* to treble, triple.
tripoter *vt* to fiddle about *ou* around with.
triste *a* sad; (*couleur*, *temps*) gloomy.
tristement *adv* sadly.
tristesse *f* sadness; (*du temps*) gloom(iness).
trognon *m* (*de fruit*) core.
trois *a* & *m* three.
troisième *a* & *mf* third.
troisièmement *adv* thirdly.
trombone *m* trombone; (*agrafe*) paper clip.
trompe *f* (*d'éléphant*) trunk.
tromper *vt* to deceive; (*être infidèle à*) to be unfaithful to.
tromper (se) *vpr* to be mistaken; **se t. de route**/*etc* to take the wrong road/*etc*; **se t. de date**/*etc* to get the date/*etc* wrong.
trompette *f* trumpet.
tronc *m* trunk.
tronçonneuse *f* chain saw.
trône *m* throne.
trop *adv* too; too much; **t. dur**/*etc* too hard/*etc*; **t. fatigué pour jouer** too tired to play; **boire**/*etc* **t.** to drink/*etc* too much; **t. de sel**/*etc* (*quantité*) too much salt/*etc*; **t. de gens**/*etc* (*nombre*) too many people/*etc*; **un franc**/*etc* **de t.** *ou* **en t.** one franc/*etc* too many.
tropical, -e, -aux *a* tropical.
trot *m* trot; **aller au t.** to trot.
trotter *vi* (*cheval*) to trot.
trottinette *f* (*jouet*) scooter.
trottoir *m* pavement, *Am* sidewalk.
trou *m* hole; **t. de (la) serrure** keyhole; **t. (de mémoire)** lapse (of memory).
trouble *a* (*liquide*) cloudy; (*image*) blurred; **voir t.** to see things blurred.
troubler *vt* to disturb; (*vue*) to blur.
troubles *mpl* (*de santé*) trouble; (*désordres*) disturbances.
trouer *vt* to make a hole *ou* holes in.
troupe *f* (*groupe*) group; (*de théâtre*) company; **troupes** (*armée*) troops.
troupeau, -x *m* (*de vaches*) herd; (*de moutons*, *d'oies*) flock.
trousse *f* (*étui*) case, kit; (*d'écolier*) pencil case; **t. à outils** toolkit; **t. à pharmacie** first-aid kit; **t. de toilette** sponge *ou* toilet bag, dressing case.

trousseau, -x *m* (*de clefs*) bunch.
trouver *vt* to find; **aller/venir t. qn** to go/come and see s.o.; **je trouve que** I think that.
trouver (se) *vpr* to be; (*être situé*) to be situated; (*se sentir*) to feel; (*dans une situation*) to find oneself.
truc *m* (*astuce*) trick; (*moyen*) way; (*chose*) *Fam* thing.
truite *f* trout.
TTC [tetese] *abrév* (*toutes taxes comprises*) inclusive of tax.
tu *pron* you (*familiar form of address*).
tu, tue *voir* **taire.**
tube *m* tube; (*chanson*) *Fam* hit.
tuberculose *f* TB.
tue-tête (à) *adv* at the top of one's voice.
tuer *vti* to kill; **se t.** to kill oneself; (*dans un accident*) to be killed.
tuile *f* tile.
tulipe *f* tulip.
tunisien, -ienne *a* & *mf* Tunisian.
tunnel *m* tunnel.
turbulent, -ente *a* (*enfant*) disruptive.
tutoyer *vt* **t. qn** to use the familiar *tu* form to s.o.
tutu *m* ballet skirt.
tuyau, -x *m* pipe; **t. d'arrosage** hose(pipe); **t. d'échappement** exhaust (pipe).
TVA [tevea] *f abrév* (*taxe à la valeur ajoutée*) VAT.
type *m* type; (*individu*) fellow, guy.
typique *a* typical (**de** of).

U

ulcère *m* ulcer.

ultramoderne *a* ultramodern.

ultra-secret, -ète *a* top-secret.

un une 1 *art indéf* a, (*devant voyelle*) an; **une page** a page; **un ange** [œ̃nɑ̃ʒ] an angel. **2** *a* one; **la page un** page one; **un kilo** one kilo. **3** *pron* & *mf* one; **l'un** one; **les uns** some; **j'en ai un** I have one; **l'un d'eux, l'une d'elles** one of them; **la une** (*de journal*) page one.

unanime *a* unanimous.

unanimité *f* **à l'u.** unanimously.

uni, -ie *a* united; (*famille*) close; (*surface*) smooth; (*couleur*) plain.

unième *a* (*after a number*) (-)first; **trente et u.** thirty-first; **cent u.** hundred and first.

uniforme *m* uniform.

union *f* union.

unique *a* (*fille*, *espoir etc*) only; (*prix*, *marché*) single; (*exceptionnel*) unique.

uniquement *adv* only.

unir *vt* (*efforts*, *forces*) to combine; (*deux pays etc*) to unite, join together; **u. deux personnes** (*amitié*) to unite two people.

unir (s') *vpr* (*étudiants etc*) to unite.

unité *f* (*de mesure*, *élément*) unit.

univers *m* universe.

universel, -elle *a* universal.

universitaire *a* **ville**/*etc* **u.** university town/*etc*.

université *f* university; **à l'u.** at university, *Am* at college.

urgence *f* (*cas*) emergency; (*de décision etc*) urgency; **faire qch d'u.** to do sth urgently; **(service des) urgences** (*d'hôpital*) casualty (department), *Am* emergency room.

urgent, -ente *a* urgent.

urne *f* ballot box; **aller aux urnes** to go to the polls, vote.

usage *m* use; (*habitude*) custom; **faire u. de** to make use of; **hors d'u.** broken, not in use.

usagé, -ée *a* worn.

usager *m* user.

usé, -ée *a* (*tissu etc*) worn (out).

user *vt*, **s'user** *vpr* (*vêtement*) to wear out.

usine *f* factory.

ustensile *m* utensil.

usure *f* wear (and tear).

utile *a* useful (**à** to).

utilisateur, -trice *mf* user.
utilisation *f* use.
utiliser *vt* to use.
utilité *f* use(fulness); **d'une grande u.** very useful.

V

va *voir* **aller**[1].
vacances *fpl* holiday(s), *Am* vacation; **en v.** on holiday, *Am* on vacation; **les grandes v.** the summer holidays *ou Am* vacation.
vacancier, -ière *mf* holidaymaker, *Am* vacationer.
vacarme *m* din, uproar.
vaccin *m* vaccine; **faire un v. à** to vaccinate.
vaccination *f* vaccination.
vacciner *vt* to vaccinate.
vache 1 *f* cow. **2** *a* (*méchant*) *Fam* nasty.
vachement *adv Fam* (*très*) damned; (*beaucoup*) a hell of a lot.
vagabond, -onde *mf* tramp, *Am* hobo.
vague 1 *a* vague; (*regard*) vacant. **2** *f* wave; **v. de chaleur** heat wave; **v. de froid** cold spell.
vaguement *adv* vaguely.
vain (en) *adv* in vain.
vaincre* *vt* to beat.
vaincu, -ue *mf* (*sportif*) loser.
vainqueur *m* (*sportif*) winner.
vais *voir* **aller**[1].
vaisselle *f* crockery; (*à laver*) washing up, dirty dishes; **faire la v.** to do the washing up, wash the dishes.
valable *a* (*billet etc*) valid.
valet *m Cartes* jack.
valeur *f* value; **avoir de la v.** to be valuable; **objets de v.** valuables.
valise *f* (suit)case; **faire ses valises** to pack (one's bags).
vallée *f* valley.
valoir* *vi* to be worth; **v. cher** to be worth a lot; **un vélo vaut bien une auto** a bicycle is just as good as a car; **il vaut mieux rester** it's better to stay; **il vaut mieux que j'attende** I'd better wait; **ça ne vaut rien** it's no good; **ça vaut le coup** it's worth while (**de faire** doing).
valoir (se) *vpr* to be as good as each other; **ça se vaut** it's all the same.
valse *f* waltz.
vandale *mf* vandal.
vanille *f* vanilla; **glace à la v.** vanilla ice cream.
vaniteux, -euse *a* conceited.
vantard, -arde *mf* bighead, boaster.
vanter (se) *vpr* to boast (**de** about, of).
vapeur *f* **v. (d'eau)** steam.
variable *a* (*humeur*, *temps*) changeable.

varicelle *f* chicken pox.
varié, -ée *a* varied; (*divers*) various.
varier *vti* to vary.
variété *f* variety; **spectacle de variétés** variety show.
vas *voir* **aller**[1].
vase *m* vase.
vaste *a* vast, huge.
vaut *voir* **valoir.**
veau, -x *m* calf; (*viande*) veal; (*cuir*) calfskin, (calf) leather.
vécu, -ue (*pp of* **vivre**) *a* (*histoire etc*) true.
vedette *f* (*de cinéma etc*) star.
végétarien, -ienne *a* & *mf* vegetarian.
végétation *f* vegetation.
véhicule *m* vehicle; **v. tout terrain** off-road vehicle.
veille *f* **la v. (de)** the day before; **la v. de Noël** Christmas Eve.
veiller *vi* to stay up; (*sentinelle*) to keep watch; **v. à qch** to see to sth; **v. sur qn** to watch over s.o.
veilleur *m* **v. de nuit** night watchman.
veilleuse *f* (*de voiture*) sidelight, *Am* parking light; (*de cuisinière*) pilot light; (*lampe allumée la nuit*) night light.
veine *f* vein; (*chance*) *Fam* luck.
vélo *m* bike, bicycle; (*activité*) cycling; **faire du v.** to cycle; **v. tout terrain** mountain bike.
vélomoteur *m* motorcycle.
velours *m* velvet; **v. côtelé** corduroy.
vendeur, -euse *mf* sales *ou* shop assistant, *Am* sales clerk; (*de voitures etc*) salesman, saleswoman.
vendre *vt* to sell (**qch à qn** s.o. sth, sth to s.o.); **à v.** for sale.
vendre (se) *vpr* to sell; **ça se vend bien** it sells well.
vendredi *m* Friday; **V. saint** Good Friday.
vénéneux, -euse *a* poisonous.
vengeance *f* revenge.
venger (se) *vpr* to get one's revenge, get one's own back (**de qn** on s.o., **de qch** for sth).
venimeux, -euse *a* poisonous.
venin *m* poison.
venir* *vi* (*aux* **être**) to come (**de** from); **v. faire** to come to do; **viens me voir** come and see me; **je viens/venais d'arriver** I've/I'd just arrived; **où veux-tu en v.?** what are you getting at?; **faire v.** to send for, get.
vent *m* wind; **il y a du v.** it's windy; **coup de v.** gust of wind.
vente *f* sale; **v. (aux enchères)** auction (sale); **en v.** on sale; **prix de**

v. selling price.
ventilateur *m* fan.
ventre *m* stomach; **avoir mal au v.** to have a stomachache.
venu, -ue *mf* **nouveau v., nouvelle venue** newcomer; **le premier v.** anyone.
ver *m* worm; (*de fruits etc*) maggot; **v. de terre** (earth)worm.
véranda *f* (*en verre*) conservatory (*room attached to house*).
verbe *m* verb.
verdict *m* verdict.
verger *m* orchard.
verglas *m* (black) ice, *Am* sleet.
vérification *f* check(ing).
vérifier *vt* to check.
véritable *a* true, real; (*non imité*) real.
véritablement *adv* really.
vérité *f* truth.
vernir *vt* to varnish.
vernis *m* varnish; **v. à ongles** nail polish.
verra, verrai(t) *etc voir* **voir.**
verre *m* glass; **boire** *ou* **prendre un v.** to have a drink; **v. de bière** glass of beer; **v. à bière** beer glass.
verrou *m* bolt; **fermer au v.** to bolt.
verrue *f* wart.
vers[1] *prép* (*direction*) toward(s).
vers[2] *m* (*de poème*) line.
verse (à) *adv* **pleuvoir à v.** to pour (down).
verser *vt* to pour; (*larmes*) to shed; (*argent*) to pay.
version *f* (*de film, d'incident etc*) version.
verso *m* **'voir au v.'** 'see overleaf'.
vert, verte 1 *a* green; (*pas mûr*) unripe. **2** *m* green.
vertical, -e, -aux *a* vertical.
vertige *m* **avoir le v.** to be *ou* feel dizzy; **donner le v. à qn** to make s.o. (feel) dizzy.
veste *f* jacket.
vestiaire *m* cloakroom, *Am* locker room.
veston *m* (suit) jacket.
vêtement *m* garment; **vêtements** clothes; **vêtements de sport** sportswear.
vétérinaire *mf* vet
veuf, veuve 1 *a* widowed. **2** *m* widower. **3** *f* widow.
veuille(s), veuillent *etc voir* **vouloir.**
veulent, veut, veux *voir* **vouloir.**

vexant, -ante *a* upsetting.
vexer *vt* to upset.
viande *f* meat.
vibration *f* vibration.
vibrer *vi* to vibrate.
vice *m* vice.
victime *f* victim; (*d'un accident*) casualty; **être v. de** to be the victim of.
victoire *f* victory; (*en sports*) win.
victorieux, -euse *a* victorious; (*équipe*) winning.
vidange *f* (*de véhicule*) oil change.
vide 1 *a* empty. **2** *m* emptiness; (*trou*) gap.
vidéo *a inv* video.
vidéocassette *f* video cassette.
vide-ordures *m inv* (rubbish *ou Am* garbage) chute.
vide-poches *m inv* glove compartment.
vider *vt*, **se v.** *vpr* to empty.
vie *f* life; (*durée*) lifetime; **le coût de la v.** the cost of living; **gagner sa v.** to earn one's living; **en v.** living.
vieil [vjɛj] *voir* **vieux.**
vieillard *m* old man.
vieille *voir* **vieux.**
vieillesse *f* old age.
vieillir 1 *vi* to grow old; (*changer*) to age. **2** *vt* **v. qn** (*vêtement etc*) to make s.o. look old(er).
vieux (*or* **vieil** *before vowel or mute h*), **vieille,** *pl* **vieux, vieilles 1** *a* old. **2** *m* old man; **les vieux** old people; **mon v.!** (*mon ami*) mate!, pal! **3** *f* old woman; **ma vieille!** (*ma chère*) dear!
vif, vive *a* (*enfant*) lively; (*couleur*, *lumière*) bright; (*froid*) biting; **brûlé v.** burnt alive.
vignette *f* (*de véhicule*) road tax sticker.
vignoble *m* vineyard.
vilain, -aine *a* (*laid*) ugly; (*enfant*) naughty; (*impoli*) rude.
villa *f* (detached) house.
village *m* village.
villageois, -oise *mf* villager.
ville *f* town; (*grande*) city; **aller/être en v.** to go (in)to/be in town.
vin *m* wine.
vinaigre *m* vinegar.
vinaigrette *f* French dressing, *Am* Italian dressing.
vingt [vɛ̃] ([vɛ̃t] *before vowel or mute h and in numbers 22–29*) *a* & *m* twenty; **v. et un** twenty-one.

vingtaine *f* **une v. (de)** about twenty.
vingtième *a* & *mf* twentieth.
viol *m* rape.
violemment [-amɑ̃] *adv* violently.
violence *f* violence.
violent, -ente *a* violent.
violer *vt* to rape.
violet, -ette *a* & *m* purple.
violeur *m* rapist.
violon *m* violin.
vipère *f* adder.
virage *m* (*de route*) bend; (*de véhicule*) turn.
virgule *f* comma; (*de nombre*) (decimal) point; **2 v. 5** 2 point 5.
virus [virys] *m* virus.
vis[1] [vi] *voir* **vivre, voir.**
vis[2] [vis] *f* screw.
visa *m* (*de passeport*) visa.
visage *m* face.
viser 1 *vi* to aim (**à** at). **2** *vt* (*cible*) to aim at
visible *a* visible.
visite *f* visit; **rendre v. à** to visit; **v. (médicale)** medical examination; **v. guidée** guided tour.
visiter *vt* to visit.
visiteur, -euse *mf* visitor.
visser *vt* to screw on.
vit *voir* **vivre, voir.**
vitamine *f* vitamin.
vite *adv* quickly.
vitesse *f* speed; (*sur un véhicule*) gear; **boîte de vitesses** gearbox; **à toute v.** at full speed.
vitrail, -aux *m* stained-glass window.
vitre *f* (window)pane; (*de véhicule, train*) window.
vitrine *f* (shop) window; (*meuble*) display cabinet.
vivant, -ante *a* living; (*recit, rue*) lively.
vive *int* **v. le roi**/*etc*! long live the king/*etc*!; **v. les vacances!** hurray for the holidays *ou Am* the vacation!
vivre* 1 *vi* to live; **v. vieux** to live to be old; **v. de** (*fruits etc*) to live on; (*travail etc*) to live by. **2** *vt* (*vie*) to live, (*aventure*) to live through.
vocabulaire *m* vocabulary.
vodka *f* vodka
vœu, -x *m* wish.

voici *prép* here is, this is; *pl* here are, these are; **me v.** here I am; **v. dix ans que** it's ten years since.

voie *f* road; (*rails*) track; (*partie de route*) lane; (*chemin*) way; (*de gare*) platform; **v. sans issue** dead end; **sur la bonne v.** on the right track.

voilà *prép* there is, that is; *pl* there are, those are; **les v.** there they are; **v., j'arrive!** all right, I'm coming!; **v. dix ans que** it's ten years since.

voile[1] *m* (*tissu*) veil.

voile[2] *f* (*de bateau*) sail; (*sport*) sailing; **faire de la v.** to sail.

voilier *m* (*de plaisance*) sailing boat, *Am* sailboat.

voir* *vti* to see; **faire v. qch** to show sth; **fais v.** let me see; **v. qn faire** to see s.o. do *ou* doing; **je ne peux pas la v.** *Fam* I can't stand (the sight of) her; **ça n'a rien à v. avec** that's got nothing to do with.

voir (se) *vpr* (*se fréquenter*) to see each other; **ça se voit** that's obvious.

voisin, -ine 1 *a* neighbouring; (*maison*, *pièce*) next (**de** to). **2** *mf* neighbour.

voisinage *m* neighbourhood.

voiture *f* car; (*de train*) carriage, *Am* car.

voix *f* voice; (*d'électeur*) vote; **à v. basse** in a whisper.

vol[1] *m* (*d'avion*, *d'oiseau*) flight.

vol[2] *m* (*délit*) theft; (*hold-up*) robbery.

volaille *f* **une v.** a fowl.

volant *m* (steering) wheel.

volcan *m* volcano.

voler[1] *vi* (*oiseau*, *avion etc*) to fly.

voler[2] *vti* (*prendre*) to steal (**à** from).

volet *m* (*de fenêtre*) shutter.

voleur, -euse *mf* thief; **au v.!** stop thief!

volontaire 1 *a* (*voulu*) (*geste etc*) deliberate. **2** *mf* volunteer.

volontairement *adv* (*exprès*) deliberately.

volonté *f* will; **bonne v.** goodwill; **mauvaise v.** ill will.

volontiers [-ɔ̃tje] *adv* gladly.

volume *m* (*de boîte*, *de son*, *livre*) volume.

volumineux, -euse *a* bulky.

vomir 1 *vt* bring up. **2** *vi* to be sick.

vont *voir* **aller**[1].

vos *voir* **votre.**

vote *m* vote; (*de loi*) passing; **bureau de v.** polling station, *Am* polling place.

voter 1 *vi* to vote. **2** *vt* (*loi*) to pass.
votre, *pl* **vos** *a poss* your.
vôtre *pron poss* **le** *ou* **la v., les vôtres** yours; **à la v.!** (your) good health, cheers!
voudra, voudrai(t) *etc voir* **vouloir.**
vouloir* *vt* to want (**faire** to do); **je veux qu'il parte** I want him to go; **v. dire** to mean (**que** that); **je voudrais rester** I'd like to stay; **je voudrais un pain** I'd like a loaf of bread; **voulez-vous me suivre** will you follow me; **si tu veux** if you like *ou* wish; **en v. à qn d'avoir fait qch** to be angry with s.o. for doing sth; **je veux bien (attendre)** I don't mind (waiting); **sans le v.** unintentionally.
vous *pron* (*sujet, complément direct*) you; (*complément indirect*) (to) you; (*réfléchi*) yourself, *pl* yourselves; (*réciproque*) each other.
vous-même *pron* yourself.
vous-mêmes *pron pl* yourselves.
vouvoyer *vt* **v. qn** to use the formal *vous* form to s.o.
voyage *m* trip, journey; **aimer les voyages** to like travelling; **faire un v., partir en v.** to go on a trip; **bon v.!** have a pleasant trip!; **v. organisé** (package) tour; **agent/agence de voyages** travel agent/ agency.
voyager *vi* to travel.
voyageur, -euse *mf* traveller; (*passager*) passenger.
voyelle *f* vowel.
voyou *m* hooligan.
vrac (en) *adv* (*en désordre*) in a muddle, haphazardly.
vrai, -e *a* true; (*réel*) real; (*authentique*) genuine.
vraiment *adv* really.
vraisemblable *a* (*probable*) likely.
VTT [vetete] *m inv abrév* (*vélo tout terrain*) mountain bike.
vu, vue *pp of* **voir.**
vue *f* (*spectacle*) sight; (*sens*) (eye)sight; (*panorama, photo*) view; **en v.** (*proche*) in sight; **de v.** (*connaître*) by sight.
vulgaire *a* vulgar.

W

wagon [vagɔ̃] *m* (*de voyageurs*) carriage, *Am* car; (*de marchandises*) wag(g)on, *Am* freight car.
wagon-lit *m* (*pl* **wagons-lits**) sleeping car.
wagon-restaurant *m* (*pl* **wagons-restaurants**) dining car.
waters [watɛr] *mpl* toilet, *Am* men's *ou* ladies' room.
w-c [(dubləә)vese] *mpl* toilet, *Am* men's *ou* ladies' room.
week-end *m* weekend.
western *m* (*film*) western.
whisky, *pl* **-ies** *m* whisky, *Am* whiskey.

Y

y [i] **1** *adv* there; **allons-y** let's go; **je n'y suis pour rien** I have nothing to do with it. **2** *pron* (= *à cela*) **j'y pense** I think of it; **je m'y attendais** I was expecting it; **ça y est!** that's it!
yacht [jɔt] *m* yacht.
yaourt [jaurt] *m* yog(h)urt.
yeux *voir* **œil.**

Z

zèbre *m* zebra.
zéro *m* (*chiffre*) nought, zero; (*dans un numéro*) 0 [əʊ]; (*température*) zero; **deux buts à z.** two nil, *Am* two zero.
zigzag *m* zigzag; **en z.** (*route etc*) zigzag(ging).
zigzaguer *vi* to zigzag.
zone *f* zone, area; **z. bleue** restricted parking zone; **z. industrielle** industrial estate *ou Am* park.
zoo [zo] *m* zoo.
zut! [zyt] *int* oh dear!